My Side

ALSO BY RUTH GORDON

Myself Among Others

# MY
# SIDE

THE AUTOBIOGRAPHY OF

# Ruth
# Gordon

HARPER & ROW, PUBLISHERS

NEW YORK, HAGERSTOWN, SAN FRANCISCO, LONDON

FIRST EDITION

*Designed by Gloria Adelson*

Library of Congress Cataloging in Publication Data

Gordon, Ruth, date
   My side.
   Includes index.
   1. Gordon, Ruth, 1896–      I. Title.
PN2287.G64A295 1976      792'.028'0924 [B]      76–5124
ISBN 0–06–011618–8

76 77 78 79 80 81 10 9 8 7 6 5 4 3 2 1

For my son, Jones

*Illustrations follow pages 122, 154, and 346.*

# Chapter

re you careful what matinee you go to? One I went to changed my whole life. Up in the balcony of the Colonial Theatre, two rows from the back and pretty far over to the left, my voices spoke to me. Joan heard hers at Domremy, mine came through at the corner of Boylston and Tremont, Boston, Mass. They turned *The Pink Lady* hit song into a second-violin accompaniment to what they were telling *me.* Onstage, beautiful Hazel Dawn sang:

> "Dream, dream, dream, and forget
> Care, pain, useless regret"

and above it my voices: "Go on the stage, Ruth, *go on the stage!* Be an actress!"

I had gone into the Colonial the average human being beset by worry, doubt, questions. When I came out I had taken off for the horse latitudes and have never lit since.

"Be a nurse." "Be a secretary." "Be a wife." "Be a lady." That voice was Mama's.

"Be a physical culture teacher." That voice was Papa's. "Go to Sargent's Physical Educational School, Snuggy."

"I don't want to."

"What *do* you want to do?"

"I don't know."

I didn't, but I knew I didn't want anything to do with bloomers, Indian clubs, sneakers, dumbbells.

"I'm going to New York and be fast for a year," I told people, but that was to keep attention focused until I could find out how to be rich and dazzling and a somebody. All my high school class were going to Radcliffe or Wellesley or Simmons Business College, but where did they teach how to get rich and be fascinating? I found out when Anna Witham came back from boarding school for Christmas. Her mother bought us tickets for the matinee at the Colonial Theatre and before the curtain fell on the pink sequins, pink ostrich feathers and beautiful Hazel Dawn, my voices had said to be a part of all that.

Rattling home over the Old Colony Railroad tracks, I sat beside Anna. Across the aisle, her mother's handsome, sexy, hawklike profile told no secrets, but Wollaston said *she* was fast. Was it because she'd divorced Anna's father and married Mr. Homer and *before* they were married someone said they saw them lying in the grass in that open land by Massachusetts Field School?

When the baby was expected, Mr. Homer's Aunt Lois said she'd leave them her fortune provided they called the baby Lois.

"It's probably a tumor," said Mrs. Homer, "but either way I'll call it Lois." Whose mother talked like that?

Baby Lois had the only string of real pearls in Wollaston and a golden rattle, gift of Aunt Lois.

Up in Anna's big room, that looked out through snowy birches, light from the fireplace flickered over the wallpaper's red roses, Anna and I under the covers.

"In Kansas City," she said, "the girls say if you love an actress, you can write her a letter."

Why tell how many times I rewrote:

> For
> Miss Hazel Dawn
>   Star of *The Pink Lady*
> Colonial Theatre
>   Boylston Street near Tremont
>     Boston,
>       Massachusetts

I didn't trust it to a letter box. I took it to our post office. "Hello," I said to Postmaster Burns. To God: "Please get my letter to the Colonial Theatre, Boston, a distance of only seven miles, as You well know, but in *time*—it's all my life."

My letter was on its way; now how would I get on mine? How would I drop out of Quincy High and go on the stage? Would my voices tell me the answer?

"Don't be helpless," urged my mother. She was a believer. Was it from her I learned to believe? Papa was an atheist, but the believer won. I was christened at St. *Chry*sostom's Episcopal Church. Some people call it St. Chry*sos*tom's. The saint was born in Constantinople and even a believer like Mama could wonder why Wollaston named our Episcopal church for a Turk.

I didn't wonder till I spent a winter in Edgartown and there we have plenty of time to wonder, plenty of time to look up things. In Larousse it said he was persecuted by the Empress Eudoxie, who found him a redoubtable adversary, but she was redoubtable too, only *he* stayed redoubtable three years longer than *she* did. She died. Admired for his eloquence, he became famous as Golden Mouth.

"Life is real! Life is earnest!" wrote our Longfellow. He could have gone further and said, "Also hard to explain." Mama had been the secretary of Mr. Edward Atkinson, who ran a wholesale sugar business, and Papa was foreman of the Mellin's Food factory; I was a few months old and what were they doing taking that long walk across the tracks to Hancock Street, named for John Hancock, not the insurance company, to a church named for some oddball? Was it because he was Golden Mouth? A good omen for a future actress, but too hard to get there. Left alone one Sunday morning, I went across the street to the Congregational church. Never write off a believer!

"What happened to Ruth?" Papa looked here, Mama looked there, my half-sister Clare went around asking neighbors, "Did you see Ruth?"

Mama remembered little Charlie Ross disappeared and was never heard from! "Clinton, tell the fire station to ring the lost-child alarm." The fire station didn't have to; I crossed the street, arms full of Sunday School books and a card with a gold star for being three years old.

Soon I was selected to be in the church historical pageant. I rehearsed my lines sitting on a cold chamber pot. Mama taught me a verse about the *Nina,* the *Pinta* and the other one, that saw red berries float on the water. Was it the cold chamber pot or forgetting the other one's name made me dislike Mama?

3

Mama didn't swerve from being Episcopalian, but believed that joining the Congregationalists was less dangerous than crossing the railroad tracks. Papa believed there was less danger if I stayed home. Is the atheist always the loser? Every Sunday, Sunday school; Easter I sang in the cantata, for the fair I made fudge, the garden party I helped with the grab bag, once a week we sewed stuff for missionaries in Labrador, I signed up for the Temperance League. "I pledge never to take intoxicating liquors. Ruth G. Jones."

"A church has no goddam right to influence a minor," warned Papa, "but you take a drink and you broke your word."

It worried me, but I'd signed my name.

It worried Papa that everything went up but his salary. We moved around the block to 41 Marion Street, still on the hill. Then everything went up some more. We moved down on the plains to 14 Elmwood Avenue. Mama felt sorry, Papa said he didn't give a damn. "Everywhere you walk in this town you wind up in a swamp."

From 14 Elmwood Avenue St. *Chry*sostom's or St. Chry*sos*tom's is just across the tracks, but I still didn't go. Papa read a man got his foot caught in the switch, the signals changed and he went through life on one foot, so I stayed Congregational till I noticed Unitarians were the fashionable ones.

Kindness of postman Mullin, on our dining room table lay a square white envelope with dashing handwriting:

*Miss Ruth Jones*
*17 Elmwood Avenue*
*Wollaston, Mass.*

Mr. Mullin had paid no attention to the 17 and delivered the letter to 14. Why was our house 14? Why care? If it's for you, you get it, and I got Hazel Dawn's letter!

"I'll send you a copy of my letter if you send me a copy of yours," I wrote to Anna.

"She didn't write me."

Either you're lucky or not; if you're *not,* work on it, be a believer, drop common sense! Blue-eyed Anna Witham, living in a big red house on carefree Grand View Avenue, but Hazel Dawn didn't write to *her.*

If the Colonial hadn't opened in 1900 with *Ben Hur,* would I be an actress? If C. M. S. McClellan and Ivan Caryll hadn't written *The Pink Lady,* would I have heard my voices? If Mr. Tout hadn't gone to bed with Mrs. Tout and had Hazel Dawn, would I be an actress?

4

I believe so.

Why?

I'm a believer. If *The Pink Lady* hadn't rung a bell, something else would have. Four years after I saw it, what bell was that that kept ringing? What was so cold in my hand?

"Five o'clock, dear. Want a second call?"

"No, thanks." What was cold was the receiver. Be careful what matinee you see or you wake up on a one-nighter in North Dakota on a road tour with *Fair and Warmer*.

North Dakota trains leave at 5 A.M. or 5:30 or 6:02. They don't know about P.M. In North Dakota they don't worry about your window; both Dakotas nail them down. My small brass alarm clock jingled and died with a feeble whir. Can you sprint? Before you play the Dakotas, learn. When the bell rings, dash for the radiator and trust it will send out a reassuring hiss. When the pipes knock that's *good,* unless it's during the show in your quiet scene.

Wrapped in my thick bathrobe, I stumbled down the hall.

"Bessie's in." Gretchen faced the dark brown door with the white china WOMEN. She played the part of the comedy maid that Olive May played in the New York company. She gave a thump to the door. "Hurry up, Bess." Her heavy black hair hung down in a braid, her face was crumpled with unslept sleep, blue velvet robe worn last season in a touring *Twin Beds,* looked it. "Bess, the line's growing."

"I had to wait, now *you* can." Bessie Brown's muffled voice lacked sympathy.

Is this what people mean when they say life on the stage is hard? "Last season with Maude Adams I played one-night stands, but good ones, and we traveled in her private railroad car."

Gretchen knocked. "Bess, hurry up."

"In Chicago I played the Blackstone Theatre. That's the most fashionable one in Chicago."

"Bess, you're in the toilet, not Marshall Field's."

The door opened. "Hi, kids."

Bessie grinned at me, shivering. "You look like something the cat dragged in and *you*'re only twenty."

Down the hall shuffled our stage manager. "Where's Men?"

"Turn left."

He shuffled off.

Bessie looked discouraged. "Four men in the cast and two of 'em nances. I should've stayed with the Robert Mantell Company."

North Dakota mornings speed up dressing. Throw off woolly bathrobe and into cold pink satin Bon Ton corset, extravagant and who saw it? Lace it tighter, quicker than in New York, knot the strings, pull on cold pink satin bloomers, cold blue Kayser silk shirt, pin on blue crocheted bag holding two hundred and thirty dollars saved. Slosh cold water from cold pitcher around in mouth, pack toothbrush in washcloth stamped COMPLIMENTS OF THE FORT PIQUA HOTEL, PIQUA, OHIO. Was that where we took the Interurban over to see the Dorothy McKay Company play their *Fair and Warmer* matinee? They were better than we were and we came back discouraged. Terrible when somebody's better than you are.

Pack bottle of Orris tooth powder, pack Cuticura soap. Hotel soap worth taking?

JAMESTOWN HOTEL
FAIRY

Take it. Hook up blue-green changeable taffeta petticoat, colder than pink satin pants, pull on tango-color wool dress Mama made me my senior year at high school, button the cold nickel buttons in the dining room. Pack bathrobe, rub hands with Frostilla, pack bottle in old chamois glove, pack hotel towel? JAMESTOWN HOTEL on a blue stripe down the middle. Pack it. Dab on Azurea face powder, then wrap in nightgown. Few drops Djer-Kiss perfume, pack Pond's cold cream.

A soft knock. "Orange or prunes, darlin'?"

"Orange, buckwheat cakes and maple syrup, sausages well done, *very* well done, coffee with thick cream. Say 'Thick,' Billy, say *'Very* thick.' "

"All right, darlin'." Billy Dorbin was the leading man. His galoshes clomped down the uncarpeted hall.

Pack lavender satin bedroom slippers I made in Wollaston, lace up beautiful tan boots that gave me the terrible blister, take Marshall Field coat off hanger, pin on blue velvet tricorn. Brown calfskin gloves in coat pocket, turn light off and down the hall where Billy'd gone, down to the lobby, my suitcase banging against each step of the wooden staircase. The lobby clock said five-thirty.

"Checking out." In Wollaston I'd never heard the expression and now in Jamestown I say it.

"Name?"

"Ruth Gordon."

"Dinner last night? Breakfast? Bus to the depot?"

"Yes."

"With bus, two seventy-five. Good house?"

"Great." In show business you have to lie.

"What's your next stop?"

"Devils Lake." I couldn't lie and say Minneapolis. This wasn't the train.

"Set your bag on the pile. The driver'll put it on the bus. Heavy weather up north."

"Our audience comes right through blizzards. The blizzard in Minneapolis we sold out." Sound better than Mankato?

I followed the smell of sausages and buckwheats to where Billy had his *Variety* on the chair. "Here's your orange, baby." He put a napkin on my lap.

Across the table, Grace told a traveling salesman, "We just do these one-nighters temporarily. We pick up the big time in Duluth."

"Funny a great liar's not a great actress," mumbled Billy, mouth full.

"Think I'm learning?"

"You *had* to, darlin'. There was only one way to go." You have to talk with your mouth full if you're catching a train. "That first show, I said I gotta ask her if she has the key to the curtain. Was it Hillsboro?"

"Hillsboro I *joined* you; I opened in Circleville. Their curtain had a key?"

"With Maude Adams didn't they say stuff like that? 'No show tonight; they lost the key of the curtain'?"

"You mean people just make it up?"

"It's a saying like 'Pictures on a broom' or 'Whistle in the dressing room and the one near the door gets fired.' Never whistle backstage, darlin', even if *you're* not the one near the door."

"Buckwheats." The waitress put four in front of me. "You were cute and *he* was killin'." She pointed to Billy. "Y' shoulda had more of a crowd. This town's dead. I'm goin' east, Grand Rapids."

"Is this *thick* cream?"

" 'Off the top,' he said. Someone has a farm in Philadelphia sent me some scrapple—ever try it?"

"In Philadelphia, with Maude Adams, I played the Broad Street Theatre."

The room clerk looked in. "Bus for Northern Pacific."

"A dime or fifteen, Billy?"

"Dime." He put one in front of my place, one in front of his.

"I'll pay you on the train."

At the station, the stationmaster was talking to our company manager, Mr. Ryder. "Your train's running four hours late. Hook your scenery on this freight comin' in."

"Want to give a show tonight?" Mr. Ryder asked us. "We travel caboose or we don't make the stand." If you don't make the stand you don't get paid.

"Oh, I *like* a caboose!" said Grace in her high-comedy voice. Last season she'd played Chicago in *Nobody's Widow.*

Do you long for faraway places? Did I like traveling all day in a day coach or do I like thinking about it? Did I like sitting up all night? Did I like giving a show Sundays if it was a Sunday town, playing extra matinees if it was a town liked matinees? No *extra* money, but money held back when we didn't make a stand.

In Wollaston, people work regular hours for regular pay at the end of the week. Factories and offices close Sundays and holidays and by midnight or even sooner, everyone on Grand View or Winthrop or Elmwood Avenue is asleep, but not in Pierre, South Dakota. The Chicago & North Western pulled out with us and dropped us off in Huron at 2 A.M. They unhooked our scenery car and rumbled on to Duluth.

*"Nobody's Widow* never had jumps like this!" sneered Grace, and climbed on the rickety bus. "Where's the fool stopping?" she demanded. "Do they call *that* a station?"

"Two-hour-fifteen-minute layover," said Mr. Ryder.

Do you love the faraway places? Do you love a station with no heat, no water, wood benches, one weak light? Oscar Johnson, who played the part that Ralph Morgan played in New York, filled his Sterno pan with snow and made tea. We all unpacked our collapsible cups.

"Lie down, darlin'." Billy Dorbin turned over a bench with iron armrests. Upside down it had a flat surface. My brown coat with the rabbit fur patches covered all but my tan boots. John spread his *Saturday Evening Post* over them like a small wigwam. Had anyone in Wollaston ever put the *Saturday Evening Post* over their boots? Had anyone slept in the station? Maybe send the Quincy *Ledger* a note: "Miss Ruth Gordon, daughter of Mr. Clinton Jones, formerly of 14 Elmwood Avenue, slept in a station in South Dakota." Maybe add, "She sleeps in a different hotel or station every night." Maybe tell how I nearly missed the train in Sault Ste. Marie. Is that what people mean when they say don't go on the stage, it'll ruin your health, break your heart, and you'll wish you were back in Wollaston living a normal life, loved by some good man?

And why not be loved by some good man in New York and only take to the faraway places *sometimes?*

From Sault Ste. Marie the train took us down to the Straits of Mackinac, where Huron meets Lake Michigan. There we had to catch the boat across the Straits, then take a train to our next stand, and that was the morning my little brass clock didn't go off!

Why didn't Billy call me? Why didn't Bessie or Grace? In show business they can forget you. Sound asleep one minute and the next I was throwing on my clothes! Was it a nightmare? Throw everything in the bag.

"Bus left."

"The bus *left?*" No breakfast, but that's not why I was crying. *Was* I helpless? If you're helpless, you don't make trains.

"We'll hurry," said the trolley car conductor. He had white hair and an old bristly mustache.

*"I've got to make it!"* Tears kept snapping out of my eyes. Most tears roll down; these flew out at right angles.

"You get out now and run. This is near's we get."

Before he stopped I jumped off. Is that what they mean when they say life on the stage is dangerous?

Way, way, way, way, *way* off, John and Mr. Ryder and Billy were arguing with the train conductor. What's the fastest anybody ever ran? If you're late for the train leaving Sault Ste. Marie you run faster.

"Hurry," screamed Grace. No *Nobody's Widow* voice today. Nobody in the second gallery would say "What?" to *her!*

Billy came running toward me, thick blue overcoat flapping, hat jammed down on his head. He grabbed my suitcase, pulled me faster. The train whistle screeched, wheels rolled, but our bunch wasn't helpless. John reached out and hoisted me aboard. The *Fair and Warmer* company slid out of Sault Ste. Marie with its leading lady.

Did Hazel Dawn ever run for a train? Did Maude Adams? Was this what Papa meant when he said, "What makes you think you've got the stuff it takes?" Did he mean could I make the trains? Did he mean would I know what to do if I got stuck in a snowbank? I wrote the news to Wollaston.

*December 8, 1916*

Dear Katherine,

Nobody in Wollaston ever saw snow like I'm in. I don't even know where we are, except it's Minnesota. Our train got snowed in on our way

9

to Albert Lea and I pray we make it. Every night in a new town and every night after the show I pack my trunk. Did I write you I bought a Taylor? It's in our baggage car with the snow piled on top. In the tray I pack my satin slippers and my silver first act ones, my makeup box and toilet articles. I fold my dressing gown across. Did I tell you our trunks go in our own private baggage car with our scenery? Our own crew are the only ones touch it. They handle my trunk very carefully, it's the only new one. Each side has R.G. painted on. On top is our sticker:

FAIR AND WARMER CO.

THEATRE

After I get packed, I go over and eat at the Candy Kitchen or a Greek restaurant. Billy always knows the good one to go. He's our leading man and you'd love him.

The conductor just came through and says we're really stuck. When you see the postmark you'll know where I am.

Love,

Ruth

No knowing where or when I'd mail it, so I put it in my suitcase till we got somewhere. It got dark. We wouldn't make Albert Lea, so one-eighth of sixty dollars gone. One-eighth of sixty a week is . . . ? Everybody was figuring one-eighth of what they got paid. In show business nobody tells anybody their salary.

"Want my *Variety,* darlin'?"

"I saw it."

"Hungry?"

"No."

A candy salesman passed out barley sugar bears and chocolate creams. That was dinner.

"They're sending us an extra engine," said the conductor. "I'm keeping the steam up; we should be all right."

Everybody slept, swapped magazines, read, slept, read, talked, compared. Mr. Ryder was rerailroading us to Winona, the next stand after Albert Lea.

It got light and we all went outside to look. Snow forever. It stretched on and on. Not a house in sight, but from far off came a man on snowshoes, two pails hanging from a yoke. It was a farmer with a basket of sandwiches, sausage patty between two slabs of farm bread, each slab as big as a loaf. In the pails was milk.

"Fifty cents apiece," he said.

Everybody said it was a gyp and wouldn't pay it.

It startled him so he asked what would we?

10

"Thirty-five cents," said Grace.

He gave her a sandwich and a cup of milk.

"It's good," she said.

We all paid him the thirty-five. It *was* good.

After that we went out again and Bessie snapped a picture of everybody in a row. The sun was melting some of the small icicles; the big ones were there till spring.

Chug chug. The new engine had come.

Bessie snapped a picture.

Winona that night, then leave Minnesota, cross the Mississippi over to Wisconsin.

"Better towns," said Billy. "You'll see, darlin'."

"Oh, I played Milwaukee and Madison. I *love* it." Once you've toured nobody can tell you a thing. Touring actors know all about everything.

"Wisconsin's nearer to Chicago; they're used to shows. You'll notice the difference."

The town of Ripon was nearer to Chicago, but not used to shows. We were only changing trains there after a layover where we'd planned to sleep in the hotel. Our train pulled in, our scenery car got unhooked, puff went the engine and took off. 1:30 A.M. a railroad station is lonely and can get lonelier when the hotel is full.

The stationmaster reproached us. "They *wrote* you to don't come. Number nineteen don't pull in till 7:04 and I close up now." He looked at a fringe of silhouettes. "Anybody take these good folks home?" What were they doing on a station platform in that cold?

"I can take two," said a husky voice.

Mr. Ryder looked at me. "You and Gretchen."

Mama had warned, "Never have anything to do with a stranger," but 1:30 A.M., hotel full, is no time to think of your mother.

"I can," said another voice. That took care of Bessie and Grace.

In show business, talk to strangers and once you talk to them they're not strangers.

The only lights we saw were the ones on our bouncing car. It stopped at a lighted house. A woman in a woolly wrapper, hair in a braid, opened the door.

"Never speak to a stranger and women are worse than men." Mama meant strangers in the East; she never got west of Hornell, New York.

"They're show folk making the 7:04 for Fond du Lac," explained husky-voice. "No room at the Ripon House."

11

"Are you hungry, girls?"

"No, thank you," said Gretchen.

Up steep narrow stairs to a room with a low low ceiling and a high high bed. "You'll be warm; it's a feather bed." Ever sleep under goose feathers in Wisconsin? In a stranger's house whose name you don't know? In the morning did they offer you a glass of milk, warm from the cow, then drive you to the depot? Did they charge forty cents?

Unless your mother was in show business, disregard what she says. In show business, talk to strangers or you don't know what's going on.

"Who's casting?" you ask a stranger, also looking for a job.

"Selwyns. Road companies for *Fair and Warmer.*"

To 41st and Broadway and up the elevator to Selwyns. "I'd like to see someone about *Fair and Warmer,*" I tell a stranger.

"Go in. Mr. Selwyn will see you." That stranger may be starting you on a road tour, and you're the leading lady.

At a big desk sat another stranger, who looked like a Palmer Cox brownie that had got tanned at Great Neck, Palm Beach, French Lick and Saratoga. "Sit down," he said. "What did you have in mind?"

"They say you're putting out a lot of companies of *Fair and Warmer.*"

"Hey, you'd be good in that."

"I just closed in the Maude Adams Company. *Peter Pan* and *The Little Minister.*"

"Was Maude Adams nice to you?"

"Perfectly lovely; we had a wonderful season. Miss Elise Clarens in the Maude Adams Company says she thinks I'd be good in *Fair and Warmer.*"

"Have you seen it?"

"No, not yet."

"Can you tonight?"

"Oh, *yes.*"

He buzzed. The office boy looked in. "Two at the Eltinge for her for tonight."

"Oh, *thank* you, Mr. Selwyn."

"Call me up, tell me what you think. Not too early." He winked. "Bye-bye."

Miss Clarens said she'd be delighted to go with me. We walked over to 42nd Street. Seats were next to the last row on the side.

"Have you ever seen Madge Kennedy?" asked Miss Clarens.

"I saw her in *Twin Beds.*"

"She's a perfectly lovely actress. I think you'll get the part. Madge Kennedy isn't like other ingénues. She looks as though she came from good people. There aren't too many of us, my dear."

Miss Clarens was the most well-bred one in the Maude Adams Company. Why had she singled me out to be charming to? Was it because I told her how well-bred *I* was?

The lights dimmed, the curtain rose, John Cumberland and Madge Kennedy made the audience laugh right through three acts.

"If only I could get the part!"

"You will. Who has that well-bred charm?"

"If only!"

"Even your *hair* is the right color. Most actresses have blond rinses or henna, but you have that naturally lovely light brown that doesn't come out of a bottle. Thank you, my dear, for a pleasant evening."


"Not too early," he'd said. I waited till ten!

"Mr. Selwyn's not in."

"When do you expect him?"

"Try around eleven." Click.

At the Hotel Richmond a phone call cost ten cents. Try a little *after* eleven. "Mr. Arch Selwyn, please."

"Who's calling?"

"Ruth Gordon."

A pause. "He isn't picking up his phone."

"Please tell him Ruth Gordon called. I'm at—"

Click.

Sixty cents later. Go over to the Selwyn office? "Mr. Arch Selwyn, please."

"Not in."

"Would you please say Ruth Gordon was here to see him."

"Spell it."

"R-U-T-H  G-O-R-D-O-N. He gave me two seats to *Fair and Warmer* last night and wants to know what I thought."

"Uh huh."

Another ten cents? "Bryant 4100."

"Selwyn and Company."

"Mr. Selwyn."

"Mr. Edgar Selwyn or Mr. Arch Selwyn?"

"Mr. Arch."

"Gone for the day."

Seventy cents. Write a letter?

HOTEL RICHMOND
West Forty-Sixth Street
off Fifth Avenue
New York
Egbert B. Seaman

Dear Mr. Selwyn,
    I tried to phone you but—

Miss Clarens said she was sure I'd hear from him. Seven companies and I couldn't get in. What happened to luck? What happened to things going right?

My two hundred dollars saved in the Maude Adams Company had shrunk. A dollar and a quarter a day for a hotel room mounts up. Inquire at that boardinghouse where Gladys Gillen said everybody went between jobs? She'd played Wendy in *Peter Pan* and had stayed at Martin's Theatrical when she was job-hunting. Said it was good, said Mr. and Mrs. Henry Martin were in the Social Register. I walked over to West 45th Street.

The row of brownstones all had their windows open. City-colored curtains sagged in or out. At 227 the door was open, but it didn't seem right to walk in. I rang. Across the street, the lights on the Booth Theatre were going to spell:

**THE FALL OF EVE**
**with**
**RUTH GORDON**

but that would be nine summers later. "I won't mind waiting five years to be a star," I'd written in my Wollaston diary.

"Whyn't ya walk in, hon?" asked a tall, rangy colored woman, head tied up in a towel marked HOTEL FLANDERS. "'Y' comin' to stay or look?"

"I'm Miss Ruth Gordon, and I've come to see Mr. and Mrs. Martin."

Her attention wandered across the street. "What'd I hear opens there with somebody featured that useta live here? They move once they sign up. Didja just close with a show?"

"Yes."

14

"Occupy the parlor."

"Good afternoon, I'm Mrs. Martin." Hot as it was, she wore black silk. Its high neck and long sleeves took no notice of the thermometer. Mrs. Martin sat on her horsehair sofa; above her was a big oil painting of stony-faced sheep. "What do you require?"

"What are your rates?"

"We have a large front room vacant in 231 at eighteen dollars, a hall bedroom, second floor, in this house at twelve. That includes meals."

"Twelve dollars!" I'd thought it would be cheaper.

Mrs. Martin nodded her marcelled white head.

"I'll take it."

The running water was in the bathroom at the end of the hall, the boarders were agreeable, the meals were good. When the bell rang twice in the lower hall that meant a phone call for someone on the second floor. Everyone on the second floor looked over the banisters. *Something* had to turn up!

It turned up at Selwyn and Company, that had cost me all those telephone calls.

"I'm sorry I didn't see you in the summer; you'd be a darling Blanny." Mr. Klauber reached his hand out and patted mine.

"Oh, thank you. Mr. Selwyn gave me two tickets to the play."

"Then forgot about you?" He smiled a friendly smile.

I smiled back.

He squeezed my hand. "I hope you're not busy. Are you?"

"No."

"Because I think you can still have the part."

Ever have your heart beat so loud it drowned out sound? Was he continuing?

"Do you mind one-night stands?"

"Oh, I *love* them."

"Oh, yes, Miss Adams plays one-nighters, so you've seen what they're like."

"I like them *best.*"

He laughed. "Would you be able to join the company—what day are we? Today is Saturday." He looked at the calendar. "Sunday, Monday —do you think you could take the train Tuesday night?"

"Oh, yes."

"Do you think you could learn the part?"

15

"Oh, *yes.*"

He laughed and squeezed my hand. "I think you could. You're very young, aren't you?"

"I was twenty last week."

He squeezed my hand. "Shall we read a little scene?"

"All right." When I'd read for Maude Adams I'd gotten the part in *Peter Pan.*

He got a script and opened it. "We'll read from this. Stand here." He pointed to a space beyond his desk. "It's with your husband in Act One." He gently put his lips to mine.

I had to have the part.

"You're sweet. Shall we begin?" He leaned over and covered my mouth with his lips. His tongue went slowly in, out, in.

"Kiss Blanny," said the stage direction. Was that the way a husband kissed? If it's in the part, isn't it all right to? *Isn't* it? Is it?

"You'll be lovely. Take the part home and learn it. I'll have our director, Guy Bragdon, work with you Monday to show you the business, then Tuesday you come up to see me and get your contract. The part pays sixty dollars a week. I'll let you know what town you join the company and we'll have your ticket and sleeper on Tuesday. You're a darling and—"

His phone rang. "Hello . . . Oh, yes indeed, put him on. . . ." He motioned me to the door. "Get my secretary to give you the part of Blanny and tell you what time Mr. Bragdon will rehearse you on Monday."

I was out the door. I was the leading lady of *Fair and Warmer!* Sixty dollars a week! Sixty dollars! The lead! At Martin's Theatrical nobody had a job, but *I* did!

> *227 West 45th Street*
> *New York*
> *November 6, 1916*

Dear Papa,

At last I have wonderful news!!! I knew about it Saturday but did not dare write. Remember the first of the season I wanted to go out in *Fair and Warmer,* a play that stayed in New York for a year? They put out seven companies it was such a success and now the girl in the third company is being replaced because she is not young or pretty enough and Saturday Mr. Klauber of Selwyn and Co. gave *me* the part and told me to get familiar with it. It is the *lead* and is seventy-nine pages long! I learned it

16

Sunday. Just drank coffee all day with a wet towel round my head and don't know what time it was I could say all the lines and fell into bed. Today I had a trial rehearsal at the theatre and signed my contract. Now prepare!!! They are supplying all my costumes and paying me *sixty dollars a week!* Isn't that wonderful? Tomorrow I take the train to join the company in Hillsboro, Ohio. They are doing one-night stands in Ohio. Imagine what a tremendous undertaking it is with so little experience. They gave me a wonderful director. I rehearsed from 8 to 10, then 12 to 1:30. He could only get the theatre to rehearse in at those times and tomorrow I take the train at Pennsylvania Station, sleep on it and late Wednesday afternoon, get off at Hillsboro, Ohio. I will be able to pay you back pretty soon now, you certainly were dear to send me so much. I will send you our route as soon as they give it to me. Did I say I am playing the *lead?* Only my second year, Papa, and I am a leading lady! I took my contract over to the manager of the Empire Theatre where we played *Peter Pan* and he says it is all right.

Lots of love,
Ruth

The company was nice, the girl who was leaving was nice, everybody was nice, but I was no good. I thought the performance would *never* get over. Nor the night. Terrible scare to play a long part and not have it go.

7 A.M. the company stood scattered along the platform of the N & W railway station; the waiting room was too hot. Gretchen Doty and Bessie Brown and I stood together. We didn't talk about last night. Had it been stage fright? Not enough rehearsal? Not knowing how? Would I be better tonight in Chillicothe?

The crew lounged around the scenery car till it got hooked onto the train. From time to time they looked over at the company. Our company manager looked worried. Later I found out his expression didn't mean anything, he looked worried no matter what was going on, but how could I know that in Circleville?

"You must be dead, aren't you?" asked Gretchen.

"Awful ordeal," Bessie moaned.

I was no good and they knew it and I knew it. Where would I find someone who would show me how?

John Winthrop came over. "Anybody see the notice? By the time I got down there were no more papers." He knew the patter.

"All gone," Bessie said quickly.

In *Peter Pan*, *The New York Times* had said, "Ruth Gordon is ever so gay as Nibs." When would it happen again?

17

Gretchen got the subject changed. "That's your best tie, John, why wear it on the train?"

John smiled the heavy smile he smiled on his entrance. "I want to impress our leading lady! She'll be a star on Broadway."

He was no good onstage and worse off.

The company was no good either, but knew what they were doing. I was no good and didn't.

A tall, dark, heavy bulk of a man came down the platform. His saturnine features were emphasized by a night's growth of beard. Claude Giroux played the Express Man in Act III. "Want to compliment you on a very lovely performance last night. Hearty congratulations. Very fine!"

He seemed to *mean* it. He hadn't *run into* me. He bowed and joined the crew down the platform.

"Train for Chillicothe; company coach last car."

I hoisted my suitcase up the high steps. I didn't expect anyone to carry it for me; that means you're sleeping together. I pushed it behind the cindery red plush seat. Circleville started to disappear. I'd never never come back there, but dreadful notice or not, I was a leading lady and tonight I had another chance in Chillicothe, another the next night in Wapakoneta, another in Sandusky, in Van Wert, in Tiffin, Lorain, Elyria, Findlay. That's as far as our route said and one day this company would say, "I was with Ruth Gordon when she was breaking in. We could tell she was New York."

Gretchen or John or Grace Hayle or Bessie Brown or Claude Giroux could count on me. They could count on two seats in the orchestra at whatever theatre I was starring. On my tour Billy or Grace or John or Gretchen would be with me, Claude Giroux could count on a good part.

"Mind if I sit with you?" It was Billy Dorbin, who played John Cumberland's part.

"Do. Was it sheer *agony* for you last night?"

"Oh, nothing gets *my* goat, but *you* were in plenty of trouble."

Still well-bred, like Miss Clarens. "I was nervous at *first*, of course."

"You were nervous right through, darlin'. Glad we weren't playin' Wyoming—they take a shot at you *there.*"

"Oh, I don't know."

"You said a mouthful, darlin'—y' sure *don't.*"

I just stared.

"And don't cool me off with those big brown Julia Sandersons. *I* was the one pullin' you out of the soup!"

I dropped stardom. "Oh, *dear.*"

"Everyone's made a horse's petoot of themselves; it's in The Book of Revelation. It says, 'If you're on the stage, y' got to.' "

"I thought I was going to be all right."

"Y' will be, but not last night. The laughs you stepped on!"

"Do you think I will tonight?"

"No, because I'm tellin' you, don't. You don't know what you're doin', but out here in the sticks is where you find out."

"Oh, Billy." I clutched his blue woolly overcoat sleeve. "I thought I'd never get *through* it!"

"That audience could've beat us with rubber hoses. Circleville must be Quakers, they were so forgiving."

*"You* were wonderful. Oh, show me *how.*"

"Do it forty years, darlin'. *Until* then, you're goin' to get away with it—you got somethin'. Even doin' everythin' wrong in the book, you got somethin' big-time. And the know-how you learn out in these jerks."

"What're jerks?"

"Where the freight train doesn't stop, just slows down for the engineer to jerk the water pipe open and the man on the caboose closes it. A jerk town, nobody from the management's lookin' at you, so no pictures on the broom."

"What's that?"

"A tryout house, after the first show, if the manager wants to fire you he comes back and hands you your pictures that were out front, but in Perth Amboy the manager did that to Hermione and Herndon, and Herndon hit him with his shoe. After that the manager held out a broom with the pictures on and stayed the other end of the broomstick. It's gotten to be an expression, like when you get paid, you say, 'The ghost walked.' Want half?" He held up a five-cent Hershey almond bar.

"Oh, thank you. I didn't eat breakfast."

"Nobody could."

Never go back to Circleville, never tell anyone when you fail and don't give up lying till you go better.

19

*November 26, 1916*

Dear Katherine,

I was so glad to get your darling letter. Honestly, your belief in me is the most wonderful influence I can have. I hope you always have it and that I may fulfill it always. I am happy I did when I opened so great in Circleville. I want you and Wollaston to be proud of me and I pray to God every night and work all the time. Voice, everything. The manager of the company told the stage manager to let me create and "ad lib." That means put in business of my own and little offhand speeches like stars do.

Why send word back to Wollaston I was having trouble playing my part as *written,* without thinking up "little offhand speeches"?

On some of my lines, I get such big laughs they give me a hand and I have more than doubled the curtain calls. Four with the company, then the leading man brings me out for the rest. I do a curtsy instead of just bowing.

I'm afraid that was true.

My gowns are perfect! Act I, an evening gown. Act II, a negligee. Act III, another one. They cost about three hundred dollars. The skirt of my evening gown is heavy white satin with four tiered overdresses of white chiffon, edged in fur and embroidered in silver and crystal beads. The bodice is white, embroidered in silver, and silver lace short sleeves and a crush-girdle of peacock velvet. I wear cloth-of-silver slippers, toes very pointed.

A *beautiful* dress. I didn't have to lie, I only had to draw a picture.

My second-act negligee is heavy peachblow crepe de Chine with overdress of white chiffon hemstitched in silver thread and a broad peach sash. I'll draw it next page.

I did.

My last-act negligee has a delicate pink satin petticoat with rows and rows of hemstitching and a ruffle on the bottom of pink chiffon. Over that is turquoise chiffon with ruffles of antique cream lace, the pattern worked out in rosebud wreaths. Turquoise ribbon around the waist with wreaths of roses on the streamers and I wear pink satin slippers. It is just like Madge Kennedy wore in the New York show.

20

True.

I may get a maid. The firm gave me a contract including a maid's railroad fare.

I have so much to tell you, darling. I had rather an awful time with Mr. Klauber, who engages all the people for Selwyn and Co. Too much personal interest in me, but I managed to keep him down without making him like me any the less.

And maybe he wasn't all that taken with me?

I told him I thought he had been so nice to give me this wonderful chance when I had had such a tiny bit of experience and he said, "Well, you've been a sweet child, too, and this is only the beginning of the nice things this firm is going to do for you."

The leading man, Billy Dorbin, told our company manager, Mr. Ryder, that if he had *my* future, he would go out of his head with joy.

Well, dear, write and tell me about everything.

Lots of love,<br>Ruth

| December | 4 | Logansport, Ind. |
| --- | --- | --- |
| " | 5 | Richmond, Ind. |
| " | 6 | Crawfordsville, Ind. |
| " | 7 | Frankfort, Ind. |
| " | 8 | Wabash, Ind. |
| " | 9 | Lafayette, Ind. |
| " | 10 | Sunday travel |
| " | 11 | Anderson, Ind. |
| " | 12 | Urbana, Ill. |
| " | 13 | Elwood, Ind. |
| " | 14 | Hoopeston, Ill. |
| " | 15 | Beardstown, Ill. |
| " | 16 | Burlington, Iowa. |

All true!

That was Friday in St. Marys. Next morning we pulled into Fremont at 9:10. The crew threw their bags in a truck, unloaded our scenery car to set up for the Saturday matinee, the company piled into the Fremont House bus. The horses snorted out steam and clattered off past frozen cornfields, houses with frosted windowpanes, and stamped into the whir of State Street. Energy crests on a Midwestern Saturday. People hurried in and out of the sprawling three-story Fremont House, weathered to molasses color. The inside was molasses color too. Worn leather chairs all occupied; the hotel kept its lobby hot. Everybody relaxed, nobody told anybody not to smoke, not to spit in the brass cuspidors, not to read the paper. A sign on the big double doors to the dining room announced:

BREAKFAST 7 to 8:30
DINNER 12 to 1
SUPPER 6 to 7

WE MEAN BUSINESS
NO STRAGGLERS ADMITTED

The sweet smell of pancakes still hung over the lobby.

"You with the show?" asked the clerk.

"No," I said. "I'd like an outside room with running water. How much?"

"Three dollars per day American Plan, dinner, supper, breakfast. How long you with us?"

"Tomorrow morning."

The clerk slammed down on a bell, gave a key attached to a five-inch board to a fat bellboy. "Sixty-five."

"How much?" whispered Billy.

"Three."

"The Mrs. Potter Palmer suite?"

"American."

" 'Have y' the rent?' 'No.' 'Then over the cliff!' " He staggered, fell over the cliff on a molasses chair.

"With the troupe?" the clerk asked him.

"Not me."

Some hotels refused actors, but traveling salesmen were acceptable. Actors might make a racket, steal the towels. Thanks to the Robert Mantell tours, Bessie Brown had a towel from every state except Vermont.

My three-dollar outside room looked onto the side street leading to State. Stores, people; a horse with a heavy plaid blanket stamped and looked for someone to get into the buggy.

Billy had told me where the good Greek restaurant was. Nineteen years in the business and never played Broadway, but knew every place in the Midwest where they served a good meal. This was his first time in a show out of New York. Usually he worked out of Chicago in a last season's Broadway hit sometimes paid for, sometimes cribbed. A stenographer went to Cohan's Grand, the Studebaker, Powers, the La Salle, took down the play in shorthand and the agency booked it in tank towns and jerkwaters where nobody checked to see if it was cribbed.

At the table by the window he sat reading *Billboard* and eating a Spanish omelet. "They're great here, darlin'—smell it." He held his plate under my nose. A whiff of onions and tomato. "This one's not as good as the one in Alliance. In Van Wert, don't go in. Dirty. Bucyrus *looks* good; the food's greasy."

If you woke him up and asked, "Sandusky?" he'd say, "Rathskeller, I'll show you." He never knew the address, only how to go there.

"Have half of my orange." He passed it to me, dipped his spoon in the glass of water, rubbed it on the coarse napkin. "We'll get a good house tonight. Fremont's a good stand. Room good?"

"Uh huh. I have to get some shoes."

Crash from the kitchen.

Billy did a take. "Mrs. Astor dropped her earring. Just a saying. Go over to the Walkover." He pointed out the window at people hurrying by. "Saturday's no good for our matinee, but stores'll be full, everybody buying hockey sticks or pants or getting a haircut or shopping for Sunday dinner."

"Saturday matinee in Boston is always full. Katherine Follett and I, when we went to a matinee we had to write and reserve seats. How much do I owe?"

"I pay for the orange, you pay twenty-five, Spanish omelet." He jotted it down on *Billboard*. "Ten cents toast, five coffee, ten tip and I'll leave ten. Gimme fifty-five cents."

"God, it's expensive!"

"But good. The next good is Mrs. Howland's Home Cooked Meals, Upper Sandusky."

"Upper Sandusky's *below* Sandusky on the map."

"Walkover is State Street down a block, the corner."

"What can I do for you, young lady?"

"I must have some tan boots, soft leather, and good-looking. *Please* don't show me the kind that come up too high."

He unbuttoned my black kid boot.

"Do you have *dark* tan? I'm size three B."

He slid the ladder down the wall and from the top shelf picked two white boxes.

"In New York I always get my shoes at Slater's." The richest girl at the Three Arts Club had gotten hers there.

He drew out a beautiful dark tan laced boot, soft leather, just high enough.

What fun to buy something! I hadn't bought one thing to wear since July.

His shoehorn slid it on.

"Where can I buy really good brown silk stockings?"

"Malley's, across the street. It used to be Andrews and Malley, but Mr. Andrews passed on."

"Do they have Onyx stockings?"

"I believe they have. Will you wear these or shall I wrap them?"

"How much are they?"

"Six-fifty."

"Six-fifty!"

"Feel how soft."

"Please wrap them. I'll wear them after our matinee. I'm at the theatre here."

"I'll have to tell my wife I waited on an actress. Is the show good?"

"Big success. In Chicago, when Francine Larrimore leaves, I'm taking over her part at the La Salle Theatre."

I went across to Malley's, formerly Andrews and Malley.

"Onyx, one pair."

"One ninety-five." She handed me change and put the stockings in a box.

"Which direction is the Fremont Opera House? I'm playing there."

"Two down, turn left." Not impressed that I was an actress.

What if I *looked* more like one? The Eccles girls, who were Hazel Dawn's cousins, said Hazel Dawn rinsed her beautiful blond hair in camomile tea.

"Your hair smells funny," said Gretchen. "Like a drugstore on a rainy day."

"I want it lighter."

"It's no lighter, just smells."

"Have a peroxide rinse," advised Grace. "It gives a dandy highlight and just the rinse, it won't look hard."

"I wish I had red hair."

"Have the beauty parlor put henna on. Marinello is good; they have a shop in every town and not expensive."

The train wandered through the frozen brown farm belt. Grace watched it sway past. "When do we get there, Mr. Ryder? I think I'll cook a dinner."

"Layover at Wabash three hours, pick up number thirty-two at two-sixteen, due into Peru 4:04."

Had Grace said, "Cook a dinner"?

"Oh, I do it every tour. John, you and Mr. Ryder get the bags over to the other station and we girls'll do the shopping."

"Cook a dinner on the layover?" I asked.

"Oh, sure. Somebody'll lend their house."

"But how would you know who?"

"Look along the streets. I can always tell. I wish Sandy was here. That's why he loves me—my dumplings."

Mr. Ryder engineered the suitcases to one end of the platform. "Where'll we meet?" asked John.

"The post office. Gretchen and Ruth'll get you."

Up a street full of small houses, Grace looked. Nothing struck her; she turned the corner. The houses looked the same, but in front of a buff-colored two-story house she stopped and studied it. Gretchen and Bessie and I waited on the sidewalk, she rang the bell. The door opened, she talked to a woman, then went in.

"That means she didn't say no," said Bessie.

Grace came out. "I'll be back in about twenty minutes," she told the woman who'd opened the door.

"How much?" asked Bessie.

"Two dollars and leave everything the way it is. The store is one block over."

I was impressed. "Do you know what you'll cook?"

"Sure. What looks great at the store."

"Farm stewers?" she asked the market man.

"How many pounds y' need?"

Grace poked chickens, pinched breastbones, told the man, "Two two-pounders'll be enough with dumplings."

"How'll I get my damn costume on?" moaned Gretchen.

"Two bunches of carrots, two pounds of medium white onions." She bought pastry flour, coffee, cream, butter, sugar, shortening, lemons, eggs. "We'll have a lemon pie. Sandy'll swoon when I write him."

Things got under way. "Find the post office," she directed Gretchen and me. "Bessie'll help me, you and the boys can set the table."

Around the dining room table sat Billy, John, Oscar, Claude, Mr.

Ryder, Bessie, Gretchen, me. Grace, not a hair out of place, face well powdered, dished up stewed chicken, onions, carrots, dumplings, cut the lemon meringue pie, poured coffee, offered the heavy cream, while we passed plates to and fro.

It was gorgeous and it was over. Dishes washed, kitchen immaculate, everybody took turns going upstairs to the bathroom. The two dollars paid and off to the station, bags out of checkroom, board the company coach on the train to Peru, Indiana.

Tacked up on the call-board was the new route. A *two*-nighter? Eau Claire, Wisconsin, for *two* days? Maybe that meant big-time!

Eau Claire! Two nights in the same room! Send out laundry, relax. The show went fine. Everybody would sleep late; no call.

Next night before the show, John knocked on my dressing room door, didn't say, "Are you decent?" Just opened it. "Play the show fast, dear," he said. "Fast. We have to get through in a hurry."

"Why?"

"Go right through the laughs."

"I never heard anything so absurd!"

"Get a wiggle on, dear." He went down the hall.

I went next door to Billy's dressing room. He opened the door a crack. "Go like a son of a gun, darlin'." He looked down the hall as though he expected somebody.

"But what's the reason?"

"John had word to, so we'll do it, huh?" He put his arm around me and we went out to the stage.

"It'll spoil the performance."

"Oh, no; helps a show sometimes."

Three musicians in the pit struck up "Alexander's Ragtime Band," and before it finished, the curtain rolled up with a clack and John, in white tie and tails, tossed his stick and silk hat to Gretchen, rattled off his first lines as Grace made her entrance talking faster than John or Gretchen.

"The audience doesn't know what they're *saying*, Billy!"

"Betcha a nickel I can talk faster than you can." He didn't wait for his cue, made his entrance on Grace's speech and started his scene with John.

"The audience won't know what it's *about!*" I whispered to Bessie, watching from the wings.

The final curtain rang down at nine-thirty, an hour and a quarter early. Every time the audience laughed, one of us said our line through the laugh and the next speech went for nothing. What must they be saying? I knocked on Billy's door. "Are you decent?" I opened the door a crack.

John was packing Billy's trunk. "He had to get over to the hotel."

"What we did to that audience was the worst thing I ever saw. I'm *never* going to do that again!"

"You're right."

I stalked back to my dressing room. That audience must be tearing us to ribbons. Talk to Gretchen? Hers and Bessie's trunks were locked, the room empty. All the rooms empty. Walk over to the Sugar Bowl? No one from the company. The Greek Candy Kitchen? No one. Were they having a party in someone's room? Were they sore because I didn't like going fast? I bought an apple and a box of ginger snaps. "Ring me at five A.M. and at five-fifteen," I told the telephone operator.

Next morning John was paying his bill. "Hello, dear."

"Nice not to ask me to the party?"

"What party?" He took his change and made room for me.

"Two nights."

The clerk riffled through papers.

"Everyone was tired and went to bed."

"One-fifty daily rate, to show folks one-twenty-five. Your bill's two-fifty."

I got out a two-dollar bill and a one.

"Always get rid of a two-dollar bill," advised John. "Everybody's at the Sugar Bowl."

Everybody was at one long table. Everybody but Billy.

"I told her everybody went to bed last night. She thought we had a party."

"I was dead," said Gretchen. "Anybody see the paper?"

"This was our two-day stand, goose," said Bessie. "The notice was in yesterday."

"Did Billy get called?" I asked.

"Yes, dear."

Why did John and Gretchen whisper?

"Something happen?"

"What?" asked John and Gretchen together.

"You look funny."

"It's too early. God, I wish I was a New York actor, stay in bed till noon."

Grace smoothed her bust. "Lillian Russell says get up the minute you wake up is what to do for your figure, but when I get in a New York show I'll get up in time for half-hour." She yawned. "What time's rehearsal?"

I looked astonished. "Rehearsal?"

"Show needs brushing up." Did John look sort of distracted?

A cold draft as the door opened. "All aboard, folks," called the bus driver.

Down at the station a policeman was talking to Mr. Ryder.

Gretchen whispered to Grace. The train pulled in, we got on the last car, the policeman got on too. He didn't talk anymore to Mr. Ryder, just sat looking out the window.

"Isn't this *our* car?" I asked John.

"Yes, dear."

"Why did the policeman get in?"

"Oh, hell, she's got to know." Grace leaned over the back of my seat. "He stays with us till we get out of Wisconsin. Billy made a pass at the banker's son. It's why we played the show fast. The police got talked into letting him do the show, then give him the summons after. Mr. Ryder told them the curtain comes down at ten-fifty, but last night it came down an hour and a quarter early, Billy ran out the stage door so now the policeman goes with us to see he doesn't come back in Wisconsin. Monday we cross over into Michigan. Billy'll be there, in Ishpeming."

Something fell over the transom. Three red roses stuck out of a twist of green wax paper. "Want to go where's good for dinner?"

It was Billy's voice. I waited.

He waited.

Three roses waited.

I opened the door.

Back of him the prisonlike long brown hall stretched out behind his blue nubbly overcoat, derby, round face with a question for a look.

"Wait till I get my coat."

"I'll put the roses in your water pitcher."

Red roses on Anna's wallpaper, red roses in the Ishpeming water pitcher in my brown room. Everything brown except three red roses and Billy's beaming face. "Mrs. Mason makes good chicken fricassee she serves in her parlor."

"I'm ready." Great to have someone you can count on. He could count on me, I counted on him. Great! Once, years later, when I opened the door to my guest room at 60 West 12th Street in New York, my feller wasn't there. No suitcase, no nothing. Only two patent leather evening pumps, each pointing in another direction.

Suddenly I was listening. My voices had come to West 12th. "It's over."

"There's a way to handle everything." Thus spake Zarathustra. You have to get past the moment. If you want to, you will, but you have to work on it. No jumping out of the window, no laying down on the railroad track, no head in the bake oven, no pill-popping all the pills. You have to work on getting past the moment, and that's work!

I never thought of trying any of the above, but I nearly dropped dead once. In Alpena, Michigan. That same Michigan where I nearly missed the train. This time I hadn't missed anything, but just before Saturday matinee the closing notice went up.

When you come in the stage door, first thing is look at the call-board. Always the list of the next town's hotels. Maybe next town treat yourself to a private bath and before you see what hotel it is, the paper says: "SELWYN AND CO. SHOW WILL CLOSE."

Could a show close in *Michigan? Everyone* had figured *Fair and Warmer* would certainly play its way east. Pick up dates we hadn't played in Ohio, Pennsylvania, upstate New York, two months of them at *least*, and there on the call-board:

> **SELWYN AND CO.**
> **SHOW WILL CLOSE**
> **NEXT SATURDAY**
> **IN**
> **NEW CASTLE, PA.**

Close in April and no casting before August?

"*Nobody* closes in Michigan." Billy turned to Grace. "Did you ever?"

Next morning was our start east. Grand Rapids.

"She's no Madge Kennedy," the paper said. I didn't send it to Wollaston and have always hated Grand Rapids.

Next stand, Battle Creek, home of Grape-Nuts or Corn Flakes. Billy's sister came over from Kalamazoo, where she ran the Cadillac agency. She brought an orange-frosted layer cake. It was good, but we felt so awful.

"Why not play Kalamazoo?" complained Billy. "I do business there."

Jackson for a matinee and night show, then Bellefontaine.

HIGHEST POINT IN OHIO, the sign said.

"Bellefontaine you never do business," said miserable Mr. Ryder.

Friday Coshocton, last Ohio, then Pennsylvania, then the train to New York, then "No casting, come back in August."

**SELWYN AND CO.**
**NEW CASTLE**
**LAST PERFORMANCE**

The house was full, but not good laughers.

*"Last* act," called John. Usually he called, "Act Three." The night a show closes, it's *"Last* act."

The last curtain came down, not much applause, we took one bow and the curtain stayed down.

"They didn't believe a word of it," said Billy. "Don't send out your laundry."

"Why would I? We closed."

"It's what they say when the show folds, darlin', a saying like 'Don't whistle in the dressing room.' *Don't,* even if New York actors tell you it's guff; you listen to your Uncle Dudley."

"Costumes ready?" John was collecting the wardrobe.

I handed him my Act I evening gown and my Act II and Act III negligees. In the tray of my trunk I put the hotel towels over my makeup mirror, packed my own silver bodice. Where was it? I just took it off. Took it off, hung it up, put on my dressing gown, where was it? Goodbye, silver bodice; it closed in New Castle, Pa., with the play.

The tag on my Taylor trunk said:

Miss Ruth Gordon
Hotel Richmond
70 West 46th Street
New York

# Chapter

————⋯⟨∞⟩⋯————

# 2

In my blue crocheted boodle bag I had four hundred dollars. At the Richmond my room was twelve dollars and twenty-five cents a week. The window that looked toward Fifth Avenue over the Deauville Hotel roof also looked at the bathroom window of the room next to mine. A man who occupied the room for a few nights wrote messages on the end of a roll of toilet paper, unrolled it enough to let it fly into my window.

Pull the window down and draw the shade. Rise above it. If I'd wanted everything proper I wouldn't have left 14 Elmwood Avenue. Forget trifles and hope *this* time I could stay. Wouldn't a leading lady get a job?

Nothing at Selwyn and Company.

Nothing at Cohan and Harris.

Nothing at Al Woods.

Nothing at Packard's Agency.

Nothing at George C. Tyler.

Nothing at Smith and Golden.

Nothing at Will Harris.

Someday they'd say, "Come right in and sign; you're just the type."

Until then, write to Katherine Follett how great I was doing. The paper, white linen folded over and engraved in dark blue. And the address:

HOTEL RICHMOND

70 WEST 46TH STREET

NEW YORK

E. B. SEAMAN

PRESIDENT

*Saturday, May 9, 1917*

Dear Katherine,

Thank goodness *Fair and Warmer* closed so I could get to New York in time for the Papa Joffre celebration! Terrible if the show kept playing and I missed *that!*

Why tell the truth unless it's good?

The Avenue looked simply wonderful with all the Allies' flags and in front of the Public Library at 42nd Street a stately Arc de Triomphe.

Why don't you run over here and visit that rich friend of your mother's? Or that actress Bessie Valentine I never heard of? Maybe she has an apartment. If she's still with the Sothern and Marlowe Company they lay off for the summer. It would be great if you came over. Everybody is here. Last night I went to the most fascinating home, the sister of the first Mrs. Marshall Field gave this dinner. She is also the aunt of Admiral and Lady Beatty of England and the dinner was in honor of Sir Cecil Spring-Rice. It was wonderful to hear first hand what they are doing over the water.

Some days you have to lie. Getting turned down gets discouraging. NO CASTING on the Cohan and Harris door. "Nothing until July," said Oliver Morosco. Nobody casting, nobody inviting me anywhere, so why not invite myself?

I've been working hard at the Stage Women's War Relief and also for the Actors Fund Fair where I was asked to sell tickets at the Fulton Theatre. Quite an honor!

They asked Violet Heming, Lola Fisher, Phoebe Foster, but who does it hurt to move things up a few years? Eventually they asked me.

I've got a crush on New Yorky clothes, so I indulged myself at Franklin Simon's and who do you think I saw? Billie Burke! I guess you wonder if I can afford to go where she goes! Well, I'm extravagant and I bought the most adorable lid, black Milan straw trimmed with a black ostrich tip. You'll adore it. *Try* and come over. Newell Vaughn left two weeks ago with the Princeton unit to drive ambulances in France. Isn't it dreadful everyone enlisting? Newell looked very cute. He could be crazy about me, but I'm only interested in Jack Morgan. He and his brother Percy are in the aero fleet. Percy is quiet, but Jack is a smash. I'm glad Clift Cornwall is at Fort Myers, Washington, in the Officer's Reserve Corps, so I don't have to explain him. The richest boy in Chicago, Jack Wentworth, is accepted for aero service. Mr. Saint-Gaudens, that gave me my job in *Peter Pan*—I adore him—went to Plattsburg. Vive l'Amerique! Who are you crazy about? Write me. And Katherine, do something for me. In Boston, go to the Cort Theatre box office and say, "Is this the company of *Fair and Warmer* Ruth Gordon is with?" Then write and tell me what they say. About a hundred boys at Harvard did it and lots of Jack Morgan's friends at Yale. It'll mean a great piece of advertising for me with the Selwyn office. Do it and ask anyone you know to. If they haven't time, they can phone, but better to ask. Write the results, dear.

Love,<br>Ruth

Mornings I heated water on my Sterno, stirred G. Washington coffee into a tumbler, spooned in some evaporated milk, ate a sweet bun. After breakfast did my washing, hung it on the towel rack, dressed and went job-hunting. Someone said Miss Clarens was at the Richmond, but I hadn't seen her. Grace Hayle was at the Hotel Van Cortlandt on 49th Street, but when I called she was always going out with Sandy. Gretchen was with her family in New Jersey, Billy went to Kalamazoo till casting picked up. Maybe go over to the library for books?

In the lobby a stout gray-haired lady spoke to me. "Are you new?" asked Anna Wheaton's mother. Anna Wheaton was the Hotel Richmond's celebrity, star of *Oh Boy* at the Princess Theatre, and I was talking with her mother!

"I was here last year. I just closed on tour."

"What were you out with?"

*"Fair and Warmer."*

"With Madge Kennedy?"

"Oh, no. I played her part. Madge Kennedy plays the first company, Francine Larrimore the second, then me." Did she believe me?

"I'll let you meet my daughter, Anna Wheaton." Does a star's mother get lonely too? "We have a beautiful suite on the sixth floor. Where're you?"

"I'm on the ninth."

"What number?"

"Ninety-one."

"Does it clear the Deauville roof?"

"Oh, I can see Fifth Avenue."

"Did you have dinner?"

"No."

"I have mine around at the Rotisserie. Want to go Dutch treat?"

We walked around the corner to Sixth Avenue.

"Don't put me by the door. My daughter, Anna Wheaton, in *Oh Boy,* says for me to not get put in a draft."

"How about a nice table the back?"

"Where the waiter comes out? Don't think I'm fussy—it's my daughter."

"How's this?"

"When my daughter comes, you can put us where she can be noticed. Pay *her* the attention; I like to eat dinner like anybody."

An old waiter came over. "Now, ladies."

"I take chicken white meat. And separate checks. My doctor tells me white meat only. And a little extra butter."

"Certainly! *Cer*tainly! Young lady?"

"Chicken dark meat."

"Dark meat, gravy."

Chickens dripped and turned on the spit and got browner.

"I had a piece of fish for lunch. Fish make you thirsty?" Mrs. Wheaton took a big drink of water. "I went with Anna, she ordered a lot of shoes. 'Send a bill,' I told Carcion and Manfré, 'before you cut into anything.' A name like Anna they rook. They all pay her attention like you'd think they didn't have a thing else to do."

The waiter was back with the order.

"You *sure* that's all white meat, because I don't come back places I get stung!" She poked around with her fork. "You're right."

"You like anything, ladies, sing out."

Mrs. Wheaton put a piece of bread in the gravy. "It upsets Anna, but nobody comes here and I like it. My dinner comes to fifty cents if they don't stick me for the extra butter. Your dark meat's forty, we'll give him a quarter tip."

Anna was friendly, but too successful to sit around with us. In their sitting room with the blue velvet furniture I felt close to success. Tossed around were Anna's beautiful, expensive things.

"Don't talk to me about clothes; Anna's been buying all afternoon."

34

Enjoyable just to hear about it.

"At Harry Collins, no less! His things would look good on you. Well, your day will come. Harry Collins paid her attention till you'd swear he didn't have a thing to do and he's bigger than Hickson's or Giddings or Lucille. That's what Irene Castle told Anna. Did I tell you she and Vernon came to see the show? I haven't got any feet left; want to go to the Rotisserie or Mr. Kelly's Tea Room?"

"Which would you?"

"Did I take my lithia tablet? Mrs. Kelly talks to me; we'll go to the Rotisserie. Lock that window on the fire escape; Anna left her star sapphire right in sight of the night maid! It was the night maid pointed it out to me. On the bureau! With all her success, she's unspoiled. Did I tell you I went with her to the doctor? 'Mrs. Wheaton,' he said, 'you can be proud, she's a sweet little virgin,' so I don't like to be hard on her. Last night she was out with Will Stewart. William Rhinelander Stewart, no less. Oh, she made me laugh! Coming up Fifth Avenue, they got out of Will's limousine and played leapfrog over fireplugs. *Millions* he has, and his mother way up the ladder, but Anna treats him like anybody. They all love her, you should hear Jerry Kern! Is today Friday?"

"Friday."

"Pay night." She sat on the blue velvet couch by the phone. "Hello, dear, get me Miss Wheaton's theatre. . . . Oh, you're new. Well, that's all right, I'm Anna Wheaton's mother, Mrs. Wheaton. . . . I *thought* you'd get a thrill. Did you see it? . . . It's sold out, but I won't forget you when and if . . . Yes, get the Princess Theatre . . ." She turned to me. "Lovely girl on the switchboard, we'll talk to her after dinner. Hello, Princess, let me talk to Jimmy. . . ." She put her hand over the phone. "Unless I remind her, Anna'd leave her pay envelope on her makeup shelf for the cleaning woman to walk off with." Her hand came off the phone. "Jim, darlin', tell Anna before she goes anywhere after the show to bring home she-knows-what." She rang off. "I have all her money here." A beaded black velvet bag hung from her arm. "A bank could fail. Did I tell you Fred Almey proposed again? For that box of orchids he leaves the standing order for at Thorley's, you and I could eat dinner at the Rotisserie and Mr. Kelly's Tea Room *and* pay the rent. Oil gushing in Texas somewhere, so what's he care what twenty orchids cost? For Anna he's a big lovable shaggy-dog hick. 'Don't tell *me*, Fred,' I tell him, but they like to. Yesterday Eddie-on-the-elevator brought me up twenty-five pounds of Maillard's chocolates Courtney Burr sent me. I could've been sick if Adelaide, my oldest daughter—you met her—didn't take it home. Ready?"

June changed to July. In Wollaston we'd take our lunch to Wollaston Beach, have a swim, have a clambake if we waited till the tide went out. At the Richmond I washed, pressed, read, went the rounds, wrote letters, and at night I went to see a play if the manager honored my professional card.

RUTH GORDON
Charles Frohman Management
*Peter Pan*
*The Little Minister*

I'd had fifty printed in Old English lettering and there were a lot left over. After *Fair and Warmer* I didn't order any new ones.

"Do you honor the profession?" If the show wasn't a hit the company manager wrote "Pass Two" on my card and I gave it to the box office man, who punched holes in a ticket, and the usher seated me far back, on the side.

When Mrs. Wheaton wanted to go, Anna told somebody to tell somebody and two passes were at the box office.

"Do you mind the first balcony?" asked Mrs. Wheaton, not sure whether *she* did. "The New Amsterdam you think you'll fall over, but the Casino you don't. Anna's got me passes to *The Blue Paradise,* with Vivienne Segal. She's had a hard time! *Beautiful* voice, but not popular like Anna's, it's good for operetta. Well, some people like that. Her mother says Vivienne's lovely to her." Mrs. Wheaton held her program up like a screen. "If you don't like the show, don't say so; we may be sitting next to Shuberts' cousins."

Saturdays nobody honored the profession. Even in summer, even if they didn't sell out, even if they were closing. Another bad thing about Saturday is the offices are closed. Saturday in Wollaston you plan what to wear to the lawn party, the clambake, the fair, the trip to Paragon Park, but at the Richmond you feel lost. A bus ride costs ten cents, a walk wears out shoes, so about all that's free is the Public Library.

The elevator's metal basket cage creaked slowly down. "Mrs. W.'s gone out," said Eddie.

"Yes."

"Up to her older daughter's. Everybody's going out; I didn't have time to do anything." He looked at a tray on the floor piled with stained coffee cups, a pitcher of dirty cream, sugar. The elevator creaked to a stop in the lobby. Warm weather made it smell of cabbage and nothing happening.

Out on 46th Street, but which way? Left to Sixth Avenue? Maybe right? On the corner of Fifth Avenue Dreicer's window featured tiaras. Would a manager notice me if I wore one? Stroll in. Not too interesting, but didn't cost anything. Velvet-lined cases glittered, walnut walls softened the shine, a white-haired man studied a string of pearls. For his wife? For someone he kept? How does that get arranged? If he offered me an apartment with a maid and dresses from Harry Collins, would I? Would he smell like eau de Cologne? Would he say when he's going to visit or would I have to be ready all the time? And after, does he get up and get dressed like the maid says Mr. Tyler does when he stays in Miss Clarens' room at the Richmond?

The clerk wrote down where to send the pearls.

The white-haired man's elegant walking stick was like a decoration as he walked down Fifth Avenue with the air of one who owned it. At Sherry's, the doorman bowed and he went in. If he was keeping me, I'd go in too.

Sherry's was on the downtown west-side corner at 44th Street. The downtown west-side corner at 42nd is the Public Library. What a difference! Sherry's doorman bowed, the librarian scowled. Did being homely make her frown? Why did the place smell like rubbers? Why were rubbers better than eau de Cologne?

Take the volume with *A Doll's House, Little Eyolf, Hedda Gabler,* take *Salome* by Oscar Wilde. A library card allows five nonfiction and why does nonfiction include plays? Take *L'Aiglon.* Maude Adams acted that. Sciotto's *Voice Culture?* Maybe *Theatre* magazine?

HOTEL RICHMOND
70 WEST 46TH STREET
NEW YORK
E. B. SEAMAN
PRESIDENT

*Saturday, July 16, 1917*

Dear Katherine,
    Don't faint, but somebody white-haired has fallen for me. I don't know how far I'll let him go.

What's so great about looking out the window at the Deauville roof?

> Katherine, I know you're broad-minded so probably all you're thinking is "White-haired?" Tonight he's taking me to the Follies and afterward to the Frolic and I don't need to ask you, dear, could Fred Atwood do that? Or Fred Shenkelberger? Or Fred Rollins? And, of course, evening dress! I may or may not accept his proposition, but if I do, it will be on *my* terms. Some of us are sweet little virgins and some of us may not want to be, so put *that* in your pipe and smoke it!
>
> Love,<br>Ruth
>
> P.S. Tell everyone I'm popular.
>
> R.

At Packard's Theatrical Agency, Miss Mason was nice. "Nothin' today, *dear*," she said, but she said it nicely.

Even Miss Humbert, the head of Packard's, went out of her way. "Come in." She motioned me through the wooden gate.

Was this my chance? I'd played the lead in *Fair and Warmer*, but a lot of ingénues had. Red-haired Zaina Curzon opened with our company, then left. Grace said the rich man who was keeping her got the Selwyns to send her on the road so she'd get sick of acting and she did. She or the rich man paid her fare back to New York *and* her sister's, who toured with her as chaperone, *and* dark-haired Nesta de Becker's, who replaced her. Then Nesta got replaced by me.

"Just wanted to see what you look like," said businesslike Miss Humbert, and I was out through the wooden gate again. Probably it would lead to something. Try Chamberlain Brown and brother Lyman?

"Nothing."

Mr. Seymour in the late Charles Frohman's office?

"Busy."

Selwyn and Co.?

"Mr. Klauber's not seeing anyone."

At the Longacre they were casting for William Collier's road tour. "You can read for the part."

I did.

"Thank you," they said, and didn't call back.

The Shuberts?

Only musicals.

Mr. Winthrop Ames?

"No plans." Miss Helen Ingersoll guarded his Little Theatre office.

"Is Mr. Ames casting?"

"No."

"Would you let me know when he is? I'm at the Hotel Richmond."

Try the Lyceum.

"Mr. Daniel Frohman doesn't produce anymore."

Second floor at the New Amsterdam, Mr. George Tyler?

"Out of town."

Mrs. Wheaton, sitting in the Richmond lobby, didn't take up time with "Hello" or "How are you?" She was old and came to the point. "You can go with me Sunday. Anna has to be at her producer's, Ray Comstock, for the weekend, she hates the country and told Bert to drive me to get her after breakfast Sunday afternoon. Ray might take a shine to you, put you in a show. Far Rockaway's his summer place and you'll get seen, everybody'll be there, they're crazy to get with Comstock, Elliott and Gest. Morris Gest is different, more Russian, but Billy Elliott the girls go crazy over. In *Madame X* he played Dorothy Donnelly's son and stole the show and is a star, but doesn't like to be, so he and Ray and Morris Gest formed their company and the first show, *Very Good Eddie,* at the Princess, ran forever, but *Oh Boy* they tell me will do bigger."

Except for Maude Adams and Billie Burke, it was the first time I saw actors I'd seen on the stage. Broadway's most beautiful chorus girl, Justine Johnstone, blond, dazzling, careful to stay in the shade, was talking to Anna and Billy Elliott. They looked sick of the country.

"Introduce Ruth to Ray, Anna."

Anna's clear, loud voice called out, "Ray, here's someone could play Marie Carroll's part when you send out the road company."

Ray Comstock came over. The two producers I'd seen, Winthrop Ames and Archie Selwyn, looked important. Ray Comstock looked small and thin and glad that Anna wanted to talk to him.

"How do you do, Mr. Comstock."

"Just say 'Hello,' " said Anna. " 'How do you do' they say in Podunk."

"Hello," I said.

Ray Comstock laughed. "Do you always take direction?"

"Hello," I said again.

Ray Comstock looked me over. "Have you seen the show?"

"Anna ought to tell *you* what to say! Didn't you know *nobody* can get in, Mr. Comstock?"

"*I* can."

"We could come tomorrow," said Mrs. Wheaton.

Did you ever see a Princess show? Music by Jerry Kern, just what you wanted to hear, lyrics by P. G. Wodehouse that were smart and funny and what you'd say if you could. Only six chorus girls, but each one was the toast of the town. Justine Johnstone! Marion Davies! Whoever was pretty, *they* were prettier.

Knocking your eye out was Anna, Marie Carroll, Hal Forde, Tom Powers, plus Edna May Oliver to make you laugh, and in the second act, when someone turned over a sofa, Dorothy Dickson and Carl Hyson rolled off and went into their dance! All the dresses by Lucille, in private life Lady Duff-Gordon; if you couldn't afford one, you copied it.

> "When it's nesting time in Flatbush [sang Anna],
> We will have a little flat
> With a welcome on the mat
> Where there's room to swing a cat . . ."

Not pretty like pretty people, but vital and sexy and chic as a *Vogue* drawing, with a figure that anything looked great on. The dresses by Lucille looked twice as great.

> "At the *opera,*
> I *go* with Freddie.
> To a mus-*i*-cal show,
> I *go* with Joe.
> I golf with Dick and Ned.
> And *dance* with
> Tom and Ted.
> And at the *races*
> And other lively places . . ."

When Anna sang it, nobody doubted she did all that, nobody doubted she had all those beaux. What a show! What an evening! I certainly *would* be right for the Marie Carroll part!

> "I want to be
> A good little wife
> In the good,
> *Old*-fashioned way . . ."

Marie Carroll looked like a Quincy Mansion School girl, ladylike, brown hair, small, everything just right and as though it always had been.

"You'd be good," said Mrs. Wheaton.

Under my door, a letter from Papa. "I'll dock Thursday morning on the Fall River Line. I won't get in the way of job-hunting, but you have to stop for dinner. Leave word at the Hotel Calvert, West 41st off Broadway, what time you want it and I'll be downstairs in your hotel."

He waited by the elevator, looking out of place.

"Stand off and let me look at you."

The only place he didn't look out of place was on a ship. Was he sorry he gave up the sea for married life?

Eddie and the clerk stared at him.

"You look good. I'll let you navigate."

"Did you ever go to a rotisserie?" Mrs. Wheaton was having dinner at her daughter Kitty's, so we wouldn't run into her.

"Lead the way. Nobody cooks like your mother and I don't expect they will. Your mother was unmatched among women—*remember* that, Ruth. Do you hear from Wollaston? I guess the boys you know are in the war."

"A lot come through here and call me up." *Would* Ray Comstock call up? Would I get the Marie Carroll part? "Fred Atwood did and Loyal Safford and Fred Shenkelberger." Could I sing as well as Marie Carroll? I could dance as well. Didn't I in *Peter Pan?*

"This war's an awful thing."

"Oh, it hasn't meant any change for me."

Papa put down the French bread he was buttering. The blue eyes that had searched so many seas searched *me.* "I hope that isn't so."

"Sure it is. I don't let it touch me."

"I don't believe that, daughter." Once a nonbeliever, always a nonbeliever.

The waiter put the check in front of Papa. He left ten cents.

I felt embarrassed. "Is that enough?"

"It's enough to show I know tipping's no good, a man's employer should pay him. Money's not a favor. You earn it or you don't."

When his back was turned I added fifteen cents. Theories are for people who don't get that waiter the next night.

"You getting along? Your four hundred holding out? You didn't write where you keep it."

"I hide it." We strolled over to Broadway.

"Use it too, I guess."

"I don't waste it. All I bought on the road was a coat. When I joined the company I was wearing Mrs. Parssons'."

Papa stopped short. "You didn't have a coat?"

"Only my old navy blue from school that made me look like a hick."

We turned up Broadway. The shops were open, lots of windows with bright lights.

"I'll buy you a dress."

"Oh, I don't need anything."

"I'd like to; it's been a long time since I bought a lady something. I regret I couldn't do for your mother. Your mother was a fine woman, Ruth." He stopped in front of an open door. "How does in here strike you?"

"I honestly don't need anything."

He led the way. "We're looking for a dress for my daughter."

"Oh, we have lovely ones." Both saleswomen took charge.

Papa didn't take to them. "Slow down. We're going to buy."

I picked out a navy blue. "Do you like this?" It was wool with satin sleeves and yoke, across the waist red and blue embroidery.

Papa nodded. "How much is that?"

"Only fifteen dollars."

"Will you take a check?"

"You bet! You got an honest face."

Papa took two bills out of his billfold. "I didn't come in to be insulted."

"I didn't mean—"

"Trot it out."

She handed him the box. "You got a lovely father, dear."

We walked down to 42nd Street and around the Times building. Three blocks farther, at the Princess, would they give me a chance?

"I'm taking the Fall River boat tomorrow."

"It was great to see you and thanks for my beautiful dress." How could I jabber away to Mrs. Wheaton and Billy Dorbin and Gretchen and Grace and find it hard to know something to say to Papa?

"Any chance of you coming my way?"

"I have to get a job, Papa."

42

"When you get through punishing yourself, you and I can set up a home. This hotel don't strike me as anything you'd miss. Fourth of July I took a bunch of carnations over to Mama. I wrote, 'From us.' Your mother was a fine woman, Ruth." He hugged me and went.

Eddie sat beside the elevator. "Mrs. Wheaton says to call her."

"Princess Theatre tomorrow at four; they'll hear you sing."

When Schirmer's music store opened I was waiting. " 'I Want to Be a Good Little Wife,' please."

Telephone the Three Arts Club. "Three Arts Club, does Valerie Deuscher still live at 85th and West End Avenue?"

"Endicott 1973."

Did I phone Papa at the Hotel Calvert?

"Val, this is Ruth. . . . Val, I've got an audition this afternoon at the Princess Theatre, they want me to play Marie Carroll's part in the Chicago company, can you show me how to sing 'I Want to Be a Good Little Wife'?"

Up at 85th and West End, singing, breathing, listening to Valerie, then, "Once again."

Down on West 39th the crowd at the stage door spilled into the alley.

"Tell them you're Anna Wheaton's friend." Valerie had come along to drill me up to the last minute. "Say you have an appointment arranged by Anna Wheaton."

"I *can't.*"

"You're *supposed* to; you have a four o'clock appointment. *Announce* yourself."

Terror had set in. "If I see Mr. Comstock I will."

"Please let us pass," said Valerie to a couple ahead. "We have an appointment."

"Don't we all!"

Valerie looked at her watch. "I'm giving a lesson at five. Remember where I marked to breathe."

Valerie Deuscher was a successful concert harpist who also knew about singing and being a friend. "You'll do it," she said, and went.

Was everybody scared?

"Is Ruth Gordon there?" called a voice.

My heart went faster. "Yes." Tough with Papa and *now* was when to be.

"Let her through." A young man guided me up the flight of iron stairs onto the stage. Who was sitting there? Was Ray Comstock?

The young man was speaking. "Anna wants you to meet Jerry Kern."
He led me to a gentle-looking man. "Mr. Kern, this is Ruth Gordon that
Anna spoke to you about."

He gave my hand a gentle squeeze. "We'll hear this young lady next,"
he told the man at the piano, and led me over, then looked at me gently.
"What will you sing, dear?"

" 'A Good Little Wife.' " Was that sound *my* voice?

"What key?" asked the man at the piano.

"The same as the sheet music." Back of my new dress, my hands
trembled out of sight.

"Are you ready, dear?" asked Jerome Kern.

I nodded. Where was my courage? Where was my confidence? Hadn't
I played the lead in *Fair and Warmer? Some* of the notices were good.
Didn't Billy Dorbin say I'd improved?

*"Louder,"* I told myself. It still came out weak.

"Thank you," said Jerome Kern. "You have a sweet voice, but not
strong. You'll need more experience. Thank you for coming, dear. It was
nice to meet you."

"Next!" shouted the young man who had guided me to opportunity.
In show business there are no goodbyes; you make it or they say "Thank
you" and "Next." On the iron stairs the crowd was bigger. Would *they*
all hear "Next"?

Down the North River the Fall River boat was getting ready to leave.
I didn't call Papa, but I did wear his dress. Was it retribution to knock
out a believer?

"Jerry Kern told Anna you need experience," said Mrs. Wheaton.
"Even with know-how, a musical's hard. That's why they pay Anna all
those hundreds of dollars and go crazy over her."

People were signing for road companies, no one said would I go?
Nobody said to come back. Sundays nobody said anything. Make
coffee, eat a sweet roll, read the *Times* theatre section, where *everyone* is
doing well.

"Can I do your room?" asked Nelly.

"Come in."

"Eat your food and read, I'll be out in a minute; Sunday I don't
sweep."

She made the bed, hung two towels, emptied the wastebasket into the
big one she kept with her. "Anything more, dear?"

"No, thanks." I gave her a quarter for the week.

"Oh, thank you. I'll see who's up. Maybe Mr. Fred Tyler; he's the room below. 'Don't Disturb' is on *her* suite till noon, but sometimes he goes out of there early. He's nice, tips well. Well, I'll go chase myself out of here."

"See you tomorrow." The door closed.

The door flew open. It was Nelly, white as the towel over her arm. "He shot himself."

"What?"

"Sitting on the toilet, he shot himself."

"Who did?"

"Mr. Fred Tyler. Dead on the bathroom floor, bills all round him. All over the floor."

Mr. Tyler! Rich and fashionable and a somebody. In *Peter Pan* he'd played Smee, and fought us Lost Boys on the pirate ship. Had acted how many years with Miss Adams? Should I call up Miss Clarens? I called Angela Ogden and she called the Maude Adams Company.

All Sunday they came in and out of the Richmond lobby. Last summer we'd said goodbye on the train from Springfield, Illinois; now they were in the Hotel Richmond lobby because life had gotten to be too much for Mr. Tyler.

When *does* it? Can it be *just* bills? Can it be no casting? Can it be a wife on Shelter Island and Miss Clarens in a suite at the Richmond? Bills all over the bathroom.

"Poor everybody," says Leonora Hornblow. "Poor everybody."

My only bill was for the current week. At the Richmond you paid weekly or got out. The owner, Mr. Egbert Seaman, was thin and cold and stylish and didn't run a hotel for his health. Twelve dollars and fifty-five cents was all I owed, but my blue crocheted bag was getting flat.

West on 45th Street, back to Martin's Theatrical. Martin's might be lucky for me; it was where I got *Fair and Warmer*.

"When do you want to move in?" asked Molly, who could answer most questions and at the same time run the switchboard. "Mr. Martin's asleep and Mrs. is somewhere."

"Tomorrow?"

"Shoot yourself."

"What?"

"Short for 'Suit yourself.' Hall bedroom, second floor front, in two-thirty-one."

The dinner gong thonged at six o'clock. In hot weather nobody dressed except for meals and job-hunting. A wrapper if the door was open, or hotel towels from the road. A petticoat meant extra washing, but I had to slip one on under my rotten-looking light blue voile from Stern Brothers' dollar counter. "Poor everybody."

"They said you were back." Mrs. Bryant, who was a permanent boarder, was already seated at her table.

Mr. Bryant said a silent hello. He played background to his wife.

"Minnie said you're at my table." Her seat was next to the 45th Street basement window. Outside, skirts and trousers passed. Mr. Bryant sat to one side of her, I the other.

"Three people more tonight," announced Minnie, and rattled ice in the pitcher. "Sound cool?"

Mrs. Bryant held up her glass. "Fill it to the top; I don't want any half a glassful. Who's the three?"

"Edna Hibbard an' her mother an' feller."

"Edna back! Well, well, well! *Don't* give me soup, Minnie, unless it's cold soup. Is it?"

"Hot."

"Mrs. Martin must figure it's a good night to save on soup."

"I'll have some," apologized Mr. Bryant.

His wife leaned back and stared at him. "You must have a hide like asbestos! How can you eat hot soup? Minnie, Mr. Bryant's a mystery."

"None for me," I said.

Mrs. Bryant took over. *"Now.* What are you going to give us nice?"

"Cold salmon salad or beef loaf."

Mrs. Bryant looked aghast. "Beef loaf a night like this! If I told my daughter, Mrs. Budlong, I was eating beef loaf this weather, I *doubt* if she'd believe me."

"Beef loaf," Mr. Bryant interjected as though maybe it wouldn't be noticed.

"Oh, I don't want to even listen to him! Salmon salad, Minnie. Canned, I suppose?"

"Uh huh, but not the cat's."

"Well, thank God for small favors! Ice tea, not too strong. My daughter's having it out on her veranda on the Cliff Drive at Newport. When people *here* eat beef loaf it's teatime for Newport."

Mr. Bryant's face wore an expression that hoped it wouldn't look like an expression.

"Salmon salad and ice coffee," I told Minnie. She ambled off.

"Wonder who Edna's feller is this season? Was she here when *you* were?"

"No, but I know who she is. She's been playing the lead in the Coast company of *Fair and Warmer."*

"Did you hear she had a baby?"

"How *could* she? Her company just closed."

"Oh, that wouldn't trouble Edna. I wonder would this be the father?"

Minnie put a bowl of tomato soup in front of Mr. Bryant. "Lady of the house feel like salmon now or when *he?"*

"Now."

Minnie moved leisurely away.

"Edna got married *once,* but it didn't amount to anything. She's got a little boy she could've palmed off on her husband, but she didn't. Little boy lives with her aunt in Detroit, or *is* it? It's out West somewhere and maybe not even her aunt. With Edna you never know. Mrs. Hibbard showed me his picture. Nice little chap; looks like Edna."

"But how could she have a baby and play *Fair and Warmer?"*

"Leave it to Edna. I'll be glad to see her—I always love what she wears. Her mother can do anything with a needle and travels right with her, of course. *Very* refined, *very* lovely and seems not to know what's going on." She stopped and listened. "Edna?"

"Hi."

An enchanting-looking girl came down the stairs. Behind her, a young-looking, white-haired, pretty lady. "Nice to see you back, Mrs. Hibbard." Mrs. Bryant and Edna kissed.

"Harlan, this is Mrs. Bryant. Oh, hello, Mr. Bryant. This is Harlan Tucker."

Would Martin's Theatrical dining room floor open and let me disappear?

Mrs. Bryant pointed at me. "This is Ruth Gordon." She leaned over to Harlan. "What did you say your name was?"

"Hi," said Harlan. "We know each other."

"Oh, hello." Did I sound casual?

Edna gently bit his ear.

"We were in dramatic school," I said, lamely. I'd never seen a girl bite a fellow's ear. Had it been only two years since Marian Gray said, "You know who's mashed on you? Harlan Tucker. I have to talk to you; come home to lunch."

The American Academy of Dramatic Arts speech teacher looked up from his book. "If you are not too engaged, Miss Gordon, let us hear *you* read."

Why blush? Was it because I wasn't doing well?

" 'I wandered lonely as a cloud—' "

"To say the letter *o,* purse your lips," said Mr. Putnam. "Think of roundness. We will start with you tomorrow, Miss Gordon. Note my *o* in tomorrow. Not tamarrer. Class dismissed. Good morning. Not marning."

Marian Gray put her arm around me. "Who cares about stuff like that?" For *her,* dramatic art meant a New York winter and meet a young man with prospects. "If I talked the way Putnam says, I'd lose every beau." Until she met the one with prospects, she practiced on future discards. "Thursday is the big ball at the Park Hill Country Club. Daddy's a member. This one's an Advertising Ball, where you get samples of everything. It's in the spiffy part of Yonkers, a half hour on the el."

In the old-fashioned white-woodwork lobby of the Wellington Hotel sat a few residents, looking.

"Any mail for me?" Marian smiled at the desk clerk.

"Your mother took it up, you pretty thing."

Marian laughed. She looked prettier when she did; it was good practice. She gave the elevator boy a sweet look. "Feel like taking me up, Georgie?"

"You're the only one I do feel like."

"Aw, don't let this place get your goat!" For practice she squeezed his arm.

In front of a door, midway down the white-woodwork hall, she stopped. "Yoo-hoo, Mama, it's a burglar," then she whispered to me, "Don't tell I squeezed Georgie's arm."

Mrs. Gray opened the door.

"This is Ruth from school, Mama."

"Come in, dear. I got lovely sliced ham from Sam's across the street."

"Mama, the whole last hour my stomach kept rumbling."

"Ruth, would you say a thing like that? I've got buttered toast and heavy cream for the coffee."

"At The Three Arts Club we have *blue* cream—it's revolting."

"Why, what's blue cream?"

"Milk they skim the cream off for Miss Seaborn's coffee. She's the director and someday I'm going to have my banker put money aside so

48

Sundays the girls get thick yellow gobby cream you have to coax out of the bottle with a fork."

"Don't you love to hear her talk, Ma? She's coming to the Advertising Ball with us. Ma, this is kind of private."

"I'm not listening. I'm carrying dishes in the bathroom."

"Ta ta." Marian lowered her voice. "Tucker told Johnson he's mashed on you. You know I'm playing around with Johnson."

Tucker was the stunningest boy at the Academy. What a piece of news! Act as if it was nothing. I took a *long* swallow of coffee. "What did he say?"

"Loves to watch you go up the steps on the platform, says when your skirt slides up he sees your adorable legs. Hicks, his roommate, says so too. They share a room with Oscar Johnson up on Columbus Avenue and are going to the ball with us. Oscar's taking me." She winked. "It's not serious, but he certainly knows what to do with a girl." She winked again. "I mean if a girl knows what to do with *him!*"

"My dear!"

"Hey, are you *really* innocent or is it just put on?"

"Put on."

"That's what *I* said! Hicks hasn't asked anybody so he'll take you, because Harlan's got Ethel Remey on his hands. He *asked* her a month ago, but now he'd like to go with *you.*"

"My dear!"

"Of course, he *has* to go with Ethel, but he's *pash* about you."

"But if he's with *her?*"

"Hicks'll bring you, then Tucker'll show how mashed he is except for the darn first and last dance, when Hicksie boy will snuggle *you!*"

I wasn't doing well in class, but the stunningest boy in the whole school felt pash! *"When* is it?"

"Thursday. Meet at six, the el platform; evening clothes, of course— it's a formal ball. Ma'll give you a note to The Three Arts Club. We'll get back later than midnight, but she'll chaperone us. Want to see my dress?" She laughed and jumped up. "I'll put it on. Mama, we're closing my door. We have to rehearse a scene."

"Not loud; they made a fuss at the desk."

"We won't." The door to Marian's room slammed. "Tucker says when you were doing your scene yesterday from *Outcast* and you were taking off your— Look, you're blushing! Oh, *show* me how! It's a great tease."

49

Thursday! I scrubbed out the fifth-floor bathtub and let hot water trickle. The Three Arts Club water didn't run.

"Dog, you've got flowers," shouted Louise Davidson through the bathroom door. "Want 'em in the tub?"

"In my room, dog."

From Harlan or Hicks?

Back to my room, wrapped in my lavender-flowered kimono Mrs. Wetmore had given Mama and Mama had given me, towel, soap dish and washcloth in hand. Louise Davidson breezed down the hall. "Why the bath, dog?"

"Going to a ball at Park Hill, dog."

"Pee-*oo!* Wish I was. What you going to wear?"

"White net with the Dresden sash."

"Pee-*oo!* Hear about it tomorrow."

On the gray seersucker bedspread were pink rosebuds and forget-me-nots with a paper lace frill and long pink ribbon streamers. "Looking forward to tonight. Hicks."

A man's man, but knew how to charm a girl.

"Anybody home?" The door flew open. Dotty Forbes pointed to the flowers. "From Miles Standish or *Truly*-loves?"

"Miles Standish. His name is Hicks."

"Hicks what?"

"Just Hicks."

"Everybody else has two names."

"He's different."

"Think you might get wild about him?"

"He's sort of stately." We hugged each other. Why?

Over my shoulder, Dotty saw white kid slippers I'd taken out of their tissue paper. "Why graduation day? Wear my gold satin." She rushed out and back. "From Slater's!" The toes were like daggers, heels really oo-la-la.

"What if someone steps on them?"

"If True-love is so pash, *he* won't, and why would Hicks if he's stately?" Into each other's arms again.

"My overshoes'll get them dirty."

"Take my carriage boots, slob!" She was out and back with gray velvet carriage boots edged with squirrel.

"Tomorrow, remind me to send for mine." If you haven't got carriage boots, next best is say you have.

White net graduation dress slid over my head, wriggled into place. "Dresden sash or not?"

"Not."

"One Hicks downstairs," called manly Vera.

"Be right down." Carriage boots over Slater's gold slippers. "Hand me my coat."

Dotty looked in the closet, then rushed out and in. A rose broadcloth evening coat with a squirrel collar was around me. "Hurry up. Hicks'll be carted off—Denise is on her way down."

We rocked with laughter, hugged. Denise was operatic and wore amber beads.

"Hicksie isn't going to be a man's man much longer! Bring me home a menu. I'm starving, but I can't face another brown betty."

Everything lovely, then one month later, Louise Davidson called down the hall, "Harlan Tucker's downstairs, dog."

"Thanks, dog."

Why couldn't I hold on to him? The Advertising Ball had been great, the night he took me to see *Milestones* great, then a terrible cold and when it was over, so was Harlan Tucker. Should I call down I had another? Wasn't he getting rid of me the way he got rid of Ethel? Now he was crazy about light-yellow-haired Miss Annette de Willoughby.

Slouched into the giant's chair in the hall, he looked stunning. "We'll meet Hicks and Johnson and Marian at the el." He rushed me out the door.

*"And* Miss de Willoughby?" I didn't say out loud.

Marian and the expert Johnson and Mrs. Gray looked out the waiting room window.

Hicks came running up the el stairs with Miss Yellow Hair. Did Ethel feel sorry when she saw *me* run up those stairs? Did *I* feel sorry now? Tucker was stunning and could go to hell! Right through life he'd go for Ethel and me and blond Miss de Willoughby and *I'd* go right to the top!

Tucker and Hicks fussed over Miss de Willoughby until I wanted to throw up. Pale blue velvet cape and pink tulle dress! Revolting! My red crepe de Chine with a slit skirt, ravishing! And it really was.

The orchestra lit into "Chinatown, My Chinatown." Last month, Harlan's jacket button left a blue bruise on my breast, tonight another couple could have danced between us. Suddenly I had a dip. How long since somebody danced too close? "It's a hard life," said Mama. Was this what she meant?

51

"Weren't you in the Midwest company of *Fair and Warmer?*" asked Harlan.

"Poor Edna!" Mrs. Hibbard shook her head. "Drinking that fizzy stuff, she blew up and had to stop playing a week. Did you?" In *Fair and Warmer* two leading characters had to drink a lot and the property man supplied the fizzy stuff.

"I was out a week, but it was a blister on my foot."

Mrs. Hibbard nodded. "Prob'ly all that water."

Edna leaned across Harlan. Her hand was on his thigh. "I heard you were great."

Not only enchanting-looking, but generous!

"What'll we eat, darling?" She squeezed Harlan's leg and her dark sapphire eyes promised something lovely.

She could have him!

Clearly, she *did*. His eyes were promising her, too. She leaned against him. "Did you get past Klauber without?"

"Edna!" Mrs. Hibbard looked at Mrs. Bryant and gasped.

"Mama, an ingénue has to."

Her mother smiled at me. "Edna loves to shock people."

"Shock, hell. *Did* you?"

I could feel my face turn scarlet.

The dark sapphire eyes appraised me. "How didn't you?"

"I waited on the sidewalk till he went out to lunch, then told the secretary I'd never make the train if she didn't give me the contract and ticket, then ran down the five flights of stairs."

"Those stairs'll be worn out with virgins. Klauber doesn't like maidenheads in a company."

Mrs. Hibbard smiled at Harlan. "She's showing off in front of you."

"Fellers have an easier time," said Mrs. Bryant.

It was Harlan's turn. "Ever see Chamberlain Brown?"

"Agent," explained Edna. "Whoopsy, but sweet."

Her mother pointed at me. "You shouldn't talk like that in front of her, Edna; she's too young."

"No one's too young that worked for Selwyns. If it isn't Klauber, it's Archie's flat-top desk. Who's staying here?"

"Nice-looking boy from *Peg o' My Heart* Southern company, the Davenports, closed with Otis Skinner, a baroness that's German, but says she's Swiss."

"Ever see Marian?" asked Harlan.

Edna didn't wait for my answer. "Were you crazy about each other?"

*"I* was, but she couldn't see me for dust."

Edna leaned over and brushed her lips against his, then looked at me. "He's mine now."

We all laughed, she did it so prettily. So feminine, so frivolous!

The summer got hotter. Sam Harris, Sam Forrest, Arthur Hopkins stayed in Great Neck and played golf. Mr. Dillingham stayed in Europe, Al Woods stayed in Europe. Even when they all came back, could I get a job looking dowdy in dollar dresses from Stern Brothers?

If it ever got cooler, the navy blue Papa bought me would look pretty. Ninety in the shade now; how would my money hold out till it got cool? Sometimes you just don't know *what* to do. Luck has to get in and help. I took a straw cushion from the pile in the hall, put it on the front steps and waited. When everything else fails, try your luck.

"I got Edna all packed." Mrs. Hibbard stood in the doorway, cool, unworried, pretty. "I'm glad she bought that Taylor trunk; the tray lifts easier." She put a cushion next to me. "That show coming in the Booth they offered Edna; it tried out in Asbury. Edna'll do better taking out *Fair and Warmer,* then Thanksgiving, Bill Le Baron is putting her in *Rockabye Baby.* Catchy title for a musical." White-haired, slender, pretty as Edna—didn't *anything* ever ruffle her? "Anything in sight?"

"Well, nothing definite."

Edna came out with a cushion.

"You shouldn't sit here in your wrapper, Edna," she said, serenely.

Edna winked at me for no reason, tossed her cushion down and sat on it, wrapper skillfully wrapped around her. "Harlan left for Atlantic City; their dress rehearsal's tonight. What happened to that baby-doll part *you* were up for?"

"The Baby Talk Lady. They want a blonde."

"What kind of part is it?"

"She's flirty. She's come to visit a girl and all the boys in town are wild about her."

What reckless impulse had made me buy Booth Tarkington's book *Seventeen?* A lot of money to lay out, but at the library I'd have to wait weeks and the *Times* said it was going to be a play.

"They won't get a blonde."

"Why not?"

"Because the way you tell it she's smart. Do you know a blonde that's smart?"

Was Gladys Glover? Was Catherine Johnson? Was Miss de Willoughby? *They* were all blondes, and they weren't. "A girl in a vaudeville act with William Gaxton they're thinking of."

*"Very* pretty, no personality. *You'll* get it. Make Mason send you."

"She says blondes are all they'll see."

*"Make* her send you. *Tell* her to."

Mrs. Hibbard eyed my Stern Brothers dress. "You better buy Edna's two ginghams she's not going to take on the road. I don't know why I just washed and ironed them. You better buy them and get that part."

"I'll throw in my yellow straw I bought in Philadelphia's Wanamaker's. I paid eight dollars."

"Edna must like you. Have her two dresses," she encouraged, "and the yellow hat for five dollars."

Do you believe good luck moves in? On the top step of Martin's Theatrical, life changed. Three straw cushions, five dollars changing hands, bought my chance to meet Gregory Kelly, and he taught me to act.

To have a career, be lucky. If you're not, *get* to be. Never give up, ignore the facts, use everybody, and when it gets impossible, ask God for a windfall. Would I have made it if Edna hadn't sold me her yellow hat and dresses?

Yes, but I'd have had to have another windfall.

If Anna Witham hadn't invited me to a matinee?

Yes, but it was time for my windfall so she didn't ask Joyce Buchanan or Katherine; it had to be me.

Time for another windfall.

Could my luck get to Miss Austa Mason?

*"Make* her send you," Edna said.

"They want a blonde, dear." Her voice was kind, but tough.

"But what if they don't get one?"

"Well, they're looking, dear." She smiled a tough, kind smile.

"Do you think they might consider *me?"*

"Blondes, they said, send only blondes."

"But I'm not *dark."*

"No, but you're not blond, dear."

"How long do you think they'll look?"

"Till they get one."

"But they have to open *sometime,* don't they?"

"Oh, they got a date. Out West somewhere."

"Will they get a blonde by then?"

"It's not till after Labor Day."

"Send me. All they can say is no. Where will they get a blonde that's smart? Send *me*. They may change their mind and I'll be right *there.*"

She took a pencil out of her colorless light hair. "Eleven tomorrow." She wrote on a paper. "See Stuart Walker. Carnegie Hall."

*"Make* her," said Edna.

In her gingham with the thin thin brown pencil stripes and her buttercup yellow big big straw hat I looked the best I ever looked. Up Seventh Avenue on the shady side, at 56th Street I crossed over to Carnegie Hall, where The American Academy of Dramatic Arts had told me I showed no promise. "Don't come back," they said. They said it on the 57th Street side. Carnegie has two entrances; Stuart Walker's office was on Seventh Avenue. The elevator took me up and when it brought me down, I'd made it. I didn't know it right then, but I had.

"See Stuart Walker," said Miss Mason's paper.

"Mr. Walker and Mr. Kelly will see you," said somebody in the outer office, somebody big and fat.

Stuart Walker sat behind the desk, Gregory Kelly tilted his chair against the wall. Anything better than to feel you look adorable? Edna's dress showed my figure, her yellow hat dazzled. "Thank you for seeing me. I know you want a blonde, but I kept plaguing Miss Mason to send me and she couldn't bear to listen any longer so she gave me the appointment." Would Quincy Mansion School's Fentress Serene Kerlin sound like that? *"Please* don't hold it against her."

"We won't," said Gregory, adorable-looking! Dark hair, spiffy gray flannel suit, bow tie—adorable!

"What have you done?" asked Stuart Walker, dark hair, elegance his stock in trade.

"Last season I played the Madge Kennedy part in *Fair and Warmer.*"

"What company?"

"The third. Madge Kennedy was the first, Francine Larrimore was Chicago."

"Did you play Indianapolis? That's where we open *Seventeen.*"

"Did we?" I put on a blond expression. "I *think* Edna Hibbard played Indianapolis. The year *before,* I was with Maude Adams in *Peter Pan* and *The Little Minister.*"

Stuart Walker's languid brown eyes were on Gregory. "I'd love to see *you* do Peter. It doesn't *have* to be a girl, you know. Let's try it, Greg."

"It might get chaotic if I ran down to the foots and asked, 'Do you believe in fairies?' "

Stuart Walker laughed and so did I.

"He's always right," he said. "That rarely has charm, but he's the exception. Did you tell me your name?"

"Ruth Gordon."

"Miss Gordon, you're promising, but we want a blonde. This summer in Indianapolis the girl who played the Baby Talk Lady acted it very well indeed, but didn't suggest Tarkington's description. You're, of course, nearer the type."

"I think Miss Gordon would be good," said Gregory.

Stuart Walker looked at me with less warmth. "We'll let you know."

"My phone is Bryant 4245."

"You might give it to Marie as you go." He sounded bored.

"Thank you." I turned to Gregory. "Thank you." Had Edna's yellow hat and dress worked?

A day went by. Another day. Across the street the Booth Theatre lighted up. Mrs. Bryant went to the opening. When she came back I was on the front steps, thinking.

"Thumbs down!" was her verdict. "Why put on a thing like that? Can't they read? Sometimes I seriously wonder. Sit two hours in a hot theatre for that!"

"Mrs. Hibbard said it would be nothing." Were the Hibbards right about *everything?* Edna had said to make Miss Mason send me and I had. Was she right about no smart blondes?

Next evening after supper I took a straw cushion out to the steps, watched people go into the Booth. Maybe Gregory Kelly?

"You must have some pretty cute thoughts," said Mrs. Bryant. "You look pretty."

"Phone," shouted Molly from the hall. She pointed to me.

"Hello?"

"It's Gregory Kelly."

Had I *made* him call?

"Stuart chose somebody else. I'm sorry."

When your throat closes, you can't say anything.

"His choice isn't *my* idea."

I managed, "Oh, dear."

"I'm disappointed."

"Oh, thank you." Next week, September, most road companies filled, new shows in rehearsal, some theatres already open.

"We'll be together in another play."

In disaster have courage. "I hope *you* have a big success. *Seventeen* is my favorite book and you'll be *great.* I wish I could've played the Baby Talk Lady, but if I can't I wish whoever got it well. I know *you*'ll have the biggest success."

"Well, thank you."

I couldn't go back to the steps, I couldn't go up to my room. In the musty parlor the sheep stared at nothing. Was Edna wrong? Had they found a smart blonde? Was Papa right? "Any profession that did not offer me a berth after six weeks, I would not deem it wise to remain in."

*Fair and Warmer* had closed April 17. April 17 through August, *no* offers, nothing in sight. But did I have anything in sight the night *before* I got *Fair and Warmer?* Had I had any offers before that? Why let people dampen your spirits?

"Any profession that did not offer me . . ."

Why unload bum experience? Tomorrow go the rounds in Edna's pink-checked gingham, my black straw from Franklin Simon's with the ostrich tip. Maybe retrim it with pink velvet roses? Maybe black tulle for a veil? Tie it round the wreath of pink flowers, a streamer down the back? Maybe take off the ostrich feather? For August, ostrich looks too hot.

In the hall, Molly rang the bell twice.

"Yes?" answered the new man, second floor rear, double room.

"Phone for Gordon."

"I'm in the parlor." I came out of the dark, head full of pink roses and tulle. "Hello."

"It's Gregory Kelly. I let the girl go. I want you to play the Baby Talk Lady."

"Oh, Mr. Kelly."

"Can you come to the office?"

"Oh, *yes.*"

"Our manager, Harold Holstein, will talk to you."

"Shall I come right now?"

"Let's say eleven tomorrow morning?"

"Oh, *thank* you."

When the cup runneth over, say "Thank you."

Next day, the pink and white checked gingham, the hat with pink velvet roses and the black tulle streamer had snap.

"The company leaves Wednesday evening. Will you be able to?"

"I could leave now!"

He laughed. "We rehearse in Indianapolis."

"I *love* Indianapolis." *Fair and Warmer* had changed trains there. What a grim railroad station!

"Stuart's stock company plays there in the summer."

"Oh, I've read about it; I read *Variety.*"

"Stuart directs, we rehearse two weeks; most of us were in it last summer. It went well except for Lola Pratt, the Baby Talk Lady. Aggie Rogers wasn't right for that part, but she's good; she'll come along to understudy."

A sturdy young man with dark hair and mustache came in. "Am I late?"

"Yes."

What a charmer!

"This is our company manager, Harold Holstein. Harold, this is Ruth Gordon, our Lola Pratt."

"Delighted to meet you. Your salary will be sixty-five dollars a week and we pay for your costumes. Rehearse Indianapolis, open Columbus September seventeenth, play two days, then one-nighters into Chicago, open at the Playhouse, Michigan Avenue, October first. Train leaves Grand Central six-thirty Wednesday evening, first rehearsal Sunday Mr. Walker's office, Murat Theatre. Have I forgotten anything?"

" 'Sit down, Nimitz, and have some soup.' "

"What?"

Gregory Kelly smiled at me. "That's Harold's favorite story. I thought he was going to work it in."

"Sign this," said Harold, and pulled out a contract.

"Let her take it home and read it." Gregory came over to me. "I have to go. Harold will tell you what the wardrobe is." He was gone.

"Here's the list Marie typed out. When you sign the contract I'll give you one hundred and fifty dollars. You have to get four dresses, evening wrap, two hats, two pairs of shoes."

What a day! What a world! What a life!

"Any profession that did not offer . . ."

Nothing in sight and the next day one hundred and fifty dollars, a part, sixty-five dollars a week, and meet a fellow. What if I'd shot myself? The money wasted on revolvers! What if I'd got married to some good man?

"When you sign you get the one-fifty."

"I'll sign now." Wouldn't *you?*

Down Seventh Avenue with a contract! One hundred and fifty dollars to buy clothes for the Baby Talk Lady that Gregory Kelly was in love with! And I was in love with him!

*"Make* her," said Edna.

In front of the Hotel Wellington I stopped. Could I have cared? Could I have thought *twice* about today? Miss Annette de Willoughby was blond, but *she* wasn't the Baby Talk Lady. When you get there, maybe enjoy a good gloat? I enjoyed it and unfolded fat Marie's list:

Act I—dressy summer afternoon dress, hat, shoes.
Act II—dressy dress for summer evening, shoes.
Act III—day dress, summer, not fancy as other two, shoes, hat.
Act IV—farewell party dress, party cape, party shoes.

When everything goes great can you keep a clear head? That's me. A ball or a bomb I'm great, in between is when I can make the bum decisions. Today with a hundred and fifty dollars I *knew* just what to do. For my first entrance order a hat like Anna Wheaton's white organdy, made to order on 42nd Street.

In trouble, keep it dark; when it gets great, spread it around.

*227 West 45th Street,*
*New York*
*Sunday, September 2, 1917*

Dear Papa,

At last! I'm in *Seventeen* by Booth Tarkington. I am the Baby Talk Lady, the *lead.* After trying out light-haired girls they decided I read the best. It didn't happen right off. I read the part, then they telephoned they decided on an actress with blonde hair. Mr. Walker, the manager, wrote me a charming letter saying he thought my work delightful, but preferred a blonde. They tried out some more, then called and asked me to go over to the office. I talked business and signed my contract. Sixty-five a week and all my gowns. They offered me seventy-five if I'd supply the costumes, but I couldn't afford that. They are allowing me to spend two hundred dollars. They'll be beautiful.

Stuart Walker is the manager and we leave Wednesday evening for Indianapolis, the home of Booth Tarkington, where we rehearse. We open Sept. 17 in Columbus, Ohio. After that I don't know the route. We get to Chicago October 1, where they expect a run. New York the beginning of next year. Everyone is congratulating me on the engagement, my first chance to create a part.

The play was a tremendous hit when tried out in Indianapolis and of course will be a success on account of the success of the book and the author's name. They are promising me a lot of press work and that in itself is a big thing. The night I signed the contract they sent the press agent

Alta Mae Coleman over to me and tomorrow they pay for me to go have pictures taken for newspaper work.

Tomorrow was Labor Day? Make up stuff, but try and hook it into believable dates.

Now I can pay back all I owe you and it was dear of you to loan it. Please tell everyone about the part and let them know it's a good thing financially as well as artistically. Write me,

Murat Theatre,
c/o Stuart Walker Co.,
Indianapolis, Indiana

Love,
Ruth

# Chapter

## 3

I n the dining car I sat with Beatrice Maude and Lillian Ross. Beatrice
played May Parcher, the one the Baby Talk Lady comes to visit;
Lillian played Willie Baxter's little sister Jane.

"When the play tried out last summer," said Beatrice, "your part
was played by Aggie Rogers. She just graduated from Vassar, but she's
good. Didn't you think so, Lil?"

"She played the part fine, but isn't blond."

"Swell-looking and dark." Beatrice was dark herself and beautiful as
Dante's. "Men are crazy about her. Greg goes for Aggie."

Lillian chose to look out the window. The train rushed up the Hudson. At the other end of the diner Gregory sat with Harold Holstein.
Someday the train would rush up the Hudson and he'd go for me.

"Aggie'll be in Indianapolis. She's going to play the small part at the
party and understudy you."

Why an understudy? Why would I be out of the show?

The long cindery train rushed through the hot night, rushed past
cornfields and rumbled into smoky Union Station, where the *Fair and*

*Warmer* company came in from Richmond, Indiana, to catch the Illinois Central to Bloomington.

"Claypool Hotel," said Bea to the taxi. She and Lillian and I sharing a taxi wasn't extravagant, but was the Claypool Hotel? It was the best hotel in Indianapolis.

"What is your cheapest room?"

"Dollar seventy-five a day." Nobody asked if it was a narrow, dingy, high-ceilinged cell with a bed, bureau, chair, bowl and pitcher, one window on a gray court, but it was. Incidentally, wherever anyone else stayed, the Baby Talk Lady was at the best hotel in Indianapolis!

"Geiger's Candy Store is great for breakfast," said Beatrice. "Last summer we went there."

"Did Gregory?"

Her beautiful eyes took me in. "Are you crazy about him?"

"I just met him."

"Think you might be?"

"I don't know."

"I slept with him. He's great. But he went for Aggie." She looked at the menu. "Cinnamon toast and coffee with whip cream."

In Stuart Walker's office, off the Murat Theatre lobby, the stage manager arranged three kitchen chairs set close together to make a sofa, two kitchen chairs separated to make an entrance to Willie Baxter's mother's sitting room, Act I. No matter who you are, a first rehearsal is hard. Hard when you know how to act, harder before.

"Ruth, this is Aggie."

"Hi."

"Hi." Why say hi because Aggie Rogers did? Is that how they talk at Vassar, and why did I like her? Hadn't Gregory gone for her? Maybe still did?

When I rehearsed a scene Stuart Walker looked bored or impatient; I was Gregory's choice. "Cross right," he said and seemed to wish I was someone else.

I spoke my line, then crossed right.

"Cross on the *line* is the idea."

Next to being heard, to cross on the line is the first rule of acting. I knew I should, but fright made me forget to. Did Gregory wish he hadn't hired me? Did he wish Agnes Rogers had the part? She was dark and swell-looking and would she have crossed on the line? I wasn't dark, but I wasn't blond either or pretty and *didn't* "cross on the line."

The whole two weeks of rehearsals, nobody said I was good. When Gregory and I acted our scenes what did he think?

> "Oh, Lola Pratt
> Sweet Lola Pratt,
> I wonder what
> You're gazing at,"

he sang, to the tune of "Genevieve" and accompanied himself on his ukulele, but no serenades outside the Claypool, none outside the Neil House in Columbus. Was he sorry he'd engaged me?

Stuart and Gregory were at Columbus' good hotel, but the rest of us went to where Dreiser's Sister Carrie had worked. She did right to leave. Too bad she didn't find happiness in Chicago. Neither she *nor* I found it in Columbus. At the Hartman Theatre I dressed *fourth!* Gregory Kelly dressed first, but why Judith Lowry second? Did Willie Baxter's mother ever play a lead?

"Stuart's a fuddy-duddy about mothers," explained Aggie.

I liked her a lot. "Did Lillian Ross ever play a lead?"

"Heavens, no!"

In *Fair and Warmer* I dressed first, now I dressed after Gregory, Judith, Lillian. Their parts were longer and better, but *not* the lead. Why a sister and mother ahead of a leading lady? Is there happiness and if there is, can it last? Suppose that night at Martin's Theatrical, when that memorable voice said, "You can have the part," he'd also said, "but you dress tenth"? Would I have cared? Would I have even heard it? But dressing room 4 at the Hartman wasn't big enough for me and my fury. For the first forty years or so, you want everything, then is "everything" so important?

And how do you define important? Is it important when the Columbus newspaper rips you up? Their critic was worse than my dressing room. He raved for a paragraph about Gregory Kelly, raved about Lillian Ross, "but Ruth Gordon was very mannered and set people's teeth on edge."

When you go to *The Pink Lady* matinee you never think they'll print you set people's teeth on edge.

Aggie said a girl at Vassar that came from Columbus said it was a dud.

After Columbus we played Dayton for one night. Ona B. Talbot, local impresario, arranged for the company to attend a Drama League tea. That was my first theatrical social event.

A night in Anderson, one in Fort Wayne, South Bend, Terre Haute, Marion, Urbana, and into Chicago. Chicago didn't think I was too mannered. All the reviews were good and Amy Leslie said I was "pretty as a china pink." The dressing rooms were all in a row down-cellar, so when people asked to see any of us, the stage doorman said, "They're all downstairs." That made me feel better. Maybe *before* forty years, work on finding how to define important.

Gregory and Stuart stayed at the grand Congress Hotel on Michigan Avenue, some of the company went to the Virginia Hotel or the Alexandria by the bridge over the Chicago River where the buses turned to go north, Neil Martin stayed at Mrs. Newbury's boardinghouse, Aggie and I went to the Stratford Hotel, rooms on a court, but big and it *was* on Michigan Avenue.

THE STRATFORD HOTEL

MICHIGAN AVE. AND JACKSON ST.

CHICAGO

*Friday, October 1917*

Dear Katherine,

I made a hit and got all rave reviews. I'll send them when I get time. They are giving me wonderful press work. I have interviews and photos all day long. I wish you could see my gowns. Spiffy! And this is the sweetest company! I'm crazy about them and there is the loveliest girl in it, Aggie Rogers. I adore her. She's a graduate of Vassar and darling. Of course, I'm being entertained a lot and she always goes places with me, it's more fun. I was going to write you anyway, but what hurried me up was I got a letter this morning from Lowell Norris, the most obnoxious youth in the world! I didn't even bother to tell you last summer he wrote me a lot of foolishness about finding my library card in some secondhand book he bought. Of course I didn't even bother to answer it. You know how I feel in regard to him. Then here I get a letter today telling how proud he is of me and how he knew my name would be in "Lamps on B'way before long" and repeated the story of the library book, then begged me to forget the little episode which ended our friendship, all couched in such flowery terms I hope somebody feeds him poison. Don't *ever* say I even mentioned him. I've just rented a piano and love to drum on it. Tell me some easy songs I can get. In the play I sing "The Keys of Heaven." Don't you love it? I may take singing lessons.

Lovingly,

Ruth

Only the weather was cold; everybody's heart was warm. Business was good, people entertained. Neil Martin, who played Johnny Jump-

64

up, gave a Sunday night supper at Mrs. Newbury's. We all bought things.

Aggie and I made dates. Sometimes cute fellers, sometimes grand Mrs. Coonley-Ward, patroness of arts, inviting us to cream of corn soup, pickled codfish, boiled potatoes, caramel custard at the Fine Arts Club and after dinner thank Mrs. Coonley-Ward for the silver and rose quartz pin or ring she gave us, and once some scarabs.

One night I went to Aggie's dressing room; it was dark. Had she said she was going anywhere? At the Stratford I knocked on her door. No answer.

Did she go out on a date? Why didn't she tell me? Now I was alone. Maybe someone in the lobby? Maybe Otto Kruger would have come in from *Here Comes the Bride* over in the Loop. I felt grand talking to him.

No one but the desk clerk. "Did Miss Rogers leave a message for me?"
"No."

"Don't be helpless," Mama said, but didn't say to step out on Michigan Avenue. Why did I? The wind nearly blew me over. Why stay out? Did my voices from Boylston and Tremont find me on wintry Michigan Avenue and say "Stay out"?

"Hello."
I forgot the cold. "Hello."

However stunning a man can look in a heavy brown overcoat, collar turned up, is how Gregory looked.

"What're you doing all by yourself?"

What would *you* say? I said, "Did *you* ever suddenly hate someone because you were going out with them?"

"You sound complicated. Are you?"

What would *you* say? I said, "Maybe I knew I'd run into you."

He took my arm. "Taxi," he called. A Parmelee cab screeched to a stop. "College Inn."

The dance floor was faintly lit. Each table had a lighthouse to turn on when you wanted the waiter. It was famous and I'd never been there.

"Chicken à la king?"

"I love it." Should we have invited Aggie? How could we? Hadn't I knocked at her door?

"Two rye and ginger ale." That was the Chicago drink. "Let's dance." His arm went around me. How great I didn't wear the blue serge Papa bought me; my Marshall Field black silk was *really* skeeky!

The last dance and Gregory brought me back to the Stratford. Would he kiss me? The desk clerk, coat off, thick sweater, cup of coffee by the

65

hotel register, two women with dirty brushes dipped in dirty water out of dirty buckets, worn leather chairs pushed against the wall, soap smelling horrible. Was he going to kiss me?

"Let's do it again," he said. Didn't even squeeze my hand.

Down-cellar at the Playhouse, a notice was on the call-board:

**CHICAGO ENGAGEMENT**
**OF *SEVENTEEN* ENDS THE WEEK**
**BEFORE CHRISTMAS.**
**COMPANY WILL LAY OFF A WEEK**
**AND REOPEN CINCINNATI.**

Holy Week and the week before Christmas, Equity lets you lay off with no pay. If you have a husband go back to him, if you have a wife go back to her, if you have a family pay them a visit. What if you haven't got anyone? The year after Mama died, Papa retired and went out to Santa Rosa, California, to see what that was like.

"Want to come home with me?" Aggie asked. "There's a sleeper after the show Saturday; we'd get to Hagerstown Sunday afternoon. We change in Pittsburgh for the Maryland train."

"I'd love to."

"Slick! I was going to miss you. Hagerstown is nice, but slow."

How could anyone miss anyone in that parlor? Lamplight gleamed, fire blazed on the hearth. Outside, but away off somewhere, lurked worry and struggle and critics that wrote you set people's teeth on edge, dark rooms on dark courts, evenings down-cellar. One night more and we'd leave for Cincinnati and dark rooms with running water. Here we each had our own white bathroom with fluffy white towels, hand-crocheted washcloth.

Mr. Rogers took my empty coffee cup. "Miss Ruth, suppose I show you my study."

"Oh, yes." I stood up and looked at Aggie.

"I want our guest for myself. Agnes, you entertain your mother. After tomorrow she will ask me all sorts of questions only you can answer." He opened the door to his study. "Sit here, Miss Ruth. I like to think this is my best chair." He pointed to a chintz armchair that wasn't *just* a chintz armchair, it was *the* chintz armchair.

"You and Mrs. Rogers would die if you saw where Aggie and I live. In Chicago we had to have electric light on all day."

"We hoped our daughter would tire of theatrical life. Need I tell you her mother misses her? I, too, but we made her a promise if she attended college to please *us,* when she graduated she should be her own mistress. Concern makes us search her letters. Can so small a part absorb Agnes?"

"Everyone said she was great when she played the part I'm playing, but it's a silly blonde and Aggie isn't. I'm not either, but closer than she is."

"Miss Ruth, you are the first professional actress her mother and I have had the pleasure to meet. Let me share a secret: I wasn't as anxious to show you my study as to get your ideas. In your opinion does Agnes seem suited to the stage?"

Should I say what I thought? Hadn't they said what *they* thought at The American Academy? "Don't come back," they said. "You don't show any promise."

"Miss Ruth, as a guest in our home, your impulse would be to praise; will you do us a favor and speak the truth?"

"Mr. Rogers, I don't think Aggie will be an actress, but *nobody* really knows. At The American Academy of Dramatic Arts they told me I showed no promise and I think they were wrong. Probably I'm wrong about Aggie."

"You may be, but I'll confide in you. Her mother and I have somewhat the same feelings."

"Then it doesn't make me seem mean?"

"How much easier for you to tell us Agnes shows talent! What stands in her way, Miss Ruth?"

"Well, *I* think she's wonderful-looking, but she's not any special *type.* She's not an ingénue like Madge Kennedy or a leading lady like Ethel Barrymore or Maude Adams, so *that* leaves character parts, but character parts don't look like Aggie."

"Aside from looks, do you believe she has talent?"

"I saw her in *Gods of the Mountain,* the Lord Dunsany play Stuart Walker put on for special matinees in Chicago and *nobody* seemed very good. The play was sort of like a play at school, but when I hear her at understudy rehearsals she sounds like at college."

"Would you think experience could train her?"

"Maybe. She's awfully ambitious; she wouldn't want to play just *small* parts."

"Are there instructors for the stage?"

"I think a great director has to fall in love with you. I don't think there's any other way."

"A solution perhaps one can't count on."

Cinder-stained Cincinnati slipped past. It looked like old scenery left standing.

"Take your bags, miss?"

The porter carried my suitcase, I carried the chintz knitting bag Aggie's aunt gave me for a Christmas present. A chintz knitting bag showed you were doing something for the boys. "Sinton Hotel," I told the taxi driver. It was the best. Without Aggie I didn't feel like going to a run-down one.

Up clicked the taxi meter, and no Aggie to split the fare. *Should* her father have asked me? Could Papa talk *me* into staying home? Maybe she wanted to stay home?

"I'm not coming back," she had said, next morning. "I feel awful to let you down."

The taxi skidded up to the icy curbstone. The best hotel was as gray as the city and as old. When I registered, the clerk handed me a note.

> Rehearsal call
> 2:30 Sunday
> Line rehearsal
> Sinton Ballroom
> Opening tonight 8:30

The bellboy unlocked the dark brown door of a dark brown oblong slice with one window that looked on a side street wide enough to let two trolleys clang past.

"Electric light all day," I told Mr. Rogers. I hadn't lied about that or about anything. He'd asked me, I'd told him.

Wipe the bureau drawers with the hotel towel, put tissue paper in. Had her father told her he talked to me? Put away the ashtray and cards to advertise massage, hairdressing, tailor and valet service. Put away pincushion with brown, black and white thread, two needles and three pins stuck through a button. Put the Gideon Bible on the closet shelf, unpack pink linen bureau scarf I made on train trips on the Maude Adams Company tour. It had a band of real filet lace each end and in the center an unaccountable ink spot. Cover it with my white monogrammed mirror. Arrange underwear, stockings, nightdresses and handkerchiefs in the tissue-paper-lined drawers. Wash my hair? On a Sunday morning in Cincinnati what else does an actress do? I made a lather with the pure castile soap and washed.

Even though I scrubbed it, the bathtub smelled like borax; shake in a handful of 4711 bath salts. The crystals melted into fragrance, get out Roger & Gallet violet soap, lie in scented bath. The phone rang.

Ringgg.

Could it be Gregory? Never since Martin's Theatrical, so why in Cincinnati?

Ringgg. Rehearsal call? They left it in the box.

I slithered across the carpet to the phone by the bed.

Ringgg.

"Hello? . . ." Only Harold Holstein.

I pulled the bedspread around me. "Of course I got in; I got in at crack of dawn. Think I'd forget you? . . ." He wasn't terrible-looking, just no fun and no sex appeal. "Yuh, Aggie felt dismal about it, but for a *lot* of reasons she decided to stay home. I'm certainly going to miss her. Weren't you a little bit mashed on her, Harold? . . . Come on, you *were.* . . . Dinner tonight? Love to. . . . Downstairs six o'clock. All right, honeybunch, ta ta." I wiped soap off the receiver with the corner of the bedspread. Food was supposed to be great at the Sinton; so what if Harold kissed me? I got back in the perfumed water. What if Gregory did?

*"Make* her send you," said Edna.

Could I make Gregory kiss me?

Next morning before I was awake the phone rang. "It's Mary Miller. Remember me from the Academy?"

I remembered she was the one who lived at the Plaza and was rich and snooty to everybody and didn't want to be an actress. Once when we had to rehearse a scene she kept looking bored at me. "What are you doing here?" I asked.

"I live here, sweetie, I mean I used to; it's where our family is, but Mother and Granny and I lit out. Remember? We live at the Plaza. I came back here for Christmas and just read your name in the paper. My dear, it's a spiffy review!"

"Oh, good."

"I'd love to show you a good time, sweetie. Want to meet me in the dining room, one o'clock? It's pretty short notice, but I'll see who I can scare up."

She scared up an "older man, but a charmer, you'll adore him. The ones our age are in the war, but you'll love the Tom Melishes. He *loves* parties, his wife Lawson doesn't, but will come along."

Tom was tall and good-looking and overweight. "Will you let us give a supper party after the show tonight?"

I liked him and Lawson. Her dress *had* to be from Lucille. Anna and Mrs. Castle might go for Harry Collins, but give *me* Lucille!

"The Melishes are *crazy* about you, my dear, and Lawson's not at all easy to know. Tom's the one who gets the ball rolling. Eleven-fifteen in the supper room? I'll see if I can get Deedy Kohlsaat, he's *great* fun and young and snappy-looking. I'll look around for some others."

Cincinnati was the way I meant it to be—compliments, attention, great food, swells, orchids, phone calls, parties, lie in bed all morning or in a perfumed bath, nobody economical, everybody probably fast. Maybe write to Wollaston? Tell Gladys Bain. She had more go than about anybody.

> *Hotel Sinton*
> *Cincinnati, Ohio*

Gladys darling,

Cincinnati is your speed! Everybody *really* skeeky, rich and wear silk shirts *every* day and don't know there *is* a church! After the show last night, the Tom Melishes gave a nifty supper party for me. He's married, but adorable, and she's not as come-hither, but fun.

At everyone's place a corsage of *white orchids!* You know what *they* cost!

Dessert was pistachio ice cream the shape of a Christmas tree with spun sugar to look like snow. While writing this I'm waiting for Deedy Kohlsaat, who's coming in his Simplex racer to drive me across the Ohio River to Kentucky! They were *shocked* I'd never seen it. Deedy is *your* type. Princeton and full of it, dark hair, dark dark eyebrows and those *eyes!*

> Love,
> Ruth

P.S. I'll write after I see Kentucky.

*Seventeen* wound up its Cincinnati engagement. Closing night the Tom Melishes gave a party in the Sinton supper club; corsages were green orchids. "Ruth G." and "Maude S." in silver letters on everything. Everybody but me knew Maude S. was a great race horse. "Say farewell to Ruth G. and honor Maude S.," the invitations read.

"Do you *have* to play Detroit next week, sweetie?" asked Mary. The rich speak a different language. "Everybody *adores* you here; they're all coming to New York to see you. Couldn't you come over from Detroit for New Year's?"

"I can't."

"Oh, damn! In New York, where do you stay?"

"On West Forty-fifth, Martin's Theatrical. I'm superstitious."

"Sounds perfect; what is it?"

*"Great* theatrical boardinghouse across the street from the Booth Theatre, where *Seventeen* is going to play. That's Winthrop Ames' theatre, the best in New York, and right *opposite* is Martin's; *everyone* stayed there one time or another. Mrs. Martin is in the Social Register, by the way."

"My dear! I can't wait to see it. Don't forget I'm at the Plaza. It's deadly, but Granny and Mummy stay there."

Opening nights in New York are terrible. Gregory had a nosebleed after the Act I curtain calls and Judith Lowry had to hold ice on his neck. "Roll a piece of toilet paper," she told Stuart. "Wad it under his upper lip." Did that happen to Hazel Dawn opening night of *The Pink Lady?* To Maude Adams opening night of *Peter Pan?*

In spite of my beautiful pink ruffled organdy, my twelve-fifty pink hat, my knees shook so I had to sit down. Floppit, the little white poodle I carried, shook right through all four acts. What did *he* have to be nervous about?

The notices were all right and *Seventeen* settled down for a run. To help the war effort, a theatre had to be dark one night a week, plus Sunday. Tuesday night was the Booth's night to save coal.

*Seventeen* was going to run through the summer even though Gregory had left for Indianapolis to act in the new play Stuart had written, *Jonathan Makes a Wish.* Paul Kelly, who played George Crooper, now was promoted to Willie Baxter. Our new George Crooper was Ben Lyon.

"What's your salary?" Stuart had asked him.

"Two hundred and fifty."

"This part pays fifty."

"I'll take it," said Ben.

He was all right, so was Paul Kelly, but he didn't have Gregory's charm. One night at the College Inn and that was it. Did he ever look across the street from the Booth? There was a message for him on my window sill, a plant covered with white blossoms and tied with a pink satin bow I'd bought to show the Booth stage door how popular I was. For "stage door" read "Gregory." Now he'd left for the Murat summer stock season, where Margaret Mower was the leading lady.

"Don't be helpless, Ruth."

What if I wrote to wish the new play well? What if I wished it "well, but not *too* well, because I miss you in this play"? I got out my parchment letter paper with "R.G." engraved in gold.

"Letter for you," called Molly.

Postmarked Indianapolis! Thanks for wishing him well in the new play and "more thanks for wishing me 'not *too* well' so I'd come back." What did *that* mean? Did *he* mean—? Read it again.

Four letters from Gregory. Four from me. Why tell the times I read them? *Then* the day came; he was back! A scorcher, the sun cooked West 45th Street. For the late afternoon rehearsal would my stylish black taffeta look ridiculous? After summer stock in Indianapolis, wouldn't he love that New Yorky black? Did Margaret Mower wear a dress like that? Did the Woodstock Country Club debutantes? Do you figure out stuff or leave it to fate? Fate's got a lot to do; I say give a hand. I turned the pink satin bow toward the Booth. A pink satin bow suggests flowers sent by fellers; would he give a damn? He had written me four letters.

Dip the rhinestone pin in alcohol, polish it with toilet paper. The safety catch is what can make a rhinestone bar pin look like diamonds.

Bathe, toss my old Japanese kimono into the closet, one day throw it away. Some things last forever. Mrs. Wetmore had given it to Mama and Mama gave it to me to wear in the Unitarian church's *A Trip Around the World*.

At Martin's nobody but the boarders saw my old Japanese kimono. Across the street pale pink pussy-willow taffeta and a chiffon one over peach crepe de Chine hung in my dressing room. I still dressed fourth, but the things in my dressing room looked like dressing room 1. I took the crystal stopper out of the Quelques Fleurs bottle. Houbigant had created it for the Empress Eugénie. Had it worked all that well for her? The crystal touched under my arms, over my breasts. Was that what the Empress Eugénie did? On Anna Wheaton's bureau at the Hotel Richmond stood the same kind of squat oval crystal bottle with opaque pink and blue flowered label, QUELQUES FLEURS D'HOUBIGANT lettered in black. Did Anna put it on her breasts? Was she a virgin like the doctor said and why is *that* great?

I kept my everyday stuff on one side of the bureau drawer, the other side the pretty things. Two bust bodices copied from Mary Miller's. Broad Cluny lace with bands of net sewn along the edges for satin ribbon to run through and tie in a bow beneath the breast. New pink satin knickers, new black chiffon stockings. Put them on.

"Do you like the Astor Roof?" asked Gregory. After the Roof we could have gone across the street to Martin's, but we didn't. He took my hand, we turned up Broadway, crossed on 46th Street, walked past the Hotel Richmond, crossed over and Gregory unlocked a door. The letter box said:

ALTA MAE COLEMAN

PIERRE COLEMAN

Up four flights of stairs, another key unlocked another door. Through the windows came the orange glare of Times Square. Gregory found the switch. Did Alta Mae and Pierre know their room looked better before they found the switch?

On the right was a studio bed. Alta Mae's? Pierre's? Or was his the one on the left? If you're married why two beds?

The door closed, I was in his arms, his lips were on mine. I was the one.

"Stay."

"I better go."

"Why?"

"It's late."

"I thought you'd stay." His arms were around me. "Stay."

That was how trouble started.

"Stay."

If I went back to Martin's the door would close, he'd stroll up 45th. To whom?

"Stay. Stay and you sleep there." Did he point to Alta Mae's? "I'll sleep here." Pierre's?

One bed for him, one for me?

He turned off the light and kissed me. His hand moved over the taffeta dress. "Where?" he whispered. His fingers found the hooks. Terror like opening night. And excitement.

The black taffeta dress dropped to the floor. A year of hoping, a year of willing it; did trouble have to come out of this? Did it *have* to? People said it did. Why *did* it? I slipped out of his arms into Alta Mae's bed. Why sleep apart? He slid in beside me.

"Don't."

His arms held me.

"You said."

"You really mean it?"

"Yes."

He lay a minute, then slid out of bed. I could hear the cover pulled down on the other one. Pierre's?

Would he come back?

Light, regular breathing.

Why did I cry?


One more week and *Seventeen* was closing its New York engagement. We went dancing every night after the show. Up at Reisenweber's on Columbus Circle the band blared out:

> Just a baby's prayer at twilight
> When lights are low . . .

Couples fox-trotted and held each other close. More uniforms than not. In the dim lights, hands strayed.

> Poor baby's tears
> Are full of fears . . .

Gregory's arm was tight around me, my head on his shoulder.

> And the mother in the twilight . . .

The trumpet blared out plaintively, everybody got closer, everybody got a little more woozy. Liquor and feelings and how long before overseas?

Gregory was a beautiful dancer, style, form. Princeton boys had more action, they went forward, also up and down. Princeton boys got their money's worth. You knew you were dancing. "Let's be careless," I whispered.

He held me closer. "Let's go home."

*Lenox Hotel*
*Boston, Mass.*
*Monday, October 24, 1918*

Dear Papa,

*Seventeen* opened here tonight and I guess everyone wished we hadn't. The house was very unenthusiastic. It looks like a failure, everyone is terribly discouraged. I'll send the notices tomorrow.

I'm at this hotel and have a very nice room. It's pretty far up Boylston Street, but I like the walk after the theatre. I don't have to come home alone as most of the company are here.

74

Most of the company were Gregory and I.

It's funny to be in Boston with you in Santa Rosa. It's the first time I've ever been here and you weren't. Don't think of moving into that boardinghouse if you like where you are better. If you need anything let me know. What's mine is yours. For the road I get seventy-five dollars a week. Write soon,

Lovingly,
Ruth

At night the hall was deserted. In the morning did the maid see Gregory go back to his room? She was Irish and jolly and Gregory knew how to tip. Would she tell about us? Would the Lenox put us out?

The play didn't go well, but these days what counted were the nights. Was I good? I would be. Was I as good as the other girls? I would be. What made me know I could learn?

The Boston run ended. We opened in Providence. What doctor? Last month it hadn't happened. Gregory found out the name of one who was old and lived in a house behind lovely trees losing their yellow leaves. Outside his office window were the bare branches of an apple tree.

"I feel quite sick to my stomach sometimes."

"What have you eaten?"

I told him.

"Is your period regular?"

"Yes, as a rule, but this time I'm late."

"Could you be pregnant?"

"Oh, no."

"It sounds like it."

"Oh, no. Could you give me something to bring on my period?"

"No."

Gregory had said there was something to take, but you had to have a prescription. Could I ask him for a prescription?

He looked stern. "If it's poisoning, it would have been more severe; if it's something you ate, be careful for a day or so. Are you married?"

"What?"

The doctor didn't bother to repeat. "That's all."

In the outer office, the girl said, "Five dollars."

When a girl gets caught, hard to find out what to do. Gregory said hot baths might work and there was a drug named ergot. It needed a prescription, he got it. It didn't work, just made me sick.

After Providence, the Bronx Opera House. Gregory went to Frank, the carpenter of a show he'd been with. Frank told him a doctor up on West 110th Street. Gregory went up and talked to him.

He wouldn't.

Frank asked around and said, "Try the doctor on West Seventy-third and Columbus Avenue."

Gregory asked him.

He wouldn't, but the nurse in his office would. Gregory said I needn't play the Saturday matinee and went up to rehearse the understudy. On the way to Columbus Avenue I stopped at Western Union.

NIGHT LETTER

CLINTON JONES
314 WEST 4TH ST HOTEL SHERMAN
LOS ANGELES CALIFORNIA

DEAR PAPA WOULD HAVE WRITTEN BEFORE BUT HAVE BEEN ILL WITH PTO-MAINE POISON AM ALL RIGHT NOW BUT HAVE BEEN MISERABLE ALL WEEK AM GOING TO GIVE YOU GREAT SURPRISE WISH I COULD TELL YOU INSTEAD OF WRITING HAVE BEEN ENGAGED GREGORY KELLY TWO WEEKS BUT KEPT IT SECRET HAVE DECIDED BE MARRIED SUNDAY AND ANNOUNCE IT AFTERWARD IT SEEMS SUDDEN BUT WE ARE ANXIOUS BE MARRIED AM TERRIBLY SORRY YOU NOT HERE AND SINCE YOU CAN NOT COME WE WILL HAVE NOBODY WE GO ON TOUR RIGHT AFTERWARD LETTER FOLLOWS WILL WRITE CLARE LOTS LOVE

RUTH

From Western Union I went up to the nurse's room on Columbus Avenue. I gave her fifty dollars and her knife cut in, no anesthetic.

She got me into a cab and told the driver to go to the Great Northern Hotel. Gregory was with me between the matinee and the night show and sat up all night with me. Next day was our wedding. "Do you think you can?"

I was too weak and we postponed till Monday morning. Gregory helped me put on my wedding dress, black broadcloth, the neck and sleeves edged with a narrow band of white ermine. A black wedding dress sounded New Yorky, I thought, and drew a picture for Mrs. Petrie to copy. Gregory, adorable, worried, hooked it up. He helped me put on the beautiful new beaver coat from Giddings that was his wedding present. "Sit down a minute."

I did.

Out on 56th Street, Gregory told the taxi the address of the church.

A priest who admired Gregory was going to marry us. He had had me sign a paper swearing that all our children would be brought up Catholic. That was all right; I didn't plan to have any and Gregory said we didn't have to.

The church looked almost as dark as my dress. The priest wore black, so did Gregory's mother. His father and Stuart Walker wore dark suits, Gregory's was navy blue. No flowers. Things looked as drastic as *The Dybbuk*.

Penn Station and a drawing room on the train to Baltimore. Five hours later Gregory wrote "Mr. and Mrs. Gregory Kelly" for the first time at the Hotel Belvedere. That night *Seventeen* opened with a weak Baby Talk Lady, next morning the doctor came. He said I must stay in bed all week. Gregory wrote out a telegram:

CLINTON JONES
HOTEL SHERMAN
314 WEST 4TH ST
LOS ANGELES, CALIF.

MERRY CHRISTMAS AND LOTS OF LOVE GREGORY AND I WERE MARRIED YES-
TERDAY

                                                                    RUTH

Wonderful, clever Dr. Iglehart behaved as if I'd been married for years and had had a butchered abortion, but hadn't he read about our wedding? Didn't he see the big picture of us in the Baltimore *Sun?*

Washington next. Not exactly our honeymoon, but it was my first time there where Mama and Papa registered Mr. and Mrs. Clinton Jones for the first time at the Ebbett House on October 16, 1895.

Gregory registered us at the Willard. At the Belasco Theatre, the opening night went well and afterward we had supper served in our room.

Next week Cleveland, another first; I'd never played there.

77

# Chapter

————⋘∞⋙————

# 4

*Statler Hotel*
*Cleveland, Ohio*
*Wednesday, January 15, 1919*

Dear Papa,

After my telegram I thought I would write right away, but remember I was ill in Providence with ptomaine poison and the next week in New York I still felt badly. Saturday I didn't play either performance and had the doctor. He said ptomaine with complications and prescribed rest and medicine. Monday I felt enough better to get up and get married and go to Baltimore. We were married at 10:30 and left on the 12:00. I felt shaky, but managed to play Monday night in Baltimore, then the trip and excitement were too much, so the rest of the week I stayed in bed and the new understudy went on.

I'm feeling fine now and never have been so happy.

Write soon.

Love,
Ruth

*Seventeen*'s tour was coming to a finish. It was June, the Philadelphia heat was fierce, Broad Street smelled of doughnuts. Cauldrons of fat

78

bubbled in front of the Ritz where we were, and across the street at the Bellevue Stratford the Salvation Army was having its drive. Saturday night finished the season, Sunday morning leave for New York and the Algonquin, Monday night see the *Ziegfeld Follies,* Tuesday night leave Grand Central on the Bar Harbor express, the start of Gregory's first vacation. He'd waited twenty-six years to take one.

When he was four, his mother put him to work as little Mina in *Rip Van Winkle* with Joseph Jefferson. Jefferson was finishing his career, Gregory was starting his. Was it work or the attack of rheumatic fever he had when he was two that made the Army classify him 4-F?

Sometimes when we were walking, a passer-by sneered, "You ought to be ashamed of yourself, not in the Army."

Sometimes a policeman said, "Let me see your card, buddy."

Gregory took it from his vest pocket.

"Uh huh." The policeman handed it back.

Our walk was silent for a while.

Now he was on his first vacation. When the Bar Harbor express stopped at the Boston and Maine Railroad station called Newcastle and Damariscotta, it would be five weeks before we went out to Stuart's company at the Murat. Until the Holly Inn opened in Christmas Cove, we'd stay at South Bristol's Thompson's Inn.

Philadelphia had been too hot, South Bristol was too cold. When the sun went down there was nothing to do and no place to go, so we went to bed. At the Lenox or Willard or Ritz or Thompson's Inn, bed was lovely. When the Holly Inn opened, we moved over there. Still cold, but now some days it was warmer; then came more fog, more east wind to make us shiver.

Up the hill, midway between the Cove and South Bristol, the rich lady of Christmas Cove, Mrs. Miles invited us to her big house for a cup of tea. A girl from Chicago named Mary Rogers was visiting her. She and Mrs. Miles were friends who had different ways of expressing themselves, but felt the same. Mrs. Miles knew everybody took advantage of her; it gave her a wary look. Mary Rogers smiled all the time she wasn't laughing, and didn't trust anyone. Not even Galli-Curci. "I know her," she said, and laughed.

"Why are you laughing?" asked Gregory.

"In Italy, my sister is a big opera star, but Mary Garden keeps her out of Chicago."

"There's a lot of meanness in opera," stated Mrs. Miles.

"Now my sister's married to the concertmaster so maybe she'll get in." That made her laugh.

"What's her name?"

"Vera Bugbee, but she uses her husband's name, Vera Devries."

At the Holly Inn, a new guest checked in—bald, red-faced, short, stocky; he walked like a man catching a train. At dinner he'd changed from old khaki pants and sweat shirt to rumpled white ducks, faded blue blazer. He stopped at our table. "Hi, I'm Tommy Russell. I used to be on the stage; I was the original Little Lord Fauntleroy."

Gregory and Tommy laughed. I gasped. "You're *Annie Russell's* brother!"

"Her summer place is over at Pemaquid."

"I'd rather meet her than anybody!"

"We'll go over one day. I'm here for fishing, gin-making and drinking. That doesn't fit with Pemaquid."

"She was great in *She Stoops to Conquer!*"

"Yes, she was. Want to come down to my room under the piazza? I just made a bathtub of gin."

We followed him. "Do you act anymore?" I asked.

"No, my partner and I have the Feragil Gallery on East Fifty-seventh between Madison and Park." A New Yorker doesn't add New York. Where else would a New Yorker live?

Vacation was over. Gregory had liked it. Now a car took us back to Damariscotta and Newcastle, the Damariscotta River flowing between. Parlor car seats on the express to Boston, from the North Station taxi to lunch at the Whipples' stately Touraine Hotel, Boylston at Tremont Street, where I'd heard my voices. Whatever you ordered at the Touraine Hotel became a memory.

Late afternoon to the South Station; in our drawing room to Chicago, en route to Indianapolis. Four tracks down, the train to Wollaston was getting ready to pull out.

"Do you need all those clothes on?"

I was in his arms, no clothes in the way, only us. Later the moon looked in. Lovely! Always the scare of being caught, but probably not. Lovely being married, lovely making love, lovely with the moon looking in.

When the cup runneth over, say thank you. It doth not run over long. Indianapolis was hotter than Philadelphia. Hotter than anywhere. We stayed at a small hotel called The Haugh, pronounced "Whore." Clean and close to the theatre and that's all you could say for it, but that's enough when you play summer stock. We were rehearsing *Nothing but the Truth.* At last I'd be wonderful.

"The way to be wonderful is get a wonderful part," Gregory had said. "The way to have personality is get a part that has personality."

That described my part. I'd have personality, I'd be wonderful, and to *look* wonderful I'd ordered a wig at Gustav Satler's in New York, where Mary Miller's mother and grandmother had theirs made. "They don't like a beauty parlor, sweetie. They like to send out the wigs."

Mine was redder than Vivian Wessel's hair. She'd played my part in the Willie Collier Company.

"Play the straight lead," Gregory suggested.

"Why? Vivian Wessel made the hit. Why not make a hit like Vivian Wessel and look dazzling in a red wig?"

Why must things go wrong?

"You wouldn't be pleased if you were out front," said Gregory. "The wig does something to your face."

"It cost a hundred and fifty dollars!"

"Scrap it."

Too bad I couldn't scrap my performance. Through tears I asked, "What's wrong?"

He was too loving to say.

"Nobody even *likes* me." Tears. Is this what people mean when they say the stage is a hard life? Tears and nobody thinks you're good and a hundred and fifty dollars for a wig?

Gregory's arms went around me. "Some people are better at serious acting, some are better at comedy. I don't think you're a comedienne, darling; you're a leading lady."

"But I want to play *this* kind of part."

"You're a heroine, darling, not someone funny."

Did he want to say, "Give up"?

He was great in the Willie Collier part, even with my performance to handicap him. When I was on, it was like intermission; when I was off, he scored.

Next week, *Leah Kleschna* with Margaret Mower playing the title role. Gregory and I rehearsed *Piccadilly Jim,* adapted by Guy Bolton from P. G. Wodehouse's novel, to be produced by Stuart in New York for next season.

Even at night Indianapolis didn't cool off. We strolled slowly back to the hotel. *"You* play parts that are funny and parts that are serious—how did *you* find out how?"

"I've been doing it since I was four, darling."

"Could you *always* or did you have to learn?"

"I had to learn. Tommy was the actor; he could *always* do it. I learned from Mrs. Fiske and before that I got jobs because I was Tommy's brother." He covered my lips with his mouth. In the fierce Indiana heat we stood like one person. "Let's get home," he said.

I'd learned to make love; could he teach me acting? If Mrs. Fiske could teach *him,* could he pass it on?

The sheets were hot, but it didn't matter.

Afterward, we lay there.

"I've got a worry."

"No acting lessons." He pulled me close.

"No. I'm pregnant."

"Oh, darling."

"Five days."

"Oh, that's nothing."

Did the other girls have irregular periods?

We made love again.

"Do you think we were careful?"

"Yes, darling."

"This morning I felt dizzy."

"The heat?"

"I love you." I clung to him and relaxed.

In Indianapolis everybody knew Gregory, he was a favorite. How would he find a doctor?

A taxi drove us past fine houses, past smaller ones, and stopped in front of a bungalow with shade trees. "Doctor is at Walther's Drugstore," said a woman. "It's closed for Sunday. Ring the bell."

A pleasant man opened the door. "Come in," he said. "I thought we'd be better off here. Is this the young lady?"

"This is my wife."

"Well, pleased to meet you. We'll go in the back."

There was a cot, sharp instruments, a table with a pitcher of hot water, a basin.

"Mr. Kelly, you wait in the store."

Gregory kissed me.

The doctor closed the door. "Now, just try and relax. That's not easy, but you try. It'll hurt, but try and bear it."

Unbearable. What could we do? Could I go through this? *Could* I?

"I'm about halfway now. Don't tense up more than you have to." Sound of a snip.

Pain.

"That's all. You lay down the rest of the day and you'll be all right. Come in, Mr. Kelly. My wife sees all your shows."

"Thank you." Gregory had his arm around me. "Want to wait a little?"

"Oh, she's all right to go. You got your taxi out there. That'll be fifty dollars."

The nurse on Columbus Avenue had charged fifty, also.

"Is there some way we can prevent this?" I asked.

"Why, sure—have a lot of babies. That's what you were *meant* to. Let Kelly support you and you raise the kids."

In *Piccadilly Jim* I played a governess who looked pretty. I wore pretty dresses and my own hair and when the curtain fell it was hard to remember I was in the play, but at least nobody said I set their teeth on edge.

"You were good," said people, then turned to Gregory: "and *you* were great!" I could hear it before they said it.

Gregory comforted me. "Nobody could play your part any better."

"I don't want to play this part, but when I had a good one I couldn't do it. Help me."

"Why do you want to be an actress, darling?"

"I have to be! I *will.*"

"But you get in such despair."

"Help me. You have to, like Mrs. Fiske showed *you.*"

"But when I tell you, you resent it."

"That's a side of me I can't help."

"Any time you change your mind—"

"I won't."

"Any time you want to, we'll have a wonderful life."

"I'd kill myself."

"Don't do that."

"If I could just get some personality! You said I would when I had a good part."

"When you play it right. The part was comedy; you're not going to be a comedienne. You're a leading lady, little feller."

*Seventeen* reopened Labor Day, we toured until Thanksgiving.

"You're good; and Mr. Kelly, you're *great!*"

Tears, anguish.

"It's the *part.*"

Tears.

"Give up, darling."

Anguish. "I *won't* give up. I *won't.* Why does everybody knock me, even in damn places like Duluth where they should be glad any damn person *comes* here? They take a *paragraph* to say I'm no good."

"Critics don't take account of the part."

Tears.

He held me tight.

*"Don't* tell me to give up."

"I won't."

"Never?"

"Never."

"Even if I'm terrible, will you be *for* me?"

"Yes."

"Promise?"

"Yes."

His handkerchief dried my eyes.

"If I could just get in that list of 'others in the cast,' but newspapers take a *paragraph* to knock me." Tears.

"You're so hard on yourself. The good notices don't give you much pleasure and the bad ones destroy you."

"I can't help it. I *will* be great."

"You said you wished you could just get into 'others in the cast.'"

"Help me."

In Minneapolis, we left *Seventeen.* The company continued to the Coast; Tommy Kelly played Willie Baxter. We were off to New York, to the Algonquin, to rehearsals for *Piccadilly Jim.*

"We play Christmas week in Wilkes-Barre," said Stuart.

Gregory looked startled. "Wilkes-Barre's a one-nighter!"

Stuart looked bleak. "That's what the booking office has given us."

"What about trying the Klaw and Erlanger office?" I asked.

"I'm with the Shuberts."

"What do they offer *after* that?" asked Gregory.

"They'll give us their new Washington house for New Year's week."

"Not the Belasco?"

"Their new."

"The Shuberts built a Washington theatre?"

Stuart looked pained at being pressed. "It's one they're taking over."

"The National?"

"The Garrick."

"That old burlesque dump?"

He became the well-bred Kentuckian. "I have no idea."

Some shows have luck, some have trouble. *Piccadilly Jim* had trouble. The next best part to Gregory's was the rich old man. Stuart engaged James Bradbury; salary, four hundred a week.

"Hey, that's a lot!" said Gregory.

"You'll need his support, Greg; the play's on the weak side."

"I only got two-fifty for Willie Baxter."

"That's Bradbury's salary and we need him."

First rehearsal. James Bradbury brought a lot of color. Everybody felt it. A good choice for the rich man. When we stopped for lunch, Gregory and I and Stuart walked over to Childs; food delicious, also quick.

"Anything but the vegetable soup," I said. "I had it every night when I was job-hunting."

When we got back to the theatre, outside the stage door was the stage manager. "Mr. Bradbury handed in his part." He held out the blue-covered pages and a Lambs Club envelope.

Thanks, but I don't believe I would be worth the money.

James Bradbury

Stuart was furious. It's tough when someone important walks out. "Marie."

Fat Marie came.

"Where's our second list?"

"In Indianapolis. You told me we were set."

"Well, go to Indianapolis and get it. At your own expense." Stuart was on the boil.

"What about William Sampson?" How did Gregory think so fast? Had he hoped Mr. Sampson would play it?

"He's nothing like Bradbury."

"But good."

"Get William Sampson," Stuart said to Marie, and left us.

Marie made a face at him.

"We'll read-in the Bradbury part," Stuart told the company. "I wasn't satisfied with his performance; his beefiness seemed to overpower Gregory."

Gregory looked as though *he* wasn't satisfied with that remark.

"We'll try for someone not so weighty."

Trouble. Everybody sensed it. Everybody felt insecure. Everybody scowled. Mr. Sampson walked on stage and everyone relaxed.

Small, thin, every gray hair in place, perfectly cut blue suit, white shirt, elegant dark tie, he impressed by his total perfection.

"Mr. Sampson will join us," Stuart announced. "We will go through the first act. Does that please you, Mr. Sampson?"

"Sure."

He didn't sound like an actor. He sounded like people.

The stage manager explained which kitchen chairs were the doors, which the windows, which the desk.

"Ready?" asked Stuart.

There was a stir, stage right.

"Oh, Mr. Bolton." Stuart went over to him.

Why hadn't he come to Indianapolis?

Mr. Sampson, pince-nez on, looked over his part.

"You were wonderful in *Be Calm, Camilla,*" I said.

"Good part. This one isn't."

Gregory saw trouble. "It *plays* better than it reads. We did it in Indianapolis this summer."

"Who played it?"

"Aldrich Bowker."

Mr. Sampson thought about that. "He must be good."

"Gregory says people are good if they have a good part."

"Everybody doesn't know that."

Stuart walked center stage. "This is Mr. Guy Bolton."

"Don't let me disturb you. Please go on."

Can a voice sound luxurious? Guy Bolton's sounded like Monte Carlo, Palm Beach, the Ritz. Why go to Indianapolis in the summer just to see your play? In summer it's Newport, Deauville, Saratoga, Southampton, depending what month you're discussing.

"Greg," said Stuart.

Gregory took my hand.

"This is Gregory Kelly." Stuart looked at me as though he'd just met me. "And the *recent* Mrs. Kelly."

"Sorry not to have been much help. I've been in Palm Beach. It's hard to come away from." He turned to me. "Don't you find it so?"

Stuart wasn't interested if I did. "*I'm* from Kentucky," he said. "That's as far south as I care to go."

"Kentucky-bred has a right to be snooty. May I watch? I shan't stay long."

Stuart turned to the company. "Act One from the beginning."

The day after the author's visit, fat Marie passed out new pages.

"Call the act," said Stuart.

"Watch Mr. Sampson," Gregory told me. "Watch everything he does. You can't tell how he does it, but watch." Then his cue came. Gregory knocked on the seat of a kitchen chair, made his entrance and said his line.

" 'Well, that's not very welcome news,' " Mr. Sampson read from his part.

" 'I'll wager—' "

"Hold it, Greg." Stuart motioned to the stage manager. "Give Mr. Sampson the new lines Mr. Bolton wrote."

"Yes, sir."

Mr. Sampson took a pencil out of his vest pocket. "What's the line?"

The stage manager politely held out the script.

Mr. Sampson adjusted his pince-nez and read, " 'Well, that's about as welcome as an ice cream freezer would be to an Eskimo in—' Oh, I can't say that stuff."

There was a moment.

Did Stuart dread another Lambs Club letter? "Let's omit that," he said. "Greg, give Mr. Sampson his cue again."

No more Lambs Club letters.

Train to Wilkes-Barre. If you don't live there, don't go there for Christmas. Cold streets, gray weather, gray indoors. A stand can offer two surprises: the theatre or the hotel is good. The hotel was. We checked in Saturday, nothing to do till dress rehearsal Sunday. See the play that was closing here? It was a war play starring William Harcourt. We watched it from stage box right. Stage box left, Bolton and Wodehouse watched. The first scene over, stage box left was empty.

"Harcourt'll expect me to come round; I knew him when I was with Mr. Belasco." A reference to Belasco made Stuart feel even *more* above us.

"Good God, I pity you!" Big, ruddy, white-haired Harcourt shook his head. "This is a dog town—why are you here a *week?*"

87

Stuart and Gregory and I walked back to the hotel through cold black streets, not much to say.

"Life on the stage is hard," people say. We didn't say that, but we could have. Very appropriate to anyone playing Christmas in Wilkes-Barre.

In the lobby sat Bolton and Wodehouse, staring.

"Shall we have something?" said Stuart.

Bolton looked at Wodehouse, who looked as if he might burst into tears.

Stuart dealt with the situation. "We'll feel better once we get to work. The crew starts setting up at eight, at ten a line rehearsal in the ballroom."

Wodehouse looked astonished. "This hotel has a ballroom?"

"Ah, yes; all hotels have ballrooms, don't they, Greg?"

"I'm afraid so."

Stuart pointed to what had been the bar. "Let's go in."

A listless waiter was leaning on a small table.

Can *you* fool yourself? I can. "Mr. Wodehouse, a hot lemonade gives you quite a kick."

"It *does?*" He was more astonished.

"Want to try?"

"By all means."

Too bad. It didn't succeed. Nor did the play. Bolton and Wodehouse left for New York. "We'll come to Washington," said the note.

Wilkes-Barre, day before Christmas! Gregory looked through the frosty window at a diamond bracelet. "Let's go in."

"Seven hundred and fifty dollars," said the salesman.

"It's quite small diamonds," I said.

"But all perfect."

Why are small diamonds always perfect?

"Try it on." Gregory fastened it. At Tiffany's he'd bought my wedding ring, a circlet of square diamonds. From Cincinnati's elegant Ratterman's came my specially designed platinum engagement ring, the solitaire from Mama's engagement ring set in flowers of diamonds.

"Let's think," I said.

We walked down the cold street. "It's yours, little feller, if you want it, but it doesn't look like your other things. I like everything for you to be first-class. Why don't I give you a bond that'll cost the same amount?"

"Why don't I give you one too?"

"I never took a bond from a girl, but I believe I will." He kissed me. The shoppers didn't even look and in 1919 people didn't kiss on Main Street in broad daylight if this gray day could be described as broad daylight.

That week had to be rock bottom; then came New Year's at Atlantic City and *that* was rock bottom! Ever see Atlantic City in January?

> The something waves dashed high
> On the stern and rockbound
> Coast . . .

This coast was sandy.

Icy winds cut along the boardwalk. We risked a walk, nearly strangled, went back to the Traymore. Our hotel was deserted. So was the Globe Theatre. The shape of a bowling alley with rows and rows and rows of seats that no one had ever had to count, because no one had ever sat in them.

"After Wilkes-Barre, Washington," Stuart had said, but the Shuberts had canceled us in favor of a New Year's vaudeville show and tossed us into the Globe.

Just past the theatre, up the boardwalk, was a big sign:

POLA NEGRI

IN

PASSION

"Who's Pola Negri?" Would a picture called *Passion* warm us up?

It didn't. Nor the other three people in the theatre.

At ours, Stuart called a rehearsal, made some cuts, and we ran them.

"Can't hear you, Gregory." Stuart's voice rang out from behind the last row, wherever that was. It startled everybody.

Gregory and Mr. Sampson stopped the scene and Gregory looked out front. "What?" he asked.

"I can't *hear* you," repeated Stuart.

"Come down closer."

The wind blew us back to the Traymore. "We better make some plans, little feller."

"He'll get *nowhere* without you!"

"Funny, but I don't know who to tell I want a job."

"Talk it over with Mr. Sampson?"

Mr. Sampson came back with us to the Traymore for supper. He was staying at the small Apollo Hotel, where Belasco always stayed, next door to Atlantic City's *good* theatre, the Apollo. "I heard around the Club Tyler's sending a company of *Clarence* to Chicago. Would you go?"

Gregory and I looked at each other. Play a part in a second company? Great for me to follow Helen Hayes, but should Gregory follow Glenn Hunter? We looked at each other. Diamond rings, a diamond watch, a beaver coat, bonds use up money. It was January 2, not the greatest date to get in a new play.

Mr. Sampson poured milk on his corn flakes, then noticed the elegant waiter hovering. "We don't need you," he said with that clipped accent inherited from his grandmother up in Maine, who'd inherited it from *her* grandmother, who was half Indian. "I'll ring up Bill David tomorrow. Around the Club, they know what's going on."

Ringgg.

What time was it? Was it North Dakota? Had we left a call?

Was it daylight?

Gregory fumbled for the phone. "Yes," he said sleepily, then woke up. "Oh, hello, Mr. Tyler."

That woke *me.* Gregory shared the receiver with my ear.

"I understand you're getting loose, Kelly."

"Yes, sir."

"I'm putting a company of *Clarence* into the Blackstone Theatre for a run. Would you and your wife want to play the Glenn Hunter, Helen Hayes parts?"

"Well, that sounds interesting."

"It's goddam interesting to me. I've got a helluva booking and I'm missing a Bobby and Cora. Did you see the play?"

"We loved it."

"It's Tarkington at his best, and nobody's best is better than Tark's. I need a yes or a no right away, Kelly, and even before I talk business with you I'll say I prefer a yes."

"When would you go into rehearsal?"

"Monday."

"This *coming* Monday?"

"I'm not cast, but I won't let any goddam actors keep me out of rehearsal when I have an open booking at the Blackstone Theatre. What do you say, Kelly?"

"We've got to open next Monday in Washington at the Shubert Garrick."

"That burlesque house? You better quit those goddam Shuberts and come with Klaw and Erlanger."

"I'd like to, but we can't walk out."

"A helluva idea! *Why* can't you?" He laughed. "Look here, Kelly, I'll play ball with you. Sunday you and your wife get the morning train out of Atlantic City, I'll call rehearsal for one o'clock. Sunday night, take the sleeper to Washington, open that rattrap Monday, take the sleeper back to New York and I'll call Tuesday's rehearsal at nine-thirty, then you and your wife take the two-thirty that gets you to Union Station at seven. Have dinner on the train, play your lousy show and the two performances Wednesday, and take the sleeper, I'll call Thursday rehearsal at nine-thirty, take the afternoon train to Washington, after the show get on the sleeper, take the afternoon train back for Friday's show, play your lousy two on Saturday, close, take the sleeper, rehearse Sunday morning and next week leave for Chicago. I'll give you five hundred a week, first billing; your wife one-fifty. Talk it over with her and call me, Bryant 1113. Remember I'm counting on your goddam show closing! Don't let me down, Kelly! Goodbye."

That night, the Globe call-board had the closing notice. The show would fold next week in Washington. Gregory phoned George Tyler and I confided our plans to Catherine Proctor, the Canadian actress who the season before had made a hit playing Laurette Taylor's mother in *Happiness.* Now she and I were sharing dressing room number 1, kindness of Gregory.

"Helen Hayes' part is great. What a joy to be in a play that plays! You'll keep these lovely clothes?"

"They cost a lot."

"You *must* keep that evening dress."

"It cost a hundred and sixty dollars. Henri Bendel had made it to order."

"How much will they sell it for?"

"A hundred."

"It's steep, but pay it. A dress you'd most certainly regret."

*Piccadilly Jim* ended its Atlantic City agony, Sunday the company took the train to Washington, Gregory and I left on the early morning train for New York.

We checked into the Algonquin. Would I be good? Gregory had taught me a lot, would I be good? It was comedy, but Gregory said this kind of comedy I'd be all right. Was that because I told him I would?

I *didn't* tell him I wasn't sure I knew how to scream the way Cora Wheeler did in the second act. Maybe before rehearsal see if I could and not wait till Act II to find out.

"Don't be helpless."

I got Gregory to go down to the lobby, then in our bathroom, facing toward the buildings on 45th Street, door closed, I screamed. And screamed. How terrific when you try and can!

For rehearsals I dressed my best. That's for beginners. Only the great Blanche Bates wore sable, full-length, with a garlic bud or two in the pocket—she liked garlic to nibble on—toque with a bird of paradise and a square emerald ring the size of a one-cent stamp. To please Guthrie, for the first rehearsal only, Katharine Cornell always wore her broadtail coat over a dress. After that, sweaters and skirts right up and through opening night and mostly through the run.

Maude Adams wore dark wool. A dress or suit? It was something with a hat and scarf and in winter a coat of dark gray soft fur called moleskin.

At Old Vic rehearsals Edith Evans wore a black and white checked jersey suit that had seen service, cherry satin one-strap shoes that had had it.

For *Ethan Frome* Pauline Lord wore a coat with a collar pulled up over her chin, a cloche pulled down over her eyes, and took off neither hat nor coat. You had to guess when it was your cue, unless she gave you a sharp reminder: "Well, go on!"

But that was for people who'd made it. To rehearse *Clarence* I walked out of the Algonquin in my navy blue elegant wool dress, vest, collar and cuffs of powder blue taffeta, from Blum's grand Michigan Avenue shop. It had cost a hundred and fifty dollars! In 1919! It was worth it to look like an actress.

Down 44th Street to Sixth Avenue, up Sixth to 45th, we turned left and midway in the block was the Hudson Theatre stage door; we went in a little ahead of one o'clock. A short and momentous walk.

"Kelly, you play it *your* way," said Frederick Stanhope, the director, then before Gregory could say the line, Mr. Stanhope said it the way Glenn Hunter did.

Gregory was dismayed. "When *I* say it, I sound like nothing, he hits it so hard."

You wonder how you live through some directors.

Mr. Stanhope left me alone, except for: "Speak up, dear, the Blackstone's a big house." "Don't drop the end of the line, dear. Don't punch it, but get it over."

You wonder.

Five nights on the sleeper, three dinners in the diner, four suppers at the Union Station lunch counter, five *Clarence* rehearsals at the ideal Hudson Theatre, six nights of *Piccadilly Jim* at the awful Shubert Garrick, the company feeling blue. Stuart didn't speak to us, I paid a hundred dollars for the sapphire blue velvet evening gown, and the final curtain fell.

"Last act," called the stage manager, and it was.

Some talk that Stuart would reopen with "somebody more suited; Greg is out of his depth."

Nobody believed it. Everybody wrote letters and called up Packard's Agency and Chamberlain Brown, read *Variety* to see who was casting what.

At the Union Station, Mr. Sampson had farewell supper with us. We sat at the lunch counter.

"I'll have corn flakes," said Mr. Sampson.

"I love you," I told him. "I loved you the first rehearsal when you said, 'It would be about as welcome as an ice cream freezer to an Eskimo. . . . Oh, I can't say stuff like that.' " I reached over and kissed his ear.

"Hey, cut it out. I've got a wife in New York!"

"Oh, by the way, where do you live?"

"No 'by the way.' We live at the Hotel Seymour. They don't soak you like the Algonquin."

We hugged and kissed and walked down the cold platform to the sleeping car. At the gate Mr. Sampson waved.

Was I going to be good? "Gregory, *will* I be good?"

"Yes, but don't be in love with pauses. You get a cue, then you pause and think. *Once* in a while surprise the audience and speak right away. Prevents monotony. A long part, it's hard not to get monotonous. And pauses are monotonous! Mrs. Fiske said, 'If you're not going well, try cutting out all the pauses. The result is refreshing.' " Gregory would help me.

# Chapter

## 5

Someone helping. Ever since *The Pink Lady* I'd looked for someone to show me how. The Academy hadn't, Mr. Stanhope wasn't, Guy Bragdon hadn't; maybe the nearest I came to practical help was in Wollaston, when I walked over to Woodbine Street with a clipping from the Quincy *Patriot:* "Mrs. Ethel Malapredo is visiting her sister, Mrs. F. M. Dooley of 25 Woodbine Street, Wollaston. Until Mrs. Malapredo returns to the stage, she is thinking of giving lessons."

Would she think of giving me some? Number 25 stood behind a sagging picket fence. Inside, someone was playing the piano and singing.

I rang again.

Someone walked heavily toward the door. It was opened by a stout brunette with remarkably high coloring. "Yeah?"

"Does Mrs. Malapredo live here?"

"What about?"

I held up the *Patriot.* "I'd like some lessons."

"Well, you're pretty cute; wait till I tell that bum when he comes home. Come in."

I hesitated a minute.

*"I'm* Mrs. Ethel Malapredo—didn' ya hear me singin', f' Chris'sake? Come *in;* I'm not doin' anything." She led the way into a dismal room. "Ever been in the Parker House? Well, this is nothin' like it." Light blue scrolled wallpaper had turned dingy, the asparagus fern had given up. "Imagine hanging on to stuff like that! Imagine having it the *first* place!" A lampshade dropped over a battered upright with curly sheet music, a wicker rocker faced a dusty tan corduroy sofa. "Sit down if you don't care what happens to your clothes; this room's on the fritz."

"The item in the Quincy *Patriot—"*

"That clown Dooley put it in. My sister's husband, the bum. He works on the paper and those other clowns added I give lessons. I guess if y' live here, y' clown around or cut your throat."

"But *might* you give lessons?"

"Y' wanna sing?"

For the first time I was going to tell someone. "I want to be an actress."

"Why not? Y' got a good shape."

It threw me, to be accepted. "But I don't have experience." Was I arguing *against* myself?

"You'll get away with it; y' kinda got something."

A real actress thought that *I* could be one?

*"Young* is the trick. Ya know anybody?"

"I had a letter from Hazel Dawn."

"Will she help ya?"

"Oh, I don't *know* her."

"Know anyone with pull?"

"No."

"What can ya do?" She smiled a lopsided smile and winked. "I mean, ya wanna talk about."

Did I have to blush?

"All ya need is a time-step. Y' can pick stuff up from the troupe. Just get to N' York and find out howta handle y'self. Wha's your name, babe?"

"Ruth Jones."

"Thinkin' of changin' it?"

"I'd like to."

"My stage name's Belle La Blue. It's good—y' can't forget it. Here with my sister I don't bother using it. Glass of beer?"

"No, thanks."

She went down the hall; the icebox door banged.

An actress had offered me a glass of beer? In a silk wrapper at three in the afternoon, with rouge on and black paint over her eyes!

"Know a song I did big?" Her voice rumbled back, followed by herself, froth beading her rouged lip. She sat down at the piano and hit it.

> "Every *day*
> The papers *say*
> There's a robbery
> In the *park!*
> So I sit *alone*
> At the Y.M.C.A.
> Singing jus' like a *lark.*
> Oh, there's *no*
> Place like *home*
> Ta da da *da.*
> But I'm afraid *to*
> Go *home* in the dark.
> I'm afraid *to*
> Go home in the *dark.*"

She swung around. "I got personality and legs. Ya live with your folks?"

"With my mother and father."

"A show I know plays Boston next week. *Puss Puss,* Jean Bedini, the old Howard. But that wouldn't be for *you.* Look, I could guy you into thinkin' I was teachin' ya, but why take your cash? Y' live near?"

"Elmwood Avenue."

"Some names! This is Woodbine, *you* live Elmwood. Get to Times Square!

"Know what I do here? Take a nap. I tell my sister, 'How can y' tell ya ain't dead?' My niece, fifteen an' very developed, last night is flyin' her tail around an' I say, 'Who is he?' 'It's the Methodist Church candy pull,' she tells me! *Her* age I been felt up by every guy in the show and the leadin' lady notices my skirt has gathers to the front and spreads word I'm in the family way, dirty tart, but it shows I wasn't down to a taffy pull! My niece has legs on her like a Knabe piano. Have *you* got good legs?" She flipped up my skirt. "Find out what to do with 'em is all the lesson *you* need. Know what I call my niece? Bessie Knabe. I guess they'll be glad when I pull out."

It was only Woodbine Street, but somebody who was actually on the stage thought I had something!

Belle La Blue and Katherine knew my secret and finally I told Mama. She burst into tears. "Oh, Ruth, *why* do you have to be so different?" All the things that had happened, but I'd never seen her in tears. "Don't tell Papa. You'll break his heart."

His heart was set on my being a physical culture teacher. One evening I surprised myself and said, "I don't want to be." It was after supper; we'd just finished dessert.

"Tell you what I'll do, Snuggy—I'll stake you to Sargent's School of Physical Education."

"I don't *want* to." The minute I said it I wished I hadn't.

"Clinton, Ruth is upset."

"What about?"

"She doesn't want to be a physical culture teacher."

"Why the hell not?"

"Clinton, some people get inspired over some things, others over *others. You* got inspired to be a sailor, not a carpenter like you said your father was."

"She doesn't know *what* she's inspired over."

"Be patient, Clinton."

He didn't look patient. "What *do* you think you're inspired over?"

I stared at the fern basket on our table. "I don't know," I lied.

"Tell Papa, Ruth. He wants to know."

Could I believe my ears? Mama, so *for* me, so understanding, so trustworthy.

"I don't want to be a physical culture teacher," I said, doggedly.

*"Why* don't you?"

"Because I'd rather be dead," I whispered.

"Ruth, don't say that. God will hear you."

The atheist brushed that aside. "God's listening to harps and trumpets and watching sparrows fall."

How did an atheist know so much about the Bible?

"God's listening to *everybody,* Clinton."

"God's listening to everybody, but I'm listening to *her.* "

Around our table hovered my future.

"God damn it, don't sit there like a dying calf. If you got something to say, spit it out!"

Mama looked at me, Papa looked at me. I couldn't look up. "I want to go on the stage."

Could he stop me? Would he hit me? Would the pause *ever* end? Had any place ever been as silent as around our dining room table?

"What makes you think you got the stuff it takes?" he asked, voice not angry, only grave.

Was it God or luck or St. Chrysostom the Eloquent, the Golden Mouth, that gave me words?

Papa heard me out, then thought. The whole room was full of silence. No train went by, no dog barked; it seemed as if *everything* had stopped.

"Everybody's got a right to a chance," he said, "and I'm going to see you get yours. Is there someplace you can go and learn? When you get up in meetin' you got to deliver the goods."

"I wrote a letter to Miss Doris Olssen, the leading lady at the Castle Square Theatre, and she thinks The American Academy of Dramatic Arts is fine. That's where *she* went and she's a leading lady."

"Where are they located?"

"They have an advertisement in *Theatre* magazine."

"Drop 'em a line, see what they got to say."

I wrote the letter that night.

14 Elmwood was full of worry. Why couldn't I be a physical culture teacher? Why wouldn't I settle down with a good man? Why didn't the Academy write me?

Worry kills you or gets solved or you learn to live with it until one day, on the corner of the dining room table, is The American Academy of Dramatic Arts catalog!

I saw it through our dining room window before I even turned our brass doorknob. The same doorknob that's there today.

Buff paper cover, dark brown lettering, very thick. In our hall chair I read the history of the Academy, the story of the founder, description of the classes, list of famous students, praise from *The New York Times,* a full page on how to get in. "Send $25 with an application letter and request the book of recitations. For the entrance examination learn one comic and one serious and be prepared to recite them to the President of the Academy, Franklin H. Sargent."

What if he didn't accept me?

Hadn't things worked out so far? Hazel Dawn wrote me; The American Academy of Dramatic Arts sent me their catalog after only two letters!

"Junior year commences October 21st. Tuition for the first year $400."

Four hundred dollars!

"Tuition for the first year $400."

*Fourteen Elmwood Avenue*
*Wollaston, Massachusetts*

Dear Sirs,

Please send me your booklet of recitations and an application blank to enter the American Academy of Dramatic Arts. I wish to join your Junior Class for next year, nineteen fourteen. I will mail the blank with the twenty-five dollars next week.

Sincerely yours,
Ruth Gordon
September seventeen
nineteen hundred and thirteen

High school days were over. Mama put my high school diploma with the things she treasured. I never saw it again. Two selections from the American Academy booklet were memorized. Mr. Sparrow carried my trunk down the front steps.

"Why don't the tag say 'Ruth Jones'?"

"Ruth wants it this way."

"Her name's Ruth Jones; this says: 'Miss Ruth Gordon, Three Arts Club, 340 West 85th Street, New York City, New York.'"

"Well, we won't bother with that now, Mr. Sparrow."

Won't bother! For seventeen years and eleven months I'd been Ruth Gordon Jones, now the rest of my life I was going to be Ruth Gordon and Mama said, "We won't bother with it"!

The Quincy *Patriot* put in a note:

Miss Ruth Gordon Jones, daughter of Mr. and Mrs. Clinton Jones of 14 Elmwood Avenue, Wollaston, is leaving for New York to go on the stage. She will appear there under the name of Ruth Gordon, named for Dr. John Alexander Gordon of Hancock Street, Quincy.

Papa bought tickets on the Fall River Line boat. Mama cut out my going-away olive green broadcloth suit, cut up the bear stole that Mrs. Brigham had given her, and made the collar, cuffs, buttons for the jacket.

"I never thought this day would come," she said. That afternoon I was going. It was the *first* time that I heard her say it. Next summer she'd say it again.

How quiet our parlor! How full of lampshades and doilies and thoughts of how to make the lightest sponge cake! The room was all Mama, except for the big black leather chair the Mellin's Food factory workers had bought Papa when he married. All of it so permanent-looking, and next summer the secondhand furniture dealer would take it away.

Looking down at our square piano was a large brown oval print of Queen Louise. Did she know how to be queen or did somebody show her?

"Mama, be *glad* I'm going; I can't ask you and Papa for things all my life."

"I hoped you'd fall in love with some nice boy."

"I don't want to love *anybody,* Mama. I got blinders on; all I see is where I want to *go.* That's my armor and my strength. Don't you always say to don't be helpless? And I'm not."

Newport Avenue sidewalk was covered with yellow maple leaves. I was walking along it for the last time. Past Mazie Hastings' house, past Anna Weston and the Weston boys', past Brazee Hall, across Brook Street. Coming out of the barbershop was Clark Boynton.

"Gladys says you're off to New York." Clark Boynton was the most attractive man in town, said Gladys.

"Yes."

Dark brown hair and skeeky-looking. He'd told Gladys I had a cute shape. The night she told me, I looked in the mirror. I didn't look bad with nothing on, but who saw me? I slipped on the lacy combing jacket Anna Witham gave me and let it float off one shoulder, one breast uncovered. Pretty, not like Muriel's brother's wife when she showed us *her* breasts. Her nipples were brown and crusty.

"That kid's got a cute shape."

Why that scary feeling? I'd pulled off the lace jacket, pulled on my nightdress and jumped into bed.

Mama nodded coolly to Clark.

*Why* that scary feeling? Delicious, but scary; why did I think of Mrs. Malapredo? "Find out what to do with 'em," she'd said. Did Mama know? Is that how she got Papa? Had she ever felt that scary feeling about Papa?

"Papa's going to give you ten dollars a week. Eight-fifty is for your Three Arts Club room and board, the rest is to buy garters and hairpins and carfare."

"I wouldn't spend money on *carfare;* I'll walk."

In the South Station, Papa waited at the gate. "You should be coming with us, Mama."

"Oh, I'm going to Ada's and enjoy myself."

Down past a lot of gates, the Fall River boat train stretched out, a line of shiny parlor cars with navy-blue-uniformed porters at the steps of each. We walked past them to the day coach, Mama's arm around me. "Write every day," she said. "You know you're still only seventeen and I'll worry." Had her face ever been such a bright pink?

"I will, Mama."

"Even just a line, you *write*."

"Annie, you ought to come."

"And if you're sick I'll come right away."

"Mama, I'm going to get everything great for you."

"Just be a good girl."

The conductor looked at his big gold watch. "All aboard!"

"Goodbye, Mama. I'll make everything up to you."

The train gave a gentle shake.

"Be a good girl." Her hat was a little over one side, the veil down. She turned away and walked toward the gate.

"Dammit, she ought to come with us."

"I'm going to get her *everything*."

He nodded. Did he think spending four hundred dollars would make me an actress?

The train rushed through red and yellow woods.

"You have your accommodations on the boat?" asked the conductor. Papa showed him.

The conductor shook his finger at me. "Be a good girl."

Why be? Does being good get people anywhere? What Mama got was Papa; did that make up for what she did without? When I said I was going to New York to be fast for a year, what had I meant?

The Fall River Line's *Puritan* was like a boat in a storybook—white decks, grand lounge with grand garnet velvet chairs and lots of them, lots of garnet velvet couches. The dining room was just as grand. Lots of white tables, lots of black waiters. We picked out what was cheapest on the menu, then I went to bed and prayed it would be calm going around Point Judith. Papa, being an atheist, stayed up. Why waste a voyage? In the early early morning we docked somewhere close to the Battery.

What a noise! What a clatter! Nothing in Boston made such a din.

Papa asked for the subway, we went down under and got out at 86th Street and Broadway. Still noisy, but different; my heart sank. A strip of *grass* ran down the middle of Broadway and there were *trees!* Tree-lined streets and grass were what I was getting away from.

West on 85th Street, we crossed West End Avenue; just ahead was Riverside Drive and midway in the block was 340. "Three Arts Club" was carved in stone. The years had changed red brick to the color of dirt, but I wasn't noticing that; I was where I was going to live in New York. Papa pushed the door open. We were in a small gray marble hall mostly elevator cage and an armchair the right size for a giant. Through an arch was the office.

"Yes?" asked a woman behind the oak rail at a roll-top desk. "Yes?" she asked crossly before we had time to say anything.

In this small dingy space I lived one of my happiest moments, but that would come next year.

"How do you do, I'm Ruth Gordon. I have a room reserved beginning today."

Crosspatch glared at me. "We expected you *yesterday*. You have to pay for your room."

"I wrote I was coming today."

"What you *wrote* has nothing to do with it; rooms are reserved from the date they're given up. The girl gave the room up yesterday. Do you expect a room to be vacant a *day?*"

"She'll pay beginning yesterday," said Papa.

It never occurred to him or to me I might not pass the examination. A buzz sounded on the old-fashioned switchboard.

"Wait by the elevator till Miss Howes comes; she's in charge. I'm Miss Schoonover, the secretary." She scowled at the girl on the switchboard. "Get Miss Howes."

Sometimes you're discouraged over practically anything, then something *really* discouraging happens and you're not. What did I care who was cross? I was on my way!

From where we stood by the elevator we could see the library. Glass-doored bookcases lined one wall, a black Mission table with curly magazines held the center spot, a black Mission oak rocker, an armchair, an opalescent electrolier overhead, a framed photo of a lady in a deaconess cap beside a drastic photo of Minnie Maddern Fiske. Down the elevator shaft came a sigh; the elevator crept down. Out stepped a tall, thin, gray-haired woman, crosser than the one at the roll-top. "I'm Miss Howes."

"How do you do, I'm Ruth Gordon. This is—"

"Step in." She gave me a push and pointed to the elevator.

Papa followed.

"Men are not allowed upstairs."

"I'm her father."

"Not allowed up."

Papa backed away. "I'll be right here. Come down when you're ready."

The elevator sighed and started. "You may use this going *up*. Coming *down,* walk. Fifth," said Miss Howes to a colored boy who didn't seem to care *where* he went.

At the fifth, he rattled open the elevator door and looked off into space.

"You needn't wait, Martin. I'm going back to my room."

"Yes'm." He watched us go down the dark hall.

Miss Howes turned the corner and opened a door, two from the end. "You're lucky," she said, crossly, "to get a single room."

What was her definition of luck? This was the worst room I ever saw. Its window was barred by the fire escape's iron rail that just missed the window in the next apartment house. Mustard-colored wallpaper and it was time to choose some more. Streaked with soot in the corners, it peeled off by the radiator. In front of the table with an ink-stained green blotter was a hard-seated, straight-backed chair. Gray seersucker covered the sagging bed. Miss Howes pushed open a door beside it. "You share the washbasin with the girl in there. You're dramatic, aren't you?"

"Yes, I am."

"We don't like loud voices."

Why talk loud?

"We have more music and art girls, but *some* drama. I hope you won't cause trouble." She looked cross and went.

I was in *my* room. In *New York!* I ran some water in the washbasin. *My* washbasin and a stranger's. I was going to be an actress—goodbye, old days. I turned off the water and ran down four flights of stairs.

Papa stood looking out of place, the way he always did.

"I *wish* they'd let you see it! The booklet says no men, but I didn't know that meant you."

"Is it what you want?"

"I *love* it!"

"Then I'll go along up to the corner. I noticed something called The Bretton Hall Hotel. You'll want to unpack and wash up."

"The appointment's at one."

"You might drop your mother a line. Tell her we didn't get shang-haied or mangled. Don't cut it short; let her know how we are."

The Broadway trolley was red. Quincy trolleys were yellow.

"I won't talk, Papa." To myself I whispered the speech from *Mrs. Dot,* one of the comedy recitations. The red trolley had reached 79th Street. I began to whisper the speech from *Ingomar, the Barbarian,* chosen from the drama recitations.

"Fifty-seventh Street," the conductor called out.

We walked east to the corner of Seventh Avenue. Carnegie Hall looked as though it had been there a long time. The Academy occupied some uneven upper floors and the theatre in the basement.

The door to the office marked SECRETARY was open. "I'm Mr. Diestel," said the man inside. Dark gray hair, an untrustworthy manner; he ran the Academy. "Mr. Sargent, our president, will conduct your examina-tion. He will ring when he is ready."

Papa, holding his hat, sat uneasily on the edge of a chair, his eyes avoiding mine.

A bell rang.

"That's Mr. Sargent. Come with me."

"Papa, please wait here. I couldn't if you're watching."

He tried to smile. "You're in charge."

The president's office looked as though nothing had or would ever change. The same could be said of Mr. Sargent, somber as his frock coat, his voice drenched with discouragement. "Have you had any stage experience?" he asked, mournfully.

"No, sir."

He stared beyond the grimy roofs of West 57th. Had he forgotten me? Was he trying to?

He broke the silence. "Let me hear what you have prepared."

"I chose *Mrs. Dot* for the comedy one."

"Ah, yes." He seemed resigned.

Day and night, night and day, I'd rehearsed it; now there was nothing to do but begin. Could I unclench my hands? Of course, forget all thought of gestures. In Wollaston my hands were part of my perform-ance. "You know you've got to marry me." Was this thread of a voice *mine?* "I must insist upon it. After all, you've been trifling with my affection shamefully. Oh, we shall be so happy, Gerald." Why did my voice tremble? "And we'll never grow any older than we are now. You know I'm an awfully good sort really. I talk a lot of nonsense, but I don't mean it. I very seldom listen to it myself." *Must* I sound so tacky? Couldn't I sound stylish? Always pretending I was; now it would be useful. "I'm sick of society." Were my knees sick of supporting me? Sit down. At home I moved around to show my cute shape. "I want to be domesticated. I'll sit at home and darn your socks and I shall hate it and I shall be so happy. And if you want to be independent you can have a job at the brewery. We want a smart energetic man to keep it up to the times. And we'll have a lovely box at the opera, and you can always get away for the shooting." Plenty of nerve when I didn't need it and now waiting in Mr. Diestel's office was Papa with four hundred dollars they wouldn't *take!*

Mr. Sargent looked out the window; the only sound was my heartbeat. How long can a pause last? "You have prepared another?"

*Ingomar, the Barbarian* was my last chance.

"Everybody's got a right to a chance," Papa believed, and he drew two hundred dollars out of his account at the Shawmut Savings Bank, raised the other two hundred on his insurance. The cash was in his pocket. At Aunt Ada's, Mama was waiting to hear. Our cat, Punk, was over at the Litchfields'. Would I let everybody down? At home I knelt on the floor and looked up at someone, but today I didn't dare to. I stayed where I'd recited *Mrs. Dot.*

Mr. Sargent's moody eyes rested on me. "Do you know any others?"

"No, sir." Defeat was mighty. What a long way I'd come to fail again.

"Do you do imitations of your friends?"

"No, sir."

"Would you like to try any?"

"No, sir."

He seemed relieved. "You will do, I think." He stood up.

*What* did he say?

"School starts Monday."

Could I believe my ears?

He opened the door to Mr. Diestel's office.

Papa stood up.

I burst into tears.

"We will accept her," Mr. Sargent said, mournfully.

The Academy secretary turned on a tight-stretched smile. "Congratulations."

Was it a lie, was it a dream? Had I died and gone to heaven? Was I going to enter The American Academy of Dramatic Arts?

"Mr. Sargent, her mother and I want to thank you for getting her started." Papa shook Mr. Sargent's hand. "You'll get a letter from her mother. She can put in words what I feel."

"Ah," said Mr. Sargent, and went moodily back into his office.

For the first time I saw four hundred dollars. It was old money. Papa counted it slowly.

Twelve years later I saw Herbert Bayard Swope's ten-thousand-dollar bill. Forty years later I saw Willie Maugham's hundred thousand dollars that his secretary, Alan Searle, carried in the briefcase in the cabin on the channel boat. Willie's hundred and Swope's ten didn't add up to Papa's. "Everybody's got a right to a chance," he'd said, and put up his life's savings.

Mr. Diestel counted it. "On Monday, be seated in our theatre by nine A.M. Mr. Sargent will make the opening address."

Papa and I floated down Fifth Avenue. Did he wonder if I had what it takes?

People stared at us. "What actress is that?" they must be saying. Olive green jacket made like Pierrot's, the skirt cut circular according to an expensive Élite pattern; black velvet hat, outlined in white ostrich, could only belong to an actress.

The Fifth Avenue bus took us up Riverside Drive to Grant's Tomb, that Papa thought I ought to see. I looked harder at Riverside Drive, where *Theatre* magazine said many stars lived, and already I lived just around the corner.

Nine A.M. Monday, sixty-one strangers and I started to learn how.

"Ladies and gentlemen, may I bid you welcome." What if Mr. Diestel hadn't accepted Papa's four hundred and I had had to take the Fall River Line boat back?

"The president of the Academy will speak to you. Mr. Sargent."

Was he keeping time to the "Death March" from *Saul?* Sixty-one strangers and I broke into restrained applause.

Mr. Sargent inclined his head and stared at some unhappy faraway. "Ladies and gentlemen of the class of nineteen fourteen, today commences our eighteenth year of The American Academy of Dramatic Arts, founded by so distinguished a theatre figure as Mr. Daniel Frohman. Let us do honor to our illustrious founder. It is you who will carry on the Academy's great tradition.

"Nineteen fourteen is a good year to find oneself in an academy. Here will be our haven."

Fifty-four years later, when the Academy honored me, I quoted, " 'Nineteen fourteen is a good year to find oneself in an academy. Here will be our haven.' "

The class of 1968 roared.

" 'Let us hope that when our school year ends in April, this dread war will be over.' "

The 1968 class laughed harder.

"I need not remind you of the great tradition of years past. Nor need I dwell on your duty to uphold it. The stage can be the scene of noble achievement or it can be an ignominious display. Bear yourselves with dignity, befitting the profession which included the great Roscius, 'who wept at his friend's grave,' reported Julius Caesar, 'and as he wept, paused to note how to bring tears and felt no less his grief.'

"Our great profession includes William Shakespeare, ofttime actor; Betterton, Kean, Garrick, Mrs. Siddons, the great Mary Anderson; countless noble others. Do them honor. Conduct yourselves with the decorum which may forever wipe out the opprobrium once attached to theatre. In the trolley cars or the elevated, do not study your part. Do not call attention to the fact that you are actors. In the fierce light of the arena be actors, in private life draw no undue attention. May the Academy help you realize your gifts, help add your achievements to the illustrious record of those gone before. God speed." Funeral-paced, he walked back whence he came, accompanied by restrained applause. I didn't see him again until the school year had ended.

"We thank our president," said Mr. Diestel, "for his inspiring message. Mr. Sargent adds to grandeur of thought, *I* take up the practical details. From the bulletin board, copy your schedules for the week. Here are further instructions: Go to Brentano's bookstore on Fifth Avenue at Madison Square. For those unfamiliar with New York, I recommend you take the Fifth Avenue bus. Buy *The Concise Oxford Dictionary*. It contains the correct pronunciation of the English language as taught in Mr. Putnam's speech class. Nothing in our curriculum is more important than learning how to speak.

"Next: Go to Berner's makeup store, address on the bulletin board. Berner's have prepared makeup boxes required in your makeup course. Bring yours to makeup lessons.

"Miss Lutz, our fencing teacher, has written out requirements for fencing apparel purchasable at Eaves Costume Company, address on bulletin. That is all, except, in the eloquent language of our president, 'God speed.' "

Every day except Saturday and Sunday, I walked from West 85th to West 57th and back. Classes let out in time for me to just make it to the Club for a terrible lunch. None of the food was a treat, but lunch was terrible. The only reason to eat it was it was included in the bill.

Breakfast was seven to eight unless you were in a play, which nobody was. If anyone *should* get a job, a tray would be left in her room at nine sharp. At midnight everybody with or without a job must be in. Miss Jerome, five-foot, brown-haired, brown-eyed, parchment-skinned ninety-pound replica of a hoot owl, locked the door and wrote a report. Thereafter, if a girl arrived, Miss Jerome rolled back the iron chain, glared like Cerberus and wrote the ill tidings to Miss Howes. Three ill tidings and you were out for good, to go to the devil or back home. They made it hard for you to let your foot slip at The Three Arts Club; the ladies on the board of governors demanded virtue. They'd all made it into the Social Register and Dun and Bradstreet, but en route hadn't *they* ever stayed out till 12:01 A.M.? If they had, they'd forgotten it.

"What if you arrive at three A.M. without a certificate to show you've been run over?" asked Dotty Forbes.

Gwen Thorpe nodded her blond head. "Or lost your mind?"

"Or got stuck in the elevated without a letter from the el?" asked Puller, who had enough muscle to unstick even the el.

I loved Anna and Katherine and Gladys, but for this year they came second to Edith and Dotty and Ruth and Gwen, Olive Templeton, Louise Davidson, Bess McAdams, Miss Frances Treat, Puller, known only as Puller, and Margaret Davis.

*The Three Arts Club*
*October 31, 1914*

Dear Kay,

Thanks for the silver lingerie clips. My birthday was quiet, but great. This place is perfect. I am wild about the girls. You would be, too. I know you wonder how I passed my exam. *Very well,* if I say so myself. I *wish* you could see Mr. Sargent! So charming, I wasn't the slightest bit afraid. My physical appearance was absolutely perfect, he said, and my personality unique. I told him my fears about being short and he said, "Marguerite Clark is petite." I'm telling you this, not because I'm conceited, but you're interested.

I presented your mother's letter to Mrs. Sawyer. I *wish* you could see her apartment. Park Avenue some say is more exclusive than Fifth Avenue and isn't Mr. Sawyer great! I could be wild about him.

School is nine to one. This afternoon Amy Dennis, a girl here, asked me to a professional matinee a friend of hers has a small part in. A professional matinee is when a company gives a performance for all the other actors playing plays to see it. Amy's friend was understudy for Patricia Collinge in *He Comes Up Smiling.* Last week Henriette McDaniels came here for dinner with a girl. When I got introduced I told her all the times you and I saw her at the Castle Square stock company. She is acting with May Robson's company.

The girl I share a washbasin with may get in the Metropolitan Opera. Think of knowing a Prima Donna! Hazel Dawn opens next month. She is in Phila. now. Miss Olssen is in Wash. with *The Misleading Lady.* José Collins opens Monday in *Suzi.* Olive Templeton called yesterday. You'd be wild about her, she's stunning!

Love,<br>
Ruth

Stunning, also frank. "Do something about your voice, Ruth, you'll put me to sleep!"

How many handicaps can a five-foot eighteen-year-old, not pretty, no connections, no talent, get away with? How far can intention take you? If you jump in and swim, sometimes you sink, but a good many times you stay afloat. Look before you leap is good advice, but when you leap, give a good one. It may be the right one or the wrong or the last one, but if you do it, *go!* Let the tombstone read: "Before *this,* I got a lot of things my way."

For instance, could you pick a school where Hazel Dawn's cousins went?

For Thanksgiving her cousins gave a dinner, and Hazel Dawn was really there! So beautiful! She had changed my whole life and when I met her I couldn't let any words out.

After dinner there was dancing. Hazel wore a slinky ruby velvet dress. When she danced it was like watching a show; when she left I felt I'd lost something. She didn't know she'd changed my life, didn't know I couldn't get up courage to talk to her.

At school I wasn't doing what I meant to. I didn't seem to fit in. Is that the way it is when you try something new? That's how I reassured myself, but then when I came home for Christmas, I didn't fit in there. We talked, but there was nothing to say. Discouraging. So was Christmas dinner. Usually we went to Dorchester to Clare's aunt and uncle, a big celebration with lots of relatives, big tree, presents. This Christmas, Clare was married and in the South. Some snippy presents came from Dorchester, but no invitation to the party. Turkey cost a lot, so we had roast pork. Anna Witham came down in the morning to bring me a present; Mama asked her to stay to dinner. I felt embarrassed.

"Thank you, Mrs. Jones, but I have to go home."

Didn't Mama know that Anna would have to be with her mother and stepfather and grandmother and grandfather? Why would she have Christmas dinner with us? After dinner I showed Mama how they taught me to put on a stage makeup. She burst into tears. Maybe I wouldn't come home anymore.

"Goodbye, Mama. Goodbye, Papa." The South Station again, but instead of the Fall River Line, I took the New York train.

The new term. Was I doing well? Mostly I seemed scared. Why couldn't I get the hang of things? Some of our class, I thought, were good; but then when the senior class gave their performances at the Belasco or Lyceum, were they like actors you pay to see?

For the end-of-term finals, everyone got one big scene. Mine was in Galsworthy's *Joy*. Mae Morrissey played my mother. She wasn't going to be an actress, she was being kept, and going to school filled up the days.

"Rehearse your scenes at home," urged Mr. Jehlinger. "Go over what you're told in rehearsal. The final plays are important."

"Girls' clubs give me the willies," said Mae. "Come home with me and rehearse."

The taxi stopped at the Hotel Belleclaire, West 77th Street and Broadway. We rode up in an elevator with looking glasses. Mae unlocked the door to a white and gold sitting room. Gilt chandelier, pale blue taffeta curtains, gold chairs upholstered in cream with rosebuds woven in, all seemed to focus on the big pale blue velvet sofa piled with rainbow silk pillows, two Kewpie dolls and a white teddy bear in a sailor suit. Beside it, a small table held a doll in lacy skirts, the phone underneath. Mae asked for room service. "Tell a waiter if he weighs in in three minutes I'll set him up a trust fund and advance him half a dollar for now. . . . Why don't you come, too? I got a cute girl with me and we can

> Sing and dance
> An' talk about
> the weather.

Sure I sing; didn' ya catch me in *The Midnight Sons?*" She laughed and hung up. "They're a good bunch, and they know who clamps onto two bits and who not."

"Do you have a bathroom here?" I asked.

"No, dear, we pee out the window. Whatta ya talkin' about? Or as old lady Putnam would say, 'Whot ah yeeou toking ay-bote?' He should get his pants off oftener." She showed me into the orchid and lace bedroom, mostly taken up by an orchid chiffon bed. "Here's the water closet. That's what we call it in Mauch Chunk, P–A., only ours was a two-holer in the yard. Fred says, why didn' we have a three-holer in case we met someone? Whatta ya waiting for—are ya scared I'll watch? I'll sing so I don't even *hear* ya."

The doorbell rang.

As I came back to the sitting room, a handsome black waiter huffed and puffed to show he was out of breath. "Didn' I get here fast?"

"You got speed, kiddo." Mae pointed to a white and gold cabinet. "Pour a little water in the bottle after; he marked it to see if I take any." She handed me the menu. "Broiler with French fries? French pastry?"

"Slick."

The waiter knocked back a slug from the bottle marked Old Overholt. "Chew a Sen-Sen."

He pulled a box out of his hip pocket, waved it and went.

"He'll be all day before he's up again. Let's do the goddam scene." She picked up her copy. "Fred tried to read it and fell asleep and I'd spiked a glass of champagne with brandy for when I want him to have some rooty-toot, but he dropped off." She flipped the book open. "Where f' Chris'sake did they dig this up? 'I *thowt* I should have more cone-fidence. I *thowt* I should be able to face it bet-tah in London, if yew came dohn heah o-penly, and *noh* I feel I mustn't speak or look at yew—' He should quit playing with himself. Anybody ever hear of this coot?"

"John Galsworthy is important."

"Fred could get me with the Shuberts, but he doesn't like me to sweat. In a musical, ya sweat, plus everybody's finger's up your snail."

My face got red.

Mae laughed. "Y' might like it. Find out."

Shouldn't I go? All right to want to be sophisticated, but not shocked. Shouldn't I leave?

"You wanna walk in from the bedroom like this room's the garden? When I go out with my pash following, I'll open the door and go in the hall; nobody's around this time of day. The book says, 'She sets her lips.' How do I do *that*, f' Chris'sake?" She tightened the Cupid's bow God had given her, to which she'd added more. " 'Walk toward the house,' it says, 'Lever following.' Here I go, followed by Hotstuff. Ya think

111

anybody gives a damn about this?"

When she was out in the hotel hall I rushed in from the bedroom. " 'Mother!' "

Mae reappeared. " 'Oh! Heah yew ah!' "

" 'Yes.' "

" 'Where hev yew bean? Yew look dreadfully hort—hev yew bean running?' "

" 'Yes—no.' "

Mae referred to the book. "What's it mean, I look at you fixedly? What the hell's 'fixedly'?" She threw the book down. " 'Wot's the mattah—yew're trembling! Ahn't yew well, deah?' "

" 'Yes—I don't know.' "

" 'Wot is it, dorling?' "

I suddenly clung to her. " 'Oh, Mother.' "

She jerked away from me. "Do I look like a mother, f' Chris'sake? I dunno if I can do this anymore. Last night Fred had me up at his goddam stone castle up at Eighty-eighth on the Drive; his mother's supposed to be in Pinehurst showin' her jumpers, only last night she wasn't. The butler runs in screamin', 'Quit humpin', Mr. Fred, your mama's comin' up the steps. She'll cut the balls offa ya.' " Mae made a face and picked up the book. " 'I cahn't reason with yew. As to whot yew heard, it's—ridiculous.' " She went over to the Old Overholt and poured some. "He's got a filthy tongue, but he did say 'Mr. Fred.' Y' want some?"

"Oh, no, thanks."

"Fred says for me to quit. 'Ya got a shape makes everybody wanna paw ya, not *listen* to ya!' "

The door swung open. "Luncheon now bein' served, ladies."

"Move your ass, Sunshine. We're starving in the midsta plenty—plenty of baloney!"

*She* didn't want to be my mother and Mama certainly didn't want to be *her*.

*14 Elmwood Avenue*
*April 21, 1915*

Dear Ruth,

I felt awful not to wash your blue batiste dress, but you said you need it for the play and the post office closed at five. I did not have time. Have it done at my expense, I sent you a dollar Saturday, registered. Did you get it? Let me know, as I hold the voucher.

Have you come around yet? Did you send me laundry last week? Let me know if you told Miss Howes the waist disappeared.

I wish I could see you in the plays. Are visitors allowed? I am going to see Katherine Follett in the senior play Friday night. We are having lovely weather. Be sure and send your professional picture proofs soon for we are anxious to see them. Your father is anxious to see you. I will send another dollar the last of the week. Have just made a cake for the Women's Exchange.

Love,<br>Mama

It takes time to learn that trouble's your best friend. You can count on it sticking with you. Learn to get in step with it; there's always plenty around. Mr. Jehlinger had said the final plays were important and I could tell I wasn't any good.

Hoot-owl Jerome put a special delivery letter down beside my dinner plate.

Mama had a stroke. Come when you can—

Was I crying about Mama? Or about my leading part that managers might see and engage me for their new play.

"What is it?" asked Gwen.

"Just some trouble."

The elevator creaked up. Maybe when I read the whole letter it wouldn't be as bad.

Dr. Adams says it may be the second stroke. The first one he thinks took the shape of a bad headache. This one, he says, has the signs of a second one. Her right side is paralyzed. She can talk, but it does not sound like her. Dr. Adams got us a good nurse. This will be a long time she'll be helpless. Dr. Adams says people recover and her age is in her favor and while he cannot exactly say, he believes she will at least have partial recovery of her speech and limbs. I left a deposit of cash at your school that will pay your fare. Her memory does not serve her and she asks where you are. It will relieve her to see you. She would not like you to come till you finish your course. You're entitled to the $400 worth. Write when and I will meet you.

Too bad this had to happen.

Papa

Would he expect me to stay home and look after her? Today Mr. Jehlinger had said his first encouraging words. "You came close to getting it today."

Should I go? Not finish?

"She would not like you to come till you finish your course."

113

*Then* would I get hooked?

"Don't be helpless, Ruth." Would she think I should stay and keep house?

Question to avoid: Should I think of what was right for others or what was right for me?

Monday morning I packed my white voile. Downstairs a letter from Mama; was Papa's letter a mistake?

*14 Elmwood Avenue*

My dearie,

I was so glad to get your letter this A.M. and hope to get your laundry tomorrow. I have made some cake for the Women's Exchange this A.M. and will send you the dollar. I enclose 10¢ for a treat. I am going to Aunt Ada's to lunch and am late, so will have to hurry. Had a pleasant time at the Women's Club yesterday. I am now at work on some underclothes for myself, but have made a pretty lace-trimmed petticoat for you.

Papa is so anxious to see you. I telephoned his letter to him yesterday. He was pleased.

Have you come around yet? Would it do any good if I wrote the Club about your waist that disappeared? I think it might help wake them up.

I will close and get dressed for Aunt Ada's.

Love,
Mama

Papa's letter had come special delivery.

In the dressing room, everyone dipped into the one can of Albolene and rubbed their makeup off. On the call-board was the list of appointments with Mr. Sargent to discuss the future.

"Ladies, are you decent?" Mr. Jehlinger's voice.

We pulled our wrappers on, Mae buttoned her blouse, we stood up.

"Very good indeed, ladies. You worked hard this term. I'm gratified. Miss Gray, I liked your Jane, you made something of it. I find you not always concentrated; today you were. Miss Gordon, your Joy was shadowy, but I think you found her. I felt she was there. Miss Morrissey, I won't delude you—you did not suggest a mother."

"Thank Gawd!"

"Now, ladies, they are waiting to clean up. There's a concert here."

Junior year was over; our great moment mustn't collide with someone else's.

I folded my Japanese kimono on top of the white voile, put the Berner's makeup box beside it. Would I use it again?

Mr. Diestel looked in. "Miss Gordon, please go to Mr. Sargent's office."

Mr. Diestel's office was empty, but I knew Mr. Sargent's door.

"Come in."

"I'm Ruth Gordon, Mr. Sargent."

He pointed to the chair where I'd done *Mrs. Dot* and *Ingomar, the Barbarian*, before Papa paid the four hundred dollars.

"I have read the reports from Mr. Putnam, Miss Lutz, Mr. Lamb, Mr. Schnable and, of course, Mr. Jehlinger, whose words bear the most weight. I saw Friday's performance." He looked at a note. "You appeared as the boy in *Strife?*"

"Yes, sir."

"Mr. Galsworthy is a fine dramatist. In *Strife* he chose the workers' side; not a popular theme, but a strong piece of dramaturgy." He looked at his notes again. "Your proportions did not suit the part of a young boy, but of the three scenes you prepared for the end of the term, you were the most convincing in *Strife*. In *The Manoeuvres of Jane* your part was small, perhaps colorless. Today I saw *Joy,* your big opportunity. You, I believe, were well suited for it. A well-brought-up young lady whom Galsworthy has placed in a good situation. This part is *not* colorless. I'm afraid you were."

Ever feel a chill start in your heart and spread?

"Mr. Jehlinger reports that you have not been difficult, nor lazy. Mr. Jehlinger says you listen and try to execute what you are taught. When all that takes place and the result is colorless, we must consider what to do about it. After much thought, we feel you are not suited to acting. You show no promise. We will not put your name down for the senior year."

The chill surfaced and turned to hate. They had agreed to teach me, now they said I wasn't suited. Were *they* suited to teaching? I hadn't said I could act; *they*'d said they could teach. They'd heard two recitations and said I would "do." Courage balled-up in me like indigestion. It was indignation. *I* hadn't failed; *they* had.

Fifty-three years later the Academy honored me. President Worthington Miner handed me the crystal trophy with The American Academy of Dramatic Arts insignia engraved. Below it:

**RUTH GORDON**

**1968**

It wasn't worth four hundred dollars, but better than being told I wasn't suited to acting.

"Never give up," I told the graduating class. " 'Never give up' sounds easy, but it isn't.

"Never give up! Does that seem funny to tell you, who haven't got started? *That's* when you have to be warned! I *can't* give up; I have too big an investment. It's when you're *starting* is when not to get discouraged. The last time I was at the Academy, the president said, 'We feel you're not suited to acting. Don't come back.' Well, you see who's standing here.

"And on that awful day when someone says *you're* not suited, when they say you're too tall, you're not pretty, you're no good, think of me and don't give up!"

# Chapter

——————⚬——————

# 6

I carried my suitcase up the front steps of 14 Elmwood Avenue, where
I'd carried it down so confidently. Up the stairs, when Christmas I'd
planned not to come back.

Mama held out her left hand; the right one didn't work. It had done
so much and now it couldn't.

"Oh, Mama."

She said something.

"What, Mama?"

"You—" It was awful, the effort it took.

"Don't try, Mama."

"You—*go.*" The effort was terrible.

"Not till you're better, Mama."

She tried to rise off the pillow. "New—" How *hard!* "York."

"Yes, Mama, but I'll stay *now.*"

On the pillow her face looked troubled and tired.

Mama's nurse patted my shoulder, then sat down at the window in
Mama's rocker, took Papa's sock out of the sewing bag and started to
darn it. "Don't bite your thumb," she said.

"It's a wart I've got." Talk about anything but the subject.

"Don't bite it. Want lamb chops for dinner?"

"Can you fix them breaded?"

"Sure."

Mama had dozed off. I went into my room. Would I get away again? The Boston train whizzed by.

"Did the school give you what you needed?" asked Papa.

"They thought I and one other girl were the best in the class."

"That's good news. Your letters sounded hopeful, but I didn't know was that for the benefit of your mother."

"No."

"Mama and I talked about floating you for the second year, but now —with her care—I'm sorry."

It was all over. 14 Elmwood Avenue was through. Mama was going to Mrs. Gould's Nursing Home in East Milton. It was money. Not enough of it; Papa couldn't swing the bills. Dr. Adams suggested Mrs. Gould's. She took invalids into her home. Papa would rent a room at Mrs. Shapleigh's, a block away from Mama, take the train from East Milton to Boston. I'd take the one o'clock to New York.

It was over. Mrs. Parssons had cooked, mended, refused to take a day off, but Papa couldn't swing it. Dr. Adams' auto pulled up beside our hitching post.

"All ready?" asked Mrs. Parssons, and helped Mama stand up.

Mama looked around the parlor. "I—prayed—this—day—would— never—come." The second occasion she said it.

Mrs. Parssons put her arm around her. "Take the steps slowly."

One foot slowly shuffled after the other. Dr. Adams held the car door open. Papa had left the factory early and was waiting at Mrs. Gould's.

"I won't say goodbye." Mrs. Parssons lifted in the suitcase with Mama's things. "You'll be hearing from me and I want to hear from you."

The car started. We watched it make the turn on Farrington, then I cried.

"Your mama has Mr. Jones and she wants to see you get started. How's your wart?"

"What?"

"Your wart, let me see it."

I held up my thumb.

"Where is it?"

"What?"

"Your wart."

I looked at my thumb, then at Mrs. Parssons.

"I wished it away," she said.

If someone could wish something away, could they wish something to happen? Had I wished myself away from Elmwood Avenue?

Papa had bought my ticket, the room was reserved at The Three Arts Club, Mr. Sparrow had taken my trunk. Sunday morning the small brass alarm clock was set for five, but I didn't wait for it to ring. It went into my suitcase, bought last year at Winship's on Summer Street. Goodbye, yellow roses on the wallpaper. Sunday, August 1, the last morning to get dressed at 14 Elmwood! This *was* the last; no more coming back again and worrying how to get away.

"I'll clean up breakfast," said Papa. "You get over to see her."

From Wollaston to East Milton is a mile, houses all the way as far as Pine Street, then the shortcut through the woods. Scary. Suppose a tramp? A murderer? Rotted planks bridged the brook; don't trip, don't fall through. Ripples in spring, in August a trickle.

The woods opened, East Milton houses ahead. On Granite Place the house next to the one on the corner was Mrs. Gould's. No one on the piazza; was I early? First door on the right, Mama's. She was dressed and waiting. "You—look—nice," she said carefully.

I bent down and hung on to her.

"Nice." She spoke better and took pride in it. "You—have—to—go," she said like a lesson. Like the Spanish lessons she gave our Marion Street neighbor Miss Turner, to pay for a trip to Bainbridge so Mama could show me where she was born.

"You—have—to—go." No concern, her feet on a low stool, on the bed a tray with a half-finished jigsaw puzzle Miss Turner had brought. It was going to be the Flatiron Building. Mama pointed to it. "New—York," she said carefully.

"Mama, I'll write every day."

She nodded. Not as though she cared, as though she agreed.

"Last time I didn't, but this time I will."

"Papa?" she asked.

"He's going to Boston to put me on the New York train. Mama, you'll hear from me every single day."

"Papa?"

"After my train leaves he's taking the East Milton train to see you.

119

Today I'm going to New York City. Remember, Mama? I'm going back to The Three Arts Club. Remember?"

"Go—*now*—so—no—hurry." She held her left arm out.

I knelt down beside her. "Mama, think about me?"

She hugged me carefully.

"Mama, write me?" Tears started down my face. "Mama, love me."

"You—look—*nice.*"

"Mama?"

She gave me a gentle shove with her left hand. "Don't—make—Papa—wait."

Goodbye Granite Place, the field, the tramp, the murderer, the rotted planks, Pine Street! Fifty dollars pinned to my corset cover, in my handbag the one-way ticket to Grand Central.

"All out."

The heat was fierce, my blue taffeta stuck to me, but did it matter? The end of the ramp was New York!

"Take your bag, miss?"

"No, thanks, redcap." Someday I'd travel with leather suitcases and a hatbox and a silver-fitted toilet case and trunks with "R.G." on the outside, a personal maid to unpack them. Right now what mattered was I'd come back, I was in Grand Central! And it was really grand.

"Take your bag, miss?"

"No, thank you, redcap." Did Wollaston know you call a porter redcap?

"Hi, cutie." A man winked. A New Yorker noticed me! Wollaston it was Clark Boynton, in New York a New Yorker winked, kept going and got lost in the crowd. Would someone help me, show me, fall in love with me, take advantage of me? That was Mama's worry.

"Don't let a man take advantage of you, Ruth."

Was it taking advantage if he wanted to sleep with me, but would teach me how to act?

Overhead in Grand Central gold stars glittered.

Exit to 42nd Street.

14 Elmwood Avenue to Granite Place to 42nd Street all in one day, but better not think about that. "Up Broadway?" I asked the conductor of the red trolley car.

"If you want me to!" Cute-looking.

"Fifth Avnoo," he called out.

Where did the Vanderbilts live? Where did the Astors? Where did the beautiful Mrs. Gould that used to be an actress named Edith Kingdon? A policeman nodded to someone in a big claret-colored limousine. Did it have enamel fittings and a crystal vase with a white flower like the picture of Billie Burke's? *Theatre* magazine said hers was pearl gray with a pearl gray chauffeur. "Sixth Avnoo," called the conductor.

The el rattled by overhead.

"Times Square."

The cute conductor did something to the tracks and a lovely smell of hot grease floated up, Times Square grease, not homemade soap grease that made our house smell.

The grease on 42nd Street smelled like tar. Who knew what home-made soap smelled like? From now on, me neither.

The sign said:

### ZIEGFELD FOLLIES

#### NEW AMSTERDAM THEATRE

The New Amsterdam was where Mama and I'd gone when she came to New York last spring. From high up in the gallery, Mama said how great Irene Castle's dress would look on me. Back in Wollaston she made it.

The trolley headed up Broadway, past Shanley's. In *Theatre* magazine, Blanche Ring said she went there every night. Maybe Joe Eccles would invite me to go. I'd wear my red crepe de Chine and pearl pendant and when I danced I'd sing the words. Did Joe Eccles know:

> First you put your two knees close up tight,
> Then you sway 'em to the left,
> Then you sway 'em to the right,
> Step around the floor kind of nice and light,
> Then you twis' around and twis' around with all your might,
> Stretch your lovin' arms straight out in space,
> Then you do the Eagle Rock with style and grace,
> Swing your foot way 'round then bring it back,
> Now that's what I call "Ballin' the Jack."

Maybe somebody would cut in. Some skeeky-haired man from Pelham Manor and everybody'd watch.

"Eighty-fifth Street."

"Wait!" I shouted.

People looked. Wasn't that what I came to New York for?

The conductor lifted my suitcase down and put his hand over my hand.

"Thank you," I said, and squeezed his hand. For practice? Like Marian Gray.

Nobody around The Three Arts Club. Martin dozed at the switchboard.

"Martin, I'm back."

"Occupy a chair. I'll get Miss Jerome."

Not much of a welcome, but did I need one?


"Go first to Packard's Agency," advised Alice Claire Elliot. "They can do a lot, if they take a shine."

They were just off Broadway on 38th Street, a small crumpled building, up one flight. People stood in groups or shifted around; at the desk an old lady jotted down notes. "Yes?" She didn't look up.

"Good morning." Until I could invent a personality, I tried beautiful manners.

"Name?" She still didn't look up.

"Ruth Gordon."

"Ruth?"

Did she want me to spell it? "R-U—"

"Last name?"

"G-O-R-D-O-N." Smile my Marian Gray smile?

"Address?"

"Three-forty West Eighty-fifth Street."

"Telephone?"

"Schuyler 2755."

"Height?"

"Five feet."

"Weight?"

"In my stocking feet?"

"What?"

"I mean a hundred and two."

"Coloring?"

"Light brown hair, brown eyes."

"Experience?"

"Stock."

"Stock where?"

"Worcester, Fitchburg." Did it sound convincing?

"Broadway experience?"

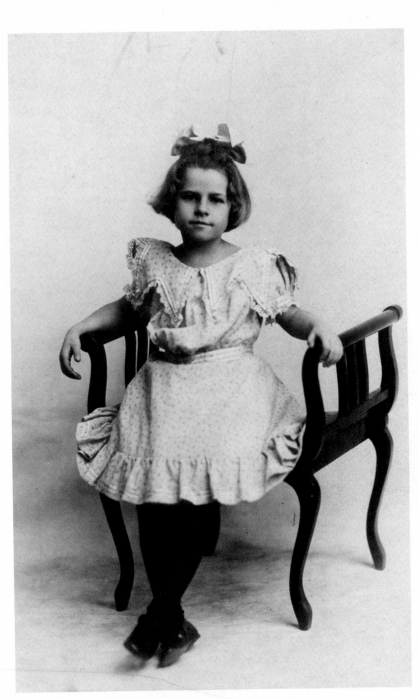

Ruth Gordon Jones, 1903

Annie Jones

Captain Clinton Jones

Elmer Chickering,

21 WEST STREET
BOSTON MASS.

James Notman Studio
270 BOYLSTON ST.
BOSTON.

Ruth G. Jones, 1912

Ruth G. Jones, QHS '14

Ruth Gordon, 1918

Mr. and Mrs. Gregory Kelly in the New York production of *Seventeen*, 1918

Ruth Gordon in Booth Tarkington's *Claren*
Kansas City, 19

Wollaston Station, 1915

"None, but—"

"Road companies?"

"Not so far."

"Age?"

"Eighteen."

"Special talents? Sing? Dance?"

"Yes."

"Which?"

"Both."

"Instruments?"

Should I tell her I could skate and fence?

"Wardrobe?"

"Yes."

"What line of parts?"

"Ingénue."

"Comedy? Emotional?"

"High comedy."

She looked up. "What?"

"High comedy like Billie Burke."

"Oh." She took a fresh sheet of paper. "Next."

"Would there be anything today?"

She shook her head.

"If I dropped in later this afternoon? Or is morning better?"

She just nodded impatiently. "Next."

A tall beauty edged me out of place.

"Name?"

I took out the list of producers Alice Claire Elliot had suggested. Across Broadway was Selwyn and Company at 41st Street.

"May I see someone in regard to casting?"

"Mr. Klauber sees for that; you can wait."

"Thank you." I sat next to a rowdy-looking character woman and a young man.

The switchboard buzzed. "Yeah . . . Who's callin' Mr. Klauber? . . . Go ahead."

On the wall, a Sarony photograph of Rose Stahl in *The Chorus Lady;* how did *she* get her first part? Who did *she* see? What did *she* say when she saw them?

Over the switchboard a picture of Marguerite Clark in *Baby Mine.* How I loved her in *Prunella!*

The switchboard buzzed. "Yeah . . . What's it in reference to? . . . I'll connect you. . . . *Theatre* magazine wants the color of Madge Kennedy's dress for the cover. . . . Go ahead, *Theatre* magazine." Click.

Buzz.

"Yeah . . . Mr. Klauber? . . . Who's callin'? . . . Spell it. . . . What's it in reference to? . . . Hold on. . . . Mr. Gaige, Claire Kummer says did her play get read? . . . Miss Kummer, you can call for your play. . . . Didn't say; just said pick it up." Click.

A beauty came in.

"Oh, hello. Mr. Klauber's on the phone. I'll show you in." The telephone girl removed the earpiece, opened the door into the passageway. A trail of perfume followed beauty.

In the outer office, three of us looked at nothing.

Out the window was the Hotel Knickerbocker, where Alice Claire Elliot said Billie Burke used to live. And Caruso and Charles Dillingham and William Collier. Ziegfeld ate lunch there.

"Mr. Klauber's busy." The telephone girl stared at us coldly. Any secrets, her eyes kept them.

"I don't mind waiting," I said.

"Not seeing."

The actor held the door open for the character woman.

"Has he cast the road company of *Twin Beds?* I think I'm right for one of the parts."

Buzz.

"Yeah? . . . Mr. Klauber can't be disturbed. Call back." Click.

"I hear there's going to be seven companies."

Buzz.

"Yeah? . . . Call the Eltinge Theatre." Click.

"Are they doing any other play?"

"All English."

"I dare say I might be—"

"Bringin' 'em over."

Buzz.

"Yeah? . . . Oh, Mr. Sherman, Mr. Selwyn wantsa know could you meet him the Knickerbocker bar at five-fifteen? . . . Tonight. . . . Fine. I'll tell Mr. Selwyn. Love ya in your show." Click.

"I'll be back tomorrow and thanks."

"What?"

"I'll be back to see Mr. Klauber tomorrow."

I crossed Broadway and walked past the Knickerbocker. If I were an actor I'd go in the bar at 5:15. "Oh, good evening, Mr. Selwyn, I under-

124

stand there's a part in *Twin Beds.* . . ."

Who next on Alice's list? "George C. Tyler, New Amsterdam Theatre Building."

"Are you casting?" I smiled like Rose Stahl's photo.

"Not just now."

The young man was pleasant. "Is Mr. Tyler in?"

"In, but busy."

Did he sound as though he wished he wasn't? "Could I wait?"

"He'll be tied up awhile."

Did he sound regretful? "Is he doing a play?"

"Not right at the *moment.*"

"Would you want to write down my telephone number? My name is Ruth Gordon."

"Well."

"I'll come in tomorrow. Nice to meet you."

Nothing definite, but pleasant. In the elevator going up to the Henry Miller office, I jotted down, "Tyler, Tues. 11."

"Good morning. Is Mr. Miller in?"

"In rehearsal."

"Is the play all cast?"

"Yup."

"Have they got the understudy?"

"Set."

"Would it be any use to leave my—"

Buzz. He went through the door marked PRIVATE.

I walked down a flight. "Good morning. Is Mr. Ziegfeld doing any casting?"

"How tall're you?"

"Five feet."

"Nope."

"With French heels, I'm five three."

"Bryant 9300 . . ."

"My name's—"

". . . 9300?"

The next office building, Cohan and Harris. "Mr. Forrest doesn't see unless y' have an appointment."

"If I wrote him—"

"Not before December. Hello? . . . Oh, yes, Mr. Forrest, no one's been in. . . ."

Next, Al Woods, Eltinge Theatre.

125

The elevator was so small only three people could squeeze in.

"Haulin' 'em up for an hour," the colored elevator boy announced, "an' nobody come down *yet.*"

"Are they casting?"

"Mr. Woods got off the *Lusitania* and lammed in here luggin' a lot a plays."

A crowd of actors, everybody talking, laughing, full of confidence; the door marked "Fred Bateman, Casting Director" banged open. "My God, it's the mob scene from *Quo Vadis!* Come in, Jay, come in, f' Chris'sake! Come in, Lou. I can't hire all youse, but keep coming round. Pop, you're too old for this pisspot."

The men laughed, the actresses made faces to show they were shocked.

"Mort, what'n hell're *you* doin' out here? Walk in the office—Al's smokin' four cigars."

They laughed.

"Blanche, doin' anything or *anyone?*"

"Not if *you* want me."

"I always want ya, but y' gimme the cold shoulder. Walk in—I wanna show ya my casting couch. The part's got two whole lines. Think ya can handle it?"

"I'll try, sir."

They laughed.

"Ya workin', Ed?"

"No, sir."

"Git inside and sign. Can y' carry a tray?"

"I can, sir."

"Sold for ten dollars! Don't bawl, I was only jokin'." He pointed to the inner office. "Write your own ticket, so long's it ain't over twenty-five. Who's left? Go home, Lola; Charlie Dillingham's been callin' ya all day. Monty, no tea drinkin' in this one."

"I can drink anything. I'd like to work."

"Beat it, you're fired. Nothing more today, folks. Who're *you?*"

I looked in back of me.

"No, *you.*" He burst into song.

> "Youse wid de feller
> Wid de open umberella
> Strollin' down Fit Avee-*noo!*"

He did a time step.

"Me?" I pointed to myself.

"Yes, Tinker Bell. When did *you* blow inta town?"

"Yesterday."

"Ain't she cute—lemme at her!"

"Lemme at *you!*" Courage shot through me. "My trouble is I can't get to anybody!"

"Your troubles are playin' the finale; step this way, baby doll!" He put his arms around me in a big exaggerated bear hug. "Ta ta." He waved to the crowd, winked, smacked his lips, the inner office door slammed behind him and me. "Hey, you're sweet." He put his lips to mine and held me close. "Where y' been all my life?"

"I don't know."

He put his lips on mine again. "Didn't I say you were sweet?" He hung on to my hand and led me into the office where actors were waiting. "Ain't she cute?" he inquired. "Looka that little shape. I betcha ya got pretty legs. Do I win?" He lifted my ankle-length skirt an inch or two. "What's under there, cutie?"

I gave a kick Miss Corlew our Wollaston dancing school teacher would have been proud of.

"Applaud, you coots, don't sit on 'em! Come in tomorrer, sign your contract."

The room went around. I put my head on his arm to steady myself.

"Whatsa matter? Hey, whatsa *matter?* Give her a shot of— Whatsa matter, kid, are y' knocked up?" He looked around at the others. "Don't looka *me*—I never seen her till five minutes! Get Al's brandy."

I opened my eyes.

"Ya scared us!"

I hung on to his arm.

"Tell 'em I'm not the papa, huh?"

"What?"

"Tell 'em I didn't get ya in the family way."

"I'm not in the family way."

"Ya wanna try? Noon tomorrow downstairs an' *first* read the part for me."

"Oh, thank you!"

"Pete!" he called to the elevator man. "Take her down nicely." He gave me a little push toward the elevator door. The door closed with a bang not as loud as my heartbeat.

127

Would I wear my white piqué with the real Irish lace and red patent leather belt or my navy blue taffeta like Mrs. Castle's or would that look too hot? My light blue linen suit? Did it get wrinkled in my trunk?

Louise Davidson looked in the laundry. "What're you ironing, dog?"

"I'm going to read for a Broadway director tomorrow and my linen got wrinkled."

"That light blue will look good."

Riding down in the trolley, I was careful how I sat. Linen wrinkles if you even think.

At the Eltinge stage door I asked, "Is Mr.—"

"Onstage." Eyes on *Racing Form.*

"There she is!"

The stage was dark except for one bulb hung from above and a pilot light on a pole.

"You read Flossie, I'll read the rest." He held out an open manuscript.

"Should I read it first to myself? That's the way we did at the Academy."

He roared with laughter. "If every little girl with a little bottom read it over first I'd be here all day. Take your jacket off; I want to see you in action."

I tossed Clare's blue linen on a chair as if I'd buy another if it wrinkled.

"Start 'Flossie peers out of the bathroom and says Shhh!' "

" 'Shhh!' " I read.

"Think where you *are,* baby! Ya got your teddy bears on an' they're pink silk an' maybe the guy's wife is in the next room. When ya come on ya surprise the sh—hell outa him! Also remember wifey. She could bean ya for givin' away stuff she ladles out for a nice livin'. What color teddies have *you* got on?"

"What? Oh, white."

"Make out like they're pink. Open the door."

I thought what to do, then moved where I thought the door was, hesitated, pantomimed opening it, remembered the wife. " 'Shhh!' "

"Do it cuter. Here, these two chairs'll show where the door is. Don't do it just scared, do it cute-scared. Act like I see every sweet little thing an' dying to get in there."

"Oh, yes."

"Go back again."

I walked up to the kitchen chairs, hesitated, then pantomimed opening the door a little way, peeked out to see who was there, first looking

128

in the wrong direction, then in the right. That was the *only* thing I'd learned at the Academy.

"You liar," Jehlinger had shouted at me when I'd made my entrance looking straight at my mother with her lover. "You liar, go back."

Why didn't he tell me, "First look in the *wrong* direction, *then* look where the person is"?

I looked where I *didn't* think anybody was, *then* the other direction and said, " 'Shhh!' "

"Better, but more petoot! Like Marguerite Clark, sweet an' juicy. Y' know what I'm talkin' about?" He came behind the chairs, tripped sweetly over to the door, opened it, gave a little wiggle and threw his chin out as though he was going to get kissed, put a finger coquettishly to his lips and said, " 'Shhh!' "

"Oh, let me try that."

"Ya want him to *do* it to ya and ya won't feel good till he does."

"Uh huh."

"Juicy."

I came through the door, did the little wiggle, lifted my chin, put my finger on my lips and said, " 'Shhh!' "

"Very nice." He leaned over and covered my mouth with his. "You're sweet. Now I'm Billy. I look at ya an' wet my pants. The wife's in her room! 'Where did y' come from?' " he whispered. A whisper that could've been heard in the Winter Garden. " 'Go back to the flat.' " Shaking, he pointed to his wife's room. " 'She's in there!' Pout the next line."

" 'Why let *her* have what's supposed to come to *me?*' "

"No, no. 'What's supposed to *come* to me?' "

"Oh, yes. 'Why should I let *her* have what's supposed to come to—' "

" 'What's supposed to *come* to me.' "

" 'What's *supposed* to come—' "

"Ya want me to come over there and spank your little ass?"

"What?"

" 'Why should I let her have what's supposed to *come* to me?' " He leaned down and put his lips on mine. "How'd you like to come back tomorrow and start fresh?"

*"Could* I? I just have to think about it first."

"Wanna take it home with you?"

"Oh, *could* I?" I'd been given back my life.

"Wanna come up my office?"

"Wouldn't tomorrow be better?"

"Oh, tonight we'll just fool around. Ring the elevator three times. Everybody goes home five-thirty. I'll come down and run ya up." His lips covered mine. "Run along," he said, but he pulled me closer and put his hand down the back of Clare's blue linen skirt. " 'Why should I let her have what's supposed to *come*—' Y' know what 'come' means? You feel sweet. Six o'clock; ring three times." He jumped off the edge of the stage and strolled up the aisle to the lobby.

I put my jacket on and went out the stage door. The doorman didn't look up from the *Racing Form*. At six o'clock would I? Could he teach me? If he could, would I? Then I could quit thinking and worrying about it. What if I liked it? What if I rang the bell at six and found out?

In show business you have to have "risk" in your soul, but if you aren't born with it, you don't get it overnight. Someday, but not at six tonight.

Sunday mornings at the Club, girls washed their hair, pressed a dress for church or to go dancing at Carlton Terrace. In the library, Minnie Maddern Fiske's picture stared straight ahead; had she ever rung three times at six o'clock?

In the theatre section of the *Times,* blond Martha Hedman smiled and looked beautiful. She was opening this week at the Belasco; had somebody taught *her* to act?

Brunette Jane Cowl, intense and handsome and opening at the Republic; had Mr. Klauber taught her? She was his wife.

William Courtenay, handsome, stern, opening at the Hudson. Smiling Otto Kruger playing at the Astor. Pictures in the *Times* were of actors already in plays or about to be. Marie Doro smiled and discussed life onstage and off. Why not tell how *she* learned?

Otis Skinner, eyes flashing, head up, announced his plans. Roi Cooper Megrue smoked a pipe and told how hard it is to write plays. Winchell Smith told how easy it is to direct. Gaby Deslys smiled, beautiful hand entwined in the big pearls King Manuel of Portugal gave her. Some people said he didn't, but who wants to listen to that? "Only Beginners Need Apply."

Was I *reading* that? Was I *asleep? Dreaming?* Why would I be dreaming? I could see Roger Wisner waiting by the elevator for Ruth Johnston.

"Hello, Roger."

"Hello, Ruth."

I *wasn't* dreaming.

## ONLY BEGINNERS NEED APPLY
### Dillingham Musical to Have
### Chorus of Untried Talent

Harry Cline, general manager for Charles B. Dillingham, says *Stop, Look and Listen,* the forthcoming Gaby Deslys show opening at the Globe Theatre, will have a chorus of newcomers. Only beginners need apply. Mr. Dillingham will engage only inexperienced young ladies. Harry Cline believes this is to be a daring departure, but well worth trying. *Stop, Look and Listen,* starring Gaby Deslys, opens at Mr. Dillingham's Globe Theatre October 16th. The music is by—

Go back and begin at the beginning!

"ONLY BEGINNERS NEED APPLY."

*That* was clear.

"Musical to Have Chorus of Untried Talent."

Who better?

"Newcomers."

Who newer? Wear dark blue taffeta with pearl gray chiffon blouse. What was I worrying about! My troubles were water under the ridiculous bridge. Or was it over the ridiculous dam?

The red trolley stopped in front of the Globe Theatre at Broadway and 46th Street.

### OFFICES OF CHARLES BANCROFT DILLINGHAM
#### ONE FLIGHT UP

My blue taffeta copied from Mrs. Castle's, skirt flaring, jacket hugging my cute shape, the broad white organdy collar copied from Marie Doro's as Oliver Twist on the *Theatre* magazine cover. My patent leather slippers with the cut-steel buckles had heels two inches high. And God bless Madame Frances for her sale of summer hats! Twelve dollars had bought this transparent black straw, its broad brim faced with flesh-colored tulle, around the crown a wreath of pink silk roses and wheat, French blue ribbon streamers; it could *make* my career! God bless Madame Frances! She changed her name to Mrs. Nate Spingold and gave Brandeis University a theatre. A nice present and so was charging me only twelve dollars for that hat.

"Mr. Cline, please."

"What about?"

I opened my black moiré bag Katherine Follett had given me and showed the clipping.

The office boy went into the inner office. Why was he suddenly tongue-tied?

He came back with a tall peroxide blonde. Golden-haired, but she meant business. "Yes?"

"I've come in answer to this." I held up the clipping.

Peroxide didn't feel like reading. "What is it?"

"It asks for inexperienced girls to be in Mr. Dillingham's show. I have no experience."

No comment and disappeared.

Great to feel confident!

Peroxide came back with a man wearing glasses.

"Yes?" he said, pleasantly.

I smiled at him. "I came because Mr. Dillingham doesn't want anyone experienced." Build up confidence like a dancer builds muscles. Show business isn't *all* job-hunting; it's some of it working on *yourself.*

"Ah, yes."

Could he see I had no experience?

"Ah, yes," he repeated, and went the same route as the others.

Up the stairs came two beauties wearing Madame Frances hats, *not* marked down. Competition? *Definitely* not beginners.

Pleasant man came back with a dashing white-haired, white-mustached gentleman who kissed one of the beauties and kept her hand while he smiled at the other. "Bring her in, Anastasia." The girls swept in.

Pleasant man smiled at me. "This young lady came in answer to our search for inexperienced girls." He smiled at me some more. "This is Mr. Dillingham."

Should I do Miss Corlew's curtsy?

"Hello," said Mr. Dillingham. "Well!"

Pleasant man took charge. "Now you've seen her, Mr. Dillingham, she and I will talk."

"Thank you for coming, dear." The great Charles Bancroft Dillingham smiled and went.

Two weeks ago I'd walked around Wollaston, *worried.* Today Charles Dillingham smiled and called me "dear." The Academy was wrong, Belle La Blue was right: I *did* have something.

"I'm Mr. Cline," said the pleasant man, "and I'll give you a note to take down to the stage manager. The chorus is onstage rehearsing; you go down and join them."

"You mean I'm engaged?" My voice came from down by the Flatiron Building.

"Yes indeed. Here's a note to the stage manager. Our director isn't in this morning. Thank you for coming."

Up the dark stairs and come down engaged!

The stage doorman waved me through.

"Have a chair," said the stage manager as though we were already friends. "The girls're learning the routine."

At a rehearsal! What a letter to write East Milton, what a letter to write Katherine at Atlantic Beach!

"I'll work with you later," said my friend, and watched the line. "Five, six, seven, *eight.* Mr. Royce likes precision."

They went over and over it.

"Once more, then lunch."

The piano gave a cue.

"Five, six, seven, *eight.*"

A hand rested gently on my shoulder. It was Mr. Cline. "We've been talking about you upstairs. Mr. Dillingham doesn't want you to start in the chorus; he thinks you'll be a dramatic actress. Your style, he said, 'is better suited to plays,' and if you start in the chorus it will keep cropping up when you get to be a dramatic star. Mr. Dillingham doesn't want to hurt the future you're *sure* to have."

I was out the stage door walking on air where other people were walking on 46th Street. Charles Bancroft Dillingham saw I was going to be a dramatic star and saved me from a false start.

I went back to the Club to put away my suit for another opportunity; it wasn't for the everyday round of offices. In my box a note. "You owe two weeks. Call my room. Miss Seaborn."

The new directress was no more understanding than Miss Howes had been. "They tell me you paid so promptly last year."

"This year I'm on my own and too proud to ask my family."

"When your board bill is behind, you can't afford pride."


Some of the girls worked as extras in the movies over in New Jersey at Fort Lee. "How do I get in?" I asked Marie Physioc.

"Come tomorrow. There's a call for the William Farnum picture."

The red trolley took us to 125th Street, transfer to the crosstown one, the ferryboat took us across the Hudson, a yellow trolley climbed the hill to Fort Lee.

We stood around outdoors. Men with hammers and planks and rope kept coming by. A man came out and said, "Go put makeup on."

We went in a shed and painted our faces yellow.

Someone said, "No eye black; you're country girls."

We went outdoors again and waited some more. Everyone looked awful.

A bus stopped. "Get in, girls." We rattled out along the Palisades. At Coytesville the bus driver stopped to inquire where.

"Further that way."

He took a dirt road and called out, "That's them."

We stood beside an auto and William Farnum walked over to us. We clustered around him.

"Goodbye," he said, waved, kissed me, got in the car and drove off.

"Keep waving," a man said.

We did.

"Back in the bus."

At Fort Lee, lined up, a hand reached out of a window and gave us five dollars. Why wasn't this a great way to tide me over? Two days a week and I'd pay my board bill! Do you think you've got it solved, then find that five dollars a day doesn't come all that often?

"You're behind again. Call my room," the note read.

Why call? What could I say? A more practical idea was eat breakfast before she came down, then go the rounds. In Wollaston when we got behind, Papa threatened to "go lay down on the New York, New Haven railroad tracks." I tried not to hear and after a while the money came in and we paid. When the money came in, *then* I'd call Miss Seaborn; until then be sneaky.

The Star Agency opened early.

"Anything?"

"Have a seat."

"Is it for Fort Lee?"

"For here."

No carfare, no ferry, keep the whole five dollars!

"Ya look like y' won't try any funny business." He held out a twenty-dollar goldback. "Go over to the Met, buy me a pair for Caruso Friday night."

"What?" I'd heard what he said, but it was unexpected.

"Bring the tickets an' ya get a dollar. Today's rainy, so no line. Also Monday wear a different garment an' ya can buy me two more. Maybe

134

a different hairdo or glasses." He reached under the counter. "Carry this music roll. Sometimes I tell 'em, 'Use a cane,' but a cane your age you'd look diseased. They don't want disease in their gold horseshoe." He handed me the bill.

"I don't do that—I act."

"Ya act this *morning?*"

"No, but I'm an actress."

"Be back in a hour an' make a dollar, Monday make another."

"I was hoping you had a call for extras."

"Extra don't pay a dollar to go across the street. Extra ya go at least to Twenty-third way over the West Side, not Broadway an' Fortieth, on toppa which it's rainin'."

"Well, thank you." I started toward the door.

He thrust the twenty dollars at me. "Be an actress the rest of the day."

"No, but thanks ever so—" I was at the door.

"Hey, Little Nemo, buy me two for *Rigoletto* an' I'll give ya a dollar 'n' a quarter."

"I would, but if I make a compromise—"

"Aw, go to hell!"

From the vestibule outside the front door, I watched Miss Seaborn go in the elevator. Safe? Wait. Safe! In my box was a letter from Mama.

> *East Milton*
> *September 29, 1915*
>
> Dear Child,
>     I was so glad to get your letter written Sunday. I count on you. Josie Babcock called on me this morning and Aunt Ada this afternoon and we played canfield. I enjoyed it. I took my longest walk today, it was clear and cold. I enjoyed it. It is quite cold tonight. My room is nice and warm. I am looking for Papa so will not write more. I have had supper and will be alone until Papa comes. Write, dearest.
>
> Mama

Write Mama every day. Remember that. Every day or almost every day. Look for a job. Get advice from Alice Claire Elliot, who was job-hunting too. She lived a few blocks away at a boardinghouse called Pelletier and Co. on West 83rd Street between Columbus and Amsterdam avenues.

"Alice, would you have an affair with a manager?"

"Somebody try something?"

135

"No, but would you?"

"It won't get you anywhere but the family way, then you never work for them again."

"What if they try?"

"Well, give 'em hope, but don't sleep with 'em. Y' know?"

"Not exactly."

"Laugh and put 'em off till you get signed, *then* fool around till they get mashed on somebody else."

"How do I do *that?*"

"Make 'em think you'd go to bed with them, *but!* You will, *but!* And don't lay down on the desk when the stenog goes home, unless they sign a ten-year starring contract at umpteen dollars!"

"How did you get *your* first job?"

"My red hair and I developed early; even as a kid I had breasts. Henry W. Savage was casting *Excuse Me* for the road, a farce, and they needed a baby-doll ingénue; Ann Murdock played it in New York and she's got red hair, so that's how they cast all the companies. Nowadays, red hair doesn't get you far—they henna theirs. It's luck or someone crazy about you and all you can be *sure* of is a lot of people did."

"Did what?"

"Get a first job. Of course, it's great if you know someone with pull. Tomorrow I'm having dinner with the lawyer for Klaw and Erlanger. He could get you in to see everybody. Why don't I bring you?"

"Alice, *would* you?"

"He's old and wicked, but attractive. He'd *like* you. Dinner is at his apartment. Hothouse flowers, not gladiolas or short-stems—red roses, violets, chrysanthemums you and I could live a season off what they cost. He could do just every little thing there is for you. I'll call his office in the morning. You're cute and he likes that. I'll make it look like you'd break a date."

"No casting today" from everybody; at the Club would there be the message?

"Miss Elliot says all right for dinner."

I rolled up my hair on strips of old silk stockings, hung out my red crepe de Chine I'd worn to the second Park Hill ball. Since then, I'd changed it to look like Julia Sanderson's costume in *The Sunshine Girl.* Layers of white net were now one layer and lowered to the tip of my pearl pendant. Change the skirt? Mama had refused to make it right. "Mama, the skirt has a *slit*—it's in the *pattern!*"

"Ruth, don't ask me to sit in the Cochato Club and hear Miss Hayward tell you your dress is too audacious for her dancing class."

Tonight *be* audacious, rip it open. I hung it on the electric light fixture, then got out the gold satin slippers Dotty Forbes had given me, the silk stockings to match. Hidden in the wool bathrobe pocket was my pearl pendant, Clare's high school graduation present.

"Need a roll of sticky flypaper?" Ida, the maid, looked in. "How's every little thing? *That*'ll drive him wild!" She pointed to my red dress.

"I'm dining out, Ida."

"That is *some color.* You'll tickle the pants off him!"

"I'm being taken to meet somebody terribly important, a very big lawyer."

"I'd like to be a little old fly squattin' on *his* flypaper an' watch the gent cave in. He can kiss himself goodbye somewhere between soup and nuts."

"He's dying to meet me."

"It'll be closer to soup than nuts."

*"Scads* of money and *very* prominent."

"Think he might set you up?"

"Ida! He's society and loves to give young people their chance, but he himself is disinterested."

"A sis?"

"Of course not. He—"

From down the hall. "Ida."

"Comin', Miss Seaborn, I'm gettin' some little old flypaper around." She lowered her voice. "Git it away from him, hon, 'steada him gettin' it away from *you.*"

Common, but nice to be told I was ravishing.

The bathroom smelled of cigarettes and talcum powder; open the window. Scrub out the tin tub with Bon Ami, let the water run, let it out, plug the stopper in, let it run in fresh, close the window. I dropped my kimono and looked in the glass. Would he fall in love, would he want to keep me?

"You're adorable! Do you know what I mean when I say I want to make love to you?"

Should I not be *too* stand-offish, give him hope?

"I gave Alice my box at the Metropolitan Opera House in the Golden Horseshoe so I could have you."

"I suppose you know I'm a virgin?"

"You couldn't be anything else. You shall have the most beautiful apartment in New York City with gold faucets, and charge accounts to order clothes, and a little motor of your own, driven by an old, old, old chauffeur. I wouldn't *trust* anyone dashing—"

"Whoever's in the bathroom, don't take all night!" Denise's voice was certainly *loud* enough for opera.

The apartment house, corner of 80th and Broadway, was tall and solid, trimmed with heavy carved stone, the entrance on 80th Street. The doorman pointed to the bronze and mahogany elevator with a long shiny black leather seat. Why did Alice wink at me?

A Negro maid, not pleasant or unpleasant, opened the door. Was she hoping the evening would be over soon?

Alice noticed my red dress and winked again. The maid motioned to the parlor. Heavy carved furniture upholstered in brocade, gold brocade drapes that looked as though they never opened. A dark painting of an autumn marsh.

"Forgive me, children." Through the gold brocade portieres strode a tall, stocky, velvet-coated man with rough features, eyes that tore everything apart. "Alice, how pretty you look! Where's the baby?"

Alice laughed her luscious matinee laugh. "The baby grew up."

The eyes tore *me* apart. "I think she should be kissed." He thrust out a powerful blue velvet arm, tilted my chin to the position he wanted it and kissed me ever so lightly on the mouth. "Oh, that's delicious. No, she's *not* a baby." His mouth covered mine and he held me tight. It startled me, then I relaxed, then I hated him, hated his apartment, his velvet smoking jacket. Why was his kiss so sweet?

Alice was laughing. He drew her roughly over to him and covered her laugh with his mouth.

Why so sudden? So harsh? So businesslike? Gladys Bain admired New York men, but him? Would she admire *him?* The maid brought in three heavy cut-glass cocktail glasses circling a massive silver shaker on a silver tray. She took no notice of her employer and Alice; was she still hopeful the evening would finish soon?

"Delicious."

"What nifty thing is that?" asked Alice, pointing to the tray.

"That's a martini for a good little girl." He filled a glass, then another.

"The baby doesn't drink anything," said Alice.

"She'll start." He held the glass out to me.

"No, thank you." Why feel unsuccessful?

"Ginger ale for our baby!" he shouted.

The maid put her head in.

"Our baby isn't weaned yet; we have to burp her on ginger ale."

"Yes, sir."

"Sit beside me, little one, and tell me why you won't drink a martini. Are you afraid I'll seduce you?" His hand beckoned peremptorily. "Alice is who I'm going to seduce." His hand beckoned, then pulled me down; his arm went around me. "Is it *you* that feels good or this pretty red silk? Alice, she's a lovely child." He put his face close to mine. "Do you know you are or shall I teach you?"

The maid brought in the ginger ale. Did she see where his hand was? A heavy hand that didn't feel heavy.

"Alice, why haven't I seen you? Has it been two weeks?" The hand moved gently.

"I thought you were miffed." She winked at me. Did she know she looked prettier when she winked?

"Why would I be miffed at you, you lovely thing?" His eyes were on Alice, but his hand moved gently up the silk over my breast.

"Look what happened!" Alice held up her glass. "It's empty."

"And mine. Be the lady of the house and pour for me." She took his glass and went over to the shaker. Suddenly his mouth covered mine, his hand explored the one layer of white net, then forced its way beneath, not gentle anymore, his rough fingers teased, then roughly his hand slid out. His mouth left mine as Alice turned and brought his drink. Did they work on signals? "Alice, would you be jealous of our baby?"

"You bet I would. Tonight she's shy. I told her what a bigwig you are. She's overwhelmed. I am, too, you know."

"Good! I can think of nothing more exciting than to overwhelm you and the baby." He turned to me. "Will you submit to being overwhelmed?"

The maid looked in. "Dinner is served."

The dining room was as heavy as the parlor. A long table, lace cover brushing the floor, twelve high-backed chairs upholstered in black leather, massive stone fireplace unaware of the small fire burning far back, on the wall a painting of a black dancer with a golden scimitar.

He motioned me to sit on his right, Alice on his left. Beyond us the black chairs went on and on. Soup came in in silver-mounted plates with dark blue dragons in the border. It was dark and salty. I hated it a little less than I hated him.

"Give me your glass, little one." He held the silver-mounted decanter.

"I don't drink wine, thank you."

"But you will tonight." It wasn't a question, it was an opinion.

"No, thank you."

"Give me your glass." That was a ruling.

"No, really."

The heavy hand slapped me hard across the mouth.

"Give me your glass."

I held it up. My mouth stung, my face stung.

He poured the glass full.

"What beautiful glasses!" Alice steered us past the moment.

"Drink."

I took a sip.

"Our baby sipped her wine, Alice." His eyes were on me. "Drink."

If only he'd drop dead! Instead, he poured more wine. "Give me your hand."

I did.

"You hate me, but learn. If someone wants to pour wine for you, *let* him. When the glass is *full,* he can't pour any more and it's *his* wine he wasted. He can't *make* you drink it."

Dessert was over. "We'll have coffee in the drawing room."

I drank a small cup.

He took out a wafer-thin crystal watch circled in diamonds. "Time for babies to be in bed. My maid will see you home."

"Oh, I'm all right by myself."

"Shall I slap you again?"

The maid came in.

"Shall I?"

"No."

He reached out and took my hand. "Take the young lady home in a taxi." He pulled me close and kissed me, then gave me a shove.

Alice smiled. "I'll call you tomorrow."

I was out in the hall, I was in the bronze and mahogany elevator with the shiny black patent leather seat, the doorman whistled a cab to the curb. We rode up Broadway. Away from that detestable, disgusting, coarse man who could have helped me and now wouldn't.

Don't cry over spilled milk. Turn the rug and get on with it.

*340 West 85th Street*
*New York*

Katherine, I pen a line straight from mine heart to thine! Movies, dear, I'm doing movies morning noon and night. Wild about them! I'm giving up all thoughts of the legitimate, I choose to be queen of the movies. So far I'm doing free-lance work. That means I take contracts with different companies and don't stick to any single one. I get a lot of attention and invites, but tonight I go to bed early because tomorrow I'm at Famous Players in *Madame Butterfly* with Mary Pickford, so no more now.

Lovingly,<br>
Ruth

P.S. I'm doing so great I can hardly believe it. It gives me courage to say no. A bigwig lawyer representing Klaw and Erlanger wants to seduce me, but I sent him on his way. God knows where he could get me, but I want to do it for *myself!*

Tomorrow I'd be an extra at Lieutenant Pinkerton's American wedding, if that's what describes "doing it for myself."

The theatre is a hard life.

Important men *say* they want to seduce you, but do they? Until some important man and I came to a decision, I made the rounds. Try Mrs. Wilson's Agency. She represented child actors, but maybe for *Peter Pan?*

"You're too old," said gray-haired Mrs. Wilson.

"I was nineteen last month."

"Only children for *Peter Pan.*"

"Are you casting for anything else?"

"Next year."

Next year I'd be even older. Why only children? When Miss Turner took me to Boston to see *Peter Pan,* even Peter was grown up. "You sure they couldn't use anyone nineteen?"

She just shook her head.

Try George C. Tyler?

Always out or busy.

Try the Cohan and Harris office?

Nothing. Some days you wonder, but then don't waste the time. Only twenty-one Novembers later the Old Vic audience chanted, "Ruth Gordon! Ruth Gordon!" Why wonder? Just keep going till it happens. Edith Evans stepped forward. "I know you want to hear our American actress." It was the great Edith Evans. She stepped closer to the foots. "But I would like to say something before you hear from *her.*" And then the great Edith said things and when she felt my hand tremble less, she said, "Our American actress, Miss Ruth Gordon." It was closing night of *The Country Wife,* a London triumph. Good if they could invent look-ahead-twenty-one-years-and-see-it-the-way-you-planned. Maybe write your senator. Who *I* wrote was Papa. "Could you send me twenty-five dollars?" Good if I could have told him about twenty-one years and great nights at London's Old Vic. Meanwhile make the rounds and don't give up. "Anything today?" "Yes," they'd say one day. Try the Greater Film Company? Nobody was waiting, so probably they weren't casting, but it was warm and no one asking about the board bill. A good place to sit. From the wall a picture smiled, across one corner in thick black ink was "Harry, darling." Another smiler in another picture signed "Harry, dearest." Another, "All the best." Four walls lined with smiles, love, good wishes, no one discouraged, how did *they* get started? Who taught *them?* Did they cover *their* summer hat with velvet and add a bunch of cherries where the velvet wasn't enough? Did *they* worry about a board bill? Did being *pretty* get them started? Being affectionate? Being easy? Did they have to go to bed with "Darling Harry"? Did they want to? Had someone taken advantage of them? How had they got through the door marked PRIVATE?

"Waiting to see someone?" A man stood in front of me. He wore a silk shirt, and his hair was white.

"I was wondering if they were casting today."

"Come in." Not old, but important-looking. Office not like an office, like a sitting room. "Sit down."

Why did I think I might cry? Wondering how those girls got in, now *I* had. Was luck coming back?

"Comfortable?" he asked as though we were equals.

"Oh, yes, thank you."

"Had 'ny experience?"

"Did you mean on the stage? Or the movies?"

He looked at me reassuringly. "Doesn't matter. How old are you? Nineteen?"

"Yes, last month. October thirtieth." Too old?

"We're thinking of making a picture here. Great notion. For the leading girl we want someone hasn't been seen before."

Did it sound as though "For the leading girl we want someone hasn't been seen before"?

"People get sick of the same old faces; we want to take a chance on a young kid."

Was nineteen a young kid?

"Something different."

"Oh, certainly."

"You say you been in pictures?"

"Some, but I'm a stage actress."

"Well, experience isn't necessary for this picture. Do you live with your people?"

"No."

"Feller?"

"Oh, no."

"Embarrassed me asking?"

"Oh, no."

"Ever live with a feller?"

"No."

"Well, read this write-up of how we're going to do the picture." He handed me a typewritten sheet. "Sit back and read it. See what you think."

The lead in a movie? It would play at Kincaid's Theatre in Quincy. Gladys and Katherine and Anna and Clark Boynton and Sylvia and Mr. Litchfield would go, Papa would bring Mama, but only August first I'd left 14 Elmwood Avenue willing to wait *five years* and now— The typewriting hit me between the eyes. "The lead is a young girl, naked. Harry Barrington is on the lookout for a young girl with a beautiful body for the title role in *September Morn.*" My eyes read it over. And over. It was like a phonograph record with the needle caught. "Naked"—"Harry, dearest"—"Young girl with a beautiful"—"Naked"—"All the best"— "Harry, darling"—"Darling"—

"You a slow reader?"

"Yes." Don't act embarrassed; I could feel him looking. "I don't think I'd be very good in it." My voice surprised me; it sounded casual.

"Why don't you?"

"Well, I don't know." I *did* sound casual.

"Any particular reason?"

"No, I just don't think I'd be right. I just *think* that. No particular reason; I don't think I just *would.*" Couldn't I stop talking?

"Too bad you feel like that; a kid like you'd be right, don't you think? Would you like to take a try at it?"

"Well, no." How calm I sounded!

"You don't think so?"

"No."

"What?"

"No, I don't think I better." I sounded as though he'd offered more ice cream.

"Without the right opportunity, it can take years."

"Yes."

"You want to get known, don't you?"

"Yes."

"You'd make a name for yourself. No experience needed, don't forget. You want to think about it?"

"I think not." Did I sound like Joy's mother or a Quincy Mansion School girl?

"What're you scared of?"

"Oh, nothing." I got up. "Well, thanks very much."

He leaned across the desk, staring. Snake's eyes, thick white hair, cold pink face, cold snake's eyes, cold white hair. "You want to turn it down?"

"Yes, thanks." Fentress Serene Kerlin would have said it like that.

"Shock you?"

"Oh, no."

"You puritanical?"

"Not particularly."

"Well, if you change your mind, drop in and see me."

"Thank you." I got the door open.

Out on 46th Street I stared in a window so nobody'd see. "You must be going *crazy*, bawling in the street; you must be going *crazy*."

Awful to hope and have it backfire, awful to be behind with your board bill, awful to get nowhere. And coming up was the end of the year. *Something* had to go right. Till it did, imagine it. Be a hit, be lucky, have something go right, have something go *great!* Have the phone ring and someone make you an offer.

# Chapter

————◦⦾◦————

# 7

"Hello, hon?" It was Guthrie McClintic's furtive telephone voice. It was Guthrie McClintic and eleven years after that discouraged night.

"Doing anything?" asked Guthrie. His phone conversation sounded as though he knew spies were listening. Or *Variety*. Or *The New York Times*.

"I'm in bed."

Guthrie laughed, using only his left tonsil. "Keep it clean, hon. Have you got a play?"

"No. Have you?"

A long pause. "Yuh." He sounded even *more* furtive.

"One *I* could be in?"

"Yuh."

"Oh, Guthrie! *My God!*"

"Keep it under your shirt, but I got one."

"Can I come right over?"

"Uh huh."

I jumped out of bed, pulled open all the bureau drawers. Even for an

145

actress who could make quick changes, I made time.

The doorbell rang.

*Dammit!* I called out the New York apartment dweller's welcome through the locked door. "Who is it?"

"Texas Guinan, lovey, with the Yacht Club Boys." It was Myra Hampton, actress friend who hardly ever had a job.

I unlocked the door and rushed back to the bedroom. "In *here,*" I shouted.

"Eloping?"

"My God, Guth's got a play! I have to go right over."

"Whoops!"

"He says it's great. Do me up, darling."

"What would you have done if I hadn't come?"

"Worn it bass-ackwards."

"*Oh,* what pretty talk! Your place is the Algonquin Round Table. Anyone ever tell you you sound like Maude Adams?"

"Hurry! You should've finished by now."

She gave me a shove. "Get going, Fortune's Fool."

"My God, a new play with Guth directing!" I stood stiff with amazement. "O God, *thank* you *thank* you *thank* you *thank—*"

"Shoes next?" suggested Myra. "I mean if you're thinking of wearing any."

"Get my new in the tissue paper under the—in the closet somewhere. Do you like this *dark* powder on me?"

"You're going to black up?"

"I don't know *what* I ought to look like. I wish I knew, should I wear my jewelry?"

"Never hurts to look solvent. These shoes cost something, I'll be bound!"

"Ring for the elevator. No, *wait* a minute! I have to take my bed jacket."

"Oh, certainly. And don't forget your whirling spray."

"What? No, I always take my velvet bed jacket; Guth keeps it so cold over there."

"*That's* thinking of everything!"

Ten minutes away was Katharine Cornell and Guthrie McClintic's house on Beekman Place, number 23. How many times had I rung this doorbell since the night Caley Bragg and the chauffeur waited while I walked up those brownstone steps and rang the bell?

146

The same Emma Wise opened the door. "How's yourself? Shoog's upstairs."

To Emma Wise, Kit was Hon, Guthrie was Shoog, or sometimes it was the other way round.

"Sitting room?"

"He's raving around *somewheres.*" She looked up the stairs. "Shoog! Where *are* ya, Shoog?"

A kind of snarl let us know.

"He's fulla the devil tonight."

I ran up the stairs and threw open the sitting room door. "Guth?"

He was on the telephone, but not furtive.

I kissed the back of his head.

"Yah . . ." he snarled, then a pause. "Yah. *Who* did? . . . Who? . . . Jesus Christ, she's older than . . . *Who?* . . . Yah. Where was Mabel? . . . Y' said that *before.* . . . But where was *Mabel?* Wait a minute. Who's that listening in? . . . Oh. Tell her to get off. . . . Yah. *Whose* play? . . . Anything for Ethel Barrymore? . . . Well, see if you can get hold of it. Don't say *I* want to read it, just say it's . . . Yah. And don't give them this address; bring it over *yourself.* Where was Clifton all this time? . . . Oh, my *God!*" He gave a mirthless laugh. "I'm working. If y' get the rest of it, ring me back."

"Here I am," I said.

"That was Winsor French. My *God,* he was at Clifton and Mabel's for the weekend, they had a terrible row, Mabel fired all the help because they used up a pound of coffee in two days and Clifton bawled her out and Mabel said, 'Go ahead and spit on me, why don't you, like y' do when there's no company.' My *God!*"

"Lovely! What about the play?"

"My *God,* what a weekend. Len Hanna brought Sidney Howard! Sidney didn't get who Winsor was and somewhere in the conversation, Sidney said to Len, 'Whatever became of that dreadful fairy married Margaret Perry?' There was a pause you could've booked in both Gish sisters in *Orphans of the Storm,* then Winsor said, *'I* am that dreadful fairy.' "

"Oh, my God!"

"Even Mabel didn't know what to say."

"My God. What about the *play?*"

"And *Sidney* said, 'Well, whatever *became* of you?' "

I roared.

Guthrie looked at me, face inscrutable. "It's great!"

"*Tell* me!"

He looked up at the ceiling. "Nothing like y' ever did." He thought some more. "Moving. I cried like a goddam baby."

"It's a *serious* play?"

Guthrie twisted his face out of shape in several patterns, then looked off into eternity. "Wouldn't say exactly serious. Audience'll laugh, but it made *me* cry like a fool."

"But underneath . . ."

"Human. What made me cry." He glared at me. "You'll be great in it. Yah."

"Who's it by?"

"Wonderful scenes, you and the boy. Love story, but all in terms of every day. Best thing he ever—"

"Who's *he?*"

"Max Anderson. Now for *Chris'sake,* don't go tell *Woollcott.*"

"My God! Are you going to do it right away?"

He screwed his mouth way over to one side; his eyes looked malevolent, as though casting a spell. "Max doesn't want you in it."

*"Doesn't?"* I felt as if I'd been hit.

Guthrie glared at me. "You'll be great."

"Why doesn't he want me? I don't *know* him."

"Says you can't be romantic."

"Oh?"

He took a blue-covered manuscript from under a sofa cushion. "Don't tell anyone you're reading it. Even Gregory."

"Of course not."

"If y' tell Gregory, tell him to keep his mouth shut. Where is he now?"

"Chicago. I don't have to tell him."

"Yah, I'm superstitious till after I get Max settled. I'll put it in an envelope so no one'll see it."

"I'm going right home."

"Your doorman might. Or the taxi."

"What do *they* care?"

He screwed his mouth up again. "Things get around and—"

The phone rang. Guthrie waited till he heard Emma answer in the kitchen, then picked up the receiver and listened. "Hello . . ." he said, and turned to me. "Call you tomorrow." He leaned over to let me kiss his cheek. "Mind if I don't go to the door?"

I went down the stairs.

"Yah . . . Mabel did? . . . Who? . . ."

Life on the stage is hard, everybody says, and they're right! Why did Maxwell Anderson, whom I'd never seen, have to do me out of my future?

"Show Max Anderson how charming you are," said Guthrie. "Let him come up to your apartment."

"My God, how can I show I'm charming?"

Guthrie consulted the stars. "You *have* to. He says he'd rather not have the play done than have you—you can only act low comedy. Let him come up and convince him."

Gregory was playing *The Butter and Egg Man* in Chicago. "Guthrie wants Max to come up so I can convince him I'm charming."

"Yes?"

"I told him I'd try."

"You really surprise me! People are nice to you and you knock 'em down, then someone insults you and you accept it. Why is that?"

"I want the part."

The elevator door opened into our hall. Tall, gentle Maxwell Anderson came in. Was he as uncomfortable as I was?

We talked about this and that and after what seemed forever, he said, "I see what Guthrie means, but I want someone pretty."

"He wants someone pretty," I told Guthrie.

"Everybody pretty turned it down. He'll have to take you—you're all that's left."

"I'd rather not have it done," said Max.

How did Guthrie get around *that?*

The elevator door opened. "Flowers." They were from Woollcott.

Dear Louisa,

Here's one of every flower at Totty's. They balked till I told them you had no taste.

Guthrie told me you got the part because every doltish ingenue turned it down. So God bless Helen and Winnie and June and Margalo and even Claiborne Foster if I can believe these old ears! Guthrie says you'll be great. God's in His heaven and you rehearse at the Booth, nobody's holding us back unless it's us, wouldn't *that* be a mess,

Joe

P.S. Ethel told me Joseph Jefferson and Mrs. Drew spent a week every summer in the Catskills where, when they were young, people called

149

them "Joe" and "Louisa." When nobody was left to call them anything but "Mr. Jefferson" and "Mrs. Drew," they went back there and rocked for a week and called each other "Joe" and "Louisa."

At rehearsals Max Anderson sat silent. He'd said his say: "If you do it with her, it'll fail."

"How do you suppose he feels now?" I asked Guthrie.

"No good. I told him we've got no third act."

"I meant about *me*. What do you think he feels about me?"

Guthrie screwed his face around. "You're going to be great. I know that, but nobody else could tell."

"How do I seem?"

"Like you're the producer's girl. I see what you're doing, but no one else could. You look like someone I'm stuck on."

I knew I was going to be good. Maybe not pretty, but wasn't the whole idea she was every cute secretary, human, not outstanding?

"God damn it, you made me cry!" Guthrie blew his nose, wiped the tears from his red eyes. *"I* know this scene is going to make the audience laugh, but *you* make me cry."

I'd made him *cry?* I thought it was a comedy scene and now I made Guthrie *cry?*

That was Guthrie's way of directing. Let you think you'd *done* it, never scared you with doubts.

He wiped his eyes some more. "It's *funny,* seeing you get a fellow to propose. Sure, that's comedy. Only *you* show the agony you feel, having to hook him that way. Funny on the *surface,* but you made it deep and terrible and moving."

*I* was doing that?

That was Guthrie's way.

If he told me that's how I *must* play it, I'd be frightened. I'd never thought about that kind of acting. Acting on the surface was what I'd learned, I never thought about *underneath*. Now I'd *done* it, I'd made him cry, and now I *could* do it, because I already had.

That was Guthrie.

*Saturday's Children* was the first real acting I ever did. Acting in the deep sense. One emotion beneath, one on the surface. Isn't that how it is in real life? At the Academy did they know that? Guthrie had studied at the Academy too, but he hadn't learned that there; he picked things up out of the air, he *felt* things. His feelings were deep, but if it suited him he could cry and he meant it. He knew how to use himself *and* the actor. Gregory taught me how to act so I wouldn't get fired; Guthrie taught me the kind of acting you remember.

One more week and open in Stamford.

"I know you're going to make a hit, and you haven't got a contract." Guthrie looked around cautiously, though everybody had left the theatre. "What're you going to hold 'em up for?" He looked up in the flies to see who was spying.

"I don't know. Gregory and I agree that if I have to *pay* to play it, it's worth it."

"Yah. Well, don't do that."

"What do *you* think?"

We paced across the Booth stage and back again. "Take five percent of the gross."

"I'd *pay* to play it."

"Yah, well, take five percent of the gross."

Sunday was our last New York rehearsal. Dress rehearsal in Stamford. Guthrie motioned me to the side of the stage. "Having Stanton see the run-through this afternoon. Play up, know what I mean? Stanton's rich, we need him."

"I always play up. Do you mean play up to Stanton?"

"Wouldn't hurt." He looked around for eavesdroppers. "I know you hate watchers, but don't act sore—this is *important.* Can't tell ya now." He took a hurried look on three sides, then stepped out of the shadow into the glare of the one big overhead rehearsal light that picked out lines on faces where there weren't any, made eyes into black sockets, lengthened everyone's nose and age. "Er—"

The company looked up from whatever they were doing. McClintic was temperamental. When he wanted to he could scream at anyone or anything that didn't suit him. He could and had. *When* was unpredictable.

"Today's our last run-through before we leave town." His voice was low, as if telling himself. He chewed each word before he said it. "Tomorrow in Stamford we get the scenery and costumes." He paused to suffer. "God help us! Tomorrow I don't expect much and God knows I won't get it! Naturally, both our sets have doors and windows to open and naturally none of you ever opened a door or closed a window. Thank *God,* there's no flight of stairs! At least you won't have *that* problem! But with doors and windows you won't have any imagination left to play your parts. That's *tomorrow.* Today is different." He fastened a baleful look on everybody. "Today is our last day *here;* I want to see some results of a *helluva* lot of work. I want to see the *play.* See the people

Maxwell Anderson wrote. They're *real* people; lemme see 'em. If anyone goes up, just keep going, the way you do in performance. No prompting, Tony." He looked malevolently at the stage manager. "And move your table back so I don't see you biting your nails. And don't eat Life Savers! And don't cough, God damn it! Oh, and, company, when you're not *on,* stay over on the *side.* Don't sit on the back wall reading the Sunday *Times* or combing your hair. And don't *eat.* Everybody stay the side you make your entrance." He coughed. Then coughed some more. That was for time to think. *"Real.* Make me feel you're *real.* Not doing a lot of business I told you and not just saying Maxwell Anderson's words. Capture the feeling *makes* you say 'em. That's acting. Acting is *you* encountering some *situation,* some problem, so we out here see someone suffer the same as *we* have, and if someone *else* has, then we can bear ours because someone's gone through it, too. We're not alone, we're not the only ones." He coughed awhile, then, impatiently, "All right, Tony." He jumped down from the stage and walked up the aisle to where Stanton was smoking his pipe.

"He ought to tour Chautauqua," whispered Fred Perry. "McClintic's a thwarted actor; he's out there praying I'll bust something so he can go on in my part. He wants to go on for everyone."

"All right, folks, settle down," said Tony Miner, politely. He came from a good family up in Buffalo. Instead of authoritative, he was polite. "Use whatever you can to approximate hand props. I'll give you the bell signals. For this run-through, doorbell and telephone bell will be the same, and Mr. McClintic doesn't want you to *stamp* your feet to show you're making an entrance. Ready now; I'll give the signal for the curtain. Everybody speak up—Stamford's not an intimate house. All set, Bill?" he inquired of his assistant, Bill Worthington. "Oh, one more thing—stick your cigarettes in the fire buckets, not on the ground cloth. I don't expect any firemen, it being Sunday, but—"

"For God's *sake!"* yelled Guthrie. "You've got a monologue longer than Jim Barton's Mad Dog Act!"

"Sorry. Curtain."

A pause long enough for the curtain to rise, then Lucia Moore pantomimed opening a door.

"Go *back!"* screamed Guthrie. "God *damn* it!" He paced up the aisle. Lucia, wondering who'd done wrong, peered out front.

Tony whispered to her, "You opened the door *in,* dear."

"Je-sus *Christ!"* Guthrie tramped down the aisle.

"Oh, I opened the door *in,* dear," said Lucia, pleasantly. "It's an open-

*out* door. I know you told us, dear."

Guthrie went up to his higher notes. "The door opens *out, Lucia! Out!* O-U-T! OUT! It doesn't open *in,* it opens *out,* f' Chris'sake! If you open it *in* in Stamford, you'll pull it off the goddam *scenery!"*

"All right, I *won't,* dear." Lucia had worked in so many productions she wasn't upset. "I'll open it *out,* dear. Look." She opened an imaginary door out. "See? *I* know."

"Well, Jesus God, *do* it, then! I have to show every goddam one of you the simplest goddam things. How to open a door! Do you need me for *that?* If *that's* directing, get the Astor doorman."

"Look, dear." Unperturbed, Lucia repeated the business. *"Out.* Our door opens *out."*

"And I'll take over *his* job at the Astor."

*"Out,* dear." Lucia did it again.

Silence onstage. Silence out front. Then Guthrie spoke, patiently. "Begin again, and Tony, move your table further back. And stop scuffing your *feet.* Don't scuff! *Out,* Lucia. *Out!* The door opens OUT!"

Behind his newspaper, Fred Perry whispered, "He'll get a hernia."

"Once again." Tony rapped his table. "Curtain!"

Lucia Moore opened the door out.

Everything went right, everybody was fine, no yelling from Guthrie, we were near the end. I stood alone and looked around me, tense with pent-up feeling. I fought back the tears.

"Actresses work up tears, but *people* try to keep tears back," Guthrie had told me.

In despair, I lay down on the narrow bed, tears held back. Around me, the hall bedroom filled up with pain.

Slowly, gently, the door opened. It was Rims.

He'd come back to me.

"And slow curtain," said Tony.

Roger Pryor and I walked off the stage.

"Jesus, you were good!" Tony whispered.

I put my hand over his.

Guthrie's voice from out front. "Time, Tony?"

"Act Three: thirty-three and a half."

The company stood around.

"You'll stand 'em on their ear, kid." Dick Barbee put his arm around me.

Fred Perry motioned to the cot. "Know what makes me bawl every time?"

"Don't *tell* me; it makes me self-conscious."

"All right, but do it in Stamford or I'll *tell* you. *Be* self-conscious; I wouldn't let you lose that business. You're going to be a star, girl. I was with Margaret Lawrence when it happened to her."

Guthrie came through the pass-door back of the box. *"Talk* to him." He motioned out front.

I'd really *done* it; he'd taught me, was patient, believed in me, now I *did* it and all he said was, "Talk to him."

"I can't look as though I want a *compliment.*"

*"Do* it, God damn it!"

"How *are* you?" Stanton had come along the passage, fur-collared overcoat on his arm.

"Hel-*lo!*" I threw on everything.

"Haven't seen you for a long time."

"Nobody's seen me. Guth is a slave driver."

"I think I'll set you up in an apartment; you're too desirable to kill." Laugh. Stanton had millions. Turn it on.

"You like this show?" The way he asked showed *he* didn't.

"It's great."

"You're great. You're going to make a hell of a hit, but you think they'll be interested in the *play?*"

"Oh, I *do.*"

"Hope I'm wrong; Guthrie's crazy about it. By the way, how does anyone get in touch with you?"

"The phone."

"Easy as that?"

Let my smile say it.

"Any interest in anyone who isn't a writer or an actor, just a business-man?"

"Why not?"

"I'm going to try you out and see." He got out a small book and pen. "Wickersham 2958."

"Where is it?"

"My apartment."

He smiled and crossed out what he'd written. "I knew you weren't interested in a businessman."

"Thirty-six West Fifty-ninth Street."

He wrote it down. "What if I call up there when I'm lonely?"

"Why would you be lonely?"

Humphrey Bogart and Ruth Gordon in *Saturday's Children*, 1927

Cecil Beaton's photograph of Ruth Gordon in *Serena Blandish*, 1929

Helen Hayes, Claudette Colbert, and Ruth Gordon in Los Angeles, 1935

Jones and his father, Jed Harris, 1936

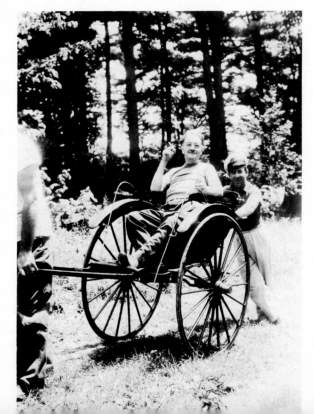

Alexander Woollcott on the
Island, 1929

Ruth Gordon and Michael Redgrave in the Old Vic production of
*The Country Wife*, 1936

Raymond Massey and Ruth Gordon in *Ethan Frome*, Act II, 1936
(*Vandamm Studio*)

Ruth Gordon as Nora, with Jessica Rogers, in *A Doll's House*, 1937 (*Lucas and Monroe, Inc.*)

Ruth Gordon with Edward G. Robinson in *Dr. Ehrlich's Magic Bullet*, 1940

As Mary Todd, with Raymond Massey, in *Abe Lincoln in Illinois*, 1939

With Greta Garbo in *Two-Faced Woman*, 1942

George S. Kaufman, Ruth Gordon, Anne Kaufman and Claude Rains, 1939

Tyrone Power, Tallulah Bankhead, Guthrie McClintic, Ruth Gordon and Anatole Litvak, 1939

"You're evading the question."

"What if you call up when you're lonely and find out?"

In Stamford, the show opened great. I went fine, except the audience laughed twice in the wrong place.

"If you do it with *her,* it will be a failure; she can only do comedy," Max had said.

I rushed out of the theatre to the hotel. No phones in the rooms. On the pay station in the lobby I got Gregory as his curtain fell. "They laughed," I said in despair.

"Tell me where."

"When Fred Perry says, 'How old are you, girlie?' "

"What's the line *before* that?"

" 'Dad, do you think I should have a baby?' "

*"Oh,* yes. Oh, that's a *hard* one! You can kill the laugh, but Anderson hasn't made it *easy* there. It isn't that the audience thinks it *funny;* it's they're surprised. Before you say, 'Dad, do you think I should have a baby?' *prepare* them. Remember how Nat Goodwin said, *'Preparation!* Always make sure of your preparation'? You have to prepare them. Make a pause. A real pause like you used to love to make all the time. Well, now *make* one. Let the audience see something is coming by your *emotion.* Stress you're in *trouble. That's* the preparation. And when you *say* it, fight back tears."

"I see. Yuh. I *do* see. Oh, *thank* you."

"How did the show go?"

"Oh, Guth is thrilled, it really did go. And I was good, but they *laughed* two places."

"That's what you're in Stamford for. If it was perfect from the start, we'd open in New York. What's the other place?"

"When I said, 'Mengel wants me to come out to dinner.' When I said that to Rims, they laughed."

"That *worried* me. I didn't want to scare you, but I worried. You're talking to Rims about the budget and somewhere out of left field you bring in Mengel's name. That one you *can't* fix; Anderson has to *help* that. Tell him he's got to *ease* it in, not throw it in. *You* can't do it without *him."*

"Oh, darling, you're wonderful, I love you, oh, *thank* you."

"What're you going to do now? Is Guthrie around?"

"He says I have to go to Dick Barbee's party. His house is near here, but I want to be by myself."

"Will Guthrie take you?"

"Oh, sure. He says if I don't, they'll all think I'm discouraged over something *they* don't know, and I have to keep up the morale for New York."

"You still open New York Monday?"

"Oh, yes."

"Well, all you've told me can be fixed in three performances, then you'll be in that wonderful Booth Theatre."

"Oh, darling . . ."

"Call me when you wake up; I'll remind you of everything we said tonight."

"I'll call you, but I'll remember. You *really* think I should go to Dick's?"

"You bet. Guth is right. And enjoy it. You've really done it, little feller."

Stanton had said he would give me forty dollars if I wouldn't read the New York notices and if I did read them I'd give him forty. I didn't need to read them. That first-night audience told me.

Next day I stayed in bed all day. Reveled.

"When you have success, enjoy it," Ned Sheldon had said to me. "It doesn't come often; enjoy it."

We were a hit, Guthrie had changed my career, I wasn't someone who could *only* be funny, I could make people laugh *and* cry. Even Max Anderson said I did. I'd taken the big step in acting, Guthrie had shown me the way.

Lovely to be a hit! Think of all the things I'd lived through. The phone kept ringing. "You're great, dear." "You're wonderful!" "Darling, have you *read* what the papers say!"

All those terrible times and now success! I knew how! I'd done it last night, I could do it tonight, I could do it tomorrow night. That is really knowing how.

The doorbell rang, in came flowers. "You've done it, babe."

More flowers. "You did it, puss!"

When it goes right, there's no business like show business.

I *knew* it would happen. I *said* it would be hard, but had I thought it would be like that day on the stage of the Eltinge: "Ring the elevator three times. I'll come down"?

The house phone rang. "I'm coming up. My God, don't you ever get off the phone?" The house phone clicked. The elevator man slid open the door. Woollcott stepped out. "Look at *this!*" He held out a dusty, crumpled wad. Was it a letter from Dickens? A letter from his first-grade teacher?

I uncrumpled it.

THE THREE ARTS CLUB
340 West 85th Street
New York

*December 22, 1915*

Dear Mr. Woollcott—

"Isn't that the goddamdest? At the *Times,* my desk drawer got stuck, I gave it a pull worthy of Sandow before Flo Ziegfeld dissipated his power with exhibition bouts, the drawer shot out, followed by this letter. You've always caused me trouble, puss! I could have fallen over and broken my fine straight goddam back!"

I laughed.

"You've got a screw loose—why should physical injury strike you as humorous? If you can stop laughing, read this."

"No."

"Read it if you don't want me to kick your teeth in."

Dear Mr. Woollcott,
I was pleased to receive your praise in The New York Times this morning. Thank you very much. I am glad you think I was good as Nibs. *Peter Pan* is my favorite play—

It's at Harvard College now. It lasted longer than the Empire Theatre. Thank God the Empire was there in 1915, its posters showing Maude Adams as Peter Pan clutching a cap with a red feather, ready to fly to the Never Never Land.

EMPIRE THEATRE

CHARLES FROHMAN
PRESENTS
MAUDE ADAMS
IN
PETER PAN
BY
J. M. BARRIE
OPENING DECEMBER 21

On December 21, ladies in evening coats, men in top hats would walk in. *Why* did Mrs. Wilson's agency say "only children"?

In the lobby, a tall, rangy colored man leaned against his elevator.

"Where are they casting for *Peter Pan?*"

"Mr. William Seymour does all casting. Get in." What a pleasant man! Why did he sound so hopeful? Didn't he know they only used children? He stopped the elevator. "Straight to the front."

A dumpy, gray-haired man was doing whatever he did at his desk.

"Good morning. Are you casting for *Peter Pan?*"

"The floor below. Mr. Saint-Gaudens."

*He* didn't say, "Only children."

At the foot of the long black iron staircase, a long dark hall, one door open, a man was reading at a desk.

"Excuse me, I'm looking for Mr. Saint-Gaudens."

"Yes."

"You're Mr. Saint-Gaudens?"

"Yes."

"Are you casting for *Peter Pan?*"

"Yes. Come on in." He pointed to a chair in front of his desk.

"Come on in"! Nothing about being "too old"? Nothing about "all cast"?

"Sit down."

"I went to a matinee of *Peter Pan* when it played Boston."

"You must have been just a little girl."

"Yes." Only nine years ago? "Do you think there's anything in it for me?"

"Can you dance?"

"I can if somebody'll show me."

He didn't turn a hair. "The part is Nibs."

Could he hear my heart thump?

"Nibs is one of the Lost Boys. Barrie's description is 'Nibs is gay and debonair.' He does the pillow dance outside Wendy's house. Remember?"

"Yes," I lied.

"Miss Adams is touring in *Quality Street,* but she'll come to New York Sunday, before she plays Washington. What's your phone? I'll arrange for you to see her."

A producer was going to telephone me?

"Do you have a phone?"

158

"Oh, I live at The Three Arts Club, 340 West Eighty-fifth Street. Schuyler 2755."

"I'll let you know what time."

Why bother with the elevator? Float down.

At the Club was a letter from Papa. Also a "Please stop by my office." One minute floating, the next back on my uppers.

*December 7, 1915*
*The Factory*

Dear daughter,

This has been a hard week and I haven't had time to write from here and of course I don't have a chance to write from E. Milton. Mama is walking better but her arm doesn't improve. Last Sunday she had a fall and hit her head on the tiled hearth and cut herself over the eye, so this week she has a black eye. She hasn't lost courage. On the whole she's more cheerful each week. Her greatest pleasure is writing to you and reading your letters. I would urge you to come this way Christmas but Mrs. Shapleigh's other room is let and money is none too plentiful. There's the chance something might happen to call you here quick but I don't see any signs of it now and think Mama is very much better than even a month ago.

I hope you're getting along all right and having a little fun out of life. Write and tell us. Anything you don't want Mama to know, write me at the factory.

Love,
Your father

So much money in the world and so little when you need it. With money, Mama could have stayed in her own house. Without money, how much longer could I hold out? Thirteen dollars and eight cents in my pocketbook, in my table drawer a board bill for five weeks. Dodge Miss Seaborn, eat breakfast before she came down, stay away for lunch, for a dime go to Drake's on 43rd Street or Gertner's next to the Empire, *big* cup of coffee topped with whipped cream. I didn't know Mr. Lindy then, but he was a waiter there, and Mrs. Clara Lindy was cashier. On every table a basket of cinnamon rolls, raisin rolls, poppy seed rolls, rolls covered with caraway seed, plain rolls and rolls with coconut frosting. Start with plain, a cinnamon to follow, top off with the coconut frosting. *Would* the Empire Theatre telephone? Why was I *sure* things would come out great? When they didn't why was I sure they would?

Was the paper in my box Miss Seaborn's "I would like to see you in my office"? Was it a notice to get out?

159

The same size paper, the same white slip *this* time said: "Be on the stage of the Empire Theatre at 11 Sunday morning."

The profession had reached out. "Be on the stage of the Empire Theatre at 11 Sunday morning"!

Things get lost, disappear, but "Be on the stage of the Empire" stuck with me in boardinghouses, road-tour hotels, the Algonquin, 36 West 59th, Jed Harris' house on East 79th, my house on West 12th, the Sulgrave, the Surrey, Faraway Meadows, our house on East 49th, our house on Cottage Street. I never mislaid it. Not even at the Great Northern or Thompson's Inn or the Holly Inn or the Hotel Wagram or the Hotel Continental or the Piccadilly Hotel or on the *Carmania* or the *Aquitania,* and today it's back on West 59th now called Central Park South.

The Empire stage doorman pointed to a passageway packed with children and mothers. The real crowd was on the stage. People squeezed out, people squeezed in. On the stage in a pool of light sat a lady. People were led up to her. I saw Mr. Saint-Gaudens cross the stage. "Mr. Saint-Gaudens!" I shouted.

He heard me.

I waved.

"I've been looking for you." He looked at my blue serge middy blouse, black half-Nelson tie, blue serge skirt, heavy blue school coat, looked pleased and took my hand. "Let us through, please," he said politely. We walked into the pool of light. "Miss Adams, this is Ruth Gordon for Nibs."

A sound of clear music.

"Would you like to hear her read?"

More clear music.

Mr. Saint-Gaudens thrust some blue-covered pages in my hand. "I'll read with you."

Why did I think I sounded good?

"That was very good." The same clear music. "Have her come to rehearsal."

"Tomorrow at two in the rehearsal room on top of the Lyceum," said Mr. Saint-Gaudens. "Bring some bloomers."

One of the many was chosen.

"Out front," said the Lyceum doorman, and didn't look up from the *Morning Telegraph.*

Snowflakes fell lazily, one here, one there.

"On top of the Lyceum," Mr. Saint-Gaudens had said.

In the Lyceum lobby, a flight of stairs went right, another went left to the balcony and there they stopped. Still do.

People were buying tickets. The box office man slapped down an envelope, two tickets sticking out; he took the money. "Next."

"Please tell me where the rehearsal hall is."

"Up those stairs. Next."

Up the stairs again, then halfway up I saw a door. Knock.

No response.

At the box office the line was longer, time was shorter; rush up and try the door again? It opened; a tall, elegant man stepped out.

"Oh, *where* is the rehearsal hall?" Why tears?

"I'll take you." Behind him was a small elevator.

"Beware of strangers," Mama had warned.

The elevator rocked slowly up, the tall, elegant man stood silent. How elegant his fur-collared overcoat, black felt hat, his gloves that held a gold-headed cane. The elevator stopped, he opened the door. "Good luck."

Someone was playing the piano. Someone came toward me. "Don't you know enough not to bother Mr. Daniel Frohman?"

Mr. Daniel Frohman! The owner of the Lyceum Theatre had helped me? Mr. Daniel Frohman had wished me luck?

"Oh, there you are!" It was Mr. Saint-Gaudens. "Did you bring bloomers?"

"I've got them on."

"All right, we can start."

Two other girls in bloomers, but didn't look right. A third looked great.

"The best dancer will get the part," said Mr. Saint-Gaudens. "We're fortunate to have Miss Chesmond teach you. Dorothy was the best Nibs ever, but she is going with a repertory company to South America, so she'll teach *you* the dance."

One of the girls was too heavy, the other two tall and spindly, and both of them were older. I was the right age and shape.

"Please play the music again," said the great Dorothy, also the right age, shape, and beautiful. "Watch me."

She danced the way I wanted to. Mr. Saint-Gaudens applauded.

"Now I'll go slow, you follow me and don't get discouraged, we'll do it and do it. You make your entrance from Wendy's house, stage center

161

and far back; all the space in front is for you to dance in. The Lost Boys and Wendy are stage left, so Nibs has the stage. Where I'm standing is *inside* Wendy's house. Miss Adams stands inside too, so you keep to *this* side, and of course, don't talk. Your cue is when you hear the orchestra." She looked at the piano player. "Please."

The piano started.

Would all the cakes Mama made to pay for my dancing school lessons pay off today?

"Never tell your father, Ruth. Papa wouldn't like it, but I want you to have advantages." On St. Patrick's Day she turned out a pale green frosted angel cake for Priscilla White's birthday. "Don't tell your father; he can only stretch his pay so far."

Mama made angel cake, sunshine cake, marble, caramel, sponge and two-egg cakes so I could have the advantages. Would I have them this snowy day?

We went over and over the steps. "Now let's do it with the pillows."

Over and over, Mr. Saint-Gaudens watching. "Kick a little higher," he urged me, and waved his long leg in the air.

The piano stopped. Snow thudded against the gray skylight.

"Now!" The music played again, then again, then *again*.

"The best dancer will get the part," Mr. Saint-Gaudens had said. The other two weren't right, but they danced better.

"Now!" We did it again.

"Can you kick a little higher?" Mr. Saint-Gaudens asked me. "All right. We better get home before dark." Mr. Saint-Gaudens pointed to the snow-banked windows. "I'll phone the results. Dorothy, my car's down on Forty-sixth Street; I'll drive you. Where do you girls live?"

"Right up the street at the St. James," said heavy Mabel.

He looked at me.

"Three-forty West Eighty-fifth Street."

"Come along." He turned to the skinny one.

"Lexington and Seventy-third Street."

"Dorothy lives at West Fifty-eighth; we'll take her first."

Huddled in the corner on the back seat, I watched Mr. Saint-Gaudens' back as he drove slowly through drifting snow. Would he phone? In front of a brownstone made into apartments, Dorothy got out and wished us well.

"West Eighty-fifth next—what number?"

"Three-forty, thank you."

I'd had my opportunity and didn't do well. This was the most discouraged I'd ever been. The car stopped. "Thank you." The car drove off. I was too discouraged to dodge Miss Seaborn. It's awful to lose hope. I lay down on my bed in the dark. What was ahead? Nothing.

"Gordon," called Gwen Thorpe's voice. "Phone."

"Thanks." What was I going to do? From August 1 to December, nothing. "Hello?"

"This is Homer Saint-Gaudens. You're the worst dancer, but you've got the part. Rehearsal tomorrow at two, same place, the salary is thirty-five dollars a week."

I couldn't say anything.

"Hello?"

"Oh, thank you."

"See you tomorrow." He rang off.

Thirty-five dollars! What would I do with all that money! Important thoughts come later. That thirty-five dollars floored me.

Everybody in the Club knew I had a job. Ida passed out the news with today's towel. Julie Muschette said her hometown paper, the Baltimore *Sun,* had engaged her to do a sketch of Maude Adams and she'd do one of me too. A Three Arts girl with a job was news! A job in the Maude Adams Company! Hope soared for everybody.

Afternoons, the Lyceum rehearsal hall. Most of the *Peter Pan* cast was in Washington playing *The Little Minister* and *Quality Street.* After the Saturday night show they'd take the sleeper. At the Lyceum were Mrs. Buchanan, who played Tootles, Miss Keppel, who played First Twin, Miss Margaret Gordon, who played Princess Tiger Lily whenever Miss Adams did *Peter Pan.* From Mrs. Wilson's Agency were two boys, Donald McClellan and Raymond Hackett for John and Michael Darling, a very little girl, Miriam Batista for Lisa. Mrs. Darling was Mary Forbes and all the animals were played by Barney Silver, young, pleasant, could do anything and did.

"Tick tock, tick tock, tick tock," intoned Mr. Saint-Gaudens.

Barney, as the crocodile who swallowed the alarm clock, slithered across the rehearsal hall.

In front of a row of kitchen chairs for Wendy's house, Barney, as the lion, fought Mr. Saint-Gaudens, standing in for Peter, lost, and fled with Peter hanging on to his tail. The tail came off and Peter presented it to Wendy, who was still appearing in Washington, so Mr. Saint-Gaudens had to present it to himself.

When the wolves chased the pirates and the Indians chased the wolves, Barney, war paint and feathers, led the Indians. Before that, he opened the show as Nana, the Newfoundland dog Mr. and Mrs. Darling employed as their children's nanny. He finished as a pirate on Captain Hook's ship and, in between, was assistant stage manager. A knock on each dressing room door. "Half hour." Wait for the thank you. "Quarter hour." "Overture." "Act One." "Two." "Three." "Four."

"Next to Dorothy Chesmond, you're the best," he told me, "and she's in South America, so:

> You should worry
> You should fret
> You should marry
> A suffragette."

"What?"

"Just a saying."

I wrote what he said to Granite Place. I mean about being the best.

*Granite Place*
*East Milton*

Dearest Ruth,

So pleased with your news. We just got the letter. Am anxious to know how you are. Don't get your feet wet, dear. Here, we are having a blizzard, snow and rain. Bless your darling heart, I wish you great success. I am proud of you.

Love from
Mama

Papa wrote from the factory.

*41 Central Wharf*
*Boston, Mass.*
*Friday, Dec. 17, 1915*

Dear daughter.

I'm truly glad you got the part in Peter Pan and are finding your mates congenial. It's easier to bring the ship into port when all hands pull together. I am sure you'll be successful. As you say, it was all luck and I hope you will be able to continue with Miss Adams. I talked to a man who was a chemist in the Massachusetts Coast Artillery and saw Miss Adams spectacle of Joan of Arc at Harvard Stadium. They had a lot of soldiers in the show, him among others. He said it was common report Miss Adams was a fine woman in every sense. I'm glad you are in such good company and under so strong a management. I didn't like you running all over greater N.Y. looking for work. Mama is very happy over it and talks a blue streak.

164

Today I bought a napkin ring for Clare's boy. It's like yours only not as heavy. He won't think much of it for a while but I thought it would be nice for him to have from his people up North.

Speaking of up North, you wouldn't know the place where we used to cut through the woods to East Milton. 3 or 4 streets are laid out and they expect to start a village in the spring. A hundred or more Italians have been at work all fall and aren't nearly finished yet. A lot of them built wigwams of pine boughs. They look funny with a stove pipe sticking out, but the ventilation must be fine. Yesterday Katherine Follett was over to call on Mama and brought her a dozen pinks which was nice of her. The first of the week Orissa Baxter sent the same only red. Katherine's were light pink. It won't seem much like Christmas this year but we will make the best of it and hope for better luck next time around. Take good care of yourself and try to please your management and when you get through punishing yourself come home to us who miss you.

Lovingly,<br>Your father

If you can't write a letter, send a p.c. and a program when you can.

Hard as it was to say "I want to go on the stage," to do it was harder. "What makes you think you've got the stuff it takes?" Papa asked, and up on top of the Lyceum, I had to prove I had it.

340 West 85th<br>New York City<br>December 17, 1915

Dear Mama,

Four days left before we open. I practice my dancing and reading of my lines from eight o'clock in the morning to one-thirty, have lunch, walk down to the theatre at two and rehearse steadily from then until seven o'clock. I guess my friends think I neglect them, but if I think about what friends think, I won't get far. After dinner I fall right into bed.

I wish you and Papa could be here for opening night. The house is almost sold out the whole engagement.

Lovingly,<br>Ruth

Sunday the scenery was going up on the stage of the Empire. Turmoil! Mr. Saint-Gaudens took us back to the Lyceum. On Monday, the whole company was onstage, dress rehearsal in the evening.

Granite Place

Dearest Ruth child,

I'm thinking of you a lot today and wondering how you are with such strenuous rehearsing. Miss Turner brought me the book of Peter Pan and

I shall begin it at once. Mrs. Andrews called and left a small bundle for Xmas and one for you. Josie Emerson sent me a dozen carnations and they are lovely. It's quite blowy and chilly and will be cold tonight. Bless your brave self, you are so persevering.

Love from
Mama

The pain was terrible. "Oh, Ida, tonight is opening night."

"Gin helps."

"I never had any."

"Miss Lister has something. Cramps make her yell every month."

"I've got Penny Royal."

She studied it. "Smells like hell, but if y' never had gin don't start. Maude Adams wouldn' like ya doing your dance soused."

Could I do the pillow dance with that stab?

"Drink this."

The cramps twisted through again. "It's going to make me throw up."

"Hold your nose an' swallow."

What if the pink pajamas showed a spot?

"Quit being a virgin helps. After the show gets open, let some feller get *you* open. That stuff doin' ya anything?"

I nodded.

"After I brush up the rest of the rooms, I'll heat some more." She started out. "Oh, here." She pulled a letter out of her pocket and slit it. "No money order, just a letter."

Dear Ruth child,

Papa got your letter and answered it, enclosing $5. Did you get it? He took me for a walk this morning and bought some Xmas cards which I mailed today. Is it Tuesday you are going to open in *Peter Pan?* I would give anything to see it. I think of you. We both send love.

Mama

She fixed it so I could be an actress, even to seeing I had Penny Royal. It worked. Inside the hollow tree upstage right I listened for my cue. The Lost Boys sat on the ground cloth and talked about mothers.

"On Christmas and birthdays I remember my mother best," said Slightly Soiled.

"I'd like to give my mother a checkbook," said Tootles.

That was my cue to step out of the tree and say, "What's a checkbook?"

Everything went well, the pillow dance was well applauded, Miss Adams fought the lion, we all fought the pirates till they jumped overboard, up in the treetops Miss Adams waved to Wendy flying home and the final curtain fell. Second Twin, First Twin, Slightly, the original Tiger Lily and I climbed the black iron stairs to our second-floor dressing room.

"You've made a creditable beginning," said Angela Ogden. High praise from one of the company's most admired members.

Back at the Club, a knock on my door; Julie Muschette carried in her supper tray. "I'll have it with you. You were fine."

On our trays, a curled-up cheese sandwich, a glass of milk and one unready pear. What was that different taste? Not a pear like *people* eat, a *first night* pear for an actress.

When my head hit the pillow, did I dream? "Sherry's? . . . Reserve a table for Miss Ruth Gordon, the pillow dancer from *Peter Pan.*" Somewhere a door was pushed open. "Read about yourself!" Edith McClellan shook a newspaper at me.

"I'm not awake."

"Be that as it may, *The New York Times* says, 'Ruth Gordon is ever so gay as Nibs.' "

Bess McAdams rushed in. "You're off in a cloud of dust, girl!" She waved the *Times.* "They didn't like Wendy, but 'Ruth Gordon is ever so gay as Nibs.' "

Louise Davidson stuck her head in the door. "Dog, you made a hit! You going to write and thank the critic?"

"I don't know who he is."

"Julie knows things like that."

I lay back on the pillow that had heard my groans. Now it heard praise! Send a copy to Mama and Papa. And Katherine. And Mr. Sargent? "You show no promise. Don't come back." One to Mr. Diestel. Mr. Jehlinger. When things go right, enjoy it. That's the cushion that lets you take the bumps.

In my box a letter from Papa.

*The Factory*
*Tues. A.M.*
*Dec. 21, 1915*

Dear Ruth,

I am sending you by express a box from Mama, also $5. Merry Christmas and every success in *Peter Pan.* Your part sounds hard, but I have no doubt you'll pull it off all right. When you write Mama don't ask her if I got a letter from you, she thinks there must be some secret in it. If she sees in the paper any accident in N.Y. she thinks you must be in it. I have to make her believe you can't be on ferry boats and subway trains and in the Bronx and on Staten Island the same time. She gets bothered but she's making a slow but sure gain. She received several packages yesterday through the mail. Also one for you. I forwarded it in your box. Also a package from "Little Jack of Durham" contents unknown.

Christmas will be rather gray for her. I'm with her all the time after I get my dinner and a smoke. If you have a chance send us a program. You know how much we'd like to see your opening night tonight. I have no doubt you'll have at least a part of the success we both wish for you.

With lots of love,
Your father

Run over to Amsterdam Avenue, look in the library to see if the other papers said things. None did; only the *Times* reviewed it.

Julie Muschette brought in her sketches. "They're all Maude Adams except one of you. Would your hometown paper pay five dollars?"

In this room that had been full of worries was a drawing of me that maybe the Quincy *Patriot* would print and my great *New York Times* notice.

Dear Mama and Papa,

Well, it's all over and you can be proud of me. I wish you could have been there. That was truly the only thing missing. It was the worst day of my life and the greatest night. No matter how old I live I will never experience such emotions. I'll begin from the worst, it was my period and, Mama, you know what pains I have, but nothing could equal yesterday. Thank fortune I had a good sleep although how I had the courage to, the night before my first opening night, I don't know! I really think I am wonderful. But this horrible pain woke me up. I could just groan and our good colored maid looked in. She asked me if I ever had gin. Mama, I *didn't* drink any. Ida fixed me some of the Penny Royal tea from Wollaston. I thought I would throw up, but I didn't and it worked.

That was my terrible day. My night made up for all that and for all the rest of my life. In a big envelope I am sending you something will prove why. I don't care how hard it is or how terrible, I would rather be an actress than live. In other words, if I could not be an actress, I would gladly take my life. I can say that without fear because I *can* be an actress and *will* be, as proven by what it says in the other envelope. Papa, I know you like the Boston Globe, but wait till you see this envelope!

At the Empire Theatre I dress one flight up with Angela Ogden, who kind of slips me little hints of what to do, without exactly letting on she's doing it. Also in the dressing room is Miss Keppel, who is sweet and subdued. They are all too old, except me, to play the Lost Boys, but most of them are friends of friends of Miss Adams or been with her since the year one. Angela Ogden is a very wonderful actress who, they say, stole the show from Miss Adams when they played *Quality Street,* so Miss Adams won't put that one on any more, but will revive *The Little Minister* where Angela has a nice part that's no competition. Well, I better get back to opening night. Did I write you I wear a suit of sort of like teddy bear fur? It goes all over me except my face and is quite hot and cumbersome, but the Lost Boys have to wear them. Well, the curtain went up and I thought I would die of fright, but the scenes in the Darlings' nursery are before I come on, so I recovered. Our scene started in the Never Never Land and I was in my place inside the tree trunk when I heard my cue and came out and said my line and got a huge laugh. I was so pleased. They tell me no one ever got that laugh before, so it made quite an impression.

All went swimmingly. It was a very fashionable audience, all the Fifth Avenue set. Miss Adams is a big society draw. They said all the men wore silk hats and white ties and tails and the ladies were quite decollete and heavily jeweled. After my dance Miss Adams beckoned me to take three bows and our orchestra leader Henri Deering stood up and applauded. Gratifying after all I've been through. And Miss Adams has no jealousy like Alice Claire Elliot says many stars have. My cup runneth over and I guess when you read this, yours will, too.

Then came the final curtain with Miss Adams alone in the treetop house after having waved goodbye to Wendy who flew home and everybody including the cast in the wings were crying when down came the curtain to thunderous applause and we all took our rehearsed bows, then rushed back and stood in the wings. That means just out of sight in the scenery. Miss Adams took one of her calls alone then came over and said "Nibs" and led me on and while the audience applauded she broke off a rose from the immense bouquet that had been passed over the footlights and handed me a long-stemmed American Beauty rose that must have cost I don't know how much and I will treasure and preserve forever.

Well, that's about all. All the people in our dressing room including those I mentioned and Mrs. Buchanan, quite a swell, and Miss Clarens, extremely elegant, told me I had made a most auspicious start. And when you see the other envelope, you will note they are right.

Your loving actress daughter,

Ruth Gordon

(A name you will one day see in lights)

December 22, 1915, my favorite day of my life.

R.

"Your hometown paper has pride in a native daughter on Broadway, don't they?" asked Julie.

"I guess so."

"If they buy the sketch is a good way to find out. I found out the critic's name. Roger Woollcott."

On the crumpled monogrammed paper Katherine had sent me, my letter to Woollcott ended,

> I would rather be an actress than anything, so your praise was very encouraging.
>
> Yours truly,<br>Ruth Gordon

For Woollcott, no personality, no gush. "Well, thanks."

"For what?"

"Giving it to me."

"Get your dung-forks off it! I just let you *look,* to remind you of your lost virtuous youth. I suppose you *were* virtuous when you wrote it? It reads like a permanent virgin! I'm glad—I speak only for others—you found the bend in the road. From reading this prim tribute who could prophesy that nine years later you'd storm the elderly set at Palm Beach's Royal Poinciana as the sidekick of Lou McGuire?"

# Chapter

⸻⊷⸻

# 8

Had it been nine years since Gregory and I had invested our money in Booth Tarkington's and Harry Leon Wilson's play *Tweedles?* It paid back praise, but no money, so Gregory took the first offer, *King for a Day*. The leading lady was as flat as my part in *Piccadilly Jim*, so we agreed I should wait for something better. Lou McGuire said come to Palm Beach with her till Bill came and she'd pay the expenses. Bill and Lou and Gregory and I had dinner the night before we were leaving and Bill borrowed five hundred dollars from Gregory so it evened out. Bill didn't pay anyone back.

Palm Beach's Royal Poinciana Hotel was splendid, but lonely. Everybody knew everybody, except us.

"We have to keep circulating where everyone can see us," advised Lou. "That's how things happened when Marge and I were here; we never hit the room except to change our clothes."

We hung around the lobby, looked at this, looked at that, looked at a pink chiffon hat in the shop.

"Hello."

Someone spoke to me! "Hello."

Lou appraised him. "He's an old cutie pie. Who *is* he?"

"Messmore Kendall. A millionaire."

"How'd you know him?"

"I don't."

"Y' do *now.*"

"He knows Anna Wheaton. I didn't think he'd remember me."

"See what a little nerve does? Hang around the lobby is the way Marge gets going and nobody had a whirl here like her. What kind of a millionaire?"

The phone rang.

"My God, a phone call!" She answered in her Saturday night Sixty Club voice. "Yes? . . . Oh, yes, Mr. Kendall, she's right here." She put her hand over the mouthpiece. "Ask has he got a friend."

"Hello . . ." My Sixty Club voice. "Of *course* I remember you. I didn't think you'd remember *me.* . . . Well, thank you. . . . Oh, no, you mustn't do that. . . ."

"Let him! Pin him down to something definite."

"Oh, it's a darling hat, but I was just *looking* at it. . . ."

"Christ, *take* it if he wants to give you one. What's a hat?"

"You're darling, but I can't let you. . . . No. . . . No, really. . . . What? . . . Oh, I'm down here with my friend, Mrs. William Anthony McGuire. That was her just now. She thinks— No, I won't tell you, it's a trade-last. . . . When you give *me* a compliment, I tell what Lou said about *you.* . . . Tonight? . . . Lou made a date for us, but let me ask her. . . ."

"My God, someone's taking us *out?*"

I held my hand over the phone. "Dinner at Bradley's and he'll bring a friend."

"Don't tell him I hocked my chastity belt—let him find out."

"Lou says she *can* break our date—it's just with a friend. . . . You'll pick us up at eight? . . . Dress, of course. . . ."

"And take it off right after."

"Adore it. . . . 'Bye."

Were we launched? Messmore Kendall—handsome, forty years our senior, lawyer for the Du Ponts, friend of General Du Pont, friend of Mr. Hearst, built the Capitol Theatre and gave grand parties in his apartment above it. Were we launched!

"Take a swig." Lou took a quick swallow and passed the Teacher's Highland Cream. "Men like it if you had a drink!"

172

"Why?"

"If he gets a whiff of scotch, he knows you play ball."

I took a swallow.

Messmore Kendall knew everybody and introduced us. The first intro was to General Colman Du Pont. Our beaux's combined age was a hundred and thirty-five? No wonder they got a great table at Bradley's, everybody bowing. Our white-haired fellows were charming, attentive. Lou and I knew *we* looked great. Could Marge have done better?

After dinner, before going into the gambling room, Lou and I went to Ladies.

Was it prophetic? I lost my diamond wedding band. "I *have* to get it back," I said, and burst into tears.

"My God, it's her *wedding* ring," said Lou. "Don't you have a plumber somewhere?"

Bradley's did. He performed some wizardry and handed me back my ring. Was it symbolic of the easy life? Is it part of a rake's progress—where there's money, there's a full-time plumber to keep reputation intact?

The phone rang all the time. "Yes?"

"Ben Maple."

"Oh, hello."

"Who is it?" Lou called softly from the bathroom.

"Remember me from the beach this morning?"

"Oh, I do."

"You were very entertaining."

"Thank you. It was fun."

"Who *is* it?"

"You're a very exciting young lady. Would you like to have dinner with me?"

"Lovely."

"Who *is* it?" called Lou, louder.

"I'll pick you up in the lobby, eight-thirty, we'll have a little dinner, then go over to a little place I have here and tomorrow I'll give you a thousand dollars."

"Can't you say his name just *once*, for Chris'sake?" wailed Lou. "Oh, what do *I* care!"

Startled, I lost my Palm Beach lingo. "Uh huh."

"Eight-thirty?"

" 'Bye."

I put the phone down. *"Lou!"*

"I don't *care* now." She was lying in the bath, jasmine bath salts scenting the air, reading *Jurgen*.

"Ben Maple—"

"Couldn't you have *said* so? Dammit, I gotta know who a person's talking to!"

"He asked me to spend the night with him."

"Over the *phone?"*

"Said he'd give me a thousand dollars tomorrow."

That caught her attention. "Said it without any *warm-up?"*

"I only *met* him this morning! Remember him? On the beach."

"What kind of a Zulu *is* he? Nobody rings up and says, 'Sleep with me. I'll give you a thousand dollars.' "

"Yup."

"Aw, nobody's got charm anymore."

"He asked me to dinner first."

"You going to?"

"Ugh!"

"Couldn't he take you to dinner, you're drinking a cordial, break it to you *then!* Isn't that only *human?"*

"He's horrible!"

"That way it's more a compliment, not like you're some commercial tart."

"My God, I think I said I *would."*

"Well, did you or didn't you?"

"I said I'd go to dinner, then after he said about the thousand, I forgot to say *no!"*

"Talking money on the phone like it's an inducement, he must feel he's some leper."

Sunday night at Palm Beach, Marge had told Lou, everybody who's anybody stays home. Lou and I went into the Poinciana dining room, where no one went even though it was charged on the bill. Only a few diners, all old except Arthur Hopkins and his wife.

"What did I tell you!" said Lou. "Sunday night *nobody* goes out."

Eight-thirty came and went, Mr. Maple got stood up, we took our time, then wandered out in the lobby. Arthur Hopkins stood there, alone. Could I know that if I'd gone to bed with Ben Maple I might have saved myself a lot of heartbreak, but is saving heartbreak what makes

174

an actress? Maybe find out. I don't think they teach that at dramatic school.

"Mr. Hopkins, do you remember me?" I'd been to his office a lot of times; no encouragement. A long walk from the door to his desk, then: "Is there anything for me in *Good Gracious, Annabelle* for the road?" He shook his head. The long walk back to the door. That was on West 45th Street.

At the Royal Poinciana, "Yes, dear."

"I guess I shouldn't tell you." And then I told him the Ben Maple story.

"Let's go out."

"I'm with my friend Mrs. William Anthony McGuire." She was talking to Herbie, a guy who filled in.

We got into two wicker rolling chairs. Arthur told the men where to take us.

The trip lasted four years.

In Palm Beach it was just a promise; his wife was there. "We should have separated long ago." He bought a drawing room for me to New York. "Tell the porter to make the lower up with two mattresses. Going through the Carolinas the roadbed is rough."

"I'll tell him."

"I wish I were sharing it with you."


*King for a Day* opened in Detroit. Gregory and I stayed at the Statler. Across the Circle was the Wolverine.

"Is there a letter for Mrs. Kelly?" The postmark was Palm Beach with no return address. I read it. Read it. Burned it.

After Detroit, Chicago for a run. Gregory engaged our same room at the beautiful Blackstone Hotel, where we'd stayed when we played *Clarence.* Where we'd had fun and were a success! Fun to buy a diamond and platinum bracelet with flexible links. Gregory bought it at Spaulding's on Michigan Boulevard; I bought him a thin thin platinum watch, gold letters, gold hands. Fun making love, fun living at the Blackstone, fun to buy a fifty-dollar pink rose-petal hat at Marshall Field's, wicked but fun to order a black satin toque at Jacques on Michigan Avenue, a bird of paradise sweeping off and curling under my chin! A hundred and fifty dollars, but it made me look the way an actress would like to.

Fun to go to the Opera Club and have people say, "Gregory Kelly and Ruth Gordon in *Clarence* at the Blackstone Theatre"; to the College Inn,

175

where we had our first date. Now we danced close, then went back to the Blackstone, where he didn't say good night and disappear up Michigan Avenue, but got closer. Fun to be in love, fun to live in style, to walk into the Blackstone's elegant lobby, into the mahogany elevator up to the stately wide hall that led to our small five-dollar-a-day room looking out at a slit of Lake Michigan.

For five dollars we could have had a big room at the Congress, but the Blackstone, when Mr. Tracy and Mr. John Drake ran it, was an event. Food, service, the real linen sheets and towels, the basketweave chair edged with mahogany that was the toilet. The Blackstone Hotel stood for luxury that only the Drakes could think up.

Thornton Wilder said the dining room, white walls and crystal chandeliers, was the most beautiful in the world. At one end, a small balcony where musicians played pretty music while everybody looked beautiful and behaved. Lovely flowers, fine china, silver; at the head of the velvet stairs to the entrance, a white damask-covered table, on it a sugar masterpiece. Easter it was a sugar bunny with sugar baskets of sugar eggs, Christmas a sugar Christmas tree, Thanksgiving a sugar gobbler with sheaves of sugar corn and a sugar pumpkin. Between holidays, sugar flowers or fruit or angels, whichever one sweet Praxiteles was pleased to concoct.

Gregory was teaching me to act.

Endless talk, discussion, corrections, questions, explanations, until I burst into tears and threw the script across our room. Gregory picked it up and comforted me and on we went. I'd gotten wonderful notices. Doc Hall in the Chicago *Journal* said, "She will be a star in five years." "She is star quality," predicted Charles Collins in the *Post*. Percy Hammond said extravagant things. A rave from Ashton Stevens. Everybody knew Gregory was terrific; I was the surprise. That was for opening night, then came the other performances. Opening night I happened to do it, but didn't know what I did.

"You're hammering," said Gregory.

"Don't tell *me*. Charles Collins says I'll be a star. Percy Hammond says— Don't tell *me*—I know what I'm doing."

George C. Tyler came back to Chicago to see the show. For confidence I had a martini.

"She's ruining the show," said Tyler, and gave me my notice.

Didn't Charles Collins, hadn't Doc Hall, but George Tyler was the one who had the say.

Gregory went to him. "She was nervous with you being out front."

"Why should she be? I told her she was fine opening night."

"Let me see what we can do; give her a chance, then come back."

He needed Gregory. "All right, Kelly, but she's ruining the show."

Tears, the manuscript thrown, agony and *gradually* improvement. *Gradually* Gregory taught me to know what I was doing and why. *Gradually* he showed me how.

"If I can find someone to teach me, I can learn."

Mrs. Fiske had passed it on to Gregory and now her pupil was passing it on. "Hold it all together, don't let pauses in. A pause is hard to act around until you really know how; hold it together."

The next performance, I tried what Gregory had taught. "Was *that* it?" I asked.

"Don't stop after a scene and discuss it. Discuss it after the play. You can't act and criticize too."

Exciting to become an actress, exciting to be married, exciting to hear Mr. Tyler say, "You're very good."

The weather turned warm, the company was booked to play through the summer on the Coast—Los Angeles, San Francisco, up north to Portland and Tacoma, where Harlan Tucker came from, and Seattle, home of Guthrie McClintic. On the way back, fill in with bookings until Labor Day, then St. Louis, Cleveland, Indianapolis, where Mr. Tarkington could see us. For the tour, no raise in salary, because it would be an expensive railroading bill for a two-set show, a fairly large company, and in summer, except for San Francisco, business would be off.

"We won't ask for more salary," Gregory wrote Mr. Tyler, "but we would like a drawing room for the sleeper jumps."

"Fine, but there are times that might be impossible," wrote Mr. Tyler, "so don't make it part of the contract."

"Fine," wrote Gregory.

Out of Chicago, a sleeper jump to Grand Rapids in a drawing room. The end of the week it was deducted from Gregory's salary. Mr. Moxon, the company manager, showed Mr. Tyler's letter: "Note, Kelly does not insist on a drawing room."

Gregory wrote a letter. Money refunded. What couldn't get refunded was our wariness of Mr. Tyler. If it had been Klaw and Erlanger or the Shuberts we'd have been on guard, but rosy-cheeked, blue-eyed, plump Mr. Tyler? It was like distrusting your grandfather, who turned out to be Foxy Grandpa.

We headed for the Coast with a stop at El Paso for one night. We hired a car and took a look across the border, Juárez. First time out of my native land; glad to get back.

Two nights in Phoenix. Hot! Transom *under* the door to let in the hot air. Glad to leave Phoenix for one night in Tucson. Loved it. Before the show, we took a taxi ride out on the mesa. Cool. What air! Loved it.

Leaving Tucson in the Fred Harvey diner, we ordered alligator pear. A first. Oh, my!

Los Angeles a week. We played the Mason Opera House and stayed at the grand Alexandria Hotel, danced to the new band, leader Paul Whiteman, playing "Whispering." Saw Charlie Chaplin dancing. Thought we saw Mary Miles Minter. National Pictures sent for Gregory and we met their grand star, Katherine MacDonald. Conrad Nagel invited us out to his house in Beverly Hills and the taxi we went in had a cloth-of-gold lining.

Didn't get San Francisco. Two weeks. Papa came. He and Gregory liked each other.

San Jose a night. Dashing Jack Morgan drove us to his house in Palo Alto. House? Mansion. Some people are *never* satisfied; I thought it would be more so.

Sleeper after the show to Sacramento.

Up the coast to Oregon. One night at Medford. Portland. I bought a chiffon-trimmed satin nightgown for eighteen dollars. Easy come, easy go.

Tacoma. Home of Harlan Tucker. Let it be. No connection, but I forgot my lines. Gregory kept right on. And I went on, but kept thinking, "I forgot my lines." It seemed so horrible that it made me cry. I kept on, but I cried, then couldn't bear it, took a chair, put my head down and cried.

Cora was a spoiled kid and the audience thought it was acting; they laughed. Gregory signaled for the curtain to ring down.

Stage manager Collamore went out and announced, "Miss Gordon has a nervous breakdown. The understudy will go on." Understudy was seeing a movie.

"Miss Gordon has recovered from her nervous breakdown," announced stage manager Collamore, "and will continue." I cried on and off during the evening. Good that the next week the company had a layoff. Gregory and I took the train to Lake Coeur d'Alene in Idaho.

We played Vancouver. Didn't like it. Crossed the Canadian border and played Victoria. Great! That old grand hotel made us feel as though we were in England, where we had never been.

In Cheyenne there was a storm and all the lights went out. We each had to carry a candle to light us while we played the show.

Heading back from the Coast, we ran into full summer. Terrible heat, mostly travel in day coaches, windows open, soot and grit pouring in. Out the window, the world had turned into hot green cornfields, not a breeze stirring; even the corn silk lay limp. Sun, dry earth, sun, cornfields, sun, dry earth, everybody wilted.

Hastings, Nebraska. A bus had a sign on it: "FREE RIDE TO THE HOG FAIR."

Gregory and I got in. Four others from the company were aboard. What else was there to do?

Hot, exhausting, but we were in love. Now it was cold and I was in love with someone else. At the Congress Hotel I picked up letters postmarked Palm Beach, read them, read them again, got rid of them.

"He's fat," said Lou. "You really go for Arthur Hopkins? Or do you think he can put you in a show?"

"Both."

"He's a chaser." Lou was really cynical. Maybe he was and maybe he wasn't and didn't he say he was unhappy with his wife?

His office on 45th Street was the lower floor of a brownstone next to the last house of Martin's Theatrical, which was no more.

"He's expecting you," said his secretary, and opened a door.

"Hello, dear."

The secretary closed the door.

Palm Beach, then the letter at the Wolverine, then letters at the Congress. Did I love him because he could do something for me? In bed I didn't remember that.

An offer for *The Goose Hangs High,* by Lewis Beach. It didn't bother me to turn it down; Arthur was in rehearsal with *What Price Glory* and when he phoned he was free, I wanted to be.

"I can't come to the Algonquin anymore, dear. It's like an annex of Great Neck and Eva has found out."

Eva was Mrs. Hopkins. Great Neck was where they lived and where her friends reported in. She was on the rampage, vowed she'd get me.

What did that mean? Hair-pulling? A shoot-out? Alienation?

"I don't know why I haven't done something," said Arthur, and took a suite for us at the Claridge Hotel. Didn't Great Neck know about *there?*

In a behind-the-arras love affair there's a lot of waiting for the phone

179

to ring. When I was pretty sure it wouldn't anymore, I went over to Lou McGuire's second floor front at the Crillon.

I rang the bell.

No answer.

The door wasn't quite shut. "Lou?"

She looked out of the bedroom, half into her new black Milgrim dress. "My God, who do you think called up? Harry!"

"Who?"

"The cute guy I'm mad about and never got started with. He's downstairs having dinner with his girl. She's Phoebe Lee."

"My God!"

"He said have coffee with them, so come on."

"You don't want *me.*"

"I told him you were coming. He said, 'Bring her.'"

"What d' you s'pose she's like?"

"You saw her, bare-ass."

For the *Follies* Act I finale, Phoebe Lee drew the blue velvet curtain across the stage, bare from the waist down. At the corner table in the Crillon restaurant, her blue velvet suit showed the lines of her long, fantastic figure, her red hair showed under the Reboux cloche. For Sunday, she wore her *short* diamond necklace.

Ten years later in the ladies' room of London's Savoy Grill I cried, "Phoebe!"

She walked toward me, murmuring, "I'm going straight."

Hugs and kisses.

"Don't tell on me. I'm married. Claude Graham-White!"

In 1912 I'd watched him at the Squantum Aviation Meet. Mama and I had taken a trolley over. We couldn't afford to go in, but stood out in a field and saw an airship go up and stay up. It was Claude Graham-White from England and we saw it! Like everybody, we made Graham-White sandwiches—one slice of graham bread, one slice of white.

In the small, elegant Crillon dining room, Harry jumped up to greet us.

Lou smiled and winked. The wink was from the old Chicago days; she was getting rid of it.

"This is Phoebe Lee."

"This is Ruth Gordon."

Phoebe gave no sign of being sociable.

Harry pulled out a chair. "Put your satchel there."

I laughed and sat down. He was cute. I saw what Lou meant.

"Still know how to play 'Nola'?" he asked her.

"What's 'Nola'?" Miss Lee had found her tongue.

" 'Nola,' baby. 'Doodly *do,* Deedo, dee*do!'* 'Nola.' What you shake it to!"

"Says who?"

"Says me, you li'l snooky-ookums."

She laughed a broken-glass chorus-girl laugh. "God, I can't get sore at you."

"Sure you can."

She leaned over and kissed him on the mouth. Then looked across at Lou. "Y' saw it, kid."

We laughed.

"How about a cordial?" Harry snapped his fingers.

"Yes, Mr. Davison?"

"Phoebe?"

"Apricot brandy, imported."

Harry looked at me.

"Kümmel, I guess."

"Louie? I mean Lou."

"Damn right." Phoebe gave him a look.

"She's married, baby doll."

*"Was!* I threw him out."

*King for a Day* wasn't for New York. It played its run in Chicago and closed. Gregory signed to co-star with Madge Kennedy in *Badges* when the new season began. For now, he was offered the juvenile part in a movie starring Richard Dix at Famous Players Studio on Long Island.

"Me away all day will leave you stranded, little feller. Let's buy us a car. We'll have a chauffeur and you can go for rides."

Mornings I drove with Gregory to Long Island City, then rode off to explore places. Great Neck, where Arthur lived; Oyster Bay, where President Theodore Roosevelt had lived. I'd seen pictures in the Sunday paper. To Long Beach to see the Castles' Castles-by-the-Sea. Every ride was part excitement, part guilt, part enjoyment, part despair. It used up time.

Sometimes I'd tell Beverly, our chauffeur, to go back to the Algonquin the quickest way. Maybe I was missing a phone call. Back at the hotel I'd look at the phone and *will* it to ring. *Wish* it to be Arthur. Sometimes it was.

In the lobby of the Algonquin I saw Mary Pickford, Douglas Fairbanks, Ethel Barrymore, Mr. John Drew. Everybody drifted in, drifted out. I recognized them, but didn't know anyone until I ran into the new Mrs. Robert E. Sherwood, who had been Mary Brandon in Indianapolis. She'd hung around the Stuart Walker stock company eager to make friends, went on one week in a small part in *Leah Kleschna.* Except for that, everybody brushed her off. Undiscouraged, she came to New York and got the lead in *Welcome Stranger,* which was a big hit. In a hit you make friends; one was movie critic Sherwood. Mary, five feet tall and fat; Sherwood, skinny and so tall he got turned down by our army and joined Canada's Black Watch. Years later I asked him why he married Mary. He kicked his feet and never found an answer.

At the Murat Theatre stage door, I didn't bother with her. In the Algonquin lobby it was, *"Hello,* Mary!"

"Will you come to Bob's birthday party?"

That was the beginning. She got me in with F.P.A., Mr. and Mrs. Herbert Bayard Swope, Neysa McMein, Dorothy Parker. Charlie MacArthur I'd already met in Ned Sheldon's room at the hospital in Chicago.

"Thank you, Mary, darling, for inviting me. Could you and Mr. Sherwood have dinner with us Sunday?"

"We're going to the Swopes' for the weekend."

"Would you want me to drive you?" When *you* see an opening do you know it?

"Bob's coming later, but *I* want to go in the afternoon."

Beverly drove Mary and me out to Great Neck, to the Swopes' big white house looking out over Manhasset Bay. On the big broad piazza, Mrs. Swope was pouring tea. A cup of tea and compliments got things moving. "Why don't you and your husband come out tomorrow," said the great Pearl Swope.

Was I in?

"Come to lunch."

"What time?"

"One?"

That "one" with a question mark was no accident. Gregory and I got to Great Neck ahead of time, drove round until one minute to one and shot up the Swopes' circular drive. If you're not in, you're prompt, but how could we know "prompt" at the Swopes' was when *they* said it was? Nothing to do with the clock.

"Take two hours," Gregory told Beverly.

"Yes, sir." He and our Packard disappeared.

The house looked restful.

Why not? No one was up.

The black maid who had served tea yesterday greeted us. She thought someone would be down soon. F.P.A. drifted out, was cordial, then gave his attention to breakfast.

"Would you like to see a paper?" asked the maid.

We'd seen them, but to look occupied, read them again.

Sherwood showed up, reasonably pleased to see us. Two more house guests appeared. At two-thirty, Mr. and Mrs. Swope brushed through. "Got everything you want?" asked Swope as he helped his wife into their limousine.

She looked at us, bleakly. *"You*'ll have a better lunch than we will. Nobody leave." They rolled off.

Lunch was served at three. Around five, the Swopes were back. Did they remember they'd met us? To get in is not always easy.

Come and see Dotty in 703–704. Charlie.

The note had been left in our box.

Propped up on pillows, Dotty Parker lay in bed, holding court. "Know the stuff in the seam of your coat pocket?" she asked. "That's pfuff."

"Why, so it is," said Charlie. In four years he'd write *The Front Page.* He and Benchley and Don Stewart—friends didn't say the Ogden—and June Walker sat around in the suite Charlie had engaged. The door opened and shut, people came and went, someone ordered a club sandwich, a waiter brought more coffee.

Charlie twisted his forelock and looked anxiously at Dotty, white as the pillow. "What have I done to deserve all this?"

Benchley held up his hand. "Some of us are too young to hear."

How did this lead me to become June Walker's sidekick? What did she see in me? June was a beauty, a success, a real actress; what could *I* contribute? She knew George Jean Nathan and invited me to meet him at a Sunday night party. Her apartment on East 50th between Park and Madison was a walk-up, four flights, but then it was grand. The walnut cabinet had been given her by Vincent Astor. When friendship lapsed and she needed money, should she ask him, she asked me?

"Of course."

"I did what you said," she phoned me, "but he said, 'At this time it wouldn't be convenient.'"

She gave a dinner for John Barrymore. Out of a list of guests, he okayed Robert Benchley and me. Bob and I climbed the four flights, John Barrymore was there. Dinner was good, but the four of us didn't meld.

Bob and I drove off to the opening of *Annie Dear.* "What happened?" asked Bob.

"Was everybody too anxious?"

June and Barrymore came to the opening, but not together.

That whole evening, everyone was too anxious, including all of us watching Billie Burke in *Annie Dear,* her first musical in New York.

If things didn't work out for June, something else would or somebody else did. She phoned. "We'll drive out to Caley Bragg's."

"Who?"

"Caley Bragg. He won the gold cup."

"He did?"

In the car were Bessie Love and Jack Pickford, who was bringing Princess White Deer. A nothing event except for the cast, but it got rid of the afternoon until somebody offered a great part. June knew what to do about everything but her life. If she got hungry, she knew a place that made caviar sandwiches and they'd run them over. She had beauty, talent, dazzle; why didn't she make it? Until she went after Gregory she was a good sidekick. If she wanted a man, she went after him, no matter whose he was. If she wanted a part, she went after it. I'm glad I cold-shouldered her before the phone call: "Mr. McClintic wants to see you at four this afternoon, The Little Theatre."

"Thank you." I hung up. "Guthrie McClintic," I told Gregory. "To come to see him. I always think he *hates* me!"

"Maybe you're wrong."

"When he was casting for Winthrop Ames, before I even *asked,* he said, 'No. Nothing.' "

"Maybe he changed."


On West 44th Street was Winthrop Ames' Little Theatre. He built it and it was as different as its owner. Other theatres were red velvet and gold, with balcony and gallery. The Little was wood-paneled, no balcony or gallery. It was as elegant as Mr. Ames' family home at Carriage Works in Massachusetts, the depot named after the Ames business.

"I'm Miss Ingersoll, Mr. Ames' secretary. I'll show you into Mr. McClintic's office." She opened the door. "Mr. McClintic, Miss Gordon."

"Hello. It's a comedy."

My heart sank.

"There are two parts; I don't know which is for you. Both good; one is bigger. Blanche Bates is the star. Can you come over to my house tonight? I'm going to read the play. The authors'll be there and Miss Bates and some of the actors."

"Yes. What time?"

"I was coming to that. I hope you pick up your cues that fast. Nine o'clock. Twenty-three Beekman Place."

"Thank you."

The Little Theatre is two blocks west on 44th Street from the Algonquin. Up in our suite, Gregory was waiting.

"It's a comedy." Despair filled my voice. Memory of *Nothing but the Truth.*

"Oh, my God!" He hadn't forgotten.

Who could?

Gregory left for *Badges,* I got ready for my date with Caley Bragg. With Caley it was always the Colony, black tie and dress up. Yellow organza over cloth-of-gold, red satin ribbon worked into appliquéd gold lace bands. Only Lucille could put stuff like that together. Red velvet Bergdorf Goodman cape with velvet and cloth-of-gold ruff, cloth-of-gold lining. Normal for the Colony, it could be a surprise at Guthrie McClintic's.

Caley picked me up in his foreign town car, small, elegant, looked handmade. "I thought we'd do the Colony."

"Great, but, Caley, at nine I have to be at Guthrie McClintic's house, he's got a divine comedy he wants me in and he's going to read it to me."

"Oh, boy." Caley didn't give a damn about a part or a show, but he knew he was supposed to say something. Also do something. He reached over and kissed my lips. He didn't give a damn if he did or didn't, his interest was fast boats, but kissing was like punctuation. You used it every so often.

At the Colony, Gene Cavallero bowed us in. "Mr. Bragg's table." First on the left, champagne bucket beside it, white orchid spray at my place.

"Caley, you're a dear."

"I guess so," he said. "Caviar, oysters, what's your pleasure?"

"Oysters." Lou McGuire had said Marge said it's sophisticated to turn down caviar.

Lovely dinner. With Caley there was nothing to do but eat. He thought about his fast boats, I thought about 23 Beekman Place. At

185

nine, his foreign town car pulled up in front, his foreign chauffeur opened the door, another kiss. Tonight was his lucky night! Caley wasn't a sis, but he loved to get to bed early. He liked me and liked to be seen out, but not often. Just often enough, like punctuation.

The chauffeur and Caley waited while I went up the high brownstone steps. First of a long series of steps.

A tall colored woman opened the door, didn't ask who I was. "He's up one, to the back." She shut the front door and called, "Shoog, one more on the way."

Those steps, for a lot of us, were "on the way."

Everybody was squeezed into the back parlor that overlooked the East River.

"Oh, hello," said Guthrie. "This is Miss Bates. Blanche, this is Ruth Gordon."

"So pleased to meet you." And she was. The first thing you felt about Blanche Bates was warmth.

"She's for either Katie or Delight."

What kind of part is called Katie? Or Delight? Or did he *say* that? Or did the champagne make it *sound* like he did?

"I'm not going to introduce everybody, but you're in the same room with Charles Waldron, Sylvia Field, Eliot Cabot, John Emery, Virginia Chauvenet and the authors, Mary Kennedy and Ruth Hawthorne."

"Hello," I said, glad I was dressed so beautifully.

Guthrie read the play. I listened for every time Delight or Katie said anything. Miss Bates was Mrs. Partridge, Delight was her daughter, Katie was a rich debutante friend of Delight's. Why Katie? Katie's a hired girl's name. Why Katie for a debutante? That sounded funny, a rich girl named Katie. Maybe that would be good.

"Which part do *you* think?" Guthrie asked me.

"Oh, I wouldn't play *any* but Katie."

"What I thought!" he said, triumphantly. "Blanche, she likes Katie."

"She'll be *great!*" Blanche Bates thought everything would be great; she was *for* things. She sailed through trouble and pleasure on a surge of things-will-come-out-*right!* And why not? Hadn't *Madame Butterfly?* And *The Girl of the Golden West?* And *Under Two Flags* and *Nobody's Widow?* And *The Famous Mrs. Fair?*

"Sylvia's perfect for Delight." Guthrie felt good about tonight. Never about tomorrow. "We start day after tomorrow; they'll call you up and talk business and where and what time." I had a job. It was comedy, but maybe a part named Katie?

186

First rehearsal we sat around the table and read. I wished I'd stuck to my Congregational church pledge never to touch alcohol. Delight talked on and *on*—why had I gone for Katie? Because a part has an odd name doesn't make a hit! Or *does* it? Anyway, *I* did. And after *Mrs. Partridge Presents* everyone knew I *could* play comedy.

In the spring, I left *Mrs. Partridge* to try out Anita Loos and John Emerson's *The Fall of Eve* in Stamford and Washington. In the autumn it would be done in New York. And still another offer! In our small tenth-floor-front sitting room at the Algonquin sat Lynn Starling, author of the script in his lap. Off in the corner, far away as he could get, sat the play's dark, resentful-looking producer, Jed Harris.

"I don't *really* think I'd like to do it," I told them. "The next thing I'm in I want to be featured and I don't really think the part in your play is big enough to be featured."

Why should the producer look baleful? Didn't I have a right to an opinion in my sitting room?

"But you *could* be featured. Couldn't she, Jed?" Lynn Starling turned to his producer and got an inscrutable smile.

"I'm not *urging* you to feature me. I wouldn't *want* to be, unless the part was worth it, and I don't think it is."

"Why be featured?" The voice from the corner sounded like a malediction from a tomb.

The author leaped in. "Just think it over, read it again. You'd be marvelous."

"Oh, I think I'd be good, but I must think of myself. You *really* better get someone else."

The producer was halfway to the door.

"Are you sure we can't persuade you? *Some* way?"

The door was open. "Come on." The producer had disappeared down the hall.

"I'm miserable." Lynn offered his hand. "And if you *do* change your mind, give us a ring."

I smiled. "Good luck."

In the mirror, my new Lanvin dress I'd bought at Lanvin in Paris showed me I was a success. Was that producer sore at success? Why hate me in my own suite? If he felt that way, why come? Lynn Starling really wanted me and showed it, the play wasn't terrible or anything, but it had good parts for *everybody*. The leading part wasn't even the lead and no pretty clothes. For a *great* part, that wouldn't matter; this wasn't even big enough to be featured. Let him sneer! I wanted to be *featured,* and I was going to be. Let *him* rise above his name in lights; I'd left home to be a star.

How was it *he* had a success and I didn't? Lights over the Booth Theatre spelled:

**THE FALL OF EVE**
**WITH**
**RUTH GORDON**

I didn't make a hit; we closed in a month. Other lights spelled:

**JED HARRIS**
**PRESENTS**
**WEAK SISTERS**

They got praised, it ran.

Offers came in, but none I wanted. What *did* I want? Success. This season Gregory had it. *The Butter and Egg Man.* Opening night, Woollcott invited Charlie Chaplin to sit with him. Chaplin said Gregory was great. Woollcott wrote he was and so was the play. George Kaufman wrote it and it was a hit. Gregory had come into his own.

We changed addresses. Up in 1010 was a mouse. I was lying down, something tickled my neck, I brushed the lace ruffle and brushed off a mouse. Two days later, we moved into a grand apartment at 36 West 59th Street. Couldn't there be a mouse up there? There could, but there wasn't.

From the tenth floor at the Algonquin to the tenth floor overlooking Central Park. With beautiful crewelwork curtains at the French windows, fine furniture, a colored maid, Esther, who cooked us fine meals, why call up Arthur? A long time had gone by; was he still crazy about Wanda Lyon?

"A chaser," Lou called him. Maybe he'd given her up.

"I've moved."

"Oh, where are you?"

"We have an apartment at 36 West Fifty-ninth."

"I'd like to come over."

I hadn't stopped being in love.

"I should have gotten a divorce," he said, "but I didn't." Did he *think* it or just keep on saying it?

Did it give *me* the idea? I went over to the St. Hubert Hotel, next to the Great Northern. Their suites were ugly and expensive. Maybe not get a divorce.

So much for principle!

"I want to be a good person," I said to Arthur. Was that like his "I should get a divorce"?

Maybe with him and me both it was sending up a trial balloon? First put out a feeler, then dip your toe in. Anything happen? A start. A seed. The first root. Arthur never got a divorce. What about me? I haven't made it yet, but I've improved.

At the Island, Woollcott and I sat on the dock looking up at the stars. When did he become the one to share unbearable secrets? "How did you know?"

"When I saved my new dress to wear for someone else and didn't even know who the someone else was."

A pause.

Stars streaked across the sky. One fell down back of Hydeville.

"You think it's final?"

"Uh huh."

"You sure?"

"I was in love with him, then I loved him, now I like him."

"You think you might *not* like him?"

"Not Gregory."

"What about Arthur?"

"I'm pregnant."

Dr. Roller wasn't as awful as Columbus Avenue or Indianapolis. He was more scientific, but he gave no anesthetic. Was that to get you away from the premises fast? Pain that was unbearable, then terrible weakness.

"Get up," said the nurse. "You're all right to walk out. I'll have the doorman get a taxi." Were she and the doctor glad to be rid of me? If I came back for a lost glove, purse or pride, would they deny they'd ever seen me?

Down Broadway to West 59th Street; at 36 I paid the driver and got out. Walk the few steps across the sidewalk, two steps up to the front door; they weren't easy. I rang for the elevator and waited. Out on 59th Street, traffic was skimming along. In the middle of it was our Pierce-Arrow, top down, Gregory driving. He looked like that night at the College Inn. Like the night when he came back from Indianapolis and

189

we were in Alta Mae's and Pierre's beds. Added to his dearness was the sense of the indignity I'd done him. Why couldn't I love him? "I sort of ache all over."

"Think it's a cold coming on?"

"Tomorrow I'll be better."

"Can I get you anything?" So *for* me, so understanding.

"Maybe I'll snooze."

"Do." He kissed me.

I started to cry.

"Don't cry, little feller."

Why did I love someone else? Did *he?* Who wrote letters in that stylish stub-pen handwriting? Was it that pretty blond Chicago debutante he did a number with in the Junior League charity show? Did he have girls? The phone rang. "Hello."

"Are you all right, dear?" It was Arthur.

"Oh, *yes.* Fine."

"Thought you would be. Well, dear, I'll call you tomorrow. I shall miss you." He hung up.

Where were the thoughts about unfairness?

"I shall miss you."

"No sexual intercourse for two weeks, then be careful," said Dr. Roller.

Two weeks! Would Arthur wait?

"I shall miss you."

Would he miss me for two weeks?

Our year was up in the grand apartment with the grand crewelwork curtains. Four hundred dollars a month was too much; we'd rent an unfurnished one on the fifth floor at one hundred and ninety-five dollars and furnish it.

"Spend five thousand," said Gregory. I meant to, but it came closer to seventy-five hundred. It was beautiful.

*The Butter and Egg Man* had closed its great New York season and gone on tour. A success!

I was a success at the Booth. Easter week, *Saturday's Children* played a matinee every afternoon. Exciting to be admired, be a hit, be praised, have money, know I could act. Exciting to have a love affair, beautiful clothes, diamonds, made-to-order fur coats from Bergdorf's, an ermine for evening, a sable stole for daytime, invitations to places to wear them! Everything I left home for. Everything my voices had promised. Praise, popularity, parties. After the Friday night show was Grace Hendrick's party. It wasn't the greatest. Two guys who seemed carried away by Grace's mother—we all called her Aunt Jo—a Columbia professor smitten with the idea of meeting an actress, Grace's rich Uncle Pomeroy, who gave her the impressive moonstone and ruby necklace, a fairy friend that was something or other, but what could that get Grace? Beautiful, rich, in the Social Register—why this bunch? "Goodbye, darling, I have a matinee tomorrow." Great to get to bed early. Pillows propped up, I struggled with the Arthur Machen book everybody was talking about. Plow on! If *everybody* could, couldn't I?

The phone rang. The hands of the little gold clock that Arthur, *not* Machen, had given me were at ten past two. "Hello?"

"Pittsburgh calling."

Pittsburgh must be Gregory. He shouldn't call this late before a matinee day. "Hello. . . . Yes, this is she." Who was *that* voice? A man's voice. Why didn't Gregory call *himself?* "Yes, I'm she. . . . *Yes,* darling. . . ." It was Gregory talking. "Oh! Oh, how dreadful; will you have to be out of the play? . . . Oh, dearest, how *awful!* What hospital? . . . You're there *now?* . . . Oh, Gregory, I'll take the sleeper tomorrow night, darling. . . . Of *course* I will. . . . I *won't* be tired. Oh, darling, I'm sorry. Look, just relax, don't worry. That's *terribly* important—don't worry about *anything.* Tomorrow night I'll be on the train and in the morning I'll come right to the hospital. . . . The *minute* I get in Sunday morning. Oh, darling, I wish I could be with you *now.* Have they got you a good nurse? Thank goodness we don't have to worry about *money!* . . . No, no, we've got *lots.* Have the very best of everything. . . . Gregory? . . . Gregory? . . . Oh, yes, Doctor. . . . I'm sorry. I didn't mean to talk to him so long. Tell me . . . Can he hear you if you answer me? . . . Well, answer yes or no. Is it serious, Doctor? . . . Oh . . . Oh, how terrible! I'll take the morning train, I won't wait to play the shows. . . . You think he'd *know* tomorrow is Saturday? . . . If he'd *know,* then my not playing the play would let him know he was . . . Yes, I will. I'll be there Sunday morning and come right to . . . Doctor, do everything there is to be done; the very *best.* . . . Yes, I do realize, but . . . May I call you in the morning? . . . Dr. Murphy. Allegheny 2424. Doctor, give him my love."

I was shaking. I got out of bed, stumbled out to the dark sitting room. Central Park's lights winked like stars in a backdrop. A heart attack. We'd always known it could happen, but never thought it would. When Gregory got the insurance we knew the stiff premium was because his heart was bad. In Pittsburgh and all alone. Stop shaking. That wouldn't do any good. The thing to do was take charge—of myself, of Gregory, of stop shaking. That was the first step out of this bog. Step two was get through the night. Maybe better news in the morning. Aren't doctors alarmists? Don't they have to be, in case? God, please don't let it happen. On my knees in the dark sitting room, lights rolling back the black and flashing across our wall. "God, please let Gregory live. God!" Was I summoning Him to the room? I wasn't shaking anymore; *tomorrow* was what counted. Get ready for it, blot out *now,* go to bed. What I could do for him was to stop shaking and go to sleep. Turn out the light, close my eyes. "Oh, darling, I wish I'd been better. I *wish* I'd been; I will be." Hot tears, hot and salt. I'd make everything up to him *somehow.*

At the Booth, Sunday had been our goal. For Easter week we were playing six matinees, six night shows over, Sunday was the day of rest.

"I'll have Leonard get you on the sleeper," said Guthrie. "Drawing room? Compartment?"

"Compartment."

After the show, he went down to Penn Station with me. "Club sandwich?"

"All right."

We sat up at the counter in the Savarin lunchroom.

"Club sandwich and give me some cheese. What is there?"

"Roquefort?"

"Naw. What else?"

"Cream cheese?"

"Naw. Ham on rye."

"My God, poor Gregory."

"Yuh."

"And all alone."

"Yuh, but you'll make the show Monday?"

"Yes."

Early in the morning in Pittsburgh is earlier than anywhere else. "St. Francis Hospital," I told the taxi. We rode and rode. Nothing to look at. Nothing. Every time I played here the show never went.

The elevator let me out at the third floor. Down the quiet corridor came nurses bringing breakfast trays. Hushed breakfast trays. A door was open. Inside was hushed. A door shut. Some apparatus rolled by on rubber tires. Things happening, but hushed. Outside some rooms were flowers. Quiet flowers. I opened the door to 301. Gregory was propped up on the pillows. White. White like no white I ever saw.

"Darling."

The nurse woke up.

"I'm Mrs. Kelly."

"Oh, come in."

I *was* in. Arms around him.

"Hard on you after last week." A whisper? It was a man who dreaded his heart.

"Oh, I slept on the sleeper. *You* know I always do." In a sleeper we were both in the lower berth.

"Would you like some coffee?" asked the nurse. "I'm going to get some."

"Thank you." I looked at Gregory. "Can you have something?"

"He's had his fruit juice; he won't have anything till doctor comes. Dr. Murphy will be here any minute. He knows *you*'ll be here." She turned to Gregory. "We're glad to see her, aren't we?"

Gregory smiled a white smile.

Dr. Murphy and I stood in the quiet corridor. He was young and tall and thin and reassuring. I knew he was good.

"It's serious," he said. "That doesn't mean hopeless, it means it's serious. He's a good patient. He's cooperating. And he *has* improved."

"Will he—" I couldn't go on.

"Get well? I most certainly expect he will. His age is *for* him. Thirty-three is young. His heart has been a problem, as you know, since childhood, but he's gotten along and I expect he'll continue. He'll need a lot of care."

"When I got off the train, my legs were shaking."

"You have to take it a little easy yourself. I know the strain you're under and how hard you work. Gregory was worried at your coming, but he wanted you to. He's not a selfish man, is he?"

"No."

"I thought as much. You must go back on the sleeper tonight?"

"Not if he needs me."

"It would frighten him if you stay out of your play."

"I can come back *next* Sunday."

"That will give him something to count on."

Gregory dozed off. Then woke. Then dozed off. When he woke, he just looked at me. He didn't need to talk; he needed to see me.

"You must be tired," whispered the nurse.

Gregory woke. "What time does the train leave?"

"Ten o'clock, but I can get on early; it makes up here. You'll be sick of me by eight."

He nodded in agreement.

We didn't fool each other. We spoke the same language.

"I'm coming back next Sunday."

He shook his head.

"All right, I won't."

His brown eyes looked startled. I leaned over and put my cheek against his. "I love you."

His hand reached out.

"Next Sunday."

Hand in mine, he fell asleep.

# Chapter

## 9

"There was a time when every Saturday night someone died," said Angela Ogden, who had thought I was promising in *Peter Pan*.

In East Milton, Mama died Saturday.

In New York, Gregory died Saturday. The night before, Gerald Brooks' limousine had waited on Madison Avenue outside the Harbor Hospital. Gerald was taking me to early dinner at the Marguery so I could get to the theatre. At the Harbor Hospital the nurse always knew where I was.

"Shall we start with caviar?"

"No, just one thing. Lobster salad?"

Gerald ordered.

"At Martin's Theatrical, Edna Hibbard said, 'God, imagine having all the lobster salad you want!' "

"Who was Edna Hibbard?"

"She'd been in *Fair and Warmer* and I wished I was like her. When we walked up Broadway she'd say, 'Hello, Cliff.' 'How're you, June?' 'Hi, Phil,' and I wished that *I* could get to know people to say 'How're you' and 'Hi.' *Now,* a lot of times I put my hand up to straighten my hat so I won't have to say 'How are you?' "

"When did you change? When I first saw you around the Swopes', I thought you were pretty frosty."

"Oh, I wouldn't be frosty to *you.* I've always been nice to millionaires. Success doesn't change that; success changes being free with your address and your phone number. When we *first* got a phone and the book had our names in it, 36 West Fifty-ninth Street, Wickersham 2958, I couldn't wait to say, 'My name is in the phone book.' Managers would know where to offer me parts, authors could say, 'Be in my play,' fellers could make a date."

"Have you had dates with a lot of fellers?"

"Then I noticed *successful* people don't have their name in the phone book. I had ours taken out."

"Good! When new men want to phone, it's 'unlisted number.' I'm crazy about you, you know that?"

"Great to get in the book, then great to get out. Things go round 'in earth's diurnal course.' Did people ever use words like that? Diurnal's great, but it got lost."

"Everything changes. Languages, weather, the female figure. God, it was awful when girls tried to look flat-chested! What did *you* do?"

"I pinned an Algonquin towel around to flatten me out."

"My God! Well, I'm glad *that* changed."

"Does everything have to?"

"Certainly. Tennyson used to be a lion, now he's as in demand as a Spanish war bond. I paid a helluva price for a first edition I couldn't get rid of today. When are you going to go to bed with me?"

It was early. Nobody in the Marguery dining room. I put my lips against his. *Never* was the answer, but not the answer yet; he was useful.

"Phone call for Mrs. Kelly."

I followed the maître d'.

"This is Dr. Goodridge. . . ."

"Yes, Doctor. . . ."

"You know he is very low. . . ."

"Yes. . . ."

"I just feel I ought to . . ."

Did he *have* to put it in words? "They told me at the hospital. I'm going to the theatre, but they know where to reach me. At the theatre they know I may have to go immediately. . . ."

"Yes. Well, I wanted to be sure you knew."

"Yes. Thank you. . . ." Why thank him?

A subject so shattering. Words so polite.

Gerald stood up.

"It was Dr. Goodridge, letting me know."

"Can I do anything?"

"No."

After the play, I went out to the Swopes' as usual, came in around noon.

After the matinee, Arthur stopped by the Booth. "Go up in my car." His chauffeur opened the door of the Isotta Fraschini.

A hot July afternoon, the hospital was quiet, everyone taking it easy. Gregory watched me come in. So frail, so white, so tired.

I sat beside the bed. The nurse went out. He lay propped high on pillows. I ate dinner beside his bed.

He opened his eyes and looked at me. A long look. "Sometimes I worry about you, little feller."

A man dying had time to worry about me?

"Shouldn't you be getting to the theatre?" It had been our life. Gregory protecting, guiding, helping, teaching. That never ceased. Now, between matinee and night, that care of me was ending.

"Shan't I stay?" I asked the nurse.

"He'd know you didn't go. That would scare him."

Could that scare a man who was dying?

Gregory opened his eyes and looked at me, that same long look. "How's our horse doing?"

"Fine." The only time we'd ever *talked* about a horse was the time we went to the British Derby and he chose Captain Cuttle, because Steve Donahue was an American jockey.

He closed his eyes again; no worry from the horse. The Derby was the only race we'd ever been to—was he remembering that happy day?

The day nurse packed up her things. "Well, goodbye."

How could anyone be so cold-blooded?

The night nurse was nice. She looked at me inquiringly. I looked at my watch, framed in diamonds. When Gregory gave it to me I thought the diamonds were small, but like everything else at Ratterman's, they were perfect. They and the shape, the works, the black ribbon, perfect.

Gregory looked off beyond me, a world of sadness in his voice. "Morgan Farley."

Morgan had played Big Bruvver Josie Joe in *Seventeen* and now was announced for the lead in *An American Tragedy*. Had Gregory wanted that part? Thirty-four years old and had had the bad heart since he was little. Was it the rheumatic fever? Was it the fierce attack of croup? The doctor had put a gold pipe down his throat; it saved his life.

At four, he'd acted with Joseph Jefferson in *Rip Van Winkle.* Rip woke after twenty years' sleep, tried to get up, couldn't make it, looked at the audience and said, "I guess I got de rheumatics."

On the ground beside him lay his gun. He picked it up, it fell apart. Jefferson showed it to the audience. "I guess my old gun's got de rheumatics."

Gregory remembered Jefferson's gentleness. Gentle with his gun, spoke gently to the audience, gentle with the little four-year-old starting to be an actor.

At five, Gregory went on tour in *The Rule of Three.* Mrs. Kelly dreamed of making a fortune. Her idol was Hetty Green. She put the children to work, put the money into real estate. Tommy and Gregory ate bread and milk when they should have eaten heartier things. Up late, then home to bread and milk. Now all that knowledge, that know-how, was going. He was asleep.

"Call me," I told the nurse. "You have the backstage number." She wasn't heartless like the one that packed her book, slippers, sweater, pills.

Around the corner on 61st Street, people were going into the Colony restaurant. A taxi stopped; ten minutes later I was at Shubert Alley. A hot night again, most of the audience still on the sidewalk. As I paid the taxi, I saw David Belasco and his assistant, Mr. Curry. David Belasco! A career could leap ahead because of Belasco. A leap like Guthrie had helped me to take. Too bad Belasco had to come tonight.

At the stage door, my maid, Margaret Bellinger, was waiting. Same stage door Gregory and I had gone in and out for *Seventeen.* Same stage door I'd gone in and out for *The Fall of Eve;* same stage door I went in opening night of *Saturday's Children* and came out a hit.

In the dressing room, Margaret had everything ready. "Dress first. If there's time, make up." Whatever happened, Margaret was calm.

I got into the turquoise-blue crepe dress, Margaret put a towel across my shoulders, another on my lap. Cold cream and rub it off, pat on Leichner Number 5, then Number 2, then a little moist rouge to give definition to the cheekbones. Work in Leichner's eye shadow, Margaret was ready with the powder puff, with the right amount of powder. "What did they call?"

"Fifteen minutes. You got time." She offered the ivory-backed baby brush to brush off surplus powder. "Eyebrows," she reminded, and handed me the brown pencil.

Tony Miner put his head in the door. "You all right?"

"Yes, she is." Margaret saved me from talking.

"All right to call the act?"

"Yes," said Margaret.

"How's my hair?"

"All right. You wore your shoes out after the matinee, so they're on. Pin your orchids." She handed me the spray of purple orchids the script said my boss, Mengel, sent. They arrived every day from Gerald.

Margaret pointed to the tumbler seven-eighths full of cloudy water. "Aromatic spirits of ammonia," she reminded me.

"If it's in the middle of a speech you *call* me."

"I will."

"In the middle of a *word.*"

"I will."

Tony took the curtain up. The scene with the Halevy family started. I crossed back of the drop to stage center, entrance to the family sitting room.

Out in the dim, hot theatre sat David Belasco. Would I be lucky?

Overhead in the flies hung the old droopy white horse used in *White Wings.* Stacked against the wall was left-behind scenery, tombstones of other shows.

Act I over, Act II rolled along. Roger Pryor and I played the long fight scene, then Fred Perry came on. "Dad, do you think I should have a baby?"

They had never laughed since Gregory showed me how.

Fred Perry left. Roger came on to play the short scene to end the act. He came straight to me, put his arms around me the way Guthrie directed, but Guthrie didn't direct him to *shake.* His *hands* shook, his *body* shook. How fast he talked! How much time was there to the end of Act II? We raced, Tony dropped the curtain, Margaret came through the first entrance, with the cloudy glass, I downed it. Margaret covered my second-act costume with a coat over my shoulders, gave me my purse.

Everybody seemed frozen. Crew, company, doorman stood still. They seemed painted on. Not Lynn Farnol. Our press agent took my arm and rushed me to the taxi waiting at the stage door. On 45th Street we turned up Eighth Avenue, going like a fire engine. If there was a red light we went through it; if there was a traffic cop, Lynn jumped out and told him. We were there.

At the Harbor, everything was quiet. I'd never been there at ten-thirty. No visitors, night nurses settled down; patients slept, with or without help, lights low.

Under an oxygen tent Gregory gasped for breath. For air. For the air we take for granted. The air wouldn't come.

Sunday morning I drove in from Great Neck. Why did 36 West 59th Street seem the place to touch base between the Swope houseful of weekend guests and Campbell's funeral parlor to make the arrangements? The elevator stopped at the fifth floor. In the sitting room, Margaret Bellinger was waiting.

"How did you know I'd come here?"

"I took a chance."

At Campbell's, the man in charge had one string to his bow: to be reassuring.

"Will you want a bronze or a silver coffin? *They*, of course, last forever."

How do they know? Forever hasn't happened.

"Or if you don't want to incur *that* expense, we offer oak with a guaranty for one hundred years."

How do they know? "Oak," I said.

"You made a *good* choice. With or without brass handles? I *think* you would want brass handles?" He waited, reassuringly.

"Yes." For no reason I looked at Margaret. For no reason she nodded.

"Silk-lined?" It was a question he felt sure of the answer, but he offered an out. "Rayon?"

"Silk."

"The difference in price is not worth any other decision." He wrote it down. "And shall we have a pillow? The effect of being asleep?"

I nodded.

"A pillow." He seemed reassured himself. "You will supply the wardrobe?"

"Yes."

"May we have it by four this afternoon?"

"I'll bring it," said Margaret.

"Soft collar or starched?"

"My husband wore soft collars." Gregory's beautiful shirts were always white, always soft collars, always French cuffs.

"*Perfectly* all right." He wiped out any thought of starch and tried to

200

make me feel I was doing well. "A soft collar if it's what *you* want, Mrs. Kelly. Now, may I suggest pine boughs?" He nodded yes as he asked it. "Pine boughs to line the aperture? Freshly dug earth people find troubling; lined with pine boughs can be a comfort, not to see the empty hole."

I nodded.

"Though I do not as a rule offer suggestions, I *would* like to urge the electric crane."

Had he said "electric crane"?

"An electric crane is less *noisy,*" he reassured. "Ropes have a tendency to squeak."

A good way to judge a man, Papa thought, was how he handles rope and string.

"Yes, the crane."

"I think that's all. I'll total it up. Will you supply the flowers or leave it to us to arrange floral tributes?"

"I'll have a blanket of roses sent by the Fifth Avenue Florist."

"And shall we arrange for flowers for St. Malachy's or will Mr. Kelly's friends?"

"I think so. May I have the total?"

In the car I told the driver, "Woodlawn Cemetery."

Margaret Bellinger looked out the window while I opened Campbell's bill. How do people afford to die? My *Saturday's Children* pay check yesterday was for six hundred and forty dollars. It wouldn't pay Campbell's. The bill was twice what Gregory and I had spent on our first trip abroad.

> *Algonquin Hotel*
> *New York*
> *March 23, 1922*

Dear Papa,

  Can you believe it? I can't. But we are going to England and Paris. I can hardly believe it! You've been all round the world so that doesn't mean much to you, but the two places Gregory and *I* want to see are London and Paris. We worked hard for it and feel we earned it. I'll write you letters all the time. Maybe not every minute, but postcards so you see where I am. We signed a contract to tour all next season in *The First Year* and that lets us feel right about going. We're with Mr. and Mrs. Miles and sail on the *Carmania,* one of the smaller Cunard Line boats, but Mr. Miles loves it. It goes to Liverpool. From Liverpool we take the train to Mr. Miles' boyhood home in Bristol. His sister lives there in a house he bought her, her name is Mrs. George Pratt. Write me care of her and she'll know where we are. I think her son's name is George Pratt, Junior. Mr. Miles is going to hire a car and drive us all over England before we go to London. Once we see London, he thinks we'll never bother with the rest. Gregory and I worked out a budget and will stick to it. Quite a long letter, but I want you to understand and not worry if we will end up in the poorhouse. Of course, in London and Paris we'll learn a lot from their actors there.

Love,

Ruth

*The First Year* was the play that Frank Craven had said he was writing for us when we were playing Chicago with *Clarence* and Frank Craven was starred in *Going Up.* We'd had after-the-theatre suppers together; he told us his new play was for us. Maisie Craven said my part was great!

"John Golden will star Frank Craven and Roberta Arnold in Craven's new play *The First Year,*" announced *The New York Times.* It would open at Mr. Ames' Little Theatre.

"It was for *you,*" said Frank, "but the show I was *going* to do didn't work out."

We signed to tour with it for the season *if* we could play it for two weeks at the Little Theatre in New York. Our contract was for seven hundred and fifty dollars a week.

After a week of rehearsals with Frank directing, I cried so, Gregory went over to the Lambs and said to take back the contract. Frank was willing, but said producer John Golden must decide. He and Gregory went over to talk to him.

"I don't want people giving back my contracts," snapped John Golden. "I have to see a rehearsal."

I don't know why we rehearsed downstairs in the Little Theatre lounge, but I know I felt bitter. So damn hard to learn and I dreaded slipping back.

"Don't talk baby talk," Frank kept saying.

I wasn't.

"It's left over from that part you played in *Seventeen.*"

"*I* don't hear it," said Gregory.

Down in the Little Theatre lounge, I felt doomed. I hated Frank, I hated John Golden, rich, powerful, staring at me, I hated my bad luck.

We rehearsed the fight scene between me and Gregory. I *really* fought. Was I fighting my fate?

The scene ended and I exited.

"Jesus!" said John Golden.

I thought he meant he agreed with Frank. I turned and glared at him.

"Jesus, you're *great*. Play it two weeks here and when you tour I'll give you Winchell Smith."

Winchell Smith was the director every actor would work for free— he could show you how. No one turned down a chance to be directed by Winchell Smith.

That would be for September. For April, we lived through horror with Frank. He never let up. At the dress rehearsal, I had to pick up a breakaway vase and throw it at Gregory. It *looked* like heavy pottery, but was made of paste. I knew it had to be handled *carefully*, but I didn't know you had to touch it only with your fingertips. It broke in my hands.

"Well, we'll have to use another." Frank looked furious. It was as though I'd broken a costly treasure, but the property man made these. They had dozens stacked up. "If you used as much power in your part as you used to break *that*, you might get somewhere."

That was 1922. Could I know that in 1937 he'd come backstage after *The Country Wife*, full of praise, then send me three costly rare books, *Theatres of Paris?* In Volume One: *"For Ruth Gordon, a great star, from Frank Craven."*

The dress rehearsal finished. We would play our first performance that night. "Have you anything to say?" asked Gregory.

"You won't get a laugh." Frank walked up the aisle and out of the theatre.

Anticipation and reality, *must* they be far apart? Reality was Woollcott at a matinee with George Kaufman; they thought I was fine. Reality was seven hundred and fifty dollars a week. Reality was opening Labor Day in Perth Amboy, New Jersey, followed by New Brunswick, where our room was over a bakery. Reality was one-nighters through New York State—Albany, Oneonta, Onteora, Norwich, Amsterdam, Rome, Gloversville, Syracuse. In Syracuse I decided never to be constipated again and never have been.

Nothing left in New York State, cross into Pennsylvania, skip Philadelphia and Pittsburgh, but not Johnstown, where they had the flood, not Hazelton, where the miners' faces were black coming out of the mines and still black next morning when they went down again. "Cleanliness is next to godliness," they say. Had godliness overlooked them? New Castle, where we had closed. Into Maryland to Cumberland, to Hagerstown, but no Aggie Rogers, to Frederick, Easton, Salisbury, but no Baltimore. Through West Virginia into Virginia. Bum hotels, train trips, fair hotels, train trips, train trips, train trips, train trips. The theatres? Draw the veil. Draw it on about everything except our great plan when the season ended. Anticipation and reality and somewhere add recollection. Recollect the Abraham Sisters' Cake Shop in Richmond, the crocodile in his tank in the Hotel Jefferson lobby.

PLEASE DON'T POKE HIM
WITH YOUR UMBRELLA.

Reality would be North and South Carolina, Georgia, Florida, Alabama, Mississippi, Louisiana, Tennessee. Wouldn't that earn us a trip abroad—so why not take it first? The future wasn't rosy, but bankable.

To go to Europe I bought a suit from Dobbs on Fifth Avenue. Elegance, with no effort to impress, was Dobbs' trademark.

A tugboat eased the *Carmania* out into the Hudson River, Gregory and I waved like people wave in the rotogravure section. I knew I looked lovely in my light blue satin hat with the pleated brim, light blue fuzzy tweed dress with white silk shirtwaist, collar, cuffs; very Quincy Mansion. Who looked more elegant? And when I waved goodbye, could people see my square-cut diamond wedding band from Tiffany's, above my platinum engagement ring, and falling below my white silk cuff the flexible diamond and platinum bracelet? There was nobody to wave goodbye to, but I waved and thought: One day I'll be in the paper. There was a picture of us waving in the paper. Somebody sent it to Papa.

The weather was fine, but nobody had told us about the ship's concert. "To benefit seamen," said Mr. Miles. "You must be prepared to give."

On *our* budget?

"A pound each."

A lady from second class played a piano solo. *Very* long. A cockney routine from the engine room went on and *on.* A wrestling match by members of the crew. A contralto sang two numbers and two encores. A collection. Until the sum was counted and announced, the cellist from the ship's orchestra played a solo. The purser told anecdotes, two girls did a Highland fling, the ship's orchestra played "God Save the King," we stood up, exhausted. "Too long," said Mr. Miles.

"Look out your porthole," said Mr. Miles. "You can see Ireland."

We dropped anchor in Cork harbor. The tender came out to take passengers and let loose a bunch of Irish newsboys shouting, "Pee-*ape-*

ers!" Old ladies offered Irish lace and bog-wood trinkets. Was that what we thought getting to Ireland would be? Sometimes you don't know what to make of things.

Liverpool in the morning. It had taken eleven days. We hadn't made any friends, we had better food at home. The tea was good, but we drank coffee. We'd lost one pound sterling a day on the ship's run. Maybe a first trip is to find out *how,* then use in conversation. "When *I* went abroad." "When *we* were in Europe." "When *we* landed in Liverpool."

Liverpool was a city soaked in grey. In the grey station-hotel dining room, grey soup, grey meat, grey tapioca pudding. Three thousand miles, then tapioca pudding.

"It's good," said Mr. Miles. He'd planned to enjoy it and did.

In the grey station, a grey porter trundled our luggage to the train for Bristol, where Mr. Miles had been brought up. His father had been organist at Bristol Cathedral.

Through grey scenery to another grey station, Bristol. "Grey" is how they spell it over there. A word they have plenty of practice in spelling. Mr. Miles' sister had engaged a room for us in a bed-and-breakfast lodging house. Three thousand miles to sleep in a sagging grey bed. Under it, a cold grey pot. On the commode was a cold grey bowl and pitcher of cold water! Too disgusted to unpack, we went over to join our friends at a crumpled house in a block of houses mashed down from the top, their sides pushed closer.

At the dining room table were Mr. and Mrs. Miles, with five old friends, his sister Mrs. Pratt and George, Junior. We had roast beef and cauliflower. In restaurants cauliflower is full of bread crumbs or white sauce, but at Mrs. Pratt's it looked like a bunch of white violets steamed fresh in its leaves. For the first time in my life I felt homesick. Mama had said I'd be and I never was, but that cauliflower made me think of Edward Sheldon's play *Romance.* The leading lady loved white violets. *What* was I doing in Bristol? After dinner, George Pratt walked us back to our bed-and-breakfaster, more dismal than we'd remembered.

Next morning, strong tea for breakfast, cold toast in a stand, bitter marmalade, sliver of poor butter. We moved out to a grand-looking hotel in the part of Bristol called Clifton. Still bowl and pitcher, but grand-looking.

Is Bristol for people who live there? For a visitor it's hard to remember. Is there a Whiteladies Road? Is there a Gloucester Terrace? I don't remember what river flows in our out, but I remember our first time in an English theatre! Walk *downstairs* to the orchestra floor! Coffee trays *passed* to you in your seat at intermission! Drink coffee right in the theatre? You knew you weren't at the Blackstone or the Colonial!

CYRIL MAUDE AND BINNIE HALE
IN
THE DIPPERS
PRELIMINARY TO ITS LONDON ENGAGEMENT
ONE WEEK

Cyril Maude had triumphed in London and New York in *Grumpy*. Binnie Hale was a dancer, strictly an English favorite.

"You won't like English theatre," said Mrs. Miles. "You have to pay for a program and *have to* tip the usher a bob. That's what they call their shilling."

Did we care?

"They call their orchestra seats stalls. Don't ask me why."

We went *down* the stairs, the usher sold us programs, Mr. Miles tipped her a bob and bought a box of chocolates.

"Coffee in the interval?"

He booked it. What a pleasant idea!

The Dippers in the play were a dance team, but Cyril Maude wasn't a dancer. When he and Binnie Hale did their turn, you knew he wasn't ever going to be.

"What did I tell you!" said Mrs. Miles. "You won't like English theatre."

*London* theatre was what we wanted to see, but Mr. Miles said, "See England first."

The morning we were setting off in the Vauxhall, how did the bowl slip out of Gregory's hands?

"Two guineas," said the hotel clerk.

Mr. Miles was indignant. "They could *not* have a bowl worth two guineas. Demand your money back; they're taking advantage of Americans."

Was Gregory's hobby "Avoid trouble"? He said he would when we came back, but he knew we wouldn't come back. We'd be in London.

The Vauxhall's springs were through; it shook us from Bristol to Beau Brummell's damp house in Bath. At the spa, we drank nasty water.

At Cheddar we went through the chilly cave and were glad to come out. For lunch they served free cheese. After lunch we took off. *Two places were behind us!*

"Services will be at St. Malachy's, eleven o'clock tomorrow," I told Margaret. "I won't go on tomorrow night."

"Your understudy didn't wear *your* dress; she's got her own."

The London *Times* announced Irene Vanbrugh to appear in *Trilby* with Lyn Harding. Violet Vanbrugh was already in a play. "God, please get us to London."

He did.

First, Great Malvern and drink the waters, then to Hindhead.

"You'll see the Devil's Punchbowl, the highest point in England," said Mr. Miles. "You'll never forget it." He drove up a hill to a big leafy hollow. He stood and stared in.

My mind wandered. "Did you read the Casino de Paris burned down?"

That sprung us. Mr. Miles knew how to run up seven million dollars, but he didn't know how anyone looking at the Devil's Punchbowl could say, "The Casino de Paris burned down."

"Well, Sam, they're interested in theatre."

He just shook his head. "Looking at the *Devil's Punchbowl!*"

"Sam, everybody isn't like *you!*"

"I'll drive you to Folkestone, where you can take the boat to France. You'll be in Paris the same night."

The Casino de Paris had burned down, but had speeded up our visit to Paris!

"Some of the boats are English, but some are French," quoth Mrs. Miles. "The English are the reliable. Remember the hotel I said in Paris?"

"The Wagram."

"They pronounce it Vagram—*W* is *V* in French. It's a convenient location and they don't soak you. Paris is an acquired taste."

"Why aren't French boats reliable?"

"Oh, they may be. The Wagram is Rue Rivoli, where you buy good things, but don't get taken in. I *like* Paris, but that doesn't mean I trust them."

Dear Papa,
     This postcard is the hotel we're spending the night before we cross the English Channel tomorrow. I know you crossed it lots of times, but tomorrow we will. Our budget is working out. Next will be a postcard from Paris!

Love,
Ruth

The crossing was perfect. So was the French train that rolled out of Boulogne, past Abbeville, past Amiens, through Picardy that "Roses are blooming in." Our first-class carriage had beautiful upholstery with coarse white lace covers where a head might rest. The Wagon-Restaurant served a perfect dinner topped off by a pyramid of vanilla ice cream with a liqueur flavor.

The train screeched and stopped short. It was Paris! Everybody rushed! Everybody talked at once and all the time. Three years of French at Quincy High, where my mark was E for Excellent; now I didn't understand a word. Three years of Chardenal Grammar, memorizing *"La Cigale Ayant Chantée,"* translating *"Le Voyage de Monsieur Perrichon";* now would people understand me say *"Porteur!"*?

He took the bags. "Taxi," Gregory told him. He had never taken French, but the porter understood. Gregory tipped him. It didn't work. We couldn't understand his words, but he meant "Not enough."

"Don't overtip," Mrs. Miles had warned. "If you do, they disrespect you."

Gregory's tip silenced him. Was it disrespect or pleasure? "Hôtel Wagram, Rue Rivoli." He said the *W* like *V* to the taxi driver.

A blank.

I helped. "Hôtel *Vag*ram."

Blank.

Together. "Hôtel *Vag*ram."

Blank.

Spell it? "Double vay-ah-jay-air-ah-em."

"Va-*gram!*" he screamed, and stepped on the gas. William James says, *"Behave* brave and you *will* be." I behaved *terrified.* We rushed at other taxis, stopped just short of destruction. Carts, wagons, hansom cabs, buses, trucks rushed at each other and us. Horns honked, drivers screamed until we stopped short in front of Mrs. Miles' choice. Another Bristol bed-and-breakfast lodging! We went to bed in the only boring bedroom in Paris, small, colorless, looking onto a cement wall, but in bed in Paris, do *you* look out the window?

Next morning, God or my voices told us to go down the Rue de Rivoli to the Rue Castiglione, into the courtyard of the Hôtel Continental.

"Too grand for our budget?"

"Ask."

*"Parlez Anglais?"*

"Yes."

"Have you a room?"

"With or without *salle de bain?"*

"Without."

"Running water?"

"Please. How much?"

It cost a few francs more than the Wagram. Our *Seventeen, Piccadilly Jim, Clarence* bags moved out of the Wagram to our fine room at the Continental. We'd unpack later, after we looked for theatres. We read their names off the kiosk: Michodière, Edward VII, Palais Royal, Vaudeville, Gymnase, Théâtre de Paris, Folies Bergère.

"Folies Bergère?" we suggested to the concierge.

It was a taxi ride, then noise, people pushing, we pushed. Inside, a blonde with red red lips and black eye makeup spoke to Gregory.

"What's she saying?"

"She wants me to come with her."

In the show some girls had nothing over their breasts. Not even *one* layer of net like my red crepe de Chine. Rosy tips stuck straight out!

Breakfast at the Continental was coffee, a croissant, pats of sweet butter, strawberry jam, a jug of hot milk instead of cream, then back to bed.


Our budget was all right until I saw a hat in the Rue Castiglione, corner of the Rue St. Honoré! It came to thirty-five dollars. Flowery and made me think of Priscilla White's Paris hat her aunt sent to Wollaston. This one was just as pretty. When thirty-five dollars was my salary in *Peter Pan,* hadn't I wondered *how* would I spend it?


"Comédie Française?" suggested the concierge.

"Perhaps not."

Perhaps he could get us into the musical comedy *Dedé.* "Maurice Chevalier 'ad success at the Casino de Paris. Alas, it burn down. 'E is now star of *Dedé.* Americans like 'eem."

"He'd make a hit in America," said Gregory.

He made a hit everywhere!

"You will like the new revue with Spinelli," suggested our concierge.

The theatre was smaller than the Princess. The chorus only four girls, but *what* four! White frilled little-girls' dresses, broad sashes tied in whopping bows, each sash a different color—light blue, red, pink and yellow.

Spinelli, not old and probably never young, chic as paint, which she wore a lot of, her clothes the latest that Paul Poiret thought up, jewels ad infinitum. A dazzler!

Notre-Dame was beyond us and so was Sacha Guitry. We knew we should see the church and we knew Guitry was somebody we *must* say we'd seen.

"Perhaps a cabaret your last night?"

"Yes," said Gregory.

"Le Perroquet is new, Place Pigalle. It is where they go in Paris. I will try for a table for two." He didn't ask if we wanted a table for four; he knew tourists don't know anyone.

Our doorman told the taxi, "Le Perroquet, Place Pigalle."

It was next door to the Guitry play, so for once we knew where we were. Next door to where we were last night.

Not large, not small, beautiful, every table had a silver bucket, champagne *de rigueur*. Did we have enough money?

If we ate no food, gave a small tip, it would leave enough for the taxi to the hotel. A dish of almonds and a quart of champagne got Gregory soused. "Bravo!" he called to an actor from the Guitry show he didn't think was any good, but how novel to recognize someone!

The actor lifted his glass. Gregory lifted mine and finished it. I paid the check, tipped the waiter; we staggered out leaving hard looks. What could we do? We'd spent our Paris budget. Only memories, programs to take with us—the handsome favor from Le Perroquet got left in the taxi—but we'd seen Paris, forgot Whiteladies Road, never thought of the Devil's Punchbowl!

At the Gare St. Lazare. Our tickets read Calais to Dover. "Boulogne to Folkestone," we'd said, but the concierge raised his eyebrows. "Calais–Dover," he said. The way he said it left no discussion.

A lot of passengers looked tired, but Gregory was the only one who looked pale yellow.

"First call to lunch."

Gregory didn't lift his head off the lace-covered gray cushion.

Dover's white cliffs looked whiter than from Folkestone. At the dock was the fine train to London, the royal coat of arms on our first-class carriage. Tea, buttered toast, scones, Bath buns, cake with currants the waiter called Dundee cake. Gregory felt up to it.

"Should we go to the Cecil? It's on the Strand near theatres. Mrs. Miles says it's next to Simpson's, the good restaurant for a budget."

Our train pulled into Victoria. London at last! Victoria not like the Gare St. Lazare free-for-all roughhouse; in Victoria they hurry at a steady gait, trains go without a hysterical shriek. The porter, a steady chap, piled our bags into a stately taxi, accepted two shillings with no feeling.

"Hotel Cecil, the Strand," said Gregory.

Our taxi took off at a sensible pace on the wrong side of the street, but the Vauxhall had got us used to it.

"Buckingham Palace!" I shouted.

"Your first time here?" asked driver.

"Oh, no!"

"The Mall looks very well this time of year."

"It does indeed." Mr. Putnam would give me a good mark.

"Trafalgar Square. We made good time."

"Gregory, there's a *theatre!* The Adelphi!" From our map we knew Covent Garden and Drury Lane and the Aldwych were up the streets. *What* were we stopping in front of? Mrs. Miles had done it again— another one-nighter.

The hall porter showed us up to a bedroom that looked out on a wall. We looked at the bowl and pitcher and remembered we weren't in Birmingham or Lynton or the West Country; we were in London and tomorrow we'd find a hotel.

We walked up some Strand and down some. Not like what we'd thought, but there was Simpson's. Should we take a last chance? It had been a long day.

What a roast beef! What a wagon it rolled up to our table on!

"Underdone or well?" The waiter could have stepped off a page of *Nicholas Nickleby.* He served us roast potatoes and steamed greens. "Bit of the crackly?" Knife poised.

How *good,* how *cheap!*

"What sweet will you have?" Another wagon with a deep-dish apple pie he called a pasty, a milk pudding *we* call a custard, boiled fruit, a jug of thick thick cream. We had it on our apple pasty.

One night at the Cecil, then luck again! The Piccadilly. Pretty bedroom *not* against a concrete wall, running water, next door the w.c., two doors down the bath. A maid ran the tub and handed out a big hot towel.

"We are Piccadilly Hotel, Piccadilly," read our wire to the Mileses, care of Mrs. Pratt.

Two days later the phone rang. "We're here at the Piccadilly." It floored us. Two seasoned travelers took *our* word?

*May something, 1922*

Dear Papa,

I can hardly believe I walked around Piccadilly Circus. We spent last night at the Cecil Hotel, but it was no good. This morning we moved to this hotel. The lobby is even handsomer than this postcard.

Love,
Ruth

Before any sightseeing, we booked seats at the theatres. Seymour Hicks in *The Man in Dress Clothes. He* was the show. Later, when I was *in,* people said, "Seymour Hicks? Oh, you mean Steal-More-Tricks." That's what *they* said. Claude Rains said, "When I was blackballed at the Garrick Club, notoriety from my divorce, it was Seymour Hicks who came over to me and said, 'You've suffered enough, y' poor bugger, what'll y' have to drink?' Seymour Hicks ended the blackball, bless him."

*He* was great, but his company? Was that London acting?

Mrs. Miles brought a letter mailed to Bristol. Papa wrote about the times he'd made port in Liverpool.

I answered on a postcard showing Piccadilly Circus.

Dear Papa,

Mrs. Miles brought your letter. I guess Liverpool is different if you're there with a cargo. We love London. They have such a lot of theatres. Right now Mr. Miles is going to show us the Bank of England. He's determined we see all the sights. It's on Threadneedle Street. Will write when I get home.

Love,
Ruth

Mr. Miles showed us Dick Whittington's house, the Tower of London with the Beefeater guards outside, crown jewels inside, and dungeon for the poor princes. I remembered not to say we had seats for *Sally* at the Winter Garden, starring Dorothy Dickson, but a pleasure to remember we did.

He showed us London Bridge and I thought about Dorothy Dickson when she'd been in *Oh Boy* at the Princess. Her slippers came from Carcion, Manfré and when I could afford to I had had a pair made to order to match my grand blue velvet dress Bendel's made for *Piccadilly Jim.* Mr. and Mrs. Miles and Gregory and I stared at London Bridge; did *each* of us see something else?

At Westminster Abbey, Mr. Miles showed us "O rare Ben Jonson."

I let enough time pass before I asked, "Where does Sir Henry Irving lie?"

We fed the pigeons in Trafalgar Square. Mrs. Miles said everybody had to.

Tonight we were going to see a *big* star, Charles Hawtrey, playing in *Captain Applejack.* Marion Lorne, American wife of the American author, was his leading lady. Could we help it if we thought Wallace Eddinger in the New York company was better?

Mr. Miles took us down Fleet Street to lunch at the Cheshire Cheese, Dr. Johnson's hangout. Mrs. said she didn't care about history, but we *must* go to Liberty's. Their things looked just like the table cover Miss Turner brought Mama. Mama thanked her, but said privately, "Why would she pick out *that?*"

"The best department store is the White House," said Mrs. Miles, and showed us through it. No temptation, our money was for theatre tickets, tonight the great Meggie Abanesi in Galsworthy's *Loyalties!* Great and you couldn't tell how she did it. *How* could I be like that? How could anybody?

Houses of Parliament, then Adelphi Terrace, where furnituremaker Adams brothers lived, where James M. Barrie *still* lived! Was it where Barrie wrote *Peter Pan?* Where Shaw wrote *Fanny's First Play* I saw in Boston at the Park Theatre on Washington Street?

God's mercy is shown in different ways and one is to get people tired. The Mileses gave up and we continued on to the Ritz for tea. We didn't want any, but wanted to see the Ritz. So quiet! Were we early? Were we late? The wrong day? Grand front desk, impressive corridor, stately dining room. We knew the hotel was for stylish people, but none of them were around. A step up through a wide arch, tea was being served to a table of ten. Plenty of empty tables; why did the maître d' put us next to them? They stopped talking, looked at us, and chatted on.

"Duke of Marlborough," I whispered. No one in the dining room but us and the ten others with a duke and his duchess, Boston's Gladys Deacon. We might have been at their table, every word was so clear. *"One* day a month I eat only fruit," said a blond young man who looked

213

like Leslie Howard in *Just Suppose*, who looked like the Prince of Wales in the rotogravure.

The waiter offered a silver tray of pink, white, chocolate pastries in frilled paper. All ten stopped talking and stared. The lady he offered it to took her time and across the table the duke stood up, reached out with his fork, speared a chocolate éclair, brought it safely to his plate and sat down.

Dear Angela,

Tea at the Ritz today. Remember the matinee days in our dressing room? Remember David Torrence brought the big squashy no-good chocolate éclairs? Today at the Ritz they were great.

We are going to a revival of *Quality Street*. Fay Compton is playing Miss Adams' part. I don't know who plays yours. They said you were great!

Love,

Ruth

The British Museum held a lot of things; our thoughts were on *Tons of Money* at the Aldwych. A tourist says "the Aldwych." After several trips, you learn to say "Aldwych." Learn to say Rafe for Ralph Lynn, co-starred with French Yvonne Arnaud, like nobody anybody ever saw before. Ralph Lynn was like our William Collier. The *show* was the funniest we'd ever seen.

London in May you catch the fever. We booked seats on a Cook's motor coach to the Derby at Epsom Downs! First race for both of us.

"Bring a hamper," Cook's warned. "That's the only way you'll eat."

Eight A.M. the bus left Piccadilly, return that evening. All London was going; travel would be at a slow pace. When all London would be coming home, travel even slower. "We suggest the hamper come from Fortnum & Mason's in Piccadilly," suggested Cook's.

What a suggestion! A salesman in frock coat recommended cold chicken, buttered Hovis bread, fruit of choice, a pint of claret. Pint of claret! What a recommendation!

"All aboard!" shouted Cook's man in the blue uniform with gold trim. "Epsom Downs."

Green countryside rolled by. What a day, what a trip, what a countryside! Then traffic started to slow down and nearly came to a stop. Look at who was in the limousine, who was in the pearl-grey touring car. Maybe downs are fields; that's what the coach turned onto. Gypsies all around. Ribbons, beads. "Give a penny to the baby, dear, bring you luck, dear, give a penny to the baby."

The coach pulled up behind our grandstand. Everybody gave a penny to the baby.

"After the last race, we assemble here," warned Cook's man, and directed hampers be handed down.

Our seats were just right, everybody lovely, lunch the best, with a bottle of *claret!* First time at a race and it's the Derby! Need I tell you we won?

Gregory bet on Captain Cuttle, Steve Donahue up. He didn't know the horses so bet on an American jockey. Our win was two hundred and fifty dollars! What a *day!* Even worth missing a play that night.

Our last night, Gerald Du Maurier in J. M. Barrie's *Dear Brutus.* It topped the Derby. His acting was what people leave home for, it was all the things that aren't at home. Even his name! Could anyone at home be named Gerald Du Maurier?

Is the first trip abroad more for anticipation and recollection? It was time for recollection, time to go home. Too soon? Perhaps not. There had been quite a lot of indigestion, quite a few wet feet, worry would our money hold out, an overdose of Mrs. Miles' recollections, Mr. Miles' relentless guidance—but seeing Gerald Du Maurier put us ahead!

We were sailing home on the *Aquitania,* the Cunard Line's stylish ship. Passage cost more than the *Carmania* and Mr. Miles liked the *Carmania* better, but thought we should see the *Aquitania.* Our lowest-price cabin was inside, below decks, just big enough for us to fit in, but it *was* the *Aquitania!*

"What boat were you on?"

"The *Aquitania!"*

Everything was elegant, even the boat train. At Waterloo Station, shiny automobiles, taxis, lorries converged. Up the Waterloo Road was the Old Vic, where I'd make my London debut, but that wasn't for another fourteen years, October 1936. The *Aquitania* boat train left on a May morning in 1922. How many carriages! First class, second class, third. For our first trip, Mr. Miles consented to go first.

First class we tore out of Waterloo Station, never slacked our pace through all Hampshire, where Marjory Pinchwife, the wife in *The Country Wife,* came from. In 1922 I'd never heard of her, but at the Old Vic that was the part I played.

The train didn't slow down until we slid alongside the Cunard docks in Southampton.

"There she is." Mr. Miles pointed to the biggest ship afloat.

How high, how mighty! And to be able to say we went on it!

"The first night out, don't dress for dinner," warned Mrs. Miles.

On the *Carmania,* we had dressed only for the ship's concert.

"And not Sunday, but every other night." No matter what she wore she looked the same.

Gregory's tuxedo had been made to order at Wetzel's on 43rd Street, two doors east of Fifth Avenue. Some said Earl Benham was the best, some said Wetzel. Gregory's was dark dark blue.

"Black looks rusty," said Wetzel.

It had satin lapels and a satin vest.

He'd also ordered a heavy brown overcoat, ready to wear next winter. With his derby, he'd look stunning!

On the *Aquitania* you could get lost, she was so big.

"What did I tell you!" said Mrs. Miles.

"Why does Mr. Miles like the *small* boats?"

"Perverse."

At lunch, served before the ship sailed, we stared at the vast dining room. Time goes by. In 1938, when Robert and his wife Madeline, and Mary Sherwood—daughter of Mary Brandon Sherwood, now divorced —and I came home on her, we thought she was a cozy boat.

"It's got no warmth," said Mr. Miles. "The *Carmania* is *my* kind."

Mrs. Miles studied the passenger list. "No notables, so *we*'ll get some attention."

"Ship's pool?" asked Mr. Miles. He bet the five-pound one.

We bet the one-pound on the *Carmania* and always lost.

On the bulletin board in the smoking lounge were the white papers numbered one to ten. Printed at the top of each,

ONE POUND    TWO POUND    FIVE POUND    TEN POUND

Only one open. It was the five-pound paper.

Gregory wrote "Gregory Kelly" opposite the number 8.

Next day at lunch, Mr. Miles, Gregory and I were seated. Mrs. Miles joined us. "You didn't win—they just posted the run."

Five pounds gone! "What was the run?"

"Four, ninety-two, so two won."

*Not* number 8.

The steward wrote our order. "Anybody on eight? That's the winner." That was the number of knots the ship had made that day.

Gentle Gregory gave a look, just a look, then rushed to where they paid off.

On a budget, to win fifty pounds!

"You must give ten percent to the smoking lounge steward," said Mrs. Wrong Number.

"I *won't*," said gentle Gregory. And he didn't. You can push a gentle person and push him, then don't.

We didn't meet anyone, no one met us, the trip was smooth, the ship's concert more stylish, but as tiresome as the *Carmania*'s.

My light blue tweed had looked absolutely right. My three evening dresses stood up to anybody's and just enough for the trip. First night, don't dress, second night, cornflower Bendel's, third night, cherry velvet from Chicago Blum's looking *great* now my legs were straightened, fourth night was Sunday and we knew not to dress, fifth night, captain's dinner, I wore the silver brocade I'd bought from Mary Miller. That was the last night to dress; we knew not to dress the night before docking.

Up before Sandy Hook, watch pilot come over the side, watch the Statue of Liberty, watch tugboats maneuver, dock, and we were back from our first trip abroad!

When people would ask, "Have you been abroad?" "Oh, heavens, yes." We could have *said* it, but it's more authentic to do it.

New York City mid-May, rehearsals not till mid-August. A lot of Algonquin bills before Perth Amboy, Labor Day. The phone rang. "Have dinner with Sam and me tonight. We'll have it here—we're sick of gadding about."

"Here" was the Great Northern, reminder of "grey" Bristol, reminder of the black day before our wedding. The dining room might have been Bristol. Was that why Mr. Miles stayed there? "What are your plans?" he asked.

Great Northern food tasted like Bristol except for the good cauliflower. Theirs didn't have green leaves and was dank. Mrs. Miles made coffee upstairs. Was that thrift? "Sam wondered if you'd like to come to the Cove. We drive up Friday."

In Liverpool we'd have said no, Bristol, no, the Charles Kingsley country, no, Hindhead they wouldn't have asked us. The day of the five-pound pool, no, but New York with no money coming in? "Would you like to?" Gregory asked.

"Love to."

"June is cold, but the house is warm."

We piled the bags into Mr. Miles' Buick. They didn't have any; Christmas Cove was their home. Mrs. Miles and I got in back, Gregory got in front. Mr. Miles drove off. If you spend the night at the Elton

Hotel, New Britain, Connecticut, make the best of it.

Up early, off to Portland, Maine. Countryside, more countryside; what I wanted was scenery by Gates and Morange, scenery builders, who built scenery to look like country. Late afternoon we drove through the leafy parts of Portland and drew up at the Lafayette Hotel. It had been there a long time and seemed to expect we'd like it. Uncle Sam did. When did I start calling him Uncle?

Up early, ride through Falmouth Foreside, through Brunswick with the college, through Bath with the beautiful houses, ferry across the Kennebec to West Woolwich, through Wiscasset with Tucker Castle, at Newcastle cross the bridge over the Damariscotta to Damariscotta, head down to the coast, cross the bridge at South Bristol, pass the Summit House, pass the house where the man made checkerberry candy wafers in his kitchen, pass Miss Otis' with the roses, down the hill and turn left through the Mileses' gate, up their road through spruce and balsam and bayberry and blueberry, with sweet fern and sassafras now and then.

At the back door, Dennis Little waited just where he'd said goodbye last year. He hadn't changed expression. Maybe not since the house was built.

When the Mileses first visited Maine, they had stayed at the Christmas Cove House, run by Dennis' brother, Wilbur Little. People called Dennis "Dennis," but Wilbur Little was *always* "Wilbur Little."

Up the Mileses' stairs came Dennis with our bags. After each step our hearts went down. A long summer and at the end of it Perth Amboy. Is that what I left home for? What had Perth Amboy in common with *The Pink Lady?* Maybe sit it out; doesn't the circle always come round? It always has, so why not always *will?* World without end, amen, and until then eat breakfast, have conversation, get tanned, enjoy the fog, eat lunch, clear the table, wipe dishes, make our bed and then, thank You, God, it happens!

"Telephone for Gregory," called Mr. Miles.

It was a telegram phoned from Rockland, the nearest Western Union office. "Would like be partner Tarkington play *Bristol Glass* stop can give it week's tryout here second week July stop can give first-class production stop Robert McLaughlin Manager Ohio Theatre Cleveland Ohio."

"Please say it again," said Gregory.

"Would like be . . ."

Pack the bags for Cleveland! Goodbye, Christmas Cove! Goodbye, fog and blue sky and Pemaquid Point and lobelia; hello, Cleveland, and the Ohio Theatre! Hello, our friend Leonard Hanna, who, when he died, left thirty million dollars to the Cleveland Museum, but who now lived in the grand Euclid Avenue house.

The cup ran over. We were *at last* going to be in *Bristol Glass!*

Thornton Wilder said, "I don't know if there's a God, but we all know *something*'s out there."

Out there and helping. You don't think so? Start over.

"After Cleveland, we'll get McLaughlin to be our partner for New York," said Gregory. "We'll save our *First Year* salaries and produce it ourselves."

"What could we spend money for in the places we'll play!"

"I'll buy a cheap suit, save my good ones."

"I'll buy a cheap suit, too. Save my blue fuzzy."

"Won't Cleveland be hot?" asked Mrs. Miles. She'd miss my help in the kitchen. After all she and Uncle Sam had done for us, and now we were running out!

Well, that's show business. You're house guests till you get a job.

Gregory wrote Mr. Tarkington to ask if he'd agree. Dennis brought a pale green envelope from the post office. On the flap was engraved: "Seaward, Kennebunkport, Maine."

Dear Kelly,
   I trust your judgment. Do as you think best.
   Susannah and I would like you and Mrs. Kelly to come to Seaward for the weekend, Friday after next. We hope this fits in with your plans.
                                        Aff'ly,
                                        Booth Tarkington

Phone the station. "Reserve two Pullman seats on the Rockland-to-Boston train stopping at Kennebunk."

Mrs. Miles believed everybody lets you down, but accepted it and rode up to Damariscotta with us; she'd like the ride. At the end of the station platform where the parlor cars would stop, Dennis put our bags.

"Goodbye, Ruth. Goodbye, Gregory."

"Goodbye." I didn't call her Mrs. Miles; I didn't call her Auntie Bob; I didn't call her Bob the way Mr. Miles did; I certainly didn't call her Isabelle.

"Goodbye," said Gregory. He didn't call her anything, either.

Where our bags were, another pile was piled beside ours, two people standing there. Could it *be?* It was Annie Russell and her husband, Oswald Yorke!

"Miss Russell!"

She was actress enough to act pleased. Mr. Yorke's acting gift was less, he looked stuck with it.

The train roared in. *One* parlor car! I sat on the arm of the next chair to Annie Russell's. To sit *in* the chair would have been pushy; on the *arm* suggested I wouldn't stay. Did she hope or did she know better?

"Biddeford. Kennebunk next," called the porter.

"Please remember us to Tark. I knew him when he was married to his first wife."

He was on the platform. Tall, handsome, elegant dark blue jacket, white flannels, Panama! Beside him stood chauffeur Chick.

"Mr. Tarkington, there's Annie Russell!"

She was smiling out the parlor car window.

He waved his Panama. London's Major Barbara waved to the Hoosier author of *Monsieur Beaucaire.*

"I won't mind waiting five years to be a star."

Eight years and I *still* wasn't a star, but was waving goodbye to one and shaking hands with a legend!

Mr. Chick turned up the winding driveway. Formal flower beds, pines; everything that was Tarkington's was touched with elegance— gray-shingled Seaward, the red brick house on Pennsylvania Street in Indianapolis, the staff who ran them. In May they left Pennsylvania Street and came east, mid-November they closed Seaward and went west. As Mr. Chick stopped the car, white-coated black butler came out, black maid in black taffeta and white organdy followed, took our coats, our bags disappeared up the back stairs.

In the big hall waiting to kiss us was beautiful Mrs. Tarkington. To her left, the dining room, its long oblong table with silver bowl of flowers on lace. To the right, the drawing room, agleam in late afternoon sun. Beyond, Mr. Tarkington's study; book-lined walls, ship models, treasures. Treasures in every room.

Midway up the stairs was a wide landing; the stairs turned and went up. Ours was the first guest room, everything in it pretty.

"Dinner will be at seven. Booth likes to dine early at Seaward. Come down before and have a cocktail with me in the drawing room. *Oh,* you look so pretty! Why don't *I* ever find a suit that color blue?"

"It's from Dobbs."

"You have beautiful taste, Ruth. Doesn't she, Gregory? Booth *loves* people to wear pretty clothes." The door closed.

We were at the Tarkingtons' and admired!

For dinner, Mr. Tarkington changed into elegant brocade jacket and dark trousers. Mrs. Tarkington wore a long dress, soft and rippling. I wore my Boué Soeurs embroidered batiste with real filet lace over black taffeta.

I looked as elegant as Seaward. My square-cut diamond wedding ring, bought with money from Mr. Tarkington's *Seventeen*, ditto my engagement ring, diamonds clustered around Mama's diamond, my platinum bracelet, a diamond in each link, bought with money from Mr. Tarkington's *Clarence*.

"Oh, Booth, don't they look beautiful!" Wetzel had made Gregory's white flannels and double-breasted blue jacket. "What do you drink?"

Mr. Tarkington lit a long cigarette, "N.B.T." stamped in black on the cigarette paper. "I won't offer you one. I remember Mrs. Kelly thinks they're too strong."

Perfect dinner, perfectly served. Gamin, the big black French poodle, sat at master's left, I sat at the right. Butler and maids served, Mr. Tarkington talked, Mrs. Tarkington laughed, we relaxed, *everything* was going right, *everything* was just how I meant it to be.

Mrs. Tarkington poured coffee in the drawing room. "Tomorrow night Ken and Anna Roberts will come and Hugh Kahler and his wife. They're so anxious to see you again, but Booth and I wanted you to ourselves tonight."

That darling lady! White hair done high, pink cheeks, brown eyes, beautiful dark eyebrows.

"Oh, you look so lovely, Ruth. I *wish* Booth wasn't against powder!"

After coffee, Mr. Tarkington led the way to the study. "Let's talk about *Bristol Glass.*"

We told him we thought Robert McLaughlin would give it a good production, then we three would like to produce it in New York.

"That will be expensive."

"We want to do it."

"Harry Wilson and I will do our share. Put us down for minimum royalty. Harry will insist on that. For Cleveland, *no* royalty; we'll waive that for tryout," said the first novelist to win two Pulitzer Prizes—*The Magnificent Ambersons* and this spring, *Alice Adams.*

A breeze from the sea, a breeze through the pines, organdy curtains fluttering, wake up? Sleep some more? Ring. A gentle knock, a pretty maid came in in a pretty light blue cotton dress and pretty white apron. Not off the counter, but made by Mrs. Tarkington's seamstress in the sewing room on Pennsylvania Street. "Good morning." She drew open the curtains, raised the shades, brought a pillow to go behind me. Brought one to go behind Gregory, straightened the covers, folded back the satin eiderdown, went out.

A knock, another maid, another pretty light blue cotton dress and apron. She carried a breakfast tray for me. Behind her, another maid carried one for Gregory. Pretty flowers on each tray. First maid came back with the Boston *Globe* and the Portland paper. Like a scene in a play? Just like, except breakfast was better.

Mrs. Tarkington came out to the garden wearing hat, gloves, lovely smile. "Come with me to town; we can visit."

Mr. Chick drove away from the Port and into Kennebunk.

"Take us by the Wedding Cake House, Chick."

Behind its white picket fence with high carved gateposts, the pale yellow brick mansion sits close to the street. Over it a white wooden-lace frosting. At each corner carved white pillars taper off in delicate pinnacles above the roof. A lace arch frames the front door, another arch with frosted pinnacles goes over the second-story middle windows. Who thought of the dark blinds that look through the lace? Who thought of the shape? Who thought of a wedding cake house?

Wherever we shopped, Mrs. Tarkington introduced us with "You remember them from Booth's *Seventeen*. Ruth was the Baby Talk Lady and Gregory was Willie Baxter. Weren't they *wonderful!* And *we* saw them in Indianapolis in Booth's *Clarence. Oh,* they were so darling!" She laughed with pleasure at the memory.

We drove over to Kennebunk Beach. "It's such cold water I never try it. Would you want to?"

Cold-water bathing we'd done at Christmas Cove. We sat on the beach in front of the Tarkington bathhouse.

Later we waited in the drawing room and a few minutes before one, Mr. Tarkington came briskly down the stairs. He breakfasted in his room, then wrote in the upstairs study. At lunch, he engaged Gamin in conversation. Gamin moaned, barked, yelped, kept silent, listened. After coffee in the drawing room, Mr. Tarkington asked would we come for a drive. Did anyone ever say no?

He sat in front with Chick. "My long legs won't fit in the back," he explained.

We drove past the grand new hotel.

"It's called Breakwater Inn. I call it Break Father Inn."

"They don't care *what* they charge," chipped in Mr. Chick. "Summer people are damn fools."

Shouldn't he add, "Present company excepted"?

We drove past Ken Roberts' house. "He and Anna live out here in lonely splendor. I don't know why lonely is enjoyable, but Ken says it is."

Pines and rocks lined the shore, glimpses of white sand, glimpse of a fine house.

Maine's firs and rocks and water made the Indianapolis doctor send Mr. Tarkington to Kennebunkport. There had been a slow recovery from diphtheria. The doctor said there was only one spot to regain his health. One! Kennebunkport. Not York Harbor to the south, not Biddeford farther north, only Kennebunkport would cure him and he "must devote six months." Each year he devoted six months.

The drive ended at his dock. Would we like to go out on the *Zantee?* Captain Thirkle bowed us aboard. He handed Mr. Tarkington a yachting cap and stowed away the Panama.

"Are the whales around today, Captain Thirkle?"

"I dunno's they be; a whale don't like nice weath-ah."

Mr. Tarkington took the wheel, steered past the outer harbor, no whales, we turned back.

Do you love it when a boat turns back? I take after Mama. Any time I step off a boat is pleasure.

"We'll have tea, Captain Thirkle."

We left the *Zantee,* named for Susannah T., and went up the gangplank of the old schooner, permanently berthed. Captain Thirkle served tea in the cabin.

"Harry and I think *Bristol Glass* will go, but in rehearsal if you have problems, feel free to suggest changes, Kelly. Rehearsals bring surprises. I'm glad Mrs. Kelly has a part at last, no baby talk to worry her. I'll be anxious for word from Cleveland. I'm sure it will go."

It did. Get through *The First Year* tour, give our notice in Nashville. Our contract didn't let John Golden give *us* notice, but *we* could, provided he knew six weeks ahead.

"How is it you can give me notice and I can't?" he asked.

"That's because Frank Craven promised us Chicago and now *he's* going to play it."

Perth Amboy to Nashville, the money saved, and back we came to New York. We cast Frank McGlynn for old Tweedles, Fred Perry for old

Castleberry. No expense spared. Bob McLaughlin booked the Blackstone Theatre in Chicago. We booked our room at the Blackstone Hotel. It opened and didn't go. Another summer to get through, then in August, with a change of name by Tarkington, *Tweedles* opened in New York and *at last I got good notices!* In the New York *Herald,* Woollcott wrote: "In addition to the gentle, blinking, immensely engaging Kelly, one must certainly mention Miss Gordon who has a genuine and forthright actuality which is immensely nourishing to a play like this and who, at times, can fill the brief love scenes with the shining light that is all one needs by which to see what goes on under Juliet's balcony."

"Miss Gordon's hands actually seem to blush," wrote former sports writer Heywood Broun, now drama critic for the New York *Tribune.*

John Corbin in the *Times* wrote, "Gregory Kelly and Ruth Gordon are truly and saliently artists."

Gregory had taught me to act, he'd planned the Indianapolis Stock Company to give me experience, he toured in *Clarence* and *The First Year* so I could learn, he got *Tweedles* to New York so I could get started. That was *his* side of the ledger. Tomorrow was the funeral.

Dear Gregory, it didn't come out even.

# Chapter

## 10

July was over. It was mid-August. *Saturday's Children* ran on. I was living at the Swopes' in Great Neck. I rang for breakfast, then sat up in bed. Through the branches of Pearl's honey locust, sun sparkled on the green water that ebbed and flowed along the shore of Long Island Sound. Beneath my door I saw an envelope with Woollcott's writing.

Lamb girl,
  Ben Franklin felt it worthwhile to sit down an hour and figure out his day. Is that what you do?
  Who would you say is smarter, you or Ben? He did it with no clothes on. I leave that to you.

                                                            Little Nemo

Mae knocked and came in. "Morning, Miss Gordon." She unfolded the legs of a tray, placed it over my knees. "I brought you the *Times* and the *Tribune.*"

"Lovely. Anybody up?"

"You're first, Miss Gordon."

"Yoo-hoo." Pearl's mother looked in.

"Hello, Mimi."

Swope had said God pity them if they ever went on trial and Mimi was called as witness.

"Come in, Mimi." I unfolded the pink linen napkin to match the clover breakfast china.

She came in.

"Hello, duchess." Woollcott leaned in the door.

She laughed. "Hear what he calls me? I'm just leaving. Come talk to Ruth." She went out.

"Oh, horrors, must I?" He leaned over and kissed me. "Hello, Blossom."

"What a beautiful robe!"

"Helen Keller brought it to me from Calcutta. Why don't *you* ever bring me something?"

"I will."

"How's the show going?"

"Great."

"How's your peace of mind?"

"Frazzled."

"Arthur?"

"Yuh."

"Want to marry me?"

"No, thanks."

"At least I haven't got a wife."

"Why does everything have to be so *complicated?*"

"You complicate *yourself.* If anyone's normal, you run. What about marrying *me* and turn rational? You don't love him. He's actually quite repulsive. Ever happen to look at him?"

"Of course."

"Little, fat, opinionated, the shape of Buddha. You're crazy about his *achievements* and the fact he gives you a complicated existence. You know what you are? A goddam puritan in love with the *idea* of a love affair. If Arthur ever asked you to marry him you'd leap off in nine directions."

"I would not."

"All *you* ask out of life is trouble! The fact his wife is out looking for you with a bowie knife makes that small-time Massachusetts heart of yours go like the band at the Cotton Club. I really must remember not to see you anymore. When I think of your idiotic, twisted infatuations, it's enough to give me the Egyptian crud."

"What's enough to give you the Egyptian crud, Lamb Boy?" Myra Hampton looked in.

"You."

Myra looked over toward me. "What's biting Albert the Good?"

"Stop flexing your muscles at me. I find you devoid of charm."

Slender, exquisite, pale auburn hair; her wispy light green chiffon negligee showed more than it hid.

"Why can't Pearl get someone to come down here that has some faint *remnant* of allure? I wouldn't put it past her to be trying to turn us all into fairies!"

Myra feigned astonishment. *"Aren't* you one, darling? The *on dit* is—"

"Stop lisping that Sweetbriar French! Just because you were the first lady of Montclair, New Jersey, don't expect people to be nice to you *here!"*

"Myra." It was Heywood's voice.

"Yes, pet?"

"Come and see *me."*

Alec poured a cup of coffee from my tray. "If you married me, you'd be free to do as you please."

"Darling, that's an awful thing to say."

"Why? You'd do it anyway, so why not say so?"

"I never want to get married again."

"Find someone *really* makes you miserable, you'll want to."

I found him. It took from August till February.

"Want to meet me at the Ritz Hotel in Atlantic City?"

"All right."

Watch those all rights! Two words, then red roses float in the bathtub and a sea gull flies through the window.

Mama believed it meant death if a bird flew in the room, but forty-seven years later, Jed Harris and I are still alive.

"Parlor car seat, Washington to North Philadelphia Sunday afternoon," I told Union Station in Washington.

In New York, Jed's secretary handed him his ticket to North Philadelphia and *two* tickets, drawing room, to Atlantic City. *One* to North Philly? *Two* to the shore? Railroad tickets helped his secretary put two and two together.

Who'd help Jed wake up in time to catch the train? He ran over his list of trusties and phoned his mother in Newark.

"Ringgg, ringgg" went his private phone, and when the Washington train came to a stop, he was looking out North Philadelphia's station restaurant window. Kiss, coffee, drawing room, Atlantic City!

"You're making a *big* mistake," warned Pearl and Herbert Swope.

Hadn't people said that when *they* went off together?

Never listen to what people say. People say anything. Maybe it's considerate to *give* them something to say.

Jed and I gave them something. It had started the year before Atlantic City. Bea Kaufman and I were coming out of the 44th Street Theatre. "Hello, darling." Bea kissed the producer of Broadway's biggest hit, then remembered me. "Do you two know each other?"

Why look pleased?

Bea laughed. "Glad you wore that green velvet coat?" Bea had a wicked laugh.

I didn't look pleased that summer day when he'd come to the Algonquin and I had on my dress I'd bought at Lanvin.

"Hello, dear."

What made *him* look pleased? Is becoming a Broadway legend good for the disposition? He smiled at me.

I smiled at him.

"Come with us, darling." Bea was for fellers. When it was over and they went for somebody else, she did too. "We're not going back for the last act; the second made us puke." To steer things toward intimate, Bea threw in words like "puke."

He smiled.

She smiled.

I smiled.

Did he smile at Bea or me?

If you don't think it's you, get out of show business—you've got an inferiority complex and that's not what they pay to see.

"Ask me some other time." He smiled at *me,* then waved the most beautiful hand in the world and, blanketed in loneliness, strode down 44th Street to the Broadhurst, with the big electric sign:

### JED HARRIS
**PRESENTS**
### BROADWAY

Bea watched him disappear. "I'm mad about him."

I *would* be. That had been winter. In August, George Kaufman phoned.

"Come for dinner Wednesday. Bea's away and Jed Harris is coming. A lot of people don't like him. He thinks he's Napoleon—and I think he is too."

Out on cold 44th Street Bea smiled, Jed smiled, I smiled, then in August George asked us to dinner, then in March Jed gave me a present. For the Boston run of *Saturday's Children* he said I must stay at the new hotel, the Ritz-Carlton.

> *Ritz-Carlton Hotel*
> *Boston*
> *March 29, 1928*

Darling Alec,

When you come to Boston, stay here, it's great. Jed has given me a suite for the two weeks we play. *Saturday's Children* opened last night and today I took the 2:10 to Wollaston. Don't ask me why. Am I looking for something? The South Station is still murky, only today I love it. Is it because I'm not part of it? We joggled past Savin Rock station, now boarded up, Frost's Coal Yard, Neponset still gives me a scare, Tubular Rivet and Stud factory is still back of St. Chrysostom's, Green's Pond is still there, sometime I'll tell you about—maybe not. The Howes' house is still painted dark red. In front of it a train ran into a freight car full of groceries, they scattered all over the place, everybody went and got some. 14 Elmwood has kitchen curtains. We never did. I got off the train on the station side where I used to watch for our great Lady Dedlock that you'd have gone for, the station platform was the only place anyone saw her. Intrigue you? The only place, then she'd get into Mike McGrath's hack and clop-clop over the railroad bridge up Grand View Avenue. (Later Mike bought a Reo with black rubber curtains for when it rained.) Chug-chug over the railroad bridge, but in that brief glimpse I saw the lady's long sweeping sealskin coat with the sable collar and muff. In the autumn, her velvet jacket with braid and real lace jabot, a turban with bird of paradise drooping over her left ear, at her waist, violets like you send me, darling.

With her was her husband, suggesting the Algonquin Club, Saratoga races, prizefights where somebody becomes world champion.

His hat was nifty green velour, the only man in Wollaston who wore gloves, his waterproof so stylish most people wouldn't get it wet. Who is it we know that's queer for shoes? His were russet! I asked Mama if she'd like Papa to look like him.

"Of course not."

"Why?"

"He looks like a man who only eats planked steak."

You're so good at mysteries, tell me why *you* think no one ever saw them except chug-chug over the bridge up Grand View and disappear under the porte-cochere into their dark green spacious house? No one ever went in but them, and they went out only to take the train. Why was that? And if no one went in, how could people know the faucets in her bathtub were 14-karat gold?

No one ever said that about anyone else's faucets. People said they had had friends, then one day Lady Dedlock stood naked at her window and let the man next door look at her! He was a deacon and after that the church asked him not to be. Wollaston never spoke to the Dedlocks, the ex-deacon moved to another street and no one spoke to him either.

Today I looked at her house and wondered. Someday you come with me and we'll guess which window she stood at. Would you have stared? Who was the first lady you ever saw naked? Where did *she* stand?

I asked the man at the ticket window for a time table, he said he hadn't one. I pointed to the pile.

"Those are only good for today and tomorrow."

Didn't it occur to him that anyone might want to make a quick turn around out of Wollaston?

I crossed the tracks, went through the turnstile. Why a turnstile? Walked as far as Miss Gorham's, when someone asked, "Which way is Fayette Street?" I was wearing my expensive red suit from Sklar and Wagner's like Pearl's, my Henri Bendel hat, my shoes that actually *are* from Thayer, McNeil. When did they drop Hodgkins? I told her to turn left on Brook, then two blocks and that was Fayette. I'm a New Yorker, but do I still look Wollaston?

> Love,
> Louisa

*Saturday's Children* had started its road tour, same cast except for Roger Pryor. Roger asked for a raise, they wouldn't pay it, he signed for *The Royal Family.* Nobody wanted to go on the road so they had to take Humphrey Bogart, who wasn't as right for the part and got the same salary as Roger would have gone for. Well, that's show business. Our first stand was Boston and it gives an idea of what the notices were if I wrote Alec, "We opened last night," then described a trip to Wollaston.

Time went slowly in my grand suite at the Ritz, no fuss made over me, what about write Clare? What would she write *me* if I wrote her that New York's most successful theatrical producer was paying for my suite?

*Saturday's Children* played Providence. Was everything all right? Had I ever been this late?

"You go to Atlantic City," said Jed. "I'll meet you there."

He was working on *The Front Page* and he couldn't get there. I came back to New York.

Terror again. It was certain. Arrange with Dr. Roller.

*Saturday's Children* played at the Forrest Theatre for three weeks and closed. In Atlantic City *The Front Page* opened for a tryout. Terrific. Everybody knew it would be a hit.

Next on Jed's schedule were rehearsals for *King's X*. He would direct. Everybody knew that would be a hit, too.

Guthrie was still sore. "It was all set, then they gave it to *him.*"

"Would you have had *me?*"

"No."

"Then you can't blame me."

"I'm not blaming *you.* I'm blaming *them.*"

Jed adored it. I thought it was great except my character's name was Cissaly, but that was the authors' child's name so get to like it.

For the father, Jed engaged a fine musical comedy actor, George Mac-Farlane. For the mother, Elizabeth Patterson. She'd played Willie Baxter's mother when Stuart took Judith Lowry out of *Seventeen.* Darling Roger Pryor left *The Royal Family* and we acted together again. Phyllis Povah had a good part, Osgood Perkins was in it, the opening was in Asbury Park. Everybody happy, everybody confident, cast great, play a gem. Poor Guthrie lost it, but he wasn't going to have *me,* so thank God, Jed got it!

A lot of New York drove down for the opening. Pearl and Herbert Swope, Noël Coward, Edna Ferber. The curtain rose on George MacFarlane reading his paper and talking to his wife, a quiet scene. Jed admired it; he'd orchestrated it as a lull. One of those lulls that come in a day of home-life irritations. A lull.

Someone laughed at something, George MacFarlane pricked up his ears. The lull was over. He took off.

"He used that newspaper like a bladder!" raged Jed. "Slapped himself with it, belted the dog, struck his wife."

The audience laughed, kept laughing, laughed when I broke down and said I was pregnant. When Osgood said something sympathetic to me it was a roar.

The final curtain came down and Pearl Swope and Herbert came backstage. "Wrong audience," said Herbert.

"They're the kind of people that go shopping in their bathing suits," said Pearl.

Noël came back to the hotel with us. He sat cross-legged on the floor of Jed's faintly Moorish suite in the Berkeley-Carteret. "Write it off," he said. "Your work is su-*perb,* Jed. Ruth, you're *too* good! Leave it *here.*"

"He's right," said Jed, and sailed for Europe. I cabled Woollcott and Harpo to expect me at Antibes, wherever that was.

We played the last half of the week at Long Branch, moved to Atlantic City, to the *good* theatre, the Apollo. At the Friday night performance, Osgood Perkins rushed into my dressing room. "I *killed* that laugh!" he said, triumphant.

"How *did* you?" We were all trying.

"I stood downstage in that dark spot."

"Yes."

"I turned back-to."

"Yes."

"And I said it so they couldn't hear."

Saturday night we closed. At the matinee, Margaret Bellinger handed me a cable from Paris.

BEST WISHES BIG HIT. CHARLES DILLINGHAM.

Well, that's show business.

The company chose to take the 7 A.M. train back to New York, the same one Gregory and I took for our first rehearsal of *Clarence*. We filed into the company coach, all of us gloomy; we'd all been so confident.

How did Guthrie feel that gloomy Sunday? The play was wide open for anybody to take it over, but he didn't. The Theatre Guild did.

Jed's office booked me to sail on the *Majestic*. What a good idea! Or was it? "Is anything worse than a nice long rest after a great big flop?" I asked Noël Coward.

"Nothing, dear."

We were both wrong. The visit to Antibes was like Dorothy's trip to see the Land of Oz.

Cables came from Jed in New York. He'd sailed back from Europe. *The Front Page* opened in New York on August 13. Jed's superstition about superstition—he liked 13. And New York liked *The Front Page*. A triumph.

Back from Oz, I read plays. Nothing. Then Jed decided he'd produce *Serena Blandish, or The Difficulty of Getting Married,* by A Lady of Quality. Sam Behrman had made it into a play. It had been sent to me by other managers, but with Jed it was different.

Woollcott rang up. "How are rehearsals, puss?"

"Jed said Mattie asked him today who he was getting to replace me."

"Why would he ask that?"

232

"Nobody ever thinks I'm much in rehearsal. I guess I rehearse the way Mama made my dresses. She'd study Butterick's tissue paper pattern, then put it on the cloth and cut it out. That's how it *looked,* but in her mind's eye was the finished dress. At rehearsal they don't see my finished dress, but I do, and when I get to the audience, *they* do. The actors worry, directors too; Guth's the only one doesn't."

*Serena Blandish* opened. William Bolitho wrote his New York *World* column about the opening night. "A wave of chill dislike for someone permeated the house. Was it for Jed Harris? For Ruth Gordon? For whom?" Bolitho asked. It was the first opening night since *Seventeen* that had scared me. So did something else. Could we have been so careless? Could I go against fate this often? Did I want to? I didn't. Who was the doctor Pearl Swope said was great? Was the great Dr. Austin Gray a gynecologist? I looked in the phone book. "Dr. Austin Gray, 64 East 54th Street."

Consult him? I couldn't consult Jed; he was off to Florida.

"Dr. Gray's office? . . . This is Mrs. Kelly. . . . K-E-L-L-Y. . . . May I have an appointment to see Dr. Gray? . . . No, I've never been to him. Mrs. Swope told me. . . . Tomorrow at three?"

Tomorrow was a matinee day.

"Would it be possible to make it day after tomorrow? . . . Oh, thank you. Thursday at three will be perfect. . . . My number is Wickersham 2958. . . . 36 West Fifty-ninth Street. . . . Thank you. Goodbye."

Jed had come back from Florida. "How do you think you're going to keep it a secret?"

"I'm not."

"Not what?"

"Not going to. I hate secrets."

"You mean you think you're going to *announce* it?"

"Not announce it, but I certainly don't want to keep it secret."

"Do you want it in the paper?"

"No, but I want to tell my friends."

"How do you think you'll keep it *out* of the paper?"

*Serena* had closed because Jed said I was beginning to show. Was it that, or had business fallen off?

It was a secret. Nobody knew. I was going abroad. Nobody knew that, either. I was going to have the baby and I was going to have it someplace far off. Berlin? Someplace where I didn't know anyone.

"You don't know what you're doing," said Jed.

I certainly didn't.

The phone rang.

"The cribbage game is at Alice's. You have to come, Blemish. Harpo has to do something about his ridiculous family and can't come till later. You're worse than useless, but we need you. Dinner, Colony, seven, I have to run."

The phone clicked.

Neysa McMein, Alice Duer Miller, Harold Ross and Woollcott had already started on the great hors d'oeuvres. Jack Baragwanath, Ray Ives, Raoul Fleischmann chose curry soup Waterbury, named after the great polo player who'd flung himself out the Pullman window.

Outside on 61st Street, Cepetti waited in Alice's car to whiz us to her grand apartment in the Campanile. He didn't know a car could move any other way. He came to a short stop just before he hit the East River and we went up to Alice's grand second-floor living room hanging over the river. The grand buffet, laid out to last a long evening, was Dean's chocolate cake towering over homemade chicken salad and sandwiches.

"I'll take Blemish," said Woollcott.

Alec played to win. I'm not lucky at cards or clever and hate games except Authors and Pit. We were playing against Alice and Ross. Alec led a card that was a signal, but I didn't have the card. When I played the one he *didn't* want, he gave a snort. The hand finished. "Why the goddam hell if you didn't have the ace didn't you play the goddam two?"

"I made a mistake."

He went into silence, glared at the table cover.

Alice dealt, Ross led, I played. Woollcott shook his head, but I didn't have what he wanted. The hand finished, Woollcott threw down the cards. "I'm through." He stormed out of Alice's into his own apartment next door.

Alice gave a little surprised laugh and gathered up his cards.

"I'll never speak to him again!" I said, and went home. It was two years before I saw him.

Again the *Aquitania.* Jed and I were to sail, then he got a strep throat. It was responding, but the doctor said he must postpone.

"I will too."

"No. You go."

"I'd rather wait."

"You really show. I'll come on the *Île de France.* It sails two days later.

I'm sending Victor and the car ahead to meet you at Cherbourg, drive you to Le Havre. You'll be there when I get in. On board ship, stay in your cabin. I tell you it shows."

"If it's a rough passage, stay in bed till it calms down," advised Dr. Gray. "Otherwise a sea voyage will be good for you. Will you take the boat train from Cherbourg?"

"I'm going by car."

"Good. Here's a letter for you to take to Dr. Bouffe de Saint Blaise in Paris and here's one just came from Dr. Gros. He's head of the American Hospital; you'll like him. As soon as you're settled in Paris, go to see him. His office is Avenue Foch. Here's my letter to introduce you." He handed it to me. "You'll like him. I know I said that before, but I want to stress it. Perfectly lovely man. He headed the Lafayette Escadrille in the war, or did I tell you that? He writes that he'll make everything easy for you. In his letter—where is it?—he says 'Dr. Bouffe is the best. Eighty-one years old and nobody to touch him. Nobody even anything like him or ever will be. There's no one to take his place. You've read his book, of course. I call it the best on childbirth. And what a dear man. Very small, a marquis, elegant as his name would suggest and does not know a word of English. Will Mrs. Kelly be able to speak French?' I wrote him you could."

"I'm going to get a teacher. Mademoiselle Gaudel. She's written a grammar."

"That's fine. Now what more can I do for you?"

"You're an angel."

"Not at all. And you'll write how things go. Will you take an apartment?"

"I suppose so." Suddenly I felt frightened. How *would* I live? "I haven't really worked it out."

"Will you be alone?"

"No. He's coming on another boat."

"Does he know my name?"

"No."

"Well, you'll manage everything. I expect to hear only good news."

"Thanks again." We shook hands and I was out on East 54th Street. He'd changed my life.

"You'll manage everything," he'd said. How confident! Does *confidence* make things go? It got me on the Wollaston train to knock at doors in New York.

"I expect to hear only good news," he'd said.

Confidence led me to a door that was open and I was "ever so gay as Nibs." I knew how to do that, but would I know how to take a Paris apartment? It would be different if it wasn't a secret. Would Jed change? Would he get a divorce? Would he marry me? Dr. Gray was confident, but did *I* know the next step?

I walked over on 54th Street to Fifth Avenue. The afternoon was cold for May. October would be cold too; Dr. Gray figured the baby would be born October 13. Jed liked 13. Wasn't 13 lucky? He chose the thirteenth to open *The Front Page*.

"How soon after October thirteenth can I come back?"

Dr. Gray looked thoughtful. "I wouldn't be in a hurry. A little baby can travel, but give it time. Two months? Two months in Paris isn't a dreadful fate. October thirteen to November thirteen to December thirteen, then home for Christmas." When Dr. Gray said it so serenely, it sounded all right.

At a pay station, I called Plaza 2424. "Mr. Harris . . ."

"Mr. Harris isn't taking any calls."

What did *that* mean? Was Judy there? Go up and knock? What if I heard Judy's voice?

"You'll manage everything."

Confidence. How do you get it and how do you hold on to it?

The *Aquitania* again, grand and somber.

"Stay in your cabin . . . it shows."

I stayed in.

Because Jed said to? Because it *entertained* me? It seemed so above it. Harry Miller once traveled second class so he wouldn't run into Alice's friends. Pearl Swope knew somebody who never left the cabin and on arrival looked as if they'd been to a cure. And didn't it show you crossed the ocean a lot if you didn't even bother to get up?

The weather made it easier, gray fog and a choppy sea. The passenger list had Bill Tilden as its somebody. How did Gregory and I know him? Was it when Bill played Alfred Lunt's part in *Clarence* one Sunday night for a benefit? Gregory and I went backstage to tell him how good he was. Did we know him before that? We saw him a lot of times since.

"I didn't know you were on board." Nobody on deck but Bill and me.

"I'm not listed. I'm staying in bed this trip."

"Very wise; it's not a good crossing."

That one short walk and I didn't appear again until gray Cherbourg. Victor came aboard. That made me close to Jed. "They let me put the car a good place on the dock, but nobody heard of driving Cherbourg to Le Havre, Mrs. Kelly. I guess we'll find it."

My trunk went to Paris to the George V Hotel, suitcases and I went in the blue Lincoln touring car with young Italian-American Victor.

Victor and I drove off. With Michelin maps we were doing it. Through Arromanches, Cabourg, back of Deauville, Trouville, on a ferry so small the blue Lincoln seemed to hang over, Honfleur, cross the Seine on a bigger ferry into Le Havre. Did we get lost or was that the route?

The Hotel Frascati was old, but not too old, and it looked out on the harbor.

"You can see Mr. Harris' boat come in from your window," said Victor. "I'm in a hotel a couple of blocks away."

Two days till the *Île de France*. Victor drove me into Le Havre; it didn't appeal. What kind of a mood was that?

"The country's pretty. Want to go for a drive?"

We drove through May greenery. Every once in a while we came out on the Seine or the sea.

Posters advertised a show, sort of a circus vaudeville. I couldn't go alone. "Get two tickets," I told Victor. "You come with me." It made him nervous, but he did. It had a lot of pantomime we understood and some we pretended we didn't.

The *Île de France* came in early, early. The car was in front of the hotel. Sometimes ships don't allow visitors aboard, but the *Île de France* didn't care. People were coming off, luggage following. I didn't know where to look, so I looked in all directions. Chic, dazzling, talking to an attractive girl, Jed saw me and shook his head. I went back to the car. Why didn't I keep going?

He came, smiling, as though he hadn't seen me on the boat. "Darling, are you all right?"

"Fine."

"Someone's coming with us." Some man from the boat sat by me, Jed sat in front with Victor.

At Rouen we were blocked. "It's Pentecost, they say," said Victor. "They're celebrating and roads are shut off to the cathedral."

Jed chose a place for lunch. One of his talents wasn't choosing a restaurant; the Hofbrau was no good. If you were in Rouen would you choose a hofbrau?

"Find out what Pentecost is, Victor."

"It's to celebrate summer coming and the crops, Mr. Harris."

In the cathedral music played, bells rang, choirboys sang in a serpentine, priests wore white dresses with lace like Boué Soeurs used to make. They carried trays of flowers with wheat sprays and loaves of shiny bread.

"You look beautiful," said Jed.

"I do *not* look pitiful."

"Beautiful," he said again.

I knew he said "beautiful"; I wanted to hear it twice.

In Paris, Jed was going to the new Hôtel Raphaël, Avenue Kléber, a block from the Arc de Triomphe. He'd said we couldn't stay in the same place, so after Victor dropped him, I went to the George V. I'd been there the summer before on my way to Antibes and on my way back. Then it was all going to be fun; this time, get ready for when it happens.

Jed warned me not to ask questions. "People are smarter than you think. And find an apartment. You shouldn't be here. I'm going off and you've got to be settled."

I looked at the ads in *Figaro,* wrote down real estate agents' names and addresses. Some spoke English, some didn't. One advertised they were anxious to find Americans a Paris home.

"You're too damn particular," said Jed. "Get something."

It got hot. Also discouraging. I didn't see one I liked, whatever the price. I asked Dr. Gros. What a good man! What a good office! On the right side of the Avenue Foch coming toward the Étoile, cool and as though it had been there for ages.

"Have a glass of white grape juice."

It wasn't chilled, just cool. Just great. Like Dr. Gros. There were no worries. He and Dr. Austin Gray had confidence.

Everything was arranged, my room was booked at the American Hospital, Neuilly; it looked out on the garden. "You'll be happy there, lovely place, I've got you the best nurse in the hospital, the best nurse in France."

"Is she French?"

"French and speaks perfect English. How do you get on with Dr. Bouffe?"

"I have an appointment for next week. I wanted to see you first."

"Good. You'll like him. I told Dr. Gray he doesn't speak English, but you speak French."

"I study with Mademoiselle Gaudel."

"I hear she's excellent."

"As soon as I find an apartment she'll come there."

"Paris is full of lovely apartments. You'll find one."

Agencies sent me here and there. Nothing I wanted, but at least I found out where I *didn't* want to live. No to the Avenue Wagram, Boulevard Haussmann, the Left Bank; yes to the 16th Arrondissement. It seemed convenient.

Convenient to what? I wasn't going anywhere, I didn't know anyone. Why convenient? Convenient to my *soul.* When Marilyn Miller married Jack Pickford they got married at the *mairie* in the 16th. I'd met Marilyn once and Jack Pickford once; I would *like* to be in that neighborhood.

"What are you looking for?"

"A place that looks livable, *not* on a courtyard, on a nice street, clean, with a maid's room."

"For how many?"

Was it for me and Jed? Me and Jed and baby and nurse? Was it till mid-December?

"You'll manage everything. I expect to hear only good news." He'd said I could do it and now I was doing it.

Mid-December or *longer?* Whatever there's a shortage of, it's not questions.

Then, a day like any other, I walked down the Avenue Henri Martin to where it ends at Boulevard Lannes. Cool, shady; on the left the Bois, cool, shady. On the right old, elegant apartment houses, a *hôtel particulier.* The apartment house on the corner had a crescent driveway, a black iron fence and shrubs. I rang the concierge's bell.

*"Avez-vous quelque chose à louer?"* No sign out. Why did I ask?

*"Oui, Madame. Entrez."*

You *have* to have luck! I was home. 67 Boulevard Lannes was home from June to mid-December.

"You'll manage everything."

I had. Twelve rooms on the second floor. In Paris, they call it the first. *Our* first is their *rez-de-chaussée.*

Who was it said, "How do I know what I'm looking for till I find it?"

I found it. Looking out on the Bois was the drawing room, library, master bedroom, another bedroom. A medium-sized bedroom and a little little bedroom, all beautifully furnished. Antiques. Two bathrooms and a w.c. Two more bedrooms looked out on the big courtyard. A big dining room. A big kitchen with no refrigerator, but cold-closets that really kept things cool.

The front door was wide; handsome pale thick wood. It opened in two sections into a spacious hall. A Spanish family was giving up the apartment in two days. It was owned by Mme. Grünbaum-Ballin.

*"Voici son adresse,"* said the concierge.

Mme. Grünbaum-Ballin lived near the river. Slender, gray-haired, a widow with children; the Boulevard Lannes apartment was her income.

"It is three hundred and fifty dollars a month."

"I would like it through December."

"How many in your family?"

"I am alone."

"Isn't that a very large apartment for one?"

"No. What references will you want?"

Dr. Gros arranged for the social one, Bankers Trust vowed I'd pay the three-fifty.

"No one ever *heard* of anyone paying anything like that for a Paris apartment," said Jed.

It was my money, what did I care what "anyone" paid? And was "anyone" in my spot?

In *Figaro* I noted an employment agency and came away with two treasures. Élise, from the Savoie, was cook. Marcelle, an angel, was the maid. Neither spoke a word of English.

Mme. Grünbaum-Ballin was right—it *was* a big apartment for one. In 1929, was June unusually long? Élise taught me to read French. She said to read the newspaper over and over till I didn't have to translate it into English. Every night, after she finished in the kitchen, she came to the library door. *"Tout va bien, Madame?"*

*"Oui, merci, Élise."*

*"Ça fait lourd."*

*"Oui."*

*"Alors, je me couche."*

*"Bonne nuit, Élise."*

*"Bonne nuit, Madame."*

She did the shopping and was able to retire when I left. That's all right. I didn't need the money, I needed someone pleasant to cook my meals, and *be* there. She and Marcelle never took a day off. Two weekends I went to London and they were free.

For dinner, Élise made green soup, a roast, vegetables, a pudding. Nothing tasted great, but *she* was.

For August, Jed went back to New York. That month I didn't speak any English.

After dinner, I read in the library. A knock. Élise, smiling, stood in the doorway. *"Tout va bien, Madame?"*

*"Oui, merci, Élise."*

*"Ça fait lourd."*

*"Oui."*

*"Alors, je me couche."*

*"Bonne nuit, Élise."*

*"Bonne nuit, Madame."*

Once she showed me a coffee tin full of tobacco. *"Pour les malheureux."*

*"Qu'est-ce que c'est?"*

She pointed to my ashtray full of cigarette butts. *"Je garde tout ça, ôte les papiers et voici du bon tabac pour les malheureux."*

I smoked and "unfortunates" finished what I left. That was Paris, summer of 1929. In St. Tropez, June 1, 1954, I smoked my last cigarette. I hope *les malheureux* have stopped, too.

At 67 Boulevard Lannes, cigarette dishes overflowed. In August, they overflowed more than ever. Cigarettes and thoughts were my company; what if I wrote some thoughts down? The Bois with all its green—did that bring Wollaston back? I wrote a story about my father and his feeling for Woodrow Wilson. In the story he was Mr. Clement. Mr. and Mrs. Clement lived in a place like Wollaston, in a house like 14 Elmwood Avenue, didn't have a daughter that needed four hundred dollars, but the memorial for Wilson did. Mr. Clement pledged it. "Wilson Memorial" filled up a lot of August.

To fill the rest of the month, I wrote another story. My father and Christmas. It came back clear as I looked out. Did I look *in,* not out? Outside were a few passers-by, a soldier loafing at the Caserne in the Bois to the left of the library window; why did that make me think of how Papa hated Christmas dinner in Dorchester? Lots of people at dinner, but he remained alone.

In Paris, August is when Parisians leave; only strangers are in Paris. Stores close, doctors and dentists disappear, the dry cleaner leaves, neighborhood shops pull the shutters down. At the corner of Avenue Victor Hugo and the Rue de la Pompe, the *pâtissier* had left for vacation; bees buzzed around in his window. In Paris there were nobody but tourists. They didn't come up to the Avenue Victor Hugo. I could walk there. For visits to Dr. Bouffe, Rue Balzac, I took a taxi. Rue Balzac is just off the Champs Élysées near the Étoile, near the Carlton, near the Chambord, near the D'Albe; I'd run into somebody. Americans would be on Boulevard des Italiens where the newsstand sold *Variety* in front of the theatre that had been Réjane's, now the Paramount. *"Prends un taxi,"* I told Marcelle, and showed her *Variety. "Je veux."*

*"Tout de suite, Madame. Rien d'autre?"*

*"Non, merci, Marcelle."*

September, but no change from August. Then one night a taxi stopped, I looked out, Jed got out.

When it gets as terrible as it can get, something good happens. He came back.

He had a suite at the Chambord, but the master bedroom at Boulevard Lannes was his.

"I can't stand that green soup every night and you can't come out."

Good nights he was in the master bedroom. Other nights I wondered. He and who were at the Chambord?

Over at the Hôtel d'Iena were his mother, Mrs. Horowitz, and his sisters, Mildred, Sylvia, and Florence. They were back from a trip to Vienna, where he was born and where his people still lived.

A taxi stopped. Jed got out with his sister Mildred. "She'll come and stay here with you. I want her to first take Mama back to New York, then she'll sail back. I don't know where *I'll* be, but I'll feel all right if she's here."

Before she sailed, she came to see me alone. "Here's a present." She handed me a white tissue paper package. It was a knitted white jacket and cap. "It's not from me."

"Who?"

"Someone."

"Your mother?"

"She's not supposed to know, but she does."

With the lovely clothes from Fairyland, the most elegant shop on the Faubourg St. Honoré, went the present for Miss Jones.

"Call her Jones." That was Jed's idea. Why did we take for granted the baby would be a girl?

"Jones?"

After that, instead of talking about the baby, we talked about Miss Jones.

Any month is beautiful if things go right and any month in Paris is beautiful even if things don't. Of *all* the months the most beautiful is October. It starts to get dark early and that's when I started my walk. Dr. Bouffe said two miles every day. From Boulevard Lannes I turned right onto the Rue Adolphe Yvon or left onto Avenue Henri Martin and headed for the Avenue Victor Hugo.

"Flat heels hurt my feet," I said, but did they or did I think French heels looked pretty? Chestnut leaves dropping down looked pretty. At the Étoile, I turned round and walked back.

At 67, Mildred and I talked, read, talked, played a little two-handed bridge, talked. Ten o'clock. We yawned and went to bed.

"Jed wants me to ask Dr. Bouffe about being late."

"You feel all right?"

"Great."

About three I got up. Everything had seemed to slip down and a bucket of water poured out. "Mildred," I called.

"Yuh."

"Mildred, I think it's starting."

"How do you know?" She was wide awake and in charge.

"In the book it says a lot of water comes out. It has a name, but that's what it is."

"Yes?"

"And just now, everything seemed to slide down."

"What time is it?"

"When I got up it was three."

"Shall I get a taxi and we'll go to the hospital?"

"What do you think?" Neither of us even thought of calling Jed at the Chambord.

"Should we wait and see?" asked Mildred.

"All right."

"I'll crawl in bed with you, so you don't have to holler if you want me."

All those weeks and now would it really happen? Scary things I think are never going to catch up with me; I'm surprised when good things don't catch up quicker.

"What does the book say *next?*" Mildred went to the sitting room and brought it back.

Under the eiderdown, I told myself not to get scared.

Mildred had the book open. "After the ploosh, it says, '*Thereafter* will come the first labor pain. Pains will be spaced far apart, but this is the warning and if you plan to go to a hospital, you would do well to—' "

"Ow!"

"Pain?"

I nodded.

"That's it then." She read: " 'you would do well to get under way.' What time is it?"

"Now it's five."

"Any pain?"

"No. Do we know we can get a taxi?"

"Élise says there's one, night and day, Boulevard Flandrin by the Métro. Any pain?"

"No."

"Bag packed?"

"Yes."

"Anything you can think of more?"

"I don't think so."

"Pain?"

"No, maybe it was a false alarm."

"But the ploosh! What're you going to wear?"

"My blue Irene Dana's the only one I can get into. Ow!"

"Bad?"

"No, but as though it means it."

"I'm going to get Élise up." She pattered down the hall to the rooms on the courtyard. "Élise! Élise, *Madame veut aller à l'hôpital.*"

*"Ah, mon Dieu!"*

In no time we heard her go out the door.

Everything went according to the book except the hospital never heard of me.

"Fill out these papers."

"Go to hell," Mildred told them. "Where's her room?"

The pains were awful; I hung on to Mildred's hand. No Dr. Bouffe.

"He'll be here," said the intern. They wheeled me into the delivery room. Would the baby be born without Dr. Bouffe? The door opened, a murmur from those around. I opened my eyes. Dr. Bouffe, small, elegant, reassuring, stood beside me. *"Bonjour, Madame."* He shook hands. *"Comment ça va?"*

French conversation, smell of chloroform, unreality, way *way* off voices. *"Un garçon."*

I'd said I wanted a girl. A boy was what I wanted, and dreaded to say so for fear it wouldn't be.

When I woke, Mlle. Valentin, the day nurse, was in my lovely, square, peaceful room. I was thin again.

"Where's the baby?"

"He's sleeping nicely. I will bring him in for a feeding."

"Is he all right?"

"Perfect. Beautiful baby."

Dark soft hair, blue eyes, long eyelashes, a rosy tan as if back from

Palm Beach. He looked at me as though he planned to remember me. Serious, but did his eyes laugh?

"For a new baby," said Mlle. Valentin, "he's very dignified."

At noon Mildred called Jed.

October sixteenth was a lovely day. A Wednesday. The baby was born in the morning; Wednesday matinee could have gone on. If you're in show business, you think of things like that. Irrelevant in this case, but the result of all those Wednesday matinees.

Jed called up in the afternoon to see how things were. Mildred gave him a good report.

"He's dignified," said Mlle. Valentin. "I call him The Judge."

Jed liked The Judge. He was likable.

"He'd like to take him," said Mildred.

"What does that mean?"

"Adopt him. You know. *Have* him."

"You mean keep him?"

"He's going to drive to Spain. Maybe live there. He'll get an Isotta-Fraschini limousine and have it custom built with a crib in the back."

Anybody know the statistics on how many fathers have an Isotta Fraschini built with a crib for their son?

"No."

"No, what?"

"No, I won't give him up."

Across the square, peaceful room I could see the yellow trees on Neuilly's Boulevard Victor Hugo. Some days start all right, then bomb.

"I *said* you wouldn't. He's waiting at the Chambord."

The Chambord where I'd left to go to Boulevard Lannes, the Chambord where I came back, stood under the trees, looked up at Jed's suite and wondered. Victor stood beside the door of the blue Lincoln. He opened it, Judy got in.

*"Suivez l'auto bleu,"* I told the taxi. At the Bank of Westminster, Place Vendôme, Judy got out and went in.

"When you can't do anything about anything, go home," my voices told me. *"Soixante-sept Boulevard Lannes,"* I told the taxi.

"Tell him no," I told Mildred. The windows looked out at Neuilly, but I saw Spain in a custom-built Isotta with a place for Jed and The Judge.

"Jones Kelly," the birth certificate read. I had the only two copies. At the *mairie* of Neuilly there was no record. Dr. Gros saw to it that I had both sets of papers.

Down the hall, in the glassed-in nursery with the other babies, was The Judge. Some were crying, some slept, some were smiling, some howled; The Judge looked up at the ceiling as though alone and reading something there.

"This morning I took him for a visit," said Mlle. Valentin.

A clench.

"The Shah asked to see him."

"The Shah?"

"The Shah of Persia has the suite next to you. He heard about the American baby."

"What's the Shah of Persia doing here?"

"He's been here almost a year. You will see his entourage in the hall. He keeps a *hôtel particulier* in Neuilly, where his meals are cooked by his chef, then brought here in his big black limousine by his chamberlain."

"His—?"

"His chamberlain. Poor man, he must taste everything first. Everything. Outside the Shah's door is a guard, day and night."

"But why is he on the maternity floor?"

"His life was threatened and for refuge he endows the maternity ward. He guarantees every expense. He is charming. When he had a— something wrong with him, I was his nurse."

"Good-looking?"

She was silent.

"His meals are cooked at his own house?"

"I tasted some. Poor man, he is lucky he has not much appetite."

"When I walk in the hall, will I see him?"

"You will see his chamberlain and the people he has around him, but the Shah? No. He thinks The Judge very handsome. 'He has beautiful eyes,' he said. Well, he has. That child has the most interesting eyes I ever saw. His expression is serious, but his eyes laugh at me. His look is full of thoughts, but his eyes laugh. His eyes laugh at you, too."

"Did his eyes laugh at the Shah?"

"No. That was surprising. He looked at the Shah and his eyes did not laugh. It was the first time I saw his eyes serious."

What happened to Spain? Jed sent for Mildred's husband, Cappy, to go with him, they loved it, and returned. The next return was to New

York. Two weeks after The Judge was born, the stock market crashed. Everything had been soaring, then thud. To get on a boat to go home was hard.

"Get home," cabled everybody's business guide, but couldn't say how.

"Down, down, down goes everything," screamed the papers. What boat left next? How to get aboard?

My phone rang. "Mr. Stanton Griffis to see you."

My heart stopped. How did he know? Should I refuse to see him? Should I see him and trust him? "Let him come up."

"How did you know I was here?"

"While I was waiting, the nurse took a call and I looked over her shoulder at the reception desk list and read: 'Mrs. Kelly.' "

"Does everyone know?"

"No. There's talk and questions, but no one *I* know knows. How are you?"

"Great. Please don't say anything."

"Not if you don't want me to."

"I don't."

He'd brought flowers for me, angora sweater and hood for the baby.

"I'm hoping to sail tomorrow morning. You've heard?"

"Yes."

"Anything I can do?"

"Jed's trying to get on a boat."

"Tell him he can share my cabin, if he needs to."

He didn't need to; he got one.

*"Le bébé, quand peut-il voyager à New York?"* I asked Dr. Bouffe.

When he was a month old, he went down to the passport office, Boulevard des Italiens. Mlle. Valentin put on his long batiste dress and crepe de Chine coat.

*"Quel bébé! Quel enfant!"* The photographer was enraptured. *"Pourquoi un passport, Madame?"*

Mlle. Valentin told him the father was in the diplomatic corps and they would perhaps travel. "No need to tell everything," she told me.

The Judge came home drowsy. Why not? His only other time out had been to visit the Shah.

At the American embassy, Dr. Gros filled out the papers, and arranged for only nurse and baby to show up. Across the photo, where it says, "Bearer of the passport," Dr. Gros wrote: "Jones Kelly. American citizen. 4 weeks old."

Andrée Valentin said it would be good for me to stay at the American Hospital a month. No hurry, no rush, everything serene, food great, I could think and wonder and plan. Things happen you don't plan for; Andrée ushered in the staff doctor.

"That baby has to have a hernia operation."

"What!"

"The baby has to have a hernia operation."

Andrée stood behind the staff doctor, looking serious.

"Do you wish us to choose the surgeon?"

I didn't even know what a hernia was. "Who is the best?"

"Do you wish Dr. de Martel?"

Andrée nodded.

"Yes."

Six weeks old. I watched him being wheeled into the elevator, Andrée at his side.

"It isn't a serious operation," she said, "only for a kid that young. You can't take your eyes off them."

How many hours did she sit beside his crib? Ate something, but with eyes on The Judge. "In the operating room all the students are allowed when Dr. de Martel operates. He is our greatest, Dr. Thiérry de Martel. Everybody with white masks, all standing around like an amphitheatre, all the lights, The Judge the center, he looked so little. Dr. de Martel came in. All the students bowed. Dr. de Martel bowed, then looked at The Judge. 'What a moving experience,' he said. 'Who knows? This could be Victor Hugo.' I *like* that man. He is not only the greatest, but he has some feeling."

Monsieur Harris was leaving 67 Boulevard Lannes. Bags packed, labels read "First Class," the cabin number, the deck, the ship, the destination, the date. To travel by ship there's a lot to do, plus figuring tips, end of the trip.

Élise rushed out to the Boulevard Flandrin for a taxi by the entrance to the Métro. Jed, Mildred, Cappy and I drove off to the Gare St. Lazare. He'd forgotten to bring his mother something; I gave him my string of amethysts Harpo had given me last Christmas. Harpo's present, but I chose them. Each Christmas he and I exchanged presents, then met the next day and together exchanged them for something we wanted.

"Think about coming home. You'll hear from me." He kissed me. Then he kissed Mildred. The train started, he leaned out till it was lost from sight. I thought he should have kissed me *after* he kissed Mildred. Do you look for trouble?

Out at the American Hospital, where the Shah and The Judge were in residence, it was goodbye. The Judge looked beautiful, eyes gray, no longer blue, worn-out hair now growing in. Goodbye, but not for long. Mlle. Valentin and he would come to New York, but that had to be arranged for. Secrets take their time. A two-month-old baby has to have things right for him. Here he was in a beautiful room, the hospital garden was good for a breather. In New York, arrangements must be made, no questions asked, and find the perfect doctor. Also find a part in a play, things cost money.

Goodbye to 67; the grand Vuitton trunk had gone. It had cost two hundred dollars, made to order *chez* Vuitton, Champs Élysées. Pearl Swope said it was the greatest luggage. During lunch hour when I went in, old Monsieur Vuitton was alone in the store. He wrote the order in his book: "Madame Ruth Kelly." Every trunk they made was in the book, a sketch and description. That had been in June, soon after Dr. Gray was sure I'd manage. Had I?

Early morning boat train rushed through the frozen land between Paris and Cherbourg, pulled up along the dock. A sign said:

**CARMANIA DELAYED**
**SAILING TOMORROW**

Ever spend the night in Cherbourg? In December? As guest of the Cunard Line? Everybody was assigned a room at the hotel by the dock. It looked like a barracks. I felt scared, alone.

"You and Mildred share a room; I'll take the single," said Cappy.

Knock knock! "Five o'clock. *Carmania* will sail five-thirty."

The bags had all gone direct to the ship. Mess hall poured a bitter black something, passed out Cunard croissants and, "All aboard!"

A December crossing is anybody's business; ours was smooth. Long, but smooth. Nobody on board we knew, nobody who knew us. We played three-handed bridge and looked for icebergs.

"Only in summer," they said. And *finally* they said, "Halifax tomorrow."

Ever tie up at Halifax? The twenty-second of December? It was like a scene that went too far. You couldn't believe a word of it. Icicles like spears, iced ropes, iced docks, iced decks, iced gangplank. A country of

249

ice and snow, colder than the Dakotas.

No customs on the dock for Americans, customs when you cross the U.S. border. The ship would continue on to New York, but to throw off reporters we took a train to Montreal. It ambled through Nova Scotia, New Brunswick. How long can scenery stay the same? However long it takes; *then* Montreal! Spend the night and Christmas Eve take the sleeper to New York, Jed's strategy to throw reporters off.

Cappy and Mildred and I squeezed into a sleigh. Under the buffalo rug we rode up Mount Royal, came back and ate grand food at the Ritz. Went sightseeing on Catherine Street, went in Mappin and Webb's and Jaeger's we'd known in London, then ran out of money. I took my passport and a Guaranty Trust checkbook, and went to the hotel manager's office.

A bearded gentleman asked me to sit down.

"I'm back from Europe and my letter of credit is used up. So are my traveler's checks, but I have an account at the Guaranty Trust on Fifth Avenue in New York and here's my checkbook to show my balance."

"Do you want to cash a check?" he asked.

"Yes, I do."

"Well, why didn't you say so?"

He cashed my check for a hundred and fifty dollars. Why shouldn't he? When he did I felt successful.

Customs man was ready at the station, so we needn't be wakened at the border. I showed him my Irene Dana coats, dresses, beautiful Chéruit pink tulle with the green sash, black lace Chéruit, shorter in front, blue and pink grosgrain belt, Persian-printed velvet day dress with short drawers to go under it edged with matching velvet, my wraparound black faille with red coin dots, all from Chéruit, Place Vendôme. Splurge like Anita Loos! What a pleasure to order, to have a waistline! Even to pay duty, and see them again in the Montreal station.

# Chapter

————⋯⋅◦⟨∞⟩◦⋅⋯————

# 11

N
ew York!
36 West 59th Street!
Jed was living at the Madison Hotel at Fifty-eighth and Madison. Dinner in his sitting room, lobster Thermidor. Why was that?

"The Guild wants you for Phil Barry's play *Hotel Universe.* It's not right
yet, but you should do it."

I'd never been with the Theatre Guild. They did plays that maybe no
other manager would do, their subscription was for three weeks, they
didn't pay as much salary as other managers, but it was impressive to
say you were in a Guild play and Phil Barry wrote beautiful comedies.
Not always hits, but always his. Always his own man. His *Holiday* was
a great success for Arthur, his *Paris Bound* the year before that.

"This one *would* be his best," said Jed, "but he won't wait to get it
right."

"Why?"

"He says he has to have a play on every season and it's December.
He wants it on. *He* doesn't think it's right, either, but he thinks he can

251

get it right in rehearsal. It's not that kind of a play. I let it go and the Guild bought it."

They paid me five hundred dollars a week. No one featured in a Guild play, not even the Lunts. Philip Moeller would direct.

"He won't know what it's about, but you have to do it," said Jed.

Lee Simonson did the scenery, a terrace, south of France. Did I play Dorothy Parker? That's what they said. The part was Lily Malone, an actress who cut her wrists a lot and wore diamond bracelets to cover the scars.

First rehearsal was Sunday. They hadn't signed my contract. The Guild wasn't businesslike; a contract got signed sometime or other.

"I won't rehearse," I told the Guild.

"You have to," they said.

"My run-of-the-play contract isn't signed; you could fire me."

"We won't."

Would I take a chance on myself?

"It's the weekend. Terry's in Westport, Lawrence is God knows where, Warren is—"

"I'll take a chance."

"Sunday afternoon, Guild Theatre rehearsal room."

Now the Guild Theatre is the ANTA.

Take a chance. *Really* take a chance—go looking awful? A part that's supposed to look chic, look awful and *see* if you'll be wonderful? Put it to the test. Dyed black dress with no jewelry and what would look *really* terrible would be my brown hat. Brown hat, dyed black dress, no jewelry, brown shoes with black stockings, I showed up at rehearsal looking like a freak. All wasted; the Guild never knew what anybody had on. Lawrence Langner noticed if you were a pretty girl, but I could have looked like Gaby Deslys and Phil Moeller wouldn't know it. Nor Helen Westley, who *normally* dressed the way I looked today. Nor banker Maurice Wertheim, nor Terry Helburn, nor Lee Simonson, whose admiration was the scenery of Appia.

Theresa Helburn, Lawrence Langner, Lee Simonson, Maurice Wertheim, Helen Westley sat back to the windows behind Phil's table and chair. They were the Theatre Guild board. Assistant to Phil, Herbert Biberman, sat next to Phil. Facing them, in a semicircle, sat Glenn Anders, Phyllis Povah, Ruthelma Stevens, Franchot Tone, Earle Larimore, Katherine Alexander, Morris Carnovsky, Gustav Roland and I. Wandering in back of us was Phil Barry, doubtful, talented, terrified.

"We'll read," said Phil Moeller.

That's all I remember.

Next day, my contract was signed, I wasn't fired, and I was late for rehearsal for the only time in my life. I walked straight up to Phil. "Will you marry me? It made me late trying to get the courage to ask you."

"Yes," he said. We hugged and kissed and loved each other forever after. It was an admiration affair, not sex.

Rehearsing a scene, Phil would sidle up to me. "Are you all right?" he'd whisper.

"Yes," I'd whisper back.

"Y' know what you're doing?"

"Yes."

"Good."

*He* didn't know, but trusted me. He and Guth, though Guth *also* knew what I was doing.

All day, *terrible* fights. The Guild, so full of prestige, and where else were there such fights?

"When you say that, dear, you're crying," said Phil Moeller. I started to think about tears.

"When she says that, she's laughing," said Phil Barry. If the rehearsal room split in two and a white horse drove out, Phil Moeller couldn't have looked more astonished; then he shrugged. "Well, you wrote it, so you ought to know."

On it went.

The first place we played was Newark, a routine place to open, or Brooklyn at the Shubert Montauk or the theatre in Stamford. At Newark it went well enough.

"Changes needed," said Rouben Mamoulian, who directed for the Guild and came over to take a look.

What changes? Nobody quite knew, and we went to Buffalo.

Franchot Tone invited the company to his home right by Niagara Falls. Pretty distracting; I liked the Buffalo Statler better.

Terry Helburn and Lawrence Langner came up to see where Phil's rewriting had gotten us. After rehearsal, Terry stopped me. "Oh, Ruth, I'm catching the midnight, so tonight when you start to do the dance and turn your ankle, really do a dance and then break down. Let me see it tonight."

Phil's Lily Malone had started as a ballerina who hated her father because he drove her so hard—nothing but lessons, lessons, up on your points! Going back into Lily's memories, the "Naïla" ballet record came on and instead of doing just one step, then an ankle twist, I'd have to go back into *my* memories and do a dance. Try my Dorothy Quincy dance I did in Mrs. Frost's pageant at the Wollaston Unitarian Church? My "To a Wild Rose" dance I did at the charity affair on Mrs. Faxon's lawn? For Lily Malone? Never mind was she Dotty Parker; she was written as someone entertaining. What dance would *she* do tonight? Would she do a version of the Charleston routine Harpo taught Myra and Gregory and me to do at Woollcott's birthday party? Woollcott forgot to ask for it. I tried the Charleston routine to the "Naïla" ballet and did my Kosloff gestures.

"That dance is good," said Terry. "Keep it in. I didn't know you were a ballet dancer."

Only one slip-up. I forgot Harpo was coming opening night. The Theatre Guild first-nighters, Phil Barry's swell friends filled the Martin Beck Theatre. Harpo on the aisle, row C, said he thought he'd piss himself!

Eight months old, The Judge steamed up the Hudson on the *Île de France.* Some days after, he crossed *under* the Hudson to meet his grandmother. In their room at the Plaza Hotel, Andrée dressed him in a white piqué suit from the Faubourg St. Honoré, elegant white piqué coat with bonnet to match. He held up a hand, she slipped on a white cotton glove, he held up the other. Did he think they were off to the Bois, where babies in prams waved gloved hands at each other?

Whatever he thought, anybody would have to think a lot of *him.* Beautiful dark hair poking out from under the bonnet, Palm Beach coloring that set off his big eyes, lashes to make anyone envious. At the 58th Street entrance, his father's limousine waited to take The Judge to Newark with his Aunt Mildred. Andrée Valentin and I kissed him. He waved his gloved hand with a jaunty air and no regret.

*"Sois sage, Coco!"* Andrée reminded him. It was their first parting.

June was getting close to July. He'd summer in Greenwich at the Kent House, overlooking Long Island Sound. Pearl Swope knew about it. I went out to look. Pearl was right; it was perfect.

Andrée liked it. Jed liked it. The Judge liked it, but he liked everything. Aunt Mildred liked it and Cappy did, so did Aunt Florence and Aunt Sylvia. So would anybody, because when, on rare occasions, Pearl Swope said a thing was perfect, it was.

The notice was up at the Martin Beck. *Hotel Universe* was going to close. Probably Jed was right—it should have had more thought, a play to meditate over.

*Who's Who* could have meditated too. In how many editions did it say I played "the part of Idly Malone in *Hotel Universe*"? Either you get things right or you don't.

Someone who gets things right is Helen Hayes. "Come visit us in California. Charlie and Ben are going to work on *Rasputin*. Charlie's rented a big house in Beverly Hills and we can see all the movie stars."

The Judge and Andrée were content and thriving in Greenwich. What was Jed doing? He said to go, he'd follow.

"I'll come."

At 6 P.M. the *Twentieth Century* slid out of Grand Central, smooth as a pussy willow. Hardly a sound. They rolled up the red carpet from the Pullmans to the gate. What a train! What porters! What service! What peach ice cream in the summer! Averell Harriman liked peach ice cream and he had his say about running the New York Central.

At nine next morning, the *Century* slid into Chicago. Step off and get pushed, shoved, shouted at. La Salle Street Station must have studied with Paris.

In Chicago, July is hot, but not too hot to look in the Michigan Avenue windows. Past the Congress Hotel, where we stayed when *Seventeen* came back to Chicago and played the Chicago subway circuit. Past the street where next to the Congress side entrance was Moffatt, who took sepia pictures of stars. I posed in my beaver coat, big floppy velvet hat I got married in. For a few poses I borrowed a friend's Japanese spaniel. He helped me look like a star.

Look in at the Auditorium Hotel. Two hot weeks in 1916 I'd stayed there on my first visit to Chicago with the Maude Adams Company; now it's Roosevelt University. Next to it, the Fine Arts Building, where Mrs. Coonley-Ward invited Aggie and Lillian Ross and Bea Maude and Judith Lowry and me to bland dinners at the Fine Arts Club on top of the building. In the lobby, the entrance to the impressive Studebaker Theatre; at the far end, the entrance to the Playhouse, where *Seventeen* had played.

Hurry past the Stratford Hotel. The columns of the People's Gas Building, where Dr. Ryerson had his office. Where I'd persuaded him to operate on me.

"I'm not a beauty doctor."

"But I'm bowlegged."

"Why, I saw your play. I didn't notice!"

"But *I* notice it; it's all I think of. Every looking glass, every window I look to see if it shows."

" 'Jim has bowlegs,' we said in college, and that meant he was *strong.*"

"It's different if you're an actress. I can't think of anything else. What if I get a part where I have to wear a ballet skirt?"

"When do you want it done?"

"When can you do it?"

He looked at his book. "December twenty-first."

Five years before, on December 21, was the opening night of *Peter Pan.*

Like the *Twentieth Century,* but with its own personality, Santa Fe's *Chief* was also great. Food you loved, polite porters, and passing by the windows, geography. The *Chief* made its first stop, then rolled slowly across the Mississippi River into southern Iowa and stopped at Fort Madison—get out and walk up and down. When was the last time I walked in Iowa? What show? Actors go to Iowa only with a show or if their families live there. My last time was when *Clarence* played Burlington in the late summer of 1919. Today was 1930, July.

All aboard, the *Chief* picked up speed and rushed through Missouri woods and cornfields. "First call for dinner." After dinner, out of the night shone Kansas City. Everybody out, walk around the cavernous station, see trains for Arkansas, Oklahoma. Those and Montana are the only states I've never been in.

I bought a postcard of Kansas City's grand Muehlebach Hotel, where we stayed when we played *Seventeen* and had our photos made by Strauss-Peyton in the lobby. Men's pictures were all the same and girls were loaned the huge white ostrich feather fan for some poses, for others a real American beauty rose, for others Peyton showed you just how to hold your hands. No matter what you looked like, in a Strauss-Peyton taken by Peyton you came out a beauty. There was no Strauss anymore. In *Clarence,* we bought the back cover of *Variety* and used our Strauss-Peyton photographs. Beneath me with the rose and Gregory looking a vision ran excerpts from our great notices. What Ashton Stevens said, what Percy Hammond, Amy Leslie, Doc Hall, Charley Collins. The ad cost a hundred and fifty dollars—a pleasure to see on the stands! A pleasure to mail around.

The *Chief* pulled out of Kansas City and tore across Kansas as though it never heard of an accident. They put on another engine and toiled up the Rockies to Trinidad. Everybody out to walk up and down and exclaim at the air. The train rested. At Raton, everybody out again while the train rested some more, then wound cautiously down to Albuquerque, twenty-minute rest. Passengers for Santa Fe made their connections.

Across the border to Arizona. At Winslow walk up and down in some more clean air. At Flagstaff everybody who hadn't gone to bed got out and got right back in. Cold. The *Chief* started down. Down some more, down, then clunk, grind, stop, shake, the sign said Barstow. Cars unhitched and hooked on the train going north to San Francisco.

"Open your window?" asked the porter. The *Chief* lolled through seven million orange trees, some in blossom, some with fruit.

People who know get off at Pasadena and drive to Beverly Hills, but I didn't know. The MacArthurs' car met me at Los Angeles' Union Station and drove me to Beverly Hills, Camden Drive, 810, a big white Spanish house rented from Marie Prevost, movie star!

"Tonight we're going to a grand party," said Helen. "Billy Haines has a new house and he's asked *everybody!* Dinner is with place cards, but he didn't know about you, so we'll have dinner here first, then go."

Charlie drove us off into the night.

A maid opened the door, voices, voices, voices all talking at once. Helen leaned over the balcony rail, looked down on endless small tables, centerpieces of piled-high gardenias lit by candlelight. "Hello," she called, and waved. It was terrifying; everybody looked beautiful. Pearls and chiffon and white arms, lace, tulle, everything expensive. My Chéruit dress was expensive, but too sedate.

"This is Ruth Gordon," said Helen.

Pretty faces, beautiful faces, handsome faces, famous faces looked up and called, "Hello."

Why not ease in *unnoticed?* I guess Helen figured why should we? In *Coquette* she had made a bigger hit than anybody, Charlie was coauthor of *The Front Page,* I'd made a hit in *Hotel Universe.*

Billy Haines made room for us at his table. "Ruth, this is Lil Tashman." *Ziegfeld Follies* beauty, now in the movies.

She looked at me. "What did I hear about you?"

"I was just in *Hotel Universe.*"

"What did I hear?" Beautiful Lil Tashman looked over some facts scattered through her blond head. A play wasn't one of them. *"What* did I hear?"

Helen broke in. "This is Mrs. Patrick Campbell, Ruth."

The great Mrs. Pat!

"Are you sort of bad?" Lil asked me.

"Isn't everybody?" put in Mrs. Pat. She must have been great in comedy. Everybody laughed.

"What was the divine play you were in?" asked Joan Crawford.

*"Serena Blandish."*

"No, *Hotel* something."

*"Hotel Universe.* We just closed."

"That's ridiculous. What did they close it for?" asked Joan. "Do you know Eddie Lowe?"

"Hello."

"He's my husband," said Lil. "What do I know about you?" Her beautiful white fragile face looked hard at me.

"Ruth, this is Polly Moran."

Maybe she'd talk and stop those questions.

"Let's go upstairs," said our host.

Jeanette MacDonald held out her arms to him. "Let me hug you."

"Watch that arm-white—I rented the suit." He took us on a tour. In his bedroom, Lil was sitting by the bed. *"What* did somebody tell me about you?"

"Why do you keep saying that, my dear?" asked Mrs. Pat from the small sofa by the fireplace. "It doesn't add to the gaiety of nations."

"It would if I could think. She's *bad,* really bad."

Luck came with me to Beverly Hills. Charlie felt like fighting David Selznick.

"We have to go," said Helen.

Should I go back to New York?

"Look up, not down," believed our Unitarian Church Lend-a-Hand Society. "Look out, not in. Lend a hand."

The phone rang. It was Jed. He asked Helen if he could come out. "Yes," she said.

In September he was going to star her in Liam O'Flaherty's *Mr. Gilhooley.* So far nothing in sight for me.

> Look up, not down,
> Look out, not in.

Look out for Lilyan Tashman, improve at miniature golf. Every evening Helen and Charlie, Jed and I played the course back of the Beverly Wilshire Hotel. Some afternoons Helen and I walked down to practice.

One Sunday afternoon, we drove down to Ernst Lubitsch's in Santa

Monica. Jed admired Lubitsch's films so much he came with us. Some people go out and some don't. Everybody worked hard, but nothing worked. A dreadful afternoon!

"I'll never urge Jed to do anything again," said Helen. "He really *tried,* but he's like Garbo. They say she really can't go anywhere."

Jed was going back to New York and urged me to fly with him. I'd never flown and was scared to. And scared not to.

"Take a short flight before," advised Helen.

Charlie twisted his forelock. "How about Tijuana for the weekend?"

Fly down Saturday afternoon, have dinner, gamble, not gamble, next day go to the races, fly back Sunday night, Monday morning take the plane to Kansas City, Pullman to Chicago, morning plane to Newark. Only the mail planes flew at night; all passengers went by train.

First time on an airplane. The first one I saw fly was in 1912 at the Squantum Aviation Meet; now I was flying to Tijuana! I wasn't afraid. Down at San Diego for the border officials to see that we weren't smuggling plants or seeds, up again and down at Tijuana.

"Look," said Helen.

I turned. Her pointed finger caught my nose and opened a blood vessel. I left the airport bleeding, but I'd flown!

We were shown to two bungalows in the hotel garden, we strolled around, then Helen and I unpacked and went to find Charlie and Jed. Dinner, what became of the evening?

Next afternoon, to the races. Mexican horses ran contrary; I lost. Helen and I packed. Jed and Charlie paid the bill.

"Taxi."

"Where to?"

"Airport."

"Last plane went."

"What!"

"Border closes five P.M."

"But we have to take the morning plane to Kansas City."

"Sorry!"

Charlie twisted his forelock. "Could you drive us to Los Angeles?"

The taxi man laughed.

"Could you?"

Anything outlandish interested Jed. "Let's go." He shoved me toward the cab.

The taxi man got practical.

"Only to the border."

"What then?"

"You like go San Diego get plane?"

"Yes."

"Get in. Taxi meet you other side of border, go San Diego." He went to a phone, came back. "Get in."

After a while, the taxi left the road and took off across a field.

"Where are we going?" asked Charlie.

"Border," said taxi, and bumped on till he came to a barbed-wire fence. "Out." He pointed through the barbed wire to a beat-up gray car.

Charlie twisted his forelock. Helen and I were two five-foot question marks. Jed decided to go.

"How do we know who he *is?*" I asked Jed.

"We don't. San Diego?" he asked the gray car.

The driver pulled two sagging barbed wires apart and we crawled through. The Tijuana taximan threw our suitcases after us. In time, we rattled into San Diego. The airport was closed.

"Closed?" asked Jed, fiercely.

"Closed. Nothing out till morning." No debate.

Would gray, beat-up drive us to L.A.?

Dubious, but he would.

Gray car took off. Gray car's brake was bad. "It won't go. You owe me—"

We paid. Was it bad or was he sick of us? Now what? An elderly couple were getting into a sedan. "Where y' going?"

"L.A."

"Hop in."

"Hop in?"

"That's where *we're* going. Y' won't get a car this time of night."

Helen, Charlie, Jed and I squeezed into the back seat. Suitcases on our knees or under our feet. We could only feel, not see. All around us thick fog had set in. What did our host use for eyes?

"How can you see?" asked Helen.

"I'm the sheriff."

Not a direct answer, but it made us feel safer.

Midnight came, went, the fog didn't change. Our plane was scheduled to leave Burbank at 6 A.M. Had we packed? Of course not.

"Our lay-ast auto trip was to the Gray-and Canyon," said the sheriff's wife. She had a voice that made me think of cracked dishes. "Bears roamin' loose, one big brown feller loosened up our trunk and the rascal hay-ad his paw in our jar of honey. They go for tourist food. When he

saw us comin' he just looked as much as to say, 'What d *'yew* want?' An'
it was *ow-er* honey."

"I was glad he didn' tackle *me,*" said the sheriff.

"Oh, he wouldn't; they're jes' nice. They *like* tourists. Give 'em nice
stuff to eat."

It was 5 A.M. when they drove up Camden Drive into the driveway.

"Cancel the plane," counseled Charlie. "Go tomorrow."

We did. The sheriff and wife came in and sat down awhile, not to put
too abrupt an end to our friendship.

Next day no breakfast. At 6 A.M. the plane zoomed up. Shortly after,
corned beef sandwiches and pickles were passed. Some of us are only
human; I threw up. Even if the plane hadn't fallen all over the sky I'd
have been sick.

Across the aisle, Jed occasionally turned a disgusted glance at me
holding the container. What did I care? There's a time to be dazzling and
sexy, but not when a plane tosses, leaps, falls, shivers, shakes. If I had
to die, all right, so long as it stopped. If I lived I promised God never
to fly again. What can you do if you're a liar? First the temperance
pledge, but since then I've had a few; now I promise God, but I'm up
in the air time and time again. Maybe biblical times you could stick to
the truth, but did they?

The plane came down at Wichita. Why not stay there? Jed bought a
paper and got back on the plane. I tagged along. Between Wichita and
Kansas City we shot the rapids. Not a doubt but what we were doomed.
It got dark, from the wing I noticed flame. It was exhaust, but how
would I know? They pass out corned beef sandwiches, but don't discuss
a flame.

Kansas City, down we came, taxi to the train for Chicago.

"I'm never going on one again," I told Jed.

"What's the matter?"

How obtuse can you be! "In Chicago, I'll take the *Century,*" I said.

"I will too. I don't like Newark."


Connecticut had agreed with The Judge. He laughed and pulled himself up in his playpen on the rolling Kent House lawn.

"He's bright, that kid!" said Andrée.

At a compliment, he jumped up and down.

"He never cries. He's good, that kid."

He looked happy and beautiful.

"Does he eat all right?"

261

"That kid likes good food!"

Everything at the Kent House was good and people weren't nosy. For visits to Dr. Schloss, a car and driver brought Andrée and The Judge to New York.

"That kid is healthy. Dr. Schloss was pleased."

Jed had an apartment on Park Avenue. I went back to mine at 36 West 59th. Three French windows opening onto Central Park made it cooler but in the summer *all* New York is hot.

"Hold for Arrival" was written on the envelope from Thornton Wilder. I'd picked him up in front of the Booth Theatre at *Uncle Vanya*. What luck it's a play with intermissions!

> Dear Bella,
>     Here are four empty sheets of paper. Enough to write the Gettysburg Address. Enough to write "To be or not to be." Enough to write the Twenty-third Psalm.
>     What will *you* write? The same with your day, what will you do with it? Make it memorable, regretful, wasted, fulfilled? Think it over.
>
>                                                                         T.

What I'd do with my day was find a job. Rent at 36 West 59th was a hundred and eighty-five dollars and fifty cents a month, a week at the Kent House was one hundred and forty dollars, Andrée's salary was eighty a week, Sarah Thorpe cooked and took care of the apartment for thirty-five. Then bills for food, phone, electricity. Find a job.

Find one, but there's no sure way *how*. Woollcott said Bayard Veiller took *Within the Law* to the Cohan and Harris office at 8 A.M. and it was closed. Al Woods was next, but still locked up; nobody at George C. Tyler's. Veiller turned down Broadway and went into the building at 41st Street. Edgar and Arch Selwyn's doors were closed, but general manager Crosby Gaige was so unimaginative he was at his desk.

"Here's a play," said Veiller.

Crosby read it. When the Selwyns showed up around eleven, Crosby had the contract made out for them to sign. *Within the Law* made Jane Cowl a star, the Selwyns' bank account shot way up, and all because Crosby Gaige came to work early.

That was how Jane Cowl got a part; how would I? The phone rang.

"Darling, ride out to Piping Rock. Laddy's polo team is playing," said the silky voice of rich *rich* Janie Sanford.

All the latest dresses, white flannels, blue jackets, but would *that* pay Andrée and Dr. Schloss and West 59th Street?

262

A voice from the next box. It was Gilbert Miller. "What are you doing, dear?"

"Watching Laddy play polo."

"No, dear, I mean have you got a play? I'm opening the Miller with Molnar's new comedy, *One, Two, Three,* with Arthur Byron, and I need a curtain raiser. Mind you, we're in rehearsal with one, but if I had you, I'd drop it and use Molnar's *The Violet.* Do you know it?"

How beautiful can conversation get!

"Any profession that did not offer me a berth after six weeks, I would not deem it wise to remain in," wrote Papa. Did he mean Piping Rock?

"Marvelous part for you, dear. You'd be marvelous! Francisca Gaal played it in Budapest. Molnar wrote the part for her, she scored an enormous hit. Where are you staying? I'll send it round. Did I tell you? Arthur Richman made the adaptation. Where do you live, dear?"

"36 West Fifty-ninth Street."

"I'll send it round in the morning. I have to know right away, dear."

*One, Two, Three* and *The Violet* opened at the Lyceum in Rochester. We were a hit. Arthur Byron was stupendous! So were our prospects. On Saturday, Miss Hattie in the box office made me a box of fudge and went down to the sleeper with me. She talked about the old days, all the performers that had pleased her. For each she made a box of fudge. We had played *Seventeen* there and *The First Year,* but *The Violet* was my first fudge.

Opening night at the Henry Miller Theatre, the curtain came down on *The Violet.* Applause, applause, applause. Through the pass-door came Gilbert, looking distracted. "My God, the curtain raiser went so great, can *One, Two, Three* follow it?" Then he glared at me. "I don't know whether to kiss you or kill you!"

I was sure of *One, Two, Three* and Arthur Byron; I rushed over to the Broadhurst, where Jed was rehearsing Helen in *Mr. Gilhooley.*

"How was it?"

"A hit."

That was as far as their interest went. Next morning's papers liked *The Violet* and slammed *One, Two, Three.*

"In the midst of life we are in death," was David Torrence's line as a church elder in *The Little Minister.* He could have been talking about show business, instead of trouble in the parish of Auld Licht.

The notice was up for *The Violet* and *One, Two, Three.* Every night Arthur Byron came early to talk while I made up. His aunt was the fabulous Ada Rehan. New York thought so, London thought so, Mr.

Sampson thought so. Arthur, as a little boy, thought so. He'd seen her act with John Drew in the Augustin Daly Company that Mr. Sampson had been a member of. "The perfect Katherine, incomparable as Rosalind, a triumph as Peggy in *A Country Girl,*" Mr. Sampson said. *A Country Girl* was the David Garrick version of Wycherley's *The Country Wife.* When the Daly Company played abroad, Mr. Sampson said, London and Paris loved her as much as did her native land. In my dressing room, Arthur Byron told about her and Daly's Theatre. I'd never seen her, but my first year in New York, I'd seen Arthur Byron in *The Boomerang.* Belasco starred him, Wallace Eddinger, Martha Hedman, Ruth Shepley. "Perfectly played by everyone," they said, but I thought Arthur Byron was best.

"Will you do the Theatre Guild play?" I asked. They'd made an offer to him and me. I didn't like my part and said no.

"Oh, no."

"Good part."

"No, I won't do it."

"Got something better?"

"No."

"Then why not?"

"I don't like The Theatre Guild."

I *did* like the Guild, but I knew what he meant. They came to a rehearsal after a company had rehearsed a week and whispered right through. If they saw Phil Barry *writing* a play, would they have whispered? Why do people feel actors can put up with stuff? They have and they can, but it doesn't make it easier.

"I worked with them once," said Arthur. "Once was enough."

A lot of actors felt that way and got over it. Did Helen Hayes? After the dress rehearsal of *Mary of Scotland* she was sitting onstage, the final curtain down. Terry Helburn rushed on. "Where's Helen?" Terry asked her.

Helen told me, *"I thought: She's so carried away with my performance as Mary she doesn't remember who I am. 'I'm Helen,' I said, and she said, 'Not you—I mean Helen Menken. Isn't she wonderful?"*

Life on the stage is hard. "In the midst of life we are in death."

*Midnight* opened without Arthur Byron and me and ran forty-eight performances.

On!

Darling Thornton,

I woke up this morning singing, "Oh you great big beautiful doll."
What would Goethe say? What would Heine? What would Miss Freud's
Pa?

Love,
Bella

P.S. Anxious!

The season waxed. When would I get an offer I wanted?

At the Kent House The Judge celebrated his first birthday. Up in his
room, we had the birthday cake from Dean's, the gorgeous Fifth Avenue
caterer, their shop where Rockefeller Plaza is now. After Rockefeller
Plaza came to be, Dean's moved to 57th Street, now Bonwit Teller's
Hermès boutique, then to East 54th Street, then to nowhere.

The birthday cake read: "Happy Birthday, Andrée, Jones, Mildred,
Cappy, Ruth." All of us with October birthdays, but we celebrated on
The Judge's, October 16. The Judge walked or maybe staggered. Several
heard him say "Mama." His Aunt Mildred and Andrée were convinced
he said "Papa." A great day, presents galore! Celebrating were Aunt
Sylvia, Aunt Florrie, Aunt Mildred, Uncle Cappy, Aunt Andrée and I.
Next move was to the Alden Hotel, Central Park West in the early
Eighties. The Kent House was closing its season.

Jed moved into 36 West 59th Street with me until he found a house
for us all. At the Alden, The Judge and Andrée had a sitting room and
a bedroom overlooking the park. The Judge had his toys, brought with
him from Au Nain Bleu, additions from F.A.O. Schwarz. Christmas came and Jed still hadn't found the house. At the Alden, a big
Christmas tree, ornaments bought at the Galeries Lafayette for that first
Christmas tree in Paris at l'Hôpital Américain. That had been a small
one; this went up to the ceiling. From F.A.O. Schwarz came lovely
ornaments and Mildred and I popped corn and strung it in garlands to
toss over the balsam branches the way Mama had done it in Wollaston.
Andrée made little bags of white tarlatan sewn with red yarn and
gathered with yarn strings. We filled them with candy to hang on the
branches. Striped candy canes dangled, up top was Père Noël from Paris,
wearing a long spun-glass skirt.

The Judge's grandmother held him up so he could give a gentle shove
to one certain blue tinsel ball he admired. He watched it swing back and
forth; when it stopped, he did it again. And again.

"Put him down, Mama," said Mildred.

"He likes it," said her mother.

Someone gave him a drum to beat.

"Give it to me, Coco," said Andrée.

He looked troubled, but did.

"Never give a child a toy that makes a noise," advised Andrée. "That's the one they like best."

Another The Judge liked was a wooden armchair Mildred gave him. He carried it around the room.

"Sit in it," said his aunt.

He looked surprised.

She showed him what she meant.

He tried it, then stood up and carried the chair around the room, wreathed in smiles.

Mornings he and Andrée went to Central Park. The Judge had outgrown his grand English Marmet carriage; he had a new go-cart. Andrée liked New York. She liked it because Altman's carried Dr. Deimel's Swiss underwear for babies; linen net that absorbed perspiration, and cut like a B.V.D. Also Dr. Deimel's fine flannel nightdrawers. She liked New York because Mrs. Sinsheimer, a former patient, lived at the St. Regis. Best of all she liked Dr. Oscar Schloss. "That kid's lucky to have *him* for his doctor."

January over, February over, no offers for a play, but Jed had found a beautiful five-story brownstone in a block of handsome houses on East 79th. All the houses are there today except his, number 135. It was an unfurnished sublet.

Kit's friend Mrs. Tonetti recommended Fred from Palisades to paint the rooms. He was doing it fine. Jed and I took a taxi to see Fred's work.

When Fred had painted everything beautifully, Jed moved in. He brought along with him his only possessions, his handsome maple four-poster bed, a magnificent desk and chair, a Vuitton trunk from Paris, the red lacquer chest from *The Royal Family.* Was the grand piano from *Coquette?* From the Alden came The Judge's crib, his chair he'd carried around, his Paris trunk, other acquisitions.

Jed and I went to auctions, got beautiful Lowestoft plates from the Rita d'Acosta Lydig collection, a blue morocco-bound *Life of Casanova,* endless volumes of the Babylonian Talmud.

Andrée's room was fourth floor front. The fourth-floor-front hall bedroom was The Judge's. My room was fourth floor back—the same floor on the garden side. Fred painted it sky blue. White linen drapes hung at the windows. Jed's room was beneath it, walls papered in Geodetic Survey maps, his fourposter with the four pineapples, his patchwork quilt. A fine maple chest of drawers we'd bought down Third Avenue. A chair or two from someplace.

Third floor front was the big library, books from the auctions there. Books, more books; books were constantly acquired. On the mantel over the fireplace, an early-American brass-trimmed wooden clock we'd bought at auction. Solid, a beauty, and kept time. Jed's massive flat walnut desk from the Rue Jacob in Paris stood between two windows looking out on East 79th, walnut armchair to match.

On the second floor, the drawing room furniture was the grand piano lit by two beautiful vivid blue French wall brackets belonging to the owner. They flanked Jed's gold-framed mirror over the fireplace and that was it. Margaret Bellinger made pale green satin damask ceiling-to-floor drapes that drew back over Brussels net curtains. Fred painted the walls white. It was like a room Turgenev might have described to Pauline Garcia.

The dining room, rear second floor, had a temporary table and chairs until we got the real ones. Jed told Fred to paint the walls sunshine yellow. No curtains. Dishes and food came up via the hand-pulled dumbwaiter. When it stuck, the maid rushed down the circular back stairs to the kitchen. It didn't stick very often and mostly we preferred trays in the library.

On the ground floor was a fine hall, curving staircase that started with a big crystal ball.

When Jed first took me to see the house, I said, "It's Ted Coy's house." After Clifton Webb's party at the Sixty Club, Jeanne Eagels and Ted Coy had invited Gregory and me to come back to his house. When he unlocked the front door, the first thing I had seen had been the crystal ball. Now neither the crystal ball nor anybody could tell where poor Ted Coy was.

The Judge, Andrée and I were moving in. Sarah Thorpe came with me to cook. A maid was recommended by Helen Stallings. Did Helen know she was partial to gin? We didn't. One day, under the influence, she sneaked The Judge over to show him to Mrs. Stallings. When fired, she rubbed number two all over the front door. Then the next night did it again!

Jed engaged a detective to stand across the street all night. His report read: "At 11:15 Mr. Harris came in with a girl. No one used the door again."

The "girl" was good at setting up a house. One of my gifts.

Summer. Jed was going to produce *Wonder Boy*. A rumpled copy of *The Church Mouse* was sent me by William A. Brady. Why rumpled? That was the Brady office. His help was Miss Healy, great, but could she do it all? Sometimes a script got rumpled.

The play was no good, but the part was.

"Do it," said Thornton.

Jed read it. "Thornton's crazy."

"Do it," said Thornton. "Seventy-ninth Street is loaded with perfectionists. Say yes, then you and I get in the car and Isabel'll drive us up to New Hampshire, clear our heads, come back full of zest."

Isabel is Thornton's sister.

JAFFREY the sign said. I hadn't been there since the week with Auntie Etta and Auntie Sue in 1910. "Want to stop for tea?" On the veranda of the Shattuck House, folks rocked and stared. The old hotel clerk said, "We don't serve tea." The old bellboy glared.

On to Peterborough and the MacDowell Colony. Isabel turned into a driveway and stopped. A gardener was leaning on his rake.

Thornton leaned out. "Do you remember me? I'm Thornton Wilder. I was in Oriole Cottage."

Light broke. "Why, how *are* ya, Mr. Wilder! How are ya?"

"Finely." Thornton beamed.

As we drove away, I asked, "Is 'finely' right?"

"Oh, no. I just wanted to make him feel comfortable."

We drove along a winding driveway. Thornton showed me the cabin where he had written *The Bridge of San Luis Rey*. At lunchtime, they put a tray in the open window so as not to disturb thought. We stopped at Edwin Arlington Robinson's. He came out and was pleasant. We left, drove into town and took rooms at the Peterborough Inn.

Sunday morning, we drove out to a pine grove. Thornton read his one-act play aloud. Isabel and I sat on a log, Thornton sat on a big rock and read. Why didn't I like it? Could New Hampshire air be *too* clear?

In the evening, we drove over to Mrs. MacDowell's Sunday night supper. The writers came from their cabins, Mrs. MacDowell greeted them in a long no-period dress, gauze scarf thrown around her throat, cut-steel bead tassel at each end. Supper was cocoa and jelly sandwiches. Is that what Mr. MacDowell had Sunday nights? Is that what he composed "To a Wild Rose" on? Would he have liked the dance I did to it at the Quincy Hospital Benefit Pageant on the Henry Faxons' sweeping lawn?

On the drive home from New Hampshire, sharing the rumble seat with Thornton, wisdom flowed from Peterborough to Northampton, flowed through dinner at the Wiggin Inn. Think it over, then sleep. Next morning wisdom flowed down the Saw Mill River to East 79th Street. Wisdom, confidence. " 'The arrow wants to reach its target,' Bella. Don't stand in the *way*."

Rehearsals were in the rehearsal room at Mr. Brady's Playhouse on West 48th Street. No new-fashioned reading around a table; we got on our feet and did the play. Author Ladislaus Fodor was not around.

"Who adapted it, Mr. Brady?"

He looked to see who was listening, put his hand over his mouth and whispered, "Frederick and Fanny Hatton, but don't tell anyone or that'll be our first knock."

Talk about discouraged! What a play! What was Thornton thinking of!

"I told you so," said Jed.

*Oct. 7, 1931*
*Hotel Niumalu*
*Honolulu, T.H.*

Dearest daughter,

I am so glad you at last found a play you like and I hope your leading man turns out better than you anticipate. Things happen like that. I sometimes signed on with a skipper I didn't relish then he turned out well enough. This letter will reach you about the time your play opens and brings my best wishes for your success. I shall be glad to hear what the *Times* has about you and *A Church Mouse*.

I read the book *Bridge of San Luis Rey* of Wilder's and liked it and have started to read *Cabala*. I have been in Lima a number of times going there from Callao which is the port nearest to Lima which is inland about sixteen or eighteen miles as I remember it. I saw my first bullfight there which I thought was very exciting.

The weather must be getting better for you than when it was so hot. I have worried because you have not been away this summer and it has been such a hot one. I went to see Will Rogers in a picture that was very funny last week. Today I have been to the Navy Yard at Pearl Harbor and had a good time. I should like to see the bridge across the Hudson. From the pictures, it must be a marvel. I don't suppose you care much about those things.

Take good care of yourself and don't get shot up or anything and don't forget to write often. I am well and getting quite a bit of fun out of life.

Thanks for the clippings.

Much love,

Father

"Fix up your part," said Ralph Nairn. He'd played the wonder-butler in *The Play's the Thing*. *"You must."*

Somebody had to. It was the first writing I ever did on a play.

Over the Playhouse the sign read: A CHURCH MOUSE.

"Did you change the title, Mr. Brady?"

"Yes, to come first in the ABC listing."

I told Jed.

"Tell Brady maybe I'll call *Wonder Boy* 'A Alte Wonder Boy.' "

Brady nodded. "If they do, I'll change it to 'A A-One Alte Church Mouse.' It's going to be first."

In Central Park, The Judge spoke his first sentence. He was carrying his favorite three poker chips, a red, a white, a blue, a boy snatched them out of his hand, he looked at Andrée, aghast. "Bad boy takes pretty bundins. Shock-*ing!"*

Once he got the idea, his comments multiplied. At the orthopedic shoe store a little boy howled.

Jones studied him, then commented to Andrée, *"Vilain garçon!"*

They were going to sail back on the same ship, the *Île de France*. We couldn't get another renewal of Andrée's visa. No use to try for the quota; it was small and always full. Andrée had to go and where would we find someone good? The Home Bureau recommended by Dr. Schloss didn't come up with an ace. What if Jones went back with Andrée? It would only be temporary.

Andrée's friend Miss Earle knew of an excellent *pension,* number 5 Rue des Belles Feuilles, a few steps from Avenue Victor Hugo where the bee had buzzed round in the *pâtissier's* window. It was also near the Rond-Point de Longchamp, where there was a toy store Jones loved; also near enough to walk to the Bois.

Goodbye again. I had to play the matinee, so Jed's lawyer, Joe Bickerton, who had met them, would bid them bon voyage. The embassy passport that Dr. Gros had arranged had not run out; he still would travel as Master Jones Kelly. For the passage over, his fare was sixteen dollars, the rate for a passenger under one year old traveling first class. For the return trip the fare was increased to half rate. The week after his second birthday, he embarked on his second Atlantic crossing. He waved goodbye and got in his papa's car. Going places made him merry; dark eyes sparkled, Palm Beach coloring grew more vivid. The car turned onto Park Avenue. I took a taxi to the Playhouse.

By the time the matinee was over, the *Île de France* had cleared Sandy Hook, had dropped off her pilot, next stop Le Havre. The same *Île de France,* the same Le Havre where I'd met Jed that May morning of Pentecost.

*A Church Mouse* got roasted, but played at Mr. Brady's Playhouse through the winter. *Wonder Boy* closed.

The author was astonished. "Every minute was so perfect."

"The trouble wasn't with the minutes," said Jed. "The *hour* hand was wrong."

Nothing was wrong at 5 Rue des Belles Feuilles. Andrée's letter said the crossing had been exceptional, The Judge had seen his first movie, a silent with titles. "When the picture stopped for the title to come on, he shouted, *'More!* Do again!'"

*A Church Mouse* closed when the weather got warm. I went up to Mount Vernon and played it a week in Chamberlain Brown's stock company. Every night, Louise Groody rode up with me on the train. She was going to play *A Church Mouse* in some other Chamberlain Brown stock company productions. Star of *The Night Boat* at Mr. Dillingham's Globe Theatre, star of *Hit the Deck!* at the Belasco.

A hard life, but maybe her mother told *her,* "Don't be helpless." When the money went, she canceled the eight direct wires to Wall Street, moved out of the Savoy Plaza, took the train to Mount Vernon to see how to play Susie Sachs around the summer houses.

*May 25, 1932*

Dearest daughter,

Your letter came yesterday morning and I reply by return of post which leaves here at 6:30 P.M. today. I have no relatives living as far as I know except a half-brother in Elmira, N.Y., and I doubt if there is anyone in Orleans now living would know me. The house in Orleans where I lived as a boy is diagonally across the street from the hotel, the Nausett House, and fronted a small graveyard. There was a man named Amos Hurd who was a Selectman in Orleans but he must have been six or seven years older than I, so no doubt has gone aloft with the rest. Today Orleans like all the towns on the Cape has been taken over by people from a distance. Young people of my time left as soon as they could, there being no industries to hold them. Many went to Brockton to work in the shoe factories.

The place where you cracked your head was just over the line from Orleans in the town of Eastham. In my boyhood days it belonged to Capt. Heman Smith, a famous whaling Capt. with the pet name of Greasy Heman.

I am having a suit of clothes made and sending a sample. We are to have a stock company here next month. They open with Church Mouse—see clipping.

You don't answer my questions. This is the third time I ask if you have to pay tribute to some gangster gang in N.Y. also if you have investments in stock at the present time??? Three ships built in Quincy for the Matson line will call here. The captains and officers of which are well known to me.

85°–75° are maximum and minimum here in the summer but with the trade winds blowing, it don't feel uncomfortable. As a matter of fact, I get chilly when the temp. drops to 70°. I am in fair health and hope you are as well. I think you have gotten the picture ere this, also a case of Poha jam. Best wishes and many Alohas from

Father

Don't forget the address and *use* it. What is your telephone number? I might need it.

The library windows were open. The curtains fluttered out to 79th Street. Was I reading? It looked as if I was, but I was listening. Would a car stop? Would *the* car?

A car stopped.

It wasn't.

A car stopped. Was it?

It was. Jed looked up. "I brought Woollcott home for a game of cribbage."

End of two years silence.

We took up where we left off. Didn't waste time to discuss the rift. He loved me, I loved him, I could tell him, he could tell me. How often do you find an intimate!

On a ship, on the Island, in a taxi, at Voisin, we could tell things. I loved him, he loved me, he was glad when Jed made me miserable. I'd broken with Arthur; wouldn't I break with Jed?

"Doubleday, Doran wants me to write my autobiography," I told him.

"The cut or the uncut version?"

Mr. Mueller led us to Woollcott's table. He waved across to Peggy Talbot.

I waved, too. "I thought it was Nelson Doubleday being sweet, but he didn't know about it. It's Ted Roosevelt. He took me to lunch at the River Club. Interesting to get an offer."

"Interesting to whom?"

"Me. What could I call it?"

" 'A Withered Ingénue Whose Foot Slipped.' "

"What *could* I?"

"From your endless horror stories about yourself, what about calling it 'Ouch'? Want to come up to the Island? I have a drawing room on the Monday train."

The Island wasn't Woollcott's; it was just the way people referred to it. Its owners were Harpo, Neysa, Ray Ives, Howard Dietz, Raoul Fleischmann, Alice Miller. No one said no to an invitation. Charlie MacArthur said it was like a summons to be on the jury—you showed up.

A soft black sky, white Vermont stars, Ethel Barrymore leaned back on the gondola cushions. Some memories poured out. "Sarah Bernhardt did things her own way! All the actors contributed to a gold laurel wreath to be presented to her onstage at the Empire by Uncle Jack. Each leaf was engraved with a donor: 'Maude Adams,' 'Billie Burke,' 'John Drew,' 'Otis Skinner,' 'Minnie Maddern Fiske,' 'Henry Miller,' 'William Faversham,' 'Elsie Ferguson,' 'Marie Doro,' 'Nazimova.' Uncle Jack made a beautiful speech and Madame replied in that *voix des larmes!*" Ethel laughed.

Something awful was coming; the Barrymores were happy in disaster.

"Her engagement was ending. There was a knock at the dressing room door. 'The man from Cartier is here, Madame.' "

Another tribute?

" '*Madame, je suis désolé de vous déranger, mais la couronne d'or n'est pas payée.*'

" '*Pas payée!*' The *voix des larmes* changed.

" '*Non, Madame. Est-ce que Madame veut régler les comptes?*' He pointed to the unpaid-for gold wreath standing, *place d'honneur*, beside her dressing table.

"Madame flung open the window, picked up the golden wreath with

273

all the famous names and flung it out onto West Fortieth Street, where the evening commuters rushed west to the subway kiosk or east toward Grand Central Station. Who got the golden wreath? By the time the man from Cartier got out, curved around matinee ladies waiting for the divine Sarah, the golden wreath was on its way to Newark, Stamford, Pelham Manor, Yonkers or wherever."

Woollcott turned to Howard Bull, punting us hither and yon. "Home, James. Miss Barrymore has depressed me. Where was *I?* Doing something honest, I'll be bound. If only Fagin had taken a shine to *me,* I could have been an artful dodger and the wreath been on *my* mantel."

Ethel laughed her throaty laugh.

"Remind me to have Cartier's Jules Glaenzer notify me the next time you actors pay a fourteen-karat tribute to each other. I'll write Marie Belloc Lowndes for her theory; nobody can beat her on mystery."

Before *Hotel Universe* closed, Will Harris had sent me Zoë Akins' *The Greeks Had a Word for It.* It had three good parts; the part modeled on Polaire, French actress, was for me. I turned it down.

Zoë pleaded with me. She'd written *Morning Glory* for me and I didn't want to do it; now this. "Would you play Jeanne?" she asked. The whole point of Jeanne was she was a beauty like Jeanne Eagels, but Zoë wanted *me* in her play so for her I'd become a beauty.

Will Harris got annoyed. "Why won't you?" he asked. "Why are you so obstinate?"

"Because I'm great."

Will Harris looked as though he'd be glad to get rid of me.

Next morning, the elevator man brought me a telegram.

JEEZ YOU ARE GREAT.

Will had sent it after the *Hotel Universe* curtain fell. I'd provoked him into coming to see me. A surprise to know you could have "Jeez" in a Western Union message. Also a surprise when *The Greeks Had a Word for It* was a hit. I should've listened to Will and Zoë.

Jed put on *The Inspector General.* Only John Anderson on the *Journal* reviewed it well. He'd made the adaptation. He read it to Jed on the phone.

"Rewrite it," said Jed. "They all knocked it."

Seven performances, but it let Billy Dorbin become a New York actor. Nobody noticed him except me and 45th Street's St. James Hotel, who had tided him over between road tours. After years at Upper Sandusky, Sault Ste. Marie, Battle Creek, he could say he acted on Broadway.

"What part did you play?"

"Another constable, but on *Broadway!*" Two weeks' pay thanks to Equity, but they played only seven performances. What does that tell? The next week *King Lear* played four.

In the spring, you can get restless. In any season you can, but spring encourages it. Was it restlessness made Jed produce and direct *The Wiser They Are?* The idea was to do it on the cheap and see. Maybe it would go. Maybe. Thornton said 79th Street we were all such perfectionists, so let's see. Get Margaret Bellinger to do the dresses, have Osgood Perkins and me play the leads. First time for Osgood in a romantic lead. Could a romantic lead use a valet? A letter was delivered to him at rehearsal.

*New York*
*Feb. 20. '31*

My Dear Mr. Perkins,

I beg you will excuse writing this letter to you because I could not see you personally as I have been tried several times at the Club.

I think perhaps you have remember me as I was with Mr. Roger Pryor for few years as his Valet at theatre.

I have left him September last which he played at Masque Theatre "up pops Devil" at time I was sick which I don't feel so happy as I have been with him it seems me he has changed in his way and I could not work if I am unhappy but I will do anything whatever may be if only I am happy to work that is my nature.

It's too bad he was such a nice gentlemen now I can't be with him.

Since then I have been with Mr. Spencer Tracy until he left Last Mile for Los Angeles.

Now I have heard of about new play which you are the Star in Mr. Harris production.

I wonder can you use me for your valet in the theatre and I shall be so glad to work for you and I am sure you would satisfactory my serves.

Much appreciate if you let me hear from you when you need a man.

Hoping to hear from you. With sincere wishes for you health and every success.

Good luck always.
Respectfully your's,
Henry Kurasaki
"Little Japanese"

Is that how my French had sounded to Élise and Marcelle? And why would I choose *The Wiser They Are* instead of *The Greeks?* Was it because the part was called Trixie? Did I fall for Trixie the way I fell for Katie in *Mrs. Partridge?*

Scripts got delivered and got said no to. "No," I said to *Springtime for Henry.*

"Don't you want to think it over?"

"No," I said. It ran for more than a year and Helen Chandler made a hit. I never went to see it, but Jed dropped in time after time to watch Nigel Bruce.

Guthrie sent me *Distant Drums.* I didn't like that pioneer woman or what she did. It opened at the Belasco Theatre and lasted no time with Pauline Lord in the part. If Pauline couldn't make a hit, who could?

Jed produced and directed *The Fatal Alibi* with Charles Laughton. It ran three weeks.

June Walker was hired for my part in *Collision.* In Rochester stock, I'd played it eight performances, in New York it ran seven.

*Another Language* ran and ran; I hadn't wanted to play it. Dorothy Stickney did.

I said yes to *A Church Mouse* and ran six months, but John Mason Brown wrote "Why does she choose such trash?"

*Here Today* I loved, but the public didn't.

Why no to *When Ladies Meet?* Selena Royle played on and on at the Royale.

No to *Autumn Crocus.* Pat Collinge said yes, and it ran on for months.

Jed worked on *Twentieth Century,* then everybody had different ideas and Jed got out. He worked on Max Anderson's *Both Your Houses,* but didn't like Max's ideas. It played a hundred performances for the Theatre Guild.

"The next thing offered, I'll take," I promised myself. Would I?

Ding-a-ling.

"Hello."

"This is Alfred de Liagre."

"What?"

"This is Alfred de Liagre."

"You sound as if you're saying, 'This is Alfred de Liagre.' "

"I am."

"Oh, you are?"

"I have a play you like."

That didn't mean I did. When an agent sent a play I said I liked it;

it cut the conversation. If I said no, they'd explain how the author's going to change it.

"Which play is it?"

*"Butter No Parsnips."*

Talk about "hoist on your own petard," whatever that is; but I certainly have one, because I got hoisted. Of *all* the plays I didn't like, I didn't like that the most.

"The next thing offered, I'll take." Thoughts of all the bills helped me not to turn that promise into a lie. "I'll be right down to see you. Do you have an office?"

"In the Chanin Building, Lexington and Forty-second."

"Who's the director?" Maybe they couldn't get one.

"I am." He was? With that stylish voice?

"Who'll produce it?" Maybe they couldn't get anybody.

"My partner and I."

"Who's your partner?"

"Dick Aldrich."

A clean sweep. Who'd ever heard of Richard Aldrich or Alfred de Liagre? And the author's name was Gertrude Tonkonogy!

The office in the Chanin Building looked new and empty. No posters because they hadn't done any shows.

"Draw up the contract," I said.

Their first poster attract you?

ALDRICH AND DE LIAGRE
PRESENT
BUTTER NO PARSNIPS
BY
GERTRUDE TONKONOGY
DIRECTED BY
ALFRED DE LIAGRE

What a pact I made with myself! Did the very next play have to be *this?*

"You must be insane," said Jed.

"We're going to fix it." At the Chanin Building every day, De Liagre and I made changes.

"What will the author say?" I asked.

"Oh, she's very agreeable. It's about her family in Brooklyn and she wants to get it on. How about Cissy Loftus for Mrs. Rimplegar?"

"Good." What made them think they could get her? Famous Cissy

Loftus! Toulouse-Lautrec had made her a poster!

"Yes," she said. Had she made a pact with herself too?

"Do you like the title?" asked de Liagre.

"Of course not. How about 'The Sky Is Falling'?"

"What?"

"What Chicken Little said."

"Who?"

"Chicken Little."

"Who?"

*I'd* never heard of de Liagre, *he'd* never heard of Chicken Little!

"Do you like 'Three-Cornered Moon'?"

I didn't, but it became the title and opened at the Cort Theatre, where the first attraction to open had been Laurette Taylor in *Peg o' My Heart.*

Right after my opening night, our fifth-floor guest had an opening. He was an actor who came to see about a job and told a story that made Jed indignant. "Move into my house," said Mr. Hospitable.

Coming downstairs, I met a gaunt young man coming up. "Who are you?"

"Joe Losey. Mr. Harris said I could have a room on the top floor."

Jed said he'd worked as a waiter in the Actors Soup Kitchen and been accused of eating a piece of pie.

"Did you?" Jed had asked him.

"No, I didn't, but I couldn't prove it."

"Tell 'em to go to hell, and don't go back there." He gave him a key to 135.

Did he also get him the job to direct Albert Bein's *Little Ol' Boy?* It was a play Jed worked and worked on with the author, then gave it up. It opened across the street from *Three-Cornered Moon* at Mr. Brady's Playhouse. In the cast was a young actor making his debut and later we met and got married. *Little Ol' Boy* didn't run, but led to things. Our guest gave up his room, returned the key and became famous director Joseph Losey. The young actor became Garson Kanin.

# Chapter

───⦿───

# 12

Number 135 came to an end. Was it money? Bad luck? What? It hadn't worked out. Jed was on the ocean; Maxie Boy—son of *The Barretts of Wimpole Street*'s cocker spaniel, Flush—and I moved to the Barbizon-Plaza, The Judge was on the Rue des Belles Feuilles, the real estate agent had the key. A lot of troubles, a lot of failures, good times, the reunion with Woollcott, evenings with Thornton, the session when Jed and Guthrie discussed *Richard III* all night. It didn't work out; get on with the next.

At the Barbizon-Plaza, first thing in the morning, someone shoved a package through a transom in the bottom of the door. It was called Continental breakfast. I could sit on my bed and there, at arm's length, was breakfast. Everything in the whole room I could reach from the same spot.

"What's it like?" Woollcott phoned from the Bulls' house at Bomoseen, up in Vermont.

"Hot, but I open the transom under the door, it lets some air in, and I take off my dress."

"And I suppose you first slip off your *left* sleeve, then you slip off your *right?* People have only so much time, puss, let's get to something interesting—will you marry me?"

"No."

"When are you sailing?"

"Saturday, the *Bremen,* second class."

"Is that a boast? When you come back you could do worse than come up here. Harpo's coming and Lederer, Alice when she gets back, and Neysa. I might as well be saddled with you."

In the star dressing room, where Laurette had dressed for *Peg,* my bags were lined up. Maxie Boy looked anxious.

Final curtain, bows, goodbye. A taxi took us crosstown to the North German Lloyd pier. Maxie Boy shook a little, and I did too; that taxi was all the home we had.

The *Bremen* second class was deluxe. The crossing was uneventful, nobody famous except George Arliss and Mrs. They were in first. Mr. Arliss and I had been on the Equity Council, but had never met. When he'd played *Disraeli* in Boston, Clare had taken Mama and me to a matinee. His leading lady, Violet Heming, was advertised to sell Red Cross seals at Slattery's elegant Tremont Street store; she got the first money I ever gave to charity. Red Cross seals from an actress's hand? The contribution was twenty-five cents, half the price of a gallery ticket.

At Cherbourg, a tender came alongside for passengers debarking.

At the foot of the gangplank, Jed was waiting. "I thought I ought to come and warn you—he doesn't speak a *word* of English."

"But he *did.*"

"He doesn't now. And he never stops talking, but it's all French."

We got a compartment on the boat train to Paris. "They'll come to the Chambord this afternoon."

"Were you out to number five?"

"Yes. It's all right, but I thought we better see him where *we*'re in charge. He runs everything. Andrée'll bring him, around four."

Jed had a sitting room and a bedroom. I had a bedroom adjoining.

*"Mademoiselle Valentin est en bas."*

*"Faites la monter."*

The Judge walked in, chic, beautiful, well. His eye lit on Maxie Boy. Rapture! *"Regardez le petit chien-chien!"* He squeezed him; Maxie Boy's eyes bulged.

*"Doucement, chéri, doucement!"*

It was true, he didn't speak English. When we said anything, he smiled a dazzling smile and looked to Andrée to interpret. The rest of the time Maxie Boy had his attention. *"Regardez sa mise en plis!"*

Andrée laughed. "He says, 'Look at his hair-set.' " Maxie Boy's coat had a natural wave.

*Hotel Chambord*
*Paris*

Dear Joe,
>Do you miss me? I miss you. The Bremen was not the France.
>"Where are you going to stay?"
>"I don't know."
>"St. James et d'Albany?"
>"No."
>Remember?

Love,
Louisa

P.S. I'm *still* not at the St. James et d'Albany.

It was 1925. The beloved S.S. *France* rolled and rolled.
"Where are you staying in Paris?" Alec asked.
"I haven't thought."
"Send a wireless to the Hôtel St. James et d'Albany. You can't arrive in Paris mid-June with no reservation."
"I'll go to the Ritz."
"What makes you think you can get in?"
"I will."
"Send a wireless. I don't want to taxi you all over Paris. I want to ditch you."
"Why don't I go where *you* go?"
"You can't. I go to the Daunou."
"Why can't *I?*"
"It's a bordello."
"Why are *you* going?"
"It's also a newspaperman's hangout. Send a wire to the St. James et d'Albany."
"I'm going to the Ritz."
The Ritz wirelessed they had nothing.
"Go to the St. James et d'Albany."
"I'll go to the Crillon."
"Send a wireless."
Nothing.
The *France* pitched closer to Le Havre.

"Go to the St. James et d'Albany."

I wirelessed the Continental, that Gregory and I had adored. Why hadn't I thought of it?

Nothing.

"Wireless the—"

But the *France* had tied up.

Alec glowered. "Remind me never to travel with you."

On the boat train he read, I looked out the window and loved everything in France except the St. James et d'Albany, which, until Woollcott recommended it, I'd never heard of. A taxi to the Daunou, he dropped his bags and I was glad we didn't drop mine. Around the corner to the Rue de la Paix, into the Place Vendôme, where the Ritz *still* had nothing. Down the Rue de Rivoli to the Crillon; still nothing. Alec gloated. *"Now where?"*

"Plaza Athénée." Stanton Griffis had stayed there.

"We have nothing, but would you like us to inquire?"

"Yes, thank you."

Woollcott's face was one big I-told-you-so.

"Do you know the Hôtel Carlton around the corner on the Champs Élysées? Very good and they can take you. They have only a suite; it's twenty-five dollars a day."

"She'll *take* it!" shouted Woollcott, and laughed and laughed and laughed.

The sitting room had a balcony looking down on the Champs Élysées; a huge bedroom, a huge bath. I couldn't afford it, but it was *not* the St. James et d'Albany.

I'd only be in Paris from Saturday to Saturday. Gregory was trying out *The Butter and Egg Man.* The following Saturday on the *Mauretania* back to New York.

Dinner in Montmartre and after dinner Alec and I strolled the little streets. "Tomorrow I have seats for Raquel Meller; I may take you."

"My God!" Raquel Meller was Spanish, dark, beautiful, somber, remote, a legend.

"I may. I may think of someone else."

We drove in a hansom cab, then we were there, crowds pouring in, everybody excited. Inside was Spain. The lights went down, curtains parted, there was Raquel. "Who'll buy my violets?" she sang in throaty Spanish, then tossed small bunches across the footlights.

We drove back to the Boulevard des Italiens, to a certain *terrasse* where

Woollcott had gone for years. They welcomed him and sat us at a sidewalk table.

"Good God, what's *that?*" He pointed to a café-au-lait limousine as big as a hearse. Out stepped Marc Connelly and a correct young lady.

"What are *you* doing here?" asked Woollcott.

Marc seemed astonished by the question. "I'm just back from Wien."

"Wien! Why do you call it Wien?"

"Because that's the way *they* call it."

"And where are you now? Paree? That's the way *they* call it. And when you go to Florence, do you say, 'I'm off to Firenze'?"

Marc and the young lady went to a table inside.

Alec thought about some things, then said, "I'm leaving tomorrow."

"Where are you going?"

"Antibes."

"Where?"

"Antibes."

"What's that?"

"It's on the Riviera."

"What's its name?"

"Antibes."

"Is it French?"

"*Now* it is. The name is Roman."

"Why are you going?"

"I'm sick of it here. And you."

The week in Paris had been arranged so I'd meet Anita Loos and John Emerson to choose the costumes for their play *The Fall of Eve,* opening early September in New York. The Emersons were at the Hôtel Mercédès, Rue de Presbourg, that starts at the Champs Élysées, two blocks above the Carlton. Anita and John were on their annual Paris trip to choose her own beautiful clothes at Chéruit, Place Vendôme, and none black. "John doesn't like black." She chose a black billowy evening dress spangled with tiny silver stars. *"Bleu marine,"* ordered Anita.

For my costumes, they liked Lanvin. Manageress Viola Krauss took charge. Two afternoon dresses, two coats, a peignoir. There was no choice; you could close your eyes—all Lanvin clothes were beautiful. The decision was a chiffon in Lanvin green, the color of new lettuce after you peel off the outside leaves. It was knee-length! Thank you, Dr. Ryerson. Thank you, Gregory. That week before Christmas, when we'd checked in for one night at the Congress Hotel, how could we know dresses would get to be knee-length? All we knew was that the next afternoon we'd check into the Presbyterian Hospital, with the operation scheduled for next morning. They were going to allow Gregory to sleep on a cot in the same room with me.

We had a great dinner at the Congress, finished off with their pale chocolate ice cream, then off to see Willie Collier in *The Hottentot*. We laughed as hard as when we'd seen it in New York. It was a risk to go, *nobody* must know we were in town, the operation was to be kept a secret. An actress to have her legs broken, then put together straight? Secrecy was why the Congress; we hadn't stayed there since *Seventeen*. The room clerk was a stranger and Gregory registered under an assumed name. The next day, we rode west in a taxi. Rode forever, came to el tracks and stopped at a grimy brick building, shown to a room level with the el tracks.

"Is this the best?" asked Gregory.

"This is millionaires' row."

We unpacked.

Would you know what you'd want for an operation? I'd made a bed jacket of peach taffeta, the neck and sleeves outlined with white marabou.

"You can wear your own nightgown tonight if you want to," said the nurse. "They'll be in to make tests."

Two trays came in. Was it the dinner or didn't we feel hungry?

A young intern came in. "I have to take some blood." He did, then looked disappointed. "Oh, I have the wrong tube." He went.

The el clattered by, the intern came back, took some more, studied the tube, looked troubled. "What did I do *now?*" He went.

On the third try, he got it.

On the operating table, as the anesthetist was putting the cup over my face, Dr. Ryerson came in. "Are you nervous?" he asked.

"No."

He felt my pulse. "No, you're not." He sounded surprised.

It would be weeks before I'd walk again, months before I'd walk the way I could now. Right now I could get off the table and be as well as I'd ever been, which was perfectly well. Most times on an operating table there isn't that choice. But *was* it a choice? I'd be well, but I'd have bowlegs. Long skirts were the fashion, but *I* knew. It's hard enough to be an actress without handicaps.

"Are you nervous?"

"No." What made me nervous was to have a handicap.

284

Somewhere in a fuzzy world the el rattled by. "Gregory?"

"He went in town to get things," a voice said. "He'll be right back. Lie on your back, remember." It was done. I was back in my room with the el rattling by, under the covers two plaster casts from my waist down, my feet enclosed like a child's nightdrawers, like our Lost Boy costumes in *Peter Pan*.

"Any pain?"

"Just sickish." My back felt as if I'd been lying on it long enough, but I'd have to lie on it four weeks. Four weeks is a long time to have to wait to turn over.

"Will I *surely* walk again?" I'd asked Dr. Ryerson that day I'd come to his office.

"Nothing in surgery is sure. Once you use a knife, there is always an outside chance, but as sure as surgery can be, it is sure you'll walk. It will be a clean cut. That heals better than if you're run over and bones got splintered or mashed, but even when that happens the bones heal. Look at David Warfield—seventy-five when he got run over, a complicated smash, but he's walking. How old did you say you are?"

"Twenty-four month before last."

"I'll make a clean cut, the big bone sawed, the small bone I break. You will have a scar on each side of your leg, of course. They will be there the rest of your life."

"How big?"

"About two inches for the big bone. An inch for the small. It will gradually become less, but it will always be there. Whiter than your skin and a straight line."

"But my legs will be straight?"

"They will."

Encouraging to remember that, the more my back hurt. What was I reading? Headline on the front page of the Chicago *Examiner:* BREAKS LEGS FOR BEAUTY'S SAKE.

Ashton Stevens, the drama critic, had run into Gregory on Michigan Avenue that afternoon of the operation. "What are you doing in Chicago?"

Gregory's answer had been evasive; Ashton looked into the possibilities. What led him to the Presbyterian Hospital? He never would tell.

Dr. Ryerson was dismayed. I was hysterical. Talk about embarrassment! The world was different then; everybody didn't tell everything, there were still secrets.

There was only one *good* result. That afternoon, a Christmas tree was brought into my room. "Merry Christmas. When you feel like it, let us meet. Edward Sheldon."

The famous playwright was a patient in the hospital. That's why I chose the Presbyterian when Dr. Ryerson asked which I preferred, the Presbyterian or the Passavant. Did I choose the Presbyterian because I thought Edward Sheldon would choose a good hospital or because I hoped it would let me meet Edward Sheldon?

Gregory wrote a note and Christmas Eve a four-foot laurel wreath, tied with a red satin bow, was hung on my hospital screen. "For you. Ned." Rich, handsome, a Broadway legend. He wrote *Salvation Nell* for Mrs. Fiske *before* he graduated from Harvard. When he graduated he wrote more plays. His great success was *Romance* for Doris Keane, then illness struck him. Some said bone disease, some said Doris Keane. She bore Howard Gould a child and Ned was an invalid, legs paralyzed.

The headline had brought me the start of a long and great friendship; the rest was hell! Newspapers called up from all over the country, a crank burst into my room to see if I was alive, special delivery brought a smudged pencil-scribbled letter. "I will give the letters you wrote that critic to your husband if you don't leave $500 at the drugstore corner of Decatur Ave and Elgin Street."

I burst into tears.

"That's nothing," said Gregory. "Just a poison pen letter."

I'd never heard of one.

Mail poured in, some sympathetic, some nuts, some asking advice how they could do the same, some asking for money, and all the time my back hurt. No pain from my legs until they changed the sheets. Nurse rolled the undersheet up close to the cast, then jerked it. I screamed.

Gregory said, "Let me do it." He rolled it, then eased it.

When Dr. Ryerson slit the casts, the bones of one leg had slipped, from the nurse jerking the sheet. Dr. Ryerson molded it straight again and taped up the cast. "Your back still hurt?"

"Not as much."

"It'll go away. I wish the newspaper story would; I get mail from all over the country. My wife is horrified. I'm *not* a beauty doctor."

One day I was eased onto an operating trolley and taken to x-ray. "Afterwards, could we stop at Mr. Sheldon's room?" The nurse arranged with his nurse. Gregory wheeled me in. The handsomest man we ever saw was sitting up in bed. "Dear Miss Gordon, what courage!" That beautiful voice! "Mr. Kelly, what a pleasure to meet you." Early January, 1921, our friendship began at the Presbyterian Hospital. It continued in New York.

"Please dine with me," he'd wire, and the reply was never no. Not from me or from anyone, and Ned knew everyone.

Once Thornton asked me, "Dear, if *you*'d been an invalid for sixteen years, how many people would plead to see *you?*" Thornton didn't wait to hear my answer. "And do you ever get a telegram from him *breaking* the date?"

"Yes."

"And did you notice Mrs. Pat Campbell was in town or John Gielgud?"

"Would Ned do that?"

"It's happened to you, it's happened to me. He can always get *us*, dear, but after sixteen years wouldn't you and I be wondering how we could scare up a visitor?"

Beside Ned's stately bed, dinner for one was served in Ned's stately upper Madison Avenue penthouse that he'd never seen. Paralyzed, then the illness attacked his eyes; a black satin mask covered them. He couldn't see, he couldn't move, but he could laugh, he could talk, he could listen, he could help you.

"Your hearing is in danger," his doctor had said one day. "There's a chance you will lose it."

Ned didn't answer. Doctor wondered had Ned heard.

"That would certainly limit my contacts."

The French windows of his penthouse looked down at Campbell's funeral parlor a block away on Madison Avenue. The black mask covered his eyes. "Hold me, I'm going," he called out to his orderly. The funeral wasn't at Campbell's; it was at St. James' Episcopal Church down Madison, too far to see from Ned's penthouse.

Famous cover artist and dazzling *femme fatale* Neysa McMein rang me up. "Let's sit together. I'll meet you outside."

In the transept the coffin looked like Ned's stately bed, except a blanket of roses was where we used to sit beside his India print bedspread.

"I didn't know you knew Ned," I whispered to Neysa.

"Why wouldn't I?"

A good question. Ned knew everyone. Our legacy was his spirit. He left his friends wisdom, courage, the example of how to ignore defeat.

Before Blue Cross and Medicare and Medicaid, hospital expenses were fierce. Help came to us in Chicago.

"Wanted on the phone, Mr. Kelly."

It was Mr. Tyler. "I'm doing a comedy called *Dulcy* by two new writers, but they're good. George S. Kaufman and Marc Connelly—they've got talent. I'm putting Lynn Fontanne into the name part and want to co-feature you as her brother. We open for three days at English's Opera House in Indianapolis, then Chicago for a run at the Cort. I understand your wife is in the hospital there. Rehearse ten days, then play the three in Indianapolis and you're together. I'll pay you your *Clarence* salary."

"I'll call you back," said Gregory.

Thirteen days! Thirteen mornings and afternoons, thirteen marshmallow salads, thirteen evenings and nights!

"What do you think, little feller?"

What *could* I think? Thirteen hospital days are longer than thirteen days at the Blackstone, and cost even more, and no six hundred and fifty dollars each Saturday.

"By the time you're ready to leave, we'll move to the Blackstone."

We didn't mention expenses. We'd never asked Dr. Ryerson's fee.

"If you think you'll be all right, I'll say I'll come if he pays *both* our *Clarence* salaries."

"All right."

He went down to the phone.

Thirteen days! It would be the first time we'd slept apart since the Lenox Hotel in Boston.

"I'll get six-fifty."

"When do you go?"

"Day after tomorrow."

Every day a letter came, every day I wrote him.

"After *Dulcy*, let's have an Indianapolis stock company of our own," wrote Gregory. "We could take English's Opera House. I'm as much a part of Indianapolis as Stuart is—why leave it all to *him?* Be thinking of what parts would be good for you. Great experience and you know how I always want to direct."

Something to look forward to. Something to get me through all those sixty minutes.

One afternoon, a note from Edward Sheldon. Wearing my peach

taffeta bed jacket, I was moved into a rolling chair, legs straight out, and the nurse rolled me down to his room. Lenore Ulric was just leaving. Belasco's star Lenore Ulric! Dark, curly hair, pointed face, big eyes, hot husky voice from the bottom of her throat or maybe from her bottom. Sensuous, talented, secret—everything about Lenore was secret.

Ned introduced me to her, then to a young man. "This is Charlie MacArthur, my brother-in-law. His brother is married to my sister Mary." Young, good-looking, charming, Charlie left when Lenore did. Edward Sheldon said he worked on a newspaper, was brilliant and going far. Then he asked about Gregory. How were rehearsals? He said he'd taken an apartment in New York and would leave for the East. "Are you all right here?" So elegant, he made *me* feel like a somebody. He was sitting up in bed; my rolling chair was placed beside him. "People wonder how you can make do in a hospital, but I never am able to finish what I plan."

In all the years he behaved as if everything was perfectly fine.

Gregory's letters said rehearsals were all right. He thought Howard Lindsay was a good director, but too conventional. Lynn was going to be good, George Kaufman and Marc Connelly were good. George Kaufman *worried* all the time. One letter was titled "Reminder—when *Dulcy* plays English's, I'll discuss us playing stock with the manager."

Did I need a reminder? Love poured through the letters.

In Indianapolis the show went well. After the Saturday night performance, Gregory took the Chicago sleeper and was in my room before I was awake.

Breakfast over, the hospital doctor dismissed me. Gregory rolled me down to the elevator, nurse carrying my suitcase. It felt scary. So quiet up on millionaires' row. I'd even got used to the el and didn't hear it anymore. Gregory and the driver lifted me into the car and off to the Blackstone, the same room we had for *Clarence*. Five dollars a day, but we loved it and the food and the service, the elegance, and *everybody* put themselves out for us.

February 20, 1921! For the opening, Gregory carried me up the stairs to the upper stage box; the Cort didn't have lower boxes. Frightening and exciting. I wished I were opening too, but it had been worth waiting for; when I did open, my legs would be straight. I hadn't stood up yet, but next day I must start to practice walking with crutches. Practice in the room at first, until I could get the knack, and the masseur must massage my legs back to health. They were like pipestems and blue. That would be tomorrow. Tonight I was upper left box at the Cort, audience pouring in to see:

DULCY

WITH

Lynn Fontanne and Gregory Kelly

A COMEDY IN THREE ACTS

BY

George S. Kaufman and Marc Connelly

At the Blackstone, Dr. Ryerson was shown up. He explained how to use the crutches. Now I must walk. What if? A crutch under each arm, I started across the small room. My feet were asleep, legs went limp, nothing responded. And how uncooperative crutches are. How sort of disgustingly pathetic. Would people know I wasn't a cripple?

"You must use them for two weeks." With Dr. Ryerson everything was definite. He took his hat and coat and left.

"Try again," said Gregory. "Pretend you're in a play."

I burst into tears.

"Look in the looking glass, don't look at the crutches. Look at your legs."

They were straight!

On the Faubourg St. Honoré, Lanvin's Viola Krauss had read the script. If *The Fall of Eve* didn't go, the costumes would! John and Anita and I celebrated with luncheon in the Ritz garden. Hattie Carnegie was there and every American in Paris with pull and money. The food terrific, the garden beauty itself.

"That fellow has a *pink* shirt!" I exclaimed.

Anita looked across the garden at a handsome, thin young man lunching with a party. He wore a pink starched-collar shirt.

"That's the new London star," said Anita. "He wrote *The Vortex*, he and Lilian Braithwaite starred in it. Noël Coward. He's all the rage."

"They're going to open early September," said John. "They're at the Henry Miller. Did I tell you we're at the Booth?"

*Seventeen,* my dressing room up a flight; *The Fall of Eve,* my dressing room number 1. That was the summer of 1926; the summer of 1933 things were only so-so. "You stay in Paris," said Jed. "I'll go to London." When he left the Chambord, I moved to the Hôtel d'Iena, where Mildred and her mother and sisters had stayed.

Andrée and Jones and Maxie Boy and I walked in the Bois.

Some afternoons, we went to La Ferme de Champs de Courses, near the Longchamps race track. Their own herd of cows grazed there and milk was served at little tables under the trees. One day Sacha Guitry noticed Jones. *"Joli garçon,"* he said.

Andrée went to pieces.

Jones was three, a *force majeure* who ran their world and let Andrée believe *she* did. His supper was served in the sitting room, its windows looking out over the rooftops. Maxie Boy, on the window seat, withdrew into his own world. Andrée placed a bowl of Pablum in front of Jones, a carafe of milk, a shaker of sugar. *"Sois sage, Coco."*

*"Oui, Tante Andrée."* He smiled his dazzling smile.

"You have to say that kid is good." She went out to do something in the other room.

Jones watched her, then lifted the shaker, shook out enough sugar for four.

"Jones!" I said.

He smiled and shook.

"I'm going to tell Aunt Andrée."

Andrée came in.

He smiled his dazzling smile.

*"Mange bien, chéri."* She smiled back and went.

He turned his handsome head toward me. "You are going to tell Aunt Andrée!" Perfect English.

Jed was at the Savoy in London. I was joining him. A few days and we'd sail. Maxie Boy was sailing too; he hadn't thrived in Paris. His pretty white fur all came off his belly. I took him to a Faubourg St. Honoré vet who couldn't speak much English, but made me understand Maxie Boy had some kind of uric acid. "Make for him a *tisane* of trees of the carrot," he prescribed.

Andrée did and also made him white linen pants from a soft old handkerchief to protect his sore skin. When the Belgian Line's *Red Star* docked in France, Cook's would put Maxie Boy on board to be cared for till we boarded at Southampton.

Jones and Andrée were off to Switzerland, where they'd spent the last summer at Vallorbe, in the canton of Vaud, French-speaking and only barely across the border.

"It agrees with a kid, Swiss air. He needs it, this one. His tonsils give him trouble and Swiss air is good for that."

He didn't travel light. He even carried his own bathtub.

"It's useful," said Andrée. "Where would I pack his toys?"

When Mama left Bainbridge, Georgia, her things were in her zinc trunk; when Papa went to sea his things were in a gunny sack. I spring from wanderers and I'm a wanderer. My things were in a Vuitton trunk marked 710 North Walden Drive, Beverly Hills, California, care of Mrs. Charles MacArthur. I inherit wandering. My father's people wandered over here on the *Mayflower.* Thomas Rogers landed, took a look and died, but his family wrestled with the Plymouth winters and eventually moved down Cape Cod to Orleans, where they made Papa's life awful.

Being a wanderer, I'm quick to take off. Visiting Helen, Jed phoned to come back. "Fly," he urged. Jed had said he'd meet me at Newark, but wasn't there, so I went to his suite at the Essex House. I woke him. He was sorry he hadn't met me, but glad I came. Then that night when we were cooking hamburgers, a girl phoned. He *must* come to California. She'd seen *Poil de Carotte;* it was the greatest movie she ever saw. We had a fight and he checked out. To get past *that* moment, I went to Mountain Lakes, in New Jersey. Mildred had a house there for the summer with Cappy and their baby, Nina. Then I wandered back to New York. At Penn Station the taxi driver asked "Where to?" and I heard myself say, "Waldorf Astoria." It was an inside five-dollar-a-day room. I took it by the day and stayed on for a year. If I wandered, it was in the neighborhood. Some afternoons, I wandered east on 52nd Street to Woollcott's apartment in the Campanile.

"Come in, Blossom." He was dictating to Leggett Brown.

"Will you be long?"

"Read this. Rebecca West sent it this morning—the woman writes like an angel. Here, improve your mind. Where was I, Leggett?"

" 'Stephen Foster gave the world its—' "

"God, you read like a metronome."

"It's to counteract the Karo in my master's voice."

"Shut up, Brown. 'Stephen Foster gave the world its true heritage, the heritage of human experience. Empty pockets, tattered clothes, hungry bellies and love in the heart'—no—'heart full of love. He died friendless in the gutter, three cents in his pocket, and on the back of his overdue board bill was scribbled the notion for his new song, "Kind Hearts and Gentle People." ' Go away, Brown. Puss, you look blooming for one approaching thirty-seven."

"Ever get sick of everybody?"

"Continually. Who'd *you* get sick of?"

"Mary Brown Warburton."

"Where'd you find *her?*"

"I was at her place. She asked me."

"You're not usually so obliging."

"Jed wanted to go."

"Who else was she boring?"

"Ted Healy, Jo Pickering, Ethel Russell, Earl Carroll—"

"Why, that's the kind of people you meet in Macy's toilet."

"Then Jed got too insulting, so we went home."

"How are you, Blossom?"

"I don't know. I may go somewhere."

"Where?"

"Why do you *like* everybody? You're unnatural."

"That's the pleasantest thing that's been said about me in years!"

"You like Lucy Drange and—"

"Well, good God, she was my first-grade *teacher!*"

"I don't even know mine's name. Yes, I do, Miss Thayer—she had an amethyst pin and came to the Ritz to see me when I played Boston, but do I tell you about her?"

"Puss, you're a mess today."

"I don't like Jed, either."

"Want to come up to the Island?"

"No."

"Alice and I are going to Saratoga, spend the night at the Grand Union, drive over next day. If you never saw the Grand Union you should."

"No."

"Do you good."

"I'm sick of— I don't know what I *am* sick of. I think I'll go off by myself. When are you and Alice?"

"Tomorrow. Drawing room on the *Saratoga Special.* Cepetti meets us in Saratoga with Alice's car."

It's nice to be wanted. "I'll go."

I loved the Island. It was different from any other part of my life. Different from any other parts of anyone's life, I suppose. Not easy to get to. The *Montreal Express* left Grand Central at 9 A.M. and sometime after lunch stopped at Whitehall, where Joe Hennessey was waiting on the platform. The train rushed off toward the Adirondacks; Joe threw the suitcases in the car and drove away through green green fields. The lower Green Mountains were far enough in the background not to be oppressive. Through Hydeville, Fairhaven, Castleton to the lake. In the motorboat waited Howard Bull, behind his ear a dahlia, sometimes a pumpkin flower. Three minutes to Neshobe Island. Woolcott's dogs, Duchess and Pip, raced down to the dock to see who'd arrived, Woollcott padding behind them. Greetings, remarks. "Harpo's here. And Lederer. They're playing croquet. Ethel Barrymore's coming tomorrow, so she has the good room. Bea Kaufman's in the old house; she's got her feller, Charlie someone. Or was that last year? Whatever his name is, you can't avoid meeting him. For some reason, Neysa's taking a nap."

Cocktails on the terrace at six, dinner in the dining room at seven, Margaret holding sway in the kitchen. Winters she held sway in Fairhaven Grammar School, fourth grade. If dinner was steaks, Joe broiled them in the fireplace and Margaret cooked the rest on the coal stove. Coming up the path might be Howard Bull bringing things, Richard Carver Wood taking pictures.

After dinner, Howard Bull punted Alec and his chosen in the gondola he'd ordered sent to him from the Chicago World's Fair. Indoors, card games went on. Nobody under any condition left the Island, nobody read a book. Was that a rule? Backgammon, cribbage, bezique, poker, hearts, casino, bridge, no reading.

After the gondola ride, Woollcott disappeared into his room with Duchess and Pip.

The phone company had pleaded to lay a cable free, but Woollcott said, "No telephone."

You never knew who would show up. Otis Skinner drove over from Woodstock, Vermont, for lunch; so did Dorothy Thompson. Ted Roosevelt dropped down in a seaplane from Oyster Bay, Long Island; David Ogilvy came from London with a Rebecca West intro. Bill Fields and Francis Robinson came from New York to set the publicity for autumn and winter lecture dates. *Anybody* arriving would be no surprise.

Woollcott tried to force everyone into the lake before breakfast. Nobody went in but him and Pip and Duchess. They jumped in and out all day. Breakfast was on the long enclosed piazza, windows open; no one ever thought of breakfast in bed. Woollcott sat at the head of the table. When anyone woke up, they came in. A twelve-cup coffeepot was the gift of Lewis and Conger, grand store that had everything but enough business. Their building stands on the southwest corner of 45th and Sixth Avenue. Nothing has ever taken their place; I wish they'd done enough business.

Breakfasters were served cups of coffee by Margaret. The favored were offered a cup of Woollcott's. Probably those twelve cups were what killed him. He said if that's the way he had to go, he would, and when the doctor told him he would, he didn't change. When he spent a fortnight at the White House, as guest of the Roosevelts, he said, "It's just like the Island." We frequenters interpreted it to mean that coffee flowed freely at all times.

The Island comforted a lot of us. So did the White House. I can't say the same for the Waldorf. One room, five dollars a day, and no offers. Plays were sent, but none I believed in. Plenty of invites. An invite from Woollcott to go with him to the first night of *As Thousands Cheer.* I think he invited me right after Irving finished the first number.

"Don't forget September thirtieth, puss."

Who'd forget it? It was *the* opening—everybody had to be there.

Moss Hart wrote the sketches. It was staged by Hassard Short, who'd made a hit as a silly ass with Laurette in *Peg o' My Heart,* opening the new Cort. Forsaking silly asses, he'd become the top musical comedy director.

Woollcott called for me at the Waldorf, we dined at Voisin and went crosstown to Irving Berlin and Sam Harris's Music Box. What a world to be part of! Marilyn Miller, beautiful and gifted Clifton Webb astonishing everyone. Everyone knew he could dance, but to be so remarkable in the sketches! Ethel Waters stopped the show. Helen Broderick floored us with Moss's funny lines!

After the Music Box, everybody went over to the Élysée, where Clifton and his mother, Mabel, were living. By breakfast time, a few took off to Reuben's, but the party stuck together through Sunday. After dark, Clifton's valet, Ramona, went down to Times Square to pick up the first edition of the *Times.* By then, Helen and Mabel Webb did not see eye to eye. Helen withdrew from all conversation except to throw in an occasional "Up your ass, Mabel."

"You've got a filthy tongue, Helen. I won't bother to reply."

"Up your ass, Mabel."

"Some people don't know when they've gone too far!"

"Up your ass, Mabel."

"If I didn't have on my Hattie Carnegie, I'd come over and spit in your eye."

To divert the ladies, Moss suggested, "Let's call up Irving."

"Up your ass, Mabel," said Helen, coldly. "Don't be a buttinsky."

"Do you like Greenwich, Moss?" asked Clifton. "We're stuck with a house there."

"Up your ass, Mabel."

Ramona came back. "A raveroo! The *Times loves* you," he said to Clifton. "He says Miss Broderick's the best!"

"Up your ass, Mabel."

Ramona looked blacker than usual. "Up yours, Miss B."

Nobody remembered when everybody went home, nobody remembered when everybody became friends, but *everybody* remembered *As Thousands Cheer* was the greatest!

October. The phone rang and rang. Invites. Max Gordon sent *Spring Song*. I didn't like it, but maybe do it? "Ten percent of the gross and a thousand dollars guaranty."

"I won't give you a guaranty." He hired Francine Larrimore. If I'd waived the guaranty would I have got married in 1933 instead of 1942? Garson Kanin was in the play. What happened to luck?

The phone rang. An offer or an invite? It was Billy Dorbin. "How're you, darlin'?"

"Fine. Want to have dinner?"

He did. How long since I'd seen him? It was 1933. *Fair and Warmer* closed in 1917. He looked exactly the same.

The Waldorf headwaiter showed us to a pink-damask-covered table.

Billy glanced at the menu and shuddered. "I'll have a roll and some relish."

I laughed. "I'm flush—let's eat."

*"Plat du jour* for me. That's the blue-plate, isn't it?"

"What is it?"

"Steak Stanley, with fried bananas."

"You really like it?"

"You bet, darlin'. Remember that place Oscar Johnson found, had the twenty-five-cent dinner, the dessert was sliced bananas, three slices. Didn't you think Johnson would get somewhere? Looks, sex, know-how?"

I thought of Marian Gray.

"I guess he dropped out. This year the Depression's got everything on the blink. I'm lucky over to the St. James Hotel. I been a little back on my rent and y' know *most* places are 'Have ya the rent?' 'No.' 'Then over the cliff!' but not the St. James Hotel. If you ever get a chance—don't go out of your way—but if the opportunity arises, give 'em a plug."

"I'll give them a plug and you something to tide over. What could you use?"

"Oh, no, darlin'. Eat a roll till the blue-plate."

"How much do you owe the hotel?"

"Never mind."

"Would *you* stake me if I needed it?"

"No."

"You would. How much?"

He buttered both sides of the roll. "Would you miss sixty?"

"I'll cash a check at the desk."

"That's not why I came to dinner."

"Anything in sight?"

"No, but something will. I missed the August casting; I had to stick with my sister Mary."

"Kalamazoo?"

"Oh, sure. I couldn't leave her with *that,* her hubby a murderer. Did you read it? My name, everything. Where *were* you in July? Every July I go out there till it picks up here in August, then do the rounds, and the night before I was leaving, her hubby, George, and I are sitting on the porch and Mary is in the dining room doing accounts. Remember she runs the Cadillac agency? She brought the books home. There sit George and I, shoes off, when a car pulls up and a cop gets out and says, 'You're arrested.'

" 'I am?' I says, trying to think. And he says, 'Not you; *him,* ' and points to George. And that's the first I or Mary knew he'd been tartin' it up! Every week, on his sales trips, he's tweaking the garters off this widow, her husband left a fortune in Galesburg real estate, then finally George got tired of her and chops her up and scatters her along the New York Central track! Know what caught him? The laundry number on her britches. They found a half-inch tape with the number on and the police traced it to a certain laundry and the laundry looked up that number and George'll eat the rest of his dinners in the Michigan penitentiary. Michigan don't have capital punishment."

Thanksgiving? No offers. Christmas? Presents, no offers.

The phone rang.

"Hello." Invite or offer?

It was Theresa Helburn. The Theatre Guild had a part for me.

"We can't pay but three hundred."

297

"In *Three-Cornered Moon* I got—"

"You can't go by what you got last year. This is the Depression. The salary is three hundred dollars. This play can't make money—it has eighty-seven speaking parts and a lot of scenery, but the Guild has to do it."

*They Shall Not Die* was about the Scotsboro trial. I was Ruby Bates, called Lucy Wells in the play. At rehearsals, there were more and worse fights than *Hotel Universe;* Phil Moeller and author John Wexley fought all the time. *Loud* fights, *loud* rebukes, *loud* insults. Phil Barry's were veiled.

It was my first emotional part, one big scene. Claude Rains had the long part, New York lawyer Samuel Leibowitz, called by another name. In rehearsals Claude was colorless; it could sink the play. His seven-page speech, he droned. Everybody worried. He was the pivot of the whole play. Opening night I sat behind the backdrop waiting for the scene to be over. Claude's summation blew the roof off! Even that frosty Guild first-night list had to loosen up and cheer. It's the only time I ever saw an actor wait till opening night to wrap up a show.

Back to the Waldorf with the big flowers from Helen and Charlie, pretty flowers from Isabel and Thornton, beauties in a box marked Thorley's "with love from Kit and Guthrie." Mary Chess bath oil from Lillian Gish, a smoked ham from sister Dorothy. Among the telegrams was a crumpled hotel envelope with sixty dirty dollars folded in St. James writing paper. "Much appreciation. Love to my star. Billy D."

The notices were tepid, we'd close after the three weeks subscription. Nobody casting this late in the season and the season was 1933–1934! We felt terrible. Actors, stage manager, crew, ushers would be out of work, the Royale would go dark.

After a matinee, a knock on the door. It was a handsome young man with unusual blue eyes. "I wrote a play for you to be in."

"Thank you."

He gave me a thin, rather dilapidated script. I read it on the train going to look at a house in New Jersey Jed heard he might like. I read half, then preferred the scenery.

Coming home I'd seen the scenery; finished the play.

Dear Mr. Odets,
   Thank you for sending me your play. I don't think I'd be right for it.
   Good luck.
                                                          Ruth Gordon

"Was it much rewritten from the script you sent me?" I asked him at the Belasco Theatre, where everybody was trying to get in to see *Awake and Sing!*

"Not rewritten at all."

Stella Adler made the hit of the season and I was waiting for the phone to ring.

Clifford Odets said to me once, "I wonder what good comes to a banker from his troubles. Troubles can't make him a better banker."

For us creative people, troubles may be our best equipment. Maybe all those forget-it moments are for learning emotional acting. In *They Shall Not Die* my big emotional scene came in the second act. Despair, in a rocking chair, in the front room of our cabin. I had to pour it out to someone. It was my mama who heard me. The performances I *really* did it, my mama, Helen Westley, moved her rocker downstage to have a better look.

One day, beneath the window behind me, some of the crew were having a discussion. Would it ruin my scene if I was distracted? I wasn't secure enough to act *around* distraction. Don't ruin your scene, I told myself, and left my rocker. Helen watched. What was I doing? I leaned out the window. *"Shhh!"* I told the talkers, and came back to my rocker.

Helen was hazy about some things, but knew *this* wasn't in the text. She left her rocker, looked out the window, saw the crew hushed, came back, sat down, and said, "You did just right."

The receipts were going down.

"Everybody take half of what they're getting," advised Jed, "and you and Claude and Linda Watkins and Helen Westley work for nothing."

"Remind me never to go in a play with you," said Claude. "Next you'll ask me to *pay* to act."

The performances were electric, any scene *less* than perfection we all felt awful; we were going for a miracle. The first-act scene in the cell was on, the boys and Linda and I herded together, the sheriff and his men talking. Back of the cell, an usher whispered, "Miss Gordon, here's a phone message."

The curtain came down, Linda Watkins picked up a loose door and went after a startled usher. "Don't talk to her when she's *acting!*"

We had to close. "You can't work for nothing," ruled Equity. "It's against the rules. You have to get minimum."

The summer stock at Dennis on Cape Cod asked me to do a week of *Serena Blandish.* How could they stage it in a week?

"Cable for you."

The Waldorf bellboy brought it up. Papa had had a heart attack. He was in Honolulu Hospital. Friends were taking charge. Could I come?

Do *you* know what to do about trouble? Lillian Gish does. She came over right away. She decided on two cables. One to Papa, in case he was conscious; one to the doctor: did they need funds? She wrote them out. What organization! "They must tell *you* what to do. Then you can decide, but *get* the facts." A remarkable friend.

The bellboy brought a cable.

CAPTAIN JONES DIED PEACEFULLY HIS WISHES ARE HE BE CREMATED ASHES SCATTERED OUTER HARBOR.

Another.

WISHES CARRIED OUT CAPTAIN JONES EFFECTS BEING SENT YOU.

# Chapter

## 13

Jed was abroad. He sent word he was sending Jones and Andrée to New York. They'd sail on the *Manhattan,* second class. Money. I'd gone second class, but Jones hadn't. Maybe it was all right. They'd arrive end of May. I'd rent a house for us to live in; a little boy ought to live in a house with stairs and a garden. What would be good for the summer? The Kent House was no more. Should they share the Mountain Lakes house that Mildred and Cappy had taken? Mildred said it would be great to have them. I'd pay half the expenses. The house was rented beginning Decoration Day weekend; until then I would rent a suite at the Gladstone, small, elegant family hotel on East 52nd Street off Park Avenue. Swope's brother Gerard and his wife wintered there and Pearl Swope said it was good.

Order a limousine to bring them to the hotel, Mildred and I would meet the boat, Helen Hayes and daughter Mary would come in from Nyack to have lunch, Mildred would bring Nina. When they're still plans, everything goes right.

The *Manhattan* was due to dock early morning. The night before, I went down to Barrow Street to Mildred and Cappy's for dinner. Jed's mother was there. They'd just pressed the dress Nina would wear to-morrow. Pink linen; Edna Ferber had brought it from Paris.

What a day tomorrow, to welcome them at the ship! For four years and eight months no story had broken; what reporter would notice us in the crowd?

"You didn't get an extra pass, did you?" asked Cappy. "I don't have appointments until late—I could come with you."

"A pass?"

"A pass!" said Mildred. "Did we *get* a pass?"

I reached for the phone.

"What're you doing?"

"Hello, Waldorf. Head porter, please."

Cappy looked astonished.

Mildred looked hysterical. "My God, what's the matter with us!"

"Porter, this is Ruth Gordon in 520B. I need two passes to meet the *Manhattan* tomorrow."

"What's he say?" Mildred *was* hysterical.

"It's *terribly* important. I have to. . . . You're *sure?* . . . There's no *way* you could . . ."

"No?" Mildred didn't really have to ask. The look on my face was enough.

"I'll call Swope."

"My God!"

Mrs. Horowitz's gentle face looked surprised. "I thought two smart girls like you would have a pass." It wasn't criticism, just statement of an old law.

"Oh, hello, Mae, it's Ruth Gordon. . . . Thank you, Mae. Is Mr. Swope there? . . . Oh . . . Do you know where I could reach him? It's urgent. . . . Oh . . . Well, thank you, Mae."

"What?"

"On the *Twentieth Century,* going to Chicago for the fight."

"Call up Dick Maney. Here, let *me.*" Mildred took charge.

"But should we?" Could a press agent keep a secret?

"We've *got* to. Jones and Andrée are more important than publicity. Dick, it's Mildred. Listen, Dick, we've got to get down to meet the *Manhattan* and Ruth hasn't got passes. Could you get some newspaper to? They *must* have loose passes lying around. . . . Well, Dick, we *have* to. It's Jed's little boy coming in. They *can't* get off the boat alone. . . . All right, call me back. We're home."

"What's he say?"

302

"He'll call up Stanley Walker at the *Tribune.*"

"My God!"

"Dick'll handle it. He's press relations for Jed, isn't he? *Trust* him."

Mrs. Horowitz nodded. "You and Jed have to trust *someone,* or else remember to get passes."

The phone rang. "Yuh? . . . He can't? . . . You *sure* he can't? . . . *Sure?* . . . What time? . . . My God! He'll be there. And you'll take care of no . . . Okay, Dick. Be seeing you."

"What?"

She hung up. "Cappy, you have to be at Pier Five at six tomorrow morning. Stanley Walker'll have a newspaper pass for you. You'll go down the harbor and board the *Manhattan* and come back to dock with Jones and Andrée."

"My God!" His expression was something!

"Well, Ruth can't."

Mrs. Horowitz still looked astonished. "I thought two smart girls would have passes. Maybe it's *better* Cappy goes."

Mildred and I pressed against the wire barrier that held back the people with no passes. The *Manhattan*'s passengers were coming down the gangplank. Way off in the section under V, did we see Andrée? Did we see Jones? She looked the same, he looked foreign. Tan herringbone tweed overcoat. Brown cap. Brown *French* cap, not a beanie like American kids. More the shape of a yachting cap.

Cappy pointed toward the wire barrier. Andrée and Jones came over. He was agreeable, not impressed or rattled. "Ma*ma?*" he asked with a French accent.

Cappy was seeing their bags through customs. Andrée and Jones went back for her to sign the papers.

I rode to the Gladstone with them, Mildred stopped off at Barrow Street to get Nina, Helen arrived with little Mary. Jones was pleased to have new admirers, Mary and Nina were pleased to admire. For once, Andrée let things rip. Luncheon had been ordered ahead. Festivity wore out everybody but Jones. Born convivial, energy enough for a dozen, the celebration could've started all over again and gone on with no end.

"The boy without a limit," Mrs. Horowitz had described *her* boy Jed.

Andrée and The Judge liked the Gladstone, loved Mountain Lakes. The house was pleasant, sprawling, old. Jones had a room, Andrée had a fine corner room, I had a nice room for the week I was there. In the morning, Nina and Jones and Maxie Boy went with Aunt Mildred and me to the lake for a swim. Home again, lunch, naps, festivities for the afternoon, Cappy arrived for dinner on Friday.

Saturday night, he and Mildred and Andrée and I drove over to Lake Hopatcong. In the pleasure park was a novelty. "Come in and cut your own record. Greet your home folks," shouted the barker. "Make a record they can play on their phonograph and hear your voice!"

"I'll make one for Jones," I said. "We'll put it on his phonograph and he'll think it's going to be 'Snow White' or 'The Three Little Pigs,' then it'll be *my* voice."

I paid the dollar. The barker showed me into the tent, started the machine, I sang out:

> "Jones was a *little* boy.
> *Lived* at the Gladstone.
> *Came* on the *Manhattan*—"

I covered the ground, then did a finish, picked up the record and came out.

A crowd applauded.

"They broadcast you over the loudspeaker; it went all over the park."

Things that can happen to a secret!

A little boy should live in a house. Get a house with stairs and a garden. Down around Washington Square they couldn't cost as much as 135 East 79th Street had. The agent showed me 60 West 12th Street, a four-story red brick house with dark green blinds; a saffron-colored cornice finished off the roof. It was part of a row of houses that belonged to the Rhinelander estate, the land was the original Rhinelander farm. Tony Sarg, famous for his puppets, was the present tenant and loved it.

Do *you* know right off when a thing is it? On the ground floor was a big kitchen, two windows that looked out on 12th Street. A back door opened into the back hall, a door led down-cellar. It was *it!* Between the kitchen and the dining room was a bathroom, opposite was the pantry. A little boy should have a garden. The dining room was on the garden. In the west wall, a fireplace; the east wall, a flight of stairs led up to a hall with a hall closet and a French window on the garden. At the other end of the hall was our front door. It was *it!* A little boy should live in a house with stairs.

Except for the narrow hall, that floor was one long beautiful room, two French windows on 12th Street, two French windows on the garden.

From the front hall a flight of stairs led up to a landing, turned, one step up to the next floor. My Paris Vuitton trunk going around that turn would prove a trial to all future expressmen. A bathroom with a window was at the garden end of the hall, the other end a hall bedroom, one window that looked out on 12th Street. Marble fireplaces were in the two bedrooms. Between the rooms were shelves and closets.

The top-floor hall was square, off it a bathroom with one window that looked on the garden, a bedroom with two windows on the garden, a small inside room for storage with an iron ladder to the roof, two bedrooms on the 12th Street side, one small, one large. I signed a lease from September first for two years, at two hundred dollars a month. They'd repaint all the walls white except for the hall; it was papered with old ecru wallpaper showing soft brown balcony scenes with a scroll under, saying "Romeo and Juliet." Varying with the balcony were scenes from three other plays. Tony Sarg had said there was no record of when the paper had been put on.

The garden had a high board fence and one tree, higher than the house. Some sturdy old privet bushes were the rest of the garden. We'd plant bulbs and grass and more bushes and what else?

"Come with me to California?" It was Helen on the phone. "Charlie isn't coming."

"When do you go?"

"Day after tomorrow on the *Twentieth Century*. Charlie'll come later. Mary'll go as far as Chicago. She's going to Libertyville to stay on the farm with Mary and Alfred MacArthur and her cousin Georgianna."

Andrée and Jones were fine at Mountain Lakes. Maybe in California I could get into a movie. Helen was going out to do *What Every Woman Knows* at M-G-M.

"Yes, I'll come." We met at Grand Central information booth.

Charlie had come to see us off. He was waiting at the gate. He twisted his forelock and seemed uncomfortable; had they had a fight? "I'll be out soon," he said.

Goodbye, goodbye. We were off. M-G-M gave Helen a drawing room. She liked the upper.

"You *sure?*"

"Maybe it's because I'm used to it. When we toured, Mother always had the lower."

"Did you bring a warm dressing gown?" I asked. "Remember Dorothy Gish says the new air cooling can freeze us."

"I can hardly believe it, but I did."

Dorothy was right. Memories of damp linen handkerchiefs on our faces to keep the cinders off were a thing of the past. We had to leave our car and warm up in a car where the air cooling was more moderate.

In Chicago, Ernie Byfield was at the station. We were going to stay overnight and take the *Chief* the next day. Ernie took us to his hotel in the Loop, the Sherman House, where Gregory and I had had our first date at the College Inn. Ernie took us up to the seven-room suite on the roof, Chicago traffic clanging all around us. We left our suitcases and were off to the World's Fair.

At the World's Fair Theatre was *The Merry Wives.* Helen and I had our photo taken, arms linked with Mistress Page. No Mistress Ford?

Next morning to Marshall Field's for big linen handkerchiefs in case Dorothy was wrong. Mine was white with a border of red and yellow stripes. Why should it stick with me since 1934 when so many sensible things didn't?

Fanny Brice was on the *Chief* with her brother Lew and several Chihuahuas. Marjorie Moss of Moss and Fontana was going to California to die. Riding through the desert, Fanny said, "Let's go and visit her."

Fragile, dark-haired, gardenia white skin, no longer young, dazzling but never beautiful, she sat propped up in her berth. An ermine bed jacket made her even more ethereal. *No* one ever did such adagio leaps. A feather guided by Georges Fontana.

"Show us your loot," urged Fanny.

Marjorie told the maid to bring her jewel case. Over the Santa Fe bedspread were diamonds, emeralds, pearls, rubies. It was Camille. Even the consumption. Eddie Goulding did everything there was to do for her, but she had to die. Terrible to see grace and beauty go; no one could do what Marjorie Moss and Fontana did. And at the end she became Mrs. Goulding.

Our temporary address was the Beverly Wilshire while we looked for a house. Saw the one Laura Hope Crews had lived in, rented one owned by Walter Pidgeon. It was on North Walden across from the one Helen had had the summer she made *Another Language.* This one not as grand. No pool. Helen's bedroom suite faced the driveway, my room the other direction. In between was a spare room. A room downstairs for the housekeeper-cook. Her name was Girlie Johnson. She was black, with shingled peroxide-blond curly hair, and drove an old black coupe with

"Girlie" in Old English lettering on the door.

The night we moved in, Helen gave a party for her mother and Charlie's sister, Helen Bishop, who were sailing next day on the cruise to the Orient, a present from Helen. That was our only party. Next day Helen started work.

Irving Thalberg had taken a poll whether people wanted *What Every Woman Knows* to be modern or period. Why is that the way to decide?

Brian Aherne played John Shand, Gregory La Cava was the director. He referred to Irving as The Pagoda. "I've been summoned by The Pagoda," he'd tell Helen. He and she got along fine. One Saturday they went fishing. All the time I'd known Helen and never knew she fished.

"Love to," she said. A girl with plenty of talents.

Another Saturday, Irving and Norma gave a grand party for Helen at their Santa Monica house. Everybody! The Goldwyns, the David Selznicks, Clark Gable, William Powell, Fredric March, Myrna Loy, the Charles Laughtons. The place card next to me said "Mr. Lubitsch." He acted so crazy about me I went over to Helen at the Thalbergs' table. "What Lubitsch is it?" I whispered.

"Ernst."

I'd met him, but that was a nervous occasion; now here he was acting crazy about me. Could this be the *real* Lubitsch? There was only one! There only *will* be one!

"I'm having a housewarming next Saturday. Will you come?" he urged.

"I'm Helen's house guest. Can she come?"

"Of course."

The Thalbergs' dinner went smoothly until the forty-piece orchestra got in the sitting room and bottled up the dining room door. We couldn't get out. Irving looked at Norma. She'd done it again! Did it bother Norma?

Monday brought our invite to the housewarming. I went to Magnin's and bought a dress. Magnin's sent over a lot for Helen.

Saturday The Los Angeles *Times* gave the list of the two hundred and fifty everybodies invited, including us. After the guest list, they ran the menu. The Lubitsch touch?

Girlie Johnson drove us to Bel Air. At the mansion, everybody was going in or getting out of their car. My place card was beside Walter Wanger's, grand movie producer. Before he was, Woollcott had taken me to lunch with him, something to do with Dartmouth, where he'd gone. I forget what it was, but I didn't forget he was married to Justine

Johnstone, one of the beauties who'd been in *Oh Boy*. I'd read in the paper that when they got married he made her give back all her jewelry. In Wilkes-Barre, I told that to Guy Bolton, who looked as though she hadn't given him back his. "He *did?*" was all he said.

"Why aren't you in pictures?" Walter Wanger asked me.

"I *want* to be."

"Who's your agent?"

"I haven't got one."

"You have now. Phil!" he called across the table. "This is Ruth Gordon. You're her agent." Out West, they don't fool around.

"Fine," said Phil Berg. "Come to see me Monday."

The Berg-Allenberg Agency was beside the Beverly Wilshire Hotel. I signed a contract and met Bert Allenberg. It's so easy, once you get to the right housewarming.

Over at Paramount, they were getting ready to do *Ruggles of Red Gap* for Charles Laughton.

"You'll be great as the widow," said Charles, and told Paramount to hire me.

Paramount said I'd better make a test.

"Nonsense," said Charles. To me he said, "Do it to humor them."

Bert Allenberg arranged the deal, to be signed after the test. "Fifteen hundred dollars a week." It didn't occur to me there'd be an *if*.

Helen was excited, I was excited, Charles was complacent. Director Leo McCarey made the test. Charles said I'd be great, but I didn't feel great. Why was that?

"You'll be very funny," Charles said.

I didn't *feel* funny; everything I did felt like nothing.

"Feel all right?" asked Leo McCarey.

Could I say to a director, "I feel like nothing"?

Bert Allenberg and I went over to Paramount and looked at the test. It looked like nothing. They hired Zasu Pitts. Charles felt bad, I felt bad, Helen felt bad, Bert Allenberg said, "I don't see you in that part. We'll do better."

The phone rang. "Bert Allenberg. Edgar Selwyn would like to make a test of you at M-G-M."

"Terrific!"

"He can do what he wants—his wife's sister is Pansy Schenck, married to Nick Schenck, the president. Edgar said you're a wonderful actress. Could we go over and see him this afternoon?"

When Selwyn and Company had produced *Fair and Warmer,* Edgar was their president. I'd never met him, but later on I'd see him dance by at the Sixty Club with his wife, Margaret Mayo, who wrote *Baby Mine,* that ran and ran and ran.

Then Margaret Mayo divorced Edgar for a young man, who left her. That destroyed her. They said she lived alone in the hills up around Croton; one day she died, all alone.

Edgar married beautiful Ruthie Wilcox; she and Pansy had done a sister act. For Edgar nothing went very well. He'd been a successful leading man, a successful producer, joined up with Sam Goldfish to form Goldwyn Pictures, then he ran out of luck.

He was kind, gentle, defeated; Ruthie was tough, sure, ran things.

"Helen likes movies, doesn't she?" asked Edgar, softly. He'd directed *The Sin of Madelon Claudet* and Helen won the Oscar.

"Oh, yes."

"You would, too." His voice was not insistent, just treading water. "You'll be great. We'll make a great test, not just rush at it; this will be a real one. One part comedy, one emotional. You can do both and we'll show you can."

For the emotional, he decided on my scene from *They Shall Not Die.* For comedy, he picked a scene from *The Wiser They Are.*

"I'll get Franchot Tone to play it with you. We'll rehearse it as though it was a play we were opening. I'll rehearse the electricians till I get one who'll know how to light you. We'll test cameramen and makeup people. This is going to be *good,* Ruth." Was he convincing himself? Once the head of powerful Selwyn and Company, what had brought him down? Margaret Mayo and the young man? Ruthie? Maybe a combination. Not everybody can take it when a *lot* of things go wham.

We rehearsed for two weeks and when Edgar shot it, it was good. The scene with Franchot was all right, but the scene from *They Shall Not Die* was *it.*

"M-G-M wants to sign you," phoned Bert.

"My God!"

"They want a seven-year contract with options. They'll start you at seventeen-fifty with a four-week guarantee."

"My God!"

"My God!" said Helen. "But what about your Theatre Guild contract?"

309

They'd signed me to open the Guild season in the great London success, James Bridie's *A Sleeping Clergyman,* early October, rehearsals after Labor Day.

"Fine," said Bert Allenberg. "That gives M-G-M time to get a good vehicle for you. You don't want to rush in; let them find the right thing."

He brought the contracts over. In Helen's sitting room I signed and signed. Could I believe I was going to be a movie star? Could I believe I was going to get $1750 a week?

Dinners and parties took on a new tone. No matter how the conversation started, it got around to "I signed with M-G-M!"

"I signed with M-G-M!" I said to Al Newman and his wife, Beth. They were giving a dinner for Helen.

"I signed with M-G-M!" I told Charlie Butterworth. After dinner, he and his wife, Ethel, and I had settled down together, but Helen got stuck with a bunch that didn't interest her. From where I sat, she could hear me say, "No!" Then some more from the Butterworths, then "No!" Then the Butterworths. "No!" On and on.

"What on earth did you keep saying 'No!' about?" asked Helen on the way home.

"Their robbery! It was night and the bell rang. 'Western Union,' a voice said. Charlie and Ethel were in bed. Ethel didn't have a stitch on. And the robber said to get the jewels and Ethel said could she put something on and he said, 'No.' "

"No!" said Helen. I guess she sounded like I had.

"Anyway, she was getting all the stuff together, Charlie watching from in bed. He didn't have anything on, either, but he stayed under the sheet, and finally Ethel got it all out and the robber liked her and said, 'I'll let you keep one thing for a keepsake,' and Ethel said, 'Oh, thank you,' and picked out the big square diamond ring Charlie gave her, and the robber laughed and said, 'Nothing doing,' and went off with the whole lot."

"No!"

Was it about one in the morning that our front doorbell rang? Scared to death, I opened my bedroom door. Helen had opened hers, scared. We stood wondering what to do.

Girlie Johnson, wrapper around her, shuffled to the door. "I won't open 'less they tell me who they are," she muttered.

Helen and I held hands and stared.

"Who are you?" called Girlie.

"Western Union."

310

She opened the door and it really was.

The telegram was from Charlie MacArthur; he would arrive Saturday.

"Oh, good," I said. "The Laughtons want me to drive up to Arrowhead."

"You don't have to."

"I *want* to." I was pretty sure there'd been a something and this would be a good time for them to be together. I phoned the Laughtons. "I have to come with you to Arrowhead."

"You do?"

"Charlie MacArthur's coming and I want to be out of the house."

"All right." Did Elsa sound reluctant?

"They *insist,"* I told Helen.

Brownie arrived back from her cruise and asked about Helen.

"She's doing the railway station scene," I told her. "Charlie wired he'll get here tomorrow."

"What else did he say?"

"I didn't read the wire."

Brownie looked at it. " 'Back Saturday and we'll fly to the High Sierras.' Oh, isn't that *inconsiderate* of him, dragging her off some fool place!" She reread it, and looked embarrassed. "Oh, I guess it's a form of speech."

"She's the best," said Gregory La Cava. Helen had to do a scene of uncontrolled laughter. Any idea how hard that is? They rehearsed, but Helen isn't much of a rehearser. Was Lew Fields right? When she was beginning in his company of *Old Dutch,* the director complained she wasn't any good.

"She's like me," Lew Fields told him. "She waits till there's two dollars in every seat." That was when Helen was five; did she still wait?

"Ready?" asked La Cava.

"Ready," said Helen.

The cameras rolled.

Uncontrolled laughter, on and on.

Gregory La Cava was thunderstruck. So were the rest of us.

"Something went wrong," said the cameraman. "Could we get another take?"

Gregory groaned.

"That's all right," said Helen.

"Oh, my God, to *lose* that!"

"It's all *right.*"

"Ready?"

"Ready."

"Camera."

When they say "Camera," that means this may be a take, and that means two dollars in every seat.

"Camera."

Uncontrolled laughter on and on. And on. *Exactly* like the first take. I'd come out to watch Helen and learn. Everybody can't *do* uncontrolled laughter. Everybody can't do a lot of things Helen Hayes can.

Summer goes fast when you're having a good time. I was having a good time. A Theatre Guild contract, an M-G-M contract, helps you have a good time.

Helen went to the studio, I went to lunch or shopped or where I got invited. George Oppenheimer gave a do for Myrna Loy. What a nice couple I met there! Mr. and Mrs. Jack Haley. I knew Jack Haley was a musical comedy star and Mrs. Haley was beautiful. Why did I give a long talk on no alimony? I was against it. If you took it you were dreadful, I explained, but that didn't hurt the liking that had sprung up between me and the Haleys, who turned out to be the Paleys, and she'd just gotten divorced from Bill Hearst. "Come to lunch tomorrow," she said.

"I will."

"We're staying at my mother's." She gave me the address. "One o'clock."

At Walden Drive, Helen was asleep; I tiptoed in. What a fright! On my pillow, a pink ball and a carving knife with a note! What maniac had been at work? What debauch had taken place? What would the note demand? "If the party's still on next door," wrote Helen, "cut this in two and let it get soft. It's wax to stuff in your ears." Talk about a happy ending!

The rooms at 60 West 12th Street were getting painted white. In Mountain Lakes, Jones and Andrée were getting ready to come to New York. In Hollywood, I went to Max Factor's to order four wigs for the four different people I'd act in *A Sleeping Clergyman*. Four people in one play isn't easy; it doesn't hurt to have four good wigs. Maybe they don't go along with that in academies of dramatic art, but until I hear their hints, four good wigs for four different people don't make playing them any harder.

On my last night, Ernst Lubitsch invited Helen and me to a sneak preview of *The Merry Widow.*

Remember Chevalier? I'd adored him when Gregory and I saw *Dedé* in Paris. I adored him the afternoon Norma Shearer invited Helen and me to meet him at her sister's, Athol Hawks. I don't think I said more than that I'd seen him in *Dedé,* but in Union Station I sent him a telegram before I got on the *Chief.*

In the next drawing room was Grace Moore, going to New York for the gala premiere of her movie, *One Night of Love.* I'd met her when she was in the *Music Box Revue* and chummed with Ruth Goldbeck, later Ruth Valambrosa. The summer I was trying out *The Phantom Ship,* Grace and Ruth showed Gregory and Charlie MacArthur a great time in Antibes. And when I was in Antibes visiting Woollcott and Harpo, Grace had her villa at Cagnes and came around to look over the field.

She'd been to *The Merry Widow* preview, but hadn't thought to wire Maurice. Next day at lunch, I showed her the wire the porter put under my door at Albuquerque. It was from Maurice!

"Just *what* did you say in your wire?" she asked, admiringly. Grace liked people who didn't let the grass grow.

In Chicago, publicity called for Grace to go out to the Fair, before boarding the *Twentieth Century.* "Come with me." We were in and out, photos snapped in the theatre where *The Merry Wives* played, like Helen and me on the way west, then back to our drawing rooms, now hooked onto the *Century.* That was the brief blissful period when you traveled in the same car coast to coast. "Cattle don't change trains, so why should people?" asked Mr. Robert Young, a railroad tycoon with some sense. Why did he have to kill himself?

"I'm going to stay in my room and read *Entirely Surrounded,* Charlie Brackett's new novel about that island and Woollcott and all the people. I have to look rested for the photos tomorrow. Where will you be in New York?"

"The Waldorf."

"You have to come to the premiere. Would Jed Harris?"

"I hope so."

I was at the Waldorf; 60 West 12th looked great, but not ready. Another two weeks? Isn't that about normal, when you move into a new place?

Jones and Andrée moved into the Grosvenor Hotel, Fifth Avenue at 11th Street, and then would you believe it? The house was ready ahead of time! We moved in. Everybody had a home at last. White walls, Shakespeare wallpaper, flights of stairs, a garden. Everybody had a room of his own, a cook and a maid looked after us, a handyman came every day and I had not one, but *two* contracts.

From California, I'd written Mildred to go to Mme. Jacquin's Agency and get a French cook. She got the greatest. Young, pretty, small, exquisite, perfect disposition, *great* cook, Suzanne from Mur-de-Bretagne, Côtes-du-Nord, spoke fluent English, though she'd been over here only two years. Her husband was *saucier* at the Biltmore Hotel. They'd known each other from childhood, came to America to make their fortunes and did.

Every day, Suzanne arrived at nine; every other Sunday after one o'clock dinner, she was off. And one afternoon a week. Irish Katherine Waldron got Jones and Andrée their breakfast and cooked dinner for us the evening Suzanne was off. Katherine was tall and hearty. She and Suzanne were friends right off.

On October 16, Suzanne baked the first of a long line of Jones' birthday cakes. It was angel with white frosting, six candles, one to grow on; in pink icing Suzanne wrote HAPPY BIRTHDAY JONES. It rested on the centerpiece Mrs. Brigham had embroidered for *my* first birthday cake at 41 Winthrop Avenue, Wollaston, Massachusetts. Sixteen more had rested on it. Round in shape, it was embroidered with a wreath of wild pink roses, the edge scalloped in white, now turned cream.

For Jones' birthday, Mary MacArthur came in from Nyack, and Nina came, from Barrow Street. Stephen Pascal came from next door. A good party.

Up at the Guild Theatre, *A Sleeping Clergyman* wasn't as good. The Theatre Guild brought over Ernest Thesiger for the part he created in London. Good. They *didn't* bring Robert Donat, whose performance made history. That wasn't good. It wasn't good that we opened cold. It could have used Bobby Donat and a few weeks out of town. Lots of difficult costume changes, wig and makeup changes, scene changes for lots of scenes.

Opening night, us chickens ran in and out of all those places, when not rushing in and out of costumes, shoes, wigs, and slapping on another Leichner grease-paint base. Three weeks later, the Guild general manager, Warren Munsell, knocked at my dressing room door. "We're closing next week," he said.

"Good." Done *right,* I bet it could have gone. I knew it would happen but even when you know stuff it doesn't keep it from being a major jolt.

"Ready for M-G-M," I wrote Bert Allenberg. "After Christmas, please."

DELIGHTED THEY WILL BE READY FOR YOU. BEST BERT

Forty performances for all that scenery, all Bridie's writing, all those costumes, wigs. At the last Saturday matinee, Jones and Andrée came. It was his first time in a theatre. Their seats were first row balcony, center.

"What do you think of your mother?" someone asked him.

"She's very good."

He'd entered City and Country School, 12th Street, in the next block. Jed had tackled Miss Caroline Pratt, the invincible head of it, and she succumbed. The school had its full quota, but when Jed finished, Jones was enrolled in the first grade.

Did he like it?

He didn't say.

60 West 12th was working out. "You have to have a dog," phoned Woollcott. "That's my present to the new house. Joe'll drive us out to Mount Kisco to Blanche Saunders' Carillon Kennels."

The house would have a dog. Poor Maxie Boy had come back from Paris, gone to Mountain Lakes, been stolen, and rewards offered never brought back Maxie Boy. Miss Saunders showed us a big black French poodle she'd helped to enter this life. Fourteen years later, as he left it, she held his paw. Definition of a friend?

"I'll call him Sacha," I said, "after Sacha Guitry." Darling Sacha. He didn't take riding off with strangers lightly. Parting with Miss Saunders he didn't take lying down. In the back seat of Woollcott's car, he threw up. Joe Hennessey walked him on the country road. He slipped his loose collar and tore off toward Mount Kisco. Did Joe sprint after him? Did he turn Woollcott's car and head off the new dog? However it happened, he was in the back seat again.

Farther along, Joe stopped and we bought four gallon jugs of cider at a road stand. Every so often a cork blew off. Once all four blew together.

315

Alec and I worked over them like a pair of Swiss bell ringers.

In front of number 60, shaking with apprehension, Sacha stepped out cautiously. Inside, he rushed around looking for Miss Saunders. We let him loose in the garden, but it wasn't Mount Kisco. In the hall beside the kitchen was the back door, at the other end, the door to the cellar; the doors were old and air came in. For the night, Sacha was left there with a bowl of water and an old comforter. In the morning Katherine Waldron looked in. The comforter was torn to pieces—there wasn't one square inch. Poor Sacha!

"Let me take him back for a month," said Miss Saunders. "I can train him."

When Sacha saw her, he jumped like a performing pony. Woollcott had paid a hundred dollars for him and after one night he went back, was away for four weeks, then with us thirteen years. A friend, a lesson in goodness, in endurance. We could all learn from Sacha.

For Thanksgiving, Suzanne roasted a great turkey. My last family Thanksgiving had been at 14 Elmwood Avenue, the turkey from the Mellin's Food Company. Around the table were Aunt Emma, Uncle George, Papa, Mama, me. Around the 60 West 12th table sat Cappy, Nina, Mildred, Andrée, Jones, me. Everybody exclaimed over the turkey, it was the finest. Everywhere in the four-story red brick house it smelled like Thanksgiving.

For Christmas, Andrée sewed white tarlatan bags to hang on the tree, filled them with Christmas candy and sugar pincushions. Mildred and I popped corn to string and throw across the branches. The Christmas ornaments from the American Hospital, the Alden, Rue des Belles Feuilles, came out of their wrappings, new ones added. The same menu as Thanksgiving, the same cast, presents for everyone. Edward Chodorov, author of *Wonder Boy* and *Kind Lady,* sent Jones a big red automobile with pedals to push, a real glass windshield and a horn. Only one word for it: gorgeous.

"Eddie has to take it back," said Jed.

I had to agree.

Jones looked surprised. "Why can't I keep it?"

"It would make other children feel bad that they didn't have one."

He looked thoughtful.

The automobile went back to Schwarz's. Did Jones ever think of it again?

Goodbye, goodbye. All aboard for California! The S.S. *Pennsylvania*
sailed early January. Jed's sister Sylvia was coming with me as my
secretary.

Ice-cold wind blew the ship into New Jersey, but the tugboats shoved
us downstream. It was noon; the steward looked in. "Want anything?"

"Could you get this fan out? It almost covers the porthole."

"You'll need it."

"We will?"

"And how!" He took off.

The next day was still cold, then the morning after, we sailed past
Morro Castle into spring. The ship would tie up in port all day.

At the Havana docks, the sun beat down on our ship, then staged a
violent sunset. We slipped past Morro Castle into the Gulf of Mexico.

"Rough till we get near Panama," said stewardess, and she knew what
she was talking about. Sylvia and I took to our berths. The next morning, we found out what the electric fan was for—it was to keep us from
suffocating. Central America over on the right, South America on the
left, and damp heat, getting damper and hotter.

Ahead of us, the white *Caronia* was going through the locks. Cole
Porter, Howard Sturges, Linda Cole Porter, Monty Woolley, Moss Hart
were in the lock ahead of us. The white *Caronia* rose and sailed on, on
its way around the world. Then we rose as if our ship had turned into
an elevator. On the canal banks, machines called mules pulled us along.
Who thought up locomotion like that? Off in a bog was rusty machin-
ery, graveyard of France's efforts. What happened?

We left the Caribbean at Colón and when we came out it was the
Pacific. The ship docked at Panama City, and then four more days on
board. Even the Roderick Towerses of Philadelphia unbent. Everybody
invited everybody into the bar for a morning sherry. The handsome
Smitherses gave a wild-duck dinner. They'd brought the ducks from
Maryland, where they'd shot them. Steam by Honduras and eat Maryland wild duck!

The ship put in to San Diego for a day ashore. The Smitherses asked
Sylvia and me to lunch at the Coronado Beach Hotel, then Tijuana.
Goodbye, Tijuana, I won't be back. Not a knock, just saying there are
places I like better.

San Pedro was our destination.

Jed was on the dock. He'd rented a house in Beverly Hills. Helen had
sent her car. She was filming *Vanessa*. I'd hired a car and let the Smi-

therses use it to go to Altadena. Jed sent the baggage with Sylvia in Helen's car. We took off in his.

Ever have nothing go right? M-G-M was pleased to see me, said they'd certainly look for something. "Great you're here." They ran the Paula Wessely film *Masquerade*. "Would you like to do the English remake?"

*Would* I!

They retitled it *Escapade* and did it with Luise Rainer.

Everybody friendly, everybody lovely, and came up with a B picture. I'd rather they'd have been terrible and cast me in *Escapade*. The one for me was made from a play that ran one night in New York. My part was a phone operator.

"A phone operator could be interesting," said Charles Laughton.

Why didn't I listen? Why didn't I take a chance? I rang up the producer. "Bernie, my window is open. I'll jump out if I have to play that."

"Come over and talk."

Una Merkel played it; it was no good, but might have led to something. I should have listened to Charles.

"Come over and stay with me." It was Ruth Chatterton on the phone. Nothing was going right for her, either.

Her career was on the blink, so was mine, her love life gone to hell, so had mine, her finances zero, so were mine, but gallant Ruth behaved as though it was still the grand days. She ordered grand clothes from Howard Greer, mornings she rode her five-gaited saddle horse in the Burbank hills that looked down at Warner Brothers' studio, where her salary had been eight thousand dollars every week.

"Why don't you ride, Ruthie?" she asked me.

The stables rented me a fourteen-hand horse; we trailed along after Ruth. I'd never ridden, but why not?

Home to an exquisite lunch in her *small* dining room off the walnut-paneled grand dining room for dinner parties. When old buddies from the boat came to call, their eyes opened on a tour around Ruth's table, set for a dinner party. Place cards for Ronald Colman, Jascha Heifetz, Grace Moore, Maurice Chevalier, Kay Francis, Dolores Del Rio, Noël Coward, Cary Grant, Charles and Pat Boyer, Frances and Nate Spingold, William Powell, Carole Lombard! Something to write home about!

In the afternoon, we drove out to Mines Field. Pilot Bob Blair gave

Ruth a flying lesson, then me. Go up in the clouds and maybe when you come down there'll be a phone message: "You got an offer!"

We flew Bob Blair's open Fleet. Lessons went so well that Ruth bought her own Stinson. Nights when there was no dinner party, we boned up on flying. A vector: what is it? Describe the fuselage. What is a 720? What is the theory of gliding? When would I get a job?

Invitations, but no offers. Western Union delivered a telegram:

MISS RUTH GORDON
704 N. PALM DRIVE
BEVERLY HILLS
CALIFORNIA

BE AT M-G-M FOR LUNCH ONE O'CLOCK TO MEET MICHAEL BALCON THURSDAY
APRIL 3. LOUIS B. MAYER

Was M-G-M sorry? I wrote out my reply. "Dear Mr. Mayer, you must have the wrong Ruth Gordon. I'm the one M-G-M had a contract with and we never met. Ruth Gordon."

Ruth was in her bathtub. I read her Mr. Mayer's, then mine. She laughed.

"If you'd rather not have it sent over your phone, I'll go out and send it."

"Oh, I don't give a damn about that, but maybe you shouldn't."

"I certainly will. I've worked for a lot of people, but I at least *met* them. He didn't even bother to *meet* me and I was there *four* weeks!"

Years after, I was telling his daughter Edie.

"He'd never see it," she said. "They wouldn't give him a message like that."

He didn't see it, but it made *me* feel better.

"Why *should* she?" said my father, when I wouldn't kiss Mr. Dollaber, the boss of the Mellin's Food Company. It made Mama cry, but Papa understood. Papa was forty-one, I was three, but he saw my point of view.

"Give me a kiss," said Mr. Dollaber.

"No," I said.

Coming home on the train, Mama was still tearful. "Oh, why *couldn't* she, just to be nice?"

"Why *should* she?" Papa thought things out for himself.

319

Ruth's new Stinson was delivered. Shiny black like dancing-school slippers, it had a yellow trim. Early one morning she and I and Blair took off for Mexico. Maybe when we came home there'd be an offer.

Did we *want* to go to Mexico in a single-motor plane or was it the way things were going? Did we give a damn if we got there? I never thought of killing myself, but there were times I wasn't all that careful. Leland Hayward said, "When everything goes to hell and you don't care, that's when the plane *doesn't* crash, when the ship *doesn't* sink, when your car *stays* on the road." He ought to know, because when Lola divorced him and married another guy, people said Leland jumped off the *Aquitania* and got fished out. He said he didn't, but who would make up stuff like that? If people say a guy jumps off a boat, I bet he did.

Flying lessons afternoons, dinner party at night or dinner for us two and study the manual, mornings on that Burbank horse and afternoon, evening, morning in despair.

Bert Allenberg rang up. "M-G-M wants you to do a little part in Joan Crawford's picture. It's good, but only two sides and they won't pay you. They say you got four weeks' salary and didn't work."

"Tell 'em to go to hell."

"You sure?"

"Sure." Maybe I'd have made a hit. Which is worth more, your pride or a hit?

"Will you star in I. A. R. Wylie's *A Feather in Her Hat?*" Columbia Pictures asked Ruth.

There were three weeks before they'd start shooting. Ruth told Rita, her secretary, to book her on Pan Am for Seville and the Easter bullfights, then signed to do the film for Columbia. If you stay with it, things shape up. She flew to Seville, I took the *Chief* to Chicago. In Chicago, Thornton asked me to marry him. I loved him, he loved me, but we weren't in love. Why did he ask me to marry him? He knew the one I wanted to marry didn't ask me and he thought somebody should.

After the two days in Chicago, visit Leonard Hanna in Cleveland. He met me at the station and we drove to dinner at the University Club. On the way out to his house in Mentor, he stopped at a raffish night-club. After the show we came out and the car door had been pried open, my mink coat gone, also my fitted suitcase that Gregory had had made at Tiffany's, my grand wardrobe for being a movie star, bought at Gervaise.

Sunday night, Leonard put me on the train to New York. Ever travel

Cleveland to New York with no luggage? It feels funny. Or is funny the word?

It was May again. Why is it that when you're out of a job, it's May? And who casts shows in May?

Jones and Andrée and I went to Dr. Schloss' office. A regular checkup.

"I want to talk to you," said Dr. Schloss.

Andrée and Jones went to the outer office.

"Miss Valentin must go."

"Must *go?*"

"Must go. There's a definite attachment."

"Must *go?*"

"Oh, yes."

From his birth they'd been together—why *not* an attachment? Isn't that what everyone's looking for?

Andrée was leaving. No more struggle with Immigration to get her stay extended. No more needing Swope to help.

"An attachment," said Dr. Schloss, and it was all over.

Who'd look after Jones? I couldn't take him on a summer stock tour, he couldn't stay at 12th Street through the heat.

"A definite attachment." How I wished *I* had one.

"Are you interested in camp for Jones?" phoned Miss Hartman. She taught first grade at City and Country School.

"He won't be six till October. Isn't he too young?"

Miss Hartman came over to discuss it. "It's a new camp we're starting at Lake Mahopac."

"Where's that?"

"Westchester, near Brewster. It's for little children."

Was this what to do?

"We can't get a permit, Andrée; they won't renew."

"I'll have to go, then."

"Yes."

"And my boy?"

"Miss Hartman says there's a wonderful camp for little boys. She'll be there."

Andrée looked resigned. "I'll get him ready. He'll need things for camp."

The room above me was Andrée's. Was she asleep or was she troubled too? She'd been born on a Greek island where her father was doing engineering. She graduated from the class of 1914 at the American Hospital in Neuilly. Now she was going back.

Across the hall from Andrée was Jones, born at the American Hospital and *not* going back. Was he asleep or did *he* know his world was changing?

Down 12th Street, a phonograph was playing, someone's dog barked, how would I handle everything?

"You'll manage," said Dr. Gray. Would I?

"Our Father Who art in Heaven, hallowed be Thy Name. Thy Kingdom come, Thy will be done, on earth as it is in Heaven. Give us this day our daily bread and forgive us our trespasses as we forgive those who trespass against us. And lead us not into temptation, but deliver us from evil, for Thine is the Kingdom and the Power and the Glory for ever and ever, amen. God bless Mama and Papa and make me a good girl, God bless Jones, God bless Gregory and help me, God, I need money, help me."

"Don't be helpless, Ruth," urged Mama. "You'll manage everything," said Dr. Gray. Now would be a good time to start. Start with my money worries; they'd gone on all my life. In Wollaston, Papa was in despair, Mama trying to cope. At The Three Arts Club, the board bill and Miss Seaborn's dunning note. At the Hotel Richmond, at Martin's Theatrical, the board bill blues, then Gregory and no money worries until we bought the Packard touring car and engaged a chauffeur, Beverly. We sold the Packard, picked up a secondhand Pierce-Arrow, Gregory learned to drive, and no more money worries.

Gregory left me sixty thousand dollars. In *Saturday's Children* I earned 5 percent of the gross, no money worries, but now they were back again. Where would money come from?

"God, let me get some money. God, You have granted so many wishes, help me, dear God, please help."

The radio stopped, shadows from the tree in the back garden splattered over my white bedroom, over the white and pink Venetian mirror I'd bought when Gregory said we could spend $5000 to furnish 36 West 59th Street and we spent over $7000.

A dog barked, sleepily.

"Shut up," shouted a man.

Why did I feel calm? What had happened? Hadn't I lived through worry before? Confidence rushed back. I had a career, I had health, a lot of responsibilities, but a lot of experience. Thirty-nine years' worth, not one easy year, but isn't that the way with everybody that's trying to get somewhere? Nothing had flattened me out; I'd get going in the next round. Money always had gotten solved, so why not now?

The dog barked, less sleepy.

"Shut up!" I shouted.

The hired car was out front. Andrée and Jones and I drove off.

He looked so little.

It would have been heartbreaking, except that he had no qualms about leaving. He welcomed a new life. The camp was not great, but good. We saw the cabin where he'd sleep. He liked it. Andrée put away the clothes she'd outfitted him with.

The little boy Andrée had spent *every* day and night with for five and a half years was at Lake Mahopac with strangers and she would sail for France. There are more questions than answers, but what kind of people have no attachments?

"Goodbye, Mama."

"Goodbye, Jones."

"Goodbye, Aunt Andrée."

"Goodbye, Coco."

Act as though it was nothing.

"Goodbye."

"Goodbye."

"Goodbye."

End of a chapter.

# Chapter

---◦∞◦---

# 14

Up on the top floor at 60 West 12th, nobody in Jones' room, nobody in Andrée's, Katherine Waldron played the radio softly in her room, Thornton and I sat on the front steps. They'd baked warm in the sun all day. *Too* warm for Sacha. He flung himself down on the threshold and went fast asleep. A great moon hung low over 12th Street. If it hung over the stage, the director would have called to the electrician, "Too yellow. Throw in more straw."

"Are you all right?" asked Thornton.

"Yes. Sometimes I'm lonely."

He looked astonished. *"Isn't that interesting!"*

What an odd reaction, Thornton so sympathetic.

"Anyone intelligent as you doesn't get lonely."

"Is that true?"

"Oh, yes."

"Maybe I'm not all that intelligent. If I was intelligent why haven't I gotten further?"

"How far you get isn't possible to put in the present tense. Cézanne's family stashed *Mont Ste. Victoire* in the barn so neighbors wouldn't see it. Did *he* ask where *he'd* gotten? Or did he know enough to not stop and ask?"

"What if somebody looks back and finds they've been wrong all the time?"

"That's called demonology, Bella."

"Isn't it good to find out?"

"*If* you've got the strength to, rise above it. Ever read Matthew Arnold?"

"Sure."

"Remember 'The Scholar Gypsy'? Wandering in his own world, then his wandering brought him back to the old haunts. He came to 'the causeway chill,' looked back and saw the 'line of festal light in Christ Church hall'—and remembered the many years since he'd left there, searching.

" 'Dreamer, the years you search are gone,' old Dr. Arnold said. Or words to that effect."

"Demonology?"

"They're not gone. Leave time and timetables to whom it may concern, Bella; go and wander. There are places never shown on the maps at Quincy High. Without wandering, a Quincy girl of no particular gifts —your *own* words, dear—couldn't have gotten from the Old Colony railroad station to Grand Central to Charles Frohman's illustrious Empire Theatre to do a pillow dance as the 'ever so gay' Nibs, where *The New York Times* drama critic welcomed your performance with Sir James Barrie's *own* adjective—'Nibs is more gay and debonair.' "

"Barrie said Nibs was gay?"

"From 14 Elmwood Avenue to the Empire stage is feeling, hope, intention. Arnold *couldn't* say where the Scholar Gypsy had gotten and we can't say where *you* have, except your wandering has brought you to sit here tonight."

"But shouldn't I *look* at what I'm doing and maybe change? I'm not finished till I'm up at Campbell's. By the way, I'm not going. I went to Helen's lawyer and made a new will: 'No funeral.' "

"Well, as I said so beautifully in *The Woman of Andros,* funerals require genius."

"Funerals for theatre people, nobody knows what to wear. They show up in polo coats and eleven o'clock in the morning nobody's up. Do *you* look any good at eleven? Well, of course, you look awful *all* the time.

You get yourself up, a cross between the absent-minded professor and 'Brown of Harvard.' Don't you want to do something about it? Being eccentric is over."

"I'm flattered at your interest, Bella."

"What would *really* be eccentric is be normal."

"But what is your definition of 'normal'? Normal is like no scenery. What *is* it? Not Cornelia Skinner's black velvet drapes, not steam pipes on the backstage wall, but, dear, we may not solve that this evening and you left us at your funeral."

"At my *non*-funeral."

A couple strolling by stopped and kissed.

"Do Christian Scientists have funerals? *They* don't ever face the facts and neither do Campbell's. Campbell's book a minister that never went to a show, never heard of anybody! 'Our dear sister Ruth Jordan,' he begins, then is stumped. He can't refer to your good notices, he can't tell the story of your life, that the obituaries got all wrong."

"Could you get McClintic to stage it?"

"At least he'd use all pink lights so people wouldn't look like they're auditioning for the next service."

"And think how lovely *you*'d look!"

"I'm not going to."

"What will you give us instead, dear?"

"My will says to turn up the heat, like on a stifling matinee day. The hotter it is, the more it'll seem like backstage at the Booth. The heat'll only be up a notch further and the lights brighter; I'm used to bright lights."

"Dear, I suddenly feel happier. I daresay it's the bright lights."

"Is cremation deductible? It's a business expense."

"What business is that, dear? By then, you're no longer in business."

"Depreciation of wardrobe? Publicity?"

"Dear, when thinking about where you've been, where you're going and what you're doing, why begin with the finale?"

"Probably because I never learned to think, so I don't do it in sequence."

"Gertrude Stein thinks chronology is of no interest."

"But *she* knows how to think. I *think* I'm thinking, but actually I'm planning and wishing and worrying."

"Verbs of desire and despair take the subjunctive, dear. Ever think why you can *talk* an hour, read an hour, but can you *think* an hour?"

"Maybe if I planned a subject?"

"Try 'Why do people dislike each other?' "

"*Do* we? Do *you* have enemies? I don't. Maybe nobody gives enough of a damn about me."

"You're being too modest, Bella."

"Do you know anybody does?"

"The girl that Gregory went for, then you married him?"

"That was eighteen years ago!"

"Do you think she feels dispassionate when you make a hit opening night?"

"How long can anyone nurse a grievance? The longest I ever held on to one was thirteen years."

"Your nature drips with forgiveness, dear."

"I'm furious over what happened *yesterday* and *last week,* but how much more can I handle? I bet Aggie'd be *pleased* to bump into me."

"I wonder."

"I'm *sure* she would."

"Dear, all of us haven't your great nature."

12th Street and Elmwood Avenue operated on a low budget for everything but trouble and dreams. Trouble always hung over us. To keep plugging, we had to keep dreaming. At Elmwood Avenue, would Papa lose his job? In 12th Street, would I get one? Would the electric light bill be more than last month? That was the same at both addresses. Would Papa get mad because Mama hadn't planned ahead to order everything from S. S. Pierce and had to run up a Backus grocery bill? That worry I didn't have. If Esposito's bill seemed too big, Suzanne shopped at the A & P and paid cash. At Elmwood Avenue would Papa catch a cold? At 12th Street would I? Would the coal bill ever get paid? That went for both Elmwood Avenue and 12th Street; both had a coal furnace. Would Papa scrape up money to pay the insurance? Insurance had been denied me. Cappy was sure he knew a firm who'd take me on, we went up to see them, but then they told Cappy no, because of the baby when I wasn't married. *Figurez-vous!* But that's what they said. Could Mama persuade Papa to let us have a telephone? In show business you have to have one. How could I get to be an actress? I had. Would Papa put his foot down? He didn't. Would Miss O'Neill my beloved Latin teacher find out we weren't rich? That we did *not* have a butler? That Mama and Papa were *not* going to get a divorce? Why had that struck me as stylish? Would Papa get his old malaria back from Punk, our cat, sleeping on the register? At 12th Street we had registers, but no Punk. Would Punk jump over Papa's leg when told to? Would Papa hurt Aunt Emma's and Uncle George's feelings when they stayed at our house Thanksgiving? Would the Mellin's Food Company *surely* give Papa his bonus at the end of the year? Would Papa *not* measure the rays of the sun with his sextant on the sidewalk in front of our house when everyone might be looking? Would I get to talk to Miss O'Neill? Would Hazel Dawn answer my second letter? Would The American Academy of Dramatic Arts ever send a catalog? Would the sponge cake be light? At 14 Elmwood Avenue, dreams. At 60 West 12th, they were still coming.

Time off from bills and worries, Papa's dream was to get out of Wollaston, where he said every place ended in a swamp; to get on a boat, *any* kind, but a sailing vessel preferred; to never be sick. "Waterhouse up on the hill can afford to have a cold, but if I do, the factory could say they don't want me." To have Mr. Dollaber not find fault before the year was out and refuse him his bonus necessary for the insurance premium, to afford to buy a bungalow across the tracks, to put me through Sargent's School of Physical Education to become a physical culture teacher, to have Woodrow Wilson be president, to afford to take the *Scientific American,* to steer clear of the law, to sleep through Christmas, to invite Mr. Gourley and Mr. Carroll from the Boston Young Men's Christian Union to our house, to hear Mr. Carroll recite: "Life's a funny proposition, don't you know." To get a Sunday afternoon ride on a tugboat in Boston harbor, to sit in the pilot house on the Boston to Bath boat, to have a dish of raw oysters at the Boston Market Oyster Bar, to play cribbage. Did he have other dreams he didn't talk about? Did Mama?

She dreamed I would take piano and dancing lessons, have patent leather slippers from Thayer, McNeil and Hodgkins and cloth-topped black boots for Sunday school in winter, that our tablecloths and napkins be real Irish damask with hems sewn by hand. That the hems of my dresses be hand sewn, the best pearl buttons on everything, that I'd be a good girl, that I'd never have corns, that I wouldn't be rude to Johnny Tribou and look like a thundercloud if he asked me to dance with him, that I'd grow up and marry a good man, that I wouldn't roll my stockings below my knees, that I'd invite my teacher home to dinner, that I'd say my prayers, that I wouldn't let a boy be familiar, that before she died she'd get a velvet dress. "When I was a little girl, I wished for a pony, a velvet dress and a gold watch. I got the pony and the gold watch, and I'm sure I'll get the velvet dress."

When you have to go without things, splurge on dreams. Dream you're a somebody and write your own definition. In my room at 14 Elmwood Avenue with the yellow roses on the wallpaper, I'd dream up how to astonish people, how to be pretty, extravagant, look like an actress, look fast, have great clothes, have a maid, a cook, a butler, a Scotch terrier, a lapis lazuli anything, a white celluloid toilet set with my monogram, silk stockings with no darns, be rich, be an actress, see all the plays, go as often as I wanted to on the train to Boston, get an ice cream soda at Huyler's, have bought clothes, have wider hair ribbons than anybody, have actresses answer my letters and send their pictures, have whipped cream, old-fashioned strawberry shortcake, opera caramels, Stubenrach's stuffed doughnuts filled with raspberry jam, a striped blazer, go to Paragon Park, look aristocratic like Josephine Smith, have our bathroom toilet not make a noise you could hear downstairs, have an *upright* piano, not a square, get sheet music of the shows I saw, have colored slippers to match my sashes, have money to send Miss O'Neill flowers on her birthday April 16, to be great in Latin to impress Miss O'Neill, to be like Anna Witham, to be like Virginia Portia Royall, to be like Alice Day and have a navy suit with a pale pink organdy jabot, to be like Fentress Serene Kerlin, to be like Helen Wade, to go to Quincy Mansion School, to be an actress, to have every color sealing wax, to have a moiré suit like Alice Claire Elliot, to go to New York to live, to know society people, to have plenty of partners at a dance, to not fall in love so I'd be stuck in Wollaston, to live up on the hill in a one-family house, to buy *Theatre* magazine, to buy *Élite,* to stay at the Holly Inn, Christmas Cove, Maine, to meet an actress, to sit in the first balcony and have a thick program and not go in the gallery entrance, to have writing paper from Shreve Crump & Low's or Bigelow Kennard's, to know people who live on Jerusalem Road in Cohasset, to know anyone on Commonwealth Avenue in Boston, to buy clothes at Slattery's on Tremont Street, to go to the Touraine Hotel, to have a party cape lined with real silk, to have carriage boots, to have curtains at our windows, to not live down on the plains, to get in with the Faxons of Adams Street, to get in with the Searses of President's Hill, and the Blackmers, and the Dobles, and the Hardwicks, and the Paffmans, the elite of Quincy. To have gold beads like Anna Witham's, a gold signet ring like Mr. Wright gave Martha and Priscilla or like the one Helen Wade loaned me, to be tall and have dark hair, have a beautiful bathing suit and a frilled rubber cap, have yellow ribbon on my nightgown. Mama made me one and I wore it the night we spent at the Wetmores' cottage on the beach at

Kenberma. It was so pretty Mama took my picture. Before she snapped it, she warned, "Ruth, you do realize Mr. Brooks will *see* this." Mr. Brooks ran the drugstore and developed our roll of film. What *happened?* The roll didn't come out.

Litany of longings, most of which had got left behind. *Now* would I worry if Mr. Kaufman, who ran Kay's Drugstore on the corner, saw me in my nightgown? Did the worries and dreams under the slate roof of 14 Elmwood move out with the rest of our things? Over at Mrs. Gould's Nursing Home in East Milton, did Mama know the furniture and Limoges china were sold for twenty-two dollars? The square piano for fourteen? It had been played at the Revere House when the Prince of Wales, later Edward VII, danced at the ball. Longfellow was there and Emerson; Thoreau wouldn't come. Did Mama know that August day it rode off in the secondhand dealer's cart? She'd sewn more than fourteen dollars' worth for Mrs. Moorehouse and later Miss Jeannie Hatch to give me piano lessons. It rode round the corner onto Newport Avenue and over to West Quincy. No more "Pixies' Drill," no more "To You, Beautiful Lady," no more "Too Much Mustard," no more "Sailing," which Papa sang too.

When Mama died, Papa spent fourteen dollars for a stick pin with a sapphire at Smith Patterson's jewelry store on Summer Street in Boston. Gertrude Waterhouse's cut-glass pitcher had come from there when we didn't have the clothes for her wedding. Why doesn't somebody invent no worry, more sapphire pins?

Everybody doesn't walk down Fifth Avenue with tears pouring out of their eyes, everybody doesn't have a friend who doesn't need to be told about tears, but comes through with comfort as if he *had* been told.

"You're waiting for perfection," said Thornton. We were out on the front steps again. "Up in the house at Seventy-ninth Street you and Jed closed yourselves in, a society for perfectionists. All the plans were perfect, all the theories worked, but if they became actualities, they were looked down on. Something was the matter with all of them. Safer not to *do* anything, then you don't risk failure, but, Bella, plans are meant to *test.* Perfection is part of it, but so is the *doing.* Jed's a hermit, born or self-made, but you can't be. An actress must get out and rub shoulders."

"Want to rub shoulders at Tony Perry's? She's having a party and I'm invited. Want to?"

"What kind of party?"

330

"Theatre Wing board; we're on it together. Actors, writers—you'll be a catch."

"You want to turn my head, Bella. Am I all right to go as I am?"

"With *your* name, you'll shine even with *your* wardrobe. By the way, why don't you dress better?"

"Dear, I look all right."

Up Park Avenue to a grand apartment house, up in a grand elevator, door opened by a grand maid, conversation louder than the Strand Theatre overture, we screamed hello and Antoinette Perry went into shock. "Oh, Mr. Wilder! I *have* admired you so! From *afar,* of course. Oh, you *are* my favorite! I've read everything you've ever written. It means so much to have you here under my own roof, if a Park Avenue apartment *has* a roof! I'll tell you a little secret, Mr. Wilder. Ruth can listen too, darling. Some of the things you have written are so revealing, I feel only *I* understand."

"Think of that!" Thornton did his bashful boy.

"Oh, you dear, dear man!"

Actually he wasn't bashful; he put it on for his pleasure. Sometimes he put on goodness, unworldliness.

"The little abbé," said Jed.

Sometimes he listened to troubles, ears big as Red Riding Hood's wolfy grandma, sometimes he was friend and teacher of life, literature, language, philosophy, music, art, history, and you understood it when he finished.

"Oh, Mr. Wilder, I feel so honored! Let me show you around, though there's no one here worthy to meet you."

"Oh, ma'am, you go too far!" Thornton laughed with amiable violence.

I moved off on my own.

*"Hello,* darling, how wonderful to see you." Lawrence Langner's purring voice helped guide The Theatre Guild. "Can I get you a drink, dear? How lovely you're looking! Wasn't it a shame *Clergyman* didn't go? What'll you have, dear?"

"Brandy and soda."

"Have you found any good plays, dear? You're such a wonderful actress you ought to be working all the time."

"What about what I read in the paper this morning?"

"What was that, dear?"

"That you're doing *The Country Wife.*"

"Yes, dear, we're giving it for a week this summer. Amusing play, don't you think?"

"If someone *right* does it. How can you do it without *me?*"

"Why, dear, you'd be very good."

"Of course. *Who* are you going to have play the part?"

"Why, dear, would you consider it? You wouldn't, would you?"

That was the start of *the* high peak of my career!

*"How* are you going to do it without me? Who can play that part?"

"Of course, *you*'d be wonderful. You know how I admire you. Could you be persuaded, dear?"

"How could you *think* of it without me?" Thornton had got me to rub shoulders and I had got the idea.

"Well, it's just a little summer production. It never occurred to me you'd be interested."

"You must've had *someone* in mind, Lawrence."

"Well, yes, dear, though mind you, nothing *definite*'s been settled."

"Who on earth?"

"Well, we thought it might be rather amusing to have—you remember the Duncan Sisters? We thought we might have Vivian Duncan."

"You must be *raving* mad!"

"We'd *infinitely* rather do it with you."

"Vivian Duncan's in musicals."

"Yes, I know, dear, but as you say, it's very difficult to cast. Look here, dear, let me send the play around."

"Oh, you'd better, darling. Out of charity *alone.* I'd do anything within the realm of possibility to help it succeed."

"I'll send it first thing, dear. Read it and give me a buzz."

Thornton brought a drink. "Grand eats in the dining room."

We pushed our way to the buffet. "He's doing *The Country Wife* at Westport. Sending it to me tomorrow."

"Very wonderful part for you. Who'd be right for your Mr. Horner?"

"Who's he?"

"The great role next to yours. Who do *you* think?"

"Oh, I've never read it."

Rehearsals were in the rehearsal room of the Guild Theatre, a place to give you the willies. Was *that* why I was floundering? Charles Laughton had said it was a great part for me, Thornton said it was; was it the Guild rehearsal room? Nobody *said* anything, but they didn't need to.

The doorbell rang. It was Jed back from California.

"I'm in *terrible* trouble! It's this part. I don't know how to do it."

"How *are* you doing it?"

"I know it's not right, but until I know *how,* I have to do it *some* way, so I'm doing my *Church Mouse.*"

"Oh, my *God!*" It was like a punch below the belt.

"I know, but how *should* I?"

He moved over to the sofa, pulled the lamp nearer and read the script. In California for two weeks and we hadn't kissed, he hadn't taken off his hat that everybody had tried to copy and when he gave them his they couldn't wear it at that dazzling angle.

I sat and watched. *Could* he avert disaster?

"Well, it's great! Just great! Just great! My God, it needs a director! Don't tell me Lawrence is?" He looked at me with malevolence.

"Harry Gribble."

"Oh, my God!" Another blow aimed low.

"He's no good, but I'm worse."

"Why?" He looked at me, astounded. "It's perfectly simple. She's from the country."

"Yes."

"Her husband brings her to London."

"Yes."

"He's older than Martin Beck."

"Yes."

"And not even as sexy."

"Yes."

"It's seventeenth-century London, where everybody wants a fuck."

"Yes."

"She's adorable."

"Yes."

"And wants to get her pants off."

"Yes."

"All the great cocksmen swarm around. She's sexy, bewitching, funnier than Fanny Brice."

"Yes."

"You don't know how to do that?"

"No."

"What's the matter with you?"

"I don't know, but tell me later—we open *Monday.*"

"Think of *two* things."

"Yes."

"You know that cartoon we saw at the newsreel? Mickey Mouse?"

"Yes."

"And you know about sex?" He reached over and kissed me. "You know about that?"

"Yes."

"Well, that's how to play Mrs. Pinchwife. Sex in terms of *Minnie* Mouse. Let's go to bed."

"You do know it's very funny, dear?" asked Lawrence. The day we opened he had me rehearse the letter scene in a small space back of the box office. "You do know it's the funniest scene ever written? They'll expect you to be *funny,* dear."

"Yes," I said. In the Fifth Avenue library, I'd read how Arthur Byron's aunt Ada Rehan had played it. How Dora Jordan, how Mrs. Perdita Robinson, how Mrs. Kitty Clive, Mrs. Bracegirdle.

"You'll be great," promised Ned Sheldon. "Remember to be inventive. A Restoration play calls for *invention,* invention, invention!"

*The New York Times* reviewed it. They said I was good. Up in the 79th Street library would I have chanced it? Thornton had said go out and see life and I could've gotten a knock in the *Times.* Up in the 79th Street library we could have rationalized: Why risk it?

Jed showed up at the Westport Inn. We drove over to camp.

"Jones," called the counselor on the loudspeaker.

He came out of a field looking small, thin, full of mosquito bites.

I put my arms around him and kissed him.

He responded mildly.

"What've you got on?" asked Jed.

It was a sunsuit Andrée made that had been through rough laundering.

"Let's go," said Jed. "Have you got anything else to wear?"

Jones and I went into his tent. There was a white piqué suit. Jones got into it. He was silent. I talked. He listened. Didn't contribute.

We drove over to the lake. A speedboat was tearing through the water. "Go for a ride?" Jed was for boats.

Jones looked worried.

"Come on."

I looked worried. I'm not for boats. Most of all speedboats.

The boat tore through the water, Jones and Jed and I on the stern seat. "Climb up on my shoulders," said Jed over the roar of the engine.

My heart stopped. Just holding on seemed dangerous enough. "Oh, don't!"

"What're you scaring him for? Come on."

Small figure of humanity-up-against-it, Jones chose destruction rather than shame. He climbed up on his father's shoulders and clung to Jed's head.

I couldn't look.

The trip ended. We got into Jed's car. Jones went back to camp, I to Westport, Jed drove off.

"Do you remember when your father and I came to that first camp and we all went on the speedboat?"

Jones looked off to a place no one else knew. Thirty years had gone by. "Yes," he said. "It was the worst day of my life."


A lot of people had come to Westport. Helen and Charlie came over from Nyack. "You've *got* to do it in New York," said Helen. "I'm going to talk to Gilbert."

A friend!

Jed said, "Dickie Whorf wants to direct it. He says the Shuberts might do it."

I told him what Helen had said.

"Hot air."

Not with Helen, but *would* Gilbert produce it? Would the Shuberts? Would Dickie Whorf know how to direct it? He'd been good, acting in *Three-Cornered Moon,* but that didn't mean he could direct a Restoration play. Bills from Esposito, bill for the August rent, phone bill, electric bill, gas bill; would they wait for *The Country Wife?*

The phone rang. An offer or an invite?

"This is the Dennis Playhouse. Would you play *A Church Mouse?*"

"Yes." What would the Society for Perfectionists say about that?

Stockbridge called. Would I come there?

"Yes." Two chances at disaster.

Suffern.

"Yes." Suffern? What do *they* know about putting on a play?

Mount Kisco.

"Yes."

Five hundred dollars for the week, four weeks booked, definitely two thousand dollars minus living expenses and they'd pay railroad fare, I supply wardrobe.

Were you ever in Dennis? There's not a whole lot of it. "Where's

Margaret Bellinger staying?" I asked.

"Over there."

I walked across a field toward a salt marsh where a weathered shingled cottage looked lonely. A kerosene lamp was by the window.

"Margaret?" I called.

"Here I am."

Could two people look less appropriate? My people came from the Cape, hers didn't. Hard to say who looked more out of place. "Are you all right?"

"Yes. Are you?" That was Margaret.

"I guess so." That was me.

"I guess so" describes Mrs. Whittemore's boardinghouse. Five minutes' walk to the Cape Playhouse; why didn't Margaret Bellinger stay there? Was a cottage on the salt marsh cheaper? Mrs. Whittemore's wasn't expensive. Were there no more rooms or was it because Margaret was black? In 1935, what would *you* think?

Up in my room was my Vuitton trunk to make me feel grand. In a boardinghouse room, grand things help dress it up, like Leonora Hornblow said about my phone book. I'd asked her for Claudette Colbert's address in Barbados. "And I'll give you her phone number," said Leonora. "Oh, I'm not going to call her up." "No," said Leonora, "but a phone number like that helps dress up your book."

Some of Mrs. Whittemore's boarders were actors. One, who wasn't, introduced herself as a "Washington divorcee"; one, a poetess, pasted up her poems here and there. By the front door, in ladylike handwriting on white writing paper, a poem reminded us to wipe our feet. By the double doors to the dining room another urged we be on time; one on the bathroom wall re keeping the tub clean.

Across the road, at the grocery store, they accepted telegrams. I wrote out: "Thornton come to Dennis. I would not want you to miss it. Bella."

The grocery store scribbled on a used brown paper bag: "Arriving tomorrow. Thornt."

Mrs. Whittemore's was full. I got him a room at another Whittemore's and he took his meals with us.

Opening night of *A Church Mouse* went fine. "Will you stay another week and play *The Bride the Sun Shines On?* Our star we hired can't come."

For the New York production I'd said no, Dorothy Gish said yes and got great notices. They said when she hit the groom with the wedding bouquet the audience laughed right through intermission. I had an open week before Stockbridge, it would be another five hundred dollars. Thornton said he'd stay for the opening.

The last night of *A Church Mouse* the audience shouted "Hurrah!"

That was Saturday. Monday I hit the groom with the flowers and *nothing!* The curtain came down and no laugh. What went wrong?

"The bouquet wasn't big enough," reassured the director.

Next night it was. I hit the groom. Wham! "A titter m' tit," as Bert Lahr said.

"It's interesting how last week everything you did was explosive," said Thornton, "and this week you make no connection with the audience. I don't understand it."

At least it was encouraging he didn't understand it. All those years when I'd made no connection, Gregory understood. "Comedy isn't for you, little feller. You're a heroine." But that wasn't the answer now. People said I was good in comedy. What happened? What did Dorothy do so great? Five evenings, two matinees, *not* to get any kind of a laugh, let alone one that lasted through intermission?

Thornton and I gave up wondering and indulged ourselves at lunch in the expensive Motor Car Inn. "Table for two in the garden."

Thornton was a comfort. On the beach, between swims, we discussed life and learning and people. Coming toward us, shamefaced, was our tablemate at Mrs. Whittemore's, behind him trailed his two ladies; he was their chauffeur. Looking as if he'd like to drop dead, he introduced us.

"I felt bad," he told us at supper. His ladies were at the Motor Car Inn, heard we were where he stayed and said he had to introduce us.

"Don't give it a thought," urged Thornton. "They're very pleasant."

"I felt *awful.* They had *no* right to."

"George, old feller, it was a pleasure."

"I work for 'em, and I take their money, so maybe I ought to hold my tongue, but I can't help noticing they don't show good sense."

Saturday night there were no hurrahs, still no laughs, no nothing, unless you count relief. Next stand, Stockbridge. No hurrahs there, either, but a relief to be in a show that went. The Red Lion Inn was also a relief. It was the past, beautifully kept up. Was that really Frank Crowninshield having cereal for supper or a person that Edith Wharton wrote? It was Frank Crowninshield's brother, who looked just like him, and might have been someone in a book Mrs. Wharton was writing in her study over at nearby Lenox, where her place had been called The

Mount and where there are still traces of her great topiary garden.

Mr. Crowninshield never lowered his voice. He talked to his companion as though they were alone. That was the way he had his supper. That was how he'd done it for years. In the dining room in Stockbridge, Massachusetts, at the Red Lion.

Next week Suffern, and I could live in Nyack at Helen's house. Brownie and Mary were there, Helen and Charlie were off on a toot.

At Suffern, rehearsals were in a henhouse, Bretaigne Windust directing. Very nice. A young Princeton man was the apprentice assigned to drive me from Nyack and back. An interesting talker, an interested listener; I told him he'd be a success. I not only told *him,* I told others.

"What do you base it on?" asked Jed.

"He drove me so nicely."

"What's that got to do with anything?"

"How you *do* things is what counts and all he's asked to do is drive me and he does it great."

In the last play of the summer, I saw him play a Roman soldier. He was terrific.

"Watch him," I said to Helen, who was Cleopatra.

"You're right, he sounds *real.* What's his name?"

"Joe Ferrer. His whole name is José, he's from Puerto Rico or Costa Rica or one of those and goes to Princeton."

"He's good," said Charlie.


It's always comforting to be lucky and some days it's even more so. After interviewing twelve governesses from the Home Bureau, I chose Miss Ryan. English, pleasant, not too young, not too old, and for the past three years with the Lafayette Page family in Port Washington on Long Island. Lafayette Page was really Lafayette, Junior. His father was the great doctor who had practiced in Indianapolis. He was Tarkington's doctor and Otis Skinner's when he had to have the mastoid operation. Otis and Mrs. Skinner went to Indianapolis. It was touch and go, but Dr. Lafayette Page did it successfully.

When I wanted to have my legs operated on, Gregory and I took the sleeper from Chicago to Indianapolis one Sunday and Dr. Lafayette Page told us the operation *could* be done. He said the orthopedic surgeon he'd choose was Dr. Edwin Ryerson on Michigan Avenue in Chicago.

The Page family gave Miss Ryan a fine reference. Lafey III was just Jones' age, the two girls were in their early teens. They were reluctant

about parting with their treasure, but glad she was going only as far as
12th Street.

"Come for Labor Day weekend," phoned Helen. She and Charlie
were sailing the following Wednesday for England on the new *Normandie.* Gilbert Miller felt Helen must meet with Rex Whistler, who was
doing the scenery and costumes for her new play, *Victoria Regina,* opening
in New York pre-Christmas.

Sunday in Nyack was warm. I was in my room reading. Helen came
in. "Could you come with me? Charlie can't. I'm taking our Margaret
to look after Mary, but Gilbert will pay for another ticket. Would you
want to?"

"Yes."

"Great! The *Normandie* sails Wednesday at noon."

"I'll go right home and get ready."

"Herman can drive you. When?"

"Now."

Helen had a contract for *Victoria Regina;* I had nothing. Max Gordon
wanted me to play Elizabeth Bennet in *Pride and Prejudice,* but I didn't
think the play was right. *Was* Thornton right? Was I still looking for
perfection? *Pride and Prejudice* was right enough to run a season in New
York and London. Was I hoping *The Country Wife* would get done in New
York? Jed was still talking with Richard Whorf, the Shuberts were
mildly interested. They offered a tour to start in Minneapolis; I'd have
to sign for two years. The plan was to build up the road.

Ten days in London, the grand *Normandie* both ways.

"Gilbert is paying everything except for Mary and Margaret. I guess
there'll be parties. Gilbert's giving one, maybe some others."

At 12th Street, I called up Mr. Fleischman, who lived two blocks away
and was always home and always pleasant. He came right over.

"Please bring my trunk down."

The big wardrobe trunk from the Champs Élysées bumped down the
stairs from the fourth floor storeroom to my bedroom.

Only Katherine Waldron and Sacha were in the house. Jones and
Miss Ryan were spending Sunday at Port Washington with the Page
family. Sacha's welcome was heartwarming. He and I lived on the verge
of despair that we'd get left alone. We understood each other.

On a trunk tag and on a sticker:

339

FIRST CLASS

NORMANDIE

LE HAVRE SUITE

SAILING    6 SEPTEMBER

DESTINATION    PLYMOUTH

LONDON ADDRESS    CLARIDGE HOTEL

The expressmen bopped it down the front steps, where Thornton and I had exchanged thoughts, ideas, advice, criticism, friendship. Today was beautiful; not too hot, not too cool. The ship was beautiful, too. Reporters swarmed in and out of our beautiful Le Havre Suite. Charlie and Helen were photographed with Mary and without. Every minute somebody exclaimed over the ship's grandeur.

"Do you like this boat?" a newspaperman asked Mary.

"Uh huh," she said. "The bathroom is just like Mommy's." She showed him the bidet.

The Le Havre Suite was stacked with flowers. From Nyack, Helen's gardener, Freddie, sent his best roses. He never liked to cut them, but for today he did. Flowers from lots of people, but the Nyack varicolored roses were on the table between our beds. Scattered around were baskets with fruit, candy, caviar, champagne, presents, farewell telegrams.

Mary and Helen and I were at the rail, waving. A storybook ship! Storybook by Elinor Glyn or Ouida?

Less than twenty hours, and was the boat going to tip over? Helen and I looked at each other across Nyack's roses. They'd crashed. One floated in its puddle of water; what would reporters say about *this?* Across the room, the round-topped table rocked, slid, turned on its side, rolled toward my bed like a hoop.

"You must have delayed senses," said Helen, disapprovingly. "You watched it come and didn't move till the last second."

"I didn't believe it."

A peach got loose from a grand fruit basket, rushed round the cabin like a mouse.

"Could you get it?" asked Helen.

It rushed under the bed.

"Leave it." She got up and put the roses back in their vase.

Roses and vase flew up in the air, landed in her bed and floated around in the puddle of water.

"We ought to get a picture of this for Charlie. 'After a wild night.'"

Freddie and Florence March didn't care for it, either. "They say there's not enough ballast," said Freddie. "It's leaning to a forty-two-degree angle. If it gets to forty-five, we go over. They say we should petition the captain to slow down." He pointed to the sinking porthole. Water was rushing past as though it were the Staten Island ferry. Was this the ship that yesterday towered above the New York dock?

In the Marches' cabin, the water came on scalding from faucets marked *Chaud* and *Froid*. The electric clocks on deck and in the grand salon had stopped at noon when we sailed and never ran again. At the entrance to the dining room, the gold statue of a goddess, hands outstretched, shook as though she were having a fit. Walls of the dining room, faced with Lalique glass, scared the dining stewards. "Glass does not expand," ours explained. "When the sheep rolls, the glass weel break and keel every *body!*"

It didn't, and we didn't tip over, but we weren't sure we wouldn't till we slowed down off Plymouth and let the anchor go.

London. Gilbert's Rolls-Royce limousine met us, another car took our luggage. Claridge's! A stylish man in frock coat showed Helen to a grand sitting room looking out on Brook Street, a grand bedroom, a grand grand bathroom, another grand bedroom for Mary and Margaret, grand bathroom for them, flowers everywhere.

"We want to give a party for you. When? And who do you want?" was on the card from Charles and Elsa Laughton. Theirs was a round flat dish of flowers like a rose-and-daisy pie.

"Every actor and actress in London," we said. "And H. G. Wells."

They all came to the house in Gordon Square. *And* David Garnett. *And* Virginia Woolf.

At Claridge's, a darling young man showed Helen sketches he'd drawn for *Victoria Regina*.

"Will it *really* be as beautiful as that?" she asked.

Rex Whistler looked pleased.

Gilbert took us to his production of *Tovarich*. Robert Sherwood had made the adaptation from the French. A Shaftesbury Avenue triumph. Cedric Hardwicke and Eugenie Leontovich triumphed in it.

Dinner at Adrianne Allen and Raymond Massey's beautiful Wilton Crescent house. She had been engaged to play Elizabeth Bennet in *Pride and Prejudice*. "I'm sailing on the *Aquitania.*"

"That's what we've asked Gilbert to book *us* on," said Helen.

"Good. We've got some good people on the crossing. Priestley. Do you know him?"

"Only his plays."

"Ralph Richardson. He's going to do Mercutio with Katharine Cornell. Do you know him?"

"Heard about him."

"And Michael Colefax, Sybil's son. Do you know Sybil?"

Heard of her.

"You'll like Michael."

Beautiful Diana Wynyard had a supper party for us at her flat, gave us lovely presents from Elizabeth Arden's—a mitt filled with almond paste; when dampened, good for the skin. Was that what the great London producer Binkie Beaumont used? His skin was like a cherub's.

The original Captain Hook in *Peter Pan,* Mr. Ernest Lawford, said, "You must see the Caledonian Market! You must—you can't go back till you do."

"What is it?" asked Helen.

"All sorts of secondhand things, all prices, all outdoors. Early morning is the time."

If you ever see a bogwood necklace, think of me; mine got stolen. I bought it at the Caledonian Market and twenty-one years later the New York robbers went off with it. They left a gold mirror from Cartier, they left an enamel and diamond butterfly from Van Cleef and Arpels. They left those on the floor and took the seventy-five-carat emerald, the Verdura diamond bracelet, diamond and pearl earrings, the diamond heart with the band of gold stars across it, the sapphire and diamond ring, the ruby and diamond ring, ruby and gold cigarette box in the shape of a basket of raspberries *and* the bogwood necklace. I'm glad I had it twenty-one years, I'm glad I wore it with Oliver Messel's grand, citified, gray satin gown in Act V of *The Country Wife.* Its shamrock leaves sat like a low collar where throat ended and shoulders began. I'm glad Angus McBean took a picture of me wearing it. It's now gone to Harvard with the rest of his collection.

"What's that?" I'd asked the seller.

"Genuine bogwood, m'lady. The shamrock pattern. Will you try it on?"

"How much?"

"Three and six. A bargain."

It lay on a cotton sheet spread on the ground, amid cracked pitchers, bent spoons and other fallals, a jeweler's case, open, and on its frayed gray satin lining the black necklace. Bogwood is black with no shine to it, dull, flat black.

"I'll take it."

Our ten days were nearly over. They'd been perfect. A farewell lunch with Gilbert at Simpson's, just as wonderful as when Gregory and I ate our first London dinner. Leslie Howard came over to the table. He was leaving soon for New York to do a production of *Hamlet*.

"Who's your Ophelia?" asked Gilbert.

"I haven't one." Leslie looked at me. "I don't suppose *you*'d want to play it?"

"No." What a horse's-ass thing to say! Was it the diffident way Leslie put it? Leslie was *always* diffident. Was it because he seemed to take it for granted I *wouldn't?* Mid-September and only a *faint* hope of *The Country Wife.* Too late to say yes to Elizabeth Bennet, why not say yes to Ophelia? My day to be a horse's ass!

I said no to Leslie, but never to English oysters. Nor did Helen.

"I'll send a hamper to the boat," said Gilbert.

The *Aquitania* didn't seem grand like the trip with Gregory and the Mileses, or even the trip when I stayed in my cabin. It seemed safe and comfortable and just where we wanted to be.

343

# Chapter

## 15

The trip was over. Jones liked his presents. Miss Ryan liked hers. Suzanne and Katherine liked theirs.

Jones was enrolled at Friends Seminary. His father admired Stephen Pascal next door and Steve went to Friends. Jed drove over to Rutherford Place and 17th Street and made arrangements. The school bus would stop for Jones at Fifth Avenue and 12th.

Jones and the school got along, but *The Country Wife* had struck a snag. Richard Whorf had the show all designed, but the Shuberts wanted a contract that Jed and I considered unjust. Why didn't it break my heart? Whorf's sets? Jed's idea of Whorf directing it?

Fate turned the corner at Nyack. "Read this," said Helen, and gave me an unpromising-looking script.

A promising-looking one is new, one that everyone hasn't read. A promising one has an uncurled cover, maybe red, maybe blue. It's a certain thickness. The script Helen gave me was skimpy, the dark brown cover was curly, but printed on it were it were two great words: ETHAN FROME.

"Ned sent it to me," said Helen. "I guess he forgot I'm going to do Victoria. It's a great part for you."

I'd read the novel when *Saturday's Children* played Baltimore. Jed had sent me twelve books; one was *Ethan Frome.* Mattie Silver certainly *would* be a great part.

"Ned says this isn't right, but could be with work."

How many times has *that* been said! And how many times did the work work?

The story between the skimpy, curly brown covers clutched me again. Edith Wharton's people were there in a loose impractical pattern, signed Lowell Barrington.

I took it back to New York. "Ned gave Helen a play made from *Ethan Frome,*" I told Jed.

"You can't make a play out of *Ethan Frome,*" quoth the 79th Street perfectionist.

"Ned thinks this could be. With work."

Jed read it. "All *this* script is good for is to show it can be done. Ask Ned if it's free. If I have a free hand I'll do it."

> Dear Jed,
> You have my blessings. I'm sure Mrs. Wharton will concur. When I gave it to Helen I knew she would pass it on to Ruth. Now it has the good fortune to interest you.
>
> Ned

Jed gave it to Owen Davis. Owen had written *The Detour* and *Icebound,* won a Pulitzer Prize. He'd do *Ethan Frome* in collaboration with his son, Donald. They and Jed had discussions, agreed. Jed engaged Stewart Chaney and together they worked out the production. I'd be Mattie, who'd be Ethan?

The script turned out great. Stewart Chaney's sketches fantastic. Who for Ethan?

"Do it with Raymond Massey," I urged.

"I won't."

"What will I do? I owe Helen and Lillian and Thornton. I can't keep borrowing. I owe nine thousand dollars."

"If you want to do it with Massey, take it, see if you can set it up."

I took it to Max Gordon, who had wanted me to play Elizabeth Bennet. He was a friend of Owen Davis'. Owen had told him what he was working on.

"If you can get that script from Harris, I'll do it," he said.

"Can you lend me a thousand dollars?"

"If you can get me the script."

Well, that's show business.

"Take it," said Jed.

Max handed me a check for a thousand dollars. It would tide me over.

"I'll get it into production as soon as I can find McClintic to direct it. Gilkey says he's out of town." Stanley Gilkey was Guthrie's general manager.

"Do you think Guth will do it?" I asked Stanley.

"Yes, I think he will."

Guth chose Jo Mielziner to do the scenery and costumes. He persuaded the great Pauline Lord. She reluctantly came down from her Catskill estate. He cabled Massey. Massey left Wilton Crescent.

Jo's designs were different from Stewart Chaney's. Guthrie was pleased with the scenery, but not the sketches for what I'd wear. "Come over tonight."

Up the stairs of 23 Beekman Place again. We talked, looked over Jo's sketches. His first-act costume for Mattie Silver was a skirt and middy blouse.

Guthrie screwed his face up and looked Oriental. "I see her in her best dress to come to meet her cousin Zeena. Poor people travel in their best clothes. Why do I think it should be two kinds of material?" Guth looked off into the land of his visions. "I see it in red. Dark red. Warm. Like a dress to wear to church."

"Challis is nice," I suggested.

"What's challis?"

"Thin half-wool, half-cotton, I guess."

"And for the guimpe, some figured stuff. Red, but maybe not matching red, with a dark figure."

When Mattie Silver came on in Act I, that's what she wore.

"What's that you got on?" asked Zeena. "It looks like a pair of portieres." Pauline pronounced it port*eers.*

That was my best dress. With my best dress I wore a blue enamel locket on a thin gold chain. It felt perfect. A costume is part of a performance; if it's right, you keep afloat. Mattie Silver's clothes were right.

First rehearsal was called for Sunday morning. Guthrie was late. Afternoon or morning, no matter what time, he'd have been late. Was it superstition? He weighed every move. To get out the wrong side of bed,

Lieutenant and Mrs. Garson Kanin, 1944 (*S. Balkin*)

Alexander Knox, Judith Anderson, Dennis King, Katharine Cornell, Edmund Gwenn and Ruth Gordon in *The Three Sisters*, 1942

Kay Aldridge, Philip Loeb, Loring Smith and Ruth Gordon in *Over Twenty-One*, 1944

Maurice Chevalier, Robert E. Sherwood, René Clair, Garson Kanin and
Ruth Gordon, 1948

With Loring Smith in the New York production of *The Matchmaker*, 1955
(*Will Rapport*)

With Natalie Wood in *Inside Daisy Clover*, 1966

Ruth Gordon in her Oscar-winning performance in *Rosemary's Baby*, with Mia Farrow, 1968

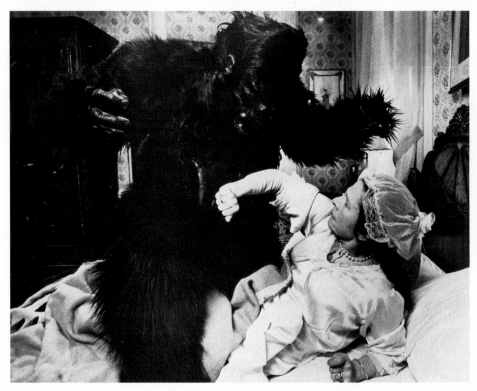

George Segal and Ruth Gordon in *Where's Poppa?*, 1970

Bud Cort and Ruth Gordon in *Harold and Maude*, 1971 (*Cinemabilia*)

Thornton Wilder and Ruth Gordon, 1969 (*The Bettmann Archive, Inc.*)

Ruth Gordon, in her dressing room, with Hazel Dawn, 1976

to walk under a ladder, to get a two-dollar bill, to have a bird fly in the room, to lose his thruppenny bit, to break a mirror, could jeopardize Edith Wharton's Ethan and Mattie and Zeena. How right! Riding over the Maures Mountains when I cracked my pocket mirror, I put it away without telling, but you can't fool luck. Seven years of bad hit me. Don't argue it; I lived the seven years and I know. And Guthrie McClintic knew Ethan Frome could not succeed if he had a two-dollar bill in his pocket, if he forgot his thruppenny bit, if he saw the new moon through glass and had no money in his pocket or saw a glove lying in the street. And maybe if he got to rehearsal on time? Then that unforgettable opening night in Philadelphia would never have been.

At our Sunday morning first rehearsal, Pauline, Guthrie, Ray and I sat on the bare stage of the Booth. It had been Mr. Ames' theatre and for a wedding present Mr. Ames had backed Guth's first production.

Guthrie liked the Booth. *Saturday's Children* had been there. This morning nothing on the stage but four chairs and a scarred oblong table.

"Shall we start," said Guthrie. It wasn't a question. It was a tonsillar thought. He listened. It seemed to bode well. "I'll read in Jotham and the other parts." He'd be the only one to enjoy this rehearsal.

Pauline pulled her hat down further, almost to her eyebrows, lit another cigarette, and retired into her turned-up coat collar.

Massey, in a fine London suit, lit another cigarette.

I lit another.

Guthrie, hat and overcoat on, muffler around his neck, cigarette lit, cleared his throat, coughed his permanent bronchial cough that through the years got no better or worse and was useful for punctuation or for while he thought what to say next.

He turned his attention to the open script, studied it, after a while looked up at the flies. "You know the scene. I needn't read the description." After a while, he looked back at the page. "This is Frome's place. 'C'mon, I'll ask Ethan 'bout drivin' you over—you won't never get to Corbury standin' there.' "

Rehearsals of *Ethan Frome* had begun and dread gripped us all. All except Guthrie; he could read in all the parts and if Massey would only lose his voice, he could read Ethan.

The prologue was over. Mattie and Zeena weren't in it. Only Massey and Guth reading in Harmon Row and A Young Man.

"Act One," snarled Guthrie. "Shall we begin, Pauline?"

"Oh, God," she sighed. Into her fur collar droned that voice that had everything in it. Nothing *stated,* but there it was. The voice of the human race that hasn't got it any good and knows it never will and continues to take it. " 'I ast you a dozen times—I done my best—but I ain't got the stren'th to do it.' "

If you could hear it, it was perfection.

Sometimes a speech struck her as too long or tiresome or irrelevant or just no good. She didn't finish it, glanced up with a querulous instruction to whoever spoke next: "Well, go on."

At the end of Act I, Guthrie looked out front and said to the Davises and Max, "You go now. Come back in two weeks."

They filed out, furious, but if you wanted McClintic you took him on *his* terms.

Guth beckoned us into empty dressing room 1.

"Good, we got rid of *them*," said Pauline.

"Have some?" Guth offered his flask.

It was Sunday noon. She nodded.

"Stanley," he called. "Glass."

In an empty, dark, dirty theatre, Stanley Gilkey handed Guthrie a clean glass. That was Stanley Gilkey!

*Ethan Frome* rehearsals were the hardest. On the bare stage, we had to imagine a scene outside the Frome house, scenes inside the parlor, the kitchen, the bedroom, in the graveyard on a hill, the scene outside the white church, the scene on the hill where the sled went down.

Without any of that, we rehearsed with kitchen chairs and benches and the one aging overhead light.

By day, we did all Pauline's scenes. After dinner, Massey and I rehearsed at Beekman Place in Guthrie's dining room.

The McClintics' dinner cleared away, a blanket was laid to protect their grand table. Woolworth silver, china, glasses were stacked ready. In the pantry was cut-up banana covered with chocolate sauce for Mattie's stew. Every night I dished up dinner, set out Zeena's red cut-glass pickle dish, welcomed the hired man, Jotham, with Guthrie reading in, admired the cider Ethan provided, ate the dinner, looked out the McClintics' window into the East River and noted it was snowin' again, would that mean Zeena'd be stuck in Bettsbridge?

"Drifts're bad," said Jotham. "As like as not this'll tie them trains up for fair!"

Nobody mentioned that would be good.

"Well, goin' home now." And Guthrie went and came back.

Mattie and Ethan cleared the table, washed the dishes in the McClintic pantry sink, Ethan dried them, touched Mattie's hand, she dropped the pickle dish, it broke. Tears and fright. It was Zeena's treasure. What would happen?

Ethan said he could get another.

"You can't." Mattie wept.

He'd fix it. Somehow the evening becomes theirs again.

"Ethan—it's been a real wonderful evenin'."

Two driven people. Two without luck.

"Good night, Matt."

"Good night, Ethan."

Curtain.

That's all. If you saw it, you'll never forget it.

We'd been rehearsing two weeks. I was in trouble. "I'm having a hard time to act with Pauline," I told Guthrie. "She doesn't *do* anything to make it hard, but I can't find how to play a scene with her. I don't feel any connection."

"Yuh," said Guthrie, and looked as if he'd left.

"Can you help me?"

He didn't seem to come back.

"Guthrie?"

"Yuh, well, I grant you she's hard to play a scene with, but if I were you, I'd find out *how.*"

Then one day we were in tune. I got her rhythm, she was terrific to act with. Guthrie was right—I had to find out *how.* Some things a director can show, some things he can only advise that opening night will come, so get ready.

From Guthrie I learned that everything must act—lights, the door closing, a bell, a curtain blowing, sounds. "After the play, when the theatre's gone dark, listen," he told me. "After *we* get through, after everything's over, after everyone's left, stand onstage and listen. A theatre has sounds."

Guth wanted the cold sound of water when Ethan got out of bed in the morning and Zeena lay watching him. Ray poured it from the pitcher into the bowl, splashed it on his face in the dark beyond the yellow light.

Rehearsals at the theatre, rehearsals at Beekman Place, and on top of everything else came Christmas!

"You can take off Christmas Eve and Christmas morning," grunted Guthrie. He begrudged saying it. "In the afternoon, we *rehearse.* The curtain goes up at the Garrick whether there's a Christmas or not."

349

At 60 West 12th, Miss Ryan and I trimmed the Christmas tree, with help from tall Katherine Waldron. Christmas morning, only halfway through the presents, I told Jones, *"Please* don't open any *more."*

"But, Mama, it's Christmas."

"But you've got too many."

"Mama!"

"Oh, go ahead." Everybody had sent him things. It seemed awful that one child had so much.

Up at 23 Beekman Place, we worried about serving the stew and eating it and dropping the pickle dish and *really* weep, *really* feel the terror, *really* feel the comfort of Ethan with nobody else there. "Ethan —it's been a real wonderful evenin'."

*Feel* it, wish it could go on and on.


Penn Station, where Guthrie had put me on the train to Pittsburgh. This time it was Guthrie and the *Ethan Frome* company taking the train to Philadelphia to open.

Check into the Ritz and off to a first *walk*-through with scenery, *not* at the Garrick, where we would open, but at the Grand Opera House, where we would dress-rehearse. It had been booked for a week for Jo to set up his hill and graveyard and the church that flew and all the rest of his scenery. At the Garrick, a show was playing, so Max booked the Grand Opera House, a theatre no one had ever heard of. We'd rehearse there until the end of the week, when the show would move out of the Garrick and our scenery would move over and our crew set it up.

Opening night at the Garrick, the play held, the scenery moved without a hitch, the church flew up into Jo's starry sky, in the lonely grave-yard snow crunched when we walked round the gravestones, the clothes felt right, quick changes went fast, everybody's makeup fine, the epilogue gray wigs looked right, the sled did go downhill, the hush out front held, while backstage six stagehands caught the sled so we really *wouldn't* kill ourselves. Ray and I slid down Jo's white velvet hill, across the Garrick stage on a greased track to six mighty men who stood between him and me getting pasted on the wall.

Everything worked except Zeena's red glass pickle dish. It did not break! It did not *break!* That could stop your heart. Your mind could go. Your legs could give out. You could die. The pickle dish didn't break. Out front, had Guthrie fainted? The Davises? Max Gordon? Apoplectic Max. And everything going so *well.* The supper scene perfect, result of

Beekman Place dishwashing and chocolate banana stew. Jotham left, Ethan and I were alone.

"Let's get the dirty dishes out of the scene as quickly as possible," Guthrie had urged. "Dirty dishes don't help a love scene. Through Ethan's speech, Ruth, get the dishes in the sink. Once they're in the water, then they don't strike us as dirty. You wash, Ruth. Ray, grab a towel and dry. I *know* that's not how it is in the script, but forget the script; I want Matt and Ethan keeping house. As though he *always* helped her wipe the dishes. The contentment after a good dinner."

Ray wiped, I washed and washed. Tranquil, no watchful Zeena. Nothing she *couldn't* have watched, but we were alone, it was *our* house, it was *our* lives, no one to badger us, no one to fear.

"Wash the pickle dish, Ruth, wash it like it's the Portland vase, whatever that is. Wash it like it's the Elgin Marbles, like it's the most precious thing in the world. It *is,* to Zeena. Wash it as though it's made of cobweb. Ray, you don't know from nothing, you're just up in Peaceful Valley. Ruth, hand it to him. Ray, all you're thinking of is the dearness of her. Your hand goes for the dish, but your heart made it go further, to Matt's hand. Ruth, you know what to do."

The pickle dish dropped.

"Ethan!" All the agony of life in that one name. Down on my knees beside the broken red glass. "Oh, Ethan." I looked at him.

"It's all right, Matt."

"But it's *broke.* It's all to pieces." Terror. "Ethan, what'll she say!"

Every rehearsal it had broken and then opening night with the critics watching, the audience watching, it did *not* break!

Down on my knees beside it. "Oh, Ethan." I looked up, terrified, terrified, *terrified!* Then Raymond Massey, six foot something and looking taller, stamped on his wife's treasure.

" 'It's *broke.* It's all to pieces,' " I cried.

Would the audience laugh? They just saw Raymond Massey smash it.

"Ethan, what'll she *say?"*

"But you couldn't help it!"

The audience was with us. They believed what they were *supposed* to see.

The play rolled on, Zeena found the broken pickle dish so carefully hidden away, then the world fell in, Ethan and Mattie said goodbye forever on the snowy hill, Mattie to take the train to nowhere, Ethan to come home to nothing.

Too much to bear.

Standing by the sled that the children had left, I said, "Ethan! Ethan, we're goin'!" I threw my arms around him, held him close.

"But where, Matt?"

My face close to his. "I want you should take me down with you."

"Down where?"

"Down the hill."

"What?"

"Down this hill so we'll never never come up again—never! Right into that big elm down there—you could do it—you could, Ethan—so't we'd never have to leave each other any more."

Ray stretched out on the sled, I on top of him. "I want to feel you holdin' me, Matt."

"Is it going to hurt, Ethan?"

"It ain't goin' to hurt at all. We're goin' to fetch that elm so hard we won't feel anything at all—exceptin' only each other." He lurched the sled forward. "Matt . . . Matt."

"I'm holding you, I'm holding you tight, Ethan."

The sled plunged down the hill. The lights dimmed. In the darkness, the audience could hear the sled go faster and faster.

In the dark, Ray and I, in a makeshift dressing room, beside where the stagehands stopped the sled, pulled on gray wigs, aged down with white grease paint over our lips, on our faces heavy white powder.

"Ready, Ruth?" pleaded stage manager Neilson.

"Ready."

Twenty years later in the Frome kitchen, the same evening as the prologue. Zeena is dozing in her rocker close to the stove. A sleigh is heard. Zeena goes to the door and unbolts it. Ethan comes in, lameness slowing each step. His face is drawn, old. A voice from the parlor calls querulously, "Zeenie! Zeenie!"

Zeena moves slowly to the parlor door, comes back pushing a home-made wheelchair. In it, Mattie, hair thin and gray and untidy, face drawn. "Zeenie, you hurt! You did that on purpose."

They had wanted to die and didn't. They lived on, crippled, bitter. "Ain't you *never* goin' to die, Ethan Frome?"

"The Fromes're tough, I guess. The doctor was sayin' to me only the

other day—'Frome,' he says, 'you'll likely touch a hundred.' "
Curtain.

Applause like we dream of. Like we comfort ourselves with when everything's gone to hell. The audience applauded and applauded. And wouldn't leave. How many curtain calls? Finally Pauline, Ray and I went up the flight to our dressing rooms all in a row, perched on the back wall. We could hear the applause go on and on. Pauline got her gray wig off, my gray wig was off, we all stepped out to listen. Guthrie, eyes red from weeping, came up the stairs. We all hugged and listened.

"They won't go till you take another bow," warned stage manager Neilson.

"My God! Even in *Anna Christie* they didn't do like this."

We put on our wigs, the curtain went up.

"What will we do about that pickle dish?" asked Ray. A man who paid attention.

"Get another kind," said Max, and sent out to Ohio to get one with cracks *baked* in, so it would break in three pieces. In a week they'd send them. They'd be perfect.

"I want a metal plate on the floor where I drop the dish," ordered Ray.

Why so fussy? The dish broke every night.

"I'm thinking of opening night in New York."

New York. Opening night. I was all right, but couldn't seem to warm up. Big strain, that part, that show; so much could go wrong. Quick changes never get easier. Moving platforms and a flying church? Everybody had to watch not to get hit. As late as Act II, Scene Three, I hadn't hit my stride!

Dinner played well. Jotham excused himself. I started to clear the dishes. Ethan helped, we talked. *Why* couldn't I get started? I washed, he wiped, his hand touched mine as I handed him the wet pickle dish, I dropped it, it didn't break. I dropped it on the *tin plate* now nailed into the floor of the National Theatre, West 41st Street, now the Billy Rose. The glass from Ohio cut to break in three parts didn't break at all and two rows across the footlights sat *The New York Times'* Brooks Atkinson. There lay an unbroken pickle dish and I had to say it broke.

Why was Ray down on his knees? Brooks Atkinson looking, audience looking, Guthrie, Max Gordon, the Davises, Ray reached back of the swill pail and brought out three pieces of red glass, placed them on the tin plate and shoved the pickle dish that wouldn't break behind the pail.

"It's broke," I cried, and I *really* cried. Despair railing against fate.

353

How could luck let a damn dish break every performance except opening night? I turned to God. "How can You *do* this?"

Did He say, "To get you started"?

"I wish I was dead! I wish't I was!" Now it was the real thing. Somebody driven, somebody pushed too far, someone who had nowhere to go. "Ethan, we're goin' down that hill, so we'll never come up again. Right into that big elm down there, so we never have to leave each other."

Thornton waited onstage till everybody had left, then we'd bring the flowers and presents and messages to West 12th.

"I was walking up and down the stage," he told me, "and someone stepped out of the shadows. It was Max Gordon. 'It's a big play,' he said. 'Isn't it?' 'Oh, yes,' I said. 'It's great, isn't it?' 'Yes. Oh, yes!' 'Is it Shakespeare?' "

At 12th Street, I opened boxes, filled vases, Thornton made notes. "Red roses: Lillian. Basket of white orchids: Helen and Charlie. Box of gardenias: 'To Mattie, from her author. Edith Wharton.' "

Darling Ned had arranged for Mrs. Wharton's instructions to be carried out. Darling Ned, he arranged for that and for this night. Paralyzed, blind, from his bed he pulled the strings that brought *Ethan Frome* to the stage.

"Old-fashioned bouquet with lace frill: Ned," noted Thornton. "Green orchids, lily of the valley: Kit and Guthrie. Yellow roses: Bob and Madeline."

The phone rang. It was Sherwood. I'd given them opening-night tickets.

"You've found my Abe Lincoln for me. I'm writing a play about Lincoln's Illinois years. Ray's a friend, but I never thought of him."

Great reviews for the play. For all of us. Mrs. Wharton didn't leave France to come to the play, but when Scribner's published it, she wrote a foreword. It ended:

> I should like to record here my admiration for the great skill and exquisite sensitiveness with which my interpreters have executed their task and to add that, if, as I am told, *their* interpreters of Ethan and Zeena and Mattie have reached the same level of comprehension, then my poor little group of lonely New England villagers will live again for a while on that stony hillside before finally joining their forebears under the village headstones. I should like to think that this good fortune may be theirs, for I lived

among them, in fact and imagination, for more than ten years, and their strained faces are still near to me.

Edith Wharton

SAINTE CLAIRE LE CHÂTEAU
HYÈRES, JANUARY 1936

A lady lived in costly elegance at Lenox, but could see.

When I wrote to thank her for the gardenias and the opportunity, I told what Mattie had meant, what the gardenias, what Ned's help. Then I told her how near I'd been to Ste. Claire le Château, a little of my own days at Le Lavandou with Jed. The afternoon trips to Toulon, to Hyères, and at Hyères the man in the bank had been so pleasant.

In answer came a long white envelope from France. Inside it, one sheet of paper, the left-hand corner engraved in dark blue with the address; above it, written by hand, the date.

*April 13, 1936*

SAINTE CLAIRE LE CHÂTEAU<br>HYÈRES (VAR.)<br>TEL: 2–29

Dear Miss Gordon,

I will follow your example and send you a typed letter. Since my illness I have found that, for some mysterious reason, my hand tires much more quickly than my head, and I could go on forever dictating letters which I used to prefer to write.

Your letter enchanted me. I had no idea that you had once been so near a neighbor, and I wish you had pushed your investigation of Hyères up to my door-step. But I hope you may still do this another time.

Meanwhile I want to tell you how much touched I was by you writing as you did of this beloved country, which so few people understand or appreciate. I have spent my winters here for nearly twenty years, and there are always fresh discoveries to be made, new beauties to be revelled in—and always in a lovely solitude, since no one else seems to care for such explorations.

How delightful it would be if I could dash over to New York to see you giving life to my poor Mattie! I quite understand what you say about the play as an embodiment of my book; but is such a transposition ever possible? I doubt it, after listening for thirty years to what people have to say to me of my novels, which always seem to turn into something different in their heads. Meanwhile the important thing is that the human and essential part of Ethan Frome *does* seem to reach your audience. I get enraptured letters from people who have seen it, and I know how largely your personification of Mattie contributed to their impression.

355

How I wish someone would dramatize its "companion-piece," my novel called "Summer," and that you would play the part of Charity Royall! But Mr. Sheldon says that a wave of prudery is sweeping over our blessed country, and that the play would shock the censor if not the audience.

I enclose a few photographs of Sainte-Claire in the hope that you may find your way there next time.

Yours very gratefully,
Edith Wharton

Business was tremendous, then Pauline got pneumonia and was out for a long time, then New York had an elevator strike.

In May we closed.

Thornton and I sat on the front steps.

"Are you all right?"

"Still lonely, but all right."

"Interesting."

"I'm all right most of the time, then sometimes it comes over me. You think I'll get over it?"

"Dear, you couldn't be lonely if you live your life. You wouldn't have time."

"I'd do a play, but I haven't got one."

"Library shelves are where *The Country Wife* was. The shelves are lined with successes."

"How do I get anyone to do them? *We* think I'm a wonderful actress, but I don't have a draw."

"Dear, all you need is a play and a stage. It doesn't have to be the Booth or the Broadhurst or the Music Box, it doesn't have to be *Broadway* —it can be wherever you step on a platform and make it become great. Try it; you can't be an actress sitting home at Twelfth Street. Sitting home narrows perspective, sets impossible standards. You've got to prove yourself. You're still waiting for perfection and it's not human to be perfect; why expect a play to be? Or a director, or an actor. You yourself said, dear, you wouldn't have done *Ethan Frome* if you hadn't had to have money."

"How do I begin?"

"The summer companies. Think how well you did at Westport. Think what it could mean to young people who could act with you and learn from you. And think what you could learn from them. Think of it, Bella! Think!"

"Ogunquit wants me to do *Saturday's Children.*"

"Do it!"

HOTTEST JULY DAY ON RECORD, read the headline on the Portland paper. The matinee had been a boiler, ladies sweated, fanned, sweated. On-stage *we* sweated. Ogunquit was to pay the 60 West 12th Street bills.

I went up the front walk to the Grahame. Inside it smelled like tomato. Was that how Martin's Theatrical used to smell?

"If you're an actress, act," said Thornton.

I rehearsed a week, played a week at Ogunquit and came back to 60 West 12th. On the hall table was a message. "New Rochelle would like you to do *Saturday's Children* for a week at the Women's Club."

Did Thornton mean I could step on the platform of the New Rochelle Women's Club and make it become great?

"If you're an actress, act," he urged. "The great Edith Evans went across the Thames and acted on the Waterloo Road at the temperance theatre Miss Emma Cons' niece runs and all London flocked to the Old Vic. Step on any stage and bring it up to your own great level."

I raised levels in Dennis and Stockbridge, then went up to Woollcott's Island to raise my own.

"I'm getting a horrid expression on my face," I told Alec. "A sweet, resigned air." We were becalmed on Lake Bomoseen. "Ever notice ladies walking down the street with a flat smile like they were going to kill themselves?" I asked.

"What's sweet about *your* face? Crab apple describes it."

"Watch it," called Howard Bull, a red zinnia back of his ear, a pencil back of the other. He let out the mainsail. Woollcott and I ducked. Duchess, the big black dog that the Seeing Eye bunch had given Woollcott, flattened out like a dog in the funny papers.

"I'm going to tell you something interesting," I said.

*"I'll* be the judge of that!"

"The only money I ever earned was writing or acting."

"What is your definition of 'interesting'?"

*"You* make a lot of money playing cribbage and croquet."

"You took Alice Miller for a quarter at your bridge club and don't tell me there's no little stock or bond garnering treasure. No Goldman Sachs?"

"Oh, I don't call that *earned.* I mean when they say 'Will you do so and so for so much per?' It's always been acting or writing."

"Why?"

"I guess I thought I'd better. Our class motto was 'Hew to the line.' "

"You told me it was *'Ad astra.'* "

"Did I? If I'd tided over by going to work at Schrafft's instead of having a grand thirty-five-cent tea there with rich Dotty Forbes, by now I might be President Shattuck."

"That sounds reasonable."

"I stick to ideals."

"A chat with you makes me feel I'm at the Cloisters with Saint Cecilia."

"Howard, turn back."

"Howard, if you know who pays you and I think you do, go twice around the Island or I will visit you in the aft or the poop or whatever the rear of this vessel is and personally tear out your entrails."

Duchess stood up, went forward. The boat was heading home.

"Aye, aye, skipper," said Howard, and tacked toward the pier.

*"Why* wouldn't you?"

"Why wouldn't I what?"

"Earn anything except by acting or writing? What else were you offered? I know what it was during your Lou McGuire days. But what else?"

"To be a relief salesgirl at Schrafft's, to stand in line at the Met for a scalper. Only once I agreed to be hired for anything but acting or writing and the lady dropped dead."

"What an effect you have!"

"I never tried again."

"I should hope not! Selfish pig that you are, it's good to hear you *once* in a while consider others."

The boat nudged the dock, Duchess leaped out. "Howard, I must say no one can circle this island in the time you can!"

Two more summer stock dates. *A Church Mouse* in Mount Kisco. *Saturday's Children* in Suffern. Helen and Charlie had gone for a holiday in England; I stayed at their house with Brownie and Mary.

In Suffern, one week the director was Josh Logan, the next week it was Bretaigne Windust. Josh asked to direct *Saturday's Children*.

"I better stick to Bretaigne. He did *A Church Mouse* last summer and he'd feel hurt if I changed."

"But why isn't it fair to give *me* a chance?"

"I think I better stick to him." Three years later he would direct *Life with Father*.

"You just don't think I'd do it well." Two years later Joshua Logan would direct *On Borrowed Time*.

"I'm *used* to Bretaigne and I'd have to get used to you."

"Oh, hell." Josh took a seat in the henhouse where Bretaigne conducted rehearsals. The hens' roosts had been removed, the place cleaned.

"Telegram for Miss Gordon—you can take it in the office." An apprentice let the screen door slam.

"Take it," said Bretaigne.

I rushed up the gravel walk to the business office in the shed. Jones was at camp; was everything all right?

"Call this number—it's Western Union," someone said.

Western Union was cross. "It's a *long* cable. It's from London August fourteenth, addressed to Ruth Gordon, care Helen Hayes, Two thirty-five Broadway, Nyack, and rerouted to Summer Theatre, Suffern, New York. It's *long*. 'Dear Ruth can you do *Country Wife* in London stop we are having production and costumes made in England from designs by Oliver Messel and are lending same to Old Vic Theatre where Tyrone Guthrie is producing play for three weeks commencing October fifth stop Guthrie would like you come London and play Mrs. Pinchwife with them stop Helen and I think this great idea stop Old Vic regulations only permit them paying you twenty pounds weekly but would personally pay your fare both ways and your expenses here stop after three weeks here we could sail back on Queen Mary October twenty-eighth bringing production and few members London cast with us rehearsing on arrival New York with new people and opening Henry Miller week November fifteenth stop please treat all details in this plan in strictest confidence stop my manager Fleischman arrives New York August seventeenth please show him this cable stop just off to Austria regards Gilbert Miller.' Shall I mail it to you?"

"Please." I floated back to the henhouse, first stop on the way to the peak of my career, thanks to Helen!

At 12th Street, our Mr. Fleischman brought down the Vuitton trunk, expressmen carried it down the nine brownstone steps where Thornton had sent me off to raise levels, citing Edith Evans at the Vic, and all at once I had plans to act with her there.

"Goodbye, Mama." Jones rushed off to catch the Friends Seminary bus. He was used to goodbyes.

"Goodbye, Miss Gordon." Miss Ryan was off to see Jones board the bus.

On the *Queen Mary,* Helen and little Mary were waiting to say goodbye.

"I must be *insane!* Go to London to play an English heroine? I must be *insane!"*

Helen nodded. "But you've got to."

A blast on the *Queen*'s loud whistle. Everybody jumped, then laughed. Helen and I and Mary hugged. "You'll be great," said Helen, then she and Mary were gone.

"Why are we always sticking our neck out?" I'd asked Helen on a Nyack walk. She was rehearsing *Victoria,* I was going to rehearse *Ethan.*

"Because we're born hurdle-jumpers."

I looked back at safe New York. Tackle the Old Vic? Tackle a London audience? Marjory Pinchwife on the same stage with Edith Evans, the unmatched actress of restoration comedy? Would London stand for an American playing an English heroine?

"You've got to," Helen had said.

Private-school bills, a house with a backyard, Miss Ryan, Suzanne, Katherine, Mr. Fleischman had to be paid. If I made it in London, my career would take a jump. Besides, what other offer did I have?

Under my stateroom door was a telegram:

BON VOYAGE BY WESTERN UNION

NAQ64 15 = NEW YORK 9 1151A

MISS RUTH GORDON

SS QUEEN MARY

BEWARE LEST LONDON TOUSE AND MOUSE YOU FOR YOU BELONG TO US THIS SIDE IDOLATRY

LORA AND BRETAIGNE

"Hello, Ruth, remember me? I'm Elizabeth Curtis. Dr. Curtis' daughter."

They lived in the first house on the left going up Grand View Avenue. I told her about the Old Vic, that I was going to be in a play there. It sounded like the lies I used to write Katherine Follett.

The *Queen Mary* sailed its uneventful trip, slid past the Isle of Wight into Southampton docks, the boat train rushed us to Waterloo.

"Hello," said Tyrone Guthrie. Could *anyone* be so tall! He and George

Chamberlain, a normal height, met me. That night, the Vic was opening its 1936 season with *Love's Labour's Lost,* directed by Tyrone Guthrie, George Chamberlain stage manager.

"Hello," I said.

They walked me to a taxi. "Claridge's," they told the driver, then went back to rehearsal.

That was hello to Mr. Guthrie. Thirty-five years later, in *The New York Times,* I said goodbye.

"Will you do the piece on Tyrone Guthrie?" asked Seymour Peck.

"No, I can't."

"Please do, dear," said persuasive Peck.

"If I don't, who will?"

"Harold Clurman."

Harold hadn't known Tony as long. "Who else?"

"Walter Kerr."

Walter Kerr never had Tony rehearse him. "I'll do it."

"Gone to Holland to see the tulips" was pasted on the door of Tyrone Guthrie's London flat one spring morning. Why not? He had time for everything.

"I don't believe we can think of anything more today." It was three o'clock in the afternoon, rehearsal had started at ten-thirty. Equity allows eight hours to think of something. Tony Guthrie did not need it.

If there was a show to be directed which would pay him a lot, he'd look hard for something else. "What play do you want to do?" he asked the Habimah.

*"The Importance of Being Earnest?"*

"I think *Oedipus Rex,"* and he flew off to Israel. The opening saw some gunfire, but the show was a hit.

At the Met he was directing *Carmen.* "Tucker," he said, "when you stab Mother Bunch, stick the knife in her womb, then pull it sharply up." The cast couldn't stop laughing.

"I had to dismiss rehearsal," he told us. "Dammit, I should never say what I mean." But on the opening night, when Richard Tucker stuck his knife into Risë Stevens' womb and pulled it up sharply, the audience didn't laugh, they gasped in terror.

*Annagh-Ma-Kerrig*
*Doohat P.O.*
*Monaghan, Ireland*
*March 8, 1971*

Ruth dear, remember me? I was once your lodger in Turtle Bay; and wasn't there something called *The Matchmaker?*

On!

We're only recently back from seven months in "Strylia" (down under to you, always so sophisticated). It was marvelous. Did us a heap of good, physically and spiritually. I forget if I told you that this time last year I was quite ill—heart. Had to Rest Complete for several months. This was accomplished without much diff. I wrote a dreadfully dull wee book (a How-to Book on Acting) and a long piece on Theatre, The Art of, for the new Encyclopedia Britannica due out next year. This kept me quiet and by the end of May I felt ready (despite pouts from m' doctor) to face the Antipodes. It was great.

Oh, in a bracket, I have to tell you that there was—in Perth, I think—a publicity lady whose name was Rosy Hayes. I called her Miss Pink Mist and she didn't see that it was meant to be funny. Jokes, down under, are apt to be concerned with sitting (fully clad) in a pot of hot porridge.

On!

I'm doing little, but there are more than enough Enquiries and Possibilities to make me feel still "wanted" and that the Wolf isn't sniffing too near the door. Might do *Figaro* in Ottawa in June; and there's talk of various projects here and there. The Met has suggested that I get up *P. Grimes* yet again in 1973. Well, that's absurd; and together with a dainty little offer from New Zealand for the same year has had to go into a file marked If Spared.

I'm now practically half-way—no, over half-way through my 71st year. God knows how old you are. Do you mind? I think I'm enjoying old age very much. It's a bore becoming increasingly inactive (and of course the more inactive you are, by twice the more inactive you do become) but I love bossing younger people around for no better reason than that they ARE younger; and I give way to practically unbridled reminiscence, much of it fictitious and most of it self-glorification.

Last night we had an invitation to go to Open or Close (it really doesn't matter) the Carrickmore Festival. I expect you may never have heard of Carrickmore or its Festival. I think it must be about the nearest thing left to the sort of event which the Athenian Festivals may have been.

Carrickmore is a village of 200 people in the wilds of County Tyrone—and that's getting pretty wild. They put up a Hall, which holds over a thousand people, and once a year they have a week of plays—amateur groups, by invitation from all over Ireland. The place is packed, nobody goes to bed, all night. After the play they sit up drinking and tearing to pieces what they have seen with the incredible acumen and malice of stage-struck Irish. This year's programme includes Arden's *Serjeant Musgrave's Dance* and *John Gabriel Borkman* besides the usual crop of native drama—Friel, Behan and so on. From what I've heard, this really is what Theatre's about—

a sort of occasion which simply doesn't exist any more in the professional situation and hasn't, I think, existed since Kean's time. The essence being an intelligent, madly keen audience which, instead of being sated with drama (breakfast to bedtime, cradle to grave—on the squire), is avidly, passionately desirous. And that does not mean uncritical adorers. Quite the contrary.

Does that describe Tony? A man contrary to his time in our theatre, who hung onto his belief? He was at odds with Shaftesbury Avenue and West 45th, but look for him in Swansea staging a play with the Drama Society. Look for him in Finland getting up a "dainty something" for the Sardine Catchers' Theatre. For any audience that he thought gave a damn, count on him peddling his wares.

"Oh dear," were David Garrick's last words.

If he had time to say it, "On!" was surely Tyrone Guthrie's.

For thirty-five years, we wrote each other. Between letters we joined up for three plays.

On!

To live in during *The Country Wife* engagement Claridge's clerk showed me to a single, inside room. A single? Inside? I called Charles Laughton.

"Tell them to give you something more spacious. Come here at six-thirty. Dinner."

He felt I *must* go to the Old Vic opening.

"You must see the theatre." He couldn't go, but Elsa could.

The theatre seemed enormous. Was that fright? People were piling in, the lights dimmed, curtain rose, and next opening night *I*'d be on that stage. On came the Princess and Rosaline, on came Biron, on they went! Tyrone Guthrie had directed it. I thought it was terrible. At 10 o'clock tomorrow he'd direct me.

"I think I'll go home," I said to Elsa.

"Back to Claridge's?"

"No, to New York."

"Oh, dear! What would Charles do? Oh, dear! What would I do if Charles? Want to practice our laugh? Anytime anyone says anything, let's laugh."

We laughed separately and in unison, like a sister act. Sister Elsa got me past the moment. I didn't go home, I went to rehearsal. If you can get by the moment, you can do anything.

I spent that night in my inside single, then Claridge's changed me to a beautiful suite.

"Hard work ahead," said Charles. "You must be comfortable."

I was. On the second floor, a beautiful, old-fashioned big square sitting room with French windows looked out onto Davies Street. The walls were pale old-fashioned pink. The bathroom was bigger than my Martin's Theatrical hall bedroom had been. The bedroom was bigger than Anna Witham's. Why think of Wollaston? It was big and square like Anna's with French windows and a "grey" marble fireplace, white walls like wedding cake frosting.

"Taxi."

"Yes, Madam." The grand doorman at the Brook Street entrance summoned one off the rank. It looked like Gilbert's limousine. London taxis are grand.

"Where to, Madam?"

"The Old Vic."

"Waterloo Road, the Old Vic," he told the driver.

We rode, then crossed a bridge over the Thames by Westminster Abbey, and rode.

"Stage door, please," I said to the driver. On the first day of rehearsal, those are terrifying words!

The stage door was off the sidewalk, no alley to wander through; directly inside was the doorman's office. "I'm Ruth Gordon."

"Yes, Miss. Take those stairs."

Theatres are sort of alike backstage, out of date and dark and hard to thread your way. Now came the frightening moment, to walk on the stage. I was on time, but Tyrone Guthrie and George Chamberlain and a scary number of others were early. Michael Redgrave was there. He had made his London debut in last night's play. He'd made a name in Birmingham rep. Everybody was introduced, everybody was pleasant and detached. An assistant stage manager, the A.S.M. they're called, gave me a small green hard-covered book with passages penciled over. This was the version we would perform. Different from the Westport one. The original is long, so productions are cut to please whoever is running things. The Westport one pleased Lawrence Langner, the Vic pleased Tyrone Guthrie.

Something happened. It was like lights had come on. A breeze. Edith Evans had come in. The stage seemed livable; someone felt at home. She changed from flat shoes to a banged-up pair of cherry satin with heels. "I expect I'll wear something similar, won't I?"

"I expect so," said Tyrone Guthrie, not remotely interested. "Messel will be along to talk about his ideas. Do you know Ruth Gordon?"

"We met in New York. Rosalie Stewart took us to supper."

She brought her to *A Church Mouse*. She was Thornton's agent and she was also Edith Evans'. Afterward, we met in my dressing room. Not a word from Miss Evans about what she'd just seen; we got in a taxi and drove to supper. I don't remember where; all I remember was no mention of what she'd seen and she kept saying, "A cairngorm. A cairngorm!" Did that get into the conversation to avoid talking about *A Church Mouse?* Now we shared the Old Vic stage. Lady Fidget and Marjory Pinchwife are rivals for Mr. Horner, but don't meet until the last scene and even then have no words together.

"Might I have Miss Gordon for a photo with the costers?" asked the press agent.

Tyrone Guthrie nodded.

I went out to the pushcarts, mashed together, selling buttons, pork, buns, neckties, fruit, shoes. A picture was snapped. That was the end of Old Vic publicity. Did the picture ever appear? They gave me a glossy and that's how I know they took it.

"Our Mr. Pinchwife is playing in Bristol," announced Tyrone Guthrie. "We won't see much of him until next week."

Only three weeks of rehearsal and no Pinchwife for a whole week?

"This is James Dale. He must leave early to get back to Bristol."

James Dale had been a triumph as suave Mr. Dulcimer when Jed brought him over for *The Green Bay Tree* at the Cort.

"He's crazy," Jed said.

That didn't make it so, unless you call it crazy carrying a door around backstage to attack the producer. James Dale and I rehearsed our scenes, said goodbye and he was off on the afternoon train to Bristol. Back in a week.

"I must be insane," I'd told Helen.

"But you've got to," she'd told me.

That's a good reminder when you rehearse in another country. At home, people get used to you, forgive you your mistakes; in a new land, they have to take somebody's *word* for it that you're good. No past achievement to give them confidence that you're going to be all right. That's looking at it from *their* angle; from yours, did you ever hear your own voice on the stage of the Old Vic Theatre? Maybe hurdle-jumpers can jump too high. A good feeling is when a scary rehearsal stops for the day. On my desk in my pink sitting room was a square white envelope with a letter from Ned.

Ruth dear,

This is just to bring you my thoughts and tell you that I hope no British obstacles have reared themselves in your path. If so, I have great confidence in your ability to sweep them tactfully out of your way.

Ned had confidence and for that other trip, so had Dr. Gray. "You'll manage everything. I expect to hear only good news."

How is it people are so sure of me and *I*'m scared?

On!

When once Mrs. Pinchwife meets her London audience, all will be well. I hope that you wrote Helen about your doctor. I know that she is going to miss you. Do you ever stop in at Gunther's in Berkeley Square? I remember their iced coffee with a large shot of brandy concealed in the depths. Very refreshing on a summer afternoon. You might take one, minus the ice, on your way home after a particularly trying rehearsal. Well, my fingers are permanently crossed until I hear that you are accepted as another Rehan.

Yours affectionately,

Ned

September 12, 1936

For ten years his fingers had been paralyzed, but not his good will and courage.

At dinner at Gordon Square, we stuck with the subject of the play. Charles' faith was like everything about him, tremendous: I would conquer London, I *had* to, he'd *told* people I would.

Would I? Would I even be *good?* Acting is hard. Only actors know *how* hard. How remarkable when it works!

I wasn't the only one worried. Tyrone Guthrie worried too. At rehearsal, he asked me, "Do you think you will be funny?"

Awful question. Awful anywhere, worse on the Old Vic stage. Confidence! Build it in till it becomes like your heart, your kidney, lung; then exercise it.

"I think I'd be funny if this was New York." Would Ned think that sounded like another Rehan? And when *she* played London did they ask *her* that? "Of course, I don't know if I'll seem funny in *London.*" Was Tyrone Guthrie ten feet tall? I'm five feet and looking down on me, he seemed twice my height.

"This part *has* to be funny. The play won't go if it isn't."

"I was funny in Westport." It sounded lame. Awful to describe how funny you *were.*

Tyrone Guthrie was worried about *me,* I was worried about our Mr. Horner.

"He's done well in Birmingham rep."

"He's handsome, but too young."

Next evening. "You still feel the same about Horner?"

"Yes. Too young for Edith Evans. Too young for me."

Next morning. Charles came to rehearsal. He was standing onstage, to one side. I spoke to Tyrone Guthrie. "Charles is watching. Please don't ask me to do my good scenes, or if you have to, I'll just mumble through; I can't *bear* anyone watching. You'll understand?"

Charles hung around, then left. At dinner, he said he'd watched to see if I was right and thought I was. He went in to talk to Miss Baylis. " 'I'll play Horner for you,' I told her.

" 'We couldn't afford you, dear.'

" 'I'll do it for nothing. I'd like to see this play succeed.'

" 'You wouldn't be good, dear. Horner is a charmer.' She's a stubborn old bitch. I can't do any more."

Any theatre in London would have taken him, but not Lilian Baylis'.

Rehearsing Mrs. Pinchwife while people ask if you're going to be funny isn't easy. It's still harder if Mr. Pinchwife is in Bristol. Substituting for him was apprentice Stefan Schnabel, in his teens and speaking the lines with his pronounced German accent.

"You'll manage," Dr. Gray had said.

"Your mail, Madam." Claridge's pageboy offered me a letter on a silver tray. From Woollcott.

GLADSTONE HOTEL

114–122 East 52nd Street at
Park Avenue
New York

PLAZA 3–4300

*CABLE ADDRESS*

*GLADSTO*

*September 21, 1936*

Dear Ruth,

Did I ever tell you the story about Maurice Barrymore's difficulties with critics? He came of an Anglo-Indian family and made his first appearance on the stage in America. Here the reviewers spoke harshly of his English accent. When, some years later, he went to London to play, the critics complained of his American accent. "Good God!" he said, "these fellows will limit me to recitations on ocean liners!"

After which affable anecdote, I beg leave to report on sundry matters here at home. Today Hecht and MacArthur are leaving Nyack by motorboat for the island. This would seem to me a wantonly arduous way to go, but, thanks to various canals beyond the Hudson, they can get at least as far as Whitehall. They are staying at the island for two weeks, making a movie out of *Wuthering Heights,* which I hope they will read soon.

I shall be a neighbor of theirs after the middle of October until June, for I have taken Feather Havermeyer's house at Snedens Landing. It's the one called, in the playful fashion of that community, The Dingdong. Anyway, it's charmingly furnished and on the edge of the water, and there's room in it for my cat, Black Neysa, and my three black dogs, the third being a transient poodle named Jalon, which is spending the winter with me while his master is in Europe. His master, by the way, is named Bob Rudd. He is one of my oldest and most charming friends. It's possible you may have met him. He teaches English Literature at Hamilton, and has gone off to Europe for a sabbatical semester. I have told him to look you up at your costly hotel, and I hope he plucks up courage enough to do so, and that if he does you will ensconce him at the Old Vic for one of the performances. He has been in a lather ever since he heard you were going to do the play, and almost got to Westport to see it there. Untie the knot in that face and release a smile. You will like him. I know you don't often like people unless they're very unpleasant, but you *would* like him.

I have been here for a week doing all kinds of business and writing immortal prose at a terrific rate, but I go back to the island tomorrow. One thing I had to do was to get the various radio offers assorted, so I have made Julian Field my agent. One of the proposals, still vague, comes through Bruce Powell, who has set himself up in the world as a broker of talent. I have made all kinds of disagreeable stipulations, agreeing to broadcast at all only if it can be done on the Columbia Network, demanding huge sums of money and complete freedom of speech, and requiring that Pearl Swope attend every broadcast.

Thursday night I filled Guthrie McClintic with expensive comestibles (flagrant paraphrase of an old Ruth Gordon expression) and in return he bootlegged me into the *Hamlet* rehearsal. I saw enough to make me feel sure I will spend November and December going alternately to *The Country Wife* and *Hamlet.* I expect Gielgud to be good, and I am sure he is going to be, but a firstrate Hamlet is no novelty in our time. It is, however, something new to see the Queen and Ophelia so richly and beautifully played.

Then I think I should tell you Moss Hart's title for the Mary Astor diary, which is to be published in book form. He thinks it should be called "Stars Fell on Mary Astor."

Good luck on the sixth.

A. Woollcott

"Do you think you *will* be funny?" asked Tyrone Guthrie again.

Funny I *hoped* to be. *Certain* I was of looking beautiful.

"Marjory Pinchwife is mousy, I suppose?" asked Oliver Messel. "Everything drab?"

"God, no. Country people are gaudy! They like colors that *show.* Mrs. Simpson would choose beige, but country-raised people would want candy *pink,* bright buttercup *yellow,* poppy *red* and trimming. People in the country like colors and trimming."

Oliver made a bright pink sketch the color of the tuppenny candy called Brighton Rock. That was my Act I dress, the one I'd begin in, the one in which I would make my London debut.

"Do you think you'll be funny?"

Next act, I put on my best dress, white heavy silk with green and red ribbons and bows and furbelows, lace, lavender satin bands with bows. "Pleated skirt," scrawled Oliver on the costume plate, "in net with ribands of Nile and cerise." On the top left hand, he wrote, "Ruth Gordon red gloves." Top right: "Mrs. Pinchwife dressing scene. Hat? Color? Material? Moiré corded silk bows, hyacinth stripes. Oliver Messel."

The scene where I rush off for an evening on the town I disguise myself, slip off my best dress and rush out in red flannel drawers and corset.

Oliver loved that. "Drawers that have ribbons and lace and rosebuds like ones made of lawn, but these will be lovely red flannel."

I'd *look* adorable, but would I be funny? Would Minnie Mouse with sex appeal make London laugh? No use harping back to Westport; would they laugh *October sixth on the Waterloo Road?*

Scenes with Mr. Pinchwife didn't get anywhere. Stefan Schnabel was good, but wrong. Confidence! Hang on to it.

The other actors seemed all right, but *only* all right. All except Edith Evans. She seemed alarmingly perfect. She liked Michael Redgrave, and her scenes with him, everyone stopped whatever they were doing and watched.

She and I hadn't talked much, then one day she said, "I have a partridge. Will you dine with me at my flat?"

Claridge's man beckoned to the grand London taxi. It rolled along Park Lane, turned left, stopped at Halkin Place off Belgrave Square. Up a flight. We ate the partridge someone had sent her, we made up talk and soon after dinner I left. What a pleasure to be welcomed, and now to bed.

369

"The letter-writing scene should be the funniest scene there is," Tyrone Guthrie reminded me. "Do you think it will be?"

"It was funny in Westport."

"If they don't think you're funny, the play won't go."

"Of course, I don't know what London will think. In New York, I think they'd think I was funny." How many times would we keep saying that? Confidence! Be sure you build it in. I started mine in Wollaston. You can't start too early.

Don't get put down; get past what people say. Confidence must be part of your equipment. Next to trouble, the biggest.

"To me you're not funny," said Tyrone Guthrie. Not meanly; just a statement of a fact.

When you hear that a week before you open in a foreign country, you *need* confidence, built in wall to wall. I put myself to sleep with extravagant encouragement, glorious predictions. I'd learned to do that at 14 Elmwood; I'd lulled myself to sleep imagining I was a star.

In Claridge's pale pink bedroom I dropped off, predicting, "They'll take the horses out of my carriage! They'll cheer! This room will be smothered with flowers! *You* will be a *triumph!*"

Costume parade was Sunday night before the opening. Dresses, wigs, shoes, but no makeup. Try the quick changes to see if they could be made. Mine could. "All perfect" is the overall description of Oliver Messel's work. To hear him talk you'd think he was indecisive, flighty, a charming dilettante, and no description could suit him less.

The semi-light of the Old Vic bare stage made us look like portraits. Angus McBean snapped his memorable photos as we moved around. Everything was calm, all the costumes pleased everybody, all the shoes fit.

"Dismiss the company," Tyrone Guthrie told George Chamberlain. It had been three weeks since we'd met at Waterloo Station. Day after tomorrow, the Old Vic curtain would go up. Would they think I was funny?

"Two dress rehearsals tomorrow," reminded George.

"George, I'll light the show now," said Tyrone.

I asked, "May I stay?" I was interested to know what he'd use.

"By all means." He looked at the stage. "Oliver's paint work is beautiful; I believe I'll just throw on all white lights. That'll do very nicely, George."

"What will that do to our looks?" I asked.

"Make you beautiful."

Beautiful, but would I be funny?

Up in dressing room 2 my dresser, Mrs. Richmond, helped me. Capable, middle-aged, unruffled, handled clothes beautifully and remained calm. She had hung up my pink dotted cotton hangings. They and she made dressing room 2 seem comfortable. Edith was number 1, turn left off the stairs from the stone passage. I turned right. Edith's was bigger. Mine was big enough.

"Half the posters will have Edith Evans' name first," said management. "The other half, yours."

"If I ever see mine first I'll leave." An American in London billed ahead of Edith Evans?

First dress rehearsal at 9 A.M., everybody dressed and ready. The Old Vic School apprentices were allowed to watch. Whatever I did they laughed and laughed. They laughed at other times, but most for me. Encouraging?

*"Next* time," said Edith, "I shall read the *whole* play. I had no idea Mrs. Pinchwife was so good a part."

Encouraging?

No comment from Tyrone Guthrie.

That same evening, 7 P.M., knock on the door. "Half hour." Tomorrow the knock and the call would be for opening night.

Out front, no one except Tyrone Guthrie, Lilian Baylis and two ladies huddled together in the first row on the left. On inquiry, it was learned they were Mrs. Gilbert Miller and Mrs. Syrie Maugham. Mrs. Miller I knew and Mrs. Maugham I'd met on the beach at La Garoupe.

"I must divorce Willie," she'd told Alec. "For Liza's sake I must. So penurious and now smiling he watches Gerald lose thousands on the Juan-les-Pins gaming table. To insure Liza's inheritance I *must* divorce."

A cold October evening and the furnace had broken down. The two ladies were wrapped in an auto rug. No laughs from or for anybody. The final curtain came down.

"We'll meet on stage at four tomorrow," said Tyrone Guthrie, "to arrange the final tableau. It won't be complicated. An hour and you'll be out. Opening night curtain at eight. Good night."

No praise, but none expected.

"Mrs. Miller will be in to see me," I told Mrs. Richmond, and waited in my soigné pearl-gray satin with discreet embroidery and black lace.

The tall black lace fontange framed my hair and face. Around my throat the black bogwood necklace. I knew I looked beautiful.

"Should I go down and show them the way up?" asked helpful Mrs. Richmond. "The Vic is not easy to find one's way."

Mrs. Richmond came back. "No one, Madam."

"Perhaps they're at the stage door?"

"I inquired. No one has been around."

"Ask Potter if anyone has been round to see Miss Evans. They may have gone there first."

I waited.

"No one, Madam."

Wouldn't Kitty Miller come back? Gilbert and Helen had put up the money for the production.

I got dressed, went past the stairs and knocked at dressing room number 1. Potter opened the door.

"Did Mrs. Miller—"

Edith's voice called out. "Come in, ducky. No one's been round. Were you expecting them?"

"They didn't *say* they would, but wouldn't you *think?"*

"Well, I expect they were cold. No furnace. They must have been anxious to get home."

"But the night before we *open,* not to come back?"

Edith read my worry. "Would you like a bite of supper?"

"Yes, I would."

Edith Evans *never* went out after the theatre. Nor did I, as a rule.

"Potter, ring up the Café Royal. Say to hold a table. We'll be along." She turned to me. "Do you like it?"

"I've never been."

"Oh, well then, you *must* go. It's where Oscar Wilde went after the theatre. It's where theatre people have always gone. Call a cab, Potter."

We drove off through the October night, across Waterloo Bridge, along the Strand to Piccadilly Circus and the Café Royal. The head-waiter was overjoyed to see the great Edith.

"What will you have, ducks?"

"What will you?"

"The chicken's very good here. I'll have that and a glass of white wine."

I ordered Welsh rarebit and beer.

"Good," she said. "Make you sleep."

The beer and the friendship helped thaw my worry. "Wouldn't you think they'd have sent *word* if they didn't want to come back?"

"Well, they don't think of things like that. I'm sure they enjoyed it and wanted to get home to bed."

"But before an opening?"

"Professional people would think of that, but not ladies."

Comforting.

"Taxi," said Edith to the doorman.

One stopped circling Piccadilly Circus and we got in. "I'll drop you back at Claridge's. I say, it's cold! Here, get under my fur coat." We both huddled in her ample coat.

At Claridge's, I said, "Want to come up?"

"Just a moment, to see you safe inside your door."

"Do you think it will go?" I asked.

*"Oh,* yes, dear! The night *before,* one always has the wind up, but we shouldn't. It's a *very* beautiful production Oliver has done, Tony's done it very well, we're a *very* good company, the play is Wycherley's best. *Oh,* yes, it'll go."

A letter slid under my door.

"It's Thornton."

"Thornton!" She'd met him on her visit to New York, with Rosalie Stewart.

"I'll read it."

"Oh, do."

> *"50 Deepwood Drive*
> *New Haven, Conn.*
> *Sept 21, 1936*

"Dear Ruth:

"Tonight or tomorrow you and our great Edith will—"

"Oh, he didn't say that! Where is it?"

I held the letter out.

"—will bring glory to the stage, and in the wings watching will be Dora Jordan and Mrs. Bracegirdle. There I was on the train from Chicago to Aleck's island and I read in the paper about your call to England and was able from Troy to send you my enthusiasm; it's just as live now, as it was yesterday at Ned's, and this morning in New York at breakfast with Aleck. All blessings on you for the sixth of October. Receiving your letter

373

this morning almost makes me mad because I wanted to get my letter to you first.

"The day you get this letter, you'll have been rehearsing hours and days. I can't get over saying it all seems wonderful. I'll be prwwlg* around for the *Times* and the *Observer* and the *Telegraph* and then the Weeklies.

"Aleck says he drove over and saw you in the Church Mouse and that it was great acting.

"In fact, everything seems to be in good shape at present except Europe and Asia. Ma has never been in better health and spirits, Isabel is blooming, Amos and Catherine are going to have a baby; Janet loves the University of Chicago; I'm fine, have resigned from the University and have every intention of becoming an author; and Aleck's well and Freud's well (I get friendly messages from him in his own hand—we're buddies) and Margaret (my cleaning-woman in Chicago) she's well; and (I forgot) *you're* well. . . .

"The only things that aren't well are Maude Hutchins and the Spaniards. They're not well at all.

"Tallulah Bankhead's play opened here in town. Poor play, but she was awfully good.

"Saw a good deal of Kit in Chicago. She incorporated some of my suggestions into *St. Joan* but she didn't catch what I was saying to her between the lines. Had lunch with Jean Giraudoux and took him to the Field Museum. Oh, what a wonderful man.

"Isn't Mrs. Otis Skinner a darlin' woman? . . .

"I've been approached about writing a radio continuity for you. I'm humble and confused about my capability, but dammit I got some lines of conversation down on paper the other day that I thought were very funny and I could just hear you flinging them radiantly about the bus. Who knows? Maybe I could. Anyway in a week's time I'll have two installments all ready to show the agent. Let's not talk about it.

"Yes, I've resigned from the University for three–four years. But I'm not a free man really until April first. Rosalie Stewart claims she's getting me a Hollywood job for October first; but no word's come so maybe I'm unvendable. And all Feb. and March I'm on a lecture-tour (my last). Maybe this fall I'll go to the Virgin Islands to write either:

1. The Widow of Monterey or

2. Geraldine de Grey or The Devil's a Fool. The first has turned into a novel, I'm sorry to say.

"My father's illness cost five thousand dollars but my lawyer says I'm still smartly solvent and I shall continue to throw money around like confetti—buying Vienna newspapers and giving my washing to the laundry and all the amenities.

"I may sound cheerful, but it's only fair to state that I'm fairly bowed down by all the nonsense that's talked in the world, oh, oh, the hit-and-miss judgments, the hit-and-run sneers, the emotional wish-wash, igno-

*"That word is prowling."

374

rance being assertive about difficult questions, oh, oh. I resigned from the University of Chicago because I couldn't endure listening to the things I had to say in public. I'm dying to hold my tongue for a couple of years.

"I shall vote for Roosevelt.

*"Gone With the Wind* has sold 75,000 copies. *Expliquez.*

"I kind of hope you'll get to like Sybil.

"Everybody, everybody* should cross the ocean to see you and Edith Evans—"

"Fancy *that! Coo!* I *say,* that's nice."

"May you have a wonderful time and a welcome and an ovation that you'll remember with happiness to your dying day.

"This is the urgent central wish and expectation of

Yr. devoted friend,

Thornton"

*"As for the smudge: stet, pardon it."

The chill was off the night! Thornton believed!

Edith went off, happy. I slept as though we'd opened to a house *rocked* with laughter!

October 6. Opening day of opening night! How get through it? How get through the day that will turn into opening night, shortly after "That evenin' sun goes down"?

In October, London is dark at four o'clock. Did it seem foreboding? Onstage stood the company. Everybody acted composed.

"It will be jelly glasses in the air," said Tyrone Guthrie, taller than ever. "Restrained mirth and a few dance steps. Ninette, where do you want them?"

Ninette de Valois of the Sadler's Wells Ballet, which also belonged to Lilian Baylis, told us to take partners, move right, move left, count it out for now, tonight the orchestra'll play it. Lift the red jelly glasses aloft and curtain will come down.

We did it twice.

"Thank you." Tyrone Guthrie nodded to George Chamberlain.

"Dismissed till seven o'clock," said George.

We scattered for nourishment.

The pub next to the stage door was too close. I walked along the Waterloo Road to the Waterloo Pub. What if I kept on going? What if I walked to Waterloo Station? Opening-night thoughts, but they *seem* real.

In the Waterloo Pub, no one was eating. I ordered a lamb chop. I must be out of my mind; what made me think I could eat a lamb chop? Did

I eat? I did something and soon I was out again on the Waterloo Road. If I turned left, I'd get to the Vic stage door; if I turned right, I'd get to Waterloo Station. Would Equity suspend me? "They can't *kill* me," I kept reassuring myself, and then I was at the stage door.

"Richmond took your flowers and messages, Madam. Good luck to-night."

"Thank you." Up the flight of stone stairs that turned at the landing, I turned right.

"Good evening, Madam." Mrs. Richmond confined her conversation to essentials.

I'd told her not to have flowers or messages around. "If any come, please hide them." Opening night I like my dressing room to look as if it were just any night.

If my makeup goes on well, I think the night will. My makeup went on well.

Knock on the door. "Act One, Scene One."

"Thank you," said Mrs. Richmond.

I wasn't in Scene One.

Knock on the door. "Scene Two."

"Thank you," said Mrs. Richmond.

I went down the stone stairs, Mrs. Richmond holding up my pink satin skirt. I went onstage. No turning back now.

In Mr. Pinchwife's London drawing room sat his elegant sister Alithea, doing needlework. I took my place, standing by the window looking out at London.

"Curtain going up," said George Chamberlain.

It rustled up. Applause. Ursula Jeans, blond, beautiful, thrust her needle through the material stretched over the wooden embroidery hoops. The applause wasn't like Thornton foresaw. It was polite, but no thunder. Ursula Jeans was liked. "The distinguished American actress"? Let's see.

Polite applause starts and stops; I didn't have to stop it. "Sister, where are the best woods and fields to walk in in London?" I asked.

Later Ursula said, "I'd expected you to be nervous, but you sounded composed. I looked up from the needlework to answer and almost forgot m' words. Your eyes had rolled back in your head so far that only the whites showed."

Scene over.

Did they think I was funny? Some laughs, but none that took in the whole house. The most was when I noticed a cockroach crawling by, lifted my pink satin skirt and came down on it with my elegant buckled shoe.

Important, Jed had warned, to show the contrast of filthy London streets and grand drawing rooms, the pox-ridden poor and the satin-clad, lace-frilled fops whose carriages splashed mud on beggars. Satin and cockroaches, frippery and neglect are the keynote. "When Wycherley wrote it," said Jed, "everyone knew that. You have to remind them."

A cockroach in the elegant drawing room brought more than Bert Lahr's "A titter m' tit," more than Joe E. Lewis' "An intellectual nod," less than Mr. Lee Shubert's "A laugh is when the whole house laughs the same time."

But did they think I was funny?

The scene in the New Exchange was on. Nothing went wrong, but nothing went great. *Why* couldn't I get started? I was playing carefully, and that's not me. Awful when you don't get started and no pickle dish that didn't break to rouse me. What would? And rouse me *now,* not tomorrow, not yesterday—*now!* That's acting! You have to do it *now.*

The letter-writing scene was coming up. I'm alone on stage in the bed. *"Do* it, do it *now, do* it! God, let me do it *now."*

He did. And that was the scene to do it in. I took off and went! October 6 on the Waterloo Road, I'm glad I did *not* go to the station! I got out of bed to look for my slippers.

"Find things under the bed," said Tyrone Guthrie. "Look for more and more. They'll think you're looking for the pot, but fool them. *Let* them think so; *you* get lost in other things. What do you want to have under there? Of course, start with finding one slipper, so they'll know what you're doing, then tell George what else you want.

I looked under.

They laughed. They knew what I was looking for.

I pulled out an Oliver Messel moiré slipper, rosette on the toe, then looked some more. They laughed. I pulled out an orange. That surprised them. An orange under the bed? They laughed. They *really* laughed. I looked again. Another orange. They laughed and I looked some more, crawled under the bed. They *knew* this was the pot. I came out with a handful of playing cards. Mr. Lee Shubert would have called that a laugh. A deck of cards under the bed? It gave an idea of what kind of housekeeper Marjory Pinchwife was. I sat down with the cards, arranged them in my hand. They laughed. When I felt like it I reached and found the second slipper. That was Mr. Pinchwife's cue to come in. The scene had gone great!

377

Pinchwife has found out Horner has designs. He makes me write the cad a letter.

The letter-writing scene.

It went!

"Now fold it up," said furious Mr. Pinchwife.

I did.

"Write on the back side his vile name," he roared, and stamped off.

With my quill I wrote "Mr. Horner" on my backside. They laughed.

"On the *backside?*" I asked the audience. I was troubled by such an instruction; had they heard it too? They laughed. I took them into my confidence. "I can't send Mr. Horner this letter." I opened it up. The ink wasn't dry when I'd folded it; it was one big illegible blot. "I can't send him *that.*" I stepped down to the footlights and held it up for the orchestra stalls to see for themselves, held it up higher for the dress circle, higher still for the gallery gods, then for the people in the boxes. They laughed.

I looked at my dreadful letter again, looked out at the audience and gave a roar of frustration that came from the soles of my feet.

They understood, laughed, applauded. Frustration is known in all countries. I dashed offstage to laughter and cheers.

Oh, my!

I dashed into the quick-change room, tore off nightgown to change into elegant pearl-gray satin. Mrs. Richmond handed me the grand black lace fontange. Nothing on but my white satin lastex pants, the flap to the quick-change room was pulled open, Tyrone Guthrie rushed in, flung his arms around me. We hugged and hugged, no one happier than Tyrone Guthrie that they thought I was funny.

The evening sailed through to total triumph. We took partners, counted the steps as Ninette de Valois instructed, the Old Vic orchestra played, we lifted aloft wineglasses half full of red jelly, the curtain rustled down.

Tony had arranged that the entire company line up, each principal to step forward. When I did, the house caved in.

"You'll have to make a speech," whispered Edith.

Up went the curtain. Cheers, applause. Each principal stepped forward. Michael Redgrave spoke. Edith spoke. My turn.

"I never made but one speech," I said, "and that was a night the theatre was on fire."

Funnier than anything yet. I was startled, shaken by triumph. I had wanted to let them know how I was unused to making speeches and it was hailed as madly witty. When things go right, enjoy it.

As we came off, Charles and Elsa were coming out of the stone passage back of the scenery; they'd stood on the queue to get in. If Charles Laughton had *reserved* a seat, word would have gotten backstage. They stood during the show so I wouldn't know they were there.

The world climbed up the stone stairs.

"I'll rush out and phone Helen," said Marc Connelly. "I can get her backstage at the Broadhurst, before she goes on."

Just as she was going to her first entrance as the young Victoria, Helen's dressing room phone rang, Marc told her the great news.

Backstage in my dressing room were Arthur MacRae and Louis and Mary Bromfield and Lady Juliet Duff. On and on they came, full of laughter and praise.

Mrs. Richmond had the boxes of flowers open. A wreath of Scotch heather was from Lilian Baylis. A small black china cat tied into the heather with a white ribbon bow. The card was engraved: *"Lilian Baylis, The Old Vic Theatre, Waterloo Road, S.E.1."* Opposite was engraved: *"Sadler's Wells, Rosebery Avenue E.C.1."* Above her name, she'd written: "A tiny offering containing a loving welcome to Ruth Gordon wishing her much happiness tonight & always." Below her engraved name was: *"C.H.M.A. Oxon (Hon.). L.L.D. Birm. (Hon.)."* Then she'd written: "The Country Wife. Oct. 6/36."

A box of roses from Edith. On the card: "All will go well, darling. Much love from Edith."

Box of flowers from Arthur MacRae. "Love and love. Arthur."

Darling Arthur. We'd loved each other since *Ruggles of Red Gap* days had given both of us trouble. Charles had got Paramount to bring Arthur over to write on the film, then forgot about him and so did Paramount. He and I had loved each other on sight. When we both got chucked, we loved each other more. "Have dinner with me at the Brown Derby?" he phoned. "I'll be humming a snatch." That was the night after I saw my test.

From Charles and Elsa, a beautiful cartwheel of Constance Spry flowers. Elegant ones from Kitty Miller. From Oliver Messel a pair of drawers made of red carnations mounted on white tulle. Scrawled on the top of some drawing paper were his directions to the florist; a sketch in pencil, beside it scribbled: "red carnations covering all over dolls draws with white lace frill." Beneath, in pencil, was: "Ruthie, darling, to wish you again all success in the world tonight & all my love, darling, Oliver."

379

From Tony and Judy Guthrie, a jar of Beech-Nut peanut butter!

Thank you, dining room of 14 Elmwood Avenue. "I want to go on the stage," I'd told Papa.

"What makes you think you've got the stuff it takes?"

"I can do it. I know I can if somebody will *show* me."

Thank you, Gregory, for the cheers at the Old Vic!

Thank you, Helen and Gilbert, for putting up forty thousand dollars to see that *The Country Wife* got done!

"I'll just drop the flowers by at Claridge's," offered Mrs. Richmond. "I expect you'll be going on with Mr. and Mrs. Laughton."

Charles asked, "Would you like to invite Edith? She's been very nice to you."

After a night of satin and lace and ribbons, Edith and I had gone back to old skirts and sweaters, Arthur wore any old kind of a suit, Elsa and Charles had dressed for the queue. Looking in on Gordon Square, would anyone think this was the queen of the London stage, the triumphant Henry VIII of films and one who next morning's *New York Times* would report "Takes London by Storm"?

Next day at our Wednesday matinee, backstage was abuzz with success. It had gone so well I didn't read the notices.

Everybody else had read them, ecstasy rampant. And on top of the notices, in the stalls sat Bernard Shaw come to see Edith, for whom he'd written *The Millionairess,* and now he'd see the rest of us when Lady Fidget wasn't onstage!

In Wollaston, I'd spent fifty cents to see Shaw's *Fanny's First Play* at the Park Theatre on Washington Street. It wasn't *The Pink Lady* or *The Sunshine Girl,* but interesting and I loved Eva Leonard-Boyne, who played Fanny. Now Shaw was out front; would he love me?

Our matinee went the same as opening night, then a knock on the door; it was Potter. "Miss Evans says would you please come in and see Mr. Shaw."

14 Elmwood Avenue to the Waterloo Road to down the hall to George Bernard Shaw.

"This is our American actress," said Edith.

When he and Mrs. Shaw had come to luncheon at the Villa Ganelon in Antibes, he had to take Alec's word I was an actress. Today he didn't acknowledge we'd ever met. He was irked that Edith hadn't signed for *The Millionairess,* but had chosen the Old Vic season instead.

"What a tiresome play. I didn't laugh but once."

Lilian Baylis' spies had reported he'd laughed continuously.

"Only when Sir Jasper said, 'Oh, thou libidinous lady,' I laughed."

He may have. No one else did.

He turned to me. "You're not funny, you're sensible. That's why they laugh." Not flattery, but a good rule for comedy? "Did you leave New York because you have so many murders there?"

"Be polite in a foreign country, but don't listen to yours get knocked," said Zarathustra.

"Goodbye," I said, and left.

"He was grumpy," explained Edith that night.

We'd been booked for the usual three weeks with an option for two more if Lilian Baylis chose. She chose. We'd be at the Vic five weeks, *As You Like It* to follow.

From the day of *The Country Wife* notices, no one could get seats for the Vic. There was talk of a move to the West End.

"Don't let's," said Tyrone Guthrie. "It has now built up a reputation *nothing* can live up to. If we move, Edith and Michael couldn't come; they're in the Vic season. We had better put it away, dear. Even if Gilbert lets you postpone the New York opening, we had better not risk it."

"I wish you were going to do it in New York."

"Gilbert hasn't asked me."

"Would you?"

"Yes, I would."

It was too late. I hadn't followed my instincts. In that final fitting in my bedroom at Claridge's, Oliver, watching Mrs. Abbey and her assistant make some adjustment, answered the phone. "It's New York."

It was Helen. "How's it going?"

"Fine, I think."

"Look, I told Gilbert you'd let him direct it in New York. He's got his heart set on it."

"I think we could have Tyrone Guthrie."

"Please have Gilbert. I told him you would."

That's the day I wasn't a star.

"A star's not someone has his name in lights, not someone who dresses in room one and gets the most money." Guthrie McClintic had said that in Stamford, Connecticut, after *Saturday's Children* opened. "A star's the captain of the ship. A star thinks of the troupe. A star stands up for the small-part people who can't go against the manager. A star sets an example. You have to come to Dick Barbee's party or the company'll think you're depressed and that *you* know something they don't know." That day at Claridge's I wasn't a star; I let the New York company down.

"Never say yes when you mean no," was Moss Hart's legacy to Garson and me.

# Chapter

———————— ··◦∞◦·· ————————

# 16

Think it over and learn not to.

Did I learn not to from that wrong decision, that New York to London phone call? Something I said yes to and meant yes was *Harold and Maude.* Ever have a stretch when everything goes right? When you can't make a mistake? That was me, except for the Los Angeles earthquake and Vincent Canby's *New York Times* review. It began when Garson and Carl Klavik and I flew to San Francisco to help me be Maude. What a start to the new year! A movie I loved, my husband I love moves his work to Nob Hill to live at the Huntington Hotel, where everyone makes life easier, and with us Carl Klavik, who knows how to do everything.

"The sun don't always shine on the same little doggy's ass," says Zarathustra. I don't know if that was his own experience, or knowledge gleaned from a friend, but the sun shone on mine the January day Garson and I said goodbye to Suzanne and Mr. Lorans and Ellen Johnson at our rented house on Tower Road, and the Carey limo, piled with luggage that hadn't been ready when Paramount Pictures' truck picked up the rest of the things, took off for International Airport, where we are faithful customers.

Los Angeles to San Francisco you can take the shuttle, but we take TWA. They pass out coffee and a sugar bun or a drink and salted peanuts, depending what hour.

"Flight attendants, prepare for departure."

Garson and I sit first row left or first row right. Not out of superstition, but because there's no one in front of us. As a rule, we work.

For years I didn't fly, then had to.

"Take four Equanils," advised Paul Schmidt, fine hairdresser, "followed by a glass of red wine."

I didn't need to write it down. The minute Paul said it, I knew it was right.

"Take a zonker of red wine so you won't scream, 'Let me out!' " I told myself. "Start the wine before they slam the door shut."

Now I take a Coke or coffee or nothing and enjoy the lanes with blue lights and red lights and wonder how the pilot knows which turn he's going to make.

Once it was a pipe dream to drink coffee five thousand feet in the air, eat a sugar bun in the clouds and look down at the beach where Jennifer and Norton Simon keep Cézanne's bright tulips painting, look down at Malibu, where Jascha Heifetz jogs on the wet sand; Trancas dunes, where Billy Wilder flies his kite; but now it's no dream.

"You carry this; I've got *this.*"

"I'll take it."

"You can't; you've got your pocketbook and the Vuitton. Is your wine in?"

"Yes, but you've got the seat."

"I can handle it."

"You've got too much."

"Just do as I tell you. If I need him, Carl can help."

Do *you* carry a lot of stuff? I carry my big dark red Hermès handbag that cost two hundred and fifty dollars at Hermès, Faubourg St. Honoré, in 1961 and has never stopped sailing or flying or automobiling and looks like a million. Of course, you could *save* a million if you stayed out of Hermès, but then you don't have a big dark red Hermès bag that looks like a million and carries the passport, two books of traveler's checks, tickets, money, change, keys, lipstick, looking glass that hasn't got broken since the Maures Mountains, comb, powder puff, good luck pieces, loose checks, Meggezones for if you cough, handkerchiefs for if

384

you blow your nose, ammonia sniffers for if you faint when they get the plane too hot. The trip I fainted I didn't say anything and tried moving to the rear, where I thought it was cooler, but I still felt funny. I came back to our front row. "I'm going to faint," I said to Garson, and sat down beside him.

"Describe how you feel."

"Like I'm going to faint," then everything went. Next thing I saw was Garson's scared face. He was standing in front of me; the stewardess held an oxygen mask over my face.

"Are you all right, darling?"

"Yes. I am, I really am." And I really was.

"The captain is going to bring the ship down at Kansas City. Are you *sure* you're all right?"

"Oh, my God, of *course!*"

The captain came and took a look. He looked like George Abbott. "You don't think I ought to bring the plane down?" How do you like that! He asks *me* what to do with a 747!

"I know she's all right," urged Garson.

"It was too hot," I said.

He picked up altitude, I drank Coca-Cola, ate some Hershey almond bars and after that I carried *two* boxes of ammonia sniffers in my Hermès and of course my American Express credit card, my Air Travel that lets me go round the world, all my airline club cards for American Airlines, TWA's Ambassador Club card, Red Carpet card for United. For twenty-five dollars a year, they buy a lot of comfort. Ring the bell at the door marked with the club symbol, it opens, sign the register, help yourself to salted peanuts, coffee, sourballs, cheese, crackers, put your hand luggage below where you hang your coat under the eye of attendants, sit up at the bar, buy a drink, go to the bathroom, phone, look at today's paper, take a few packs of matches, get the pretty girl to have your ticket validated so at the gate you breeze through. Is *that* worth twenty-five dollars? For one year?

To shoot *Harold and Maude* in San Francisco, do I need my Carte Blanche, Diners, Actors Equity, Screen Actors Guild, Academy of Motion Picture Arts and Sciences with the gold Oscar, Hertz, Shell Oil, Blue Cross? Who knows?

Why carry my voter's registration card? Maybe so I'll know where it is. In *Harold and Maude,* when Harold gives Maude the disk he printed "I love you" on, she says, "It's the loveliest thing happened to me in years," then tosses it in the bay.

"Why did you do that?" asks Harold.

"Because now I'll always know where it is."

And if I put anything in my Hermès bag, I always know where *it* is.

Plus my Hermès, I carry a Vuitton satchel with a pint or a quart of white wine in it. That was *Harold and Maude* time. Now I've switched to Jack Daniel's, but don't need to bring it. That flows everywhere.

Luggage keys I keep in a plastic bag Saks Fifth Avenue used to sell better nylons in. For my passport, I have a red crocodile case with room for my out-of-date Great Britain Labour Permit I hang on to, a nice reminder of all those times I had to check into the police station to renew my work permit.

If you had a London dresser, maybe carry along a letter from her? A thread or two of the past never hurts, so carry along a letter from Dodie Higgins, who enclosed her gold charm I wouldn't like to fly without. A letter from Heidi is good luck for me. She played my granddaughter in *A Very Rich Woman.* It was her first time on Broadway and she used Murray for her stage name and dropped the Vanderbilt. Everybody said, "How can you trust the end of the play to a beginner?" Didn't Maude Adams trust the pillow dance to me? I trusted Heidi Vanderbilt, who chose her middle name of Murray, like I chose my middle name of Gordon. Maybe people who do that are trustworthy. Carry a letter from her—she's now my daughter-in-law—two Hershey almond bars, a bar of Lindt's, a bar of Peter's so the plane doesn't have to come down in Kansas City, also a Boston Ritz Hotel envelope with three Band-Aids.

All that in my Vuitton satchel plus pocket Kleenex, extra lipstick, extra eyeglasses, sunglasses, packet of salted peanuts, packet of cheese, crackers. If you're going, go in comfort, and give a porter something to carry so he can put his kids through Dartmouth or Bryn Mawr or the Sorbonne or Oxford or Girton.

Red Hermès, Vuitton, big white canvas satchel with red "G.K." to carry my folding seat. It has a hard back, hard seat and cost three sixty-five in an auto supply place and is irreplaceable for comfort in a plane, car or where there's squashy upholstery, if you have a slipped disk. Anyone that's got one knows what I'm talking about. *How* could such a thing happen to me? So lucky, then wind up with a slipped disk!

My fourth carry-on is a Vuitton shopping bag with a legal-size pad of green ruled paper. Pentel Rolling Markers, an envelope with whatever I'm writing. I wouldn't like to get off with all that at Wollaston even if they still had a railroad station, but with a movie company you get a lot of help. Waiting at San Francisco Airport was the unit manager, who *said* he was; next came the teamster, who said what could he do?; the assistant director, who said director Hal Ashby and producer Chuck Mulvehill were scouting a location, but would come to the hotel at four Sunday afternoon with Bill Theiss, in charge of costumes.

A skycap piled luggage in teamster's truck and Carl and Garson and I got in the fine LTD that Paramount had provided for me.

"I'll telephone you Monday's call," said the assistant director. "Opening shot is Redwood City; you're in it. I'll call the hotel with the scene numbers and our spot." Every business has its shorthand.

The LTD took off. How does Carl know his way through the crazy turns out of any and every airport? Faced with something to do, he knows how. Does he have my theory of whether you know or don't, *act* as if you do?

"Going the other direction is where we go to Redwood City," he said.

Garson took charge. "Let's do a trial run this afternoon and time it for Monday so no nervous prostration."

Carl nodded. "They're giving us a Winnebago; it'll be at the hotel." Travel with a movie company!

Anybody wants to give you a Winnebago, let them, the hell with candy and flowers! Mama was on the wrong track—worry if people respect you *later;* say yes to a Winnebago. It's man's gift to man, a camper with its own steering power, inside between picture windows a couch to take a nap on; opposite, a stove, a fridge, table with two seats on either side; another couch across the back to take another nap or in case you meet a friend; a closet, a bathroom with shower, toilet and basin, electric light, air cooled or heated—go from Redwood City, California, to Christmas Cove, Maine, and never pick up a hotel bill.

"Paramount figures you'll travel back and forth in it to location and use it for your dressing room," said Carl. "The teamster says they've laid out some rugged trips."

Carl made a left up some street past a pale blue hotel that looked new and is named Jack Tar. Up the hill some more. In San Francisco, either you're going up or down. Turn right at California Street, lined with three-story wooden houses, then a bar or a store, and sweep gradually up to the grand church on one corner of Nob Hill and the grand auditorium on another corner. Cross a street that offers a precipice on the right and on that corner is the traveler's treasure, Mrs. Dorothy Fritz Cope's Huntington Hotel!

Probably for *Harold and Maude* we'd have gone to the St. Francis or the Fairmont, but thirteen weeks on a movie you need a kitchen. Movie hours don't jibe with room service or with anything but movie hours. Breakfast six days a week at 5 A.M. From San Francisco we allowed an hour to drive to location.

"Made up and dressed eight o'clock," was the call.

Location? One day Redwood City, one day Oyster Point, Half Moon Bay, Oakland, Palo Alto, Soldiers Cemetery in Daly City, the daisy fields past South San Francisco, Cabot, Cabot and Forbes' Business Park. We were there.

At the Huntington if we didn't want to order up the perfect food from the restaurant, we could have it cooked on our four-burner electric stove. The kitchen had a full-size fridge, dishes, pots, pans or whatever needed, supplied by helpful housekeeper. Table linen for the dining table was in buffet drawer in the big dining alcove.

The sitting room, newly decorated, had beautiful dark chintz, dark furniture, white walls; the big picture window looked past rooftops descending down the steep hill to the bridges, to the Pacific, to Route 1 with signs saying Daly City and South San Francisco and on to Redwood City. At night and breakfast time, auto lights formed a moving necklace. Two beautiful bathrooms, a wide hall, two beautiful bedrooms, closets to gladden the heart.

The phone rang, Carl answered. "Hold on." He turned to us. "The Winnebago's in the garage, gassed up. Think you'd want to ride out to Redwood City?"

"We better," said Garson. "Straighten ourselves out later."

"I'll pick it up shortly," Carl told whoever had called.

He brought the Winnebago around. Cable cars clanged past. They make a bright San Francisco sound. Even on a foggy day, it sounds bright. Also lively, people are squashed on the platform, on the running board, sometimes someone on the running board has his dog on a long leash. As the cable car toils up California Street, doggy lopes along beside it.

Carl drove, Garson and I sat on the couch.

"To get to Redwood City, we go back past the airport," called Carl.

When Colin Higgins wrote "Page 1, Scene 1" on a film script, what an upheaval he would cause. People left home for San Francisco, rented Winnebagos, trucks, station wagons, cinemobiles, a stretchout, a four-doored LTD, and director Hal Ashby bought a Ferrari. Colin's script said Los Angeles, but Hal Ashby thought everybody'd seen a lot of pictures of Los Angeles.

Colin had meant to direct it and Paramount let him shoot test scenes.

388

They were shot in L.A. Paramount asked Colin if he thought he did well. He didn't think so.

"Want another chance?" asked Paramount.

"Yes."

"Try again."

He did and said he didn't get it right again. Paramount sent the script to Hal, who said yes.

He said a lot of other things. He said maybe Massachusetts, maybe some other place, then hit on San Francisco. He said Maude should live in an old Pullman car instead of the apartment the script said, that Harold should drive a hearse of his own instead of souped-up cars, that he didn't know if he wanted *me*, he'd look around.

Talk about surprises! Talk about the floor coming up and hitting you. I'd thought I was *in!* In New York at Grenouille, when Garson and I were having dinner with the Merricks, at the next table sat Bob Evans and Ali MacGraw. "I've got a sensational script for you, Ruth."

"Good part for you?" I asked Ali. If she were the lead, the script would get done.

"No part for Ali at all. *You*'re the star!"

Didn't I *know* it would happen?

"Where can I send the script?"

"Tomorrow we fly to London; back in a month."

"I'll send it a month from today. Who're you with?"

"Dick Shepherd, CMA."

"Have a good trip."

Why wouldn't I? Bob Evans was vice president of Paramount, Paramount made *Rosemary's Baby.* He'd send a sensational script in a month!

"You're back?" Dick Shepherd's voice.

"Had a great time."

"Great. There's a script here for you. Don't know what it is."

"Is it from Bob Evans?"

"Arlene, who sent the script for Ruth Gordon?"

"Robert Evans."

"From Bob."

"He says it's sensational and I play the star part."

"*You* want to read it or you want me to?"

"Oh, send it *over.*"

"Arlene, send this special messenger."

Bob was right, it was sensational and so was the part. "Read it," I said

389

to Garson. "Nobody could play it but me! It's a *terrific* part, she's fantastic, big acting scenes, deep and moving, then funny, and I sing a song and dance. Talk about vitality, it leaps off the page, and she's *eighty!* Who could play it but me?"

"Nobody. Who wrote it?"

"Oh, I don't know."

Garson opened the script. "Why, it's Colin Higgins!"

"Who's he?"

"He was in *Idiot's Delight.*"

Garson had directed Robert E. Sherwood's play at the Ahmanson Theatre in Los Angeles with Jack Lemmon and Rosemary Harris. "What part did Colin Higgins play?"

"Oh, a lot of parts, and was an assistant stage manager."

"Any good?"

"Very. Johnny Rubinstein sent him. I asked Johnny if he knew any clever kids. He said, 'You bet,' and sent Colin Higgins and Flora Plumb. Colin never told me he was writing. I knew he was in Johnny's class at U.C.L.A. You say this is good?"

"Not good—*great!*"

He read it, agreed.

I phoned Bob.

He was pleased, but not surprised. "It's scheduled for the first of the year. We're looking for a director."

They found him and he didn't know if he wanted *me!*

"It's *got* to be you," said Garson. "Who else can do all that stuff and look eighty! What does *Bob* say?"

I called him.

"Leave it to me, Ruth; you'll have the part. You understand? I can't tell a director he's *got* to have someone; he has to look around. Leave it to me, let me represent you. Okay?"

Represented by Paramount's vice president, would you say I had a good chance? "Okay and thanks."

Time passed. "Garson and I are going to New York, Dick."

"How long?"

"Maybe two weeks. No word from Bob Evans?"

"I'll light a firecracker under him. Let you know. Okay?"

"Okay."

Our New York apartment phone rang. "Hello, this is Jane Oliver at CMA. Hal Ashby's in town and would like to see you."

He'd chosen me!

"He's at the Drake Hotel. Is this afternoon a possibility?"

"Sure. I'll meet you in the Drake lobby." As a rule, I like to go alone, but she sounded nice and didn't they say Hal Ashby was an oddball?

Colin had said, "Hal's wild. Long wavy beard, long wavy light hair, thin as a ghost, tall, freaky clothes."

"Freaky like what?"

"Oh, you know."

Colin was for me playing Maude. For Harold he wanted Johnny Rubinstein, wrote it for him. Johnny thought he was set, but Hal had said he didn't know if he wanted him *either.* Johnny had gone to see Hal and played some music he'd composed for *Harold and Maude.*

"He's nice, but I don't know if he's the director Colin needs. He kept referring to Maude as 'the old bag' and I *know* that's not how Colin thinks of Maude. 'Maybe it would be wild if she had a front tooth out,' Hal said."

I was right about Jane Oliver; she was nice. We went up. Hal was seeing us in a suite. Was this a sitting room or an anteroom?

"He's on long-distance," somebody apologized, "but will be right out."

Jane talked, I got restive, then Hal came out. *Very* nice, a soother. He was that way right through all those wet damp thirteen weeks. In and out of rainy cemeteries, lost in the fog looking for Half Moon Bay, sitting around on wet daisy plants, making motorcycle shots at Dumbarton Bridge, when the stunt boy went over the rail, motorcycle and all, and the ambulance took him to Peninsula Hospital, where later we shot Maude's last scene, and all through everything he was soothing. Only the morning Wes gave the wrong directions and cars, campers, commissary, Cinemobile with the equipment kept passing each other and asking the gas station for directions, Hal got mad and swore a lot. Everybody swore. A tough day ahead and we were all loused up.

At the Drake, he soothed and looked like Colin and Johnny said he did. He and another man sat facing me and Jane. He talked, I talked, we talked nicely on and on and pretty soon I thought we ought to say something. "Well, do you want me?" I asked.

Hal lost his cool.

"Well, of course I want you. *Everybody* wants Ruth Gordon."

"Thanks."

"But I'm flying to Europe tonight to see some actresses there before I finally decide."

Well, the hell with *him!* Out in front of the Drake, Jane kept protesting, "I'm stupefied. Of *course,* I thought he wanted to see you to say yes. Miss Gordon, you *must* believe me, I would *never* have submitted you to the indignity of being up for *approval!"* She and I were new to each other; she wanted to make her position clear.

"I wouldn't do it now if they *ask* me," I swore to Garson. Actors can really be sensitive.

"Who's he going to see over *there?"* asked Garson.

Word drifted back he'd talked to Edith Evans, Gladys Cooper, Peggy Ashcroft, Edwige Feuillere, Elisabeth Bergner. In New York they said Hal had talked to Mildred Natwick, Mildred Dunnock, Dorothy Stickney, everybody.

"Bob?"

"You'll get it. I'm running things."

The phone rang, it was Hal. "May I come to see you, dear?"

"Please do." Do *you* stick to threats? You can't in show business. "We're on Tower Road, 1144." Maybe that's not the number. I didn't like that house; it was a stopgap.

I opened the door. Hal looked the same as at the Drake. "Come in."

We sat down on the two chairs that belonged to *us,* not the house chairs. I bought them at W. and something Sloane and one has springs that come at you like a rectal thermometer. I gave that one to Hal. I guess I'm only human.

"Isn't that Edith Evans?" Hal pointed to Angus McBean's picture of Edith and me in *The Country Wife.*

"Yes. It's when I made my London debut at the Old Vic."

"She was one I interviewed. She's charming."

"But not right for Maude."

"No, I saw that. She saw it too. She laughed at the description of Maude in the script and said, 'That doesn't sound like me, ducky. Why don't you get Ruth Gordon?' "

There's a sensible friend!

"Well, thank you for seeing me. I think I've got what I need."

Would you believe it? That was *it!* He left. Well, the hell with him in *spades!*

"He's crazy!" said Garson. "He's *got* to be crazy. How can he interview you twice and not hire you?"

"He's crazy—I don't want anything to do with him," I told Dick Shepherd. "How could I work with anyone like that? Talk about disorganized!"

"What happened?" asked Dick.

"Very nice, then left."

"Bob tells me you've got it."

"Hal Ashby doesn't think so."

"Let me find out what the hell's going on."

A week passed. "Well, congratulations," said Dick.

"On what?"

*"Harold and Maude.* You're in."

"I'll call up Hal and say thank you."

"Got his number?"

"No."

"Arlene, get Hal Ashby's number for Ruth."

"Hal, I'm thrilled."

"Oh, yes?"

"I'm glad you chose me."

"Oh, is it all settled? I hadn't heard."

"Bob Evans told Dick Shepherd. They sent the contracts."

"Oh, I'm pleased, dear. You'll be great."

"Thank you."

"Thank *you* for being patient."

Did Colin think all that was going to happen when he wrote Maude? If it's for you, it's for you, and there's nothing anybody can do about it.

The Winnebago bowled past the airport. I wasn't used to its swing. "I don't like it."

"Ask them to let you drive back and forth in the LTD, Carl," said Garson.

"Good idea, and keep this one on location for Miss G."

We swung past the San Mateo Motel.

"That's where most of them are. Hal Ashby and Chuck Mulvehill took a house in Hillsborough; the rest are here."

"Bud Cort?"

"Yes."

Bud Cort was Harold. How many *Harolds* did Hal consider?

"They want you to test with six Harolds," Dick had phoned. "Of course, *you're* signed; it's no test for *you.* The contract won't be ready, but Paramount gives us a covering letter: you're in and consent to test with six boys, two scenes with each. Actually, the way I see it, it's *good* for you because they can match someone up to you if they see you play a scene."

All the tests were shot at Hal Ashby's house. Carl drove me up and thanks to Bob Balaban, we drove *down* another way. Bob Balaban was the first to test.

Hal's house, on the Appian Way, had a view to Catalina. The days I was there it looked into sunlit haze and down on L.A. smog, but if it hadn't been haze and smog there was Catalina.

The house, not old, not new, was built like a house someone admired in his youth. Trim dining room the size of one on a sizable yacht, the kitchen just a kitchen, but the *big* room! Down two steps, drapes, lamps, furniture like the old Capitol Theatre lounge. The stuff came with the house and had nothing to do with Hal or what was going on there: cameras, sound, lighting equipment, all sorts of movie rigs with everybody working at something, helpers rushing in, rushing out, air filled with cigarette smoke.

"Your room's all ready," a helper said. I followed him upstairs. Wasn't that what Mama warned me never to do? She said it could lead to the white slave trade; in show business it leads to upstairs. "Hal said you'd be comfortable here."

Is anybody comfortable making a test? Even with a covering letter? For semantics, write off show business.

Carl brought my clothes up and the bag with makeup to refresh the makeup I'd put on at home.

The helper pointed right. "The bathroom's next door. Okay?"

"Okay."

"It'll be a while; they're lighting. Hal's doing something, but he'll be up to see you."

"Anything?" asked Carl. "I put the lunch hamper back here, the Mountain Valley's in the canvas bag with a glass, two Cokes."

"You'll stick by, won't you?"

"I will. I'll be downstairs somewhere within call."

Getting dressed had a settling effect. I feel steadier when I get my costume on. I'd brought the one I wore in *The Loves of Cass McGuire.* For that show I had two sets of costumes. One set I hated and one that I loved. Today's was the beauty that Freddy Wittop designed because of Garson. No wonder our marriage is in its thirty-fourth year! If it hadn't been for him there would have been only the horrible costumes that were all wrong for Cass, all wrong for me.

Darling Bob Balaban didn't get the job. Did he look too good-natured,

394

too young? One out, five to go. Then two out, four to go.

Number three, not right at all.

That was all for the first day. Hope, fear, good luck, bad luck, nerves, prayers, thoughts of unpaid board bills, had circled the glare of Hal's big room. Blue haze of cigarette smoke still hovering around the camera, lights turned off but smoking, the campy Capitol Theatre lounge chairs, drapes, lamps, and somewhere three guys struck down with discouragement. "Let you know," said assistant, but we always know ahead.

Hal had soothed each one, *genuinely* wanted each to succeed. He came up to his guest room with me. "Are you worn out?"

"Oh, no."

"Tomorrow we've got John Rubinstein. Colin wants him and I hear he can really act."

"Oh, he can, I've seen him. He won the Natalie Wood Acting Award prize at U.C.L.A."

"And it looks like we'll hear Bud Cort."

"I hear he's good in Robert Altman's new one."

"I hear that too, dear, and we've got one other. Oh, I'm *sure* this time tomorrow we'll have a great Harold."

Be hopeful. You owe it to the race.

Next morning I got into my Freddy Wittop costume and went out again to the hall to see what was going on. "Hi, Ruth. I'm Bud Cort."

We kissed. It was Harold.

"They gave me the script late last night. It's dynamite."

"It's terrific!"

"I've *got* to get it."

"You will."

A head appeared up the stairs. "All ready, Ruth."

"Okay, Ruth, I'll see you." He was Harold.

Number four and I walked the Appian Way, camera on the tow truck rolling ahead, cop holding up cars. "Action," said Hal. Then, in Hal's big room, the fourth told me about his life. He wasn't Harold. Four down, two to go.

Number five. Bud and I walked the Appian Way, the scene came to life. We weren't actors remembering lines; Harold was *really* telling Maude.

"Good," said Hal. But he'd said that after the other tests. You have to, if you're human. All the misgiving that trails through a test, a director *has* to come up with a "Good." Only *this* time Hal meant it!

"Thanks, Hal." Bud didn't sound as though *he* had any misgiving. He sounded like a rich, well-bred, good-looking guy.

Up in the hall, he'd said, "I've *got* to get it." His "Thanks, Hal" sounded like he *had*.

"Action," said Hal.

We were in the campy big room, playing the scene where Harold explains his troubles, his hopes, how he tried to get his mother's attention. A deep scene, hard to do. It's hard to explain trouble. It's hard to explain anything and stay interesting.

"Breathe in," says Maude, "it's organic," and offers Harold a pipe of hash.

He breathes, lets go, the story pours out.

The four other boys knew the scene without a prompt; Bud blew. "Hang in with me, Hal," he told the director.

"Take your time," soothed Hal.

"Sorry, Ruth." Bud knew I didn't give a damn. He was Harold and if he didn't remember at Hal's, he would in Redwood City and Daly City, in Half Moon Bay, at Dumbarton Bridge and everywhere else on the Bay Peninsula. We started again. Everybody knew he was Harold.

"Sit in, will you, Hal, and I'll let y' know when I need you."

"Oh, sure," soothed Hal, and sat cross-legged just out of camera range.

Haskell Wexler, great cameraman, had set up a tight two-shot. We started, then Bud blew. "Hal?"

Hal softly said Bud's line.

Bud said it as though he'd just thought it.

The scene was over.

"You really did it," I said.

"You helped me, Ruth."

"Wouldn't you have helped me?"

"Right on! Well, I certainly hope I see you."

"You will." We kissed.

As I came upstairs, there was Johnny Rubinstein. "May I come in and talk?"

"Better not. Before a scene I like to cut off. Save our energy for the scene."

"Okay." Thin, tense, determined, hair Afro style, Johnny wore a sort of dark brown jump suit. Like Bud, like Harold, he looked rich, well-bred, good-looking, young but not boyish. Colin had written the part for him. Could he suggest "disorganized"? Doesn't Johnny have life under control, know *exactly* what he's going to do? He'd had the script longer than the others. He knew it, *really* knew it, and had planned it out minute for minute. It was like a scene with Nureyev and a partner. When Johnny stopped, I came on with my line: "As Confucius says, 'Don't simply *be* good. Make good things happen.'"

"Did Confucius say that?" asks Johnny.

"They say he was very wise, so I'm sure he must have."

The long scene continued. Johnny took off into all his trouble, hope, trying to reach his mother, his despair.

"Yes, I understand," I told him. "A lot of people enjoy being dead. But they're not dead, really. They're just backing away from life. They're players, but they think life is a practice game and they'll save themselves for later. So they sit on the bench. Reach out! Take a chance! Get hurt, maybe. But play as well as you can. Give me an L, give me an I, give me a V, give me an E, L-I-V-E, LIVE! Otherwise, you'll have nothing to talk about in the locker room."

"I like you, Maude."

"I like you, Harold. Come, I'll teach you to waltz." I hummed *The Merry Widow* waltz and we danced.

"Good," said Hal. "Just what I wanted."

"Thanks."

"I see what Colin means. That was—that was tremendous."

"Well, thanks."

"It really was," added Hal. "Ruth, I want to try some effects, I'd like to see what it looks like with no makeup."

"Fine."

"Somebody bring Ruth something to take her makeup off."

My face shone.

"That's fine, dear."

"Want to see my hair a different way?"

"All right. I *like* those braids round your head."

Coronet braids was the way my sister wore hers. This time I rolled the braids into a rosette over each ear. Cléo de Mérode had started it. They said it was because she didn't have ears, but the King of the Belgians said she did. Why wouldn't she? I read her book and *she* said she did. In Paris, I sent her flowers from La Chaume on the Rue Royale where Ziegfeld chose flowers for Anna Held. Cléo de Mérode telephoned. Is that hard to believe? But she *did!* 14 Elmwood Avenue, Wollaston, Mass., to the Rue Teheran, Paris VIII*ieme. Nothing* is impossble! She wrote her life story, I bought it, loved it, looked her up in the Paris *Bottin,* sent her flowers and she telephoned me at the Hôtel Raphaël. Two girls who made it.

Hal liked coronet braids better than rosettes. "Try one more, hair hanging down. Harvey, come in close."

The camera was wheeled up for what George Cukor calls "a great big gorgeous head."

It's the one where a face fills the big screen at Radio City Music Hall

"I want a really *hot* light," said Hal to the man up the ladder.

A whole powerhouse was turned on me. Like Blanche when that horrible Kowalski stuck the bulb in her face, only *this* was more like maybe five thousand bulbs, and no makeup, hair flying! Would that appeal to you smoking in the loge at the Music Hall, Avenue of the Americas?

"Can you make it any hotter?" soothed Hal.

"Hotter?" asked up-the-ladder. Nothing astonishes the crew.

"Or is it as hot as it'll go?"

"No. I can go higher." A crew can do anything. Hal knew that, but it's only polite to ask.

Hal said, "The no makeup and hot lights were really too much; it would be unpalatable." I guess *so!* My face would have to come out like our Congregational Sunday school sand map where Mrs. Chase pointed out Capernaum and the Dead Sea. "I'd like to come up and talk to you if you're not tired out, dear."

"No, come up."

"You're going to be fine, dear, I'm very pleased. Today was useful to bring out what's needed. Just think of Maude in terms of vitality and life and humor; don't let it drag. There were spots you let down and that's not Maude. *Harold* is the one that's down; *you* must keep it moving."

"Yes, I see that."

"I'm sure. I haven't a worry."

Me neither. Maude I *knew* how to play. "Have you made up your mind who'll play Harold?"

"No, I really haven't. Bud Cort was terrific and John Rubinstein is—what an actor! Astonishing! He did things—oh, just fine! How did you feel playing the scenes with them?"

"Good."

"How old is John Rubinstein?"

"I don't know, but young."

"We're lucky to have such a choice."

I knew it wasn't a choice. Bud Cort was Harold and Hal knew it too. "Garson and I are going to New York tomorrow, if that's all right."

"Oh, sure. Have a nice trip, dear, and thank you so much for going through all this. It of course makes my job much easier. I learned a lot today."

Downstairs everyone was puff-puffing; Hal's big room was blue. When Colin Higgins wrote "Fade in" on a pad of paper, did he think all that was going to happen before the plane touched down in San Francisco? While he was writing Harold for Johnny, could he know Johnny would play Pippin for two years in the New York musical *Pippin* because Bud Cort was going to play Harold in *Harold and Maude?*

"Certainty is not certitude," reminded Justice Frankfurter. Colin was certain Johnny would play it, I was certain I would, and all the thirteen weeks we shot the film everybody was certain *Harold and Maude* was wonderful. When did certitude surface? Was it *The New York Times* giving us a bad review? I don't believe it. I wrote a letter.

> *244 Ladera Drive*
> *Beverly Hills*
> *California 90210*
> *22 December 1971*

Dear Mr. Canby,

What a disappointment to read your review. I know people aren't supposed to write a critic and the last time I did was fifty-six years ago today. I got a good review in the December 22, 1915, *Times* and wrote the critic. It was my first time on the stage and I didn't know you shouldn't. Today I know, but I'm doing it. I wish you'd liked *Harold and Maude.* They said you saw it in a screening room with a dozen other critics. I *wish* you could have seen it with an audience. Maybe you wouldn't have liked it then, but *then* I'd feel you saw it the way it was meant to be seen. Shoulder to shoulder with people is how a play or film is written to be seen and I wish you'd seen it that way. Maybe you think this is about as important as what Lillian Lorraine said was wrong with her life when the lady reporter came to interview her. Lillian Lorraine was old and broke and living up Broadway at 96th. Some paper sent the lady interviewer up to do a piece. "What do you think happened, Miss Lorraine? Ziegfeld said you were the greatest beauty he ever had in the Follies. What went wrong?"

"He was *right.* And he was crazy about me. He had me in a tower suite at the Hotel Ansonia and he and his wife lived in the tower suite above. And I cheated on him, like he cheated on Billie Burke. I had a whirl! I blew a lot of everybody's money, I got loaded, I was on the stuff, I got the syphilis, I tore around, stopped at nothing, if I wanted to do it I did it and didn't give a damn. I got knocked up, I had abortions, I broke up homes, I gave fellers the clap. So that's what happened."

"Well, Miss Lorraine," gasped the lady reporter, "if you had it to do over would you do anything different?"

"Yes," said Lillian Lorraine. "I never shoulda cut my hair."

Well, seeing *Harold and Maude* in a projection room may strike you as no more relevant than she shouldn't have cut her hair. Forgive the letter. Maybe it's all right to do if you only do it every fifty-six years.

Ruth Gordon

Up on the Appian Way, Colin didn't know Johnny wouldn't get the job and that Saturday afternoon as the Winnebago rocked Garson and Carl and me into Redwood City, I didn't know I was going to write that letter.

"For Monday," said Carl, "the location they gave me is Maude driving Harold in a car around city hall."

"Ready and dressed and made up at Redwood City," read the call-sheet. "Location: Square where the Court House is." The call-sheet is a long typewritten sheet handed out to crew, cast, director, producer, camera, sound, wardrobe, hair, makeup. It shows who works the following day and what scenes to prepare. If your name isn't on, you have the day off. If your name has "On call" after it, you don't need to show up, but must leave word where you are and keep phoning in in case of a message.

"Don't need you till noon; you can sleep late," said the friendly assistant director, and gave me the call-sheet. "Ruth Gordon—12 noon."

"No early call," I told Garson.

"Thanks." Cold and black five o'clock is no time to get up.

In Wollaston, Mama had had to, every morning except Sunday. Breakfast for Papa so he could make the six-fifteen train to Boston to open the Mellin's Food factory at seven.

"I suppose you get used to it," said Mrs. Wetmore, who lived in the other half of 14 Elmwood Avenue.

"No, never. It's easier in summer when it's light, but when the alarm goes off, I'm never used to it."

My call was twelve noon, but in a movie company things change. The phone rang. "You're in the opening shot. Dressed and made up at eight A.M. Okay, Ruth?"

"Okay, Bob."

400

Before *our* alarm went off, I heard Minna setting the table for our breakfast at five.

I made up at the hotel, did my coronet braids, got dressed in my own warm skirt and cashmere cardigan, a must for actresses. Comfortable, warm, quick to get out of in the Winnebago when Andrea brought in the day's costume.

At six-thirty Carl came to the suite. Minna opened the door. She'd got the hamper ready with food.

Each morning when we got there, the Winnebago was spotless, warm, aired out, and on location. "What shall I give Mongo, Carl?" The last day was in sight. Mongo was a man who had put aside several careers and settled in the Bay peninsula and kept my Winnebago great.

"Give him your book when it comes out."

"But that won't be till next month."

"He won't care. If you write in it is what he wants."

"But I can give him some money too."

"I wouldn't. What'll please Mongo is you writing in your book to him."

That was the last day. The first day began with a knock on the Winnebago door. "Hi, Ruth, it's Bud." He stood on the step. "I brought you this, Ruth." A tumbler of daisies.

We hugged and kissed.

"How do you feel?" I asked.

"Dynamite!"

"Me too. I love you."

"I love you."

He rushed off to his Winnebago for Bob Stein to make him up.

I put a record on my record player. Get in the rhythm on a chilly morning. The only chill in the Winnebago was first-day scare. I turned on my Noël Coward–Gertie Lawrence record.

"You were there," sang Noël.

It turned *me* on.

"I saw you and my heart stopped beating . . ." Glamour, dazzle, someone doing it the way *you*'d like to.

"You were there . . ."

A knock at the door. "Can I come in?" Hal.

I cut off the record player.

"Are you all right, dear? Oh, I *like* your black stockings." He had the eye! "I never would have thought of it, but they look just right. It's Maude. Really Maude."

Did *he* have first-day scare?

Everybody has.

"And don't you love my boots?" I asked. They were beat-up black suede to just above the ankle.

"I do."

From Switzerland via New York's Saks Fifth Avenue. I'd worn them all last winter every time I was in New York. Snow, slush, New York streets age shoes; they looked old enough for Maude to have brought from Vienna.

"All right, dear, we'll have a good day. Everything's working for us. I'll see you over there." Blond long hair, long blond beard, spiffy brown leather jacket, combat boots, he went over to the courthouse.

Assistant director looked in my door. "Rehearsal, Ruth. I'll walk you over. We're set up, front of the courthouse. I'm Bob. Bob Enrietto."

The call-sheet opening shot was the car, Maude driving Harold, Harold startled by the way Maude took curves. It was chilly. The shops around the square were still closed, a man was unlocking one. He'd done it so often he put the key in the lock without looking. His eyes were taking in my gray-green nubbly wool coat, black Swiss boots, black stockings, old pink silk India scarf I'd worn in *Whatever Happened to Aunt Alice?*, when Gerry Page drove the car with me in it to the edge of the lake, then jumped out and let the car plunge in and drown me.

"When the lake smooths out after the car goes down," I said to director Barney Gerard, "how would it be if the pink scarf were afloat?"

He liked it, but he got replaced on the film. In the final cut, that shot was out. That's all right; I'm not a director and don't want to be. I wanted a pink scarf afloat to be a continuation of my performance. Alice stood for good against evil and the glimpse of pink would show that good survives. What survived was the old pink silk scarf around my neck for the first day of *Harold and Maude.*

"When you're driving, have it up over your head," said Hal, "so it'll conceal some of your profile. Susy will wear it in the pickup shots. That'll be useful. Not too much face seen and we concentrate on the pink scarf."

Susy would do the wild driving, the tricky curves and sharp turns Maude loved. Stunt driving isn't one of my gifts.

Andrea joined us, carrying her work kit of pins, needles, scissors, thread, tape measure, thimble, buttons—the notion counter. Cathie

Blondell carried her bag of brushes, combs, mirrors, hairpins, bobby pins, spray—instant hairdresser shop that could help her accomplish whatever director, cameraman, actors could want done to hair. Bob Stein carried his makeup trunk of everything to put on or take off a face. Bob was distressed that I didn't want him to make me up, but lived with it, and in the last scene, Maude in love and beautiful for her eightieth birthday, Bob made me look beautiful. And John Alonzo did his part with lights and camera.

People working over my face starts my day wrong. Bob would have made me look better, but I think Maude forgot eye shadow and face contour and connected with the human race.

"Let us through, folks." Bob Enrietto's voice had authority. People stepped back on the feet in back of them. Everybody made way.

All Redwood City stood across the street from where the shot was being set up.

"Coming through, ladies."

Some waved, some smiled, some said, "Who's she?"

"Didn't you see *Rosemary's Baby?*"

"Oh, is that her?"

Motorcycle cops were ready to charge, cops on foot held up the traffic. Some cars they sent down another street, some just waited. The sound truck was in place. Bob and Sid, brothers, were testing sound. In front of the entrance to the courthouse stood Chuck Mulvehill's four-door Plymouth sedan. Hal chose that for Maude to drive; now Susy and Rod were sitting in for Bud and me. Rod looks like Bud, but who chose Susy? Nineteen, adorable round face, snub nose, long light brown straight hair, she looked exactly the way I'd like to have looked. If I *had* looked like that, would Harlan Tucker have gone for Annette de Willoughby?

John Alonzo had his light meter on Susy, lighting her where I was going to sit.

"The way you light us, even that *girl* will look like an orangutan," called Pauline Lord to Guthrie McClintic in her soft, discouraged voice that could reach the last row in the second gallery. He was lighting nineteen-year-old, flower-faced Sylvia Weld, who stood onstage where Pauline or I would stand in *Ethan Frome.*

If they light it right for Susy, will *I* look like an orangutan? Trust John Alonzo. Trust Hal's eye or don't take the job. In movies, in the final cut, you're in the director's hands, so believe in him. I believed in every director but two.

"We're about ready, dear," soothed Hal. "Susy, hop out and let Ruth in. John, want to look at Ruth?" Hal helped me in. Everybody helps you in a movie. "You see the mike, dear? It's adjusted to pick up your voice, but it won't be in your way." It was fastened to the top of the windshield. "Sid thinks it'll work. He's pretty sure you won't need a body mike, but if this doesn't, he's got it ready to put on you, no trouble at all."

John Alonzo's dark, handsome face looked in the car window. "How's my sweetheart?" he asked dispassionately, and held his light meter to my forehead. Chuck's Plymouth was fastened by a thick rope to the camera truck. The camera was mounted on the back facing Bud and me, camera operator working on it. The crew was coming, going, bringing wood blocks they call apples. They took stuff here, stuff away. In the middle of the street were canvas chairs marked HAL ASHBY, RUTH GORDON, BUD CORT. Who wanted to sit down?

Chuck Mulvehill came over. "How *are* you?" Good-looking, bright face, not unlike Jack Nicholson. "Are you comfortable?"

"You bet."

"Good. We want you to be." Comfort they know about in the movies.

"Thanks for the LTD to drive back and forth in."

"The Winnebago didn't work out for you?"

"Too much swaying."

"I'll have to square it with Paramount, but that's not *your* worry. I'm glad they allowed you Carl."

"Oh, I'd have to have him."

"But it's good Paramount picks up the expense check. You pay his salary anyway, but the overage from his daily I'm glad they take care of." Talk about comfort! In San Francisco, they don't give food and rooms away.

The other door of Chuck's car opened. It was Bud. Following behind him were Cathie and Bob Stein. Did you ever see anyone look perfect? That was Bud Cort ready for first day shooting, opening shot, Scene 70.

In shooting *Harold and Maude,* Hal followed the Gertrude Stein theory: chronology has nothing to do with anything. We shot where and when and what Hal said to. Hal is his own man. Do *you* care about sequence? Not me. We don't think in sequence, we rarely talk in sequence, we don't rehearse a play in sequence, so why shoot a script that way? When I get it I learn it. Maybe everybody does, maybe nobody does, maybe it's wrong, but if it is, don't tell me. I don't like to be told things. In the *beginning* I knew I could learn if anybody'd teach me, and they did. I can still learn, but not from *telling* me.

That afternoon at the Vic, Shaw said, "You're not funny, you're sensible." I learned from that. Sensible's good, unless you're *too* sensible.

"We must have order," said Alfred North Whitehead when Professor Frankfurter left Cambridge to go on the Supreme Court. "We must have order, Felix—but not too *much* order."

That was sensible.

"Isn't it hard not shooting in sequence?" ask people.

It is and so is shooting in sequence. Everything about making movies is hard. Every day before I start, I do my whole part. Sensible? When I get to Scene 70 I know where my part has gotten to and where it will continue. Sensible? In a play, does a director rehearse Act I each day and go straight through to the finale?

"Let's rehearse, shall we?" soothed Hal. Who'd know it was first day? Everybody so contained. "You want to run the lines?"

"I don't. Do you, Bud?"

"Not me."

"All right. I'll be up on the tow car, under the camera, and for rehearsal I'll use a megaphone." Helping hands helped him up on the tow truck. "Are you all right, Ruth?"

"You bet."

"I love you," whispered Bud.

"I love you," I whispered.

"Ruth, let me see your hands on the wheel," Hal called through the megaphone.

Driving out in the LTD, Carl had shown me where to put my hands. "I have my hands *low* on a wheel," he said. "Some have theirs high."

"That's how Garson drives."

"Yes."

I put my hands low on the wheel.

Hal conferred with John Alonzo. "Hands higher, Ruth."

I put my hands halfway up, not as high as Garson's.

"Fine, dear. You can change when we're riding, but for most of it keep your hands where they are now. Bud, can you hear me?"

"What, Hal?"

"Can you hear me?"

"Oh, yes."

"Slump down a little lower. I want Ruth to dominate. You're taller, so let me see you down lower. Ruth, sit up tall as you can."

Bud slumped, I sat up.

"That's fine. Are you comfortable?"

Who's comfortable before playing a scene?

"Sound, are you ready?" called Hal.

Now it was the sound man's turn. "Tell Bud and Ruth to say something."

"Hello, Ruth," said Bud. "How y' doing?"

"Right in there."

"Okay," called sound. Was it Bob or Sid?

"Ready. We're going to start. Ruth, you know how to start the motor?"

Carl had shown me.

"I turn the key, release the thing and push my foot down."

"Right. Of course, we're towing you, but do it real, dear. All right." He nodded to the assistant director.

Assistant director spoke to Redwood City. "Keep it quiet, folks." To the outfit. "Ready. This is a rehearsal. *Quiet,* please. Let's have a bell for rehearsal."

Sound man rang a bell.

"Wait for my signal, Bud. I'll hold up my scarf. Can you see it?"

"Sure thing."

Hal held up his scarf. Our car pulled off, made a crazy turn the way the script said, Bud straightened up, but also remembered to slump.

"Boy, Maude. The way you handle cars. I'd never handle *my* car like that."

"Oh, it's only a machine, Harold." In my script, I underlined "machine" with a pencil mark and after "Harold" I put a line that drops down, reminder for me to emphasize "machine" and drop the end of the sentence.

I went on. "It's not as if it were *alive.*" In the script, Colin Higgins underlined "alive." "Like a horse or a camel. We may live in a machine age, but I simply can't treat them as equals." The script says to look over at the radio. "Of course, the age has its advantages."

The script says for Maude to turn on the car radio. "Music plays softly," it says.

I reached over to the dashboard and turned a thing. No music; they dub that in later. The camera car pulled round a corner, we passed by the back of the courthouse.

The script says for Maude to listen to the music. "The universal language of Mankind," I say, and begin humming along with the tune. Nobody said what to hum and if they didn't tell me, I'd planned to hum what I'd been playing on my record player. Acting is planning, then

406

doing it as though you'd *never* had the idea.

" 'I never re-al-*ized*,' " I sang. Forget the hum. " 'That you cared for me.' " Noël Coward's song. " 'I never re-al-*ized* that such a *thing* could *be*.' What music do *you* like, Harold?"

"Well—" He gets thrown against the door as Maude makes a sudden U-turn.

"Cut!" shouted Hal through the megaphone. "Very *good*."

The camera car pulled us back to our starting position. Everybody up on the tow car began fixing things. "How's that for sound?" called Hal.

"I'm coming over." Was it Sid or was it Bob?

Hal jumped down from his seat under the camera. He motioned for me to roll the window down. "That's fine, dear. Bud, very good. You can't overdo the fear, Bud, the way she's driving."

"I didn't do enough?"

"Just right. And no *less*. Maybe it could be a *little* more. Every corner she goes round, *really* fall over and—well, what you did was right. Just don't let down."

John Alonzo put his light meter to my forehead. "Look where you look when you turn on the radio, sweetheart."

I did.

"How's that?" John called to the man that worked the camera. The cameraman plans it, then the operator shoots it.

"Good."

John turned to Hal. "Okay if I tell her about her hands?"

"Go ahead."

"Sweetheart, favor me. Keep your hands high on the wheel, so they're in the shot. Okay?"

"Sure."

Hal looked in the car window. "You feel all right to take one, Ruth? Bud?"

"Right." I like a *take*. I never feel it's *happening* till it's on camera.

"Okay for a take," soothed Hal.

Bob Stein set his makeup trunk on the sidewalk by Bud's side of the car and did some retouch and a freshen-up. Behind him stood Cathie with a comb. Behind Cathie stood Ernest with a clothes brush. Bob did his last stroke and flick of the puff. Cathie shaped Bud's long hair. Ernest gave an expert tug to the coat collar, straightened Bud's tie. No brush necessary—no specks.

"Are we ready?" asked Hal.

A nod from everybody or a yes.

Hal climbed up on the camera tow car. "Watch for my signal, Bud; I'll wave the scarf. This is a take, so I won't use the megaphone, of course. All right, let's try one."

First shot of *Harold and Maude,* that for the next five years would be shown in New York, Boston, Dayton, Paris, Minneapolis, Edgartown, you name it; people would come up to me and say they saw it two times, nine times, thirty times, and when last heard from, Doug Strand of St. Paul, "Two hundred and one."

John Alonzo stood beside the big camera on its perch, operator got behind it, sound reached his hand into Chuck's Plymouth and tilted the microphone down slightly. "Don't forget to roll your window *up,*" he whispered. "Makes a difference to the sound."

There's a lot to think of, making the first shot of a movie. It isn't easy and doesn't get easier when you don't know how to drive a car and are driving. Good that Maude was a crazy driver.

"Keep it quiet, folks," called assistant director. "This is a take. Hold the talk or we'll have to clear the square. This one's a *take*—let's have the bell."

The boy with the marker leaned in, held it up in front of camera. Operator photographed it.

HAROLD AND MAUDE
SCENE 70   TAKE 1
CAMERAMAN   ALONZO
DIRECTOR   ASHBY
JAN 3 1972

Boy clacked his clacker and got out of camera range.
"Roll," said Hal. That meant power the camera.
"Rolling." That meant camera was up to speed.
"Action," Hal called.
The tow car started, the rope to our car pulled.
"Watch me," called Hal. We could hear him fine without the megaphone.
The tow car and the Plymouth were picking up speed. Hal waved his scarf.
"Boy, Maude. The way you handle cars."
This might be the scene they print, this *might* be in all the theatres. The first take may be the best.
"Hold Take Two and Three, print Take One," Hal could tell the script girl. Lurching round the back of the courthouse might be the lurch

they'd see in New York, Quincy, Rio de Janeiro, Tokyo, Providence, Paris, Boothbay Harbor, everywhere.

"Cut."

We'd done it. 8:40 A.M. and one was in the can.

"We'll go again right away," soothed Hal. "Sound okay?"

"I picked up that plane, but not bad." Was that Bob? Or Sid?

"Great. Bud, Ruth, that was good. *Very* good. Let's go again while we're in the mood."

"Places, everybody," called assistant Bob. "And quiet, you people." He pointed to the Redwood folks, police holding them back of the curb. "I'll have to clear the square if there's any noise and we don't want to have to do that, so enjoy yourselves *quietly.*"

Hal was in place, head below the camera lens, legs and combat boots straight out in front; John Alonzo concentrated beside the camera, operator wiping off something.

"Rolling," called assistant Bob. Riveting word!

"Speed." Another riveter.

"All right," soothed Hal.

The tow car started, the rope straightened out, our car moved, Hal waved his scarf.

"Boy, Maude. The way you handle cars. I'd never handle my car like that."

Around the square, more lurch than in Take 1.

"Cut."

Back to starting spot.

"Once again," called Hal. "Right away."

"Sound reloading," called Sid. Or Bob.

A breather. Bob Stein rushed in, towel over his arm and powder puff in hand, lip and eye liners in his pocket. He handed Bud a mirror. Bud studied himself.

"Just a little on the under lip?" asked Bob Stein.

Bud moved his face closer. Bob's liver-colored pencil did something unnoticeable that on camera would do the trick.

Cathie gave the okay signal—every hair in place.

Ernest stood like a question mark.

Bud had no question.

I looked in the auto mirror. Okay.

"Ready," called Sid or Bob.

"Ready, folks," called assistant Bob.

"Don't lose that energy you had in the last take," soothed Hal.

"That's probably the *one,* but maybe we can do this take better. Colin, you want to get up here where you can see?"

Colin was up before Hal finished. A writer is glad to be included. He sat on a pile of rope, navy pea jacket buttoned up to his throat, long hair blowing; plenty of mustache made him look like an author and helped cover his pleasant face. A lot of people don't think you're an intellectual if your face is pleasant.

"I think we've got it," said Hal after the take. "Okay, sound?"

"Okay."

"All right for you, John?"

John nodded.

"You and Bud can relax, dear. I'm going to do the shots with the doubles. Susy'll come over to your camper, Ruth; she'll need your pink scarf and coat. You didn't need to put the scarf over your head for this shot because I won't come in close on the stunt car, but the scarf's established, you wearing it around your neck."

Frightening to look at Susy! She wore the mask they'd modeled that night Garson and I drove over to the Valley, the week before we'd left for San Francisco. Bob Stein had phoned would I come over to Burbank, he had it set up to take an impression of my face.

I didn't like the idea.

"You have to cooperate," said Garson. "At least *do* it. If it turns out wrong, then fuss, but *don't* say you won't go; that's not cooperating."

Carl had left; Garson drove me. Down Sunset to Hollywood, out Cahuenga Pass, where I'd driven for *Dr. Ehrlich* and *Edge of Darkness* and *Action in the North Atlantic*. In *Action in the North Atlantic,* Humphrey Bogart and I were in the same picture and I hadn't seen him since *Saturday's Children* in 1928, when I was the important one. In 1942, Humphrey was king. No more diffidence, no more insecurity, his dressing room was like the throne room, things went the way *he* said. When he was important, he didn't try to ingratiate any more than when he'd got hired for *Saturday's Children* on our road tour because Guthrie couldn't find anyone to replace Roger Pryor, who'd asked for a raise.

"Hello, sit down," said Humphrey. That was the fourteen-year bridge. "Christ, I'm reading an awful script." He tossed it on a crowded table. "By some college type."

"What's a college type?" *My* fourteen-year bridge.

"People who say 'fuck' in front of the children."

Bud went out to watch. "My God, you can't believe it! She's a dare-devil. She must go ninety miles round the curves. Rod was so scared he thinks he'll be sick. I told him to come in my place and lie down. *I* wouldn't ride with her. She's a *great* driver. *Great.* My God, you ought to come out and watch!"

"Will she look like me?"

"I tell you, you won't believe it! If I didn't know you were in here, I'd swear it was you out there racing Chuck's car. This picture is going to be really *something!*"

Hal looked in and laughed. *"God,* can't she go! And with a mask on and looking through the *eye holes!* She says it doesn't bother her at all. God!" He was laughing with pleasure. The picture was working right.

Do *you* think people are interested in this? I do. Endeavor, hope, fear, triumph, despair, getting it right, are part of us all in life, in business, in a profession.

"Once more right away," said Hal.

"Sound reloading," called Sid. Or Bob.

"I won't have the light," said camera.

"Okay. Start on Bud tomorrow."

"It's a wrap," shouted assistant Bob. Everybody rushed in every direction. "Seven o'clock crew call, eight o'clock cast, here. 'Night."

"Everything's loaded in," said Carl.

"Good night, dear," said Hal. "I think we had a good day."

"Good!"

"Bye-bye, Ruth." It was Bud. He leaned over and kissed me. "I love you."

"I love you and thanks for my daisies."

"Oh, forget it."

"Mongo'll close up unless you want to go back to the camper."

"No, let's go."

"The LTD is over here." Carl pointed behind the courthouse. "I've got it headed toward the freeway. Starting now, we *may* miss the traffic."

"Won't it be going *out* of San Francisco?"

"We'll lose a lot of cars at the airport turnoff."

At the airport turnoff, we lost a lot of cars.

The traffic going in was no problem. Coming out, lanes were slowing down; by Daly City, cars were bumper to bumper. Pass Candlestick Park, round the hill with the Granny Goose sign, pass the warehouses and stacked-up gray buildings. Carl swerved away from Oakland Bridge signs, took a lane that spoke to him, went briefly in a tunnel and out on a lane that appealed. Off the freeway, he took some street with houses that had once been grander. Three-story wooden ones with plenty of curves, some light green, some pumpkin pie color, some the color of Postum. Up past the Jack Tar Hotel, with how many rooms, do they say? Stop at the traffic light, start, stop, into the right lane to turn right onto California Street. Will people care what street?

"If it occurs to you to cut, cut," advised Willie Maugham.

If it occurs to *me* to cut, I think it over. Were you *always* right, darling Willie? Maybe not always, but tell me who hit a higher average?

He'd arrived in New York.

"Come to dinner," I wrote him. "We are now so successful we have no engagements whatsoever, so you name the hour and the night. The place will be Le Pavillon, 3 East 55th Street as you know. Love, Ruth."

A dry martini all around.

"Shall we order?" asked Garson.

"I'd like oysters, if I may."

"Sauce vinaigrette?" asked Le Pavillon's Martin.

"Red sauce," said that clipped Ashenden voice.

"Why do you choose red sauce?" I asked.

Willie Maugham knew that life after a certain age must be contribution. He wrote *The Summing Up* to contribute his knowledge. The most trivial question he would respect and furnish his best thought.

At Le Pavillon, why did he choose red sauce?

"I prefer to eat what is accepted in the country I'm in. At Driver's off Regent Street, I don't choose red sauce; in your country I do. You're leaving an oyster. Why is that?"

"Adrian, who designed all the beautiful clothes at M-G-M, said to always leave one and hope it's the *bad* one."

A fork flashed past me and Maugham had the oyster. Also a companion one I'd forgot.

I offered him the butter dish.

"No butter," he said. "I'm bursting out all my seams." He caught sight of my emerald and fell over at a forty-five-degree angle, recovered, took my hand and exclaimed.

"Garson bought it in London."

"You must *save* your money. Very important. This"—he pointed to the surrounding elegance—"does not go on and on. One runs out of

412

ideas as one runs out of time. I haven't had an idea for years. My latter-day books are written from ideas culled from my journal. It will be coming out in October."

Martin offered him the Montrachet to taste. He made a wry face. *"Aigre."*

"Have something else," said Garson.

"No."

Garson had a word with Martin.

"Have you always kept a journal?" I asked.

"Since I was eighteen. I had thought of dropping out the early period, but decided against it. Eighteen to seventy, except for notes already used."

"Does it tell how you got to write for the theatre?" asked Garson.

"No."

"With no theatre background or contact, how *did* you?"

"That I don't know. Very early, I remember, I translated an Ibsen play."

"Did you know Norwegian?"

"No. I used a German version."

"Where is it now?" asked Garson.

"Oh, I don't know. I saw Ibsen once in a café."

Martin brought the Corton Charlemagne.

"Did *you* ever write in a café?" I asked.

"No. In the early days I came home from the hospital, had a high tea and dinner combined, then wrote."

I asked about Liza and we talked about her for a little.

Martin offered the menu. We ordered.

"Any salad?"

"I should like hearts of lettuce."

Martin suggested, *"Effrayé?"*

"No. Tight hearts of lettuce."

"Dessert?"

"No dessert."

"Stewed strawberries?" I suggested. "Fresh ones."

He was delighted. "Fresh strawberries with cream. But, Ruth, darling, you must *save* your money. Knoblock died in penury. Did you ever hear of Edward Knoblock?"

*"Milestones,"* Garson said.

Maugham nodded. "He was an American, you know. Went to live in London. Bought a house for sixty thousand pounds. If he could not get

413

a play on, he put it on with his own money. He died in penury. Charity of his friends. Ruth, have you a savings account?"

"No, but I will have tomorrow."

"Have a savings account and keep a journal. Everyone goes out of fashion, dear. Even as successful a playwright as Pinero. I talked to him at the Garrick Club late on in his life. 'They don't want me anymore,' he said."

"Ever notice how many people have a bad third act?" asked Garson.

"Your journal is your insurance. Ideas refuse to come after a certain age. What you must do is prepare for this."

"I shall open a savings account," I said, "but a journal, no. My diaries are so boring, they'd drown out all ideas. Please lend me yours."

Garson wrote something.

"What are you writing?" asked Maugham.

"I'm starting my journal. Do you think you learned about life from being an intern?"

"No. Suffering doesn't refine a person. Happiness does. Suffering brings out meanness and cruelty."

"Perhaps this isn't the place to ask, but do you believe in God?"

"I feel it's impractical. How could God look after the earth and all its people, plus all the tangle of the stars and the sun and the moon and the planets?"

"Willie, do you think I should cut my hair?"

"Oh, do. Liza had long hair, cut it short and was vastly improved. Do you know Reno?"

"Yes, but we've no plans to go there," said Garson.

"I advise you to use it for background. Cowboys, divorcées. Also go and stay in Charleston. You lead entirely too restricted a life. Go to New Orleans. You don't *see* people. You must not succumb to New York. I wrote 'Rain' quarantined in Pago Pago."

"You called it 'Miss Thompson.' "

"Yes, but now it's known only as 'Rain.' "

"Why were you quarantined?" Garson asked.

"Cholera had broken out."

Garson looked impressed. "You make it tempting. How did *Quartet* come out?"

"All right, except they missed the entire point of each story. Would it interest you to know I've sold five of my stories and received twenty thousand pounds? No tax."

"What will you do with it?"

"I gave it to Liza." He turned to me. "Dear, would you like to have no worries? I urge you to go to Max Wolf."

"What's he like?"

"So unimpressive he impressed me. When I arrived in New York after the escape from France, I was so ill and feeble I thought I should never recover. I went to Dr. Wolf and feel I owe my health—perhaps my life —to him. The Mountbattens telephone him for help from England."

Garson started to write.

"Your journal?"

"No, my doctor."

Would you cut the above? It occurred to me, but I wouldn't dream of it. Willie, darling, maybe rules really *are* made to be broken.

Scene 70 was the first shot in Redwood City; tonight it was a wrap with Scene 78. In between, all Colin Higgins' scenes got shot, everybody got a cold but me, Cathie Blondell touched up my hair at the Holiday Inn, Santa Cruz, Hal bought the black Ferrari, the stunt man went over the fence and into Peninsula Hospital, Bud had to cry without letting his nose run, Garson and I lived thirteen weeks on Nob Hill, went to New York for Avedon to take my picture for *Vogue,* and came back to Beverly Hills for the earthquake!

"It's a wrap. As soon as you can make it, wrap-up party is at Sy Silver's family's house, 2221 Presidio Parkway. See you there," announced assistant Bob Enrietto.

Everybody looked dazed. It was over. A way of life was over. The breakup.

"You're coming to the party, dear?"

"You bet, Hal."

At the Winnebago, Bud knocked. "Can I come in?"

"Come in."

Andrea, my dress over her arm, opened the door. All I had to do was zip up skirt, button sweater.

"Here, Ruth." Bud put a square package in my hand. "I love you. See you at the party." He was gone.

The blue leather box from Shreve's in San Francisco opened, on a white satin cushion was a violet pansy with a diamond dewdrop

415

set on a petal. I pinned it on my sweater.

"Everything's in," said Carl. "Will you be going to the hotel for Mr. K.?"

"He's at Trader Vic's having dinner with Mr. Rubinstein. They're waiting for me."

Ever try to squeeze into San Francisco's Trader Vic's on a Saturday night?

The man in charge saw me. "Mr. Kanin is waiting inside."

A pretty slant-eyed girl in a pretty kimono led me through the lesser rooms up to the pinnacle made known to us by Telegraph Hill's Whitney Warren.

Arthur Rubinstein and Garson were deep in talk. Two comfortable men. Garson fifty-seven, Arthur eighty-four. Who cares? Are their shoe sizes the same? Do their neckbands agree? What has age to do with a friend?

Champagne was chilling.

"Did you finish?"

"We did."

Champagne glasses lifted. Kiss. Kiss. Kiss. A toast.

"Did you say goodbye to everyone?"

"No, we're going to the wrap-up party. Arthur, will you?"

"Oh!" he groaned. "If I didn't play a concert tomorrow afternoon I would *love* it." He did his boo-hoo cry.

"You're joking, aren't you?" Garson asked me.

"No. Sy has been working on this party since we started; we can't let him down." Sy was our assistant set dresser.

"All right." Definition of a dear man.

Sy's party *looked* as though he'd planned it for thirteen weeks! As we went in, Carl in a Santa Claus suit scattered snow over us, reminder of our chilly schedule when we were mostly cold for three months. The house was strung with icicles, snowbanks in every corner, wet slickers and umbrellas here and there. A sign said, "Over here for your ginger pie and oat straw tea." What Maude served Harold the first time he paid a call.

"Organic hashish," said another sign. A hookah puffed smoke like Maude's. A tape played Cat Stevens' song that we'd just done for the closing shot. Everybody and wife or husband or girl or feller showed up.

"Look," I said to Bud, and pointed to my beautiful flower with the diamond dewdrop pinned on my sweater.

"You know what it's supposed to be?"

"A daisy."

"They didn't have daisies. I knew you'd know."

"I did."

"Did you read what it says?"

"The card?"

"The pin."

I took it off. "Where?"

"There." He pointed to the back.

Why put on glasses at such a moment? Garson understood. "Read it, Bud," said Garson.

" 'I love you, Maude. Harold.' "

# Chapter

―――――⸎――――――

# 17

Too bad *The New York Times* didn't love Maude or Harold or *Harold and Maude.* At the Coronet or the Baronet it opened and closed. The *first* time; then it got its second chance. Does everything? Some get it before others, but I bet if we hang around long enough we all get it. For some it's a long, long wait. Gustav Eckstein's play hasn't got its *yet.*

"Whew, what a play!" ended its criticism in *The New York Times.*

How *could* it? Guthrie McClintic had told me it was a superb play and I *know* Gustav Eckstein is a superb writer. That paper was wrong. I reached for the phone. Who could I call up would say the play was good? Too early to call Guthrie. *Who* would be up?

A knock at my door. Up two flights of stairs had come Suzanne with my breakfast tray, Sacha rushing ahead of her. Sacha sat beside my bed and drooled. The smell of a waffle undid him.

Good waffles for me and Sacha, good coffee, good 60 West 12th Street, a good notice for Gustav Eckstein's play is what *had* to be; read it again.

"Whew, what a play!" Brooks Atkinson had to be wrong!

At nine o'clock, who was awake enough to reassure me? I tried a number.

"Not up yet," said a maid.

"Whew, what a play!" Was Brooks Atkinson in the phone book?

J. Brooks Atkinson lived on West 12th Street.

A woman's voice answered.

"Is Mr. Atkinson there? This is Ruth Gordon."

When we got to be friends, Mrs. Atkinson said she got him out of the shower.

"Hello."

"Mr. Atkinson, I read your notice and I just want to know if you aren't the *only* one felt that way."

He didn't know what the other reviews said, but that's the way *he* felt.

For the last time in my life, I took a critic's opinion against my own instincts. What if Brooks Atkinson was right? I knew Gus wrote wonderful prose, but maybe he didn't know how to write a play. Maybe Guthrie was wrong. Maybe it would be kinder to stay away.

"I don't think so at *all,*" snarled Guthrie. "It's a beautiful, an important play."

I saw it. A miracle of feeling! Its subject, the lack of privacy. People living cooped up in one room, no place to work out despair, the indecency of nowhere to be alone, no place to hide one's feelings. *Christmas Eve* opened December 27, 1939, and closed at the end of the week.

"Darling darling Ruth," wrote Gus thirty-five years later, the stationery headed:

### COLLEGE OF MEDICINE
#### UNIVERSITY OF CINCINNATI
#### EDEN AND BELLRESHDA AVENUES
#### CINCINNATI, OHIO 45219

DEPARTMENT OF PHYSIOLOGY                    TELEPHONE (513) 872–5639

The college is moving from the old building into a huge wonderful new one—I myself deposited the words into the cornerstone. After that, homesick a little, I tore up tons of my past and found . . .

My God, Ruth, the letter you wrote me after seeing the closing performance of *Christmas Eve!* It makes up (at this distance) for the way the play did not succeed. I'm not given to weeping over letters, but, since you aren't here, I let a lump climb up into my throat.

Affection—both,

Gus

That letter came on June 17.

Not only Brooks Atkinson, but all the critics put it down.

*"How* could it fail?" I'd asked Guthrie.

Guthrie thought, searched his mind. "I ought to have prepared the audience. A play called *Christmas Eve* opening two days after Christmas sounds like a *merry* play. When you opened *A Doll's House* Christmas week, people could have thought that was a cute comedy, but it was tagged Ibsen, so everybody knew. With Gus, nobody knew. Margaret Case came in her best bib and tucker. She and Natasha and Jack Wilson had come from dinner at '21.' The audience was all like that. A holiday mood, parties before the show, after the show to another. I should have *somehow* gotten it around the play was serious. I should have opened it at a matinee. Kit *always* has opened *Candida* at a matinee. I should have done that with Gus."

Too bad you missed it. On its second chance, *don't.* And never put down failures till you see them. In show business, if you don't have failures, you didn't reach out. When Gustav Eckstein's play is done again, let's hope there won't be a war on.

"Meet me for lunch at Sardi's," phoned Jack Wilson, then rang back. "It's raining so, want to pick me up at my office and we'll go somewhere near?" Jack was John C. Wilson, who produced Noël Coward's *Blithe Spirit.*

JAPAN JOINS THE AXIS, read the headlines on the newsstand as I waved to a taxi. Raincoat, umbrella and rubbers were small protection against the gale.

Jack was waiting for me. We blew across Rockefeller Plaza. Through Jack's high-up office window the shiny sidewalks had had beauty; at close range they were slippery. The wind nearly blew us over.

In the restaurant, a newspaper lay on the hat check girl's chair. GERMANY, ITALY, JAPAN JOIN FORCES AGAINST U.S.A. How remote the Louis XIV restaurant seemed from trouble, wind, rain. Pretty people sat at the tables in pretty clothes. Didn't *they* come through the rain? The maître d' was in morning suit or today was it mourning? It was black and he was foreign. "Thank you, Mr. Wilson," he said, and left us at our table.

Gilbert Miller came over. "Well, all sorts of celebrities are here today.

420

They tell me the Archduke is in here somewhere. Of course I don't know." He left us.

Up to Gilbert's table came a foreign-looking young man, accompanied by another. "The Archduke?" I asked.

"Probably," said Jack. "Gilbert's standing up."

"And he's with a Warner Brothers dialogue coach."

"What?"

"Emergency," I called softly. Irving Rapper turned. He'd been assistant director to William Dieterle on *Dr. Ehrlich's Magic Bullet.* "Emergency" had been our company byword. Before the movies, Irving had been stage manager for Gilbert's London company of *Grand Hotel;* now Gilbert was standing and bowing to Irving's luncheon guest, the Archduke.

"Emergency," I said again.

Irving bowed and smiled. It was not the moment for royalty's host to hear "Emergency," but Irving was not one to forget a pal. He came over. I introduced him to Jack, who congratulated him on his fine cast and small but appreciative audience. Gilbert and the Archduke were conversing as politely as people in a tapestry where there was no rain, no Japan, and the Axis was something in *Vogue,* overpublicized by the Red Cross.

"Would you like me to bring him over to say hello to you?" asked loyal Irving.

"Irving, honey, quit it."

"Well, some other time then," he said, and rejoined Austria-Hungary's last ruler.

Gilbert saw his own luncheon guest to the door, then came back to Jack and me. "That was my king," he said, pulling out a chair. "This couldn't happen anywhere else in the world today, the people who are in this room! The Archduke, mind you! And you must have seen Raimund von Hofmannstahl? Who was that blonde he was with?"

"Eileen Plunkett," said Jack.

"That's right, Eileen Plunkett! And down there Lady Ribblesdale. You know who she is?"

"Yes," I said.

"You *do?"* He looked disappointed. "Well, there she is, Lady Ribblesdale. And with her, that's the Baron and Baroness de Staël. Over across the room is Lopez-Wilshaw, the richest man in Chile. That was Pierre Wertheim with *me,* the one who owned the famous race horse Épinard

421

and, of course, Bourjois perfume. And you know what he said? 'Where would you find all this? New York has become the modern Babylon.' All those famous people!"

"And me and Jack."

"Yes, dear; only I'm just naming foreigners. And I *forgot* the Maharanee of Sarawak. She's in the corner. There you are! How do you like that? The Maharanee of Sarawak!"

Jack, who had seemed to have no plans, said he had an appointment. As we drifted over to the hat check girl, Gilbert stopped and spoke to the maître d'. "This is quite a thing, you know. All these people here. You ought to have it in the paper."

I got into my raincoat, took my umbrella.

"Oh," said Gilbert, "you go out in the rain, don't you? I go underground to my office."

"I could too," said Jack, "if I wanted to."

He and I walked out into the rain. The wind whipped our raincoats, I clung to my hat. We walked past the rain-swept skating rink. The skinny trees tossing in the gale looked aimless and hysterical. Rain beat down like shot. "The Maharanee of Sarawak!" said Jack, morosely. "Why, she's nothing but an Australian tart!"

"We were going to talk about something at lunch," I said.

"I know. It's slipped my mind."


1941 and summer and not enough money to get through it. Where does money go? A mink coat and green brocade evening dress and this and that and that's where money goes, so back to summer stock.

Where? Open late June at the Ann Arbor Festival; they wanted me for *Ladies in Retirement.* Rehearse there a week, play a week, close Saturday. On Monday, get to Sea Gate, outside Coney Island, rehearse *The Little Foxes* a week, play a week. On Sunday, go to the Ocean House at Swampscott, Massachusetts, meet Alec and Harpo, rehearse *Yellow Jack* a week, play it a week. On Monday, out to Westport to rehearse a new play, Dennis King to co-star. Every week for eight weeks rehearse a week, play a week, gross earnings seventeen hundred dollars. God, in Your infinite mercy, maybe keep an eye on this distracted sparrow?

At 60 West 12th Street, I learned the Flora Robson part in *Ladies in Retirement,* and Tallulah's part in *The Little Foxes.*

"Maestro, how do you learn a score?" marveled a Toscanini admirer.

"I *learn* it," said the maestro.

That describes it. I write down all the pages *I'm* in, then how many days I have to learn the part, then divide the pages by the days. Ten days into sixty-two pages. On some I may have only two lines, on some the full page. I read the scene, then put an unpaid bill over my first speech, read the line ahead of it. Does it suggest anything?

No.

Look under the bill and read what my line is. Put bill over line, read line ahead. Suggest anything? It should.

No?

Look under bill, read line and *really* read it, put bill down. You've *got* it! Repeat till you can do that whole page, then tackle the next, and *after*, go back and do all the others learned. The beginning pages a whiz-through, the last page a struggle, but tomorrow it'll be in my head.

Before I left 60 West 12th, I learned *Yellow Jack*. Goodbye, back in two weeks for one day, then Sea Gate for two weeks. Don't think about it; get to Ann Arbor. I'd never played their theatre, never met the director, nor any of the company except Mildred Natwick. She'd been rehearsing *Three-Cornered Moon* in Mount Kisco stock when I was acting there in *A Church Mouse* and she'd asked a question about playing Elizabeth Rimplegar.

"How does the play come out?" I asked her.

She looked startled.

"Once I'm through doing a play, I don't remember it."

In Ann Arbor, Mildred and I had adjoining rooms in a building that was part of the university. Across campus, the church chimed the quarter hours. For years after, whenever Milly and I met, our salute was: "Bing, bong, bong, bing."

*Ladies* was the second play in the festival. The first was *Man and Superman*, playing the week we were rehearsing.

*Man and Superman* scenery filled up the stage of the theatre, so we had to rehearse in a hall. Director Valentine Windt said we couldn't get onto the stage till dress rehearsal. Too bad. A play needs a theatre; an actor feels better on a stage. I hate a hall.

"Phone call from Culver City, California, for Miss Gordon."

Valentine Windt said, "Take it."

It was God leading Metro-Goldwyn-Mayer to me to get me out of my troubles.

"We want you for a fine part in the Garbo film to be directed by Cukor," said M-G-M's casting director, Billy Grady. "It's written by

423

S. N. Behrman, salary two thousand dollars a week, four-week guaranty, starting date first week in July, must know later today, will pay drawing room to the Coast."

At the lunch break, I called Actors Equity in New York. What is the rule about breaking stock contracts?

You can if you pay them the salary they contracted to pay you and the salary of any player specially engaged.

After rehearsal, I could send a check for five hundred dollars to Sea Gate, the rest when my two thousand a week came in.

The company was excited. Good luck for one means good luck can strike anybody. If it happened to me, couldn't it happen for them? Exciting!

Also exciting was opening night. Act I curtain came down, the audience gasped, then screamed. I'd done it, it worked, the audience believed I was a murderess. They *saw* me murder the lady at the piano.

A year and a half later, when Guthrie cast me for wicked Natasha in *The Three Sisters,* I knew I could play it. I'd found out how at Ann Arbor. The audience would accept my wickedness.

Five hundred dollars went to Sea Gate, Swampscott agreed to release me for three hundred, five hundred dollars to Westport, every company agreed to the payoff. Dennis King said to forget it.

"Equity says I owe it; you were specially engaged."

"Forget it," said Dennis.

A friend.

No time to go back to New York to pick up stuff there. Phone calls to Miss Ryan, to Suzanne, to Katherine Waldron to find and send what I didn't have with me, and after the show Saturday the sleeper to Chicago, next morning the Santa Fe *Chief* to the Coast. M-G-M phoned that the great Adrian needed measurements to design my clothes. Wardrobe Department at Ann Arbor thrilled at contact with the man who designed all the costumes for Garbo, Norma Shearer, Jean Harlow, Joan Crawford!

"She has a good figure," George Cukor had told Adrian.

"Not anymore," Adrian told George.

*How* had I let myself put on twenty pounds?

*How* does that happen?

"Despair," says Lillian Gish. "People eat out of despair; if they're happy they don't stuff."

I never despaired, but worry puts it on, too. Adrian had to design dresses for someone five feet tall, weighing a hundred and twenty-five pounds.

"Always treat yourself as though you're going to be fitted for some great clothes," spake Zarathustra. I wish he'd spoken earlier and would also recommend a good agent.

I called up Mike Levee. I'd heard he was Spencer Tracy's agent and somebody said he was good.

He called M-G-M and got the contract drawn up.

"I'll come over to the hotel so we can meet," he said.

"We don't need to."

Years later Ray and Dorothy Massey and I were having dinner at the Stork Club, a pleasant small man came to the table. Ray introduced him.

"I used to represent you," he said. It was the first time I saw Mike Levee.

*Two-Faced Woman* made George Cukor and me friends. The film didn't help any of us connected, except me.

About everything in the picture went askew. Sam Behrman wanted to call it *Ubiquitous Lady.* He said everyone would know what it meant. M-G-M thought otherwise. Mr. Louis B. Mayer thought Garbo should wear her hair curled. Feeling ran high. The picture went out of work for two days, started shooting again when Garbo wore her hair curled. *Two-Faced Woman* over, she retired from the screen. 1941 was a no-good year. Then came December 7. What were *you* doing on December 7? I rang up Billy Dorbin.

"How ya, darlin'?" His voice sounded as though I'd called him every day since *Fair and Warmer* closed.

"Billy, I'm rehearsing in—just started—*Portrait of a Lady* and there's a part—not good enough for you, darling, not good enough at *all,* but it's a part and I wondered if you were doing anything?"

"Nope."

"We're rehearsing in the Astor Hotel banquet hall, the small one, ground floor, 44th Street side. Come over at three and I'll introduce you to Chester Erskine. He's directing."

"I'll be there. Thanks, darlin'."

Back of the rim of gilt chairs I saw Billy edge in and sit down. Was that the same blue woolly overcoat from *Fair and Warmer?* How could it be? That was twenty-five years ago. I finished a scene, went over and hugged him.

425

"Y' look great, darlin'."

"You too."

"How's it look?" He pointed to the cleared center of the banquet hall.

"Well, *you* know. Y' never know."

"Your part good?"

"I guess so. Yours isn't, but I thought—"

"I don't care. I had a bum stretch, some terrible bills, sister's opera-tion. I helped her out. Haven't worked since *Man Who Came To* last season, Midwest company. They're great to me over to the hotel and this'll pay my bill fine. Think they'll want me?"

"Sure they will. Chester's over there; I'll introduce you." We went down to the banquet table. "Chester, darling, this is Billy Dorbin I was telling you about."

"Hello."

"How do y' do, Mr. Erskine."

"The part's a butler. No particular kind of a butler. Just a butler. What do y' think?"

"Like to do it, sir."

"Okay. Sit down and watch the run-through and I'll talk to you after."

"Thank you, sir." He squeezed my arm and returned to his gilt chair.

Chester spoke to the company. "All right; Act One. I'll watch the act for cuts today—the act runs long. Try to keep going. Don't stop for lines. If you're up, say *something.* If you find you're in the wrong posi-tions, get out of 'em and keep going. All set for Act One, Dave?"

"One minute, sir." The stage manager swung three gilt chairs to-gether. That was the off-center couch to loll on. He placed another gilt chair in front of two others. That was for the luxurious kneehole desk. The space between two chairs facing each other marked French doors. A lone chair for the big overstuffed chair down left. A chair to mark the entrance to the study. Two chairs suggested the fireplace. "Telephone." Dave held up a shoe box and planted it on the chair that would be a desk. "Telephone book?" He borrowed a *Saturday Evening Post* from one of the cast. "And doors open *out.* Please get used to that. *Out!* All set, Mr. Erskine."

"Okay."

"Places, Act One. I'll give you the signal."

I draped myself as glamorously as the three-chair couch allowed. Freddie Worlock stood warming himself beside the chairs that would be the fireplace.

"Curtain!"

A pause.

The Butterick pattern for my part was Clare Boothe Luce. I looked up from the notes I was writing with no pencil on no paper. "What time is it?"

"Twenty to four," said the assistant stage manager.

"For Christ's sake!" Chester Erskine glared at the assistant stage manager.

"I'm sorry. She read it so real, I forgot it was a line in the play."

"What if she reads it real opening night—are you going to call out eight-forty?"

"Sorry, sir."

"Sorry, Ruth. Dave, start again."

"Curtain!"

"What time is it?"

Freddie Worlock looked at me angrily. "Time we faced the situation."

After the run-through I went over to Billy. "What do you think, darling?"

"They've got some work to do, haven't they?"

"Oh, yes. Chester's wonderful at play doctoring. He's one of the authors, you know."

*"Your* part's longer than the moral law."

"It'll get cut. What do you think?"

"Oh, fine with me, if they'll take me."

"I'll go talk to Chester."

"I can wait. He's got plenty to think of. I got all the time there is."


We were opening at the Majestic Theatre in Boston, where Papa had taken Mama and me to see Forbes-Robertson in *Hamlet.* Where Katherine and I had got twenty-five-cent seats in the gallery to see Olive Wyndham in *What Happened to Mary?* Two days of dress rehearsals and open Christmas night. Over at the Copley Plaza in a suite overlooking Boylston Street, Jones and Miss Ryan were putting up a Christmas tree, rushing out to buy more ornaments, sightseeing, going to a movie, buying another comic book.

Between rehearsals, one of my costumes had to be refitted, one costume changed, my shoe straps lengthened, evening-shoe straps shortened, rubber heels for Freddie Worlock's shoes. Interview with Elinor Hughes, interview with Marjorie Adams. Interview at the Avery Hotel with man from which paper?

427

I hurried out onto Avery Street, deep in slush. No empty taxi, a cold rain beating down, dress rehearsal at two-thirty. I rushed along Tremont Street. No need to dodge the puddles; my feet and legs were soaked. I could feel the cold water squish. Only a few blocks, cross Boylston, then up the alley to the Majestic stage door. Just beyond it and across the alley is the stage door to the Colonial. Had Hazel Dawn ever had to run through rain and slush? I was perspiring from having hurried so. What if I took cold? What if tomorrow night my voice was ragged? Or gone altogether? All those lines, all those words, all those changes and cuts and additions! I pushed open the stage door. Billy and some of the crew were talking with the old doorman.

"What'sa matter, darlin'?"

"I'm soaked to the skin."

"All right, darlin'." He got my wet coat and hat off as I rushed to my dressing room.

"Couldn't get a cab. *Look* at my shoes!" I was in tears—part nerves, part worry.

"Get 'em off." He was down on his knees, tugging at the squishy shoes.

"I'll lose my voice if I get a cold! I always *do*. I'll—"

"Get your stockings off."

Like a child, I undid my garters. He pulled the muddy stockings off.

"Oh, Billy."

"You're all right." Down on his knees, he took my feet in his hands and rubbed them until they were rosy.

"Billy, you shouldn't be doing that."

"Why shouldn't I? Got any dry stockings?"

"Top drawer my trunk. I'll—"

"Sit still." As efficient as a lady's maid, he had the stockings on me.

"Oh, darling, thank you. I don't know what—"

"Want your neck massaged? Get the circulation?"

"No, I'm fine now. I was scared I'd be late and—"

"You're all right. Twenty minutes before I call the act." Along with playing the butler, he'd been made assistant stage manager.

"Oh, thanks, darling."

"See ya in church!" He was out the door.

Christmas Day at five o'clock I was eating dinner in the sitting room of our suite. Our Christmas tree a thing of beauty. Likewise the holly wreaths in the windows, with big red satin bows. On the room service table a small steak, spinach, fruit compote. Downstairs in the grand dining room Jones was having turkey, Miss Ryan chose goose. My dinner before opening had to be easy to digest.

A knock at the door. "Flowers, Miss Gordon."

A dozen pink roses. "Love and Merry Christmas. Wonderful to be with you, darling. Billy."

Backstage was taut with excitement, nerves, good wishes. Actors are great. None of us thought the show would make it, but the good wishes didn't sound like that. One last sip of water, one last trip to Ladies, one last pat of the powder puff, last prayer to God, then wait in the wings. Deep breath. Cue, open the door. On! A burst of applause, the first line. It was happening. Doing it was less dreadful than the dread. The scene on the phone. I said the line for the butler to come on. There was a split second's delay. Where was Billy? Billy wouldn't miss a cue. My God, what was it? Why would Billy be late?

"Mr. Dorrance to see you, Madam." Why was the stage manager in Billy's morning coat? I went cold with fear. Only five things keep an actor from going on: forgetting to, sick, accident, death or drunk.

Billy forget? Not Billy.

Drunk? Not he.

Accident? Pray to God!

Sick? Oh, God!

The scene was going on, but where was Billy?

End of Act I. Friendly applause.

"Where's Billy?"

"He had a little accident."

"Dead?"

No answer.

"Is he?"

"He died without knowing. I didn't want to tell you till after."

"How? How did he?"

"He went out to buy a Christmas present he said he had to, came back, opened the stage door and collapsed on the stage door step. They had a doctor in five minutes, but he died instantly, the doctor said. He died happy. Meant everything being in the show with you."

Billy.

The Christmas of 1941 was no good. No other way to describe it. The play got bad notices, I broke a tooth, depression rampant. I wrote a letter to George Cukor. "Somewhere along the line I acquired a lot of character and lost something cute."

I wrote to Orson Welles. "The Mayor of Boston gave me the key to the city, the public gave me the gate."

We canceled the second week and moved to Philadelphia.

Depression rampant. Only one remedy: live through it and before forever you're jumping up and down! Christmas 1942 was the top knockout of all Christmases ever! *The Three Sisters* a hit at the Ethel Barrymore Theatre, married three weeks to Garson Kanin. It was in the Willard Hotel's small ballroom, Garson in uniform, me in my Hattie Carnegie brown and black plaid dress. We stood beside each other and a Washington judge said: "I pronounce you man and wife."

That was Thursday night after *The Three Sisters* performance at the National Theatre. I walked along Pennsylvania Avenue to the Willard, reporters and photographers walking along with me. We pushed our way through the wartime Washington crowd in the lobby.

In the small ballroom, lovely white flowers, a place for the judge to stand, a place for us, behind us stood the guests. We planned not to have any, but Garson's sister and brother and sister-in-law had come to Washington.

"I *have* to ask Guthrie and Kit. My God, I owe half my career to him!"

"Oh, sure. And Bob Russell; he and I've been together since Fort Monmouth."

"And Dennis King; he played in *A Doll's House* beginning with Central City."

"And my cousin Marion Greenbaum; she made all the arrangements."

"I'd like Alice Belmore Cliffe. She's over eighty; I feel if *she's* there, it'll *last!*"

Backstage, Judith Anderson said, "If *they're* coming, you can't leave *me* out. I'm coming whether you ask me or not." And did. And Dennis said Edmund Gwenn should.

"Felix and Marian Frankfurter, of course." The Justice found us the judge.

Upstairs, Sherwood was in his and Sam Rosenman's two-room inside suite where they wrote President Roosevelt's speeches. "We certainly want Bob."

"Won't Madeline be here?"

"She can't, but Swope and Pearl."

They were on time and stood behind us. "You don't think you could get married without *us!*" growled Pearl.

The René Clairs sent flowers from California. Woollcott called up from Lloyd Lewis' in Libertyville, Illinois. He went out there to get away from the wedding.

The judge said, "I pronounce you husband and wife." We kissed. The maître d' applauded. The guests joined in. Waiters passed the champagne and Garson and I led the way to the long table. We sat at the head and everybody sat where they sat. No one thought about protocol.

"Do you ever wear a wedding ring?" I asked Kit.

"Only in *Candida.*"

Garson designed ours. Twisted gold and platinum, one made for me, one for him. Nineteen years later he lost mine in the sand at Biarritz and gave me his. *I* wear it, but it belongs to us both.

"Do you?" I asked Marian Frankfurter.

"I never had one."

A wedding brings out a lot of things.

"Felix and I decided to get married in a hurry. The jewelry stores were closed. Felix stopped at the Harvard Club and borrowed a wedding ring. I had to give it back right after the ceremony."

A wedding brings out a lot. Guthrie pulled off his shoe and took out a thrupenny bit. "God help me if I lose it."

Sherwood rose and made a beautiful speech. We wept and loved him even more. For a finish, he sang "Just a Gigolo," coat collar turned up to characterize down-and-out.

Swope spoke and proposed a toast.

The Justice spoke and lifted his glass.

Kit left her place, came to where Garson and I sat, lifted her glass to us and fell flat on the floor. Rice is slippery.

*The Three Sisters* company rose as one. There'd be no season without Katharine Cornell as Masha; would we close after five performances?

"Are you all right, Kitty?" asked Guthrie, white as the roses in the centerpiece.

"Yes." She got up!

Guthrie glared at Judith and Dennis and Teddy Gwenn and Alice Belmore Cliffe. "I don't want anyone else to get married during the engagement; tonight's show was off."

Nobody wants a show to be off, especially one that had been such a ball-breaker to get on.

431

That was the end of 1942. The beginning had been no good. No offers, no money coming in, I had to do something. I did a lot of reading, a lot of writing:

Dear Mr. Shumlin,
    Is there a part for me in any play you are doing?
Yours truly, Ruth Gordon

*60 West 12th Street*
*Gramercy 7-2748*

Dear Max,
    If you read a play with a part for me, let me know.
Love,<br>Ruth

Dear Mr. Wyler,
    I read that you're going to direct *The Little Foxes.* Would you consider me for Birdie? My address is 60 West 12th Street, New York. The phone is GRamercy 7-2748.
Best wishes,<br>Ruth Gordon

*60 West 12th Street*
*New York*

Dear Lawrence,
    Is the Guild doing any play I could be in? I hear Sam Behrman's play is great. Is there a part for me?
Ruth

Thornton said the library shelves are full of hits. Find one. Ask him which they are. "Long distance—New Haven, Connecticut, State 0304. . . . Thornton, tell me a play to do. . . ."

"*Mistress of the Inn, Hedda Gabler.* And, Bella, I'm sending my new one to Jed. Remember the part of Sabina is yours."

Jed turned it down.

Back to the bookshelves. *Mistress of the Inn?* Thornton had said he'd make a new translation, but now his hands were full. *Hedda Gabler?* Was it her name I didn't like?

Back to the shelves! Maybe Chekhov? *The Cherry Orchard?* Nazimova had made that her own. *The Sea Gull?* Recently done by the Lunts. *The Three Sisters?* I settled down on the couch bought with Gregory's seven thousand dollars to furnish 36 West 59th. Four hundred of it went for the couch and I blocked out of my memory what its hand-blocked made-to-order chintz cover cost! For a few years the couch went to

Manhattan Storage when we all moved into Jed's 135 East 79th Street house, followed by my year in an inside room at the Waldorf, then it came out for when I rented the 60 West 12the house. How many plays had I read on that couch? That was where George Kaufman sat when he said, "Going to read the new play we wrote." "We" meant him and Edna Ferber. The play was *The Royal Family.*

That was then, now was now. *"The Three Sisters,* by Anton Chekhov."

Get a director. Jed was frying other fish; what about Lee Strasberg? I didn't know him, but I didn't know Brooks Atkinson either, and when I needed him I looked in the phone book and phoned.

"Mr. Strasberg, I want to do *The Three Sisters.* Would you want to direct it?"

He would.

"Would you want to come down to my house and talk? It's 60 West 12th Street."

We sat on the four-hundred-dollar sofa.

"I want to play Masha."

He nodded.

"For Olga, I've asked Lillian Gish."

Another nod.

Lillian would be perfect, also solvent. A good thing in a classic. "For Irina, I asked Grete Mosheim."

"I hear she's very *good."*

Very good and very rich. Howard Gould's Union Pacific money behind her. The sisters selected, we went about getting it on.

We thought, we talked, we met some more, decided to raise the money and produce it ourselves. We interested Carly Wharton, wife of John, lawyer for John Hay Whitney, also for the successful Playwrights Company. Carly hoped he'd help raise money. Lee and I went up to their grand East End Avenue apartment. John Wharton said a pleasant hello and disappeared. We three talked and talked, then met again. We had been pledged twelve thousand dollars. For a four-set show with lots of costumes and a *big* cast?

Keep going, think about what adaptation. Lee said he thought Clifford Odets was doing one.

Great! On the phone again. "Clifford, it's Ruth. Are you doing an adaptation for *The Three Sisters?* . . . May I read it? . . . Can I pick it up? . . . I'll drop by tonight."

He lived on Beekman Place, five houses from Kit and Guthrie's, where

I was going to have dinner with Guthrie. The doorman handed me the script, I walked back to 23.

Kit was in San Francisco playing Henri Bernstein's *Rose Burke*.

Guthrie and I had dinner alone.

"Are you still trying to get that *Three Sisters* on?"

"Yes, I am."

"Have you got it set up?"

"We've only got twelve thousand dollars."

"Would *The Three Sisters* be good for Kit?"

"And how!"

"I know the play, of course, but just refresh my memory. What part would Kit play?"

"Masha."

"What part do *you* play?"

"Masha, but every part is good."

"Uh huh. What adaptation are you going to use?"

"We haven't got one we like. Clifford Odets has made a new one. I haven't read it; it's out in the hall."

"Out *there?*" He pointed.

"Yes."

"You want to read it or could I?"

"Keep it."

Late that night, he called up. "I see what you mean. Would you want us to do it?"

"Oh, my God!"

"What about Lee Strasberg?"

"We couldn't raise the money."

"Yuh."

In show business, it's like the pirate ship in *Peter Pan*. The ones who didn't win went overboard; stagehands threw rock salt for the splash.

In show business, when you go overboard, you make shore and start the next!

"I'll fly out to Cleveland tomorrow and read it to Kit. She opens Monday; I'll wait till Tuesday and read it to her. She's read it, of course, but I want to read it to her *right*. It's pretty sure we'll do it."

The phone rang. "Cleveland calling Ruth Gordon."

"Yes."

"She says yes. We'll close next week in Washington. Come up at ten tonight. Talk ideas."

434

Lee understood. To get a show on takes money, so the producer is the one who has the money. Lillian and Grete understood too.

In show business everybody understands it's not easy to get the money for a four-set revival.

Guthrie didn't say hello, didn't say to sit down. "I want this to be the greatest thing ever done in the theatre. Kit agrees this should be our monument. In a sense, give back for all the theatre's given us. I talked to Alfred and Lynn. He be great for Vershinin, she be Olga! Oh, God, what an Olga!"

Kit for Masha, Lynn for Olga, I'd be Irina. In a classic play discount age. Act I is Irina's twentieth birthday party, but in a classic, you can be any age or anyone. I'd be forty-five playing Irina at twenty, but what of it? Hadn't Edith Evans swept the Old Vic audience off its feet as Rosalind when she was fifty or going to be?

"Alfred and Lynn don't want to. Come up tonight. Maurice Evans is coming; I'm going to offer him the Baron. He'll be great."

After a persuasive séance, Maurice and I were out on Beekman Place. Whistling for a taxi. Indoors there'd been plenty of "Oh, my God!"

"Do you think you'll do it?" I asked between whistles.

"Well, I may go into the army."

So go high hopes. But not Guthrie McClintic's, a forceful man. "Maurice has been assigned to Honolulu. He'd have been good, but I like Orson better."

"Will he do it?"

"I'm calling him up."

Orson would give anything to do it, always loved the play, loved Guth, Kit, Gertrude Macy, Kit's manager, loved the theatre, but alas, he had to do—

Does it matter what? It was something else.

Guthrie kept coming up with big names who would also give top performances.

The pile of bills got higher. I called up Elia Kazan. "Anything in the new play?" He was announced to direct Paul Vincent Carroll's *The Strings, My Lord, Are False.* He'd done *Café Crown,* a success; this was his second try.

He and actor-producer Alexander Kirkland came down to 60 to dinner. "It's not good enough for you," said Elia.

"We couldn't pay anything," said Alex.

"But would you do it?" said both.

The part was Iris. We were all Scottish, Walter Hampden was the star, the cast had a lot of good people and some that were going to be. We went into rehearsal at the Royale. My part wasn't good enough, my salary was three hundred a week, it could only be described as better than nothing. Interesting to watch Elia direct. He was an actor who made any part memorable; now he wanted to direct.

Walter Hampden was pleasant. Sometimes we'd share lunch across the street at Ralph's.

We all believed we were in a wonderful play, we all thought Elia was doing it fine, I got carried away and said it was like a Scottish *Our Town* gone to war. While you're doing a play, you're reasonably unaccountable. The same with making movies. Billy Wilder says he's never *heard* of the rushes being short of *great.*

One night after rehearsal, Elia and some others and I went over to Sardi's. At another table sat Garson Kanin. We'd met once at Radio City Music Hall, the opening of his film *They Knew What They Wanted,* Charles Laughton and Carole Lombard the stars. I'd gone with Elsa Lanchester; Charles had to stay on the Coast. The second time I met Garson was dinner at George Cukor's. George and I, Garson Kanin and Katharine Hepburn. Neither time struck sparks; the third time we meshed. At least we knew we were going to. Leonard Lyons and I and Garson Kanin and Simone Simon at the Copa.

At Sardi's, Garson came over to the table and asked if I could go Sunday night to *Candida.* Katharine Cornell was playing it one week for a benefit, Guthrie had directed it. It was at the Shubert and sold out, of course. Now Garson Kanin invited me. I looked at Elia. He'd told us in advance to make no plans for Sunday, rehearse Sunday night.

"It's important to me," I said.

"Go. We'll rehearse around you." The words began my new life.

I was in love again. For life.

"A Scottish *Our Town* in wartime," I told Garson. He bought a seat for opening night.

Two more rehearsals, then dress rehearsal, no out-of-town tryout. Dress rehearsal, then open, a rich man named Sheppard was producing it with Alexander Kirkland. Everybody hopeful, everybody working hard. Dress rehearsal fine; we had an invited performance. It went great. Elia came backstage ecstatic. "I know just what to do, just what cuts, just where the trouble lies."

The trouble was the producers; they replaced him next day. Alex

436

Kirkland took over, we opened and that was *almost* all there was to *that.*

Notices no good. Why did I leave 60 West 12th and come up to Sardi's to dinner? So did some of the others. I guess we knew it was hopeless and had better stick together.

"The *Evening Sun* is *great,*" shouted Mr. Sardi. He held it out to us, overjoyed.

Nobody cheered up.

"Read it," said Vincent Junior's father, host to actors *in* funds or out. "Read it—it is really *good.*"

That night we were told the manager had a scheme to continue, we must be on the Royale stage next afternoon at four. Encouraging, but what could it mean? Walter Hampden didn't know. I didn't. Philip Bourneuf couldn't imagine.

Four o'clock everybody sat in a circle on the stage where we'd rehearsed with such high hopes. Alex Kirkland led on a short woman. "This is Elsa Shroeder," he said. "She has seen the play. Now she will tell her ideas."

"If you agree," said Alex Kirkland, "you must vote, and Equity's rule is you can't rehearse after you open unless the vote is unanimous. I have John Sheppard's guaranty we will continue four weeks. If you do *not* agree, we close Saturday."

The vote was unanimous: to close.

"I was *sure* of your vote. Why wouldn't you let me?"

Was it the German accent? Was it the take-charge manner? Was it loyalty to Elia? Could she do what he couldn't? What he could have if the managers had stuck with him.

Garson had come to see it opening night, he came again on closing. Thornton came the second night. He liked the direction and said he was going to ask Elia to direct *The Skin of Our Teeth.* "I liked this, I liked *Café Crown.*"

I told him about Garson. The next day he left a long letter at the stage door. He knew him and liked him, thought him brilliant, but urged me to beware of a man "with no hobbies."

I was in love and dreaded it. What if it busted up? Garson was a big success as a movie director. I hadn't done anything successful for how long! I was forty-five, he was twenty-nine. What kind of agony lay in store? I decided to end it. He'd been drafted on the first call-up, had done basic training on the Coast and at New Jersey's Fort Monmouth. Until further orders, he was doing war work, out of uniform. Any minute, orders could carry him off.

437

June. *The Three Sisters* was definite. Booked to open in Washington the last day of November, rehearsals four weeks earlier. What would I do in between?

I had a standing invite to go out to California and visit George Cukor. "For two weeks *only,*" he stipulated. When I looked surprised, he said, "That's the limit. I don't care who it is, I don't want anybody for more than two weeks."

"I'm going away," I told Garson.

"Why?"

"I love you too much."

He thought that was an odd answer.

He thought so, but I knew me.

At 60 West 12th, Jones had said he didn't want to go to camp this summer, he'd rather stay in New York. I asked, "Would you want to go to California?"

"With you?"

"With me, then when we get there, I'll stay at Mr. Cukor's and you stay at Edward Hardwicke's."

He liked it.

Picsie and Cedric Hardwicke had rented the house on Camden Drive where I'd gone to visit Helen and Charlie the summer of 1930. A fine house, lots of rooms, a fine swimming pool. Little Edward was a year younger than Jones, but they liked each other, spent weekends together when Edward was in New York. Lady Hardwicke had said how wonderful it would be if Jones and his governess, Miss Ryan, came for the summer. Everything seemed to jibe.

I wrote George. He wrote back an exuberant welcome. I wrote again with the dates and said it wasn't just for pleasure, I needed to land a job, could he help? Yes, he could.

The house had always stayed open summers, but this summer I had to cut corners. Mr. Fleischman, who came every day to fix the furnace or empty the garbage, could come every day and look at it, but our cook, Suzanne, and our maid, Katherine Waldron, would have to go.

"Would they work for me?" Garson asked.

"Would you want to work for Mr. Kanin?"

They were overjoyed. He'd rented the lovely house at 13 Sutton Place, looking on the East River. Suzanne and Katherine were to move in and look after it. I packed my Vuitton trunk, Jones and Miss Ryan got all their things together, and down the stairs bumped the trunks, out the front door and down the steps Thornton and I had sat on so many hot and instructive evenings. I turned the key and walked down the steps, behind me unpaid bills, *with* me worry. "There comes Tom," said Miss Ryan as the taxi pulled away.

"Keep going," I told the driver. Tom was our man at Esposito's, where we bought our food. I owed them over four hundred dollars. "Keep going." Was Tom bringing another of those "Please remits"? Good the story had a happy ending. By November, Esposito and Helen and Thornton and Lillian and Dorothy Gish and Lynn Fontanne and Kit and the Provident Loan Association had all got paid.

"Don't economize," Charlie MacArthur had advised Helen. "Just earn more."

Jones and I shared a drawing room on the *Twentieth Century Limited*, Miss Ryan had a roomette. On the *Twentieth Century* a terrific dinner; the food was worth the trip. In Chicago aboard glorious *Super Chief* for California. It was Jones' and Miss Ryan's second trip, my eighth. I don't count the time I'd flown out with Jed. My eighth New York to California where I could see the scenery.

George was at the M-G-M studio but he'd sent a note. "Tonight dinner at the René Clairs, pleasure. Tomorrow dinner at Jack Warner's, business."

Business it was. That's where I got the job that got me through the summer till rehearsals for *The Three Sisters*. When I went into rehearsal I was solvent. The job that came from Jack Warner's dinner was a part in *Edge of Darkness*, starring Errol Flynn and Ann Sheridan and featuring Walter Huston, Judith Anderson and me and somewhere in smaller type Helene Thimig, wife of Max Reinhardt. It lasted thirteen weeks, it paid me fifteen hundred a week, it nearly made me miss *The Three Sisters*. They were already rehearsing when I got back to New York and Sergeant Garson Kanin, in uniform, met me at Grand Central Station. Washington a triumph and Sunday the company was off to Baltimore. Garson got a weekend pass, then went back to Washington.

The Sunday after our Baltimore week we gave a performance for the soldiers at Fort Meade.

"Garson, you have to make a speech before our performance," said Guthrie.

"Why me?"

"Yuh."

"Why don't *you?*"

"Naw, you."

439

In his new second-lieutenant's uniform, Garson told the uniform-packed auditorium about Chekhov and the company they'd see and ended with, "Natasha is my wife, so look at her the most."

*The Three Sisters* opening at the Ethel Barrymore was a triumph!

I didn't read the notices. Years later, I read Lewis Nichols in the *Times*. Jones had cut it out, mounted it, wrote some extravagant praise of his own on it, decorated it with pine cones off our Christmas wreath at the Hotel Sulgrave, where we'd moved. When Jones showed it to me I admired it with my glasses off and pretended to read. How can you explain to a thirteen-year-old son you're too scared to really read it? It was his first opening night; he was a great first-nighter! After the show, Kit was receiving onstage. He followed the crowd to stage center. "Wasn't your mother *great!*" she said.

"I thought you *all* were." Thirteen years old!

Woollcott had come to the play in Philadelphia. Saturday night after we opened in New York he died.

*The Three Sisters* triumphed until early July, then we closed in Chicago. I went to Washington, where Garson was assigned to the OSS till he went overseas.

"I've got a good idea for a play," I said. July, Washington is pretty hot to get a good idea. On some of the street corners they put buckets of salt pills to keep walkers from fainting before they got home.

Walking past the salt buckets I didn't take any, but it felt great to get back to our Sixteenth Street North West air-cooled apartment, a rarity in wartime Washington.

"What's it about?" asked Garson.

"Kind of about us."

"Oh?"

"You struggling with all the army stuff you don't really know about, but great in your *own* line, and Thornton in Miami worrying will he pass his officers training exams. He'd made it in Oberlin and Yale, got a Guggenheim to Rome, taught at Lawrenceville and University of Chicago, but now thinks he may flunk."

"Yes?"

"Me and you living in a crazy two-room apartment and I'm counting on the butcher being a fan so he'll wait on me, and spending the summer fighting off salt pills while you do God knows what in a uniform and the commanding officer tells you to have short short hair."

"But that's not a play."

"It isn't?"

"No."

Next afternoon, walking past salt pill buckets, I stopped in at the Willard Hotel.

"Come in, honey," said Madeline. "I'm washing Sherwood's socks."

I sat at the door of the bathroom while she soaped and rinsed. "Want to hear an idea?" I told her my play.

"That's good."

"Garson doesn't think so."

"I bet Sherwood would."

That night, in *our* two not *quite* so small rooms, I said, "Madeline thinks Sherwood would like my idea."

"Tell me again."

I told it.

"Well, that *is* an idea for a play. That's not what you told me last night."

"It isn't?"

"You must have enlarged on it when you told it to her. Write it; it'll be a great part for you. Audiences have seen you as Mattie Silver, Nora Helmer, Natasha; now let them see you as *you.*"

"Should I be an actress? *She* has to be a big shot, *he*'s like you or Thornton—great career given up to learn about what Thornton says he can't: vectors."

"What about have her be a famous novelist? Dashing, sexy, great-looking like Clare Luce, not a novelist, but she could be."

"Married to a newspaperman, like Ralph Ingersoll?"

An elixir for that summer, me alone in the apartment, Garson all day in the military, then both of us out in the steambath heat, where we'd meet. Fan and Bill's always let us in for dinner *if* we had it at five-twenty, before the queue on Connecticut Avenue got too long. Then we'd stroll over to Lafayette Park, sit on the bench that Bernie Baruch had conferred on earlier and talk about the play. Still twilight, we strolled up Sixteenth Street to our apartment house a block this side of Florida Avenue and I'd show what I'd written. Garson scratched out some, suggested some. "I'll give you my Texas colonel and his wife and mother-in-law at Fort Worth. It was when Burgess came over and the colonel gave me an order to bring him to cocktails; his wife *had* to meet Burgess Meredith! I *was* going to use it, but you take it." It went in.

In the morning, Garson left at seven, I went to work on a card table, where my portable Corona typewriter was permanently set up. I called

441

my character Dotty after me mixed with Dorothy Parker and Clare Luce. There was a character Swope, mixed with no one. He was the publisher who was my husband's boss. For the third act, we'd bring in a film great, a David O. Selznick. In the original script his name was David.

Evenings in Lafayette Park, we thought up names that would match our characters' real names. For Herbert Bayard Swope, what conventional first name? What grand name to follow? We flailed away at mosquitoes, thought, suggested, discussed. Robert we settled on for the conventional. The second name ought to have two syllables. Drexel won. A good sound. For Swope? One syllable and no usual name. Gow? It fitted with the Drexel. "This is Robert Drexel Gow." It sounded great onstage! In Act II, "The phone rings. 'Hello. . . . The Miami *Daily News?* Why, this is Robert Drexel Gow. . . . Yes, it is. . . . Well, that's very complimentary. Get your racing man to tell you who came in in the sixth at Jamaica—and if it isn't Wingfoot don't tell me, just hang up.' "

For a substitute for Dotty, we needed a name that could shorten to a nickname and a good last name to go with it. A name that would look good on a book jacket with a good rhythm like Edna Ferber, like Edith Wharton. What about Wharton? We slapped mosquitoes, discussed, kept our minds off how long before Garson would get shipped out.

Wharton was chosen; now what first name? Lillian shortened to Lil, to Lily? Lillian Wharton? Didn't make it. Alice Longworth's daughter was Paulina. Sounded good with Longworth; with Wharton it didn't. Paula?

Pauline?

Paula?

Paula Wharton, Polly for friends? Looked and sounded great.

The play was finished. Heat, salt pills or no salt pills, military worries, twenty-minutes-past-five dinners, the play was finished! In Lafayette Park, we'd come up with *Over Twenty-One.* I'd come from the foot-fixer. "Age?" he'd inquired.

"Over twenty-one."

Garson liked my answer. "What about that for the title?"

" 'Over Twenty-One'?"

"Spelled out."

The heat was terrible, but we had a play with a title; now what producer? Howard Lindsay and Buck Crouse kept coming up on top. The paper said they were in Washington. We asked them to lunch at the roof restaurant of the Washington Hotel, where Gregory and I had stayed the week of *Piccadilly Jim* when we weren't going back and forth to New York on the sleeper. Lunch was enjoyable; we made a date for two days after Labor Day, when Garson had been promised a leave. We'd come to New York, he'd read it at the Lindsays' house on West 11th Street, one block in back of 60 West 12th, which I'd given up the year before.

I'd known Howard since Gregory acted in *Dulcy*. I'd known Buck since he was Woollcott's assistant on the *World*, assistant and friend, along with Alison. After the *World*, he was head of the press department for The Theatre Guild.

Garson got his two-day pass and on Labor Day the *Congressional* ran off the track. Near Frankford, the station before North Philadelphia. The papers ran pictures of the tracks strewn with wreckage. People were hurt, Lin Yutang, reported to be on board, disappeared no one knew where.

"We don't have to go if you're scared," said Garson.

I went and it was scary and so were Lindsay and Crouse. In Dorothy and Howard Lindsay's parlor, Garson read the play to no response. It couldn't be, but it was. Garson is a remarkable reader. How did he keep going with no response? That takes courage. Dorothy laughed once, twice, maybe three times. Howard and Buck didn't laugh at all.

"We'll send it to Max Gordon," Garson said. "He likes you; you got him *Ethan Frome.*"

We delivered it to Max's office and went back on the scary *Congressional*.

Next morning *early*, the phone rang. "What do you want to do? Kill me? I just had an operation. I think I busted my stitches. I'm not *supposed* to laugh. What do you say to Kaufman? He's got Gypsy Rose Lee's play goes into rehearsal next week, then he could do yours. Shall I send it to him?"

George said he'd do it. Did he ever say he *liked* anything? He didn't say he liked this. "You can improve it," he said.

"Tell us."

"I'll read it again."

The mail brought his notes. We made some of the changes, some we talked him out of, some more got thought of, some changes got changed back to *before* it was changed. That's show business.

George said he would come to Washington. A big concession. He liked his Park Avenue apartment where Bea made him so comfortable, but the military only issues so many leaves.

MEET KAUFMAN 9:05 P.M. UNION STATION MONDAY, wired Max Gordon.

Washington taxis were unpredictable; there were some, but not when you wanted one. Garson borrowed a car and gasoline coupons from a friend, met George at Union Station and drove him back for a session at our apartment.

"Why's your fruit on the window sill?" He pointed to two pears, three peaches, a plum.

"To get it ripe. Stores don't sell ripe fruit."

"Oh?" he said. "When will they be done?"

"The plum's ready now. And the pears. Want one?"

"All right." A good sign. George was a choosy eater, maybe win him with fruit.

He gradually got the train trip depression out of the way, became reconciled to not sleeping in his own bed and unfolded enough to report that Max would book the play into New Haven, Boston and Washington, then New York the week after New Year's. What did we feel about Ray Sovey to design the set? "He's not inspired, but has it ready when he *says* he will, and it works. Any idea who'd be good in these parts? You'll have a hard time to get anybody for Max." Max was our name for the Garson Kanin–Thornton Wilder–Ralph Ingersoll character.

"Why?"

"That part's not good enough. Ruth'll be the whole show and that ought to be enough for the price of a ticket. Any ideas for Swope?"

Garson nodded. "We saw an actor *looks* like him. Played the National Theatre this summer in *Junior Miss*. His name is Loring Smith."

"Oh, I know who he is."

How's that for a reaction? "Oh, I know who he is." Period.

I jumped in. "The colonel's wife we wrote for Dennie Moore, if you like the idea."

George wrinkled his face up like a nutmeg. "She'd be all right."

Encouraged, Garson sprung one. "The colonel I'd like Carroll Ashburn."

"Who?"

"Carroll Ashburn. He was the leading man in Plainfield stock when I was a kid."

"Plainfield?"

"New Jersey."

"He sounds about right."

Rise above it. I hurried on. "Do you like Jessie Busley?"

444

"Good."

"For the colonel's mother-in-law she'll be great."

Did George feel we were too encouraged? "The first act's the least good. *That*'s a novelty. Anybody can write a good first act and quite often does, but *you* didn't."

"Oh?"

"No."

"We thought of the play as a whole; the first act and the second are leading up to the third."

"But the audience goes out after Act One and unless you have the ushers announce, 'Don't form an opinion,' they're likely to say it's no good."

"What can we do?"

"I wish I knew." He looked as though he never would and screwed up his face even more. "For Act Two, I might give you my icebox routine I've been saving. You could *use* it! Act Two is better than Act One, but that doesn't mean it doesn't need help. I'll probably give you my routine. Act One has to have something big at the finish, like the scenery fall in."

"What?"

"It would double the cost to have a breakaway roof, but we *might* get a curtain. Polly does the go-to-bed routine, thunder, lightning start up, and a tree falls in."

"Uh huh." Nobody said no to George S. Kaufman. If you didn't like his suggestions, you hoped they'd disappear, but the way to that wasn't to say no. The tree through the roof and the thunderstorm got written, then George decided, "Maybe the act will go without it. Unlikely, but maybe." Was it Ray Sovey's estimate for the breakaway that cooled him? Or did he decide a tree through the roof didn't seem funny?

Borrow the car again, get gas coupons. George was coming to hear new scenes, see what more to do. Ripe fruit on the window sill. Washington was cooler; Garson wore his new cashmere pullover.

George looked over the window sill display and chose one.

Garson recited the Act I changes, really selling it. To emphasize, he waved the big library shears, then stuck them under his arm.

"They'll be good," I agreed, "and don't cut your sweater."

"Don't cut your *sweater!*" repeated George, and from time to time revived it. "That Act Two scene *might* work, Ruth, and don't cut your *sweater.*"

445

In the script, I'd written Paula Wharton is dressed by Mainbocher, top couturier in New York, but he'd done stage costumes only for Mary Martin in *One Touch of Venus.*

On a two-day pass we went to New York. Mainbocher and his partner, Douglas Pollard, had read the script, liked it, and told their ideas: Paula Wharton must be elegance itself in the midst of this army-officer bungalow existence. A dress with a jacket to match when she arrives carrying her Vuitton suitcase and hatbox. When she changes into a negligee, it must be ravishing.

Nobody like Mainbocher! Dior said about him, "He does what *we* do, but *he* does it in America."

I rang up Max. "He loves it, he'll do my clothes. You do know he's *awfully* expensive."

Max shouted, "Don't tell me about the cost of buttons when I got an Act Two like *I* got!"

"He'll send you the estimate, but I do *want* him."

"Will you quit worrying? You *got* him!"

Casting was going to start. I moved from our two-room apartment in Washington into a two-room suite at the Sulgrave Hotel on Park Avenue and 67th Street. Jones and Miss Ryan had a three-room suite down the hall. Garson got there as often as he could get leave.

The phone rang. "Hello?"

"Ruthie, I'm not going to pay any lousy dressmaker thirty-seven hundred dollars!" screamed Max.

"But I *told* you—"

"Ruthie, I don't care *what* you told me. I never paid it and I won't. The whole wardrobe for *My Sister Eileen* didn't cost *half* that!"

"Max, I *told* you he was expensive but I *want* him. It's part of my character to have her wear clothes like—"

"Do you want to bankrupt me? I been bankrupt once and no more. A third act like you wrote is all y' need. Clothes won't get you a quarter!" He rang off.

What magic persuaded him? Garson? Main was engaged, the thirty-seven hundred agreed on. It was Garson, certainly not George. "Don't worry about clothes. You've got three acts to worry about; *all* of them could be better. And I know those society designers! His clothes won't work in the quick change. They may look all right at Birdie Vanderbilt's, but with a bastard pink spot hitting them, they go the wrong color and

446

your Mainbocher guy'll have the vapors."

"Not Main; he's more theatre-crazy than anyone I ever saw."

"Really? Why is that?"

"He loves the theatre."

"He *must* be crazy."

Casting went on in Max's office on top of Daniel Frohman's Lyceum Theatre, which Max and George and Moss Hart had bought. Next to the office was the rehearsal room where I'd learned Nibs' pillow dance. Garson couldn't sit in with us, but every night I phoned Washington and we consulted over what was going on.

Harvey Stephens was engaged for Max.

"You're lucky to get him," said George. "In *that* part." Producer Dwight Deere Wiman's daughter, Tottie, was engaged for the ingénue who opens the play. Tall, slender, blond, with a profile for Renoir, a nose that wasn't a nose, just something that turned up. Indescribably pretty, but all the governesses Steve and Dwight had got her had never taught her how to pronounce Arkansas. In Act I, when Roy held out his orders to her and said, "Hurry up, now, honey," she slit the envelope open; his orders read, "Crocker Field, Arkansas," but *she* read it, "Crocker Field, Ar*kan*sas."

"Arkansaw," corrected George from out front.

"Oh? Give me a pencil. My part says Ar*kan*sas."

It wasn't only that. George thought she didn't have enough experience. After rehearsal one night, he went with Garson and me to the Algonquin lobby. George ordered shredded wheat, milk and a pencil and paper. "I'll send her a telegram," he said.

How nice of him to do it personally; everybody hates to fire someone. He wrote it out, then asked, "How's this? 'Dear Miss Wiman, we are sorry we feel we must replace you. We need a more experienced actress. I am sure we can use you in some other play someday. Please return your part.' Does that cover it?"

"Yes."

" 'Best wishes, Max Gordon.' "

Tottie Wiman got replaced with Beatrice Pearson. Just great, I thought. Certain to be a future star.

"What does she take me for?" George asked.

"Why?"

"She comes out front and sits with me and tells how they wanted her to star in that desert picture, but she didn't like it, so they engaged

447

Marlene. Then she says Selznick wanted her to play Bernadette in *The Song of,* but she didn't like it. Doesn't she know *I* know she's playing a *one*-act part?"

Will wonders never cease. Everything she said was true. When David Selznick came backstage one night, he said, "That Pearson kid is good. I tried to get her for Bernadette and she turned it down."

Who was it, connected with "that desert picture," told us, "You got Beatrice Pearson—we wanted her for the lead."

Rehearsals went smoothly till Jessie Busley showed me her part and asked, "Ruth, is this line meant for a laugh?"

"Yes, it's—"

"Are you directing the show?" asked George.

That snowball helped me not to make the same mistake twice.

After two weeks I asked him, "Don't you ever pass a compliment?"

"No. You're supposed to know when you're good. I tell you when you're not." He and Tyrone Guthrie worked the Spartan method: Do it; don't look for encouragement.

"Isn't it a kick how Loring Smith looks like Swope?"

George wrinkled up his face. "Yes. I wish he *acted* more like him."

It was true. He looked like Swope and didn't have his starch or style. Didn't until opening night in New Haven, where he *was* Swope. In fact, he was about the only one who got over. "It's a failure," I phoned Garson.

Later he told me, "You nearly stopped my heart."

I thought it was. So did Eddie Chodorov. "Is there anything I can do to help?" he asked George.

When George told me, he added, "Rather giving the impression there was nothing *anyone* could do."

George and I sat up late and cut the script. "We've got to get a second-act curtain." He said it as though it was something he'd read in the Bible.

What could I say? I nodded and knew he was right.

"Don't expect to get it tonight, but it would be good if we had it for Boston. Where we *must* have it is Washington, so it plays in for New York."

Two o'clock I went to bed, exhausted, sunk. George didn't say *he* thought it was a failure; he thought it needed work. Friday Garson got a four-day pass and arrived in time for the night show. Gilbert Miller was there too, and called up next morning. "You need a second-act curtain."

"Yes," said Garson.

"Why isn't your curtain Loring Smith stamping and the window flies open? That's a big laugh."

"Yes, it is," said Garson. "I don't think it's a curtain."

"Try it?" said George.

Garson was right. Nothing.

The actor playing David O. Selznick wasn't making it. He'd been part of a vaudeville team, but didn't seem to be David O.

"Is something bothering you?" asked Garson.

"Yes," he said. "I can't act sideways."

Philip Loeb could and was engaged to come to Boston. He opened with us at the Wilbur Theatre. It went better than New Haven, but still no second-act curtain. When I came off after the curtain calls, Garson and George were beaming. "We've got it," said Garson.

George did his dance step. "Tell her on the way to the station; you don't want to miss the sleeper. It'll work."

In the hire car, Garson told me the scene.

"When a playwright needs help, it's beautiful to be married to another playwright!" counsels Zarathustra.

Washington was total hysteria! Swope dropped in to every performance. "They tell me one of your characters bears a resemblance to me. I fail to see it." He took bows right and left.

Act III opened with me in my great Mainbocher graduation dress, making phone calls. "Felix? It's me—Polly. Darling, my God, the most terrific thing! Max—he *graduated!* Do you know there were three hundred and fifty-three in the class and he graduated—you're not going to believe it, but I'm telling you—he graduated *two hundred and seventy-first.* . . ."

Justice Felix Frankfurter and his wife were there the second night. They and we had supper later in our sitting room at the Statler.

"I was going to ask your permission to do the phone call, but we were afraid you'd say no. Would you have?"

"Yes, I believe I would, but all day my phone rang with people telling me how good it is."

The week was a triumph. I didn't even mind that I had the beginning of a cold. George said to stay in bed, he'd come over. "It'll be a success," he said.

"Are you sure?"

"Oh, yes. When a show goes with audiences in three towns, it goes in New York. We *finally* got them in New Haven and Boston; *here* it went from the start."

"Wonderful how it goes!"

"I wish it was reflected in the notices."

"Garson said they were good."

"We'll need better in New York."

For the New York opening, heavy snow, then rain, thunder and lightning. George phoned, "Stay home, don't come to the line rehearsal. You know your lines."

The hire car brought me down to the Music Box early. For no particular reason I sat out on the stage with Carrie, my maid. The orchestra was tuning up to run through the overture and entr'acte music. They played "To You, Beautiful Lady" for me. Outside, the rain beat down, wind rattled something up in the flies. "They'll come in *late.*"

"Maybe not," said Carrie.

She was right. The best audience anyone ever saw came in on time. Everything went the way it was meant to go. The first act played like a dream. As the curtain fell George tore through the pass-door. "Where's the goddam trumpet player?"

"Didn't it go—"

"Where is he? He's fired."

"George, it didn't *matter!*"

The trumpet player had missed one cue and didn't blow "Taps." My next line was, "All right, all right, don't rush me," as I got my negligee off and got into bed. The trumpet player didn't sound it; I acted as *if* I'd heard it and they laughed.

"I'll kill him," said George, and looked as though he would.

"George, *didn't* it go sensationally!"

He looked thoughtful, then surprised. "Yes," he said. "It really did."

Rave notices! A sellout!

"When you have success, enjoy it," said darling Ned Sheldon. His bouquet with the paper lace frill and satin ribbons had: "Dear Ruth. Your Ned."

Garson bought advance sleeper tickets for every weekend. Some of them he got to use, some of them he didn't. Hanging over us was when he'd be shipped out. Sherwood had gone to London and said that Garson was needed in the OSS there. I lived on the edge of my own Devil's Punchbowl. We knew the time was getting close. The Washington apartment was over and we were together in New York until. The until was a Saturday night. Big week at the theatre, we'd celebrated with supper out.

"Here's a message," said the Sulgrave switchboard operator.

"Call LE 5–1000."

"That's it," said Garson.

A plunge of ice.

"LE 5–1000," he told the operator.

"Be at the armory tomorrow morning at seven A.M."

"Yes, sir."

"I'll be back," he said next morning. "Maybe something'll work out." Then he was gone.

How to get through those minutes, hours, two hours.

The phone rang. "I'm coming home."

Ruth Chatterton's husband, Barry Thompson, was the officer in charge. He ordered Garson to take another ten days, then get called.

How fast can ten days go? These ten went faster.

"Call LE 5–1000."

Next morning, he went with his equipment. "I'll be back," he said and we both knew, but he said it.

I nodded.

Thank you, God, for it being a matinee day. A matinee day, no matter what happens, you pay attention. I knew he couldn't tell me where he was or where he'd be. Pretty certain to be London; Sherwood thought he'd be most use there. But had he gone? Would he fly? Was he still in camp here? Had he left?

Toward evening next day, the phone rang. "I don't care if you're resting before the show; I don't care." It was Madeline. "Sherwood got word to me through the diplomatic pouch. 'Letters thirteen and fourteen arrived in good condition.' "

Garson was carrying letters 13 and 14 to Sherwood.

It was Sherwood's way of putting me out of misery. He couldn't send word Garson had got there. Not even through the diplomatic pouch. He *could* say letters 13 and 14 arrived and to me that would mean Garson did! It would be two weeks before the army censor would let Garson's

451

letters come through to me. Now I knew he was there in good condition. Good I *didn't* know I wouldn't see him for a year and four months.

Nothing makes that easy, but when it happens go to work.

"Write the play from your *Atlantic Monthly* pieces and your diary," Garson had urged, and helped me plot it out, scene for scene. He knew I was going to be alone a long time. "Write a scene; never mind how you get into it, just write it and find out how to hook it in later. If you worry about the feather-stitching, you'll never get on with the play. Scenery changes, costume changes—don't think how they're going to happen, just write it; get practical later."

Edith Wharton had given me the idea that I could write, Garson gave me the rules. Someone had given the rules to Edith Wharton and out of them had emerged *Ethan Frome*. When she left her own country to go to live in France, her French instructor said it would help with the language if she wrote one of her stories in French. The one she chose, *Ethan Frome*, had its first version in French. Years later, Thornton sent it to me, printed in the *Yale Review*.

# Chapter

## 18

The Sunday after Garson left, I went out to Central Park with a pad of ruled paper.

MISS JONES

Act I

The dining room of 14 Elmwood Avenue, Wollaston, Massachusetts. Our golden oak dining room table is—

Ever take a trip to the past?

"I'm going to drive out to Wollaston to see the house I was born in," I told Dr. Gundersen, thirty years later. When Dr. Gundersen says you don't need to change your glasses, that is word direct from the fount.

"I wish I might go with you," he said. A charming man.

Down Harrison Avenue blew the east wind coming off Boston harbor. It started to sprinkle. The Carey Cadillac pulled out of its space in front of the Doctors' Building at 720 Harrison Avenue, Boston, Mass.

"We'll drive out Route Three; let's turn off at East Milton. Do you know where I mean?"

"Oh, yes indeed. It's where I live. *Have* lived over forty years."

Sometimes a trip starts right. "Is the Babcock mansion still on Adams Street?"

"May be. Would you like to drive there?"

"Yes, please." The Babcock girls were Mama's first friends when Mama and her three sisters came up North from Bainbridge, Georgia, after their parents had died in the yellow fever epidemic. They went to live with their Aunt Molly Dewing in East Milton.

"It's not *there?*" asked the driver, slowing down.

"No."

He speeded up. "When they widened Route Three, I guess they took care of the Babcock place."

Funny way to put it? Route 3 had cut across the orchard where the apple trees and cherry trees had been. Bulldozers "took care of" the spirea and mock orange, "took care of" the old grape vines, the Bartlett and Seckel pear trees, their stumps pulled up so Fords and Dodges and Chevies could rush along. Gasoline smells "took care of" the autumn smells, the spring violets' delicate perfume, the summer peonies, Miss Clara's English pansies. The bees and crickets and grasshoppers had had to move elsewhere.

"We'll head over to Wollaston, but first I want to pass my aunt's house further along Adams."

"They narrowed Adams Street to make way for Route Three."

"We'll find the house." It had been yellow, now it's no color and behind it no garden in the place where Aunt Ela grew June peas that people remembered.

We turned off Adams onto Granite Place, past Mrs. Shapleigh's, where Papa's room was after he'd closed up 14 Elmwood.

Round the corner was the house that had been Mrs. Gould's Nursing Home.

*Xmas 1915*

Dearest darling,

Your letter of Wednesday came last night and made me so happy I couldn't sleep. I am very proud of you! You deserve it all you have been so conscientious. We talked of you a lot today and read your letter several times. You better take a cascaret pill. I had about 50 cards yesterday but your letter meant more than them and all the presents. I am thinking of you in *Peter Pan* tonight.

Love,
Mama

It was my second week of being an actress! Second week to go in the stage door of the Empire Theatre! To go past the doorman and up to a dressing room where my makeup was spread out on the shelf! And pretty soon another payday. And in my box another letter from Papa.

*December 29, 1915*
*East Milton*

Dear Ruth,

   Mama is not well. I have been here all day. Do you think you could come over for Sunday next? I haven't money enough to send your RR fare, but come if you can. I could send the money tomorrow night, if I go to the factory tomorrow.

Love,
Your father

Could I come over Sunday? Take the train to Boston for the *day?* I'd have to be back Monday for the performance; what could Papa mean?

   A knock on the door. The new elevator boy handed a telegram to me.

MAMA HAD ANOTHER SHOCK SHE IS UNCONSCIOUS AND PROBABLY WILL RE-
MAIN SO SHE IS NOT SUFFERING COME IF YOU CAN THERE IS NOTHING YOU CAN
DO

FATHER

At The Three Arts Club I said I was going to see my mother; I'd be back on Monday. At the theatre I told no one. Why? I couldn't. My suitcase was in the checkroom at Grand Central. I had a lower berth on the midnight to Boston. In my green broadcloth suit Mama had made for me to go to New York in, I came back.

   In Boston only some redcaps were on the South Station platform. Was Papa in the waiting room? No one sitting there; what track was the East Milton train on?

   At East Milton the snow had been shoveled off the station platform, the snowplow had gone through the street. No one in sight; had Papa missed my telegram? Mrs. Gould's was about three blocks. I pushed the bell; everything would be all right. The door opened a little. Mrs. Gould looked out. Her face said it.

   We stood there. She just shook her head and we stood there. Then I started to go.

   "My poor child," she said.

   I still couldn't say anything.

"Mr. Jones went to meet the sleeper."

She watched me down the path.

At the station, Aunt Ela came hurrying through the cold. "Your father was waiting at the South Station, but you missed each other. Take the trolley car to Aunt Ada's. He'll come back to Quincy on the next train."

The trolley rattled past the quarries where Papa and I went for our Sunday walk. *Was* I yellow?

"Hang your feet over, Ruth."

"I don't want to."

"Ruth, you got a yellow streak."

We rattled past Florence Crowell's father's grocery store at Quincy Adams, into Quincy Square, and Papa was waiting. Missing me seemed like one blow too many. I couldn't make him see it didn't matter.

He took my suitcase and we walked up Hancock Street to Whitney Road. "The service is at Aunt Ada's this afternoon. We know you have to take the train back. Mama went just as the firehouse whistle was blowing New Year's. I had my arm around her and she just rested there. She didn't know." He had to stop. "She didn't want to be an invalid. Your Christmas present came after." We started to walk. "She never was conscious after."

I'd said I'd get her things and I hadn't.

"Dr. Adams said she didn't know."

"I never did anything for her."

"You made her proud."

"I could have done things."

"You turned out all right."


At Aunt Ada's, the parlor doors were closed. In there was Mama's coffin. Bunches of flowers were around it. On her dark blue dress was the Bonwit Teller hand-embroidered net collar.

I kissed her forehead. The first time I'd ever kissed her and no response. Her life had been to respond; my response was to go. I could have kept 14 Elmwood open for her and now none of us had a home. Mama was taking leave of us from her sister's house.

Aunt Ada's front door opened and shut, people took their places on Mr. Fay's chairs. Mr. Fay's man stacked the umbrellas on the piazza. People kept their rubbers on.

"A lot have colds," Mr. Fay warned. "It's risky weather to be out." He'd placed more chairs than were needed.

The door stopped opening. Mr. Horst started the service.

456

Papa and I and Aunt Ada and Uncle Emery sat on the landing at the head of the stairs in the upper hall. Last night *Peter Pan* at the Empire, this afternoon Mama's funeral at Aunt Ada's.

It was over. Papa and I went down the back stairs and out the kitchen door. Mike McGrath's taxi stood in front of Dr. Hunting's backyard, separated from Aunt Ada's by a hedge.

We got in the taxi and waited. What were we waiting for? I looked back. Mike was helping Mr. Fay and his two men bring the coffin down the front steps. The rain was coming hard and Mr. Fay's men had their hats off. Why think of that?

Papa carried my suitcase. We walked from the track where the Quincy train had come in to the track where the New York train would leave.

"Anytime you had enough of it, I can look after you."

"Thank you, Papa."

"I guess that idea doesn't appeal. Anyway, keep it in the back of your head. How much longer can you be in *Peter Pan?*"

"Two more weeks, but after that they want me for *The Little Minister.*" A lie.

"Oh, you didn't say about that."

I didn't say about that because no one had such an idea but me. How could I make it happen? There was no part for me, but I *had* to be part of it. How could I get in?

I'd lost someone who'd always helped me do what I wanted to. If I needed help I got it and was forgiven for my selfishness. Even encouraged to be selfish if I wanted something.

"Don't be helpless, Ruth."

We turned onto Beale Street to Wollaston. Small houses close together where fields were, but I see the fields, the scraggly woods and rocks where Mama and I hurried home through snow or strolled in summer and slapped mosquitoes.

People have built their houses side by side along Beale Street, but on the left I saw Mr. Luard's small greenhouse with nothing closer than distant Pine Street. Kind, English Mr. Luard had come out of his flower shop to help me when the car hit Jill and she came limping toward me, a gentle, stricken look, front leg hanging loose. Mr. Luard, a short man, but strong, took Jill in his arms, carried her into the greenhouse, bound her leg as best he could, then locked up his shop and carried our big gentle Llewellyn setter the mile between where the car hit and 14 Elmwood.

When Papa came home he looked at mute, suffering Jill. "We'll get the veterinary."

Mama spread a sheet on the dining room table, Papa turned on all three bulbs in the chandelier. I'd never seen all three lit at once. He shoved the reading table with the two-burner Welsbach lamp closer, took off his coat and helped the veterinarian set Jill's broken front leg. It cost five dollars.

Big and slender, long silk hair flecked with black and brown, graceful, loving and so sensitive that she never recovered. The broken leg mended, but she always limped. The vet said, "A highly bred carries the memory."

At Harkness Pavilion, Garson had asked Cole Porter how he felt.

"It hurts so."

"Where, Cole?"

"My leg that's been cut off." A highly bred, he carried the memory.


At the corner of Winthrop is the new Congregational church. Why a new? Doesn't a Congregational church wear well? The house I was born in has. I've never been in it since we moved out before my fifth birthday party.

When we lived at 41 Winthrop it was buff-colored with weathered shingles; its front porch we shared with the Brighams. Now our side of the house is made into apartments. On the ground floor front, where our parlor was, is an apartment. Maybe look in the window? Kids going home from school noticed me. I walked out on the lawn to where our kitchen had been when Swedish Sandra cooked for us. The lawn sloped down to where our garden had been. Do other people come back to 41 and remember?

The kids had passed by. Should I look in the parlor window? See where Mr. and Mrs. Cartwright sat down with Mama and Papa to discuss the Cartwright boy. Did it have something to do with Clare? It was something and it got straightened out. They weren't friends of ours, just people to "bow to."

October 1, 1901, Mama and Papa and Clare and I had come out this door for the last time. I carried our big black cat, Cudah, around the corner past the Whitmarsh house to our new home, 41 Marion Street. Mr. N. G. Nickerson had raised our rent at 41 Winthrop Avenue. Papa said the N. G. stood for "No Good." Sandra wasn't coming with us; Mama would do the work. Mr. Sparrow and his boy had moved our furniture over.

School had begun the day after Labor Day, but I couldn't begin till I turned five.

"Couldn't you make an exception?" Papa had asked. "In October she'll be five and she's bright."

Wollaston Grammar School didn't make exceptions.

"Dammit, she's in her fifth *year.*"

Do you think that swayed them?

"Deprive a child of a year's learning because of a few weeks?"

Mama enrolled me at Mrs. Farrington's Kindergarten, conducted in her parlor and dining room down on Arlington Street. Carrying our lunch boxes, Louise Emery and I were trusted to walk there alone.

"Look both ways when you cross Beale Street," warned Mama. "You don't want to get run over by a wagon. Down Farrington Street, stay on the sidewalk, and cross over at Brook. Look *both* ways for the trolley car."

The trolley car from Quincy came along every hour and was in no hurry. On Beale Street, before it went down Farrington, it stopped on a siding. If the trolley from Neponset wasn't waiting, the trolley from Quincy waited. No hurry. And when it started again, who could it surprise with that noise?

"You and Louise hold hands every time you cross the street and pay attention to what you're doing. Did you tinkle?"

We lived on Marion Street for two years and I mostly remember trouble. School didn't want me, my birthday collided with the operation that Dr. Gordon had performed in our kitchen to take off that cyst or the piece of gravel in my forehead. Thanksgiving I came down with the whooping cough. Papa stayed home with me; Mama and Clare set out for Thanksgiving dinner with Aunt Emma and Uncle George in Malden.

Papa warmed up something Mama had left, if you're whooping you're not hungry. He read me the sunny Jim Jingles from our packages of H.O., short for Hornby's Oats, and I liked them more than the food. When Mama and Clare got back they brought a box of good things, so maybe "trouble" is too strong for Thanksgiving but not too strong for coasting down the school slope on my sled.

Coming home from work Saturday afternoon, Papa saw me. "You'll

459

ram your head into that elm down below; that's no place to coast."

"But, Papa, nobody hits the elm."

"If *they* do, I don't have to pay Dr. Adams. You go coast somewhere else."

"But, Papa, I won't run into the tree."

"Do what I tell you."

I never ran into a tree until Ray Massey and I got on the sled in *Ethan Frome* and *aimed* for the big elm, and then we only ran into the stage-hands. Probably Papa wouldn't have let me do that, either. Being fore-man of the Mellin's Food Company made him cautious.

In Wollaston, a two-family house with an upstairs and a down was a double house. If you had a whole floor and your neighbor had a floor, that was a flat.

For our flat at Marion Street, Mr. N. G. (No Good) Nickerson raised our rent again. Our furniture took off down Winthrop, past the school slope where I didn't ram my head, past the Unitarian church on the corner of Beale Street.

"Meet me at Beale and Winthrop," I had told the driver, and now where was he? Could a limo disappear in Wollaston? I left him at Belmont Street and Beale and said, "Meet me at Beale and Winthrop." Does *everybody* make mistakes but you? *Why* hadn't I thought I'd make a mistake? In a show, there's an either-or system; if you don't show up, there's the understudy. Why didn't I make an either-or arrangement?

The big black Cadillac whizzed up. Nobody had made a mistake.

"The parking law is you can't park the foot of Winthrop and Beale," said the driver.

Not two cars passed by, but the rule is you *can't* park at Beale and Winthrop. What a location! I couldn't go to school there until I was five, couldn't coast downhill, couldn't park a chauffeur-driven Carey limo! I hope I have no worse problems.

I got in the limo. Our grammar school is no more; where I went became a park. Eight years of hopes and fears and adventure are leveled off, grass, grass, gravel, bushes, trees grown over. And across from it, no more Methodist church. On Hancock Street is still St. Chry*sos*tom's or *Chry*sostom's, a new Congregational on Lincoln, an old Unitarian, old Baptist next to Mrs. Brigham's; *what* became of Methodist?

"Please turn down Farrington Street." No need to tell the driver to look both ways; there is no more trolley. "Turn right on the next street. That will be Elmwood."

460

Marion McCloon's house was still on Farrington. Her father had been a conductor on the Boston to Providence train and she got free rides. Do *you* envy people? A free ride anytime she felt like it to Providence, Rhode Island.

Across from the McCloons', Papa and Mama and Clare and I waited Christmas morning for the trolley to take us to Neponset, then change for the one to Field's Corner, then change for the Ashmont and Milton, that let us off in Dorchester at Mather Street. Before automobiles, we saw more life.

Walk past Uncle Dan Weymouth's to where Mather became Lindhurst Street and soon we were at Uncle Clarence Knight's grand house, almost a mansion, and Papa still with us! At intervals he had threatened to turn around and go home and now all four of us climbed the handsome steps. Uncle Clarence and Aunt Judy weren't my uncle and aunt. Aunt Judy was Clare's mother's sister and Clare's mother was Papa's first wife. Uncle Dan's wife, Aunt Abby, was *Clare's* other aunt. The Weymouths would be here with daughter Fan and her husband, Bert Marshall, whose mother also came along, also the Weymouths' older son, Frank, who worked at the Mellin's Food Company and was my godfather. His wife, Grace, would be here and the Knights' son, Harry, his wife, Mabel, their little Eleanor and baby Peggy, and Papa didn't like any of them. He didn't like Charley Brigham's frock coat he was wearing, he hadn't mentioned Mama's bear tippet and muff, he *had* mentioned he didn't like Christmas. He didn't like the trolley ride to Dorchester and didn't like the ride back to Wollaston. Starting the week before, he'd threatened to go lay down on the New York, New Haven railroad tracks. We felt sure he wouldn't, but we knew he felt bad.

Christmas at Dorchester was no more a problem after Clare married Albert Webb and they spent Christmas in Bell Buckle, Tennessee. Aunt Judy mailed Mama and me skimpy presents that let us know we weren't invited.

"Papa's happy, but I'm disappointed, I *never* would have expected it." When things didn't come out right, it surprised her and she had to read *Unity* magazine to rise above it.

The big black limo looked inappropriate on Elmwood Avenue. We crossed Fayette Street. On the right had been the dump where Papa dug up the hollyhock. Is that stealing? It was growing in the dump, but if it wasn't stealing, why did we wait till after dark for Papa to come over here with his shovel? Whose hollyhock was it—was it Wollaston's or Quincy's? Have I said Wollaston is Quincy's Ward 5?

"Anybody could dump something right *on* it," said Papa. Was that in justification?

"Why, who would, Clinton?"

"The one threw it out."

How could anyone do such a thing? Its flowers were pink ruffles edged with garnet. Papa got it up, roots and all, and planted it beside our front steps. When autumn turned it brown, he cut it back. Snow covered it, rain soaked it, and in spring it put out feelers, then grew tall. By June, garnet edged its pink ruffles again. Is that why a dump appeals to me? Because it offers promise and mystery. A park's all right if it's not too well kept, but I like an overgrown dump. Once Papa and I found an arrowhead.

"That's a valuable thing," said Mama.

"Go ahead and sell it," said the nonbeliever. It stayed on our dining room mantel, got shown, but not sold until it was swept up by the West Quincy secondhand dealer. Did *he* ever sell it? Who bought Mama's Limoges plates? Who bought our furniture? Are they still using it? Who's sleeping in *my* bed?

It was too big a bed for a modern house; why did Mama and Papa buy it? Theirs was curly birch and pretty, but mine was dark oak with a high solid headboard and a solid footboard like a fence. Sometimes Katherine Follett and I sat on the footboard. No reason. Just something to do. What had Mama and Papa in mind to buy such a big bed for ten-year-old Clare? A slender little girl doesn't need a big oak bed. All the years I was sleeping in it, why hadn't I ever asked?

Maybe it had come out of storage, part of Papa's first marriage; had he and Clare's mother bought it? Had they bought that square, solid bureau with drawers to the floor except for space enough to let a dime or a ring roll under where no one or nothing could maneuver it out? Anything lost didn't show up again until it was moved to West Quincy.

We were coming near to 14. "Stop here, please," I told the driver. "Meet me corner of Brook and Arlington." No either-or plan this time, either; too many other thoughts. I got out in front of the Litchfields' barn.

The Litchfield house faced Arlington Street. Their front porch faced our parlor windows and Mama's room. Their house and ours still looked the same. It takes me a minute before I can walk up to the luckiest address of my life. Or is 41 Winthrop Avenue? Which is luckier, the place you're born or the place where you connect with yourself? I walked out of 41 Winthrop Avenue without anything in mind, the same

462

when I walked downstairs at 41 Marion Street, but when I walked down these front steps, I was on my way.

This house, full of despair, what would I do, what would I be, and one day I had the answer. I knew. Knew what I *wanted,* knew nothing would *stop* me, learned to accept trouble, learned to live with it, learned to get what I want, learned the need for confidence and built it in, learned *not* to accept facts, learned to believe. Or did I always know that?

Over here came Hazel Dawn's letter to "17 Elmwood Avenue" written on the square white envelope. Here Mrs. Rose Parssons wished the wart off my hand. If a person can wish a wart off, does that mean a person can wish *herself* off? Off on the New York train? Over here I did that. Down these steps I had to carry my pictures of actresses and put them under bushes in the Fayette Street dump across from the dump where we got our hollyhock.

"Get rid of them," said Papa. "You don't need them anymore." The secondhand man was coming here for our furniture, except the square piano, sold separately. Nothing more could be squeezed in my trunk marked "Three Arts Club, 340 West 85th Street, New York City."

"You don't need them," said Papa.

There was no room for them except in my head. I remember them all, especially the small brownish one from Billie Burke, her dashing name written dashingly with a thick stub pen.

"You were a friend of my grandmother's," said the tall, lovely looker in a red sheath dress to the floor, long pale brown hair.

"Who was your grandmother, dear?"

"Billie Burke Ziegfeld."

Oh, my! Memory of *The Mind-the-Paint Girl* at the Tremont Theatre in Boston, all the letters written—"Dear Miss Burke, I saw *The Mind-the-Paint Girl"*—then *finally* there came a picture. *Could* it be from Billie Burke? It was! Then York Harbor with Mr. and Mrs. Tarkington to lunch with Billie Burke, then when Gregory died and I came home from the funeral, there in the apartment at 36 West 59th Street was a big basket of orchids, the card signed "Billie Burke and Florenz Ziegfeld," then Beverly Hills and Billie's house on Woodburn Drive, afternoon tea and treasures, the painting by Ben Ali Haggin that used to hang in the Empire Theatre lobby, the marriage license made out to Ethelbert Burke and Florence Ziegfeld, treasures from the great days, table set for high tea and Billie answering questions; she remembered it all with love.

"Mother said you never forgot her."

In my address book a year ago I crossed out "Billie Burke Ziegfeld, Rockhaven Sanitarium 2–4 p.m., 2713 Honolulu Ave., Verdugo City (Ventura Freeway)."

How often had I gone out to see her?

"Mother said you never forgot her."

Couldn't I have gone out even *once?*

Had Pat Ziegfeld remembered it the way it ought to have been? Can memories pay off? I hope so. The Urises have made room for some when they left space in their theatre for the Hall of Fame. We all know money pays off, but aren't memories what show business is built on?

"You were a friend of my grandmother's." That was at the opening of the Uris Theatre in New York. If the Urises didn't have a Hall of Fame at the Uris Theatre, Billie Burke's name wouldn't be carved there and I'd have had one less memory.

So many letters written to her, *then* her picture came, then it had to go to the Fayette dump.

"It's a hard life, Ruth. You'll wish you were back here."

I don't, Mama. I never did.

Upstairs in that corner room, Mama prayed I'd marry a good man.

I did, Mama, but not till after you gave up your home and your life. It comes high to be an actress.

The pictures are gone, the dump is gone, but not the window where Mama sat. A white-haired lady, with a sweet face, looked out, not at me, just looked out of her window in the Elmwood Nursing Home.

I walked up the walk. The brass "14" beside the door is the same curly 14, not 17 like Hazel Dawn's letter and postcard. It's the same fluted brass doorknob.

I looked in. A pale, white-haired lady lay flat on a bed where our marble-top reading table was with Miss Turner's table cover she'd brought Mama from Liberty's in London. The pale lady turned her head. Had I disturbed her? I went down the steps I'd gone down to go to the station, now torn down, to go on the New York, New Haven and Hartford or Old Colony train, now no longer running, to meet Papa, gone, to take the Fall River train, not operating, to board the Fall River Line boat to New York, a thing of the past. What lasts? Bricks and granite and slate roofs and weathervanes go, but a believer barrels on.

"It's a hard life, Ruth," Mama had warned. Did she think it would include a caboose? Sometimes you ride the caboose or miss the show and don't get paid, but that's show business; Wollaston people don't ride cabooses. Did Thornton Wilder? In his play *The Matchmaker*, he wrote, "Mr. Vandergelder's apprentices, Cornelius and Barnaby, exclaim, 'Holy Cabooses!' " Why "Holy"? And what was the date on the calendar that Thornton wrote down "Act I, page 1"? A lucky day when he wrote:

Act I

Yonkers. Mr. Vandergelder's hay, grain and feed store.

When Thornton sat down that day and wrote "Act I, page 1," he made a lot happen. He'd written "Act I" before and that time it had been *Our Town*. This time it was *The Merchant of Yonkers*, that later he renamed *The Matchmaker*, that later had music included and some changes in the dialogue and came out as *Hello, Dolly!*, but when Thornton wrote *his* Act I, he was writing about some Yonkers folk and two New York widows, Mrs. Irene Malloy and Mrs. Dolly Gallagher Levi, and he meant for me to be Dolly.

He'd admired a Viennese farce by Nestroy called *Einen Jux will er sich machen* and in New Haven or Zurich or Stockbridge or wherever, before he'd sat down to write this one, that Nestroy farce had got him thinking. What had got Nestroy thinking seventy years earlier was an English farce which *he* must have admired, John Oxenford's *A Day Well Spent*.

When *The Matchmaker* played Berlin or London, the critics found no resemblance to the Nestroy or the Oxenford play, but that was their privilege; Nestroy and Wilder gave their predecessor credit.

Act I, page 1 and the rest made a lot of people happy. They loved it in New York. They'd loved it in Newcastle and Berlin and London. They loved it all the way across the country to San Francisco and Hollywood, where three years after Newcastle, we said goodbye at the Huntington Hartford Theatre, July 1957. People had loved it everywhere, but where they loved it the most of all was in Los Angeles. Opening night at the Huntington Hartford nobody would go home. Everybody had laughed and cried and applauded and never since the rainy opening night at Newcastle-on-Tyne had it ever gone better. The same for two weeks, then after the performance the men from the Customs Bureau waited with hatchets and knives to destroy the great Tanya Moiseiwitsch production and costumes that had come to the United States under bond.

Backstage were George Cukor and Clifton Webb, and a redhead who just stood in my dressing room. Garson said it was Shirley MacLaine,

465

who had done *Around the World in Eighty Days.* She never spoke to me, but later when we knew her she said she couldn't go home; she had to be part of it and hang around backstage.

Crash, bang, rip, tear. The furniture at Mr. Vandergelder's barber-shop, at his hay, grain and feed store, at Mrs. Irene Malloy's Hat Shop, at the Harmonia Gardens Restaurant, at Miss Van Heusen's, that had traveled all those places those three years, now had to go. Everything except memories and one straight-back chair that had opened in New-castle, closed at the Huntington Hartford, and in between had never missed one show until the closing night. Our property man brought it to my dressing room after the last matinee. Offstage it could still hear the fourth act, played at Miss Van Heusen's, but it stayed offstage and now it stays in the parlor on 49th Street, where Tony Guthrie said, "It's an amiable play," and started Thornton's Dolly Gallagher Levi on her way.

242 East 49th Street has been a useful address. So was 41 Winthrop Avenue, so was 41 Marion Street, so was 14 Elmwood Avenue, where I got my chance to be me. Is 4 my lucky number? At 340 West 85th Street I got the part in *Peter Pan.* At West 45th Street I got *Fair and Warmer,* and at 45th Street Edna Hibbard sold me her gingham dresses and I got *Seventeen.* 4 is my lucky number.

Proust says not to blame ourselves for things we do. It's not just us, it's all our people. I'm Mama and Papa and Mama's mother and father, who died in the yellow fever epidemic, I'm Papa's father, who ran off with the Polish woman, and Papa's mother, who killed herself in a Boston boardinghouse; she didn't know what else to do.

Maybe all that helped Papa know what to do even before I left home that hot August Sunday; he began the breakup. From all the people who'd gone before him had he learned when it's over, get done with it?

This breakup wouldn't be like our move from Winthrop Avenue to Marion Street, then down to Elmwood Avenue. Those were because of the rent. Breaking up 14 Elmwood meant getting out from under. Mama had walked down the front walk; on Sunday I would and next day Papa would. All of us with different feelings. I was going to be someone, Papa was going to not be tied down, Mama was going to die.

To be on top means somebody has to be the support. If it's you on top, remember the cost. See you give some back.

Everybody lent a hand and 14 Elmwood was over.

In the taffeta suit Mama made like Mrs. Castle's, with a one-way ticket in my bag, I went out this door with the curly oblong knob and Papa locked it. Last time for me, last but one for him. With my suitcase, we walked down these six steps. Don't figure the cost. You can't. Fifty years later, when a play we were in closed in New York, actress Ethel Griffies said, "The gain was great; the loss was only money."

I could have kept a home for Mama, I could have kept house for Papa; instead I went. Mama wouldn't have, Papa didn't. What highbinder do *I* take after?

I turned down Arlington Street.

At the corner of Beale, the limo driver came over the Beale Street railroad bridge, that used to be wood.

"Cinders'll set it ablaze," predicted Papa.

Mama nodded. "Wouldn't you think they'd *do* something."

"They won't."

After Mama died and the insurance money was paid, Papa moved into a room at the old Quincy House in Boston, a short walk from the Mellin's Food factory on Central Wharf. Another winter and he said goodbye to New England and tried a warmer climate.

"Go up Grand View," I told the driver. We passed the fine sweeping Corthell lawn, that became Katherine Follett's after she married Herbert Mann. One afternoon, she invited Garson and George Cukor and me there when George was going to direct the movie about how I wanted to be an actress.

"Everybody is entitled to a chance," Papa had said, and gave me mine. Thirty-eight years later, Metro-Goldwyn-Mayer thought people would like to see Spencer Tracy play my father and paid me a hundred thousand dollars for my play about Mama and Papa and me, called *Years Ago.* M-G-M called it *The Actress;* it plays a lot on TV.

"It pays to stay alive," I said to Justice Frankfurter.

He had told me an incident that had happened after a mutual friend's demise.

"It pays to stay alive," I told him, and he admired the thought and repeated it to the bench.

The limo turned left on Lincoln Avenue, past the Streeters' yellow house.

Around the corner on Lincoln Avenue was the house where Bob Stone lived before his family bought the grand house on Grand View where today there's the high-rise. Bob? Franklin? Priscilla? Gladys? Ralph? Ernestine? Where *is* everybody?

"Turn right on Newport Avenue. We're going to Quincy."

For my four high school years this had been my route. Only a deluge or a blizzard forced me onto the trolley. School tickets were half the price of the nickel fare, but I didn't squander tickets. Down our 14 Elmwood Avenue front steps at 7:30, walk along Newport to Beale Street as Katherine came rushing down Grand View from their Park Street house. In winter, slip and slide on icy snow till we hit a plank walk beside the meadow before the Brooks Adams' stable. Quincy granite and red brick, it looked like a stable in a picture book. There were other stables in Quincy, but this was old and silent and befitted people not grand in Quincy *only*—grand wherever there were people.

"Go slow," I told the driver.

Once I'd seen the gate open and a touring car come out of the driveway, old chauffeur at the wheel; in the back sat gray old Mr. Brooks Adams, beside him an old gray lady. Hats, goggles, high-collared coats covered most of them, but no one could mistake the "apart" look. Between them sat a black Scotch terrier.

I believe in God, Jesus, Life Eternal, people, luck, my voices, myself. Pan me, don't give me the part, publish everybody's book but this one, and I will *still* make it! Why? Because I *believe* I will. If you believe, then you hang on. If you believe, it means you've got imagination, you don't need stuff drawn out for you in a blueprint, you don't face facts—what can stop you? If I don't make it today, I'll come in tomorrow.

"Drive down Adams Street to City Square. We'll go round the church and come back on Hancock Street." The place you were born in is like a book that reads different with the years. What's on the left? What's on the right? What is lost? What is remembered? What changed? On the right is still Adams Academy. Granite and red bricks like the Adams' stable. The Adams family gave it to Quincy to be a school for boys. Didn't Mrs. Abigail ask President John why not educate the girls? Didn't Mrs. Louisa ask President John Quincy? Now it's the Quincy Historical Society. The week before came a letter inviting me to the tercentennial ball. Their address is: Adams Academy, 8 Adams Street, Quincy, Massachusetts 02169.

Quincy is pronounced Quinzy. I should have mentioned that earlier. In Illinois and Florida, they call theirs Quintsy, but we call ours Quincy with a sound of *z*.

At the ball I'll wear my pink satin Givenchy I wore when I got the

Oscar. Eight years ago, but a Givenchy holds up.

The traffic light turned red. We stopped at the Unitarian Church.

Gold-domed, granite columns above the granite steps, where President John Adams lies buried beside Abigail. Beside them, their son John Quincy Adams beside rich Louisa. Ever read Abigail's published letters? Ever read John's? Often he addressed her as "Portia." She wrote how she made do through the hard Quincy winter while hubby was over in Paris trying to get the king to give us help for our revolution. That was before 1776, but in 1975 I was going to wear my pink Paris dress to our tercentenary.

Autumn of 1946, on the granite steps with the columns, Mayor Ross presented me with a scroll. A loudspeaker let all the people in Quincy Square hear what he said. My play *Years Ago* had opened in Boston with Fredric March playing Papa, Florence Eldridge playing Mama, Patricia Kirkland, whose father wrote *Tobacco Road,* playing me when I lived at 14 Elmwood Avenue. To celebrate, Quincy had arranged a Ruth Gordon Day that started with Garson and me on the train from the South Station to Wollaston.

"Wollaston," announced the conductor. His white mustache rose above an embarrassed smile at Wollaston station; acting silly, they crowded around to see a Wollaston actress.

Garson and I got off, then Pat Kirkland, then Bethel Leslie, who played the part of Katherine Follett, then Jennifer Bunker, who played Anna Witham. The mayor of Quincy waited on the station platform to welcome me and Garson and Bethel and Jennifer. Florence Eldridge and Fredric March would join us later at the Neighborhood Club luncheon. The vintage cars pulled out, banners waved, neighbors waved and lots of strangers.

The program began at North Quincy, called Atlantic when Clare got the offer to teach there. She'd taught first grade upstate in Chicopee Falls, now she came back to 14 Elmwood Avenue, paid rent for the room which was to be mine, slept in the bed that her mother and Papa may have bought when they got married. Early mornings, she crossed the tracks to Hancock Street and took the trolley to Atlantic. Sundays she crossed the tracks to St. Chrysostom's.

Today, in the big hall at North Quincy High School, the pupils were restless. Garson and I sat on the platform, the principal spoke, then introduced us. I hadn't gotten the knack of speaking to an audience, a gift that has nothing to do with acting. The principal said some flattering things, then led me to stage center. Polite applause came from the students.

"Grow up," I said. "Don't stay young, get where *you're* in charge, don't hang around school or your family, grow older! And hurry, I know what I'm talking about. If there's a shortcut, take it!"

"Ruth, try not to be extreme," Mama had urged. She should have heard me today. She'd have liked all the festivities, liked lunching at the Neighborhood Club. November, and she could have worn the velvet dress that had been her third wish. She'd gotten her first two wishes, the pony and the gold watch; now I could have gotten her the velvet dress. She'd have liked to meet Delcevare King from up on Adams Street. She didn't know him, but knew he was called Delcevare because his mom and dad, Mr. and Mrs. Theophilus King, riding to Boston in their carriage, had chosen a letter from each billboard and the letters came out Delcevare. He was at the luncheon, so was Buster Johnson, now called Howard. The Marches had grand seats on the dais, and below the salt sat Pat Kirkland, who played Ruth Gordon Jones. Beside her sat Bethel and Jennifer.

Katherine Follett, who'd become Mrs. Herbert Mann, sang "Years Ago," a number specially composed for the occasion. Following Katherine was beautiful Miss Elizabeth Irene O'Neill, who told about my looks at Quincy High, described my dresses, my hair ribbons, and requested her worshipful audience to remember.

Garson said it was like a glimpse of school. Rapt attention from her pupils, now become businessmen, dentists, wives, professors, mothers, secretaries, teachers. Everybody in the "worst class" responded the way they were told to; beautiful Miss O'Neill was in charge.

Miss Clara Thompson spoke, Miss Sally Dawes gave a talk, Mr. Ernest Collins, our principal, told what he felt. Freddie March spoke, Florence said her say, Garson rose to his feet, I said a moved thanks and the cortege moved off past all the banners and bunting to Quincy Square. Ruth Gordon Day climaxed on the steps of the Unitarian Church. Traffic had been rerouted to go around the back, none to go between the gold-domed granite church and City Hall across the street beside the old burial ground. Friends and strangers and cousins filled the streets.

Mayor Ross made his address from the broad granite steps under which the Adamses were buried. From a scroll he read:

*In tribute*
*To her record of achievement in*
*The Theatre,*
*The wide range of her creative*
*imagination and understanding,*
*her unfailing loyalty to the persons*
*and places of her girlhood*

*This*
*testimony of pride*
*is presented to*

## RUTH GORDON

*Actress, Playwright, Daughter*
*of Quincy*

*with the affectionate regard of*
*her native community*

CHARLES A. ROSS
MAYOR OF QUINCY

TUESDAY NOVEMBER 10, 1946

Mayor Ross handed me the scroll, a thing of beauty, delicate colored painting, beautiful letters.

Could Mama hear the applause? Could Papa?

"Mr. Mayor, friends: Across the street in that building there's a paper that says on October 30, 1896, I was born. Down Hancock Street is the house where Dr. John Alexander Gordon lived; he brought me into the world. For him I was given my middle name. I was christened Ruth Gordon Jones. Further down Hancock Street is Quincy High School, where I was given my education. Behind me is the Thomas Crane Public Library, where bound copies of *Theatre* magazine and the plays of Ibsen and Yeats and Synge and Shaw and Oscar Wilde inspired me.

"Down Coddington Street is Mount Wollaston Cemetery, where my mother lies buried. I'm surrounded by memories of love and kindness and help. Here I was born and raised, was given the opportunity to become what I wanted to become. May it always be the same. When I left Quincy, I had your good wishes, your good will. Today I came back

471

and they're still with me. Thank you, Mr. Mayor and Quincy friends. May I be worthy."

"Are you hungry?" I asked the Carey driver.

"No."

"Can you turn left, around the church, and go back up Hancock Street?"

"I think they'll let me."

Past city hall, no bunting today, but inside there's still:

Certificate of Birth.      Quincy, Commonwealth of Massachusetts
NAME: Ruth Gordon Jones
DATE OF BIRTH: October 30, 1896
SEX: Female
ADDRESS: 41 Winthrop Avenue
FATHER'S NAME: Clinton Jones
MOTHER'S NAME: Annie Zeighler Jones
REGISTERED January 31, 1899

James Carter, Clerk

Why spell Mama's name like that? Why wait till the last day in the last January in the century to write me in? Why let two years and three months go by before Mama and Papa got my birth certificate?

"Turn left on Coddington Street and keep going. I'm looking for Mount Wollaston Cemetery."

We drove through the gate to the cemetery. The snow had lasted; old snow was over everything. A man in work clothes came out of the snug office, said he'd show me where the plot was.

"Get in." The driver opened the limo door. "Can I pass that car?" A sand-colored sedan had been parked in front of the office.

"Back up. Y' might go in the snow and be in trouble."

In a graveyard they call that *trouble?*

We backed.

"Now go right." The man looked back at me. "Would y' know it when y' see it?"

"I think I would." I said "I think" because what actually *is* maybe isn't the same as what's in one's mind. In my mind I saw a tree, a large stone for the Crane family, small stone for Uncle Emery's father, small stone for his mother, whom I called Gramma Crane because my cousins Donald and Richard did, a stone for Uncle Emery, for Aunt Ada, for Aunt Carrie Crane, for Katheryn, my cousin who'd died when she was little.

Dr. Hunting had worked to save her, but it was meningitis and 1905. After Katheryn's stone came Mama's. Clare's mother was at Cedar Grove Cemetery, Dorchester. What had been Papa's thoughts about his final rest? A loner, who didn't believe in the hereafter, but if wrong, why spend it in Quincy?

"Up this hill," directed the man. "Recognize anything?"

In summer, it's easy to tell your own snowball bush, your lilac looks like yours, but in winter, snowy rhododendrons look like anybody's.

"Go right, then left."

The big black Carey limo looked like a car looking for a funeral.

"Stop now." He got out in the old snow. The driver got out and walked after him. Then they stopped and studied things. The man paced back and forth. "It ought to be *here,*" he called out. "It's seven fifty-two and where *I'm* at is seven fifty-five." He paced and looked. "Has it got a plank marker?"

From the limo, I shouted, "I don't know."

The Carey driver hired for the day, the man who worked at Mount Wollaston, looked for "Crane."

"Here!" The guide pointed to a big stone.

I was surprised at how grand it was.

"Benjamin Crane," he shouted.

"No," I shouted back.

"Not Benjamin?" Now *he* was surprised.

"No. Emery."

He read another stone. "Emily?"

"Emery."

He didn't know *what* to say.

"Emery, Ada, Carrie, Katheryn, and a small one would say Annie Jones."

"Here it *is!* Wife of Dr. Jones?"

"No. Annie Ziegler Jones."

He didn't know *what* to do.

Why should he and the limo driver stand around in the old snow? "I'll come back," I said. "You get in the car, it's cold. I'll come back in the spring."

"Well, it's *here.* It's just a question of looking. Here is seven fifty-*five.* Seven fifty-*two* is in here *somewhere.* This plot is Speare."

"They're cousins."

"Well, this is their plot and they're seven fifty-*five.*"

"Get in."

473

"You come back and ask for *me*—John."

"I will. Get in."

"I can walk it."

"Why should you?" I turned up the heat.

"Just drop me off, the front of the hill."

We did.

"To get back to the Square, you take Sea Street." He waved to us.

"Thanks for your help."

"You come back when it's spring and we'll find it now we know where it *is.*"

Greenleaf Street finishes at Hancock by the Woodward School.

"Turn left. We're coming to the high school. I'm going to get out here."

"I can't park on Hancock."

"Drive in," I ordered. Did I foresee that I would come back in a black shiny Cadillac limo and say, "Drive in"? Did I foresee a chauffeur in uniform helping me out of the limo? I *did* foresee I'd astonish everybody, but now I was astonishing *myself.*

Straight up the stairs to the second floor to room 24, Miss O'Neill's room. Her subject had been Latin, but she taught us ambition and how to achieve it. She taught us how to study, how to learn. The most important thing I've ever been taught, maybe the most important to teach. Once I asked Thornton if goodness could be taught. He said, "Plato said, 'Of all subjects, goodness is the hardest to pass on, but I do not despair of succeeding.'"

The door to room 24 was open, a class was going on. Twelve-year-olds lolled at their desks. Our high school had become junior high. The teacher, in his shirtsleeves, saw me looking in. "Can I help you?" he asked.

"I used to go to school here. This room means a lot. I studied Latin in here."

Is that a conversation stopper? He listened, went back in and closed the door.

To be an actress there's a lot to learn, and up front, ahead of other items, put "Learn to cope." Had I learned? Not in the room where I studied algebra or mathematics. Up at those blackboards Miss Clara E. G. Thompson made my life miserable. She made fun of me, ridiculed me before the whole class. Black despair tried to sink me, but live

474

through stuff and it will probably come out right. Maybe it takes a while. Maybe twelve years? Stick it out—it can happen. In Boston, at the Plymouth Theatre, the stage doorman handed Margaret Bellinger a box of pretty flowers. The card said:

We are in the audience. May we come back to see you after the performance?

> Three old maids,
> Clara Thompson
> Victoria Zeller
> Grace Howe

Stick it out till the box of flowers. Hang on and resentment fades. For three years I'd been Miss Thompson's target; Miss Zeller didn't take aim till I got to The Three Arts Club: "Your butler and Scotch terrier must miss you and who will tell us about your mother's divorce?" she wrote (tall tales I'd told to make an impression until I got hold of something to really impress), and now was sending me flowers. Can you forgive and forget? Forgive, yes; forget, no. Colette wrote: "Do you notice your amethyst is the thing that always winds up in your jewel box? Your diamond pin goes, your pearls aren't there, your sapphire gone, but that amethyst is *there.*" And along with that amethyst sticking with you is what you can't forget but *can* forgive.


The trip was over. Outside in the driveway the limo was surrounded. Who was going to get in? The driver stood beside it, looking off at nothing. He'd had to do it for years. I walked toward the car, the way I'd imagined I would. I'd come back and amaze the place. Everybody would look at me the way I'd looked at Marguerite Clark and Julia Sanderson and Doris Olssen and Hazel Dawn.

"Hello," I said.

A hi, a hello, grunts.

"I used to go to school here."

"When?" someone asked with no interest.

"The class of 1914." 1914 made everyone laugh. "Our class gave that stone post."

A murmur, then a girl said, "She's in *movies!* Weren't you in *Rosemary's Baby?*"

"Yes."

"You *were!*" Now it was the way I'd thought it would be.

"Will you write your name?" A girl shoved a notebook at me. "Here."

I wrote.

"What's her name?" whispered someone, then read off the notebook, "Ruth Gordon?"

Pieces of paper were thrust forward. "Will you write on mine?" We were standing beside the door that Katherine and I had walked out of on our way to the Thomas Crane Library.

"Are you in a movie now?"

"Did you see *Harold and Maude?*"

Nobody had.

*"Where's Poppa?"*

Nobody.

"All right," I said to the driver. "Goodbye." I got in.

"Goodbye."

The driver closed the door, climbed in and closed his door, started the motor. I smiled and waved. "Goodbye," I called through the open window the way Billie Burke did in the picture in *Theatre* magazine.

"Who is she?" asked a boy.

"An actress."

That was what I dreamed people would say.

"She's not pretty enough for an actress."

Jesus wept. Had something doused *His* spirits? Then I guess He got over it. You learn that on the trip.

Where does the trip start? With all those people Proust says are part of us? Did Papa pass his temper on to me? Could he help it if his father had passed it on to him? Or is it all my *own* bad temper and did the trip start with Dr. Gordon's slap? With the voices at the Colonial Theatre? With Hazel Dawn's letter? With "Everybody's got a right to a chance"? With "You show no promise. Don't come back"? With "Be on the stage of the Empire Theatre at eleven Sunday morning"? With "You're the worst dancer, but you've got the part"? With 340 West 85th Street at seven o'clock the night I walked to the 86th Street and Broadway subway station? Was it cold on December 21st? At Times Square get out and go up the stairs to the 40th Street kiosk, walk east on 40th to the Empire stage door.

"The key's up," said George. Someone was already in.

Past Miss Adams' dressing room, past R. Peyton Carter's at the end of the hall, up the long flight of black iron stairs. On the door of dressing room 3 the card said:

Angela Ogden
Elise Clarens
Margaret Gordon
Katherine Keppel
Margaret Field
Ruth Gordon

A long shelf, a long mirror. At my place was the Berner's makeup box from school, kitchen towels from Wollaston. "Hello," I said, and hung up my navy blue nubbly high school coat, middy blouse that Papa had bought me at Lombard's, ships' outfitter, blue serge skirt Mama had made; put on Mrs. Wetmore's lavender flowered silk kimono. On a hook was my Nibs costume that wardrobe mistress Sophie Eggert had brought in.

"Half hour," called Barney Silver. He had on his Saint Bernard suit, ready to play Nana. For now, the head was off.

Act I is the Darlings' nursery. In Act I, only Mr. and Mrs. Darling, their children, Wendy, John and Michael, and Nana appear. Our Lost Boys scene wasn't till Act II. No hurry, but tonight everybody did. Opening night puts on pressure like steam pipes turned up.

"Fifteen minutes," called Barney, still with his Saint Bernard dog's head off.

"Thank you," said Angela, nearest the door.

My American Academy makeup was going on, but Mr. Jehlinger wouldn't scream, "You liar, you cheat." This rouge wasn't smoothed on for *Joy* or *Strife* or that colorless *Manoeuvres of Jane*, this eyelash black wasn't for a job as extra in *The Butterfly on the Wheel* in a Fort Lee movie studio, this flick of the rabbit's foot was to take the edge off the rouge for the opening night of *Peter Pan* at Charles Frohman's Empire Theatre in New York City.

"Act One. Places, please," called Barney. Now his head was on.

"Thank you," said Angela.

Through the heavy iron door we heard Barney call, "Act One. Places, please," down the hall.

"Thank you." That was Mary Forbes' voice. She played Mrs. Darling and came onstage soon after the curtain went up. She would kiss her children good night, turn the lamps down, except for the night light, then she and Mr. Darling would go out for the evening. Then there'd be a tinkle of bells, a whir of wind would blow the window curtains, and Peter Pan would fly in the nursery window, fly to the mantelpiece and light on it, steadying himself holding on to the teddy bear hanging on the wall above the mantelpiece at just the right height for Miss Maude Adams to hold on to for a moment.

Sophie Eggert said it was the same teddy bear that had been in the original production that Miss Turner had taken me to see when it played Boston. Sophie said Miss Adams was superstitious about it. Hughie Reilly, our stage carpenter, trusted no one to put it away but himself. He locked it up after each show.

I know just how he felt. My pink teddy bear has slept in the same room with me since 1955. No one packs that bear but me, you bet! Under the same roof with me every night for twenty years except the week he went to Denihan, the costly cleaner, and came back with only his ribbon pink; most of his fur had rubbed off and what was left had gone "dirty flesh." All the way from Givan's, Brook Street, London W.1, window to our bedroom on Central Park South, with twenty rugged travel years in between.

"Look," I'd said to Garson. A small pink bear sat on a pile of table linen in the side window of Givan's Linen Store, alas no longer with us, though their pink bear is.

"I'll buy it for you."

We went in.

"I'll have the pink bear in the window," said Garson.

"Very good, sir. That will be thirty shillings."

The pink bear came back to Claridge's, one block from his Givan window. In our bedroom on the third floor looking onto the Mews, Pinkie sat in the pale green damask armchair. His mouth, embroidered in black, smiles at times, at times it tightens into worry. He has a short upper lip and a black embroidered nose, two yellow glass eyes that might strike you as small. Or is that because they're set wide apart? His ears are small, around his neck was a pink silk ribbon that tied in a bow to the side. After his trouble at Denihan's, he returned minus his London silk with wide pink velvet tied into a bow, really too much for a small face. Small, but in proportion; he's ten inches.

When Pinkie moved over to Claridge's, we were winding up our London stay. From October 1953 to July of 1954 we were planning how to get *The Merchant of Yonkers* on. By the time we went into rehearsal at Binkie Beaumont's Globe Theatre, Shaftesbury Avenue, Thornton had retitled it *The Matchmaker*. It ran from that July till July of 1955, when we left the Haymarket Theatre for a week at Golders Green and closed after a week at Streatham, pronounced Stret'm. It was somewhere near the finish that Pinkie moved into our three rooms on the Mews side that Moss Hart asked for when he booked his suite for the weeks he'd be staging *My Fair Lady* at Drury Lane. Moss wrote Mr. Van Thyne to please reserve for him the suite the Kanins had that Maugham thought the furniture was their own that they'd brought over from New York.

In the light green brocade chair near the French window Pinkie was "out of harm's way," as Mama described a place safe enough even for me. The bedroom was still reasonably clear, but our hall and back bedroom where Garson worked and the parlor were lined with trunks brought up from the basement. Room service had to maneuver the table around suitcases and black tin lockers from Paris' Galeries Lafayette, bought to move our things after a year at the Hôtel Raphaël, Avenue Kléber, when it came time to move to London. Some things were checked, "Paris to London," some were loaded into our Ford station wagon we'd brought over from New York the September before. Now, September a year later, Garson, me beside him, drove off, early morning, into the Avenue Kléber, around the Étoile and onto whatever route the Auto Club had made out a "triptych" for us to get to Calais to make the ferry we were booked on. Chantilly off to the right, where Diana Cooper has her beautiful house. Around Beauvais and 28 kilometers on to Breteuil in the Somme and 42 kilometers that side of Abbeville. Cross the Somme and head for Montreuil 37 kilometers away from Boulogne where the channel boat from Folkestone had landed Gregory and me that spring afternoon of 1922.

Boulogne-sur-Mer with the port ahead of us, concrete blocks still left from the invasion. Pass the Alfa Romeo–General Motors place, pass the Renault, leave the coast on a straight line for Calais 34 kilometers away. Glimpse of the channel again. Is it rough? The paper never says it's rough. What is the word they say? Past the Chrysler–Simca place, follow the signs that say CAR FERRY GARE DE TRANSIT.

Into town off Route 1, onto Boulevard Léon Gambetta, left turn on Boulevard Jacquard, right at Place d'Armée, pass Place de Suède over Pont Mobile to the breezy car ferry, our papers *almost* okay; does anyone *ever* have the blue one? Yellow, pink, white, green, all in order, but pssst! No blue one. Cook's man helps, someone thinks of something, a head nods and *"Passez, Monsieur."* Garson drove our station wagon with the red trim onto the Calais à Douvres ferry and when he came off he'd have to drive on the left side of the road. Left side for two years until after the week at Streatham, a suitable place to close, the theatre an uncomfortable building. Golders Green is big, but nice and you feel the audi-

479

ence. Streatham, it's like you were off in outfield and the audience was in the next stadium.

Goodbye to Eileen Herlie, goodbye to Sam Levene, goodbye to Alec McCowen, goodbye to Rosamund Greenwood, Esmé Church, Prunella Scales, Peter Bayliss, Arthur Hill, Paddy MacAlinney and wife Philomela, goodbye to some forever, others would join up in September to appear in the New York company. David Merrick and the Theatre Guild would produce it, goodbye to Binkie, who promised to come over to see it.

The station wagon had got driven to the United States Line docks at Southampton, also eight Vuitton trunks, four Galeries Lafayette black lockers, six navy blue lockers from Harrods, five white leather suitcases from Aux Trois Quartiers department store, corner of Rue Royale and Boulevard de la Madeleine. Twenty-three pieces were checked through, some marked "Hold," some marked "Cabin, S.S. *United States,* Main Deck, Cabin #. . ." something or other. I'm glad I've forgotten; it cost two thousand dollars. "Waste not, want not." Do you believe that? I've wasted and I've wanted and I've not wasted and not wanted in about the same proportion.

"You go your way and I'll go mine," Dolly Levi tells Mr. Vandergelder in Thornton's *The Matchmaker,* and that's what happened to our luggage. We checked twenty-three pieces to the ship. With us for our visit to Paris before we took the *United States* home were eighteen pieces we'd need for our ten days at the Raphaël. And in the Vuitton suitcase designated on my luggage list as HR5, Pinkie made his first trip, wrapped in Lubin's pink flannel and placed between Lubin flannel-wrapped nightgowns.

At the Raphaël he sat on the walnut and yellow-silk-paneled armchair, back to the window giving onto the Hôtel La Pérouse, corner of Rue La Pérouse, the street where Proust says Odette had her boring little house.

London to Paris Pinkie's first, then the two-thousand-dollar suite on the *United States,* where some days his chair rocked or pitched quite a lot and we stayed in bed and for dinner ate celery and baked potato.

In New York he sat in the French chair from Faraway Meadows, gray-painted wood with faded gray and pink silk upholstery. Pinkie, a spotless pink, made the chair look even grayer. His back was to the Turtle Bay garden. He sat there when the robbers came that Saturday night, yellow eyes staring. Those yellow eyes stared at the Barclay Hotel for *The Matchmaker*'s disastrous reopening at Philadelphia's Locust Street Theatre.

"I don't see the show I bought in London," said David Merrick in a melancholy voice like Poe's raven must have used to quoth.

After two weeks we moved to Boston and Pinkie, in a green silk striped armchair in room 1505 at the Ritz, turned his back on the Public Garden.

Early the morr.ing of our opening, the phone rang. It was New York calling; Victor Samrock told us Bob Sherwood had died.

That night at the Colonial, Sam Behrman was at the opening. Sam and Garson and I held our own memorial service for Bob backstage at the Colonial Theatre, where so many of his wonderful plays had played.

This morning he died.

Poor everybody.


In Boston, *The Matchmaker* found its audience again. Philadelphia's disastrous engagement was wiped out. Audiences crowded into the beautiful Colonial, their enthusiasm like London. One more week, then New York. Would New York be like Boston? Would it be like Philadelphia? Would my voice get right? It had gotten hoarse the morning Vic Samrock had phoned, "Bob died this morning."

We'd known it was serious, yet maybe it wasn't. Maybe we knew, but we hoped.

Sherwood had been my friend since 1924. A friend to me and Gregory, friend to me and Garson. "I've got to get out and do something," I said.

"But you have to rest your voice."

"I have to get out. Let's go over to the Ned Sheldon room and see my letters to Woollcott. My God, how do I know what they're about? I may've said *awful* things about everybody. How did I know they'd end up at Harvard?"

"Houghton Hall. Professor van Lenneps is the curator who wrote you. I'll get the car. You *sure* you know what you're doing?"

"I've got to get out of here."

At Houghton Hall, Garson told the driver, "We'll probably be an hour."

"Ayuh."

A library is quiet. What I needed. Down the hall was the Edward Sheldon room, given by his mother for Ned's things. Why were *Wooll-*

*cott's* letters there? There are more questions than answers, but why weren't they at Hamilton with his other things? Professor van Lenneps pointed to a shelf. "Letters from Ruth Gordon," was printed on the back of the big leather box.

What an odd feeling if you're born in Quincy to have your letters go to Harvard.

"Let me know if there's anything you want. Here's a pad and pencil, in case."

"Oh, no, we won't stay long this time."

"How's the play going? Everyone likes it."

"Oh, yes."

The professor was off.

Garson and I sat down at a long table. I lifted the lid off the box. On top was a crumpled, smoothed-out letter.

THE THREE ARTS CLUB
340 West 85th Street
New York

*December 22, 1915*

Dear Mr. Woollcott—

I burst into tears and closed the box. "Let's get out of here."

"Don't you want to just—"

"Let's get out."

"But—"

"I've got to get out."

"That's all for this time," Garson told the attendant. "We'll be back."

The car crossed the Charles River bridge. I gave Garson's hand a squeeze, leaned over and kissed him. "That's Massachusetts Tech over there." I pointed. "The play's going to be a big hit in New York. Bob thought so too."

"Yes, he did."

"Everything's going to be all right."

"Good. That's the way I like it."

"Me too."

"How's your voice?"

"Okay. We've had some great friends. Sherwood and I and Charlie MacArthur and Ray Massey were all the same age. I'm sure to be good in the play; I've got a lot of people believing in me."

482

"Let people worry about making good with you, not vice versa."

"Maybe *The New York Times* critic'll write *me* a letter instead of me writing him."

Pinkie took his gray chair in Turtle Bay for the winter and summer too, except when Garson and I'd throw a few things into a few bags and Chapman would get lost driving us and Pinkie in his Lubin pink flannel for a night at Westhampton or Canoe Place Inn, or Spring Lake in New Jersey or Atlantic City at the Shelburne or the Claridge, where Thornton stayed on account of Ada Taylor.

When *The Matchmaker* toured, in his Paris flannel he moved into Detroit's Book-Cadillac for two weeks, draw the veil! Next stop Cincinnati's Park Terrace, that Loring Smith loved so. There Pinkie sat back to the Ohio River in a suite so modern the assistant manager had to come up and show the guest how to work it. Next week at the hotel Loring loved in St. Louis, not modern at *all* and not so good.

"Maybe it's the roast beef I go for," explained Loring, "and they have Yorkshire pudding." Goodbye, that hotel, and that's final. Train to Chicago for four weeks at the Blackstone Theatre, my name in lights where Maude Adams' name had sparkled in 1916 in *The Little Minister*. Pinkie's chair was at darling Ernie Byfield's Ambassador East. Ernie had joined the majority, but his inspirations still made life pleasant for guests. Does "guest" describe sixty dollars a day for the Sarah Siddons Suite plus adjoining room?

We were such a smash David added four more weeks. Business tapered off and we went to Cleveland. The Statler chair was not what Pinkie was used to.

From Cleveland Chapman arranged for our Cadillac limousine to be driven back to New York. He rented something green and tinny for the last few days till we all got on the train back to Chicago and boarded the Union Pacific's grand equivalent of Santa Fe's *Super Chief* and all aboard for San Francisco, Pinkie's back to state after state. Floods slowed us down, but Pinkie turned his back. We didn't get into Oakland till noon and would you believe wonderful stage manager Eddie Dimond and our crew got Tanya Moiseiwitsch's four sets hung and the furniture out of its crates and perfect wardrobe mistress Marie Mann told her little white dog to sit still and be good and she had everybody's costumes ready for the curtain to go up at the Geary Theatre *not one minute behind the time advertised!*

"House lights out."

Out they went.

483

"Curtain going up," said Eddie Dimond from downstage right, at his desk with the light focused on his script open at Act I, page 1.

Onstage was Vandergelder's room over his Yonkers Hay, Grain and Feed Store. I stood offstage left, paced up and around in my light blue taffeta with a train, my lace hat and lace jacket from Berman, Ltd., Garrick Street, London. During *The Matchmaker* engagement I wore out four sets of costumes, eight Stanley Hall Ltd, Portland Place, red wigs, and had all my real jewelry stolen except the diamond ring and earrings I was wearing the night Pinkie stared ahead when the robbers heard our chauffeur unlock the front door to put flowers from the theatre and theatre laundry away and they ran up two flights and took off over the roof. If a pink bear could talk he'd have plenty to say!

In San Francisco he had a fine chair again. His back to Alcatraz and the green ship off for Yokohama.

Back to London, back to Paris, to Montecatini and Munich, to the Frankfurter Hof, where the waiter was anti-Semitic, to Vienna, where the Bristol Hotel loved us. To St. Tropez at the René Clairs', and sat back to the Mediterranean. To Beverly Hills and Santa Monica and Bel Air and back and forth and back and forth.

To England and France and England and France again and again on the *United States,* once on the *Queen Elizabeth.* To Frank Sinatra's at Palm Springs for Christmas and New Year, to Palm Springs' Spa Hotel, to Roxbury Drive in Beverly Hills, to Delfern Drive in Holmby Hills, to Merle Oberon's mansion on Ladera Drive, to Jean Negulesco's rented Camden Drive house opposite the house I'd come to to visit Helen and Charlie and gone to that first scary party at Billy Haines'. When he died the *Times* had a small obit: "Screen Comedian Dies." That was cutting it fine!

From Camden back to Ladera. "This house loves you," phoned Merle.

"We love it."

"Please come back."

"But we've leased this house for six months more."

"Can't you do something?"

"We can move back to your house, but we can't pay you three thousand a month and pay fifteen hundred for this. Should we split it? Come back and pay you two thousand. And pay fifteen hundred for this?"

"I want to be extravagant," I told Mama. Some people just talk and some people do what they talk about.

At Merle's everything in the house was beautiful and Pinkie sat in a pink satin chair. When the room got swarming with bees Pinkie's yellow glass eyes watched that too. They swarmed and buzzed and dropped dead by the hundreds behind Merle's beautiful ivory satin curtains with the moss green velvet band.

Bee men came from all over and finally chopped open the outside wall of Merle's walk-in closet that now had become a swarm-in. In the wall bee men found nearly two hundred pounds of honey the bees had stored. When the bee men got it out the bees never came back again and Merle had to rebuild her wall.

Pinkie was with us in London when Suzanne was told to show the house to people who might want to buy it. The people did and after six weeks to get set, we moved to Tower Road, where the Beverly Hills police wouldn't come when I thought a kook was breaking in. They said it wasn't in their precinct; draw the veil.

Later Carl saw two deer with big antlers that must have got caught in the bushes and vines under our bedroom window. Forest fires had driven them down from the high hills.

Pinkie sat there, the first earthquake. Not awful like the one that shook him off the chaise longue at Tower Road, but still an earthquake. The brass lamp on the desk did a jig and I said to Garson, "Where do I go? Where do I *go?*" It's the first time I ever thought of myself as 100 percent American. An American *knows* there is a place to go where he is safe. He knows it. He isn't grateful, he just takes it for granted that there is a place an American goes to to get out of danger. But the morning at Tower Lane with the brass lamp jigging Garson didn't say where the place was that an American was safe.

Not too good a chair at the Algonquin rehearsing for *A Very Rich Woman,* but you don't go to the Algonquin for the furniture.

When we rented the Feary house in Edgartown, chairs fine. At the Harbor View Hotel, only summer-resort chintz, Pinkie sat back-to to Peter Sharp's house facing out Starbuck Neck. Pinkie faced more chintz furniture.

At the Daggett house he spent two nights till we found the Feary house to rent. At Cottage Street, when we moved in for good, would you believe he's back on the Tower Road chaise longue, the same one the earthquake shook him off?

One day, writing at my desk by the window opposite the window by the chaise longue, the window rattled. "If that was California I'd think it was an earthquake."

At lunch I asked Julianne if she'd noticed the windows rattle.

She had.

"I guess it's some of the trucks or blasting."

In the next issue of the *Vineyard Gazette,* on the front page, they reported, AN EARTHQUAKE.

Earthquake or failure or whatever it is, get past the moment and get over it. Something good eventually happens.

"I can do it," I'd told Papa. "I know I can if somebody will *show* me." And at the Empire it was going to begin. 14 Elmwood Avenue was finished, Mama was asleep at Mrs. Gould's, Papa would be smoking his pipe and reading at Mrs. Shapleigh's. His fifty dollars had gotten me where somebody would show me; tonight I was going to begin.

Miss Ogden, Miss Clarens, Miss Field, Miss Keppel and I struggled into our fur suits. Miss Margaret Gordon, face painted Indian fashion, got into Princess Tiger Lily's dress with fringe and beads. "We don't have to wonder how it's going," she said. "Any other play you have to wonder, but not *Peter.*"

In Wollaston no one thought of plays *going;* we went to a play to *like* it.

"What makes you think you've got the stuff it takes?" Papa had asked me.

Act I was over, Miss Adams had flown in the window, caught hold of the teddy bear, flown off with the Darling children to the Never Never Land. Our room gave final touches—a little powder, a little *less* powder, lip rouge toned down, toned *up,* eyebrows brushed, hair tucked more securely under wig; my hair being short, I didn't wear one.

"Act Two. Places, please," called Barney in his Indian costume, beaded headband, long-haired wig.

It was beginning! I was doing what I wanted to do, what I was scared to say I wanted to, then said it. "I want to go on the stage." Would Papa hit me? Our dining room was quiet. He waited, Mama waited.

"What makes you think you've got the stuff it takes?" Papa asked.

Down the black iron stairs past Mr. R. Peyton Carter's closed door. He had to change from Mr. Darling's white tie and tails to Captain Hook's pirate costume. Past Miss Adams' door, closed. The heavy iron pass-door onstage was open. It was where I'd come through and waited till Mr. Saint-Gaudens noticed me.

The stagehands had moved away the Darling nursery. The forest was set, big trees in place.

"Places," said stage manager Mr. Willard Barton. No matter what he said, he sounded stern. "Get in your tree, Nibs."

486

"I was just going to."

"Don't *talk!*" he hissed.

In the forest, the Lost Boys formed their circle, sitting on the ground. "Ground cloth," I'd learned to say, along with "flats" for scenery, and "cyc" for cyclorama, and "flies" for way up under the roof. I went into the tree trunk. It was going to begin.

"Curtain going up," said Mr. Willard Barton.

There was a sound like the slow roll of surf at Nantasket beach, then it stopped.

"Do you think Peter will be back today?" asked Miss Field's well-bred American voice.

"Oh, yes," answered Miss Clarens' well-bred English voice. "Peter always comes back when he says he will."

"What would you give your mother for Christmas?" asked Billy Sheafe's well-bred Boston voice.

"I'd like to give my mother a checkbook," answered Miss Ogden, clear and cultivated.

That was my cue. I stepped out of the big hole in the big tree. "What's a checkbook?" I asked.

The audience laughed.

Did I have my costume on wrong? Why did they laugh? No one had laughed in rehearsal. Now the opening-night audience laughed. The very first thing I'd ever said on the stage, they'd laughed. I could do it, it had begun! "What's a checkbook?" Laughter.

Well, it's all set down. Maybe not *all,* but what counts is. Impossible to set down *all* of it; some of it has to be lived. I can set down: don't be helpless, don't give up, don't kill yourself, don't look for trouble, stuff gets in your way, kick it under the rug, stay well, stay with it, *make it come out*—but then on top of all that there has to be something that's *you* and that can't be set down.

It's been great, it's been hell, it's been short, it's been mean, it's been fair, it's been endless, it's been tough, it's been lucky, it's been selfish, it's been like Papa's charts in his closet that showed the latitude, the longitude, the coastline, the height of the mountains, the borders of countries, but not the countries themselves.

It's been a ball, it's been sad, it's been lonely, it's been hard work, it's come out right. I live in the past and the present and the future and haven't let them get me down and I wouldn't want to live anywhere else.

487

Coming up to the last page, you've gotten a little older, so have I. You know me better, and maybe yourself. Some things there's nothing to do about, some there are. A day when it all goes right, nobody has to help you handle; a day it all goes wrong, try thinking over your six worst. Would you change today for one of those? If the answer is yes, that's trouble, but remember you lived through six. If the answer is no, appreciate it and think of your six best. Maybe you're due for a seventh.

People say stuff like that is foolish. Why *is* it? Think it over. And one thing more. "I don't *care* if I have a diploma," I told Mama. I meant my high school diploma. But today, in the mail, came what I care about.

Dear Miss Gordon,
    Thank you for your lovely note.
    These words from such a great artist are a tribute indeed!
                                        Very sincerely,
                                        Vladimir Horowitz
                                        *1975 April*

# Index

491

494

Maney, Dick, 302
Mann, Herbert, 467, 470
Mann, Marie, 483
*Manoeuvres of Jane, The,* 115, 477
Mantell, Robert, 6, 22
Manuel, King of Portugal, 130
Maple, Ben, 173–74
March, Florence, 340
March, Fredric, 307, 340–41, 469–70
Marlborough, Duke of, 213–14
Marshall, Bert, 461
Marshall, Fan, 461
Martin, Henry, 14, 45
Martin, Mary, 446
Martin, Mrs. Henry, 14–15, 45, 71
Martin, Neil, 64–65
Martin's Theatrical, 14–15, 45–47,
  52–60, 71–73, 322
Marx, Harpo, 232, 234, 248, 254, 273,
  280, 294, 333, 422
*Mary of Scotland,* 264
Mason, Austa, 38, 54–55
*Masquerade,* 318
Massey, Dorothy, 425
Massey, Raymond, 341, 345, 425, 460,
  482
*Matchmaker, The,* 361, 465–66, 478,
  480–84
Maude, Beatrice, 61–62, 255
Maude, Cyril, 206
Maugham, Liza, 371, 413, 414–15
Maugham, Syrie, 371–72
Maugham, William Somerset, 106,
  412–15, 479
May, Olive, 5
Mayer, Edie, 319
Mayer, Louis B., 319, 425
Mayo, Margaret, 309
Megrue, Roi Cooper, 130
Melish, Lawson, 69–70
Melish, Tom, 69–70
Meller, Raquel, 282
Menken, Helen, 264
*Merchant of Yonkers, The.* See *Matchmaker,*
  *The*
Meredith, Burgess, 441
Merkel, Una, 318
Mérode, Cléo de, 397–98
Merrick, David, 389, 480, 483
*Merry Widow, The,* 313
*Merry Wives, The,* 306
Messel, Oliver, 342, 359, 364, 369, 370,
  373, 377, 379, 381
M-G-M, 305, 308–10, 315, 318–20, 412,
  423–25, 467
*Midnight,* 264
*Midnight Sons, The,* 110
Mielziner, Jo, 346, 350

Mildred. *See* Caplan, Mildred
Miles, Isabelle (Bob), 79, 201–2, 204–8,
  215–19
Miles, Sam, 201–2, 204–8, 215–19
*Milestones,* 51, 413
Miller, Alice Duer, 234, 236, 273, 280,
  293, 357
Miller, Gilbert, 263, 335, 339, 341, 343,
  359, 372, 380–81, 420–22, 448–49
Miller, Harry, 236
Miller, Henry, 125, 273
Miller, Kitty, 371–72, 379
Miller, Marilyn, 239, 295
Miller, Mary, 69–71, 72, 81, 217
*Millionairess, The,* 380
*Mind-the-Paint Girl, The,* 463
Miner, Tony, 199
Miner, Worthington, 115
Minter, Mary Miles, 178
*Misleading Lady, The,* 109
*Miss Jones,* 453
"Miss Thompson," 414
*Mistress of the Inn,* 432
Moeller, Philip, 252–53, 298
Moiseiwitsch, Tanya, 465, 483
Molnar, Ferenc, 263
*Monsieur Beaucaire,* 220
*Mont Ste. Victoire* (Cézanne), 325
Moore, Dennie, 444
Moore, Grace, 313, 318
Moore, Lucia, 152–53
Moran, Polly, 258
Morgan, Jack, 33, 178
Morgan, Percy, 33
Morgan, Ralph, 8
*Morning Glory,* 274
Morosco, Oliver, 32
Morrissey, Mae, 110–12, 114
Mosheim, Grete, 433, 435
Moss, Marjorie, 306
Mower, Margaret, 71, 72, 81
Moxon, Mr., 177
*Mr. Gilhooley,* 258, 263
*Mrs. Dot,* 104, 105, 115
*Mrs. Partridge Presents,* 185–87, 276
Mrs. Wilson's Agency, 141, 158, 163
Mueller, Mr., 273
Mullin, Mr., 4
Mulvehill, Chuck, 387, 393, 403, 404
Munsell, Warren, 315
Murdock, Ann, 136
Murphy, Dr., 191, 193
Murray, Heidi, 386
Muschette, Julie, 163, 167, 168
*Music Box Revue,* 313
*My Fair Lady,* 479
*My Sister Eileen,* 446

497